Articles on American Slavery

An eighteen–volume set collecting nearly four hundred of the most important articles on slavery in the United States

Edited with Introductions by
Paul Finkelman

State University of New York,
Binghamton

A Garland Series

Contents of the Series

VOL. 14

Antislavery

Edited with an Introduction
by Paul Finkelman

Garland Publishing, Inc.
New York & London
1989

Library of Congress Cataloging-in-Publication Data

Antislavery/ edited with an introduction
by Paul Finkelman.

p. cm.—(Articles on American slavery; vol. 14)

Includes bibliographical references.

ISBN 0–8240–6794–0 (alk. paper)

1. Slavery—United States—Anti-slavery movements.
2. Abolitionists—United States—History.
I. Finkelman, Paul. II. Series.

E449.A58   1989

306.3'62'0973—dc20   89–23540

Printed on acid-free, 250-year-life paper
Manufactured in the United States of America

Design by Julie Threlkeld

General Introduction

Few subjects in American history have been as compelling as slavery. This should not surprise us. Slavery affected millions of Americans, north and south. Afro-Americans, Euro-Americans, and Native Americans were involved in the system. All antebellum Americans were affected, directly or indirectly, by slavery. Slavery especially affected Americans from 1861 until well after Reconstruction. As Lincoln noted in his famous second inaugural address: "The slaves constituted a peculiar and powerful interest. All knew that this interest was somehow the cause of the war."

The goal of this series is to reprint the key articles that have influenced our understanding of slavery. This series includes pioneering articles in the history of slavery, important breakthroughs in research and methodology, and articles that offer major historiographical interpretations. I have attempted to cover all major subtopics of slavery, to offer wide geographic representation and methodological diversity. At the same time, I have resisted the temptation to reprint highly technical articles that will make sense only to specialists in certain fields. For example, I have not included a number of important slavery related articles on economics, law, theology, and literary criticism (to offer just a few examples) because they appeared to be beyond the interest of most generalists.

I have used articles from a wide variety of scholarly journals. I have also used essays and articles in edited volumes, as long as the main focus of those volumes was not slavery, abolition, or black studies. It is my hope that such books are readily available to scholars and students and will show up through card catalogues or on-line catalogue searches. For the same reason I have not reprinted chapters from books about slavery, which are often found in anthologies. With a few exceptions, I have not reprinted articles that later became chapters of books on the same subject. In a few cases I have strayed from this general rule of thumb. I have also generally avoided essay reviews of books, unless the essays go well beyond the common book review or even essay review format. I have also tried to avoid certain famous historiographical controversies that resulted in large numbers of essays being collected and published. With some exceptions, therefore, I have not included the many articles attacking the "Elkins" thesis or Fogel and Engerman's Time on the Cross. Students and scholars interested in these two enormously important scholarly works, and the criticism of them, will find a great deal on both in their card catalogues. Finally, I have also excluded articles from Encyclopedias and dictionaries. These editorial decisions mean that many famous essays and articles will not be found in these volumes. Indeed, a few very important scholars are not represented because all of their work has been in books that are directly on the subject of slavery. Finally, some important articles were left out because we were unable to secure permission from the copyright holders to reprint them in this series.

This project was made easier by the hard work and dedication of Carole Puccino and Leo Balk at Garland Publishing, Inc. A project of this magnitude would not be possible without the help of a number of other scholars, who read lists of proposed articles and discussed the whole problem of slavery with me. I am especially grateful for the help and suggestions of Catherine Clinton, Robert Cottrol, Jill DuPont, Seymour Drescher, Linda Evans, Ronald Formasano, John Hope Franklin, Kermit L. Hall, Robert Hall, Graham Hodges, Michael P. Johnson, Charles Joyner, Alan Kulikoff, Greg Lind, David McBride, Randall Miller, Alfred Moss, James Oakes, Albert J. Raboteau, Judith Schafer, Robert Sikorski, John David Smith, Jean Soderlund, Margaret Washington, William M. Wiecek, Julie Winch, Betty Wood, and Bertram Wyatt-Brown. Two SUNY-Binghamton students, Marci Silverman and Beth Borchers, helped me with much of the bibliographic work on this project. Carol A. Clemente and the inter-library loan staff at SUNY-Binghamton were absolutely wonderful. Without their patience, skills, and resourcefulness, I would have been unable to complete these volumes.

—Paul Finkelman

Contents

Introduction

It would be impossible to understand American slavery without at least some understanding of the opposition to slavery. Antislavery did not grow up exactly alongside slavery; slavery began to develop in the American colonies in the 1630s. The first protest against slavery came in 1688, when Quakers in Germantown, Pennsylvania, issued their famous remonstrance against trafficking and owning slaves. The basis of their protest was simple: "There is a saying, that we shall doe to all men like as we will be done ourselves; making no difference of what generation, descent or colour they are."[1] The religious basis of antislavery begun by the Germantown Quakers set a tone that dominated pre-Revolutionary attacks on slavery and would be followed by most post-Revolutionary opponents of slavery. The Christian injunction to "do unto others" was a powerful argument in the struggle to end black bondage in America.

Following the Germantown protest other Quakers also protested slavery. Particularly important was George Keith's often reprinted pamphlet, *An Exhortation and Caution to Friends Concerning Buying or Keeping of Negroes* (1693). Also important was *The Selling of Joseph, A Memorial* (1700), written by Samuel Sewall, a Puritan judge in Massachusetts. The most important pre-Revolutionary pamphlets were the Quaker John Woolman's *Some Consideration on the Keeping of Negroes* (1754) and the Quaker Anthony Benezet's *A Short Account of that Part of Africa Inhabited by the Negroes* . . . (1762).

During the Revolution antislavery gained new arguments and new strengths. The new arguments were based on the revolutionary creed of natural rights. As early as 1764, James Otis argued for the liberty of all Americans, black and white. "The colonists" he asserted, "are by the law of nature freeborn, as indeed all men are, white or black." He argued that any reason "given for enslaving those of any color" could be applied to Europeans and white Americans, as well as Africans. He mocked the racist assumptions of the age: "Does it follow that 'tis right to enslave a `man because he is black? Will short curled hair like wool instead of Christian hair, as 'tis called by those whose hearts are as hard as the nether millstone, help the argument?"[2] Even in England the antislavery movement found a sympathetic ear before the Court of King's Bench, where Chief Justice Mansfield freed the slave Somerset.[3] The natural rights arguments were, of course, best stated by Jefferson, in the Declaration of Independence.

The Revolution did not end slavery throughout the nation, but in the North abolitionist societies gained strength. The societies put their energies into ending slavery in the North, providing education and other services for former slaves, and protecting free blacks from kidnapping. The societies were successful in ending slavery in the North and were able to provide some institutions for free blacks.[4]

After achieving the adoption of gradual abolition statutes, or the outright end to northern slavery, the abolitionist societies concentrated on getting Congressional legislation to end the Afican slave trade. This goal was achieved in 1808.[5] After this these first abolition societies began to decline. The first wave of antislavery had ended in America. From 1808 until the 1830s there was relatively little antislavery activity, although what activity there was laid the groundwork for the vigorous movements of the antebellum period.[6]

In 1828 David Walker, a free black in Boston, published his famous *Appeal*, which called on blacks to reject colonization in favor of radical action, including violent action, to end slavery. This was the first salvo in a new, more radical antislavery movement. While few blacks or whites accepted Walker's formula of violence, most blacks agreed with him in rejecting colonization. In 1831 William Lloyd Garrison published his first issue of *The Liberator*. This signaled the beginning of a new, integrated (although predominately white), abolitionist movement, which both rejected African colonization and supported immediate abolition.

From 1831 until the mid-1840s the abolitionist movement focused on moral suasion and propaganda campaigns, such as sending massive petitions to Congress to protest slavery. Starting with the election of 1840 abolitionists became involved in politics. They were joined by people who were somewhat less radical, who have often been termed "antislavery" (rather than abolitionist). Although the distinctions are sometimes blurred, by the mid-1840s there were two wings of the abolitionist-antislavery movement. The Garrisonians rejected politics in favor of propaganda and calls for moral regeneration. Garrison himself denounced the Union and the Consitution as a proslavery compact and a "Covenant with Death." Other abolitionists, such as Gerrit Smith and Salmon P. Chase, fought slavery through the Liberty Party and then the Free Soil Party. In the mid-1850s many of these people joined more moderate antislavery northerners, such as William H. Seward and Abraham Lincoln, in the Republican Party. The election of Lincoln and the Civil War eventually brought together nearly all antislavery Americans, from the radical Garrisonian abolitionists to moderate antislavery Republicans.

This volume does not offer a comprehensive collection of articles on antislavery. Such a collection would be a multi-volume series by itself. The articles in this volume were chosen with three goals in mind. First are articles that lay out major historiographic trends, such as Merton Dillon's "The Abolitionists: A Decade of Historiography," Betty Fladeland's essay on "Revisionists vs. Abolitionists," and Lawrence Friedman's "Historical Topics Sometimes Run Dry." Second are those key articles on antislavery that provide an introduction to the major issues of the field. These include articles on Garrisonian abolitionism, immediatism, and the relationship between abolition and mainstream politics. Finally, this volume contains a sampling of the kinds of issues that historians have found important in the last two decades. Thus, there are important articles that tie antislavery to questions of race relations, radicalism, or gender in antebellum America.

—Paul Finkelman

Notes

1. The protest is reprinted in Roger Bruns, ed., *Am I Not a Man and a Brother?* (New York: Chelsea House, 1977) 3.

2. Reprinted in Bruns, *Am I Not a Man and a Brother?*? 103–04.

3. See, William M. Wiecek, *"Somerset:* Lord Mansfield and the Legitimacy of Slavery in the Anglo-American World," reprinted in Volume 11 of this series. *See also,* David Brion Davis, *Slavery in the Age of Revolution* (Ithaca: Cornell University Press, 1975) and William M. Wiecek, *The Sources of Antislavery Constitutionalism* (Ithaca: Cornell University Press, 1977).

4. Arthur Zilversmit, *The First Emancipation* (Chicago: University of Chicago Press, 1967); Paul Finkelman, *An Imperfect Union* (Chapel Hill: University of North Carolina Press, 1981). *See also* the articles in Volumes 4 and 5 of this series.

5. Mary S. Locke, *Anti-Slavery in America, from the Introduction of African Slaves to the Prohibition of the Slave Trade, 1619–1808* (Boston: Ginn and Company, 1901).

6. Alice Dana Adams, *The Neglected Period of Anti-Slavery in America, 1808–1831* (Cambridge: Radcliffe College, 1908).

Further Reading

Adams, Alice Dana. *The Neglected Period of Anti-Slavery in America, 1808–1831.* (Cambridge: Radcliffe College, 1908).

Barnes, Gilbert Hobbs. *The Antislavery Impulse, 1830–1844.* (New York: Appleton-Century Company, 1933).

Blackett, R.J.M. *Building an Antislavery Wall: Black Americans in the Atlantic Abolitionist Movement, 1830–1860.* (Baton Rouge: Louisiana State University Press, 1983).

Cover, Robert M. *Justice Accused: Antislavery and the Judicial Process.* (New Haven: Yale University Press, 1976).

Davis, David Brion. *The Problem of Slavery in Western Civilization.* (Ithaca: Cornell University Press, 1964).

Davis, David Brion. *The Problem of Slavery in the Age of Revolution.* (Ithaca: Cornell University Press, 1975).

Davis, David Brion. *Slavery and Human Progress.* (New York: Oxford University Press, 1984).

Dillon, Merton. *The Abolitionists: The Growth of a Dissenting Minority.* (DeKalb, Ill: Northern Illinois University Press, 1974).

Duberman, Martin, ed. *The Antislavery Vanguard.* (Princeton: Princeton University Press, 1965).

Dumond, Dwight Lowell. *Antislavery: The Crusade for Freedom in America* (Ann Arbor: University of Michigan Press, 1961).

Fladeland, Betty. *Men and Brothers: Anglo-American Antislavery Cooperation* (Urbana: University of Illinois Press: 1972).

Fladeland, Betty. *Abolitionists and Working-Class Problems in the Age of Industrialization.* (Baton Rouge: Louisiana State University Press, 1984).

Foner, Eric. *Free Soil, Free Labor, Free Men.* (New York: Oxford University Press, 1970).

Friedman, Lawrence J. *Gregarious Saints: Self and Community in American Abolitionism, 1830–1870.* (New York: Cambridge University Press, 1982).

Gerteis, Louis. *Morality and Utility in American Antislavery Reform.* (Chapel Hill: University of North Carolina Press, 1987).

Kraditor, Aileen. *Means and Ends in American Abolitionism: Garrison and His Critics on Strategy and Tactics* . (New York: Random House, 1969).

Locke, Mary S. *Anti-Slavery in America, from the Introduction of African Slaves to the Prohibition of the Slave Trade, 1619–1808.* (Boston: Ginn and Company, 1901).

McKivigan, John R. *The War Against Proslavery Religion: Abolitionism and the Northern Churches, 1830–1865.* (Ithaca: Cornell University Press, 1984).

Pease, William and Jane Pease. *The Antislavery Argument.* (Indianapolis: Bobbs-Merrill, 1965).

Pease, William and Jane Pease. *Bound Them in Chains: A Biographical History of the Antislavery Movement.* (New York: Atheneum, 1972).

Perry, Lewis. *Radical Abolitionism: Anarchy and the Government of God in Antislavery Thought.* (Ithaca: Cornell University Press, 1973).

Perry, Lewis, and Michael Fellman, eds. *Antislavery Reconsidered: New Perspectives on the Abolitionists.* (Baton Rouge: Louisiana State University Press, 1976).

Quarles, Benjamin.   *The Black Abolitionists*. New York: (Oxford University Press, 1969).

Rice, C. Duncan.   *The Rise and Fall of Black Slavery*. (New York: Harper and Row, 1975).

Richard, Leonard.   *"Gentlemen of Property and Standing:" Anti-Abolition Mobs in Jacksonian America*. (New York: Oxford University Press, 1970).

Sewall, Richard.   *Ballots For freedom: Anti-Slavery Politics in the United States, 1837–1860*. (New York: Oxford University Press, 1976).

Sorin, Gerald.   *The New York Abolitionists: A Case Study in Political Radicalism* (Westport, Conn: Greenwood Press, 1971).

Stewart, James B.   *Holy Warriors*. (New York: Hill and Wang, 1976).

Stewart, James B.   *Wendell Phillips: Liberty's Hero* (Baton Rouge: Louisiana State University Press, 1986).

Walters, Ronald G.   *The Antislavery Appeal: American Abolitionism After 1830*. (Baltimore: Johns Hopkins University Press, 1978).

Wiecek, William M.   *"Somerset*: Lord Mansfield and the Legitimacy of Slavery in the Anglo-American World," reprinted in Volume 11 of this series.

Wiecek, William M.   *The Sources of Antislavery Constitutionalism in America, 1760–1848*. (Ithaca: Cornell University Press, 1977).

Wyatt-Brown, Bertram.   *Lewis Tappan and the Evangelical War Against Slavery*. (Cleveland: Case Western University Press, 1969).

Antislavery

AHR Forum
Reflections on Abolitionism
and Ideological Hegemony

DAVID BRION DAVIS

ATTENTION IS TURNING ONCE AGAIN TO THE ALMOST SIMULTANEOUS APPEARANCE of industrial capitalism and antislavery sentiment in Great Britain. Since the publication of Eric Williams's *Capitalism and Slavery* more than a generation ago, the relation between these two broad forces has provoked considerable debate. Historians have discredited Williams's argument that Britain's antislavery measures were economically determined acts of national self-interest, cynically disguised as humanitarian triumphs.[1] But it has been difficult to find a middle ground that rejects Williams's cynical reductionism while also taking account of the realities of class power. In 1975, in *The Problem of Slavery in the Age of Revolution, 1770–1823*, I suggested that British abolitionism served conflicting ideological functions but that it helped reinforce, in this initial period, the hegemony of capitalist values. This view has recently evoked fruitful criticism, especially a two-part theoretical essay by Thomas L. Haskell in *The American Historical Review*.[2]

---

[1] See especially Roger Anstey, *The Atlantic Slave Trade and British Abolition, 1760–1810* (London, 1975); Stanley L. Engerman, "The Slave Trade and British Capital Formation in the Eighteenth Century: A Comment on the Williams Thesis," *Business History Review*, 46 (Winter 1972): 430–43; Howard Temperley, "Capitalism, Slavery, and Ideology," *Past and Present*, 75 (1977): 94–118; Seymour Drescher, *Econocide: British Slavery in the Era of Abolition* (Pittsburgh, Pa., 1977); Seymour Drescher, "Cart Whip and Billy Roller: Antislavery and Reform Symbolism in Industrializing Britain," *Journal of Social History*, 15 (September 1981): 3–24; Seymour Drescher, *Capitalism and Antislavery: British Mobilization in Comparative Perspective* (New York, 1987); *British Capitalism and Caribbean Slavery*, Barbara Solow and Stanley L. Engerman, eds. (New York, 1987); and David Eltis, *Economic Growth and the Ending of the Transatlantic Slave Trade* (New York, 1987).

[2] Thomas L. Haskell, "Capitalism and the Origins of the Humanitarian Sensibility, Part 1," *AHR*, 90 (April 1985): 339–61; Part 2, *AHR*, 90 (June 1985): 457–566. See also the relevant article by T. J. Jackson Lears, "The Concept of Cultural Hegemony: Problems and Possibilities," in *AHR*, 90 (June 1985): 567–93. Although my response to Haskell meets some of the criticisms advanced by Betty Fladeland and Seymour Drescher, I have tried to deal with their substantive arguments, many of which are compatible with my own views, in a different version of this article, "Capitalism, Abolitionism, and Hegemony," in Solow and Engerman, *British Capitalism and Caribbean Slavery*, 209–27. See Betty Fladeland, *Abolitionists and Working-Class Problems in the Age of Industrialization* (Baton Rouge, La., 1984); Drescher, "Cart Whip and Billy Roller," 3–24; and Drescher, *Capitalism and Antislavery*.

Because I bear some responsibility for the misinterpretations that have been given to my "thesis," I would like to take this opportunity to restate and clarify my argument and to assess some of the criticisms.

I should first point out that my hegemonic argument fills only a few pages in a 570-page volume and that it applies only to British history in a limited period from the 1790s to 1823, with some brief speculations reaching ahead to the 1830s. I did not extend the concept of hegemony to America or France, where abolition movements emerged in wholly different contexts. Certainly, I advanced no general theory of abolitionism *per se* as an instrument of hegemonic control (although I would claim it was always related to the need to legitimate free wage labor). I have never meant to suggest that abolitionism can best be understood as a device for deflecting white working-class discontent or that it was not part of the wider egalitarian and liberalizing movement I described in *The Problem of Slavery in Western Culture* (1966).

It is important to distinguish the *origins* of antislavery sentiment, a subject I discussed at length in the first volume, from the *conditions* that favored the acceptance of antislavery ideology among various governing elites. This is a distinction that Haskell continually blurs. In all my work, I have taken pains to emphasize the importance of religious sources of antislavery thought and the religious transformations that made slave emancipation a symbolic test of the efficacy of Christian faith. In *The Problem of Slavery in the Age of Revolution*, I did not say, and here Haskell misquoted me, that the "origin" of the new humanitarian sensibility lay in "the ideological needs of various groups and classes."[3] I did maintain that "the continuing evolution" of antislavery opinion "reflected the ideological needs of various groups and classes."[4] I had in mind the ideological needs generated by the French Revolution and the early Industrial Revolution, by war, nationalism, and religious revivalism. At issue are the uses made of antislavery doctrine and rhetoric as the movement pulled away from the Painite radicals of the early 1790s, won legitimacy from government ministries in 1806–07, was appropriated by the aristocratic African Institution, and was then reshaped by wealthy merchant philanthropists.

In *The Problem of Slavery in the Age of Revolution*, I dealt with Britain in the period from 1793 to 1823, decades of reactionary politics and domestic repression that should not be confused with the era of social ferment and reform that accompanied West Indian slave emancipation and the abolition of apprenticeship. The crucial question, therefore, was not why groups of enlightened British, French, and Americans attacked slavery from the 1760s to the 1780s but why this single reform cause, which attracted significant radical support in the early 1790s and which some conservatives denounced as a Jacobin front, won growing acceptance in the early nineteenth century from British political and social elites otherwise obsessed with the fear that social reform would open the gates to revolution.

---

[3] Haskell, "Capitalism and the Origins of the Humanitarian Sensibility, Part I," 344.
[4] David Brion Davis, *The Problem of Slavery in the Age of Revolution, 1770–1823* (Ithaca, N.Y., 1975), 42.

2

During the long period from the late 1790s to 1823, the British public showed little interest in the slavery issue except at the end of the Napoleonic wars. In 1814, an eruption of petitions expressed outrage at the prospect that the government would allow France to resume the Atlantic slave trade, which Britain had earlier renounced on moral grounds. This brief popular outburst drew on nationalistic pride and was orchestrated by abolitionist leaders who were eager to demonstrate to the courts of Europe that "with a single voice" the English people demanded international suppression of the slave trade. The cause served the purposes of Wellington and Castlereagh, who actively cooperated with the abolitionists. But the crucial antislavery measures from 1800 to 1823 were not the result of public pressure. Leaders of government and a few influential abolitionists were responsible for the decisions to curtail and then stop the flow of African slaves to Guiana and other foreign colonies conquered by Britain and later to prohibit the British slave trade to all foreign nations and colonies. The successful abolition bill of 1807 originated in the House of Lords; the prevailing public apathy and ignorance of the question prompted William Wilberforce to publish and widely circulate *A Letter on the Abolition of the Slave Trade; Addressed to the Freeholders and Other Inhabitants of Yorkshire.* The subsequent campaign to establish a central registry of all colonial slaves aroused little public interest, although it was seen as an essential preparatory step toward amelioration and gradual emancipation. Even in 1823 and 1824, when an organized emancipation movement got underway, the abolitionists who solicited petitions and organized auxiliary societies were surprised by the general public ignorance concerning West Indian slavery. Yet the governing elites, while still divided on the issue, had become increasingly committed to colonial labor reform. By 1833, even the Tory opposition in the House of Commons failed to rally behind the West Indian interests.[5] In pursuing the question of why colonial slavery seemed so repugnant to such groups, I should have made it clearer that by "ideology" I did not mean a fixed set of ideas and doctrines used to promote concrete class interests. When referring to an ideology as a "mode of consciousness," I was thinking of a perceptual lens, a way of viewing social reality that helps to define as well as legitimate class, gender, or other collective interests. Keeping this definition in mind, it is important to draw a distinction between the motives of individual reformers and the ideological context that gave hegemonic meaning to their rhetoric and influence.

When, in 1786, Thomas Clarkson published his prizewinning Cambridge University essay on the horrors of the African slave trade, he clearly had no intention of condoning British child labor in factories and mines. But Clarkson's proslavery opponents, such as Gilbert Francklyn and Jesse Foot, immediately contrasted the alleged comfort and security of West Indian slaves with the oppression of English workers and the plight of English children exposed to the "pestilential vapour" of factories. Francklyn pointedly asked why the universities

---

[5] Eltis, *Economic Growth*, chap. 2. Eltis argued that abolishing the slave trade and emancipating colonial slaves were contrary to Britain's economic interests but were the result of a free-labor and free-market ideology that led to the New Poor Law of 1834 and to concerted efforts to increase the productivity of labor.

did not offer prizes "for the best dissertation on the evil effects which the manufactures of Birmingham, Manchester, and other great Manufacturing towns, produce on the health and the lives of the poor people employed therein?" He proceeded to show how Clarkson's rhetorical techniques could be applied to the specific consequences of the early Industrial Revolution. Francklyn was probably not surprised when Lancashire manufacturers took the lead in 1787 in initiating the great petition campaign to abolish the African slave trade.[6] Antiabolitionist counteroffensives such as these had appeared even earlier, and they became a dominant theme of British and, later, American proslavery writing. Similar points were made by representatives of radical labor who were in principle opposed to all forms of economic and political bondage. Given the venom of the debate, no abolitionist could plead ignorance of the charge that moral outrage was being directed against oppression overseas while similar or worse oppression was complacently tolerated at home. In 1818, for example, Francis Burdett asked why Wilberforce could be shocked by the enslavement of Africans and yet support in Parliament a seditious meetings bill and the suspension of *habeas corpus*, measures that allowed the English to be seized and treated like African slaves.

In theory, abolitionists faced by these challenges could condemn all forms of social oppression and simply give priority to the slave trade or chattel slavery as the most flagrant and remediable crimes against humanity. Such a course would entail a disavowal of the claims of proslavery writers and at least a private expression of regret over the unintended consequences of extolling free wage labor. As a second alternative, exemplified by some of the radical Garrisonians and labor reformers, the abolitionists could assert that both distant and nearby evils arose from a common cause. As a third choice, they could deny any comparability between black slaves who were subjected to constant physical coercion and English workers who faced merely the threat of starvation, which was termed a "liberal motive" and a "rational predicament" by the reformer who drafted the slave emancipation act of 1833.[7]

In response to both proslavery and radical indictments of the wage-labor system, most abolitionists accentuated the moral contrast between what they conceived of as the free and slave worlds. Their greatest hope, after all, was to end the involuntary shipment of Africans to the New World and to transform black slaves into cheerful, obedient, and grateful laborers whose wants could be satisfied only by working voluntarily for wages. This hope rested on the assumption that the British system of labor had achieved a reasonable balance between freedom and order and could serve as a norm against which harsher regimes should be measured. I am not suggesting that early abolitionists were mostly conservatives who accepted the status quo and opposed domestic reforms, although some of them fit this description. But the sharp contrast they drew between British and

[6] Cited in Davis, *Problem of Slavery in the Age of Revolution*, 462–63. Because I am responding to misreadings of this book, I will take most of my examples from it. Seymour Drescher has recently drawn attention to the crucial role of Lancashire industrialists in initiating the antislave trade campaign (*Capitalism and Antislavery*, 67–88).

[7] David Brion Davis, *Slavery and Human Progress* (New York, 1984), 218.

colonial society had ideological meaning, especially at a time when there was a growing need to valorize wage labor as a universal norm, when the Industrial Revolution was introducing new forms of exploitation and suffering, and when it was by no means clear that the British working class was less victimized than were West Indian slaves.

For example, early in 1807, at a depressing stage in Britain's war against Napoleon, James Stephen the elder, who was the master strategist for the abolitionists, singled out British depravity in Africa and the West Indies as the cause for God's vengeance. Stephen specifically excluded domestic sins and proceeded to marvel over the "social happiness [that] has been showered upon us with singular profusion." "In no other part of the globe, are the poor and helpless so well protected by the laws, or so humanely used by their superiors . . . If it be as the protector of the poor and destitute, that God has entered into judgment with us, we must, I repeat, look to Africa, and to the West Indies, for the causes of his wrath."[8] Stephen was a deeply religious man who was genuinely concerned with collective guilt and retribution. We can be almost certain that he did not consciously intend to use his abhorrence of slavery and the slave trade, which he had observed firsthand in the West Indies, as a means of diverting attention from domestic suffering. Although as a boy he and his mother had lived in debtors' prison, he honestly believed, at least after marrying into the Wilberforce family and allying himself with paternalistic Tories, that Britain's treatment of its poor could not be a cause for divine displeasure. Later in 1807, Stephen played an important role in securing the abolition of the British slave trade, in a law hailed by political leaders as the most altruistic act since Christ's crucifixion and as proof that Britain waged war for human brotherhood. National pride is especially dangerous and deceptive, as Reinhold Niebuhr reminds us, when it is based on the highest achievements of human history.[9]

Haskell has argued that it is difficult if not impossible to reconstruct a historical actor's unconscious intention or to distinguish between consequences that are unconsciously intended and consequences that are unintended and even random. This difficulty, in his view, invalidates any historical explanation based on the concept of self-deception. I would reply that the concept of self-deception is so central to any quest for self-understanding or social analysis that it cannot be discredited by a kind of positivistic behaviorism. In everyday life, people continually recognize self-deception without resorting to depth psychology or finding the source of unconscious intention. To cite one obvious example, advertising agencies know they can rely on self-deception when they link cigarette smoking or the consumption of "lite" alcoholic drinks with health, slim figures, and vitality. Because the actual effects of smoking cigarettes and consuming alcoholic beverages are well known to the public, the success of the advertisements cannot be attributed simply to ignorance or gullibility.

[8] Quoted in Davis, *Problem of Slavery in the Age of Revolution*, 366–67. Wilberforce also warned in 1807 that Britain's afflictions might be a prelude to much worse divine punishment if the nation persisted in the criminal slave trade (*Letter on the Abolition of the Slave Trade* [London, 1807], 4–6).

[9] Richard Wightman Fox, *Reinhold Niebuhr: A Biography* (New York, 1985), 181.

5

A subtle complicity often exists between self-deception and externally imposed deception that produces what some historians would call "false consciousness." That term carries unfortunate connotations that lead to unnecessary controversy. But, as historians, we do need to recognize the reality of deceptive or biased consciousness—of collective rationalizations, sometimes consciously crafted, that serve identifiable interests and help convince individuals of their own innocence and virtue. Biased consciousness, which Haskell tried to subsume under the morally neutral term "convention," also shields individuals from any sense of complicity in social injustice and oppression. The abolitionists dramatized the personal guilt entailed by one form of biased and deceptive consciousness. Modern history, from the Holocaust and Vietnam War to the peril of Star Wars and nuclear annihilation, teems with examples of individual and collective self-deception. Although biased consciousness can result from ignorance as well as individual self-deception, historians should by now be skeptical of the excuse that "we never knew." Self-deception usually involves choices to screen out or discount disagreeable truths. Human beings are not passive automata wholly programmed by "society."

But Haskell ignored or dismissed a vast body of knowledge that reveals the ways in which class, gender, and social circumstances tend to guide our selective attention, control our mechanisms of avoidance, displacement, and projection, and shape the very cognitive style to which Haskell gives center stage. Sexism provides a telling example, since many American men are just beginning to realize the ways in which their language, culture, and daily conventions reinforce sexual inequalities. Sexism is seldom the result of conscious intent, but individual males benefit from the assumption that female disabilities are part of the natural order of things. Male hegemony has usually been accepted by women, who have redefined it in their own way but have found it difficult to create an alternative world. Class and racial hegemony can have similar effects, although Haskell's emphasis on conscious intention can blind us to the psychological realities we confront every day.

Historians' assumptions about human behavior are necessarily drawn from personal experience or from reading about the experiences of others. Most of us are probably aware of the complexity and ambiguity of our own intentions and may recall making choices that led to supposedly unintended consequences that we may still have intuited or dimly foreseen. Fiction offers endless variations on the themes of contradictory impulses, inner division, and the need for self-justification. Historians must engage in a dialectical process in which we strive to discover the "otherness" of the past while also making sense of past events from a present-day perspective. If we have empirical evidence that a group of historical actors believed they were advancing the interests of all humanity when they were actually promoting the interests of a special class, we can justifiably speak of self-deception. But my central concern in *The Problem of Slavery in the Age of Revolution* was not the conscious or unconscious motives of individuals but rather the social meanings and consequences of certain moral perceptions.

From the time of the Mosaic Exodus, slavery and redemption have been extremely powerful paradigms involving the ultimate questions for both individual and collective life: the passage from present misery and degradation to a land of Canaan. Apart from their religious meanings, these paradigms are capable of being extended to a wide range of social experiences with oppression and liberation or of being confined to the historical sufferings of a specific people. According to Rousseau, "man is born free—and everywhere he is in chains." But since Rousseau, at least, there has always been a tension between such generalizing proclamations and attempts to dramatize the horrors of a special instance of human bondage.

For James Stephen, William Wilberforce, and the government leaders who deplored the African slave trade and who moved toward gradualist antislavery policies, it was essential to maintain a sharp distinction between the evils of the colonial slave world and the ostensibly free institutions that had been imperiled both by French tyranny and English Jacobinism. The constant comparisons in abolitionist literature between the agony of black slaves and the smiling, contented life of English husbandmen was not fortuitous. Abolitionists repeatedly reminded Britons that the Somerset decision of 1772 had outlawed slavery in England. At a time when many of the peoples of Europe were said to be "enslaved" by French despotism, it was crucial to define England as a "free" nation—both in the sense of having no slaves and of having successfully resisted foreign domination. With the growth of nationalism in the Napoleonic era, "freedom" increasingly signified membership in a nation that had resisted or thrown off foreign tyranny. When national leaders were perceived as the protectors of liberty in this collective sense, it was more difficult to accuse them of fostering various forms of domestic oppression.

If the existence of the slave colonies allowed England to define itself as free soil— much as communist countries enable the United States to define itself as the leader of the free world—they also helped specify the nature of freedom. The African slave trade defined, by negative polarity, the conditions necessary for consensual and acceptable labor transport. On the one hand, it was unacceptable for an employer to claim ownership of the person of an employee, to sell husbands apart from their wives, or children apart from their parents. But it was acceptable, on the other hand, to buy the labor of adults or children under conditions that led to the separation of families and that made a mockery of the worker's supposed consent. Labor conditions could be seen as the effects of market forces, not human intentionality.

IN DISCUSSING INTENTIONALITY, Haskell pointed to the absurdity of blaming Hank Aaron, when he hits a home run, for allowing the ball to strike a spectator on the head. The gap between Aaron's intention of hitting the ball and the consequence of injuring a spectator is too wide to be of any significance. Haskell was primarily concerned with the virtue or blameworthiness of individual moral choice. But, if the rules of a game were constructed in a way that ensured that many spectators

7

would be hit on the head during every inning, and if it were assumed that this was simply one of the costs of the sport, we would consider the consequences culturally significant regardless of the conscious intentions of the players.

Haskell also argued that selectivity is inevitable, that limits of moral responsibility have to be drawn somewhere, and that it is therefore unfair to blame abolitionists for not attacking forms of exploitation closer to home. I should emphasize that I am not interested in blame but rather in understanding the moral ambiguities of history. But Haskell's argument reminds me of similar reasoning advanced by Serafim Leite, the historian of the Jesuits in Brazil. In praising Manuel da Nóbrega and other sixteenth-century Jesuits for protecting the Brazilian Indians from enslavement and mistreatment, Leite is forced to deal with the unfortunate fact that Nóbrega openly defended and encouraged the African slave trade. But, according to Leite, to accuse the Jesuits of injustice for favoring Indians is like condemning a person for founding a hospital for tuberculosis while ignoring the victims of leprosy. One has to draw the line somewhere. Yet selection is seldom neutral, either culturally or psychologically, as we can see in Leite's own illustrative choices of tuberculosis and leprosy. Indians were conventionally pictured as the victims of consumptive physical or social diseases introduced by whites; the African's dark skin and physiognomy were sometimes seen as a kind of leprosy, or as the result of a leprous disease for which the European bore no responsibility. Leite accepts the traditional distinction between the freeborn Indian and the enslaved African, who was accustomed to bondage and whose labor was essential for successful colonization.[10]

British selectivity, as I suggested in *The Problem of Slavery in the Age of Revolution*, must be understood in terms of historical context. The government's first interventions in the colonial labor system coincided with an urgent domestic problem of labor discipline and labor management—not yet the problem of an industrial proletariat but of an immense rural labor force that had been released from traditional restraints and controls but not deprived of the independence of preindustrial village culture. Many Britons, including abolitionists, felt ambivalent about the changes accompanying early industrialization. Tensions mounted between the advocates of hard-headed utilitarianism and the defenders of traditional paternalism or evangelical benevolence. The issue of slavery provided a meeting ground for these diverse groups and for members of different propertied classes who longed to ensure stability while benefiting from the economic changes underway.

"Because the slave system was both distinctive and remote," I wrote, "it could become a subject for experimental fantasies that assimilated traditional values to new economic needs. An attack on the African slave trade could absorb some of the traditionalist's anxieties over the physical uprooting and dislocation of labor . . . By picturing the slave plantation as totally dependent upon physical torture, abolitionist writers gave sanction to less barbarous modes of social discipline. For

---

[10] Serafim Leite, *História da Companhia de Jesus no Brasil*, 10 vols. (Rio de Janeiro and Lisbon, 1938–50), 2: 227, 246–47; 6: 350–51.

reformers, the plantation offered the prospect of combining the virtues of the old agrarian order with the new ideals of uplift and engineered incentive. Abolitionists could contemplate a revolutionary change in status precisely because they were not considering the upward mobility of workers, but rather the rise of distant Negroes to the level of humanity ... British antislavery provided a bridge between preindustrial and industrial values; by combining the ideal of emancipation with an insistence on duty and subordination, it helped to smooth the way to the future."[11] I have quoted at length from this passage because I have sometimes been interpreted as arguing that British abolitionism was a "screening device" designed to distract attention from metropolitan exploitation.[12] In actuality, I was trying to suggest a far more complex model in which the colonial plantation system served as a projective screen or experimental theater for testing the ideas of liberation, paternalism, and controlled social change that were prompted in part by domestic anxieties. As one might expect in a society as deeply divided as early industrial Britain, different audiences drew contradictory conclusions from the experiments in overseas reform. But it is difficult to deny that the abolition cause offered both national and local ruling elites an increasingly attractive opportunity to demonstrate their commitment to decency and justice.

In the passage quoted above, I was also concerned with the implications of sharply separating slavery from other kinds of coerced labor and social domination. It is noteworthy that even Thomas Clarkson, who retained much of the liberal spirit of the late 1780s and early 1790s, found nothing inequitable about coerced labor. Any state, he said, could legitimately use convicts to work in mines or clear rivers. What outraged Clarkson and other early abolitionists was the claim of personal proprietorship that justified arbitrary and unlimited authority. The slaveowner's claims contrasted sharply with those of the idealized British squire, whose authority was constrained by law and custom, and with the rights of the rising capitalist, who was content to purchase labor in the market like any other commodity.

Above all, the slave system came to epitomize an inherent and inescapable conflict of interest, a kind of warfare sublimated or suspended from the time the original captive was subdued. For a while, the more moderate abolitionists searched for means to ameliorate this conflict, hoping that an end to further slave imports, for example, would persuade masters to promote their slaves' welfare as part of their own long-term self-interest. But the continuing negative growth rate of the West Indian slave population seemed to show that the system itself was unreformable and would lead to eventual genocide. This impression was reinforced by the slaveholders' truculent resistance to missionaries, moral uplift, the abolition of Sunday markets, restrictions on the flogging of women, and other benevolent measures. The major goal of the British antislavery movement by the early 1820s was to create a natural harmony of interests between planters and black

---

[11] Davis, *Problem of Slavery in the Age of Revolution*, 466–67.
[12] See especially Drescher, "Cart Whip and Billy Roller," 4.

9

workers, a relation similar to the assumed mutuality between British landlords and tenants.

In arguing that the antislavery movement mirrored the needs and tensions of a society increasingly absorbed with problems of labor discipline, I was not saying that such needs and tensions are sufficient to explain the emergence and ultimate direction of antislavery thought. While emphasizing the importance of class and social context, I specifically warned against "the simplistic impression that 'industrialists' promoted abolitionist doctrine as a means of distracting attention from their own forms of exploitation."[13] My main theme was that opposition to slavery cannot be divorced from the vast economic changes that were intensifying social conflicts and heightening class consciousness; in Britain, it was part of a larger ideology that ensured stability while acclimating society to political and social change.

Even in Britain, where the cause won significant support from the governing elites, abolitionist thought had both conservative and radical aspects. Some readers have focused exclusively on the first part of my argument, in which I claimed that the acts of selectivity by abolitionists "helped to strengthen the invisible chains being forged at home." But I also emphasized that abolitionism "bred a new sensitivity to social oppression," "that it provided a model for the systematic indictment of social crime," and that it "ultimately taught many Englishmen to recognize forms of systematic oppression that were closer to home."[14] To illustrate the radical potentialities of antislavery thought, I quoted from Friedrich Engels precisely because he showed how abolitionist perceptions and locutions had become universalized by the 1840s: even a resident alien, with no roots in the abolitionist movement, appropriated the language and perspective of Anglo-American abolitionists when he exposed the "slavery" of Manchester's working class. As early as 1817, when Wilberforce and his friends in Lord Liverpool's cabinet feared that England was on the verge of revolution, another radical alien pointed to the connections between the oppression of West Indian slaves and the oppression of England's poor. Iain McCalman has recently discovered that Robert Wedderburn, a Jamaican mulatto whose slave mother was born in Africa, edited a London periodical, *Axe Laid to the Root*, that called for a simultaneous revolution of West Indian chattel slaves and English wage slaves. Working with Thomas Spence, Thomas Evans, and other London radicals, Wedderburn popularized a plebeian antislavery rhetoric in the taverns and hayloft chapels of London's underworld.[15]

[13] Davis, *Problem of Slavery in the Age of Revolution*, 455.

[14] Davis, *Problem of Slavery in the Age of Revolution*, 455, 467–68. Drescher has greatly amplified these themes, which do not contradict my position, as he seems to think. No doubt I should have cited more varied examples of the linkage between denunciations of colonial slavery and wage slavery, and I was unaware of the language in petitions that Drescher has discovered. It is my intention to explore this subject in a succeeding volume on the "Age of Emancipation." Drescher does not seem to deny that Wilberforce, Stephen, Macaulay, Clarkson, Cropper, Buxton, and the other national leaders of the early period were unsympathetic to the wage-slavery argument, which they associated with their enemies.

[15] Iain McCalman, "Anti-Slavery and Ultra-Radicalism in Early Nineteenth-Century England: The Case of Robert Wedderburn," *Slavery and Abolition*, 7 (September 1986): 99–117. Although

Reform causes often serve opposing or contradictory functions as innovative doctrine is co-opted by different social groups. As I have already indicated, slavery and emancipation have long been extraordinarily complex paradigms capable of almost infinite extension to both material and spiritual states. Even in the 1820s, antislavery agitation led American radicals like Langton Byllesby and Thomas Skidmore to the conclusion that black slavery was not only the quintessential American crime but that it revealed deep structural flaws allowing a fortunate few to live off the labor of the so-called free majority.[16] Yet, when radical American reformers later contended that the wage system was slavery, that conventional marriage was slavery, and that submission to any government using coercion was slavery, their rhetoric surely diluted the charge that Negro slavery in the South was a system of exceptional and intolerable oppression. Frederick Douglass was outraged in 1843 when his white abolitionist colleague John Collins asserted that antislavery was "a mere dabbling with effects" and that tolerating private ownership of land was worse than enslaving human beings. As Christopher Lasch has observed with respect to our own time, the language of radical protest was impoverished when it was appropriated by fat people, short people, old people, and other such groups who claimed that they were as much oppressed as racial minorities: "Since interest-group politics invites competitive claims to the privileged status of victimization, the rhetoric of moral outrage becomes routine, loses its critical edge, and contributes to the general debasement of political speech."[17] Likewise, an indispensable term such as "holocaust" becomes trivialized when it is extended metaphorically to every atrocity or instance of ethnic oppression.

The concept of hegemony is easily discredited by misconstruction or misunderstanding—by attacking the argument, for example, that a discrete capitalist class imposed a form of false consciousness on a passive populace, duping people with antislavery propaganda designed to divert attention from the women and children in the mills and mines. It is now clear that, by the early 1830s in both England and the United States, the abolitionist movement had attracted significant support from artisans and other skilled workers; that in England the "pressure from without" ran ahead of the elite antislavery leadership, embarrassing Thomas Fowell Buxton in his negotiations with government ministers; and that a few reformers moved from an apprenticeship in the abolitionist campaign to more radical activism as Chartists or labor reformers.[18]

Wedderburn dedicated his autobiography to Wilberforce, it is clear that Wilberforce abhorred the ideology and culture that Wedderburn represented. Nevertheless, disguised as a "stranger" and equipped with a Bible, Wilberforce visited Richard Carlile in prison and attempted to convert him to Christianity; Carlile reported that Wilberforce also talked to the imprisoned Wedderburn and declared the black to be an "honest and conscientious man." John Pollock, *Wilberforce* (New York, 1977), 258; McCalman, "Anti-Slavery and Ultra-Radicalism," 113.

[16] Sean Wilentz, *Chants Democratic: New York City and the Rise of the American Working Class, 1788–1850* (New York, 1984), 164–67, 183–90.

[17] Waldo E. Martin, Jr., *The Mind of Frederick Douglass* (Chapel Hill, N.C., 1984), 28; Christopher Lasch, "The Great American Variety Show," *New York Review of Books*, 2 February 1984, 36.

[18] For a discussion of the pressure exerted on Buxton and the parliamentary abolitionists, see Davis, *Slavery and Human Progress*, 195–202. Drescher's *Capitalism and Antislavery* emphasizes the broad-based, popular character of the antislavery movement. For abolitionist Chartists, see Betty Fladeland, "'Our

11

But these facts in no way invalidate the hegemonic argument when it is properly understood. Hegemony, as Eugene D. Genovese has written, implies no more than the ability of a particular class to contain class antagonisms "on a terrain in which its legitimacy is not dangerously questioned."[19] Ideological hegemony is a process that is never complete or total; it can be understood in different ways by opposing groups or classes as long as it limits the terms of debate, heads off more fundamental challenges, and serves to reinforce the legitimacy of the ruling groups and existing order. Seymour Drescher, who scornfully rejects the hegemonic thesis, lends it invaluable support in his description of the mass political mobilization by abolitionists that was "virtually unopposed in most areas." A perfect example of ideological hegemony can be seen in Drescher's claim that "Parliament's assessment of property claims in persons residing in the metropolis appears to have been congruent with that of the Irish chimney sweep." In France, in sharp contrast, "antislavery was clearly distinguished by an inability to combine a stable élite leadership with a mass appeal."[20] Obviously, British antislavery agitation had different meanings in 1814, 1833, and 1838, and a detailed analysis would be required to show the degree to which abolitionism stabilized or destabilized Britain's social and political order at a particular time. But a few preliminary points can be made in response to the common view of an expansive, one-directional surge of democratic consciousness.

No doubt many British workers empathized with colonial slaves and understood abolitionist principles in ways that would have deeply troubled Wilberforce, Buxton, and Zachary Macaulay. But rank-and-file abolitionists could not escape the fact that the governing classes succeeded in appropriating the cause and defining the terms of the debate. Britain's landlords, merchants, and manufacturers showed by their behavior that there were varieties of exploitation that would no longer be tolerated in England or on the high seas, and that there were forms of labor, even in the distant colonies, that would have to be brought more in line with metropolitan standards. This affirmation of moral standards helped legitimate both the existing system of class power and the emerging concept of free labor as an impersonal, marketable commodity. The emancipation act of 1833 gave assurance to Britons of various classes that there were limits to the rapid socioeconomic changes taking place: workers could not literally be reduced to chattel slavery; owners of even the most questionable form of private property could not be deprived of their capital without generous compensation.

Although the politics of slave emancipation were extremely complex, the act of 1833 fostered the illusion that the newly reformed Parliament had become an almost democratic assembly that would respond to the voice of a moral majority. The succession of antislavery victories and official commitments, beginning with the order-in-council of 1805 restricting the slave trade to conquered colonies,

---

Cause Being One and the Same': Abolitionists and Chartism," in *Slavery and British Society, 1776–1846*, James Walvin, ed. (Baton Rouge, La., 1982), 69–99.
[19] *Roll, Jordan, Roll: The World the Slaves Made* (New York, 1974), 26.
[20] Drescher, *Capitalism and Antislavery*, 46–47, 53, 75.

vindicated trust in the government's basic sense of justice. It is no wonder that, when various British groups wanted to dramatize their own oppression or lack of freedom, they complained that their condition was at least as bad as that of West Indian slaves. Defenders of colonial slavery had opened this door, and their argument implied two propositions: first, to receive attention, one had to meet the "slavery test" by enumerating horrors equivalent to those in abolitionist literature; second, because Parliament and the middle-class public were attuned to this language, the same techniques that had persuaded Parliament to bestow liberty on West Indian slaves would also bring freedom and justice at home.

In effect, the antislavery radicals were addressing the governing classes as follows: wage labor under present conditions leads to even worse misery than chattel slavery; because you responded to moral arguments in abolishing the slave trade and in freeing the colonial slaves, you should now relieve the distress of England's poor. But this reinforcement of ruling-class standards is precisely what is meant by "ideological hegemony." Denunciations of "wage slavery" were a way of expressing outrage and resentment over working conditions in industrial Britain and America. But as Christopher Lowe pointed out, there could be no lower standard than to ask that free laborers be treated better than slaves.[21] Everyone knew that white workers were not really slaves. The analogy, whatever its emotive power, invited a rhetorical response celebrating the benefits of the market and the inestimable privilege of being free to change employments. The dichotomous terms of this debate forced radicals to prove that, in some fundamental respects, wage earners were no freer or better off than slaves.

There can be no doubt that abolitionism contributed to more radical kinds of social criticism. Especially in the United States, where slavery was abolished in a cataclysm of violence, radical labor leaders and socialists found that parallels between black and white slavery retained their resonance well into the twentieth century.[22] But analogies with chattel slavery may also have retarded the development of a vocabulary that could depict more subtle forms of coercion, oppression, and class rule. To be a free worker was to be as unlike a Negro slave as possible. Most opponents of slavery equated unjust domination with a legalistic concept of property rights in human beings. This absolutist approach often made it difficult to distinguish the forms of domination concealed by voluntary contracts and the "bundle of powers" that could be exercised over nominally free workers.

HASKELL SEEMED PRIMARILY CONCERNED WITH the *moral* status of individual acts of benevolence and charity, such as our going to the aid of a starving stranger. He evidently feared that any links with class interest would inevitably tarnish the virtue of humanitarian acts by reducing them to lowly motives. His thesis allowed a place for class interest but minimized its importance when compared with his own alternative explanation: "Whatever influence the rise of capitalism may have had

---

[21] Christopher Lowe, "Ideology, Hegemony and Class Rule" (Yale Graduate School seminar paper, 1985).
[22] Barry Herbert Goldberg, "Beyond Free Labor: Labor, Socialism and the Idea of Wage Slavery, 1890–1920" (Ph.D. dissertation, Columbia University, 1979).

13

generally on ideas and values through the medium of class interest, it had a more telling influence on the origins of humanitarianism through changes the market wrought in *perception* or *cognitive style*."[23] Aside from the point that changes in perception and cognitive style are often closely associated with changing class interests, I fail to see why aiding a starving stranger is more praiseworthy when it is the psychological by-product of market forces that may also encourage moral callousness and bring starvation to the unemployed. Indeed, one can argue that we have even less reason to admire Haskell's humanitarians, since their altered perceptions seem to be the mechanistic and behavioristic result of what he himself terms "market discipline." [24]

I see no need, however, to fall into this trap of reductionism and counter-reductionism. Few historians would maintain today that abolitionists were hypocrites who consciously exploited humanitarian sentiments for ulterior aims. Few historians would argue that abolitionism was simply a spontaneous eruption of virtue, wholly unrelated to the rise of modern capitalism and the concomitant redefinition of property, labor, and contractual responsibilities. The abolitionists were neither otherworldly saints nor the agents of a capitalist conspiracy. Whatever their virtues or shortcomings, they have been vindicated by history: morally, they were right. But, like their opponents, their private moral and personal needs had public consequences that reinforced or altered relationships of power. Haskell confused the issue by conflating the hegemonic argument with the origins of the antislavery movement. The movement had various origins and was supported by different groups for different reasons. Only gradually did the British movement become hegemonic in the sense of promoting an alliance of various religious, social, and political blocs that succeeded in overriding the interests of West Indian merchants, landowners, and their conservative allies. It was precisely because the antislavery alliance could convincingly present itself as disinterested and high-minded that it bestowed moral legitimacy on the reformed Parliament, British society, and the British character.

Haskell recognized a connection between British capitalism and antislavery thought, but he posited an original and ingenious theory about the effects of the market on the understanding of causation, promise-keeping, foresight, and the conventions defining personal responsibility. Haskell's reasoning deserves more careful consideration than I can give here, but I will offer a few preliminary observations.

It should be noted that Haskell applied extremely rigorous standards to the hegemonic theory, demanding that it explain, in class terms, the origin and rise of British abolitionism. In other words, Haskell seemed to be looking for a strong causal link between some element of capitalism and the appearance of abolitionism. Any link based on class, he argued, must ultimately rely on intentionality, for which there is no empirical justification. When Haskell turned to his own alternative thesis, however, he retreated from the demand for a strong causal link.

---

[23] Haskell, "Capitalism and the Origins of the Humanitarian Sensibility, Part 1," 342.
[24] Haskell, "Capitalism and the Origins of the Humanitarian Sensibility, Part 1," 342.

His market mechanisms and recipe knowledge supply only one of various unnamed preconditions for the humanitarian sensibility and, more specifically, for the rise of abolitionism. This weak connection has no predictive power—that is, Haskell did not suggest that merchants involved in a world market were more likely to become abolitionists than were merchants confined to a traditional village clientele. But this very softness shields Haskell from serious empirical attack. For example, there can be no doubt that the market tended to teach people to keep their promises and attend to the remote consequences of their acts. But such lessons were especially useful for slavetraders, who were in the vanguard of long-distance commerce and who had to calculate costs and risks against long-delayed payment. The British slave trade flourished and indeed rose to its peak during the very period when Haskell's capitalist market was becoming triumphant. It is clear that a market mentality enabled many merchants to scorn older, paternalistic notions of responsibility and to justify virtually any practice that was good for business. Indeed, one can argue that market values tended to shrink the scope of effective human agency, as economists ascribed the misery of the poor to the effects of immutable economic laws and as people became aware of the interconnections of a global economy that fractionalized individual responsibility beyond measure. The knowledge that our economic acts are related in some way to most of the world's crime and oppression can blunt any sense of complicity. Even so, Haskell can claim that nothing is proved by the failure of slavetraders to become humanitarians. The market did not breed humanitarians but was a precondition that enabled certain kinds of people to become humanitarians.

The same reply can be given, though with much less force, to certain counterexamples. Antislavery opinion emerged in various societies including those of Virginia and North Carolina, France and Brazil. These societies were involved in international markets that required a degree of rational calculation and long-range planning. But only in industrializing Britain did this opinion crystallize into a national consensus that received official sanction. If the British pattern had appeared in market-oriented nations that had not yet shifted to a wage-labor economy, Haskell's thesis would appear more plausible. Given Haskell's criteria, a strong antislavery movement should have emerged in Holland, which was certainly involved in mercantile capitalism, in long-distance commerce, in world markets, and in complex banking and credit. Surely, the Dutch learned to attend to the remote consequences of their actions, and there must have been as many potential humanitarians per capita in the Dutch population as in Britain or the United States. Yet, despite repeated prodding from British abolitionists, the Dutch remained stolidly indifferent to the whole abolitionist campaign. Antislavery ideas excited virtually no popular interest. Before 1840, only twelve pamphlets were published in Holland on the issue of slave emancipation. It was not until 1853 that Dutch liberals succeeded in founding an antislavery society, but, according to Peter Emmer, the minutes of the annual meetings "show a complete lack of enthusiasm among its members: only seventeen to twenty of them attended." In 1863, long after slavery had been abolished in the British, French, and Danish colonies, the

15

Dutch government emancipated Holland's colonial slaves in an almost perfunctory gesture.[25]

The market theory also fails to account for the large number of women who were involved in the abolitionist campaigns of Britain and America. Clearly, women as a group were relatively removed from the kind of liberating capitalist market Haskell had in mind; married women were not even permitted to make contracts in their own name. They were not subject to a market discipline that rewarded "impersonality" and "efficiency," to use Haskell's terms, or that "taught them to attend to the remote consequences of their actions."[26] Yet women were strongly represented among the petition-gatherers, the local organizers, and the writers and distributors of antislavery literature. Haskell ignored the whole pre-Romantic and Romantic cults of sensibility and domesticity that were pitted against the brutality and insensitivity of the marketplace but that gave a powerful impetus to the abolitionist crusade. One can argue that the cultivation of empathy, which was obviously central to all humanitarian reform, arose in large part as a reaction to what Haskell termed the "nineteenth-century folklore about avaricious landlords and piratical factory owners . . . the metahistorical imagery of a class of me-first bourgeois individualists."[27]

HASKELL MADE SOME EXTREMELY INTERESTING POINTS about the effects of the market on cognitive style and recipes for action. But I would shift attention from the origins of individual humanitarian sensibility to the way that market values highlighted the evils of Negro slavery. Haskell failed to see that thinking causally, keeping promises, learning to calculate and compute, and taking responsibility for the remote consequences of one's actions is precisely the kind of behavior that slavery proscribed. How could a slave be expected to keep all promises or make responsible choices? Slavery stood in direct opposition to the virtues inculcated by the market, the virtues that English employers and ratepayers wished to instill in the English working class. This line of reasoning brings me back to class interests and hegemony—not to any rigid or mechanical notion of social control but to the broad moral, political, and cultural transformations that accompanied the triumph of capitalism.

[25] P. C. Emmer, "Anti-Slavery and the Dutch: Abolition without Reform," in *Anti-Slavery, Religion, and Reform: Essays in Memory of Roger Anstey*, Christine Bolt and Seymour Drescher, eds. (Folkestone, Kent, 1980), 80–94.
[26] Haskell, "Capitalism and the Origins of the Humanitarian Sensibility, Part 2," 550, 551.
[27] Haskell, "Capitalism and the Origins of the Humanitarian Sensibility, Part 2," 549.

The Relationship between Capitalism and Humanitarianism

JOHN ASHWORTH

SINCE AN OBVIOUS TEMPORAL CORRESPONDENCE exists between the development of capitalism and the rise of humanitarianism, historians are understandably reluctant to believe that there is no causal connection. The problem, however, is to explain, indeed to theorize, this connection. The two-part article recently published in this journal by Thomas L. Haskell is an attempt to do just that.[1] One can hardly fail to be impressed by the authority that Haskell brings to the subject. The wide-ranging knowledge, the variety of sources consulted, and the rigor of the theoretical analysis make his article a landmark in the historiography of antislavery. I have reason, nevertheless, to be skeptical about the interpretation he offers and, perhaps more important, reason to question the sociological assumptions on which it rests.

It may be helpful to begin with a brief review of the historiography or at least parts of it. First, there was the Whig view of the abolitionists. It was probably not very different from the abolitionists' view of the abolitionists. The emphasis was on progress; waves of humanitarian sentiment came lapping onto the shores of Britain and then the United States as part of the divinely ordained scheme of things. Quaint though some of their notions may seem today, Whig historians did recognize that morality and values were subject to change over time. At this point, enter Eric Williams with his attack on the abolitionists and his reduction of humanitarianism to a simple reflex of self-interest. This view has been effectively demolished by, among others, Howard Temperley and Seymour Drescher, who have shown that good cause exists for doubting whether abolition promoted Britain's economic interest. But, as Temperley has pointed out, the Williams view does at least have the merit of connecting the rise of capitalism to the emergence of the humanitarian movement. His view also explains the contrast between the abolitionists' condemnation of slavery and their tolerance of, or even enthusiasm

For their assistance in the production of this article, I should like to thank my colleagues Richard Crockatt, Geoffrey Searle, and especially Howard Temperley, my friends Greg and Christy Ludlow, and also my father, Eric Ashworth. I should also like to thank the anonymous reviewers of an earlier version, whose comments I found extremely valuable, and the editorial staff of the *AHR*.
[1] Thomas L. Haskell, "Capitalism and the Origins of the Humanitarian Sensibility," 2 parts, *AHR*, 90 (April 1985): 339–61; (June 1985): 547–66.

for, the system of wage labor then emerging. It seems to be difficult, if not impossible, however, to demonstrate the existence of a direct economic interest in the abolition of slavery.[2] But David Brion Davis, against whose work much of Haskell's article is directed, has concluded that capitalism brought to prominence a bourgeois class whose interest it was to attack slavery. This was not a simple financial interest that can be calculated in pounds, shillings, and pence but a much broader one, involving ideas about labor discipline and unemployment. With this more subtle notion of self-interest, Davis was able to explain, without resort to crude charges of hypocrisy, what he took to be the abolitionists' lack of concern with, for example, factory conditions. The abolitionists were responding to their own class needs. Davis also argued that they were not generally conscious of these limitations on their world view: they believed their ideals were universal rather than partial.[3]

This interpretation allowed Davis, like Williams, to recognize that values and morality are subject to change. It also maintained the spotlight on the limitations of the abolitionists, their special concern with slavery. In other respects, Davis has advanced beyond Williams, and Haskell justly praised him for not charging those who opposed slavery with conscious deception. Yet, according to Haskell, Davis has fallen into a different trap. Haskell's principal criticism of Davis maintains that he was wrong to try to connect abolitionism and capitalism via class interest.

This criticism raises an important theoretical point. Haskell's argument, I believe, is misdirected. Scholars now agree that it is a mistake to charge the abolitionists with conscious deception or hypocrisy. And Haskell has spent a considerable amount of time showing that it is impossible to claim that unconscious intention was present, either. For how can historians establish an unconscious intention? If an intention is unconscious, the individual is presumably not aware of its existence. How can the historian ever hope to demonstrate self-deception and unconscious intention? Showing conscious intention is difficult enough. Davis's argument is in fact incoherent. Haskell concluded, "To say that a person is moved by class interest is to say that he *intends* to further the interests of his class, or it is to say nothing at all."[4]

Although Haskell's conclusion sounds plausible enough, it must be resisted. Davis has only himself to blame for talking about self-deception and thus opening himself to Haskell's criticism. Davis ought to have focused on "false consciousness," the notion that the awareness of historical actors is incomplete, with the result that they misperceive the world around them. Historians are often, understandably,

---

[2] Thomas Clarkson, *A History of the Rise, Progress and Accomplishment of the Abolition of the African Slave Trade*, 2 vols. (London, 1808); W. P. Garrison and F. J. Garrison, *William Lloyd Garrison, 1805–1879*, 4 vols. (New York, 1885–89); Eric Williams, *Capitalism and Slavery* (Chapel Hill, N.C., 1944); Seymour Drescher, *Econocide: British Slavery in the Era of Abolition* (Pittsburgh, Pa., 1977); Howard Temperley, "Capitalism, Slavery and Ideology," *Past and Present*, 75 (May 1977): 94–118; Howard Temperley, "The Ideology of Antislavery," in *The Abolition of the Atlantic Slave Trade: Origins and Effects in Europe, Africa and the Americas*, David Eltis and James Walvin, eds. (Madison, Wis., 1981), 21–35; Howard Temperley, "Eric Williams and the Abolitionists: The Birth of a New Orthodoxy," in *British Capitalism and Caribbean Slavery*, Stanley Engerman and Barbara Solow, eds. (Cambridge, 1987).

[3] David Brion Davis, *The Problem of Slavery in the Age of Revolution, 1770–1823* (Ithaca, N.Y., 1975).

[4] Haskell, "Capitalism and the Origins of the Humanitarian Sensibility, Part 1," 347.

18

reluctant to employ this concept, perhaps because it smacks of condescension toward the past, perhaps because the word "false" is insufficiently nuanced. Yet, it seems to me, we cannot do without the concept. Otherwise, we are limited to the understanding of events that contemporaries possessed. The most important factors to them will have to be the most important for us; what they are unaware of, we will be unable to discuss. But Haskell's objection to the idea of self-deception is quite justified. The way out of this impasse lies, quite simply, in a recognition that society rather than the individual generates false consciousness. In the words of one Marxist theorist, "it is not the subject that deceives himself, but reality which deceives him." When Marie Antoinette told the peasants of Paris (never mind that the story is probably apocryphal) to eat cake when there was no bread, she was not deceiving herself in thinking that they could afford it. Rather, the nature of her involvement in society obscured from her the realization that peasants could not in fact afford cake. False consciousness, which human beings all possess to a greater or lesser degree, is not a matter of self-deception.[5]

One can say that a person is moved by certain ideals that have grown out of class interest. This knowledge may or may not be reflexive; the individual may or may not be aware of the relationship between ideals and self-interest. History often illustrates the proposition that actors are not always conscious of the forces that operate on them. It is clearly quite possible to argue that an individual is moved by class interest without showing that the individual intends to further those interests either consciously or unconsciously.

I do agree with Haskell that current interpretations that point to class interest as the major causal factor are open to serious criticism.[6] Haskell of course answered his main question, the relationship between capitalism and humanitarianism, by reference to the market and its multifarious effects. Before considering this view, let us first note that, in what it seeks to do, Haskell's argument marks a retreat from certain issues. Davis's view, despite its limitations, did tackle this crucial point about the selectivity of the abolitionists, their concern with chattel slavery rather than, as some contemporaries put it, "wage slavery." Haskell has nothing to say on this selectivity except for his demonstration that there was no conscious hypocrisy on the part of the abolitionists and his (powerful) argument against the notion of self-deception. Granting that neither conscious hypocrisy nor self-deception was present makes the question of the abolitionists' selectivity of concern more, not less, urgent. Haskell introduced an interesting analogy here. If, in a hundred years'

---

[5] M. Godelier, "System, Structure and Contradiction in Capital," quoted in Nicholas Abercrombie, *Class, Structure and Knowledge* (Oxford, 1980), 77. It is evident that no individual can ever attain an entirely "true" consciousness, just as the person burdened with a consciousness that is utterly "false" would be incapable of any rational behavior or thought. In other words, we are dealing with a continuum rather than the dichotomy that is perhaps implicit in the term "false."

[6] The major problem arises not from the concept of intentionality but from that of interest. On this subject, Haskell's words seem to me important enough to bear repeating. He referred to "the glib assumption so characteristic of modern scholarship that a person's 'interests' are readily identifiable and constitute a complete explanation of his conduct." The problem is that "the term is utterly elastic" so that "there is no human choice that cannot be construed as self-interested." To this, I would add only that this is an especially severe problem for scholars of a Marxist persuasion. Haskell, "Capitalism and the Origins of the Humanitarian Sensibility, Part 1," 351.

time, everyone were a vegetarian, would the many twentieth-century reformers who ignore this question today be deceiving themselves? Indeed, they would not, but the analogy is perhaps better than Haskell realized. If that moment were ever to arrive, a vital question for historians studying the twentieth century would be why its peoples were selective in their concerns. In other words, the historians of the future would want to know why so many of us, unlike their own contemporaries, were indifferent to this reform. Does Haskell assume that he is not entitled to go beyond the actors' own understanding of their ideas? Certainly, when he finds abolitionists who speak of what he regards as the crucial factor (the market), he seems to think these statements are especially significant.[7] Yet, if one had asked abolitionists why they were abolitionists, they would have talked a good deal about God and righteousness, a good deal about the evil effects of slavery, and very little about the spread of the market. In short, something very like the Whig view.

It is important theoretically to decide whether the abolitionists' understanding of their own ideas is definitive or not. If it is, historians must speedily resurrect the Whig view. But if it is not, we are entitled to ask Davis's question again: why were abolitionists selective in their concerns? Search Haskell's article as we may, we will find nothing that helps answer this question. All the links postulated between capitalism and humanitarianism via the market might just as easily have operated to make the conscientious reformer hostile to wage labor, too. In this connection, we can also note that abolitionists in the United States and Britain tended to be involved in many other reform causes. Why did they accept wage labor? Haskell quoted an abolitionist, O. B. Frothingham, saying that slavery, unlike poverty, was susceptible to human control. We need neither doubt Frothingham's sincerity nor accuse him of self-deception to ask why it was that he and others reasoned in this way. Haskell, far from answering this question, seems to doubt whether it should even be posed.[8]

HASKELL PRESENTED HIS EXPLANATION WITH ADMIRABLE LUCIDITY in one of his concluding paragraphs: "What, then, did capitalism contribute to the freeing of the slaves? Only a *precondition*, albeit a vital one: a proliferation of recipe knowledge and consequent expansion of the conventional limits of causal perception and moral responsibility that compelled some exceptionally scrupulous individuals to

---

[7] Haskell, "Capitalism and the Origins of the Humanitarian Sensibility, Part 2," 564.

[8] Haskell, "Capitalism and the Origins of the Humanitarian Sensibility, Part 2," 557. Historians have recently revised the assumption that abolitionists were uninterested in reforming institutions and practices that were closer to home. Many maintained an interest in a wide range of issues, and some were concerned with the conditions of the laboring poor in their own societies. Nonetheless, for all but a small minority, there was a characteristic belief that the relation between capitalist and worker either was, or could be made, harmonious; by contrast, the relation between slave and slaveholder by contrast, could not. See Betty Fladeland, *Abolitionists and Working-Class Problems in the Age of Industrialization* (London, 1984); Jonathan A. Glickstein, "'Poverty Is Not Slavery': American Abolitionists and the Competitive Labor Market," in *Antislavery Reconsidered: New Perspectives on the Abolitionists,* Lewis Perry and Michael Fellman, eds. (Baton Rouge, La., 1979). There are many comments by American abolitionists on the virtues of wage labor. See, for example, *Liberator,* 1 January 1831, 24 December 1841, 19 and 26 March 1847, 9 July 1847, 1 October 1847; *The Letters of William Lloyd Garrison,* 4 vols., Walter M. Merrill, ed. (Cambridge, Mass., 1971), 2: 167; *Emancipator,* 10 October 1839, 31 December 1840; Theodore Parker, *The Slave Power* (1916; rpt. edn., New York, 1969), 63, 116.

20

attack slavery and prepared others to listen and comprehend. The precondition could have been satisfied by other means, yet during the period in question no other force pressed outward on the limits of moral responsibility with the strength of the market."[9] That is, the market enhanced causal understanding, deepened the sense of responsibility, and thus spurred the reformer into action.

Of course, Haskell was aware of the other effects of capitalism. The market could also encourage the atavistic pursuit of self-interest. As he himself commented, "both friends and foes of capitalism often read into technical analyses of wage and price movements a very simple message: since the laws of supply and demand automatically transmute each individual's self-interest into the greater good of the greater number, no one need be concerned with the public interest."[10] This message was undoubtedly received loud and clear by many nineteenth-century Europeans and Americans. The market in this case had contradictory effects. Surely, to substantiate his argument, Haskell must show that the effects he wants to emphasize were actually greater than the opposite ones. If one demonstrates that factor f tends both to produce and to prevent result r, then to make f a significant cause of r, one must show that the productive effects are greater than the preventive ones. Nowhere did Haskell do this. He did not even acknowledge the difficulty. Yet it may be that he sensed the problem. Certainly, he was at pains to emphasize the positive effects of the market. The language he used to refer to the negative ones is revealing. He refers to "the rich nineteenth-century *folklore* about avaricious landlords and piratical factory owners" and to "the *metahistorical* imagery of a class of me-first bourgeois individualists displacing a feudal aristocracy" (emphasis added). More explicit is the remark that "it is easy to forget . . . how moderate, in the long perspective of human history, the capitalist's license for aggression really is."[11] Whether one agrees or disagrees with this statement, it hints at a major problem in Haskell's argument, a problem that was not adequately identified, let alone resolved.

Let us for the moment concede that Haskell was correct in emphasizing these positive effects of the market. Suppose that more individuals do become aware of the importance of their actions and the consequences that will flow from them. Will this be conducive to reform movements such as abolitionism? Haskell cited the case of John Woolman, the early Quaker abolitionist. In an essay in 1746, *Some Considerations on the Keeping of Negroes*, Woolman suggested that custom might have to be breached and people treat Negroes as they would themselves wish to be treated. He made it his responsibility to point out to his readers the extent to which they were implicated in slavery and the slave trade. Woolman argued that both geographical and temporal remoteness were irrelevant. Woolman recognized (as few did until the nineteenth century) "the causal relationship that exists in market

[9] Haskell, "Capitalism and the Origins of the Humanitarian Sensibility, Part 2," 563.

[10] Haskell, "Capitalism and the Origins of the Humanitarian Sensibility, Part 2," 549.

[11] Haskell, "Capitalism and the Origins of the Humanitarian Sensibility, Part 2," 549. It is perhaps necessary to add that this is separate from the (important) question of who the reformers actually were. Haskell quite legitimately disclaimed any intention of answering this question. I too am concerned with the overall societal effect.

21

John Ashworth

societies between supply and demand." Haskell quoted Woolman at some length: "'Whatever nicety of distinction there may be betwixt going in person on expeditions to catch slaves, and buying those with a view to self-interest which others have taken, it is clear and plain to an upright mind that such distinction is in words, not in substance; for the parties are concerned in the same work and have a necessary connection with and dependence on each other. *For were there none to purchase slaves, they who live by stealing and selling them would of consequence do less at it*'" (emphasis in original).[12] Haskell concluded that a man "attentive to the remote consequences of his acts in business and familiar with the intricate web of mutual dependencies that the market establishes between buyers and sellers" was naturally "among the first to see the seemingly civilized and law-abiding slaveowner as engaged in essentially 'the same work' as the barbaric slave stealer."[13] Woolman provides good evidence for Haskell. Unfortunately, it is negated by the case of Daniel Defoe, whom Haskell also cited but without seeing the damage it did to his thesis. Although Defoe "conceived of the slave trade as part of a network of cause-and-effect relationships, he drew from this in 1713 the conclusion that the slave trade was indispensable to England's prosperity." Defoe represents one who appreciated the role of the market in producing intricate patterns of interdependence but who, instead of arguing for abolition, drew the opposite conclusion: one must not tamper with its workings. This stance was anything but rare. In the United States, for example, it was adopted time and time again. To blunt the force of the abolitionist attack on slavery, proslavery advocates pointed to "the intricate web of mutual dependencies" established by the market between buyers and sellers. Too many people, too many interests, it was said, were dependent on slavery. So the complexity produced by the market could have a paralyzing effect. Once again, the consequences are contradictory; once again, Haskell supplied no reason for believing the tendencies that he emphasized were not offset by the opposite ones.[14]

In common with many other writers on the subject, Haskell seemed to define capitalism very much in terms of the market. Let us consider for a moment the South. According to Haskell, the market promoted new levels of scrupulous attention to ethics. An unprecedentedly high standard of conscientious performance was encouraged. The South had always been connected very firmly with the international market. From 1820 onward, Southerners were major suppliers of raw cotton to Europe and particularly to Britain. They were involved in the market and, at the same time, required by Southern honor to maintain high "levels of scrupulosity in fulfilling ethical maxims."[15] Yet no powerful humanitarian movement took place in the South. Not only antislavery but all the other reform movements that flourished in the North and in Britain were much weaker there.

[12] Haskell, "Capitalism and the Origins of the Humanitarian Sensibility, Part 2," 565.
[13] Haskell, "Capitalism and the Origins of the Humanitarian Sensibility, Part 2," 566.
[14] Haskell, "Capitalism and the Origins of the Humanitarian Sensibility, Part 2," 564–66.
[15] Haskell, "Capitalism and the Origins of the Humanitarian Sensibility, Part 2," 555.

Why was this? It is not easy to see how Haskell's thesis can explain this anomaly.[16]

Finally, an even greater difficulty confronts his argument. Whatever the deficiencies of the Whig view of history, which saw the abolitionists as representatives of a new and superior moral order, it did at least have the merit of recognizing that morality itself, the notion of what is right and wrong, has not been a constant in human history. Changes in morality are not the same as a judgment whether an evil is or is not bearable; I am concerned here with the prior question of whether a practice is an evil at all. This distinction is important in the case of slavery. At times, Haskell assumed that the problem of slavery is analogous to that of the starving stranger today: we all know the situation is bad, but we lack a feeling of responsibility for it and a recipe to end it. Thus he referred to "the miseries of the slave, which had always been recognized but which before the eighteenth century had possessed the same cognitive and moral status that the misery of the starving stranger in Ethiopia has for us today."[17] But is this correct? Did people always recognize that slavery was an evil? There is every reason to doubt it. Davis's earlier volume, *The Problem of Slavery in Western Culture*, clearly demonstrates that many defenses of slavery were offered and that, while some individuals and groups were convinced that the enslavement of human beings was an evil, others held the opposite view, and a third group had an ambivalent attitude. Davis concluded an excellent analysis of antiquity's view of slavery with the words: "For some two thousand years men thought of sin as a form of slavery. One day they would come to think of slavery as sin."[18]

It would be wrong to imply that Haskell was unaware of the evidence for changing morality. As he himself observed, "Although its morality was often questioned before 1750, slavery was routinely defended and hardly ever condemned outright, even by the most scrupulous moralists."[19] This statement sits rather awkwardly with the analogy of the starving stranger. Is poverty in the third world "routinely defended and hardly ever condemned outright"? The core of the problem is an ambiguity in Haskell's argument. Was he arguing that a change in values occurred so that what was once believed acceptable ceased to appear so? When he discussed earlier attitudes to slavery, that was the impression we were given. Or was he instead emphasizing a continuity of values but a discontinuity of technique and cognitive style? That was the impression offered when the starving stranger was being considered. A possible way out of this impasse would be to argue that a change in technique can generate a change in values, so that, having found a recipe or perceived a causal connection, human beings then find intolerable an evil they had previously been prepared to tolerate. Although this may seem the most sophisticated position to adopt, it tends toward reductionism.

---

[16] On Southern honor, see Bertram Wyatt Brown, *Southern Honor: Ethics and Behavior in the Old South* (New York, 1983).

[17] Haskell, "Capitalism and the Origins of the Humanitarian Sensibility, Part 1," 359.

[18] David Brion Davis, *The Problem of Slavery in Western Culture* (London, 1966), 90. Of course, there were good reasons why people were slow to condemn slavery. As Davis noted, "if slavery were an evil and performed no divinely appointed function, then why had God authorized it in Scripture and permitted it to exist in nearly every nation?"; Davis, *ibid.*, 91–92.

[19] Haskell, "Capitalism and the Origins of the Humanitarian Sensibility, Part 1," 339.

For it is clear that the relationship can easily be reversed. Having come to find an old practice intolerable, people look for a recipe to end it or discover the extent of their complicity in it. To the extent that he assumed that the process is one-way, Haskell reduced values to technique and recipe knowledge. Again using "technology" in the broadest sense, so that it includes cognitive style, recipe knowledge, and technique, Haskell offered us an analysis that comes perilously close to technological determinism.

So, there are many reasons why historians should be reluctant to accept Haskell's thesis. First, the market has contradictory effects on a sense of responsibility, and, while Haskell realized this, he did not justify his own emphasis on its positive ones. Second, even if the market makes individuals conscious of causal processes in a new way, this consciousness may serve to deter rather than encourage reform. Third, even if the reformer were encouraged by the market, we would be no nearer an answer to the question Eric Williams posed: why the selectivity of concern; why some reforms rather than others? Why reject slavery but tolerate wage labor? Fourth, no conceptual space is allotted to the possibility that changes in values may precede and even cause the changes in cognitive style and technique that Haskell outlines. Fifth, difficulties occur with certain geographical regions such as the South. This is not to deny that a market was one of the necessary conditions for the rise of humanitarianism; capitalism cannot exist without markets, and it would not be surprising if there were some connection between markets and humanitarianism. But I shall argue that the connection is utterly different from the one Haskell suggested.

AT ONE POINT IN HIS ARTICLE, HASKELL INTRODUCED AN ANALOGY of oxygen and fire: "Since capitalism [For this, read "markets," since for him they are the same thing] supplied only a precondition, no one need be surprised that the subsequent history of capitalist societies has not been greatly distinguished by humanitarian achievements. The argument presented here is not that markets breed humane action but that in the particular historical circumstances of late eighteenth-century Anglo-American culture the market happens to have been the force that pushed causal perception across the threshold that had hitherto made the slaves' misery (and much other human suffering) seem a necessary evil. One would no more expect markets continually to elevate the morality of the population than one would expect oxygen—in the absence of which ignition cannot occur—always to produce fire. Then, too, there is reason to fear that still another face of the market has prevailed in the later stages of capitalism, one far less supportive of the humanitarian sensibility."[20] This passage is highly problematic. First, Haskell recognized that the market does not necessarily and indeed has not since the mid-nineteenth century operated in this way. Yet we are not really told why. What crucial change occurred? Or rather, what was present before the change? The analogy with oxygen is incomplete. While a fire cannot burn without oxygen,

[20] Haskell, "Capitalism and the Origins of the Humanitarian Sensibility, Part 2," 563.

oxygen only rarely and in special circumstances produces a fire. What are these special circumstances?

The root of Haskell's problem, it seems to me, lies in his definition of capitalism. If we move beyond the assumption that capitalism is merely production for the market and for profit, we may be able to understand its relationship with humanitarianism more easily. It is surely preferable to define capitalism as generalized commodity production. Among these commodities is labor power. Capitalism involves not only markets but wage labor, a class of wage-laborers, in fact, selling their labor power. Markets, after all, have existed for millennia, but capitalism, according to this definition, is a more specific occurrence. In order to explain the rise of humanitarianism in general and antislavery in particular, we need to focus on the relationship between capitalist and wage-laborer.[21]

For most of human history, the status of the wage-laborer has been exceptionally low. At least some wage-laborers have been present in most pre-modern societies, and they have been a despised and hated lot. Aristotle believed that to be a wage-laborer was to be virtually a slave, and this attitude seems to have been prevalent in Europe (and perhaps elsewhere) for two thousand years after him. Christopher Hill has shown how the wage-laborer was viewed in seventeenth-century England, and it is apparent that the English, perhaps without knowing it, were good Aristotelians in this respect. It is also easy to show that early American democrats, as late as the Jacksonian era, had much the same attitude. The problem was dependence. Wage-laborers were dependent on those who paid their wages, and the word frequently used to describe the dependence was "slavish." So, when we study the rise of antislavery, it is even more striking that abolitionists should have attacked chattel slavery while defending wage labor. Why the break with the past?[22]

Whereas some historians may be tempted to make light of the growth of wage labor, its impact was actually enormous. The vast increases in material production recorded in the last two centuries have occurred in societies that have been capitalist in this sense. Apart from those that achieved industrialization at the point of the gun, no nation has modernized without wage labor on a large scale. This alone suggests that the relationship between capitalist and laborer is likely to have a profound structural effect on a society. In the nineteenth century, the effects were indeed profound. The home and family ceased to be the center of production they had traditionally been. Similarly, notions of individualism, long potent in England and the United States, came to be modified in many subtle ways. These were some of the processes by which capitalism fostered humanitarianism.[23]

---

[21] I am, of course, following Marx's definition of capitalism.

[22] G. E. M. de Ste. Croix, *The Class Struggle in the Ancient Greek World* (London, 1983), 179–204; Christopher Hill, "Pottage for Freeborn Englishmen: Attitudes to Wage Labour," in Hill, *Change and Continuity in Seventeenth-Century England* (London, 1974), 219–38.

[23] At one point, Haskell did refer to C. B. Macpherson's notion of possessive individualism, which accords easily with the Marxist definition of capitalism, but he did not follow up the point. Haskell, "Capitalism and the Origins of the Humanitarian Sensibility, Part 2," 553; C. B. Macpherson, *The Political Theory of Possessive Individualism: Hobbes to Locke* (London, 1962).

I can perhaps best present my argument by comparing abolitionist thinking with that of classical republicanism.[24] Among the key questions for all political and social theorists are these: what is the foundation of individual morality? How is social stability to be achieved? How is loyalty to the state to be secured? The classical republican tradition could not conceive of a stable society unless the vast majority of the citizenry owned their own means of production, either tools and shops if they were to be artisans or, more typically, land if they were farmers. Classical republicans wanted the informed and politically active citizen to be able to place the common good ahead of private and personal gain. The egotistical pursuit of self-interest, it was believed, would plunge a republic into anarchy. Wage-laborers lacked the independence to be able to consider the common good.[25]

Yet wage labor did emerge and on an ever-increasing scale. Not surprisingly, the rise of wage labor called into question many traditional assumptions. In societies that were changing in this way, people altered their attitudes and practices in an attempt to bring them into line with the new realities. They looked for, and found, new supports for individual morality and the social order. Among these were the family, the home, and the individual conscience. None had been previously ignored but all came to be redefined. In societies that had redefined them or were in the process of redefining them, slavery came to appear as a greater and greater evil. Thus a small but growing number of influential individuals were sensitized to the evils of slavery. As they viewed their own society differently, these individuals initiated a new hostility to slavery (and other evils, too) and led the humanitarian movement.[26]

The spread of the market meant that a growing part of human life was subject to the force of individual self-interest. But a society in which the pursuit of self-interest is universal is a society that is about to collapse. The pursuit of self-interest threatens to subvert the rules by which the game is played. Why should self-interested individuals not seek to buy the law? Why should they not sell out the nation for gain? Why should they not rob, kill, or maim their competitors? It might well be in their interest to put an end to the system by which everyone else's interest can be pursued. This, of course, is the paradox of freedom. If all are free, will not some use their freedom to end the freedom of others? A society based on the pursuit of self-interest needs certain institutions, certain practices that must remain outside the area in which self-interest can operate. This requirement perhaps explains why right-wing groups that have sought the free play of market

[24] The interpretation I am offering is in a highly abbreviated form. I am seeking to provide evidence sufficient to demonstrate its plausibility rather than firmly establish the case. Nor have I considered temporal or geographical differences in antislavery opinion. For additional evidence of some of the attitudes I am describing, see Ronald G. Walters, *The Antislavery Appeal: American Abolitionism after 1830* (Baltimore, Md., 1976).

[25] J. G. A. Pocock, *The Machiavellian Moment: Florentine Political Thought and the Atlantic Republican Tradition* (Princeton, N.J., 1975).

[26] It is not necessary to claim that the abolitionists were aware of the social origin of their beliefs. Indeed, the very fervor of abolitionism and of humanitarian reform generally came from the conviction that the ideals espoused were timeless and unconnected with any specific social formation. Although historians should take this belief seriously enough to seek to explain its origin, we need not assume that it is correct.

forces in the economy have, in a search for transcendental values, often emphasized the nation, the family, the race, and the soil. In order for self-interest to operate, there must be a sphere from which self-interest is barred.

Without ever expressing this notion in these terms, nineteenth-century Americans were fully aware of the need for a sphere in which self-interest did not operate. Behind most of the political controversies of the antebellum period lay an implicit understanding of this most fundamental problem. The tariff controversy concerned the propriety of selling labor power in factories; temperance disputed the right to sell liquor on the market. Slavery raised the question of the sale of human beings. Generally speaking, those who were willing to sell humans were reluctant to see labor power being bought and sold while those most keen to see the spread of wage labor tended to be antislavery.[27] To allow the sale of labor power was to consent to the most dramatic and far-reaching spread of market relations in society and create a need both for an area from which the market would be barred and for a morality to support the new society. The abolitionist argued that the market must be barred from dealing in human beings so that man himself, with his conscience and his "soul immortal," could become the prop for the new social order. Although these new attitudes are clearly expressed in much of the humanitarian writing of the eighteenth and nineteenth centuries, I shall confine myself to American abolitionists in the last thirty years of American slavery.

"THE WHOLE QUESTION OF THE DUTY OF OPPOSITION TO SLAVERY," declared the American and Foreign Anti-Slavery Society, "rests on the sinfulness of reducing innocent men and women, and their children after them, to articles of merchandise." The use of the word "innocent" implies an optimistic view of humanity. More explicitly, the society condemned the practice of converting "into articles of merchandise . . . beings charged with no crime, made a little lower than the angels, and redeemed by His own blood." Abolitionists frequently referred to man's "immortality" and displayed their contempt for those who blasphemously assigned to it a mere commercial value. Thus Gerrit Smith, in an open letter to Henry Clay, referred to "the abhorrent calculation of the worth in dollars and cents of immortal man," and George Bourne asserted that "to traffic in flesh and blood animated by the reasoning capacities is the greatest practical indignity which can be offered to men as immortals."[28] Abolitionists deliberately juxtaposed references to humanity's higher qualities with the language of trade and commerce in order to emphasize their utter incommensurability. This was the strategy that Theodore Dwight Weld employed in order to direct his readers' attention to the enormity of the slaveholder's sin: "ENSLAVING MEN IS REDUCING THEM TO ARTICLES OF PROPERTY—making free agents, chattels—converting *persons* into *things*—sinking

---

[27] Thus with some exceptions the Democratic party, even in the North, was more tolerant of slavery than the Whig, the party of the tariff and the factory system. See John Ashworth, *"Agrarians" and "Aristocrats": Party Political Ideology in the United States, 1837–1846* (London, 1983).

[28] *An Address to the Anti-Slavery Christians of the United States* (New York, 1852), 3, 2; *Letter of Gerrit Smith to the Hon. Henry Clay* (New York, 1839), 22; [George Bourne], *A Picture of Slavery in the United States of America* (Middletown, Conn., 1834), 35.

27

immortality into *merchandize* ... MEN, bartered, leased, mortgaged, invoiced, shipped in cargoes, stored as goods, taken on executions, and knocked off at a public outcry. Their *rights*, another's convenience, their interests, wares on sale, their happiness a household utensil; their personal inalienable ownership, a serviceable article or a plaything, as best suits the humour of the hour, their deathless nature, conscience, social affections, sympathies, hopes, marketable commodities."[29] Often, abolitionists emphasized that it was above all the human soul that must be placed beyond earthly or worldly considerations. "How can there be room for further wrong," William Alger asked, "when a soul is made a thing?" Eliza Lee Follen told her readers that "he who pretends to own a soul usurps the prerogative of the Almighty," and George Bourne argued that "as no person can possibly offer an equivalent for a human soul, no purchase could ever be honestly made of a rational being." But it was perhaps Harriet Beecher Stowe in *Uncle Tom's Cabin*, surely the most influential antislavery work ever written, who gave fullest vent to the abolitionist's sense of outrage at the attempt to make the human soul a commodity. One of the most powerful passages in the book comes when the narrator describes a slave warehouse in New Orleans. She tells the reader to expect that "you shall be courteously entreated to call and examine, and shall find an abundance of husbands, wives, brothers, sisters, fathers, mothers, and young children, to be 'sold separately, or in lots to suit the convenience of the purchaser'; and that soul immortal, once bought with blood and anguish by the Son of God, when the earth shook, and the rocks rent, and the graves were opened, can be sold, leased, mortgaged, exchanged for groceries or dry goods, to suit the phases of trade, or the fancy of the purchaser."[30] There had to be a rigid separation between those areas of life where the market could rule and those where it was forbidden.

In place of tradition, in place of the stability offered by ownership of one's farm or workshop, the reformer offered the individual conscience. It was an unfailing guide to action. It could not be repressed. Its dictates could not be reasoned away. Referring to a slavetrader, "Uncle" Tom says: "I'm sure I'd rather be sold, ten thousand times over, than to have all that ar poor crittur's got to answer for." Another virtuous character in the novel remarks, "What we are conscience bound to do; we can do no other way." Hence the sinner, as Stowe explains, turned to drink to drown out reflection and the voice of the soul.[31]

Abolitionists generally agreed on the conscience as the underpinning for society. As one of them put it, "our strength all lies in a single force—the conscience of the nation." Even though "all else" was "on the side of the oppressor," this difficulty need not provoke despair, since conscience, "that force of forces when properly instructed, is all, and always, on our side." Wendell Phillips, in the aftermath of John Brown's raid on Harpers Ferry, declared that it was not the old "gray-headed

[29] [Theodore Dwight Weld], *The Bible against Slavery* (New York, 1838), 8.

[30] William Alger, *The Historic Purchase of Freedom, An Oration Delivered in . . . Boston, December 22, 1859 . . .* (Boston, 1859), 8; Eliza Lee Cabot Follen, *To Mothers in the Free States* (n.p., n.d), 2; [Bourne], *Picture of Slavery*, 37; Harriet Beecher Stowe, *Uncle Tom's Cabin: Or, Life among the Lowly* (1852; rpt. edn., London, 1981), chap. 30, p. 467.

[31] Stowe, *Uncle Tom's Cabin*, chap. 7, p. 111; chap. 17, p. 289.

man" himself that made "Virginia tremble." Instead, Virginia "trembled at a John Brown in every man's conscience." In Theodore Parker's view, conscience was "relatively perfect" and "the last standard of appeal." Gilbert Haven believed that conscience was "employed by our Creator as His representative in the soul."[32] From this premise, it followed that people must obey their consciences. "Let every one settle it as a principle," William Lloyd Garrison exhorted his readers, "that his conscience, and not his lay or spiritual leaders, must be his commander." The conscience must "govern the movements of soul and body." To Parker, it was imperative that, having learned from his conscience "the moral law of God," man must obey it. Indeed "nothing can absolve men from this duty."[33]

These beliefs promoted abolitionism in two ways. First, they made it appear abhorrent to trade in, and assign commercial value to, the human conscience. Second, they ensured that antislavery would be pursued in an uncompromising manner and with all the righteousness of a holy crusade. Northerners were in general opposed to slavery, but those who shared this moral absolutism became its severest critics. The conscience would thus be one barrier against the destructive force of self-interest. A second was the home and the family. The nineteenth-century family as described in the novels of Charles Dickens, for example, was preeminently a refuge, a haven from the tumultuous world outside. This was the abolitionist view, too. Without the family, "the world would be nothing better than one scene of pollution and wo." It would be "a wilderness." The family brought to a man "the comfort and solace of wife and children, whatever may betide him in this rugged world." The family home was "the place where we must cultivate all the narrow virtues which cannot bear the cold atmosphere of the outside world"; it was "a sanctum wherein the world has no right to intrude, where the heart may freely expand in every possible manifestation to which Nature prompts."[34]

Abolitionists believed that the family was an essential counterweight to the spirit of selfish acquisitiveness that an increasingly commercial society promoted. At home, a man "forgets this strife, and all the hardness which the world demands of him, living quietly once more." "The effect of common toil, of intercourse with the business of men, as both are now managed," Parker noted, "tends often to harden the man and make him selfish." Yet "the sweet influence of home" was, fortunately, "just the reverse." "The sphere of a man's daily business" made few demands "on his affections, on the loftier and better sentiments of his nature," since those "he finds not necessary to attain his private ends." Home was the "school

---

[32] *Revolution the Only Remedy for Slavery* (New York, 1855), 16; Wendell Phillips, *Speeches, Lectures, and Letters*, 1st series (Boston, 1863), 273; Parker, *Slave Power*, 292; Gilbert Haven, *National Sermons, Speeches and Letters on Slavery and Its War . . .* (Boston, 1869), 9.

[33] *Liberator*, 26 January 1833; Henry C. Wright, *Marriage and Parentage: Or, the Reproductive Element in Man, as a Means to His Elevation and Happiness* (Boston, 1855), 249–50; Parker, *Slave Power*, 292–93.

[34] "Letter of Gerrit Smith to Rev. James Smylie," in *Anti-Slavery Examiner*, 1 (1837); *Mr. Allen's Report of a Declaration of Sentiment on Slavery, Dec. 5, 1837* (Worcester, Mass., 1838), 7; [George Allen], *A Report on American Slavery Read to the Worcester Central Association March 2, 1847* (Boston, 1847), 13; Theodore Parker, *Lessons from the World of Matter and the World of Man* (Boston, 1873), 197; Wright, *Marriage and Parentage*, 308.

for affection and kindly sympathy." It was in the home that "we learn the great lesson of affection, gentleness, tenderness," it was there that "a man learns to trust another, without fear," and in the home, "qualities which our daily calling does not exercise" would experience "a serious and healthful growth."[35]

Abolitionist writers portrayed the family as a potent force for good in the world. The law of conjugal loyalty was "inscribed deep in the nature of man." According to Stephen S. Foster, "the conjugal relation has its foundation deeply laid in man's nature, and its strict observance is essential to his happiness." One anonymous writer declared that marriage was "the most intimate, endearing, and sacred union, that can be formed on earth" so that "a strict and high regard for its sacredness must lie at the foundation of a well ordered and virtuous state of society." Henry C. Wright even went so far as to assert that "in their power over the organization, character and destiny of human beings, the Church is nothing, the State is nothing; religion, government, priests and politicians are nothing, compared to marriage and parentage, to the husband and wife, the father and mother." Wright believed that it was "only in a true home" that "the soul" could "attain its full development in all directions" and there "alone" that "the conscience" could "become a universe of light to guide the soul onward and upward." Theodore Parker reasoned that since "its roots" were "in the primeval instincts of the human race," "the family will last forever."[36]

Abolitionists gave close attention to the relationship between parents and children. They did not simply claim that it was the duty of parents to instill correct moral values into children but expressed a faith in the redemptive powers of children themselves. In an extraordinary passage, Henry Ward Beecher explained the process: "When your own child comes in from the street, and has learned to swear from the bad boys congregated there, it is a very different thing to you from what it was when you heard the profanity of those boys as you passed them. Now it takes hold of you, and makes you feel that you are a stockholder in the public morality. Children make men better citizens. Of what use would an engine be to a ship, if it were lying loose in the hull? It must be fastened to it with bolts and screws, before it can propel the vessel. Now a childless man is just like a loose engine. A man must be bolted and screwed to the community before he can begin to work for its advancement; and there are no such screws and bolts as children."[37] Beecher employed the language of commerce ("a stockholder in the public morality") as well as an extended metaphor that reflected the importance of technology to the age in which he lived. But it was apparent that the process he described depended on the inviolability of the family and required that both home and family be kept strictly separate from the pervasive values of commerce and finance.

[35] Theodore Parker, *Sins and Safeguards of Society* (Boston, n.d.), 209, 211–13;

[36] *Mr. Allen's Report*, 7; Stephen S. Foster, *The Brotherhood of Thieves; Or, a True Picture of the American Church and Clergy* (Concord, Mass., 1886), 11; "A Native of the South-West," *The Family and Slavery*, tract no. 37, American Reform Tract and Book Society (n.p., n.d.), 5; Wright, *Marriage and Parentage*, 276, 291; Parker, *Lessons*, 187.

[37] Beecher quoted in *Atlantic Monthly*, 1 (May 1858): 866.

In this light, slavery presented a spectacle that was profoundly shocking. "The worst abuse of the system of slavery," according to Harriet Beecher Stowe, "is its outrage upon the family." Since the master could buy and sell slaves at will and since slaves could not legally marry, slavery "breaks into the sanctuary of the home." The power the master had over his female slaves meant that the sanctity of his own family was in constant danger. Gerrit Smith claimed that slavery was "essentially and inevitably at war with the family state." Charles Beecher argued that slavery "nullifies the family" and was, as a consequence, "in direct and flagrant opposition to the law of God." He added that it "must excite his deepest displeasure." Another abolitionist declared that "the Family is the head, the heart, the fountain of society and it has not a privilege that slavery does not nullify, a right that it does not violate, a single facility for improvement it does not counteract, nor a hope that it does not put out in darkness." This writer also pointed out that "those who impose and those who suffer the bondage, alike suffer."[38]

Since the abolitionists had rejected many of the institutions of their nation, they necessarily placed a heavy burden on those that they wished to sustain. The family was preeminent among them. Abolitionists believed that the family was redemptive, a means of supplying the altruism that was threatened by the dissolvent force of self-interest. In *Uncle Tom's Cabin*, the head of one (virtuous) family spells out this function: "'Thee uses thyself only to learn how to love thy neighbor, Ruth,' said Simeon, looking, with a beaming face on Ruth. 'To be sure. Isn't it what we are made for? If I didn't love John and the baby, I should not know how to feel for [Eliza].'" By contrast, a vicious individual like Simon Legree, we are told, rejects both conscience and mother. Indeed, had Legree not rejected his mother, he would have been saved from sin.[39] Even as the family was losing its economic importance, it was being asked to assume this other role. Traditionally, writers had been inclined to view society, or at least the local community, as the family writ large. That is, rather than see the family as a refuge from society, ruled by different conventions and norms, they had often viewed society as a family. The family was society in microcosm. As these attitudes came to be revised, the humanitarian crusades of the eighteenth and nineteenth centuries gathered momentum. The heightened concern for the soul and the individual conscience, nourished within the family circle, necessarily intensified the concern for slavery, which disrupted family ties and offered many temptations and opportunities for the slaveholder to sin. (It is interesting to note that drink was also condemned for undermining the family and for silencing the conscience.) In other words, one route from capitalism to humanitarianism was via an altered understanding of home, family, and conscience. Since it was also possible to claim that slavery slowed the pace of

---

[38] Harriet Beecher Stowe, *The Key to Uncle Tom's Cabin* (Boston, 1853), 257; "Letter of Gerrit Smith to Smylie," 41; Charles Beecher, *The God of the Bible against Slavery* (New York, 1855), 3; "A Native of the South-West," *Family and Slavery*, 23.

[39] Stowe, *Uncle Tom's Cabin*, chap. 19, p. 331; chap. 13, p. 220. It is tempting to speculate that a shift was occurring at this time in the locus of moral values, a displacement away from the traditional community, in toward the family and the individual conscience and out toward the nation.

economic advance, it is not surprising that to more people than ever before it seemed an unmitigated evil.[40]

FOR SEVERAL REASONS, AN INTERPRETATION THAT EMPHASIZES WAGE LABOR has more explanatory power than one that focuses on the market. First, as I have indicated, Haskell's view makes a bit of a mystery of the abolitionists' selectivity of concern. On the hypothesis I am proposing, it ceases to be a surprise that the abolitionists accepted wage labor at the same time as they attacked slavery. Indeed, it was precisely because of the spread of wage labor that they attacked slavery in the way they did. Haskell needs to show why a set of attitudes generated by the market made the idea of a market in human beings especially unattractive. The market produced attacks on the market. But to accord causal primacy to wage labor leaves no corresponding difficulty. Second, we are now more easily able to explain a change in values. It is not necessary to claim either that slavery was always regarded as evil (as implied in the starving stranger analogy) or to assume that there is a one-way, causal relationship between changes in recipe knowledge and changes in values. Third, the problem of the South can now be seen not to be a problem at all. A lower level of humanitarian sentiment is precisely what one would expect in a society based on slavery rather than wage labor. Finally, the diverse and contradictory effects of markets in both strengthening and weakening the sense of responsibility cease to present a problem. As Haskell suggested, the market supplied the oxygen. But wage labor was the explosive. While both are necessary, it is an odd explanation of a fire that emphasizes the oxygen rather than the explosive. Indeed, it is the explosive that historians need to handle with care and attention.

[40] It was possible to condemn slavery on either moral or economic grounds, and some individuals pressed one set of criticisms to the exclusion of the other. It was more common, however, for humanitarians to employ the economic arguments, too. A complete explanation of the relationship between capitalism and antislavery must, of course, take account of this. See the works by Howard Temperley cited in note 2.

One group closely involved in wage labor that nevertheless remained indifferent or even hostile to the antislavery crusade was the factory owners of the North who depended for their livelihood on the supply of cotton from the South, a clear case of direct economic interest obstructing the process by which broader economic developments generate ideas.

Convention and Hegemonic Interest in the Debate over Antislavery: A Reply to Davis and Ashworth

THOMAS L. HASKELL

I AM DEEPLY INDEBTED TO BOTH DAVID BRION DAVIS AND JOHN ASHWORTH for reading my essay with such care and responding to it so intelligently and creatively. It is rare to have such acute critics and rarer still to have civil ones. My sense of gratitude to Davis is especially strong because of the obvious dependence of my work on his. But for his research into the problem of slavery in Western culture, the question that my article addressed could not have been formulated. Indeed, because my principal concerns have to do with changing concepts of personal agency and moral responsibility, rather than with the history of the movement to abolish slavery, I am in the position of a rude stowaway in Davis's finely crafted historiographical vessel: not only did I come aboard uninvited, I have even challenged the master's authority by proposing a change of course. For the captain to react to this impertinence by accusing me of sins no worse than "misinterpretation," "reductionism," and "positivistic behaviorism" is, I suppose, better treatment than a stowaway has any right to expect.

Cogent though my critics have been, no one will be surprised to hear that there are aspects of my argument that I think they have overlooked or misunderstood, as well as some that my original essay did not develop adequately. Because Ashworth is something of a stowaway himself (and since he seems little more content with the vessel's present heading than I am) I will examine the differences between Davis and myself before turning to Ashworth's proposal for still another change of course.

DAVIS'S RESPONSE TAKES THE FORM OF A ROUSING REAFFIRMATION of faith in the hegemonic mode of explanation, including especially the self-deception argument that both Ashworth and I find unpersuasive. But, even as Davis reaffirms the hegemonic mode, he severely narrows its scope to a single nation, a limited period, and a certain phase of the antislavery movement, its "acceptance" rather than its

A critical reading of an earlier version of this article by Martin Wiener led to important improvements, for which I am most grateful. All responsibility remains mine.

33

"origin." The effect of this shift of emphasis is to render the argument less vulnerable to objections but also far less ambitious than I and many other readers have assumed that it was originally meant to be.

In most respects, Davis seems little concerned whether we take his current remarks to be a restatement of his original position, a needed clarification of it, or a revision, a redeployment on more defensible terrain. This is as it should be, for Davis's volumes on slavery constitute one of the towering achievements of historical scholarship in our generation, and the author of a continuing project of this magnitude and high level of distinction need not apologize to anyone for changing his mind. But, on one point, Davis's unconcern gives way to a different tone: in regard to a distinction he is now eager to make between the origins of the antislavery movement and its acceptance, he says that I seriously misrepresented his original views—"here Haskell misquoted me."[1] Davis knows better than anyone else what he intended to say, but I did not misquote him. Nor can I even agree that I was mistaken about the spirit of what he actually wrote. To show that this is true and to clear the way once again for the alternative to the hegemonic argument that I am recommending, I must begin by examining the differences between Davis's original position and the one he now occupies.

The hegemonic argument, Davis now says, "fills only a few pages" of a long book and was meant to apply "only to British history in a limited period from the 1790s to 1823, with some brief speculations reaching ahead to the 1830s. I did not extend the concept of hegemony to America or France, where abolition movements emerged in wholly different contexts. Certainly, I advanced no general theory of abolitionism *per se* as an instrument of hegemonic control (although I would claim it was always related to the need to legitimate free wage labor)."[2] This is a puzzling statement. The last sentence, with its highly elastic parenthetical proviso, is its most problematical part, but the first sentence is also surprising. Far from devoting only a "few pages" of *The Problem of Slavery in the Age of Revolution* to the hegemony argument, Davis organized much of the book around it. In his own words, "much of this book will be concerned with the ideological functions and implications of attacking this symbol of the most extreme subordination, exploitation, and dehumanization, at a time when various enlightened elites were experimenting with internalized moral and cultural controls to establish or preserve their own hegemony."[3] In contrast to his original stress on the hegemonic implications of the movement, Davis now minimizes those implications, in form if not in substance, by drawing a sharp distinction between saying that abolitionism was an instrument of hegemonic control and saying that it was "related to the need to legitimate free wage labor." But what substantive difference stands behind this formal distinction? To say that abolitionism is in some degree explicable in terms of the need to legitimate wage labor is to say that it is, in that same degree, hegemonic. Everything

---

[1] David Brion Davis, "Reflections on Abolitionism and Ideological Hegemony," *AHR*, 92 (October 1987): 798.

[2] Davis, "Reflections on Abolitionism," 798.

[3] David Brion Davis, *The Problem of Slavery in the Age of Revolution, 1770–1823* (Ithaca, N.Y., 1975), 48, 49.

therefore depends on what Davis means by "related." If abolitionism is strongly related to the need to legitimate free labor, the parenthetical proviso counts for nothing, and we are right back where we began, with the claim that abolitionism is largely to be understood as an instrument of hegemonic control. If the relation is weak, then abolitionism's hegemonic implications fade in significance, possibly to the vanishing point. Where on this wide spectrum of possibilities does Davis mean to stand?

In the present article, Davis attaches great significance to a distinction between the *origins* of the antislavery movement and its *acceptance* by governing elites. The story of its origins, he says, is the one he told in the first of the three volumes he has published on slavery; it is a tale of the seventeenth and eighteenth centuries, and it concerns authentic religious impulses and radical popular initiatives. None of this, Davis now seems to believe, is much illuminated by the hegemonic argument. Antislavery took on a hegemonic character, according to his current view, only in the 1790s and the early decades of the nineteenth century, when it was appropriated by the aristocratic African Institution, reshaped by wealthy merchant philanthropists, and translated into state policy by conservative governing elites otherwise hostile to social change.[4]

Hegemony was not originally confined to this modest and unobjectionable explanatory role. Consider the following two paragraphs from *The Problem of Slavery in the Age of Revolution*. They present an arresting vision of a dynamic transformation in moral sensibility that defies any neat division into "origin" and "acceptance." Material interests are invoked to illuminate the entire transformation, not a phase of it. It is in connection with these paragraphs that Davis states that he was misquoted.

The diversities of New World slavery should not blind us to the central point. In the 1760s there was nothing unprecedented about chattel slavery, even the slavery of one ethnic group to another. *What was unprecedented by the 1760s and early 1770s was the emergence of a widespread conviction that New World slavery symbolized all the forces that threatened the true destiny of man. How does one explain this remarkable shift in moral consciousness, if it was not a direct response to an innovation of unparalleled iniquity?* Presumably men of the eighteenth century were no more virtuous than men of earlier times, although something might have altered their perception of virtue. No doubt the new antislavery opinion drew on the misgivings and anxieties which slavery had always engendered, but which had been checked by desire for independence and wealth. Yet the slave systems of the New World, far from being in decay, had never appeared so prosperous, so secure, or so full of promise.

The emergence of an international antislavery opinion represented a momentous turning point in the evolution of man's moral perception, and thus in man's image of himself. The continuing "evolution" did not spring from transcendent sources: as a historical artifact, it reflected the ideological needs of various groups and classes [my emphasis].[5]

My summary of these words read as follows: "Like Foucault . . . Davis insisted that the new sensibility 'did not spring from transcendent sources.' Rather, its

---

[4] Davis, "Reflections on Abolitionism," 798–99.
[5] Davis, *Problem of Slavery in the Age of Revolution*, 41–42.

origin, he said, lies in 'the ideological needs of various groups and classes.'"[6] The words I had enclosed in quotation marks accurately reproduce Davis's language. It is evidently my use of the word "origin" in place of "continuing 'evolution'" that he objects to, yet in his own text, the latter term presumably refers back to the previous sentence in which he spoke of the "emergence" of international antislavery opinion and the evolution of "man's" moral perception. How different is "origin" from "emergence?" How can "man's" moral perception be understood to refer exclusively to the perceptions of a British elite between 1790 and 1823?

Not a "source" from which attitudes "spring" an origin? Nothing in the original text suggests that Davis thought that the "origin" of antislavery opinion and its "acceptance" (or "continuing evolution") were distinct chronological phases centered on the 1790s or that they posed crucially different problems of explanation. Davis described, in the two paragraphs quoted above and in the adjacent pages, the emergence in many minds of an unprecedented conviction that slavery constituted an intolerable evil. That conviction, he specifically said, was already "widespread" by the 1760s. He called it a "momentous turning point in the evolution of man's moral perception" and a "remarkable shift in moral conscious- ness," and he took pains to insist that it did not spring from transcendent sources.

He originally invoked "ideological needs" to explain not just the "acceptance" of the movement by conservative governing elites after the 1790s but the entire process by which a deep repugnance for the principle of slavery spread beyond the handful of sectarians and eccentrics who first expressed it and gradually gained strength in ever wider and more influential circles. It was, in Davis's view, ideological needs that prepared a receptive audience, and this effect was being felt before the nineteenth century. "By the eighteenth century," Davis wrote, ". . . profound social changes, particularly those connected with the rise of new classes and new economic interests in Britain and America, created an audience hospitable to antislavery ideology." Although he was always extremely careful to avoid any simple reduction of antislavery opinion to class interest, Davis clearly believed that material interest affected not only the political repercussions of the new sensibility but also the emergence of the sensibility itself: in his own words, "material considerations . . . helped *both* to shape the new moral consciousness and to define its historical effects" (my emphasis).[7]

Any attempt to exempt religion from the hegemonic mode of explanation, or to confine hegemonic considerations to the period after the 1790s or to governing elites, would make a shambles of the interpretation Davis presented in the pivotal chapter of his book, "The Quaker Ethic and the Antislavery International." In that chapter, he ranged brilliantly across the entire last half of the eighteenth century and traced a multitude of interconnections between Quaker organizational skills, religious principles, and concerns about labor discipline. The fabric he wove displays no seam between "origins" and "acceptance." Eighteenth-century Quak-

---

[6] Thomas L. Haskell, "Capitalism and the Origins of the Humanitarian Sensibility, Part 1," *AHR*, 90 (April 1985): 344.
[7] Davis, *Problem of Slavery in the Age of Revolution*, 82, 48.

ers in both England and America, not a nineteenth-century British governing elite, first demonstrated that "testimony against slavery could be a social correlative of inner purity which seemed to pose no threat to the social order—at least to that capitalist order in which the Quakers had won so enviable a 'stake.'" It was also the transatlantic community of Quakers about which Davis was speaking when he formulated the keystone of his entire interpretation, the idea that "as a social force, antislavery was a highly selective response to labor exploitation" and one that "gave a certain moral insulation to economic activities less visibly dependent on human suffering and injustice."[8] If this is not the hegemonic argument, I am at a loss to know what would be.

Ambiguous though his present position is, Davis has obviously abandoned much of the territory he once claimed under the banner of hegemony. In spite of his rousing reaffirmation, a considerable disenchantment with the hegemonic mode of explanation is plainly evident in his attempts to confine it (formally, at least) to a narrower range of events. Although I am a critic of the hegemony argument and believe that some sort of retreat from exposed terrain was in order, I am not convinced that this particular move was the right one to make. The sponsors of the African Institution certainly make a more likely target for hegemonic explanation than do the Quakers, and living in Reagan's America gives us ample demonstration that clamorous attacks on distant evils can function effectively to obscure problems uncomfortably close at hand. But, by confining hegemonic considerations so narrowly, Davis threatens to tear apart the rich and subtle network of connections between consciousness and society that make *The Problem of Slavery in the Age of Revolution* a historiographical landmark.

Discovering non-reductionist ways of relating consciousness to social structure and change is, in my view, the most pressing historiographical issue before us today. And, for all its many drawbacks, the hegemony schema—self-deception and all—did enable Davis to bring the economic developments that we associate with the rise of capitalism into extremely close explanatory conjunction with the new humanitarian sensibility (especially in the lives of the Quakers) without falling victim to either of the excesses that usually spoil efforts to relate conciousness to social structure: he neither disregarded the stated intentions of the reformers nor projected into their activities any implication of conspiracy. So successfully did he navigate the treacherous divide between consciousness and society, in fact, that in spite of my reservations about hegemony, if forced to choose between Davis's original position and the present one, I might well prefer the former. It at least acknowledged the existence of pervasive links between consciousness and society in all phases of the antislavery movement and did not imply that authentic moral innovators—the "originators" of antislavery as opposed to those who merely "accepted" it—must be seen as uncaused causes. I would rather cling to the frail reed of hegemony than accept the claim that shifts of moral sensibility spring from transcendent causes, beyond the power of any social or economic analysis to

---

[8] Davis, *Problem of Slavery in the Age of Revolution*, 251.

illuminate, and then become tainted by material concerns only when they spread to the upper classes.

This is not to say, however, that I find the hegemony model adequate. It grapples with the problem of relating consciousness to society but does not carry us very far toward a satisfying formulation. In logic, if not in fact, its principal appeal ought to be to people who once construed the relation between consciousness and society in classic Marxian terms (and thus were confronted with an anomaly in the failure of conflicting class interests to generate a rising curve of working-class radicalism) but who have come to regard the classic formulation as excessively reductionistic and need an alternative that does not carry them beyond the Marxian pale altogether. Because the Gramscian alchemy acknowledges the existence of pluralism and consensus, even as it transmutes them into proof of domination, it serves—paraphrasing what Erasmus Darwin said about the relation of Unitarianism to Christianity—as a feather pillow, perfect for catching falling Marxists.[9] The fact that people other than falling Marxists, including myself, occasionally find it comforting is attributable less to its intrinsic merits than to the dearth of alternative ways of formulating the relationship between consciousness and society.

The difficulties of the hegemonic mode of explanation are notorious and need no extensive rehearsal here. Its most sophisticated defenders strive to make it more flexible, allowing that there can be "open" as well as "closed" hegemonies and that hegemony need not imply control from the top down but can "bubble up from below." When Jackson Lears writes that "even the most successful hegemonic culture creates a situation in which the dominant mode of discourse—and each visual or verbal text within it—becomes a field of contention where many-sided struggles over meaning are constantly fought out," he succeeds in accommodating the schema to the diversity and complexity of modern society but only at the expense of tacitly acknowledging that hegemonic and pluralistic societies are almost impossible to tell apart.[10]

This mode of explanation is already much too flexible. There seems to be no concrete situation around which it cannot be wrapped. No doubt the upper classes exert a disproportionate influence in cultural matters, but it is specific instances that we need to be able to identify as hegemonic or not, and the question of whether a particular social consensus is "spontaneous" or the product of ruling-class influence, conscious or otherwise, is scarcely ever open to empirical resolution. Even to hope for empirical testability is thought a gauche display of positivism in some circles, but many scholars, including some who have impeccable antipositivist credentials and are eager to see the Gramscian schema work, have acknowledged that the problem is a grave one.[11]

---

[9] Gertrude Himmelfarb, *Darwin and the Darwinian Revolution* (New York, 1968), 15.

[10] T. J. Jackson Lears, "The Concept of Cultural Hegemony: Problems and Possibilities," *AHR*, 90 (June 1985): 587, 591.

[11] Lears, "Concept of Cultural Hegemony," 579; Robert W. Westbrook, "Goodbye to All That: Aileen Kraditor and Radical History," *Radical History Review*, 28–30 (1984): 69–89; E. P. Thompson, *The Poverty of Theory* (New York, 1978), 37–50.

To adopt Davis's practice, which identifies as hegemonic any measure that reinforces ruling-class standards or otherwise stabilizes a regime, would be to make all societies always hegemonic, for any measure short of handing over the reins of power to a new ruling class can—by virtue of the more extreme concessions it forestalls—be said to stabilize and reinforce the status quo.[12] It seems unlikely that rulers ever knowingly destabilize their regimes except for the sake of what they perceive as a higher stability, and even the most dramatic concessions to radical critics can always be construed as co-optation from a standpoint still more radical. Hegemony, by this standard, becomes indistinguishable from governance. I would not claim that this unwanted flexibility renders the concept entirely unusable for explanation, but it does make it highly volatile. Like dry ice, hegemony always tends toward sublimation, becoming merely a diffuse aspect of the human condition rather than a distinct feature of particular societies that one could ever point to in explanation of specific events and actions.

Davis's reply provides a striking illustration of the tendency of arguments in the hegemonic mode to float off in directions that have little to do with historical explanation. He gives as an example of hegemony—indeed, an illustration of "precisely what is meant by 'ideological hegemony'"—the "reinforcement of ruling-class standards" that occurred when radicals were "forced" by the dichotomous terms of the antislavery debate to argue that "in some fundamental respects wage earners were no freer or better off than were slaves." After all, he observes, "there could be no lower standard."[13] Problems abound in this statement. To begin with, I doubt that "forced" is the right word here, either for the degree of restraint felt by radicals or the degree of control over discourse exercised by the rulers. Also, there is room to doubt that people who liken their condition to that of slaves thereby accept a low standard—on the contrary, by rhetorically equating one's own possibly bold demands with the slave's humble plea for liberty, one may be setting a very high standard. Consider the hyperbolic efforts by Thomas Jefferson and other patriots on the eve of the Revolution to characterize British policy as a "deliberate, systematical plan of reducing us to slavery"; surely, this rhetoric did not imply the acceptance of a low standard and neither was it evidence of George III's secure hegemony.[14]

It is in his next paragraph that Davis leaves behind historical explanation altogether and enters a dimension of abstract meanings that is quite detached from any judgment scholars might want to make about how things happened or who was responsible for them. After conceding that abolitionism served in some instances to stimulate radical protest against other forms of oppression, Davis argues that the movement also produced effects that worked in the opposite direction: "analogies with chattel slavery may also have retarded the development

---

[12] Davis, "Reflections on Abolitionism," 809, 808. It should also be noted that if, as Davis now says, "reinforcement of ruling-class standards is precisely what is meant by 'ideological hegemony,'" it becomes very difficult to see how hegemonic considerations can be confined to one country or period. This raises the question of just how far Davis means to go in abandoning hegemony.

[13] Davis, "Reflections on Abolitionism," 809.

[14] Jefferson quoted in Gordon S. Wood, *The Creation of the American Republic, 1776–1787* (Chapel Hill, N.C., 1969), 39.

of a vocabulary that could depict more subtle forms of coercion, oppression, and class rule."[15] Obviously, if anything had the retarding effect Davis describes, it was slavery itself, not the attack on it. If the reformers had withheld their attack, prolonging the life of the institution, a vocabulary suited to more subtle forms of oppression would presumably have been even slower to develop. So Davis cannot mean that in the absence of antislavery rhetoric a refined vocabulary would have developed earlier. Instead, his point, valid and unobjectionable in itself, is simply that as long as people were preoccupied by the stark oppressiveness of chattel slavery, milder forms of oppression seemed minor by contrast, and this condition, which was utterly beyond the control of the reformers, helped discourage other kinds of challenges to the status quo. This tells us nothing about why people attacked slavery, why the movement grew, or even how abolition *per se* contributed to hegemony; Davis is not in this passage trying to give a causal explanation of anything, he is merely savoring an irony, a "moral ambiguity" that inescapably attended the existence and overthrow of slavery. Such ambiguities are well worth noting as long as they are not mistaken for explanatory assertions. The danger is that some readers (all but the most careful, I suspect) are likely to come away with the preposterous impression that this supposed effect is one more of the hegemonic consequences that abolitionists unconsciously intended—that antislavery flourished partly *because* its rhetoric retarded the development of a more extensive vocabulary of oppression.

But the frailties of the hegemonic mode and the degree of Davis's ambivalence about it are of only passing interest. At the heart of the disagreement between Davis and myself is a different way of formulating the relationship of consciousness and society. That there is a relationship—that consciousness is shaped to a great extent by the social situation of the thinker—both of us take for granted. Davis construes the relationship mainly in terms of class interest and relies on self-deception to introduce a saving element of indeterminacy into the linkage between humane intentions and hegemonic consequences. My formulation, while acknowledging the reality of self-deception and not denying that interest plays an utterly indispensable role in the explanation of human affairs, directs attention instead to another factor that is generally ignored: the role played by social conventions, especially those governing causal attribution and thereby establishing the outer limits of moral responsibility. The stress on conventions and skepticism about the explanatory value of self-deception are the two aspects of my thesis that Davis finds most objectionable. Indeed, apart from his claim that I exaggerated his reliance on the hegemonic argument and his empirical complaints that my thesis cannot account for the existence of women abolitionists or the weakness of antislavery in Holland (points to which I will return), his reply consists largely of an impassioned reaffirmation of the reality of self-deception, coupled with warnings about the moral dangers of convention as an analytical category.

Although Davis misunderstands my views on self-deception, he is correct that we are at loggerheads over the issue of convention. I believe that the unprece-

[15] Davis, "Reflections on Abolitionism," 809.

dented surge of humanitarian activity in the century following 1750 can be traced to a shift in the network of conventions that govern the attribution of moral responsibility and personal agency. In my view, such conventions exist in all societies, and they are no cause for dismay: without them, no one could possibly know how to apply abstract moral prescriptions such as the Golden Rule in concrete cases. From Davis's perspective, convention and morality tend to be mutually exclusive, and all talk of convention merely shrouds in an unwholesome neutrality the evils associated with "biased consciousness"—self-deception, selective attention, rationalization, mechanisms of avoidance, displacement, projection, and so on. He seems sincerely to believe that my preoccupation with convention can only shelter evildoers from the blame they deserve and sap our will to resist palpable evils such as the Holocaust and the growing threat of nuclear annihilation.[16] These fears are misdirected.

I HAVE NEVER DOUBTED EITHER THE REALITY OF SELF-DECEPTION or its ubiquity. "The problem with self-deception," I originally wrote, "is not that it is a rare mental state or overly technical term. All of us can recall episodes in our lives when we ignored or denied what now seems the plain and reprehensible meaning of our actions— moments when, to paraphrase what Sigmund Freud said about dreams, we knew what the consequences of our action would be but did not know that we knew."[17] I argued not that self-deception does not exist but that it must be distinguished from other deceptively similar states of mind. Although the *unconsciously intended* consequences that self-deception implies are very different in moral tone and explanatory significance from the *unintended* consequences that make up much of what happens in human affairs, the two are not readily distinguishable empirically. Because every event or condition generates a potential infinity of unintended consequences (think of Cleopatra's nose or the two-penny nail for want of which the battle was lost), it is very difficult to show that a specific consequence belongs not in this immense category but rather in the special and much smaller category of consequences that are unconsciously intended. I said that this difficulty "limited" the utility of the concept for historians, not, in Davis's words, that it "invalidates any historical explanation based on the concept of self-deception."[18]

Davis and I do not disagree about the reality of self-deception but about the sort of warrant a historian needs in order to establish the existence of self-deception in particular cases. Granting, as I always have, that one of the many and often contradictory effects of the attack on slavery was to cast the wage-labor system in a comparatively favorable light, I do not find either in Davis's book or in his reply to my previous article any adequate warrant for his claim that this effect was

---

[16] Davis, "Reflections on Abolitionism," 802.
[17] Haskell, "Capitalism and the Origins of the Humanitarian Sensibility, Part 1," 348–49.
[18] Haskell, "Capitalism and the Origins of the Humanitarian Sensibility, Part 1," 349; Davis, "Reflections on Abolitionism," 801.

41

unconsciously intended by substantial numbers of reformers.[19] Davis still contends that it was and offers as example the case of abolitionist James Stephen, whose blend of sincere humanitarianism and chauvinistic patriotism does not seem to me to cast any light on the question.[20]

Davis also cites as an "obvious example" of self-deception people who respond favorably to advertisements for "lite" beer and cigarettes. "Because the actual effects of smoking cigarettes and consuming alcoholic beverages are well known to the public, the success of the advertisements cannot be attributed simply to ignorance or gullibility," he writes.[21] No doubt self-deception accounts for some of the sales of these products, but would we really want to say that it accounted for all or most of their success? Surely, the ignorance and gullibility that Davis mentions explain a large share, and different attitudes toward prudence and risk aversion—which he does not mention—explain still more. The health risks of smoking pale beside those associated with skydiving, spelunking, rock-climbing and automobile racing, yet these activities do not necessarily entail self-deception. Even daredevils need not deceive themselves; they need only define interest and acceptable risk in eccentric ways. Much less does it require self-deception to smoke cigarettes or drink "lite" beer. Human perceptions vary: some people prize forethought, others value spontaneity; some get their kicks hang gliding, others refuse to fly even in airplanes. Only at the far end of this spectrum, as we approach behavior that is plainly suicidal, do we find a boundary between realistic and unrealistic perceptions of risk that is independent of the perspective of the observer. Only there, it seems to me, can we confidently say that risk-takers deceive themselves. Human interest is less a matter of objective fact and more a matter of subjective interpretation than Davis allows. ›

A similar overestimation of the accessibility of objective knowledge is built into much of what Davis says about self-deception. For example, in summing up his discussion of the subject, he says that we can justifiably speak of self-deception whenever a group of historical actors "believed they were advancing the interests of all humanity when they were actually promoting the interests of a special class."[22] This is not a workable test of self-deception. It ignores the problem of distinguishing between consequences that are brought into being by the actors' unconscious intentions and consequences that are wholly unintended but that

[19] Davis suggests in his reply that his principal concern is not with individual motivation but with "social meanings." This is very hard to reconcile with his ardent defense of the analytical value of the category of self-deception. Self-deception is a vital element of his interpretation precisely because of what it says about the unconscious motivation of individuals. Moreover, meaning resides nowhere but in individual minds: we can speak of meaning as perceived by actors, as perceived by their various contemporaries, and as perceived by us, looking back retrospectively on events—all these discriminations are well worth making, and perhaps these are what Davis has in mind when he speaks of "social meanings." But there is no meaning that resides in society itself. See Davis, "Reflections on Abolitionism," 799, 802.

[20] Davis, "Reflections on Abolitionism," 801. A much harsher side of Stephen emerges in his plans to bring West Indian freedmen under the sway of "the rational predicament"—work or starve—but the harshness of the plan does not in itself tell us anything about unconscious motives. See David Brion Davis, *Slavery and Human Progress* (New York, 1984), 218–19.

[21] Davis, "Reflections on Abolitionism," 801.

[22] Davis, "Reflections on Abolitionism," 802.

happen, in retrospect, to serve the interests of the actors (or fit some interpretation of those interests). The word "actually" also implies in this context the existence of a perspectiveless knowledge that we rarely possess in moral matters. Morally interesting acts ordinarily are susceptible to more than one empirically accurate description, and their moral quality varies with the description given. Davis's statement tacitly assumes that all morally competent people perceive the same objective good and therefore arrive at the same description—unless they deceive themselves. To those of us who are less optimistic than Davis about the availability of objective knowledge, it is virtually a defining feature of the human condition that there is no course of action so pure that its disinterestedness and universality cannot be challenged from some plausible point of view—after all, if liberating slaves does not qualify as disinterested, what would? If no course of action is proof against the charges of interestedness, then, by Davis's test, all moral choices become self-deceptive in some degree or from some point of view. Defined this loosely, the category possesses little discriminatory power.

Davis employs an even looser test of self-deception when he speaks of the sixteenth-century Jesuits in Brazil, who strove to protect Indians from enslavement and mistreatment even while encouraging the slave trade. The historian of the Jesuits, Serafim Leite, argued that, although this choice seems oddly "selective" from our standpoint, it would be wrong to call it unjust, just as it would be wrong to complain that a person who founded a hospital for tuberculosis thereby committed an injustice against the victims of leprosy. Davis disclaims any interest in mere "blame," as opposed to the "moral ambiguities of history," but he makes much of the fact that Leite chose to mention leprosy, a disease historically associated with white prejudice against blacks, and he clearly feels that Leite's judgment on this issue is morally flawed. Presumably thinking in terms of self-deception rather than conscious bias, Davis concludes ominously that Leite "accepts" a traditional distinction that prejudicially singles out blacks as suitable for enslavement.[23]

To see how loose a standard of self-deception Davis is applying here (both to Leite and to the Jesuits), we need only turn the tables. How would we respond if a historian who had devoted his career to the history of slavery (David Davis himself, let us say) was accused on that account of unjustly and prejudicially neglecting the history of the whites' oppression of Indians? Historians' career choices, too, are selective, and certainly one predictable consequence of devoting one's career to the history of slavery is to pass up the opportunity of drawing public attention to the plight of Native Americans.[24] Unconscious intention or prejudice could account for such a choice, and no doubt a speaker for Native American interests, justifiably eager to attract attention to the cause, might feel some temptation to adopt such an interpretation, at least for polemical purposes. "If you

---

[23] Davis, "Reflections on Abolitionism," 804.

[24] The list of opportunities omitted stretches potentially to infinity, as does the stream of unintended consequences that may be said to stem from any act or omission; so the historian in question might equally well be accused of neglecting the Holocaust, nuclear annihilation, environmental catastrophe, and so on.

are not for us, you are against us" is a familiar refrain among activists competing for public support. But it is a fallacy, and, in the absence of other evidence tending to show prejudice, we would, I think, decide that it was not only invalid but frivolous to take the historian's choice of slavery as a sign of prejudice toward Native Americans. The world is overflowing with suffering strangers; choosing to help one does not signify an intention to prolong the suffering of the others. It plainly will not do to claim that people must intend, either consciously or unconsciously, all the consequences that predictably follow from their choices. Some predictable consequences are intended, some are not; the difference, though by no means entirely arbitrary or irrational, is inescapably a matter of convention and cannot be ascertained without close attention to the norms of the relevant community—without attending, in other words, to the range of meanings that a certain culture makes available to its members.

Davis's strongest evidence for thinking that the abolitionists deceived themselves about the hegemonic consequences of their attack on slavery is that some of their contemporaries accused them of exaggerating the suffering of distant slaves while neglecting that of nearby wage-laborers. Davis assumes that, even if the reformers were initially unaware that one consequence of their attack on slavery would be to cast the wage-labor system in a comparatively favorable light, these contemporary critics—proslavery writers on the one hand and radical labor leaders on the other—brought it to their attention. Once they had been made aware of it, Davis assumes that it became part of their intention, unless they specifically disavowed it. In his present article, Davis concedes that, in the face of this criticism, an abolitionist who was genuinely opposed to all forms of oppression might nonetheless have chosen to give priority to the struggle against slavery on the grounds that it was the most "flagrant and remediable" form of oppression, but Davis assumes that "such a course would entail a disavowal of the claims of proslavery writers and at least a private expression of regret over the unintended consequence of extolling free wage labor."[25] Finding in the archives no expressions of regret and taking into account the rapturous extremes to which abolitionists sometimes went in contrasting free labor with slave labor, Davis concludes that the hegemonic implications of antislavery were indeed intended, though only unconsciously.

Why should we find Davis's imputation of hostile (though unconscious) intention any more persuasive than that of the hypothetical Native American advocate above, who sought to advance a worthy cause by accusing anyone who did not embrace it of deliberately opposing it? Is that not what labor leaders like William Cobbett were doing when they lambasted the abolitionists as "the hypocritical sect of negro-loving philanthropists"?[26] Or when they complained, as the *Poor Man's Guardian* reported in 1833, that the slave worked "only 55 hours and had everything provided for his comfort" while "the mechanic of England

[25] Davis, "Reflections on Abolitionism," 800.
[26] Cobbett quoted by Seymour Drescher, *Capitalism and Antislavery: British Mobilization in Comparative Perspective* (New York, 1987), 252 n.41.

44

procured a bare subsistence by 84 hours hard work"?[27] Was anything weightier than this at stake in the accusations of selectivity hurled by the defenders of slavery? Proslavery writers certainly needed no deep insight into the fundamental continuities between free and coerced modes of labor discipline to see that it was to their advantage to accuse their antagonists of hypocrisy and to set the various components of metropolitan opinion against one another by complaining that the self-appointed protectors of the Caribbean slave cared nothing for the suffering of their neighbors. English labor leaders could not fail to see that one way of hitching their own cause to the immensely popular and remarkably successful campaign for abolition was to equate the misery of free workers with that of slaves and to pound away on the selectivity of the reformers.[28] "If you are not for us, you are against us" is a fallacy, but it is a useful one for activists competing for scarce resources.

By accepting the claims of the abolitionists' critics at face value, Davis construes as a dispassionate and objectively true report what may more fruitfully be understood as a familiar rhetorical tactic to change behavior. It is certainly true that when we disapprove of people's behavior and wish to alter it, we often can do so by disregarding their actual intentions and treating them as if the behavior in question could only signify some sort of reprehensible intention. Thus inattentive spouses are routinely accused of spurning their mates; whether the imputed intention is accurate or not is irrelevant to its tactical efficacy. The leverage this tactic is capable of producing one-to-one can be immensely magnified when large numbers of people threaten the same deliberate misinterpretation. This is what happens, for instance, when university trustees are put on notice that the small measure of stability that they have unintentionally supplied to an oppressive regime (South Africa or Russia) by investing in stocks of companies doing business there will henceforth be interpreted as an intended endorsement of that regime and all its worst practices. Deliberately misinterpreting another person's intentions is a shabby way of treating them, but this process of "creative misinterpretation," as it might be called, is no trivial charade, and any movement or political persuasion that abstained from the use of this manipulative strategy would be paying a high price for purity. Cultures can be transformed in this way, and, once the network of conventional meanings available in a culture has been rewoven, by this or other means, the rules for imputing intentionality will have truly been changed, so that what was once an unintended consequence or meaning will conventionally be construed as intentional.

But this change is not accomplished overnight—or in a year or a decade. Culture always remains an arena of contested meanings. More "misinterpretive" projects are always underway than can succeed, and few bring about the permanent transformation they aim at. Until such a project achieves a very substantial degree of success, the instrumentally skewed accounts its supporters give of their opponents' motivation remain just that—skewed accounts or misinterpretations—

[27] Drescher, *Capitalism and Antislavery*, 149–50.
[28] The wide popularity of the movement has been stressed by Drescher, *Capitalism and Antislavery*.

no matter how good the cause. To mistake them all for innocent reports of the truth would inundate historians with a flood of seemingly malicious intentions and render us incapable of understanding what is going on.

Davis's evidence for thinking that the abolitionists unconsciously intended to legitimate free labor by confining their attack to slavery consists essentially of two classes of facts: the first showing that critics advanced this interpretation (or something close enough to it to lend it credibility), and the second that the abolitionists did not take the trouble to disavow in writing the intention to legitimate free labor. Would we accept similar evidence as a basis for judgments about the unconscious intentions of political activists in our own day? Would we agree, for example, that twentieth-century liberals are guilty of an unconscious desire to foster "welfare dependency"—unless they publicly disavow it? If we accept Davis's evidence, it would seem that we should, for dependency is one predictable consequence of welfare programs, and conservatives have not been shy about alerting the public to it. Of course, conservatives, by the same measure, become guilty not only of indifference but of harboring a deliberate intention to inflict hunger and malnutrition on the poor, for these are predictable consequences of cutting back on welfare. Likewise, by Davis's criteria, feminists favoring abortion rights would stand convicted of unconsciously intending the destruction of thousands of fetuses a year, and right-to-life advocates of wanting to repress women and confine them to traditional roles. College trustees who oppose divestment would be guilty of endorsing apartheid and those who march in protest against them of seeking "easy grace." All of us who read and write about slavery, instead of marching against nuclear weapons, would manifest a latent death wish. The list could go on and on, but the drift toward absurdity is clear enough. If we demand no more evidence than Davis provides, no person or group is free of self-deception and malicious intention. Not that all of these imputations of unconscious intention are flatly false; some may be accurate accounts of the motivation of some individuals. Nor am I saying that historians should never adopt the motivational interpretations set forth by one party to a dispute. Instead, if we want the idea of self-deception to carry any analytical weight, historians need stricter criteria. We cannot make sense of human affairs if we treat all predictable consequences of human choice as intentional. Many predictable consequences are neither consciously nor unconsciously intended, and, since culture cannot be transformed overnight, many remain unintentional even when a vocal interest group is hard at work to intentionalize them.

I am wary of self-deception for much the same reason Davis is wary of convention: each of us fears that the other's approach is self-indulgent. Indignation is a powerful appetite, and nothing satisfies it so abundantly as the idea that our opponents are deceiving themselves—that, in their heart of hearts, they perceive moral issues just as we do, and know that we are right to condemn them. By imputing self-deception to those we criticize, we affirm the universality of the standards by which we judge them and set aside the disturbing possibility that the world is one in which equally competent moral reasoners can arrive at conflicting interpretations of right and wrong.

46

Davis's argument presupposes that conscience dictated a single path of moral duty in the era of abolition: opposition to all forms of labor exploitation, whether slave or free. Observing that most abolitionists confined their protest to chattel slavery, Davis wonders (in spite of his admission that slavery was the most "flagrant and remediable" form of exploitation) why they strayed from the path of objective duty. Self-deception is his answer. The question is made necessary by the presupposition that morality is in the fullest sense objective; once we give up the idea that conscience has a single message, we will no longer be puzzled by the abolitionists' failure to take on a larger task than they did, and we will feel little incentive to resort to the idea of self-deception. I will have more to say about selectivity at the end of this article, when I respond to Ashworth's criticism, but for now it is enough to observe that Davis's pivotal question—why were the abolitionists selective in their response to labor exploitation?—is prompted in large part by his apparent conviction that morality is a matter of objective fact rather than interpretation.

WHEN DAVIS WROTE *The Problem of Slavery in the Age of Revolution*, he was more appreciative of the importance of convention than he seems to be now. In spite of the prominence he assigned to self-deception, much of what he originally wrote implied, logically, not that the reformers deceived themselves but rather that their vision was confined within certain conventional limits. For example, when Davis spoke of the reformers furthering the interests of their class only "unwittingly" and said that it would have been "unthinkable" and "inconceivable" for them to recognize the hegemonic implications of antislavery, he gave us a glimpse of a kind of explanation that would not depend on self-deception or unconscious intention and would not necessarily point toward hegemonic interests.[29] "Unthinkability" does not denote self-deception but a meaning that is genuinely unavailable to the actor and is therefore not a part of intention, conscious or otherwise. Similarly, Davis's remark that "prior to the Revolution, few colonists were capable of the imaginative leap of placing themselves in their slave's position" and his observation that "neither Luther nor Calvin . . . had any notion that Christian liberty could alter the fact that some men are born free and others slaves" also acknowledge in convention a constraining power over moral judgment that Davis now seems to find worrisome.[30]

The question of whether morality can be authoritative when it is admitted to have no firmer or deeper base than social convention is, of course, a problem of immense philosophical importance. Neither Davis nor I mean to set up shop as philosophers, but in this regard we unavoidably take well-worn positions in an ancient controversy. I am not sure to what extent Davis would be prepared to treat moral obligation as an objective fact, inherent in the very nature of mankind and the world, timeless in character and therefore not dependent on human consciousness or social convention. But he is certainly closer to that honorable

---

[29] Davis, *Problem of Slavery in the Age of Revolution*, 253, 350.
[30] Davis, *Problem of Slavery in the Age of Revolution*, 279, 44.

tradition of moral philosophy, often identified with Plato and Aristotle, than I am. Although I am not at all in sympathy with the reckless, Derridean assault on "foundationalism" that is fashionable in some literary and philosophical circles, I am enough of a historicist, in the contemporary sense of that term, to believe that human morality is neither natural nor divine but a historical product, and it therefore has an inescapably conventional component.[31]

Temperamentally, Davis and I are not far apart. I lament, as I believe he does, the evasiveness of our current "emotivist" or "therapeutic" culture, in which the word "moralist" has become an epithet, and all talk about moral obligation is liable to be taken as a mask for personal preference. We agree, I believe, that a culture that acknowledges no difference between the statements "I *ought* to do this," and "I *want* to do this"—the former an invocation of objective obligation, the latter a report of merely subjective desire—is in deep trouble.[32] But there is, in my view, no help to be had outside the sphere of history and convention. Notwithstanding the persistent and sometimes eloquent protests of Leo Strauss and others, it is widely acknowledged among philosophers that three centuries of inquiry into the basis of moral judgment have shown that ultimate foundations are not to be found, in nature or anywhere else. Instead, our best hope is to demonstrate that treating morality as conventional rather than natural does not mean we are setting it adrift and leaving it at the mercy of every ripple of fashion and stray breeze of personal whimsy. Convention need not be the same as fashion, and the place of convention in moral judgment can be acknowledged without capitulating to subjectivism. Morality can, I believe, possess a constraining and even objective (at least, non-subjective) quality, even though it is conventional.[33] In one of the most widely influential books of our time, Thomas Kuhn has demonstrated that, when scholars give up the idea that scientific thinking aims at correspondence with an objective reality, timeless and independent of human consciousness, the authority of scientific knowledge is not diminished, the familiar practices of rational debate and justification among scientists are not discredited, and science remains as real, as rational, and as relevant to the conduct of life as ever.[34] I am confident that much the same can be said about moral thinking when we give up the contention that it aims at correspondence with truths that are immune to time and have origins somewhere outside human society.[35]

---

[31] A list of books relevant to this wide-ranging debate that began in literary studies a decade or more ago, and about which historians cannot much longer remain innocent, would be impossibly long. Some exceptionally lucid works are: Jonathan Culler, *On Deconstruction* (Ithaca, N.Y., 1982); Allen Megill, *Prophets of Extremity: Nietzsche, Heidegger, Foucault, Derrida* (Berkeley, Calif., 1985); Gerald Graff, *Literature against Itself: Literary Ideas in Modern Society* (Chicago, 1979); Richard Rorty, *Philosophy and the Mirror of Nature* (Princeton, N.J., 1979); Frederick Crews, "The House of Grand Theory," *New York Review of Books*, 33 (29 May 1986): 36–42; and David Hollinger, "The Knower and the Artificer," *American Quarterly*, forthcoming.

[32] Alasdair MacIntyre, *After Virtue: A Study in Moral Theory*, 2d edn. (Notre Dame, Ind., 1984); Philip Reiff, *The Triumph of the Therapeutic: The Uses of Faith after Freud* (New York, 1966).

[33] I have argued this point at greater length in "The Curious Persistence of Rights Talk in the 'Age of Interpretation,'" *Journal of American History*, forthcoming.

[34] Thomas A. Kuhn, *The Structure of Scientific Revolutions*, 2d edn. (Chicago, 1970).

[35] The preeminent work in recent moral philosophy is that of John Rawls, who specifically rejects "rational intuitionism" and identifies his own position in conventionalist terms: "What justifies a

To demonstrate the large and vital role that convention necessarily plays in our moral thinking, my original article set forth a hypothetical exercise, the "case of the starving stranger," to which Davis and Ashworth give little attention.[36] This exercise embodies the crucial anatomical features of the process that I believe gave rise to the humanitarian sensibility, and anyone wishing to challenge my thesis will find their target here. In particular, I should think that anyone who is disturbed, as Davis is, by the large role I assign to convention, would want to grapple with this exercise and try to explain what it is, if not convention, that allows us to feel that we have lived up to the Golden Rule, even though we render aid to only a minuscule fraction of those in need. This is one of the more elementary lessons taught by the case of the starving stranger: that selectivity is an utterly inescapable feature of humane action in a world that overflows with suffering. All of us, no matter how humane, confine our operative sense of responsibility within limits that fall far short of what we could do to alleviate human misery, and it would make a mockery of the idea of intentionality to say that we "intend," consciously or not, all the suffering we leave unrelieved. An immense gap exists between what a literal interpretation of the Golden Rule would seem to require and what even the best of us actually do and consider sufficient, indeed, admirable. What bridges this gap if not convention? Instead of confronting the problem, Davis brushes it aside, insisting that "selection is seldom neutral" and archly advising us to "be skeptical of the excuse that 'we never knew.'"[37]

We would all prefer to believe that our own moral judgments are a pure exercise of reason, shaped only by the immutable nature of mankind and the world and shared by all whose moral judgment is worthy of respect. It is disconcerting to acknowledge that convention, which is liable to vary incommensurably from one cultural and historical situation to another, sets the stage for judgment, establishes its limits, and channels its direction. Yet this is the implication not only of the case of the starving stranger but also of a familiar truism of moral philosophy, "Ought implies can."

To say that "ought implies can" is, obviously, to say that we do not hold people responsible for doing what they cannot do. Less obviously, the truism also means that our sense of what people are responsible for extends no further than our causal perception. At most, we feel responsible only for evils over which we believe we have causal influence (ones about which we "can" do something), and even this is an outer limit, for there are many evils that we obviously could do something to alleviate for which we do not hold ourselves or anyone else responsible. Because convention enters crucially into what we think we "can" do, the dependence of

---

conception of justice is not its being true to an order antecedent to and given to us, but its congruence with our deeper understanding of ourselves and our aspirations, and our realization that, given our history and the traditions imbedded in our public life, it is the most reasonable doctrine for us. We can find no better charter for our social world. Kantian constructivism holds that moral objectivity is to be understood in terms of a suitably constructed social point of view that all can accept"; John Rawls, "Kantian Constructivism in Moral Theory," *Journal of Philosophy*, 77 (September 1980): 519; *A Theory of Justice* (Cambridge, Mass., 1971).
[36] Haskell, "Capitalism and the Origins of the Humanitarian Sensibility, Part 1," 353–59.
[37] Davis, "Reflections on Abolitionism," 804, 802.

"ought" on "can" carries with it the further implication that convention plays a large role in moral judgment. Cause-and-effect relations pervade our thinking at every level, from high theory to the most mundane affairs of everyday life. They constitute, as one philosopher said, "the cement of the universe."[38] We do not fry an egg, drive to work, or please a lover without drawing on our fund of knowledge about the relation of present acts to future states of the world. But the fund is distinctly cultural. Cause-and-effect relations are not given in raw experience, and what we think we "can" do is very much a matter of interpretation and social convention. Indeed, it is doubly a matter of convention, for convention not only shapes our understanding of cause-and-effect relations (and thus helps define the farthest horizon of our moral vision), it also maps the entire moral landscape within that distant perimeter, specifying which of the many things that we know we could do to relieve suffering we must actually do in order to feel that our lives accord tolerably well with the moral prescriptions of our society. These are what I call our causal horizons.

Let us imagine, for example, that a great earthquake has just occurred, such as that which struck Mexico City in 1985. In a strictly physical sense, I "can" stop writing this essay, fly to Mexico City, and help save at least one endangered stranger's life by lifting debris and performing other emergency tasks. If I took literally the moral rule, "Do unto others what you would have them do unto you," this would seem to be the only acceptable thing to do, for if I were pinned beneath a collapsed building, I would certainly want others to drop their daily routines and come to my aid. Yet I continue working instead of going to the aid of the stranger, and no one accuses me of violating the Golden Rule. Why not? Because, by the prevailing conventions of my time and place, this "can" is not real, not operative. Mexico City is "too far away"; it would disrupt my life "too much." Too far and too much by what measure? Convention supplies the measure. Convention authorizes me to say that I "cannot" help the stranger, at least not in this direct way, even though, in a purely physical sense, I certainly possess the power to do so. This shared, tacit understanding that converts the "can" of physical ability into the "cannot" or "need not" of acceptable moral practice, is a large part of what we mean by convention.[39]

If ought implies can, and "can" is conventional in this sense, it follows inexorably that our concepts of moral responsibility—of what we "ought" to do—are deeply imbedded in social practice and are influenced at least in broad outline by the material circumstances, historical experiences, and technological capabilities of the

---

[38] J. L. Mackie, *The Cement of the Universe: A Study of Causation* (Oxford, 1974).

[39] One's first instinct is to think that anything that eases our conscience about the suffering of others must be a bad thing and that the path to a better world must lead away from such conventions altogether. But a little thought will show that conventions limiting responsibility in this fashion are utterly indispensable; a world without them is quite impossible to conceive. Even the perfect altruist who devotes his or her life to helping others must choose which victims to help first, and, from the vantage point of the victims not helped, the choice will appear "selective." Some sort of limiting convention is inescapable, but of course that does not prevent us from preferring a more inclusive set of limits than now prevails. A valuable exploration of this and related problems is James S. Fishkin, *The Limits of Obligation* (New Haven, Conn., 1982).

50

society in which we live. As our collective circumstances, experiences, and capabilities change, we should expect the limits of moral responsibility to change as well, though not in any simple or automatic manner. The easiest way to illustrate the point is to imagine a radical change in what we "can" do. Obviously, the invention of technology that would enable us to travel to and from Mexico City, or any other scene of disaster, instantaneously and at trivial expense would be very likely to alter the conventions governing moral responsibility in our society, making the passivity that convention now authorizes quite unacceptable, at least in some circles. If we could save someone's life by merely reaching out to press a button, we would be monsters not to do so. A more familiar example of an innovation in institutional "technology" that induces people to make a (nominally) humane gesture they would not otherwise have made is the "Live Aid" rock concert; another, of a much more substantial sort, is the creation of an organization such as Amnesty International that collects funds, publicizes abuses, and provides a new means of exerting influence. Projects of "creative misinterpretation" by large groups of people can have the same effect. Any change in the practices of our society that stretches our causal horizons and expands the sphere within which we feel we "can" act, has the potential to transform what we hitherto perceived as "necessary evils" into remediable ones, thereby exposing us to feelings of guilt and responsibility for suffering that previously aroused only passive sympathy—like the sympathy we feel today for distant earthquake victims who are "too far away" to help. This is the sort of change that I believe accounts for the emergence of the humanitarian sensibility in the eighteenth century.

Because Davis and Ashworth have rival claims of their own to advance about the determining influence that material interest exerts on moral judgment, it is amusing that each wraps himself in the tattered mantle of voluntarism to complain that my mode of explanation is deterministic. Davis throws in for good measure the all-purpose, academic perjorative of our era, "positivistic"—in spite of crediting mankind with much fuller access to positive moral knowledge than I do.[40] I plead guilty to a few overzealous rhetorical flourishes in my original essay that may have exaggerated the explanatory completeness of my scheme, but the scheme itself is not deterministic.[41] The three propositions that "ought" depends on "can," that "can" is largely defined by convention, and that convention is deeply imbedded in social practice—thus making "ought" indirectly contingent to some degree on changing social practices—will no doubt be unsettling to anyone who assumes that moral judgment is an unconditioned exercise of reason aiming at the apprehension of timeless absolutes or Platonic essences. But acknowledging these things does not subvert consciousness or reduce moral choice to a phenomenon of a lower order.

---

[40] John Ashworth, "The Relationship between Capitalism and Humanitarianism," *AHR*, 92 (October 1987): 820; Davis, "Reflections on Abolitionism," 801, 802, 809–10.

[41] I do not share the curious confidence widespread among historians today that "deterministic" accounts of human affairs must be wrong and "voluntaristic" ones right, as if the question of free will and determinism had been solved once and for all. If my account were deterministic, I would defend it as such. But it is not.

My scheme of explanation requires only that we admit that moral thinking, like all thinking, is carried on within a mutable framework of assumptions about what the world is and how we relate to it. The scheme is probabalistic rather than mechanistic, and it applies in the first instance to collectivities rather than to individuals. Good Samaritans go back as far as our records go, and I stipulated from the outset that I was not trying to explain their existence. "We are not concerned," I wrote, "with individual episodes of human kindness and decency—which I assume can occur anywhere, anytime—but with a sustained, collective pattern of behavior in which substantial numbers of people regularly act to alleviate the suffering of strangers. That, I take it, is what we mean by the emergence of a new humanitarian sensibility in the eighteenth century."[42] And that is what I set out to explain. Far from denying the authenticity of the reformers' moral outrage or rendering epiphenomenal their choices or values, my purpose has been to protest the transmogrification of all these lively and productive states of mind into monotonous shades of class interest.

If my aim had been to present a full descriptive account of the emergence of antislavery, I would of course have had to write a book instead of an article and devote much more space than I did to Evangelical piety, Quaker earnestness, the ambitions of artisans for independence, and many other subjects. My aim instead has only been to suggest a better way to conceptualize the rich body of evidence and interpretation that Davis and other specialists have already assembled and which I take as the descriptive foundation for my argument.

I have tried to identify a threshold in the perception of personal agency and responsibility, one that helps us make sense of the most striking finding of Davis's first volume on slavery: namely, that before the eighteenth century practically no one, no matter how compassionate or scrupulous, regarded slavery as an intolerable evil. To see the significance of this threshold, it is important to be clear about what was novel in the eighteenth century. The novelty was active opposition to the institution of slavery, based on the conviction that it was an intolerable evil, not recognition that the slave's lot was a bitter one. The suffering of slaves had long been recognized. John Locke, father of liberalism, who invested in the Royal African company and wrote slavery into the Fundamental Constitutions of Carolina, was perfectly aware that it was a "vile and miserable" state of being. As early as the thirteenth century, the authors of *Las Siete Partidas*, a model legal code that specifically authorized slavery and influenced later legislation in the slaveholding societies of Spain and Spanish America, acknowledged that "slavery is the most despicable thing which can be found among men, because man, who is the most noble and free creature . . . is placed in the power of another."[43] The myth of the contented slave of course propped up many a slaveholder's conscience,

---

[42] Haskell, "Capitalism and the Origins of the Humanitarian Sensibility, Part 1," 360.

[43] Herbert S. Klein, "Anglicanism, Catholicism, and the Negro Slave," in *The Debate over Slavery: Stanley Elkins and His Critics*, Ann J. Lane, ed. (Urbana, Ill., 1971), 142. Theoretical considerations aside, the document also contains the observation that the actual condition of Moorish slaves in Spain was "the most miserable that men could have in this world"; David Brion Davis, *The Problem of Slavery in Western Culture* (Ithaca, N.Y., 1966), 103, 118.

but in every slave regime some people were morally perceptive enough to recognize that slaves suffered—not only when their masters violated local standards of decency but always, even under the best of material conditions, simply because they were "in the power of another." This moral perspective, which recognized that slaves suffered and acknowledged that it was bad for people to suffer and yet tolerated slavery, seems alien to us. Why, in a culture that had long identified humanity with spiritual autonomy, and ethical conduct with reciprocity, did practically no one before the eighteenth century interpret the Golden Rule to require active opposition to the very institution of slavery? Or, to put it another way, why, in a culture that has long honored the Golden Rule, does recognition that slaves suffer have such a long history and opposition to slavery such a short one?

The answer was once sought in the idea of progress, the happy faith that civilization has its own inner dynamic, carrying mankind to ever-higher plateaus of moral knowledge and ability. We have, for good reasons that need no rehearsal here, grown skeptical of the cozy assumption that we moderns abolished slavery because of our superior insight into the requirements of morality. A second possibility lies at the level of explicit appeals, sermons, and speeches. But the answer cannot be found exclusively or even mainly here. There were many such appeals, of course, and they played an indispensable part in mobilizing opposition to slavery. Any fully descriptive account of the history of the antislavery movement would necessarily allot much space to them. Had no one ever preached that slavery was evil, it would be with us still. But to treat explicit preaching against slavery and in praise of benevolence as the sufficient cause of the widening circles of humanitarian reform activity that history records in the century after 1750—and not to ask why such preaching emerged then and why the message was warmly received—would be to beg the most vital questions. Prescription is certainly a proximate cause, but nothing bars us from inquiring into the cause of a cause: what unleashed this avalanche of prescription? What enabled an avalanche of words to trigger in turn a flood of emotion and expressive action? The rule of reciprocity that the Golden Rule embodies is so central to moral judgment that everything else that can be said by way of prescribing moral duty is gilding the lily. The idea of reciprocity was not new; it had been available in the form of biblical precept for at least two millennia, and by itself it provided an adequate *prescriptive* basis for devoting one's entire life to the liberation of slaves. If prescriptions of moral duty had been enough, the history of opposition to slavery would have begun long before the eighteenth century. That it did not suggests that the cause of the sudden surge of humanitarian activism in the eighteenth century was not fundamentally a matter of prescription, no matter how indispensable prescription may have been to the outcome.

A more likely place to look for the answer to our question lies in the conventions that define personal agency, set practical limits to responsibility, and broadly determine specific interpretations of abstract moral prescriptions like the Golden Rule. We cannot literally do for every suffering "other" what we would have others do for us, and without conventional guidelines to limit and specify our respon-

53

sibilities, we would not know what it means to "be good." The conventions that prevail in Western culture today enable us to feel that we live by the Golden Rule even though we actually render aid to only a minuscule fraction of the world's needy people—only that fraction so centrally located within our sphere of causal influence that not to help them would seem abnormal, a departure from the level of care that we routinely achieve in our everyday affairs. Our ancestors were also guided by convention, but, because the fabric of everyday affairs in which we are enmeshed is very different from the one they knew, we have no reason to think that the causal conventions that shape our operative limits of responsibility today are the same ones that prevailed two centuries ago. The causal imagination feeds on the recognition that things could be other than they are and that we know how to alter them. Behind every observation that "x causes y" is a hypothetical annihilation in which x, the cause, is imagined not to exist: "in the absence of x, no y" is the violent fantasy from which each judgment of causal relationship springs. This hypothetical violence comes more readily to us than to our ancestors. We live in a society that is rife with change, that preens itself on the range of options it holds out to each of its members, and that routinely puts in human hands dramatic powers to come, go, move, do, build, destroy, and otherwise transfigure the world that were scarcely dreamed of before the eighteenth century.

If, as I suppose, the conventions that prevailed before the eighteenth century confined what people thought they could do within much narrower limits than ours—if, in other words, their conventionally defined sphere of causal influence excluded much that ours now includes—there would be nothing surprising in their failure to take action against slavery and other evils that we construe as remediable. This difference between their conventions and ours would explain why even the most scrupulous moralists could acknowledge the misery of slaves and even feel a passive sympathy for them without feeling any obligation to take action against the institution that made them miserable—all the while being sincerely devoted to the Golden Rule. Just as causal conventions allow us to have clear consciences today about the starving strangers and earthquake victims whom we omit to help because they are "too far away," so, I suggest, a different set of conventions once made the misery of slaves seem equally far out of reach. Before substantial numbers of people could feel outraged by the very existence of slavery and take action designed to uproot it (which, again, is not at all the same thing as feeling passive sympathy or protesting particular instances of mistreatment, attitudes that leave the institution itself unchallenged), they had to be able to impute to themselves historically unprecedented powers of intervention and to perceive hierarchical social arrangements and institutional structures not as reflections of God's will or manifestations of nature's own order but as contingent, malleable phenomena open to human influence and correction.[44] This is just another, more familiar, way

---

[44] As Davis observed in his first volume on slavery, the middle years of the eighteenth century "represented a turning point in the history of Western culture. To both religious and secular writers the period brought an almost explosive consciousness of man's freedom to shape the world in accordance with his own will and reason. As the dogmas and restraints of the past lost their compelling force, there was a heightened concern for discovering laws and principles that would enable human

of saying that an upheaval had to occur in the conventions governing the attribution of causation and responsibility. One result of upheaval would have been to transform what had been perceived as "necessary evils" into remediable ones, thereby imposing on certain sensitive souls a compelling sense of obligation to remedy miseries that had in all prior human history evoked no more (and usually less) than passive sympathy, even from the most scrupulous and compassionate moralists.

Does this scheme of explanation make human beings "passive automata wholly programmed by 'society,'" as Davis suggests?[45] Certainly not. We do not detract from the honor due those hardy souls who first perceived slavery as a remediable evil by observing that equally compassionate people in previous centuries did not respond to the same facts in the same way, or by suggesting that people could not have responded as the reformers did until they felt, accurately or not, that they had knowledge of cause-and-effect relations sufficiently complex and far-reaching that they could readily imagine a course of practical action capable of uprooting one of the most ancient and interest-bound institutions in their society. To say that it took a shift of causal conventions to push people over this threshold and place slavery (and much else) on the agenda of remediable evils, making possible the collective action historians call "humanitarianism" does not reduce humane sentiments to something lower or undermine in any way the subjective sense of freedom to choose between perceived options that we all normally feel. The only vantage point from which my scheme must appear comparatively deterministic is, that of a reader who (boldly) believes that mankind is free not only to choose between perceived options but also to choose which options to perceive, for my causal explanation extends only to what people perceived the outer limits of their responsibility to be, not to the choices they made in light of that perception.[46]

To contend that the moral perceptions that were constitutive of humanitarianism did not exist before the eighteenth century and could not have become available until certain historical conditions were met is no more deterministic, in the ordinary sense of that word, than observing that a person cannot jog while seated, play bridge without a deck of cards, perform a lifesaving tracheotomy without medical training, or understand what inflation is without having lived in a monetary economy. To ask that our moral judgments and perceptions be

---

society to be something more than an endless contest of greed and power. This quest for moral assurance led inevitably to examinations of inequality, sovereignty, and servitude"; Davis, *Problem of Slavery in Western Culture*, 485.

[45] Davis, "Reflections on Abolitionism," 802.

[46] Ashworth fears that my scheme falls victim to "technological determinism" because it does not allow for the possibility that people might first feel responsible for suffering and then seek means (technologies) for doing something about it. Ashworth fails to recognize that no one can "feel responsible" (operatively responsible, as opposed to feeling passive sympathy) for suffering whose knowledge of cause-and-effect relations is so limited that he or she cannot imagine any course of action that would relieve the suffering. Responsibility presupposes possession of some threshold level of recipe knowledge, and the entire point of my scheme is to account for the crossing of that threshold. It is of course true that once a person feels responsible, he or she is then free, within limits, to seek appropriate means to relieve the pain, but the very fact of feeling responsible means that the critical threshold that should interest us historically has already been crossed. See Ashworth, "Relationship between Capitalism and Humanitarianism," 820.

independent even of conditions like these would be to ask for a sort of freedom that the world cannot deliver and that we do not need.

NOTHING HAS SEEMED MORE SHOCKING TO MY CRITICS than my suggestion that the capitalist marketplace had something important to do with the establishment of these cognitive preconditions for the emergence of the humanitarian sensibility. Their astonishment is ironic, since the role I assign to capitalism is a good deal smaller and less direct than the one Davis assumes. Instead of treating the antislavery movement (or at any rate, its acceptance by the powerful) as a refraction of class interest, unconsciously aiming at the legitimation of a new, ostensibly free, system of labor discipline, I argue that the market merely had the incidental effect of expanding the sphere of causal perception within which everyday affairs proceeded, pushing people over a threshold of perception such that the most sensitive moralists among them no longer found passive sympathy an adequate response to the misery of slaves. The point of departure for my argument was the conviction prevalent among historians that the concomitance of capitalism and abolitionism, though paradoxical, was not coincidental. Taking for granted the existence of some connection, I set out to rethink what it might be, other than class interest. My conclusion that capitalism contributed to the freeing of the slaves "only a precondition, albeit a vital one" does not assign capitalism a very large role in the emergence of the humanitarian sensibility.[47] Had there not already been a debate in progress over the relationship between capitalism and antislavery, I am not at all sure that I would have assigned capitalism a role even that large, for, unlike many of the participants in this longstanding controversy, I have no interest at all in chalking up points "for" or "against" capitalism.

From my perspective, the question that most needs answering concerns the history of causal perception: why did social problems that once appeared intractable take on, in the eighteenth century, an appearance of unprecedented plasticity? Capitalism enters the picture only insofar as it helps answer that question. After centuries during which the misery of slaves was treated with indifference, or at most as a necessary evil, something produced an outward shift in the conventionally defined sphere of causal perception, such that some unusually acute moral reasoners began finding it easy to imagine a course of action leading to the destruction of slavery—so easy that not to embark on it seemed a dereliction of moral duty. What was it that produced this crucial expansion of the sphere of causal perception within which people assessed their responsibility for the suffering of strangers?

My crucial claim in this regard is that the market was one of the major factors in the expansion of causal horizons. Pivotal though the claim is, Davis and Ashworth put up surprisingly little resistance to it. As Davis says, "there can be no doubt that the market tended to teach people to keep their promises and attend

---

[47] Haskell, "Capitalism and the Origins of the Humanitarian Sensibility, Part 2," 563.

to the remote consequences of their acts."[48] This concession is more important than Davis recognizes. Given the dependence of "ought" on "can," and "can" on conventions of causal attribution, the tendency of the market to widen causal horizons gives us a way of accounting for the concomitance of capitalism and abolitionism that relies neither on naive concepts of moral progress nor on class interest cunningly disguised as altruism. Capitalism and humanitarianism seem antithetical—and their concomitance puzzling—because of the divergence of the sentiments on which each rests. Capitalism fosters self-regarding sentiments, while humanitarianism seems other-regarding. What can account for the parallel development in history of two such opposed tendencies? The mystery fades considerably once we recognize that, in spite of their divergent properties, capitalism and humanitarianism also have something important in common: both presuppose the existence of wide causal horizons. Both depend on people who attribute to themselves far-reaching powers of intervention. Neither can flourish unless it can enlist the energies of people who display a strongly self-monitoring disposition, people who routinely allow their behavior in the present to be shaped by obligations incurred in the distant past and by anticipations of consequences that lie far in the future. People who dwell only in the present and attribute to themselves little power to alter the course of events live in a world that cannot sustain either a market-oriented form of life or the acute sensations of moral responsibility that Nietzsche derisively associated with the "bad conscience" of the humanitarian reformers. And, although humanitarianism has no means of bringing into existence the type of "conscience-ridden" personality it needs, capitalism, through the disciplinary mechanism of the market, has a very considerable power to do just that.

It would, of course, be absurd to credit the market with the power of bringing this personality type into existence by itself. The point of my previous article was to show that capitalism and humanitarianism both presuppose a population imbued with the habit of remote causal attribution and therefore that their concomitance can be accounted for without construing humanitarianism as a reflex of class interest. I did not claim that capitalism was the sole source of the humanitarian sensibility. Humanitarianism and the personality capable of sustaining it were the outcome of a "civilizing process" that extended over many centuries and resulted at least as much from religious and political developments as from anything economic. Christianity's definition of the person as a potentially immortal, but immaterial, soul, temporarily housed within a corruptible, material body, is eloquent testimony to the antiquity and the centrality in Western culture of the aspiration toward overcoming the self and transcending impulse. No market ever held out any reward for delay of gratification that could compare with that which Christianity held out to those who could learn to live for the future: eternal salvation.

At a completely different level of analysis, Norbert Elias has made a strong case for the importance of geographically extensive monopolies of physical force. Only

[48] Davis, "Reflections on Abolitionism," 811.

the emergence of such monopolies in the medieval period, he contends, permitted the crystallization of networks of functional dependence within which social constraints could achieve enough force and steadiness to be internalized as self-restraint. "The moderation of spontaneous emotions," he argued, "the tempering of affects, the extension of mental space beyond the moment into the past and future, the habit of connecting events in terms of chains of cause and effect—all these are different aspects of the same transformation of conduct which necessarily takes place with the monopolization of physical violence, and the lengthening of the chains of social action and interdependence. It is a 'civilizing' change of behavior."[49] The political rigors of living at court and taking part in courtly intrigue no doubt did more to convert warriors into calculating courtiers than either religion or any economic institution of the age could, and yet Elias recognizes that what life at court once did to induce foresight in a handful of warrior aristocrats was, in the eighteenth and nineteenth centuries, extended to a much larger sector of society by the trade networks and functional dependencies of an increasingly interdependent economy. Even then, of course, the market could shape personality to its needs only within limits established by traditional religion and morality and only within a framework of legal order and comparative political stability supplied by the state.

The market reinforced the long-term drift of Western culture toward vigorous self-surveillance and far-flung causal horizons, and these tendencies were magnified still further by contemporary events such as the scientific revolution of the seventeenth century, the dramatic technological feats of the next two centuries, and the eruption of political revolutions in France and North America. Nothing could have done more to stimulate the causal imagination or to dispel illusions of immutability (sides of the same coin) than the sight of a world of ranks turned topsy-turvy. But revolutionary acts presuppose a high degree of confidence that the world is open to alteration, and the humanitarian sensibility did not make its first appearance in 1776 or 1789. As Karl Marx observed, capitalism had long been teaching, in a subtle yet compelling way, much the same lesson about mutability that revolution taught: "All that is solid melts into air, all that is holy is profaned."[50]

Although Davis and Ashworth accept the idea that the market helped expand causal horizons, they seem not to understand that this effect in itself sheds much light on the concomitance of capitalism and humanitarianism and establishes a linkage between "base" and "superstructure" that does not rely on the concept of interest. I contend that the market, by expanding causal horizons, helped bring into existence a perceptual world in which some people—those who would have been distinguished for their exceptional conscientiousness in any case—began defining their own responsibility for suffering so broadly that they, unlike their equally scrupulous predecessors in earlier generations, could no longer witness the misery of slaves with merely passive sympathy. Attributing to themselves great

---

[49] Norbert Elias, *Power and Civility: The Civilizing Process*, vol. 2, Edmund Jephcott, trans. (New York, 1982), 236.

[50] Marx quoted in Marshall Berman,"'All That Is Solid Melts into Air': Marx, Modernism, and Modernization," *Dissent*, 25 (Winter 1978), 54–73.

powers of intervention, they also found themselves exposed to acute sensations of guilt and responsibility-by-omission for evils whose causes had previously seemed inaccessibly remote to everyone, even the most sensitive moralists.

In contrast to this explanation, in which the idea of a perceptual threshold figures prominently, Davis and Ashworth seem to believe that, in my view, the market acted unilaterally and mechanically to bring about a general improvement in the morality of those subject to its influence, converting sinners into saints. They impute to me a theory in which the market functions like a source of benign radioactivity: the closer a person is to it and the longer exposed, the greater the dosage of humane impulses—no matter what the person's values, character, religious convictions, ethical commitments, gender role, material interests, or state of mind. This is the theory that Davis evidently has in mind when he contends that my scheme cannot explain the presence of women in the antislavery movement (because they were comparatively uninvolved in the market) and suggests that my theory should lead us to expect slavetraders to have been converted to the antislavery cause (because they were directly involved in market transactions).[51]

I took considerable pains in my original article to guard against this sort of misinterpretation, especially in the "case of the starving stranger," where the idea of humanitarianism as a threshold phenomenon is developed at some length. It was the "radioactive" view of the market's function that I was rejecting when I wrote that "the argument presented here is not that markets breed humane action but that in the particular historical circumstances of late eighteenth-century Anglo-American culture the market happens to have been the force that pushed causal perception across the threshold that had hitherto made the slaves' misery (and much other human suffering) seem a necessary evil."[52] That was also the view I meant to reject when I stressed that John Woolman's pioneering antislavery work presupposed both exceptionally wide causal horizons and exceptional moral standards and yet again, when I acknowledged that most of those whose horizons expanded took the occasion only as an opportunity to pursue self-interest at a higher pitch.[53]

That slavetraders did not become abolitionists and that women often did would tend to disconfirm an explanatory scheme which held that markets uniformly induce humane behavior in those most closely exposed to them, regardless of all other influences. But the scheme I set forth holds no such thing. In view of the longstanding identification of femininity with compassion and moral rectitude, I see nothing at all surprising or disconfirming about the prominence of women in the antislavery movement (or about the prominence of people of deep religious convictions, of a comparatively rigid moral temperament, or of a fairly high level of aggressiveness and self-confidence). For women as well as men, the key question remains why indifference and passive sympathy for slaves gave way in the eighteenth century to active opposition to the institution of slavery. Anyone

[51] Davis, "Reflections on Abolitionism," 812.
[52] Haskell, "Capitalism and the Origins of the Humanitarian Sensibility, Part 2," 563.
[53] Haskell, "Capitalism and the Origins of the Humanitarian Sensibility, Part 1," 353–59; "Capitalism and the Origins of the Humanitarian Sensibility, Part 2," 565–66, 562–63.

seeking the answer to that question would have to take the stereotype of the separate spheres very literally indeed to think that women were not influenced by the market (or that men were not influenced by the domestic sphere). To say as Davis does that women "were not subject to . . . market discipline" is to construe the cultural impact of the market too narrowly.[54]

As for the idea that the market had the power to transform callous people into ethically sensitive ones, or slavetraders into abolitionists, I am unable to find any statement in my essay remotely capable of encouraging such a preposterous inference. Of course, the market did not exist in a vacuum or act on its subjects unilaterally—nothing in the universe of human affairs does. The market was only the keystone for an entire way of life, one in which radicals could be as deeply immersed as entrepreneurs and about which women could become as conversant as men. Like other complex institutions, the market determined nothing rigidly but channeled conduct by encouraging some perceptions and discouraging others. Like poems and rainy days, the experiences it induced were open to a range of interpretations, and the interpretation given to them varied with the personal history of the interpreter. Quakers, prosperous artisans, and other members of the middle class were among the earliest to adopt this way of life, and it is no coincidence that it was from among these groups that some of the earliest antislavery leaders emerged, but a person did not have to cut deals, sign contracts, dispatch bills of lading, or mobilize a work force in order to see the world in an altered perspective and experience the heightened sense of agency that is relevant to my form of explanation. Nor today is it necessarily airplane pilots and computer operators who best grasp the revolutionary cultural implications of the innovations they superintend. The market did not make anyone "good." The market does not help explain why some people conducted themselves morally but why moral conduct was redefined in some circles to include root-and-branch opposition to slavery, a problem previously construed as intractable.

Of the three efforts Davis makes to test my thesis empirically, the first two, concerning women and slavetraders, seem to me very wide of the mark, but the third is more interesting. Assuming that Holland was a strongly market-oriented society, Davis takes the weakness of the antislavery movement in Holland to be an argument against my thesis. His point is well taken: if the advance of a market-oriented way of life is what pushed Britons and Americans over the threshold into a new moral universe, why was the same effect not felt in Holland? The Dutch case is well worth further exploration, but we must begin by noting that it poses no more of a problem for me than it does for Davis. He, after all, *should* find it puzzling that the Dutch bourgeoisie passed up the opportunity to legitimize wage labor, accumulate moral capital, and bolster its own self-esteem by attacking

---

[54] Davis, "Reflections on Abolitionism," 812. To see how easy it would be to exaggerate the gender specificity of the market's impact on culture, one need only think of the centrality of the concepts of covenant and contract in English political philosophy and religion. A recent important work on religion is David Zaret, *The Heavenly Contract: Ideology and Organization in Pre-Revolutionary Puritanism* (Chicago, 1985). For a very broad construction of the cultural impact of the market, see Jean-Christophe Agnew, *Worlds Apart: The Market and the Theater in Anglo-American Thought, 1550–1750* (New York, 1986).

slavery. If Anglo-American capitalists were unconsciously attracted to antislavery agitation because it "gave a certain moral insulation to economic activities less visibly dependent on human suffering and injustice," why did Dutch capitalists not feel the same attraction?[55]

From both Davis's vantage point and my own, the Dutch case can fairly easily be distinguished from the Anglo-American one by pointing to the decidedly paternalistic temper of Dutch political life and to the very marginal role that slave labor played in the Dutch economy. Relying only on the same essay that Davis cited by the Dutch historian P. C. Emmer, we can see that the slave trade to the Dutch colonies in the New World had nearly ceased as early as 1773, not because of agitation but because of diminishing returns. About 36,000 slaves lived under Dutch control when emancipation came in 1863, and in the 1840s the trade between the principal slave colony, Surinam, and the Netherlands amounted to only about 1.5 percent of the Dutch gross national product. Even when Dutch consumers drank slave-grown coffee sweetened with slave-produced sugar, they were relying largely on imports from plantations beyond the control of their government. In the interval running from about 1800 to 1813, slavery was a "purely academic issue in the Netherlands" because during those years all of the Dutch slaveholding colonies were controlled by the British.[56]

There may be some sense in which the Dutch deserve their reputation as a market-oriented people, but, if so, their political culture in the era of abolition was curiously lacking in the liberalism that is generally taken to be the paramount political expression of market culture and capitalist hegemony. Emmer reported that "the ideology of political and economic liberalism found few adherents in the Netherlands" and noted that in 1840 the king was so determined to resist popular initiatives of any kind that he refused even to receive a petition by the British Anti-Slavery Society—one that was accepted by all the other monarchs of Europe except the Sultan of Turkey. The king seems to have been not so much concerned to defend slavery as to retain control over its eradication, for, although the details of compensation were drawn out, emancipation was taken for granted as an inevitability by the government after 1844 and by slaveowners as well after 1852.[57] My thesis would be severely challenged by evidence of a truly market-oriented society whose members continued to see slavery as nothing worse than a necessary evil, but that is not what the Dutch represent. On the contrary, support for slavery seems to have evaporated in spite of the absence of any strong, indigenous antislavery movement. The Dutch case is an odd one, and further investigation

[55] Davis, *Problem of Slavery in the Age of Revolution*, 251. Davis might argue that it was not capitalists generally who sought to legitimize wage labor but industrial capitalists, and that the Dutch bourgeoisie was predominantly mercantile. Before one could assess such an argument, one would need to know more about the Dutch economy than has been brought forward so far. Merchants need wage labor, too, and it would not be at all easy (judging from what Davis has written in *Problem of Slavery in the Age of Revolution*) to show that Anglo-American abolitionists owed more to industrial than to mercantile wealth.

[56] P. C. Emmer, "Anti-Slavery and the Dutch: Abolition without Reform," in *Anti-Slavery, Religion, and Reform: Essays in Memory of Roger Anstey*, Christine Bolt and Seymour Drescher, eds. (Folkestone, Kent, 1980) 80–83, 88–89, 84.

[57] Emmer, "Anti-Slavery and the Dutch," 85, 87, 80.

61

may demonstrate that it is a genuine counterinstance, but the evidence brought forward thus far is too ambiguous to do my thesis any significant harm. Indeed, in the absence of political agitation, what else could account for the abandonment of slavery in the Dutch colonies if not a pervasive sea change in moral perspective?

Momentarily shedding his antipositivist robes, Davis complains in the closing pages of his essay that my form of explanation "has no predictive power." Frustrated by my untroubled acknowledgment that not everyone exposed to the market was transformed by it into an abolitionist—indeed, that for many people an expansion of causal horizons meant only that self-interest would be pursued on a grander scale—Davis says that "this very softness shields Haskell from serious empirical attack." For Davis, it is a sign of the lamentable evasiveness of my explanation that "Haskell can claim that nothing is proved by the failure of slavetraders to become humanitarians."[58]

This complaint reflects not only a failure to recall what the argument is about—why two developments as dissimilar as capitalism and humanitarianism emerged in close historical conjunction—but also a failure to grasp the character of a threshold explanation. Surely, Davis does not really expect historians to explain the conduct of human beings more fully than a chemist can explain the motion of molecules—yet, when a chemist explains the boiling of a pot of water by saying that at certain threshold values of pressure, volume, and temperature, water will begin to undergo a change of state, becoming a gas instead of a liquid, we do not reject the explanation because some of the water in the pot remains a liquid, nor do we complain about the chemist's failure to tell us which individual molecules will break through the surface and enter the atmosphere—it is enough to know that some (those with the greatest velocity) will do so.

Although we have no analog in the study of human affairs to the thermometers, gauges, and scales that enable the chemist to predict when the change of state will begin, that does not prevent us from realizing that we are dealing with a threshold phenomenon and that it was only natural for the line to be crossed at a time when the market was powerfully reshaping everyday life to its needs. Being skeptical about moral progress, scholars must assume that people who lived before the eighteenth century were about as insightful and capable of moral choice as people are today. We know that they recognized that slaves suffered and also that they acknowledged the force of a moral prescription that required them to do for others what they would want done for themselves. I am not trying to account for an instantaneous or universal triumph of antislavery opinion, for, even at the moment of emancipation, some people favored the retention of slavery, many were indifferent, and most probably continued to feel only the passive sympathy that had for so many centuries marked the outer limits of response. Missing from this picture, however, is an expansion of the perceived limits of human agency and responsibility—one sufficiently far-reaching to account for the emergence of a determined network of activists and a gradual shift of opinion in their direction. Without attributing to the market any power whatsoever to make bad people good,

---

[58] Davis, "Reflections on Abolitionism," 811.

we can see that the premium the market paid for forethought and all the other habits of remote causal attribution could easily have supplied the missing piece, completing the picture, and creating a world of wide causal horizons in which slavery would appear to some people as a remediable and intolerable indignity.

What most disturbs both Davis and Ashworth is, perhaps, not the supposed determinism or limited predictive capacity of my explanation but rather its counterintuitive character. Davis's own account has a counterintuitive touch insofar as it depicts bad capitalism giving rise to good antislavery sentiment, but then its final twist, in which antislavery is shown to be shot through with hegemonic implications, confirms the reader's intuitive expectation that bad causes should produce bad effects. In contrast, my explanation requires the reader to believe that the market had one decidedly good effect, and this idea will be counterintuitive for those who are committed to the view that the market is a bad thing. Up to a point, I have no quarrel with those who criticize the market. As I acknowledged very fully in my original essay, "the market" was the favorite rhetorical resource for several generations of people intent on playing down concerns about the public interest and legitimizing the pursuit of self-interest. There may be a touch of romanticism in Davis's lament for the "older, paternalistic notions of responsibility" (which could, of course, be extremely intrusive and never hinted of any general obligation to help strangers), but there can be no doubt that appeals to the automatic functioning of the market often served to justify cold and callous relations between contracting parties, including especially those between employers and employees.[59] If the market shrank responsibility in this respect, my critics ask, how can it be said to have expanded responsibility in any other?

The answer is obvious: complex institutions like the market have multiple and contradictory effects that defy any sort of reconciliation. So, for that matter, does so common a substance as water, which cooks or cools, gives life or takes it away, enables distant transport or destroys whole towns and villages, depending on its amount, its temperature, its relation to bodily orifices, and so on. Why would anyone expect the effects of the market to be any less diverse and contradictory than those of water? And what point would there be in trying to sum up its overall impact, as if each bad effect came tagged with a minus sign and each good one with a plus? Does the scalding of John somehow cancel out or negate Mary's cooling bath? Or a thirst-quenching drink make up for a devastating flood? Because these effects have no common denominator, we have no choice but to deal with them discretely, which means that bad causes may well lead to good effects.[60]

Both of my critics seem to fear that by saying something good about the market we forfeit the right to indict the evils associated with it. I give us all greater credit for mental agility than this fear implies. Ashworth is even more insistent than Davis that the good effects I have attributed to the market could only be justified by some sort of calculus that would tote up all the market's good and bad results and show

---

[59] Davis, "Reflections on Abolitionism," 811.
[60] Compare with Ashworth's complaint that Woolman's humane sentiments are "negated" by the example of Daniel Defoe: Ashworth, "Relationship between Capitalism and Humanitarianism," 818.

that its overall impact on morality was good.[61] The project appears to me both futile and irrelevant. There is nothing illogical about attributing to the market two distinct effects: it authorized the more aggressive pursuit of self-interest in business affairs and, by expanding the horizon of causal perception, it also encouraged in some people strong feelings of guilt and anger about suffering that had previously aroused no more than passive sympathy. One would not be surprised to find individuals in whom both effects were expressed simultaneously and whose behavior toward others might accordingly meander between rigorousness in regard to people perceived as contractual equals and tenderness in regard to those—like slaves—who were perceived as suffering through no fault of their own. This is, in fact, not a bad description of a common Victorian stance toward others. Knowing that, by some overall measure, the market was, on the whole, good or bad would add nothing to our understanding of this contradictory scene. We know that water is, on the whole, good, in that life cannot continue in its absence. But this awareness does not diminish the importance of knowing that floods, drownings, and scaldings are bad. By the same token, even if we were to conclude that the market's effects on the whole were bad, this would not diminish the importance of knowing that one of them was good.

ALTHOUGH I HAVE TRIED TO DEMONSTRATE THAT the humanitarian sensibility can be linked to capitalism without relying on the much-overworked concept of class interest, I took pains in my original article to acknowledge that interest functioned as an indispensable concept in human affairs, and I noted in particular that "interests exert an important influence on belief through what [Max] Weber called 'elective affinity.'"[62] My aim has not been to supplant the concept of interest—an unthinkably bizarre project—but to supplement it and suggest that its explanatory power may be exaggerated. In his response to my essay, John Ashworth often seems to assume that my disapproval of Davis's sort of explanation, which wraps interest in a cloak of self-deception, must extend to all forms of explanation based on interest, including his own. But this is not quite so. I find much to agree with in Ashworth's essay. In its best moments, it bears a resemblance to Weber's approach, which, while denying the crude thesis that interests directly determine consciousness, acknowledges that, through the process of "elective affinity," people do adopt ideas and values that are loosely suited to their interests. Ashworth's understanding of the role of interest is not consistent, and I am not at all persuaded by his claim that antislavery can best be understood as a product of class interest, but my objections have more to do with execution than the type of explanation he is recommending.

In a curious maneuver near the beginning of his argument, Ashworth nearly succeeds in obscuring its merits (and its kinship with that of Weber) by announcing that his aim is to rehabilitate the discredited notion of "false consciousness." This

---

[61] Ashworth, "Relationship between Capitalism and Humanitarianism," 817.
[62] Haskell, "Capitalism and the Origins of the Humanitarian Sensibility, Part 1," 342; Richard Herbert Howe, "Max Weber's Elective Affinities: Sociology within the Bounds of Pure Reason," *American Journal of Sociology,* 84 (1978): 366–85.

term has a very checkered history and no certain referent, but it is often associated with the very view Weber was attacking, one that treats consciousness as epiphenomenal. This, it turns out, is not at all what Ashworth means. He means by the term only that historical actors always act on an "incomplete" perception of reality (never mind all the questions that could be raised about the singularity and objectivity of "reality" and the "completeness" of our own perception) and that historians are entitled to assign to historical acts meanings other than those the actors had in mind.[63]

Why Ashworth maintains that the assertion of these familiar propositions requires the resurrection of false consciousness is not clear to me. He evidently imagines that I wish to confine the meanings of acts to those which the actors themselves held, but this is simply not true. When I explain humanitarianism in terms of a shift of causal conventions, I am obviously assigning to the actions of the reformers meanings very different from the ones they had in mind. Ashworth apparently mistakes my concern with cultural availability for the outlandish view that only the actor's meanings count. It is of course vital to ascertain the range of meanings culturally available to past actors so that we do not mistakenly impute to them a view of the world and an understanding of self that they could not have had. But this concern to avoid anachronism in no way prevents us from contrasting the meaning the act had for the actor with the meaning that it has for us, which may be very different because we view it in retrospect and see it in light of our different experiences and priorities. Indeed, ascertaining cultural availability is the indispensable groundwork for any such distinction, and only by maintaining this distinction scrupulously can we prevent history from being a bag of tricks played on the dead.

Disregarding, then, the unfortunate connotations of false consciousness, we can see in Ashworth's proposal a scheme of explanation that bears comparison to the approach that Weber developed most fully in *The Protestant Ethic and the Spirit of Capitalism.*[64] Weber did not employ the notion of self-deception and neither does Ashworth, who is no more persuaded by this aspect of Davis's interpretation than I am. Ashworth agrees with Davis, as I do, that some of the consequences of reform served the hegemonic interests of the reformers, but unlike Davis, he treats these consequences as unintended—just as I do. Neither consciously nor unconsciously, in Ashworth's view, did any significant number of reformers intend, by attacking slavery, to advance their own interests. Here again, his treatment parallels that of Weber, who insisted on a very close relationship between the spread of Protestant religious doctrines and the advance of capitalism but who strongly denied that ministers or their parishioners had ever *intended* anything other than the glorification of God.

It is at the next stage of the argument that Ashworth parts company with both Weber and me. Although he does not regard the hegemonic consequences of reform as in any sense intended, Ashworth does believe that they must be viewed

---

[63] Ashworth, "Relationship between Capitalism and Humanitarianism," 814–15.
[64] Max Weber, *The Protestant Ethic and the Spirit of Capitalism*, Talcott Parsons, trans. (New York, 1958).

as a product of class interest. In contrast, I had argued that the very idea of "pursuing class interest," or being "moved" by it, implies intentionality, at least of an unconscious character. "To say that a person is moved by class interest is to say that he *intends* to further the interests of his class, or it is to say nothing at all."[65] This was a strong assertion and not one I would want to detach from its original argumentative context and set up as a general methodological imperative, but it does accord with Weber's practice in *The Protestant Ethic*: in his view, the contribution that Protestantism made to the advance of capitalism was neither intended nor the result of class interest. Weber held that it was a fortuitous conjunction, not any causal dependence of values on interests, that brought capitalism together with a religious ideology capable of breaking down the traditional psychological barriers that had hitherto blocked economic advance.[66]

Ashworth says at one point, in a very un-Weberian manner, that "a person is moved by certain ideals that have *grown out of* class interest" (emphasis added).[67] If the relationship between interests and values was truly like that of the acorn to the oak or the caterpillar to the butterfly, so that one grows out of the other, we would have grounds for saying that interest is the "major factor" in explaining both values and whatever outcomes they lead to in action. But the metaphor "growing out of" notoriously exaggerates both the objectivity of interest and the determinateness of the influence that it exerts on our thinking. It was in part to protest that sort of exaggeration that Weber turned to the much looser and more ambiguous metaphor of "elective affinity."

The question of how much class interest explains is finally one of degree, for neither Weber nor I deny that interests and values tend to go together and to be mutually reinforcing. In fact, my own scheme, by treating people's perceptions of both interest and moral obligation as elements of the cognitive style appropriate to a market-oriented way of life, suggests a connection between values and interests that is even more intimate than the word "affinity" implies—namely, a common origin in a set of causal conventions. But I do not believe that the values of the movement against slavery were generally produced by class interest or that the movement can be best explained in its terms. And if we focus on Ashworth's practice rather than his methodological pronouncements, neither does he—at least, not all the time.

Ashworth says that he is going to show, contrary to my argument, that the reformers were moved by class interests, even though they had no intention of advancing those interests. But the scene he actually paints for us depicts people being moved not by class interests but by consciously held values and ideals, such as the importance of personal autonomy, the primacy of conscience, the sanctity

[65] Haskell, "Capitalism and the Humanitarian Sensibility, Part 1," 347.
[66] "For those to whom no causal explanation is adequate without an economic . . . interpretation, it may be remarked that I consider the influence of economic development on the fate of religious ideas to be very important and shall later attempt to show how in our case the process of mutual adaptation of the two took place. On the other hand, those religious ideas themselves simply cannot be deduced from economic circumstances"; Weber, *The Protestant Ethic and the Spirit of Capitalism*, 277 n.84; see also chap. 2.
[67] Ashworth, "Relationship between Capitalism and Humanitarianism," 815.

of the family, and the like. True, Ashworth makes a case for the idea that these values and ideals were, in turn, related to the class interest of the reformers, but the relation he draws is not very strong, and, even if we accepted his claim at face value, it would not follow that the reformers, in attacking slavery, were "pursuing class interest" or that antislavery could be best understood as an expression of class interest. That antislavery values and bourgeois interests are not wholly unrelated goes without saying, as does the existence of affinities between them. But that is not what the debate is about. Ashworth has evidently set out to prove that class interest is "the major causal factor," the principal explanation of the movement against slavery, and in this he does not succeed.[68]

Consider the structure of his argument. He contends that the commodification of labor that attended the advance of capitalism provoked, in the middle and upper levels of society, a twofold reaction: a heightened ideological commitment to a cluster of values centering on the priority of individual conscience and the sanctity of the family and, in close association with these values, a general search for ways of setting limits to the wholesale legitimation of self-interest that the triumph of capitalism seemed to threaten. Because a strong conscience was commonly thought capable of anchoring moral judgment in the bedrock of divine law, and home and family were widely understood to be refuges from competition within which disinterested love could survive and flourish, these values were, appropriately enough, held aloft by those leading the battle to confine self-interest within manageable boundaries. As these ideological commitments gathered strength, the institution of slavery, which disrupted families and substituted the self-indulgent whims of a slaveowner for the sacred authority of conscience, came to appear ever more evil and anomalous. Finally, inspired by the vision of bounded liberty and conscientious conduct that the struggle to come to terms with wage labor had indirectly set in motion, the middle and upper classes felt obliged to rid their society of slavery, in what might be described as a paroxysm of ideological consistency. The ideals of family and conscience that they had come to venerate they sought to translate into reality, not only in their own lives, which would be unsurprising, but also in the lives of the slaves—which Ashworth should find much more surprising than he does.

In fact, I find this explanation unpersuasive (at least in its present, abbreviated form) on several different levels. Ashworth fails to establish a strong enough connection between class interests and ideology, on the one hand, and between ideology and antislavery action, on the other, to justify his conclusion that antislavery ought to be understood mainly as an expression of class interest. Still more vulnerable are certain of his assumptions. He imputes to human beings a greater thirst for consistency between values and practices than I believe they display, and he correspondingly underestimates the ease (and sincerity) with which even the most passionately held values can be interpreted so as to seem in conformity with a wide variety of practices. Most serious of all, Ashworth offers no explanation for what I regard as the defining characteristic of the rise of

[68] See Ashworth, "Relationship between Capitalism and Humanitarianism," 823–28, 815.

humanitarianism as a historical event—the extension to strangers of levels of care and concern that were previously confined to family, friends, and neighbors. No doubt slavery was an outrage against ideals of conscience and family, but it was an outrage perpetrated against the slaves, not the reformers whose behavior we are trying to explain. The reformer's own domestic tranquility obviously was not imperiled by the existence of slavery and neither was the reformer's fidelity to conscience, except insofar as he or she chose to construe the extension of benevolence to slaves as one of the demands of conscience. Ashworth gives us no reason to think that reformers could not have cultivated these values within their own circles, while leaving slaves bereft of them, just as democratic and republican values had been cultivated within the free populations of ancient Athens and colonial Virginia—or, for that matter, just as the values of hearth and home were cultivated on many an antebellum plantation. By taking it for granted that people who learn to venerate conscience and the family will naturally seek to extend those blessings from those who are near and dear to the most lowly and distant of strangers, Ashworth not only simplifies his task, he literally assumes away the central problem for which we seek an explanation.

This is not to say that Ashworth's account is without merit. I strongly agree with his suggestion that abolition was part of a broader effort to tame the market by setting limits to the pursuit of self-interest. Ashworth evidently imagines that the existence of such an effort is evidence against my thesis, but my argument has never depended on the claim that the preponderance of the market's effects on morality was good. I claim only that the market helped push people across a critical threshold of perception; whether it was on the whole good or bad may be a lively political question, but it is irrelevant to the question of historical causation that concerns us here. Having myself written about some of the quite different forms that this countermovement against the market took in the latter half of the nineteenth century, I can heartily endorse Ashworth's suggestion that the celebration of conscience, the veneration of family life, and the repudiation of slavery ought to be viewed as three aspects of a many-sided campaign to restore moral authority in the face of the market's de-moralizing impact on traditional practices.[69] Much of the history of England and America in these years could be written in terms of this wide-ranging effort at containment, some aspects of which were first described by Karl Polanyi in *The Great Transformation*, a book Ashworth does not mention but in which he would find much support for this part of his argument.[70]

Although I agree that the ideology of antislavery drew strength from these concerns about the widening orbit of legitimized self-interest in capitalist society, the relationship between this ideology and the class interests of those who

---

[69] Ashworth, "Relationship between Capitalism and Humanitarianism," 822. See my essay "Professionalism versus Capitalism: R. H. Tawney, Emile Durkheim, and C. S. Peirce on the Disinterestedness of Professional Communities," in *The Authority of Experts: Studies in History and Theory*, T. L. Haskell, ed. (Bloomington, Ind., 1984), 180–225; and *The Emergence of Professional Social Science: The American Social Science Association and the Nineteenth Century Crisis of Authority* (Urbana, Ill., 1977).

[70] Karl Polanyi, *The Great Transformation* (New York, 1944).

embraced it is much more ambiguous than Ashworth allows. In a footnote, Ashworth applauds a statement I made in my original article warning that the concept of interest is elastic—so elastic that there is literally no human act that cannot be construed as self-interested.[71] But he proceeds inadvertently to formulate what deserves to become the classic textbook illustration of the dubious practice I was warning against, by contending that a campaign to inhibit the pursuit of interest was itself an expression of interest. What can one say? Interest can never be ruled out as an explanation of behavior: measures taken to restrain self-interest may in fact have benefited some people more than others, and it is not inconceivable that some of the beneficiaries—whether deliberately, self-deceptively, or by way of "elective affinity," or even "false consciousness"—anticipated the benefit and joined the containment effort in order to achieve that benefit. But the scenario puts a heavy strain on the idea of interest. We can easily imagine a campaign against self-interest that would erect barriers selectively so as to favor the interests of the campaigners, but the campaign that Ashworth describes does not display any obvious biases. The interest he imputes to the campaigners is that of avoiding social "collapse"—an interest not confined to any one class.[72] Even if an entrepreneurial class were to conclude that its self-interest required the erection of barriers against the pursuit of interest, would not other, non-entrepreneurial, classes reap the principal benefits? Instances like this, in which people can be said to be pursuing interest even as they oppose its pursuit, should at least alert us to the elasticity of the concept and point toward the double illusion under which much contemporary scholarship labors: that interest is the only thing that explains human behavior and that, once historians have linked acts with interests that might plausibly account for them, there is nothing left to explain.

Every link in the chain by which Ashworth tries to attach antislavery to class interest is open to objection. Consider first the provocation that is supposed to have set the entire process in motion—the emergence of a class of propertyless laborers, deprived of access to the means of production and forced to sell their labor power on the market. Ashworth is very eager that his readers take this to be the cutting edge of capitalism, rather than anything as general and abstract as "the market," partly, perhaps, because it has a robust Marxian flavor and partly because it permits him to claim that his explanation solves the supposedly knotty mystery of why the abolitionists "selectively" went to the aid of slaves rather than helping exploited workers generally: the problem of legitimating wage labor, he claims, was what they were really grappling with from the very beginning.[73] This claim might be plausible if the values that Ashworth describes offered any likely solution to the problems faced by a ruling class seeking to legitimate wage labor. We could understand why the rise of a new class of unruly laborers would inspire fear of crime or revolution or provoke anxiety about the future of republican institutions.

---

[71] Ashworth, "Relationship between Capitalism and Humanitarianism," 815 n.6.
[72] Ashworth, "Relationship between Capitalism and Humanitarianism," 822.
[73] Ashworth, "Relationship between Capitalism and Humanitarianism," 822.

69

866   *Thomas L. Haskell*

But why would it lead specifically to the veneration of family life, the exaltation of conscience, and a general preoccupation with the dangers of self-interest? These are reactions suitable to people whose eyes were fixed not only on the commodification of labor and the problem of controlling an underclass but on the broader problems created by the general breakdown of taboos on the pursuit of self-interest and consequent spread of competitive relations throughout society. "The market" is a term of art referring to this very phenomenon, and, when Ashworth actually addresses the task of explaining the middle-class preoccupation with self-interest, he repeatedly speaks of it as a response to "the spread of the market" rather than wage labor—apparently unaware that this undercuts his concluding exclamation that "it was precisely because of the spread of wage labor that they attacked slavery in the way they did."[74]

Even if we could agree that reformers' heightened concern for conscience and family stemmed from their anxieties about wage labor rather than the market, Ashworth has given us no adequate reason to think that these values were novel enough or determinate enough in their implications for action to account for the attack on slavery. He argues that the increasing number of wage-laborers, hitherto viewed as a slavish class unfit for citizenship in republican society, set in motion a massive shift of attitudes and practices. People searched for and found "new supports for individual morality and the social order" in three things: the family, the home, and individual conscience. "None had previously been ignored," Ashworth assures us, "but all came to be redefined." He goes on to say that, "in societies that had redefined them or were in the process of redefining them, slavery came to appear as a greater and greater evil. Thus a small but growing number of influential individuals were sensitized to the evils of slavery. As they viewed their own society differently, they initiated a new hostility to slavery (and other evils, too) and led the humanitarian movement."[75] Much hinges on just what this redefinition of family and conscience consisted of. Ashworth tells us only that the family lost its economic primacy as a center of production and that both family and conscience gained a new significance as counterweights to the growing force of self-interest. Exactly what it was about these surprisingly familiar and undramatic redefinitions that suddenly "sensitized" people to the evils of an institution that had been tolerated for centuries is none too clear. Ashworth merely asserts, without explaining, that "the heightened concern for the soul and the individual conscience, nourished within the family circle, *necessarily* intensified concern for slavery, which disrupted family ties and offered many temptations and opportunities for the slaveholder to sin" (my emphasis).[76] Evidently, we are expected to believe that, as middle-class people grappled with the problem of wage labor by

---

[74] Ashworth, "Relationship between Capitalism and Humanitarianism," 822–23, 828. The commodification of labor and the spread of "the market" are not two distinct things between which we must choose; the former is a particular case of the latter and one that it may be important to bring to the forefront in certain contexts. My usage follows that of Polanyi (for whom the countermovement was specifically aimed at containing "the market") and C. B. Macpherson, *The Political Theory of Possessive Individualism: Hobbes to Locke* (Oxford, 1964).
[75] Ashworth, "Relationship between Capitalism and Humanitarianism," 822.
[76] Ashworth, "Relationship between Capitalism and Humanitarianism," 827.

70

appealing (never mind the mismatch between means and ends) to the values of disinterestedness, individual conscience, and domesticity, the growing disparity between their high ideals and the lowly life of the slave became so great that they could not stand it any longer.

This conclusion vastly overestimates the determinateness of values and the force of prescriptions. Values are prescriptions: when we value conscience, we embrace a prescription that tells us that the good life consists of attention to an inner voice, one that promises to bring us into conformity with the dictates of universal moral law. When we value hearth and home, we embrace a prescription that identifies the good life with the pleasures of the domestic sphere, as opposed to the cold world outside, and defines duty and fulfillment largely in terms of nurturing the next generation. Nothing in the values named by Ashworth specifies to whom these prescriptions apply; even the most ardent devotees of family and conscience need not feel any obligation to extend these blessings to slaves, or to neighbors, or to the residents of the next town, or to anyone beyond the circle of their closest associates.

Although these prescriptions regarding family and conscience were highly characteristic of middle-class people during the era of abolition, they were not distinctive. They were neither new at that time nor unique to that class. Conscience, in particular, has for centuries stood close to the heart of Christian teachings, and, if we were to look for a plateau when its importance was notably increased, the Reformation of the sixteenth century would be a better candidate than anything that happened in the eighteenth or nineteenth centuries. Family values, too, have had a long history. What redefinition of conscience and family in the eighteenth century could possibly account for the failure of earlier versions of these values, or any others, to provoke hostility to slavery? How could even redefined versions of open-ended values like these, which specify nothing inherently about their application, accomplish more toward the overthrow of slavery in a few decades than had been accomplished over a period of two millennia by the biblical injunction "Do unto others as you would have them do unto you?" The Golden Rule is the prescription of prescriptions, and it not only told people what the good life was but also to whom it should be extended. If that was not enough to inaugurate the history of active opposition to the institution of slavery, nothing in the realm of prescription could have done so.

Ashworth loses sight of the central questions. How are we to account for Davis's finding that practically no one before the eighteenth century saw in slavery anything worse than a necessary evil? Why at that time did people who were, by individual disposition, probably no more compassionate or scrupulous than their ancestors decide that an institution their ancestors had found tolerable was instead an intolerable evil and set about its destruction? I believe that they did this because of a shift of conventions, which prompted them to evaluate their responsiblity for suffering within an unprecedentedly broad arena and therefore to feel responsible for suffering that previous generations had perceived as inaccessibly remote. Ashworth can only suggest that their family-nurtured ideals of conscientious

71

behavior rose to such stratospheric heights that they could no longer bear for slaves not to share in them.

It is especially ironic that Ashworth thinks that my scheme of explanation ignores changes in morality.[77] Here, Davis is closer to the mark. He sees that the most problematical and disturbing aspect of my explanation is precisely that it puts morality in motion, by giving it roots that run no deeper than convention. What Ashworth mistakes for a failure to recognize the historicity of morality is instead my insistence that prescription and practice not be naively lumped together, as if we could predict how people will act once we know what prescriptions they embrace. There is no one-to-one relation between prescription and practice; what people do is not merely an unfolding of the values they embrace. Of course, moral practices change: no one could write about the rise of antislavery or the emergence of the humanitarian sensibility who doubted this. Prescription also changes but not in any way that could explain the emergence of the humanitarian sensibility. To explain that development, we must take into account changes in the tacitly understood conventions that shape the way prescriptions are interpreted and reconciled (sometimes very circuitously) with practices. That is what my original essay strove to do, and that is what Ashworth's alternative leaves entirely out of account.

WAS THERE ANYTHING REVEALINGLY SELECTIVE ABOUT the decision of abolitionists to attack chattel slavery rather than labor exploitation generally? One might think that the question could be shelved in view of Davis's concession ("in theory," at least) that an abolitionist sincerely opposed to all forms of oppression might nonetheless have given priority to the slave trade and chattel slavery as "the most flagrant and remediable crimes against humanity."[78] What is there to explain when people choose to attack the most "flagrant" and "remediable" of the "crimes" before them, instead of doing something else? Problems that can be described in terms this strong naturally take priority. Davis has also acknowledged that "everyone knew that white workers were not really slaves." Since no one has ever thought that mistaken identity was an issue, I interpret this to mean that everyone also knew (taking both material and non-material conditions into account) that the plight of wageworkers—an extremely heterogeneous category—was not as severe as that of slaves. Davis has also allowed that the reformers, whatever their shortcomings, "have been vindicated by history: morally, they were right." Surely, history has also vindicated their sense of strategic priorities: as the *National Anti-Slavery Standard* remarked, "the first work of the reformers . . . is to establish universally the right of man to himself." The problem of slavery "underlies all

---

[77] Ashworth, "Relationship between Capitalism and Humanitarianism," 819.

[78] Davis, "Reflections on Abolitionism," 800. Davis believes that an abolitionist who thought like this would have left a written record of regrets about the tendency of attacks on slavery to obscure the abusive treatment of wage-laborers. I wonder. One common reaction to political opponents who try to cast doubts on one's motives is simply to ignore them, on the theory that base canards should not be dignified by a reply.

other reforms . . . [for] there can be no universal reform . . . even no partial reform . . . in a nation that holds one-sixth of its people in bondage."[79]

These considerations suggest to me that, although there may be something puzzling about the abolitionists' attitudes toward wage labor and toward the poor generally, there is nothing at all puzzling about their selection of slavery as the problem of highest priority. Ashworth, however, laments my "retreat" from the "crucial" issue of "the selectivity of the abolitionists, their concern with chattel slavery rather than . . . wage slavery." Surprisingly, he concludes that on this point I have practically "nothing to say . . . Search Haskell's article as we may, we will find nothing that helps answer this question."[80]

Taken at face value, this is a most disheartening response, for it suggests that Ashworth has entirely missed the point of my essay, which from start to finish revolved around the problem of selectivity. The keystone of Davis's interpretation in *The Problem of Slavery in the Age of Revolution* was his claim that "as a social force, antislavery was a highly selective response to labor exploitation," one which—not unintentionally, but as a result of an unconscious hegemonic interest about which the reformers deceived themselves—"gave a certain moral insulation to economic activities less visibly dependent on human suffering and injustice."[81] Against this claim by Davis of an unconsciously intended selectivity on the part of the reformers, I have argued that, in a world that overflows with suffering, all humane acts are unavoidably selective. Because no possibility exists of acting unselectively, the fact that the reformers went to the aid of slaves rather than exploited wage-laborers cannot logically be taken to imply any sort of intention, conscious or otherwise, to "morally insulate" the exploitation of wage labor. To say (in the absence of more specific evidence) that the reformers unconsciously intended to perpetuate this or any of the multitude of other evils they left unrelieved is not essentially different from saying that a person who sends a contribution to Oxfam instead of Amnesty International displays an ominous indifference to torture—or that a person who makes the opposite choice thereby reveals a heartless disregard for hunger. The conclusion does not follow, except on the fallacious proposition that "if you are not for us, you are against us." As long as the question of selectivity is posed in hopes of inferring unconscious intentions, then, it is a question *mal posée*.

Ashworth, unlike Davis, rules out unconscious intentions from the start. This puts the question of selectivity on a different, and I think less vulnerable, footing, but the difference comes at a cost, and not all readers will think the cost acceptable.

[79] Davis, "Reflections on Abolitionism," 809, 810; John R. Commons, *et al.*, eds., *A Documentary History of American Industrial Society*, 10 vols. (New York, 1958), 7: 219. There has been no clear resolution of the immiseration controversy, but for purposes of argument I have assumed in everything that follows that no important difference existed between slaves and free workers at the level of the material conditions of life. No doubt some wage earners were as bad off as slaves, but the heterogeneity of the category "wage labor" makes it very likely that the group as a whole was better off materially than were slaves.

[80] Ashworth, "Relationship between Capitalism and Humanitarianism," 815–16. If selectivity were a problem at all, it would be as much a problem for Ashworth as anyone. Why would the same idealization of family and conscience that supposedly drove middle-class people to liberate slaves not also have driven them to ameliorate the lot of immiserated wageworkers?

[81] Davis, *Problem of Slavery in the Age of Revolution*, 251.

Davis posed the question of selectivity in hopes of inferring unconscious intentions; Ashworth returns to it for the sake of highlighting what he takes to be the reformer's "false consciousness" or, more exactly, the incompleteness of their grasp of reality. Instead of assuming that the reformers knew in their hearts that wageworkers were victims of exploitation and that the reformers failed to render aid because they hid that knowledge from themselves, Ashworth assumes that reformers were blinded to the facts of exploitation by their class position. In Ashworth's view, it was the nature of their "involvement in society" that kept them from understanding the real conditions of working-class life, and he takes pains to stress that this is "not a matter of self-deception" but of class-induced ignorance.[82]

This explanatory strategy has the considerable virtue of making it unnecessary to postulate the existence of unconscious intentions (empirically undemonstrable, anyway), yet it retains the claim that the reformers' conduct was governed by their class position—which, at first glance, seems to be the same thing as saying that it was governed by class interest. Like any strategy, however, this one entails certain costs. By conceding that the reformers did not know, either consciously or unconsciously, that they should have gone to the aid of "wage slaves" as well as chattel slaves, Ashworth locates the hegemonic effects of antislavery agitation squarely in the category of unintended consequences. As such, neither the reformers nor anyone else bears responsibility for them. The reformers acted in ignorance, and, although their ignorance resulted from their privileged class position, it is not at all clear how any person or group could be thought blameworthy for failing to perform a duty of which, for whatever reason, they were genuinely ignorant. Ashworth's account has a blander tone than Davis's, and necessarily so, for, in the absence of intentionality and blameworthiness, words like "social control," "class oppression," and "hegemony" lose their bite.[83] It was presumably for this reason that Raymond Williams warned Marxists that, by withdrawing too far from the claim that there is a "process of determination," they risked emptying "of its essential content the original Marxist proposition . . . Intention, the notion of intention, restores the key question, or rather the key emphasis." In order for an interpretation to be called "Marxist," Williams believed it should at least depict the "organization and structure [of society] . . . as directly related to certain social intentions, intentions by which we define the society, intentions which in all our experience have been the rule of a particular class."[84]

Anyone hoping to defend Ashworth's strategy may have second thoughts at this point and want to reopen the question of just how "ignorant" the reformers were. Perhaps false consciousness produces a sort of ignorance over which people have some control; perhaps it is all a matter of degree; perhaps they could have

[82] Ashworth, "Relationship between Capitalism and Humanitarianism," 815.

[83] The paradoxical coexistence in the Marxian tradition of moralism with doctrines deeply subversive of the very idea of morality is the subject of Steven Lukes, *Marxism and Morality* (New York, 1985).

[84] Raymond Williams, "Base and Superstructure in Marxist Cultural Theory," *New Left Review*, 82 (1973): 7.

overcome their class-induced blindness if only they had tried harder. But every step in this direction leads back toward self-deception or some functional equivalent. We mean, by self-deception, a form of ignorance that is self-inflicted and for which the self can be held partly responsible, on the theory that whatever the self can do, it has at least some power to undo. Any modification of false consciousness that would entitle Ashworth to say "they ought to have known better" would be vulnerable to all the same objections that we have already registered against self-deception.

We are now in a better position to appreciate the brilliance of Davis's formulation and see how much was at stake in it. By treating the hegemonic effects of antislavery as a result of intentions that were unconscious, Davis avoided the conspiratorial and reductionist overtones that plagued Eric Williams's interpretation of abolitionism, and yet Davis also retained a strong enough element of intentionality both to account causally for the reformer's comparative indifference to the problems of wage labor and to hold them at least ambiguously responsible for the consequences of that indifference. In contrast, Ashworth can account causally for their indifference—the nature of their "involvement in society" obscured from them the realities of the wage earner's situation—but he has no basis for imputing responsibility. Ashworth's account has victims but no villains, for he attributes the shortcomings of reform to the distortions of consciousness (something we "all possess to a greater or lesser degree") that come from our having to occupy a single vantage point in society, from which the whole can never be apprehended in its entirety.[85] The only villain is the human condition.

Ashworth's abandonment of intentionality may make his interpretation unacceptable in some quarters, but I have no objections on this point. I have argued all along that the hegemonic consequences of antislavery were unintended. The disagreement between Ashworth and myself lies elsewhere, in the reason for the abolitionists' comparative indifference to the suffering of wage earners and the poor. I have no doubt that their attitudes were shaped in part by their social position, but I am not persuaded that this is the main or the most useful explanation. I would distinguish, moreover, between class position and class interest, as two separate and possibly contradictory kinds of influence on perception and ideology. Ashworth lumps them together as if there could be no important difference between them: having accepted the idea that values grow smoothly out of interests, he naturally supposes that interests themselves grow out of class position in an equally regular fashion. There is no justification for these assumptions.

It is undoubtedly true that the reformers, because they came preponderantly from a single, affluent sector of society, had a limited experience of life and made errors when they generalized, as we all must, from their own experience to that of others in their society. Their vision was, then, influenced by their class position, just as Ashworth claims. But this is not at all the same thing as saying that their blind spots were induced by, or served, class interest. The wants, desires, and

---

[85] Ashworth, "Relationship between Capitalism and Humanitarianism," 815.

passions that drive conduct no doubt take shape within the confines of the particular perspective that a person's social position affords, but they can originate anywhere. As Jon Elster has shown, there is no reason to assume that the interests shaped by position necessarily function to reinforce that position or even that the beliefs shaped by interest necessarily serve that interest. These are matters for empirical investigation, not sweeping generalization. Wishful thinking induced by interest, for example, can be fatal to the interest that induced it, and a taste for conspicuous consumption can fritter away the wealth that sustains the taste. The idea that a social situation always induces beliefs that are favorable to the ruling class or conducive to the perpetuation of the status quo is no more plausible than the idea that bad causes always give rise to bad effects, or *vice versa*.[86]

Is it possible, in spite of everything I have said to the contrary, that the comparative insensitivity of the abolitionists to the needs of wage labor was the result of class interest? Of course. Interest can never be ruled out. There is no human act so incontrovertibly disinterested that it cannot be construed as self-interested by enclosing it within a suitable interpretive framework.[87] But the ease with which any sophomore can perform this trick should make us skeptical of its value. Trying to explain events without referring to interests would be absurd, but we can take note of the infinite elasticity of the concept and the obsessiveness of our reliance on it and then develop a certain skepticism in the presence of those of every political persuasion who take it to be the sole proper terminus of explanation.

Let me close with a concrete example of selectivity, partly to bring these abstract issues into tighter focus and partly to satisfy Ashworth's curiosity about how I would explain the abolitionist's comparative unconcern with wage labor. The example is one my critics ought to find congenial, for it lends itself readily to an interpretation in terms of class interest. My aim is not to show that such an interpretation is flatly erroneous—no such demonstration could ever succeed, in my view—but rather to display in a specific case the tendency of explanation-by-interest to terminate inquiry prematurely.

The views of the American abolitionist Wendell Phillips are especially pertinent, because, in spite of his patrician origins, he ultimately came to believe something quite close to what Davis and Ashworth assume that all of the abolitionists would always have believed if their judgment had not been distorted by class interest. In 1871, when Phillips presided over a Labor Reform convention that declared war on the entire system of wage labor, alleging that it "enslaves" the working man and "demoralizes" and "cheats" both him and his employer, he construed the problems of labor in a way that is basically familiar to us today—that is, in a way that sees through the formal liberty of abused wageworkers and situates their problems on a continuum with those of chattel slaves, acknowledging differences in degree, perhaps, but not in kind.[88]

---

[86] Jon Elster, *Sour Grapes: Studies in the Subversion of Rationality* (Cambridge, 1983), 141–66. See also Robert W. Gordon, "Critical Legal Histories," *Stanford Law Review*, 36 (January 1984): 57–125.

[87] Haskell, "Capitalism and the Origins of the Humanitarian Sensibility, Part 1," 351 n.32.

[88] Wendell Phillips, *Speeches, Lectures, and Letters*, 2d ser. (Boston, 1894), 152.

Phillips had not always thought that it made sense to compare wage earners and slaves, much less to lump their problems together as variations on the single theme of labor exploitation. Before the Civil War, like most humanitarian reformers of his generation, Phillips had found the very idea of "wages slavery" to be "utterly unintelligible," at least in the American context. In a remarkable statement in 1847, he acknowledged that manufactured articles were often the products of "unrequited labor" and that complaints against capital and monopoly were well justified in England and Europe, but things were different in America. Between the free laborers of the North and the slaves of the South, he drew a distinction so total as to stagger the imagination of any twentieth-century reader:

> Except in a few crowded cities and a few manufacturing towns, I believe the terms 'wages slavery' and 'white slavery' would be utterly unintelligible to an audience of laboring people, as applied to themselves. There are two prominent points which distinguish the laborers in this country from the slaves. First, the laborers, as a class, are neither wronged nor oppressed: and secondly, if they were, they possess ample power to defend themselves, by the exercise of their own acknowledged rights. Does legislation bear hard upon them? Their votes can alter it. Does capital wrong them? Economy will make them capitalists. Does the crowded competition of cities reduce their wages? They have only to stay at home, devoted to other pursuits, and soon diminished supply will bring the remedy . . . To economy, self-denial, temperance, education, and moral and religious character, the laboring class, and every other class in this country, must owe its elevation and improvement.[89]

These are obviously the words of a man who defined the self and its relation to the world in a manner that is extremely formalistic by present standards. Phillips seems not to have recognized any distinction between the form of freedom and its substance. He seems to have believed that a person who is physically and legally unconstrained is as free as any human being ever can be. Some of what he said resembles twentieth-century laissez-faire conservatism, but the resemblance is largely spurious, and even a reckless conservative today would be unlikely to assert in public, as Phillips unhesitatingly did, that workers need only practice "economy" in order to become capitalists in their own right, or that low wages can be raised by staying at home, or that self-denial, the ballot box, and good character form a sure path to advancement. These assertions are shot through with implications of a strongly formalist character, and everything turns on what we make of this alien element in Phillips's thinking.

The more alien an idea is, the easier it is to dismiss as ideology, but if we resist this temptation and take what Phillips said as an expression of the way the world once looked to an acute and certainly conscientious observer, we immediately discover that his attitude in 1847 toward wage labor is not at all perplexing—once we grant him his formalist premises. No matter how unrealistic we may think these premises, once adopted, they lead naturally and consistently to the conclusion that "wages slavery" is a contradiction in terms.

[89] Phillips quoted in John R. Commons, *A Documentary History of American Industrial Society*, 7: 220–21. See also Daniel T. Rodgers, *The Work Ethic in Industrial America, 1850–1920* (Chicago, 1978), 32; and Richard Stott, "British Immigrants and the American 'Work Ethic' in the Mid-Nineteenth Century," *Labor History*, 26 (Winter 1985): 86–102.

The cast of Phillips's mind will not be unfamiliar to students of Victorian culture in England and America. He wrote as if a normal, healthy, adult self was an uncaused cause, a pure point of origin, a kind of cornucopia in which purposeful activity arose out of nothing and surged into the world. To be a person, in this view, was only incidentally to be a material body, caught up in nature's endless fabric of cause-and-effect relations and fully subject to all the natural processes of growth, disease, and decay. The heart of personhood lay in the will, and the will, though not necessarily supernatural, was uncanny. The self formed a pure point of origin through its mysterious capacity of "willing," of almost magically transmuting the evanescent, inward, and private experience of desire and choice into the concrete, outward, and public phenomenon of action. More mysterious still, the resulting external acts produced consequences that corresponded with, or satisfied, the internal desires—or, at least, could do so if the will allowed itself to be guided by the dictates of reason and knowledge.

The self's ability to trigger causal chains and set events in motion meant that it was very much *in* the world, and yet, because it was always the producer, never merely the product of any antecedent chain of natural causation, it was not quite *of* this world. Every merely natural cause is a transitive link in a chain and can be construed both as cause of what it produces and the effect of some link antecedent to it—which, in turn, can be seen as the effect of some cause still more remote, and so on indefinitely. But the self in the act of willing was seen as a new, non-transitive, causal beginning, independent of everything but the First Cause and His providential order—a very special sort of dependence that even predestinarians insisted did not dilute in the least the self's responsibility for whatever it willingly did.[90] In the world of formalism, the self's every act was deemed voluntary insofar as will was in it, and scarcely anything other than direct physical coercion was thought capable of displacing the will and emptying an act of its voluntary character.

Formalism assigned such a high level of autonomy to the will that the context within which the will formed faded into the distant background, making nearly all deliberate acts appear voluntary. Circumstances, the stuff of environmentalist interpretations of behavior, counted for very little in judging what the self was responsible for. The self was responsible for whatever its activity led to, almost without regard to the circumstances surrounding choice and action. The formalist had no difficulty in recognizing that the will actively assessed its environment and inclined toward one act rather than another *in light of* various circumstantial factors, but to assign these factors causal significance and treat them as the explanation of what the self did would have been to deprive the self of the uncaused character that made it what it was. The cause (and therefore the explanation) of what people did was their choosing to do it, not the circumstances surrounding the choice. We of the twentieth century impute to circumstances a

---

[90] "Man is entirely, perfectly and unspeakably different from a mere machine, in that he has reason and understanding, and has a faculty of will, and so is capable of volition and choice; . . . so that he has liberty to act according to his choice, and to do what he pleases . . . [and so is fully worthy of] praise . . . [or] punishment"; Jonathan Edwards, *Freedom of the Will* (New Haven, Conn., 1957), 370.

power to mold and induce choice—virtually to cause it and certainly to explain it—that mere circumstances could not possess in a formalist's eyes.

These are the conventional premises defining selfhood and governing the allocation of praise, blame, and responsibility that I believe Phillips and most members of his generation shared. They account for what we perceive as his curious insensitivity to the plight of exploited wageworkers and the poor. As seen from our (not necessarily superior) vantage point, Phillips and his contemporaries were blind to an entire range of environmental factors that powerfully influence conduct yet leave people formally free to do as they please. Where we see a deceptive form of freedom, lacking substance, they saw a large and sunlit realm of authentically voluntary choice.

To a person who sees the world as Phillips did in 1847, the difference between a free worker and a slave is not a matter of degree but of quality. Phillips imputed to free workers—a class "neither wronged nor oppressed" and equipped with "ample power to defend themselves"—a degree of autonomy so great that their problems were not commensurable with those of slaves. Free workers, unlike slaves, were masters of their own fate. Even by our twentieth-century standards, there is an irreducible element of voluntariness in even the most fated of contractual arrangements: the free worker can, at a cost, always say "no" and refuse the employment contract. For a formalist, the perceived cost approximates zero because the conditions impelling the employee to accept undesirable conditions of . work are assigned little weight.

Because wage earners were thought free to rise or fall to whatever social position corresponded to their inner merit, those who found themselves in a state of misery had little besides themselves to blame. Formalist assumptions did not prevent decent people like Phillips from feeling passive sympathy for a pauper or playing the Good Samaritan in particular cases by "lending a hand" to a person "down on his luck." But there could be no general attack on the institution of wage labor or any systematic attempt to reform the institution (indeed, it could not even be perceived in a causal role), as long as reformers saw the world through lenses that made most of the poor appear to be deeply complicitous in their own suffering. Because formalists perceived the causes of suffering to lie largely in the victims' own apparently unimpeded choices (ultimately, in defects of the will), the only general remedy for their misfortunes was to help them perfect the arts of self-mastery and educate them about the predictable consequences of their actions. The lessons of "economy," "self-denial," "temperance," and "education" thus stood at the head of Phillips's list of priorities. We must struggle to appreciate that, to him and to most members of his generation, this thin gruel was not only an adequate prescription for social improvement but a trenchant identification of what on formalist premises were the vital nutrients of progressive change.

Although, on formalist assumptions, immiserated wage earners were the cause of their own misery, slaves could not possibly be cast in the same causal role.[91] The

---

[91] Here I may understate the extravagance (in our eyes) of the formalist concept of voluntariness, for at a more abstract level the question of whether people could ever be thought to have voluntarily

status of chattel property shrinks to the vanishing point every hint of voluntariness, making the slave the perfect victim, a person whose misery even in formalist eyes is untainted by any suspicion of complicity. It is for this reason that the concern for slavery displayed by Phillips's generation of reformers could be more wholehearted and vehement than their reaction to most other forms of suffering. In the eyes of an observer who makes little or no distinction between formal and substantive freedom, legally free workers bear a large measure of responsibility for their own plight, but the suffering of slaves, being wholly involuntary, is the responsibility of everyone who has any power to stop it.

We can see, then, that the different treatment Phillips accorded to slaves and wage laborers did not result from a discrete bias against wage laborers but from a system of conventional assumptions that colored his and his generation's thinking about all human conduct. This is not the place to sort out the connections between this set of assumptions and the rise of capitalism, or between those two developments and the great upheaval in the conventions governing causal attribution that made reformers of formalists like Phillips (by expanding causal horizons and thereby overcoming the chilling effect of their extravagant concept of voluntariness) and then helped shatter formalism itself. It is indeed true that formalism, like opposition to slavery, "cannot be divorced from the vast economic changes" of the eighteenth and nineteenth centuries, but neither can it be understood as a reflex, however unconscious or indirect, of those changes.[92] No doubt it insulated entrepreneurs against the barbs of conscience and public opinion as they drove hard bargains with workers too poor to "stay at home," waiting for wages to rise. But it had many effects that were not at all congruent with the needs of capitalism and may even have obstructed its path.

The formalist cast of mind was not something capitalism brought into existence. Six hundred years before Phillips was born, Thomas Aquinas defined the outer perimeter of voluntary action no less extravagantly than Phillips did. In an image that Hobbes would borrow four hundred years later, and that Aristotle had employed more ambivalently a millennium and a half earlier, Aquinas, the great codifier of Christian doctrine, insisted that even a man at sea, who chooses to throw his possessions overboard rather than risk death in a storm, is acting voluntarily. "That which is done through fear is voluntary," said Aquinas. "The will cannot be compelled to act . . . violence cannot be done to the will."[93]

---

renounced their freedom and chosen to become slaves was taken very seriously by several generations of rights theorists, beginning in the early sixteenth century. At a more prosaic level, one of the principal rationales for the legitimacy of slaveowning construed the slave as originally a captive in war, who might well choose slavery over death. See Richard Tuck, *Natural Rights Theories: Their Origin and Development* (Cambridge, 1979), 3, 49, 54, 100; and Davis, *Problem of Slavery in Western Culture*, 117–20.

[92] Davis, "Reflections on Abolitionism," 806.

[93] Aquinas and Aristotle, unlike Hobbes, recognized that the seafarer's act is of a "mixed kind" and that there is a sense in which it is involuntary. But both assigned clear priority to the sense in which it is voluntary, just as Hobbes did. *Basic Writings of St. Thomas Aquinas*, Anton C. Pegis, ed., 2 vols. (New York, 1945), 2: 234, 231; *The Nichomachean Ethics of Aristotle*, D. P. Chase, trans. (New York, 1911), 44–45 [Book III]; Thomas Hobbes in *British Moralists, 1650–1800*, D. D. Raphael, ed., 2 vols. (Oxford, 1969), 1: 55 [*Leviathan*, chap. 22].

We sense how truly alien to our own experience the perspective of formalism is when we see how literally Aquinas believed that the willing self was a new causal beginning, a pure point of origin. Turning a radically blind eye to all the environmental factors that (in our eyes, at least) shape the will and tailor life's opportunities to the imperatives of a particular social order—to all the factors, in other words, that create a gap between the form and the substance of freedom—Aquinas denied that there was anything at all outside the self, anywhere in God's created universe, that could move the will, other than its own object (the "apprehended good") and the gentle art of persuasion.

Now it is a law of providence that everything is moved by its proximate cause . . . But the proximate moving cause of the will is the apprehended good, which is its object, and the will is moved by it as sight is by color. Therefore no created substance can move the will except by means of the apprehended good—in so far, namely, as it shows that a particular thing is good to do; and this is *to persuade*. Therefore no created substance can act on the will, or cause our choice, except by way of persuasion.[94]

We are the heirs today of a revolt against formalism that bore fruit in the years 1880–1920 and inaugurated the modern era in social thought.[95] To expect people who lived prior to this intellectual watershed to share our antiformalist concept of freedom and responsibility is to project into an age importantly different from ours the deceptively familiar features of our own world. It is also to underestimate the genuine historical novelty of antiformalism, one prophetic stream of which first struggled into existence in the thought of Owen, Fourier, Marx, Engels, and a cadre of others, who were the first to criticize the highly abstract and autonomous characterization of the self and its relation to the world that came to be known in the nineteenth century as individualism. To find that the abolitionists defined freedom formalistically and were therefore more sympathetic to slaves (whose lack of independence made them perfect victims) than to impoverished wageworkers (whose formally defined freedom meant that they always bore some responsibility for their own misery) is merely to reaffirm that the likes of Owen and Marx were truly harbingers of a new age who construed the world in ways that were profoundly unconventional, which is to say, culturally unavailable to most people of their era.

Given the antiquity of formalism and its centrality in the Christian tradition, the question we need to ask about Wendell Phillips is not why he "selectively" attacked slavery and ignored the plight of wage-laborers in 1847, but why, a few decades later, he and many others abandoned the premises of formalism and adopted a far less robust concept of the self that put the entire problem of responsibility and reform in a dramatically new light. As long as we are mesmerized by the idea of interest, this question cannot even come up.

---

[94] *Basic Writings of St. Thomas Aquinas*, 2: 168–69 [Summa Contra Gentiles, Book III, chap. 88].

[95] Morton White, *Social Thought in America: The Revolt against Formalism*, expanded edn. (Boston, 1957); H. Stuart Hughes, *Consciousness and Society: The Reorientation of European Social Thought, 1890–1930* (New York, 1958); Talcott Parsons, *The Structure of Social Action: A Study in Social Theory with Reference to a Group of Recent European Writers* (New York, 1937); James T. Kloppenberg, *Uncertain Victory: Social Democracy and Progressivism in European and American Thought, 1870–1920* (New York, 1986); Haskell, *Emergence of Professional Social Science*.

If we asked Davis and Ashworth why Phillips changed his mind between 1847 and 1871, we would likely receive an answer that treats twentieth-century antiformalist assumptions not as anything mediated by convention or emergent in history but simply as reality. Davis's answer would presumably explain how Phillips managed to stop deceiving himself about formalistic assumptions that, unconsciously, he had always known were unrealistic. Ashworth—perhaps after hesitating momentarily at the thought of a change of values without any corresponding change in the interests they supposedly grew from—would presumably strive to show how Phillips managed to break the grip of "false consciousness" and began seeing things in their true light. From both vantage points, Phillips's initial opinion requires explanation, since it was an error, but his later opinion would not seem to merit an explanation because, when people give up error for truth, there is nothing to explain. In contrast, if we take the role of conventions seriously, put interest to one side, and do not press the all-too-human claim that our own views correspond with reality, Phillips's opinion in 1871 can be seen as part of a cultural transformation of far-reaching significance, one that we cannot hope to understand until we have charted the entire course of that upheaval in the conventions defining selfhood and governing the allocation of praise, blame, and responsibility that began in the eighteenth century.

The Emergence of Immediatism in British and American Antislavery Thought

By David Brion Davis

In the history of reform few slogans have brought forth such confusion and controversy as "immediate emancipation."[1] To the general public in the 1830's the phrase meant simply the abolition of Negro slavery without delay or preparation. But the word "immediate" may denote something other than a closeness in time; to many abolitionists it signified a rejection of intermediate agencies or conditions, a directness or forthrightness in action or decision. In this sense immediatism suggested a repudiation of the various media, such as colonization or apprenticeship, that had been advocated as remedies for the evils of slavery. To some reformers the phrase seemed mainly to imply a direct, intuitive consciousness of the sinfulness of slavery, and a sincere personal commitment to work for its abolition.[2] In this subjective sense the word "immedi-

---

[1] For the dispute over which American abolitionist had been the first to preach the doctrine, see George W. Julian, "The Genesis of Modern Abolitionism," *International Review* (New York), XII (June, 1882), 538, 542; A. T. Rankin, *Truth Vindicated and Slander Repelled* (Ironton, Ohio, 1883), 2-15; and the Parker B. Osborn Papers (Ohio Historical Society, Columbus).

[2] This was essentially the doctrine of the American Anti-Slavery Society in the 1830's. According to Gilbert H. Barnes, New York philanthropists borrowed the phrase from British abolitionists and interpreted it as meaning an honest and prompt beginning to gradual emancipation; but such jesuitical "gradualism in a British cloak" injured the cause, in Barnes's view, for many critics pointed out that the abolitionists must either be gradualists, in which case the slogan was meaningless, or favor instant and unconditional liberation of the slaves, which would be sheer madness. Yet the antislavery agents from Lane Seminary found in the doctrine a way of emphasizing the sin of slavery and making their cause "identical with religion." See Barnes, *The Antislavery Impulse, 1830-1844* (New York, 1933), 48-49, 66-67, 102-104, 248; Gilbert H. Barnes and Dwight L. Dumond (eds.), *Letters of Theodore Dwight Weld, Angelina Grimké Weld, and Sarah Grimké, 1822-1844* (2 vols., New York, 1934), I, vii-x. While Barnes shows that Americans were mainly preoccupied with the sin of slavery, he tends to overemphasize the British origins of immediatism and ignores the historical development of the doctrine in both countries. This criticism applies also to Stanley M. Elkins, *Slavery: A Problem in*

ate" was charged with religious overtones and referred more to the moral disposition of the reformer than to a particular plan for emancipation. Thus some reformers confused immediate abolition with an immediate personal decision to abstain from consuming slave-grown produce; and a man might be considered an immediatist if he were genuinely convinced that slavery should be abolished absolutely and without compromise, though not necessarily without honest preparation.[3] Such a range of meanings led unavoidably to misunderstanding, and the antislavery cause may have suffered from so ambiguous a slogan. The ambiguity, however, was something more than semantic confusion or the unfortunate result of a misleading watchword. The doctrine of immediacy, in the form it took in the 1830's, was at once a logical culmination of the antislavery movement and a token of a major shift in intellectual history.

A belief in the slave's right to immediate freedom was at least implicit in much of the antislavery writing of the eighteenth century. If Negro slavery were unjust, unnatural, illegal, corrupting, and detrimental to the national interest, as innumerable eighteenth-century writers claimed, there could be no excuse for its perpetuation.[4] Several of the *philosophes* held that since masters relied on physical force to impose their illegal demands, slave revolts would be just;[5] Louis de Jaucourt went so far as to argue that slaves, never having lost their inherent liberty, should be immediately declared free.[6] Anthony Benezet advanced a similar argument, asking

American Institutional and Intellectual Life (Chicago, 1959).

[3] In both England and America immediatists denied that they opposed careful preparation for full freedom. See, for example, the influential speech of Joseph Sturge at the Society of Friends' London Meeting of 1830, printed in Henry Richard, *Memoirs of Joseph Sturge* (London, 1864), 87-88.

[4] Frank J. Klingberg, "The Evolution of the Humanitarian Spirit in Eighteenth Century England," *Pennsylvania Magazine of History and Biography* (Philadelphia), LXVI (July, 1942), 261-65; Klingberg, *The Anti-Slavery Movement in England* (New Haven, 1926), 25-69; Wylie Sypher, "Hutcheson and the 'Classical' Theory of Slavery," *Journal of Negro History* (Washington), XXIV (July, 1939), 263-80; Edward D. Seeber, *Anti-Slavery Opinion in France during the Second Half of the Eighteenth Century* (Johns Hopkins Studies in Romance Literatures and Languages, Extra Volume X, Baltimore, 1937), *passim*; Thomas Clarkson, *The History of the Rise, Progress and Accomplishment of the Abolition of the African Slave-Trade by the British Parliament* (2 vols., London, 1808), I, 83-126, 185-89, 461-67.

[5] Seeber, *Anti-Slavery Opinion*, 71-72; F. T. H. Fletcher, "Montesquieu's Influence on Anti-Slavery Opinion in England," *Journal of Negro History*, XVIII (October, 1933), 414-26; Shelby T. McCloy, *The Humanitarian Movement in Eighteenth-Century France* (Lexington, Ky., 1957), 86-92.

[6] Louis de Jaucourt, "Traite des Negres," *Encyclopedie, ou Dictionnaire Raisonné des*

what course a man should follow if he discovered that an inherited estate was really the property of another: "Would you not give it up immediately to the lawful owner? The voice of all mankind would mark him for a villain, who would refuse to comply with this demand of justice. And is not keeping a slave after you are convinced of the unlawfulness of it—a crime of the same nature?"[7]

In England, Granville Sharp denounced slavery as a flagrant violation of the common law, the law of reason, and the law of God. After exhorting Lord North to do something about the plight of the slaves, he warned: "I say immediate redress, because, *to be in power*, and to neglect . . . even a day in endeavoring to put a stop to such monstrous injustice and abandoned wickedness, must necessarily endanger a man's *eternal* welfare, be he ever so great in *temporal* dignity or office."[8] Sharp, who argued that "No Legislature on Earth . . . can alter the Nature of Things, or make that to be lawful, which is contrary to the Law of God,"[9] secured a judicial decision outlawing slavery in England. Americans like James Otis, Nathaniel Appleton, and Isaac Skillman took a similarly uncompromising stand before the Revolution;[10] by the 1780's the doc-

Sciences, des Arts et des Métiers, par une Société de Gens de Lettres (Neufchastel, 1765), XVI, 532-33. De Jaucourt was simply developing the antislavery principles of Montesquieu to their logical conclusion. After arguing that Negro slavery was contrary to all natural law and human rights, he wrote: "Il n'y a donc pas un seul de ces infortunés que l'on prétend n'être que des esclaves, qui n'ait droit d'être déclaré libre, puisqu'il n'a jamais perdu la liberté; qu'il ne pouvoit pas la perdre; & que son prince, son pere, & qui que ce soit dans le monde n'avoit le pouvoir d'en disposer; par conséquent la vente qui en a été faite est nulle en elle-même. . . . C'est donc une inhumanité manifeste de la part des juges de pays libres ou il est transporté, de ne pas l'affranchir à l'instant en le déclarant libre, puisque c'est leur semblable, ayant une ame comme eux."

[7] [Anthony Benezet], *An Address to the Inhabitants of the British Settlements in America, upon Slave-Keeping* (Philadelphia, 1773), 20-21.

[8] Granville Sharp to Lord North, February 18, 1772, printed in Prince Hoare, *Memoirs of Granville Sharp, Esq., Composed from His Own Manuscripts* (London, 1820), 79. See also Granville Sharp, *A Representation of the Injustice and Dangerous Tendency of Tolerating Slavery; or of Admitting the Least Claim of Private Property in the Persons of Men, in England* (London, 1769), 15-16, 23, 41; Sharp, *Extract of a Letter to a Gentleman in Maryland; Wherein Is Demonstrated the Extreme Wickedness of Tolerating the Slave Trade* (London, 1793), 4-14.

[9] Granville Sharp, *An Appendix to the Representation* (London, 1772), 25. In 1776 Sharp argued that it was not sufficient to get slavery outlawed in England when the "abominable wickedness" persisted in the colonies. See *The Just Limitations of Slavery in the Laws of God, Compared with the Unbounded Claims of the African Traders and British American Slaveholders* (London, 1776), 2.

[10] Mary S. Locke, *Anti-Slavery in America from the Introduction of African Slaves to the Prohibition of the Slave Trade* (Boston, 1901), 19-20; Lorenzo J. Greene, "Slave-Holding New England and Its Awakening," *Journal of Negro History*, XIII (October, 1928), 523-25; Herbert Aptheker, "Militant Abolitionists," *ibid.*, XXVI (October, 1941), 440.

trine of natural rights had made the illegality of slavery an established fact in Vermont and Massachusetts.[11]

But the natural rights philosophy was not the only source of immediatism. Officially, the Society of Friends showed extreme caution in encouraging emancipation, but from the time of George Keith a latent impulse of moral perfectionism rose to the surface in the radical testimony of individual Quakers, who judged slavery in the uncompromising light of the Golden Rule. For such reformers, slavery was not a social or economic institution, but rather an embodiment of worldly sin that corrupted the souls of both master and slave; emancipation was not an objective matter of social or political expediency, but a subjective act of purification and a casting off of sin.[12]

Immediatism, in the sense of an immediate consciousness of the guilt of slaveholding and an ardent desire to escape moral contamination, is similarly evident in the writings of men who differed widely in their views of religion and political economy. John Wesley's combined attack on the opposite poles of Calvinism and natural religion could also be directed against slavery, which some defended by arguments similar to those that justified seeming injustice or worldly evils as part of God's master plan or nature's economy. In 1784 Wesley's antislavery beliefs were developed into a kind of immediatism in the rules of American Methodists: "We . . . think it our most bounden duty to take immediately some effectual method to extirpate this abomination from among us."[13] A related source of immediatism can be traced in the development of the romantic sensibility and the cult of the "man of feeling," which merged with Rousseau and the French Enlightenment in the writings of such men as Thomas Day and William Fox.[14]

[11] In Vermont, slavery was effectually prohibited by the state constitution; in Massachusetts the courts supported the claims to liberty of individual Negroes.

[12] Samuel W. Pennypacker, "The Settlement of Germantown, and the Causes Which Led to It," *Pennsylvania Magazine of History and Biography*, IV (1880), 28-30; George Keith, "An Exhortation & Caution to Friends Concerning Buying or Keeping of Negroes," *ibid.*, XIII (1889), 265-70; Society of Friends, Philadelphia Yearly Meeting, *A Brief Statement of the Rise and Progress of the Testimony of the Religious Society of Friends, against Slavery and the Slave Trade* (Philadelphia, 1843), 21-24, 44-56; Letters Which Passed Betwixt the Meeting for Sufferings in London and the Meeting for Sufferings in Philadelphia (MSS in Friends House, London): Philadelphia to London, February 1, 1759; London to Philadelphia, August 22, 1766; London to Philadelphia, September 4, 1795; Philadelphia to London, March 17, 1796; Thomas Drake, *Quakers and Slavery in America* (New Haven, 1950), 14-15, 68-83.

[13] Lucius C. Matlack, *The History of American Slavery and Methodism from 1780 to 1849* (New York, 1849), 15-20.

[14] Ronald S. Crane, "Suggestions Toward a Genealogy of the 'Man of Feeling,'"

In the light of this evidence we may well ask why immediatism appeared so new and dangerously radical in the 1830's. The later abolitionists charged that slavery was a sin against God and a crime against nature; they demanded an immediate beginning of direct action that would eventuate in general emancipation. Yet all of this had been said at least a half-century before, and we might conclude that immediatism was merely a recurring element in antislavery history.

But if immediatism was at least latent in early antislavery thought, the dominant frame of mind of the eighteenth century was overwhelmingly disposed to gradualism. Gradualism, in the sense of a reliance on indirect and slow-working means to achieve a desired social objective, was the logical consequence of fundamental attitudes toward progress, natural law, property, and individual rights.

We cannot understand the force of gradualism in antislavery thought unless we abandon the conventional distinction between Enlightenment liberalism and evangelical reaction. It is significant that British opponents of abolition made little use of religion, appealing instead to the need for calm rationality and an expedient regard for the national interest. Quoting Hume, Lord Kames, and even Montesquieu to support their moral relativism, they showed that principles of the Enlightenment could be easily turned to the defense of slavery.[15] A belief in progress and natural rights might lead, of course, to antislavery convictions; but if history seemed to be on the side of liberty, slavery had attained a certain prescriptive sanction as a nearly universal expression of human nature.[16] Men

English Literary History (Baltimore), I (December, 1934), 205-206, 216, 225, 229-30; Wylie Sypher, Guinea's Captive Kings: British Anti-Slavery Literature of the XVIIIth Century (Chapel Hill, 1942), 10, 77-85, 193-98; Thomas Day and John Bicknell, The Dying Negro (London, 1773); William Fox, An Address to the People of Great Britain, on the Consumption of West India Produce (London, 1791).

[15] [Edward Long], Candid Reflections upon the Judgment Lately Awarded by the Court of King's Bench (London, 1772); [Gordon Turnbull], An Apology for Negro Slavery; or the West-India Planters Vindicated from the Charge of Inhumanity (2nd ed., London, 1786); [Robert Norris], A Short Account of the African Slave Trade (Liverpool, 1787); Lord Rodney to Lord Hawkesbury, March, 1788, British Museum, Additional MSS, 38,416, fols. 72-76; A Few Conjectural Considerations upon the Creation of the Human Race, Occasioned by the Present Quixottical Rage of Setting the Slaves from Africa at Liberty, by the Reverend Dr. Lindsay (1788), Add. MSS, 12,439; [Anon.], Considerations upon the Fatal Consequences of Abolishing the Slave Trade (London, 1789). For one of the sources for the doctrine of Negro inferiority, see David Hume, "Of National Characters," in Essays Moral, Political, and Literary (2 vols., London, 1889), I, 244-58.

[16] This was a problem recognized by Montesquieu and Burke, among others. See

who had acquired an increasing respect for property and for the intricate workings of natural and social laws could not view as an unmitigated evil an institution that had developed through the centuries.

Though evangelicals attacked natural religion and an acceptance of the world as a divinely contrived mechanism in which evils like slavery served a legitimate function, they nevertheless absorbed many of the assumptions of conservative rationalists and tended to express a middle-class fear of sudden social change.[17] Despite the sharp differences between evangelicals and rationalists, they shared confidence, for the most part, in the slow unfolding of a divine or natural plan of historical progress. The mild and almost imperceptible diffusion of reason, benevolence, or Christianity had made slavery—a vestige of barbarism—anachronistic. But while eighteenth-century abolitionists might delight in furthering God's or nature's plan for earthly salvation, they tended to assume a detached, contemplative view of history, and showed considerable fear of sudden changes or precipitous action that might break the delicate balance of natural and historical forces.[18]

There was therefore a wide gap between the abstract proposition that slavery was wrong, or even criminal, and the cautious formulation of antislavery policy. It was an uncomfortable fact that slavery and the slave trade were tied closely to the rights of private property, the political freedom of colonies and states, and the economic rewards of international competition. Yet from the 1790's to the 1820's British and American reformers were confident that they

Fletcher, "Montesquieu's Influence," *Journal of Negro Hisotry*, XVIII, 422; Seeber, *Anti-Slavery Opinion*, 14-16, 28-33.

[17] For the influence of naturalism and the idea of progress on English theology in the eighteenth century, see Ronald S. Crane, "Anglican Apologetics and the Idea of Progress, 1699-1745," *Modern Philology* (Chicago), XXXI (February, 1934), 281-306, 349-79; Leslie Stephen, *History of English Thought in the Eighteenth Century* (2 vols., New York, 1949), I, 70-91; James Stephen, *Essays in Ecclesiastical Biography* (4th ed., London, 1860), 440-45.

[18] For the connection between gradualism and the idea of progress, see John Millar, *The Origin of the Distinction of Ranks* (3rd ed., London, 1781), 304, 320-47; William Paley, *The Principles of Moral and Political Philosophy* (London, 1785), 197-98; James Ramsay, A MS Volume, Entirely in Ramsay's Hand, Phillipps MSS, 17,780 (Rhodes House, Oxford). For the conservative approach of the Church of England to slavery, see Edgar L. Pennington, *Thomas Bray's Associates and Their Work among the Negroes* (Worcester, Mass., 1939), 10-12; J. Harry Bennett, Jr., "The Society for the Propagation of the Gospel's Plantations and the Emancipation Crisis," in Samuel C. McCulloch (ed.), *British Humanitarianism* (Philadelphia, 1950), 16-29. For cautious gradualism in America, see "The Appeal of the American Convention of Abolition Societies," *Journal of Negro History*, VI (April, 1921), 200-201; "American Convention of Abolition Societies Documents," *ibid.*, VI (July, 1921), 323-24, 363-64.

understood the basic principles of society and could thus work toward the desired goal indirectly and without infringing on legitimate rights or interests. Frequently they seemed to think of slavery as a kind of unfortunate weed or fungus that had spread through the Lord's garden in a moment of divine inattention. As expert horticulturalists they imagined they could gradually kill the blight without injuring the plants. The British reformers focused their attention on the slave trade, assuming that if the supply of African Negroes were shut off planters would be forced to take better care of their existing slaves and would ultimately discover that free labor was more profitable. In America, reform energies were increasingly directed toward removing the free Negroes, who were thought to be the principal barrier to voluntary manumission. Both schemes were attempts at rather complex social engineering, and in both instances the desired reform was to come from the slaveowners themselves. Antislavery theorists assumed that they could predict the cumulative effects and consequences of their limited programs, and since they never doubted the goodness or effectiveness of natural laws, they sought only to set in motion a chain of forces that would lead irresistibly to freedom.[19]

This gradualist mentality dominated antislavery thought from the late eighteenth century to the 1820's. Though French thinkers had been among the first to denounce slavery as a crime, the emancipation scheme which they pioneered was one of slow transformation of the slave into a free laborer.[20] Even the *Amis des Noirs*

[19] [William Belsham], *Remarks on the African Slave Trade* (London, 1790), 14-15; Thomas Clarkson, *History*, I, 282-89; II, 195, 586-87; [James Ramsay], *An Inquiry into the Effects of Putting a Stop to the African Slave Trade, and of Granting Liberty to the Slaves in the British Colonies* (London, 1784), 32-33, 40; [Joseph Woods], *Thoughts on the Slavery of the Negroes* (London, 1784), 31-32; *The Debate on a Motion for the Abolition of the Slave-Trade . . . the Second of April, 1792* (London, 1792), 12-17; *Society Instituted in 1787 for Effecting the Abolition of the Slave Trade* [Report] (London, 1788), 1-2; James Anderson, *Observations on Slavery* (Manchester, 1789), 11-23; Henry Brougham, *A Concise Statement of the Question Regarding the Abolition of the Slave Trade* (London, 1804), 57-60; Thomas Clarkson, *Three Letters (one of which has appeared before) to the Planters & Slave-Merchants, Principally on the Subject of Compensation* (London, 1807), 14-15; "Gustavus," letter to *Connecticut Courant* (Hartford), August 21, 1797; Joseph Parrish, *Remarks on the Slavery of the Black People* (Philadelphia, 1806), 40-42; *The Emancipator* (reprint, Nashville, 1932), ix; "Appeal of the American Convention," *Journal of Negro History*, VI, 332; "American Convention . . . Documents," *ibid.*, VI, 324-26; American Convention for Promoting the Abolition of Slavery, *An Address to the Free People of Color and Descendants of the African Race* (Philadelphia, 1819), 4-5. It is true, of course, that American reformers also devoted considerable attention to the slave trade.

[20] For the economic considerations behind French gradualism, see Gaston Martin, "La doctrine coloniale de la France en 1789," *Cahiers de la Révolution française* (Paris), III

feared immediate emancipation; and the French decree abolishing slavery in 1794, which was the result of political and military crisis in the West Indies, seemed to verify the ominous warnings of gradualists in all countries.[21] The years of bloodshed and anarchy in Haiti became an international symbol for the dangers of reckless and unplanned emancipation.

British abolitionists were particularly cautious in defining their objectives and moving indirectly, one step at a time. When outlawing the slave trade did not have the desired effect on colonial slavery, they then sought to bring the institution within the regulatory powers of the central government by limiting the extension of slavery in newly acquired islands and by using the crown colonies as models for gradual melioration;[22] and when these efforts failed they urged a general registration of slaves, which would not only interpose imperial authority in the colonies but provide a mechanism for protecting the Negroes' rights.[23] By 1822 these methods had proved inadequate and the British reformers began agitating for direct parliamentary intervention. Even then, however, and for the following eight years, British antislavery leaders limited their aims to melioration and emancipation by slow degrees.[24]

(1935), 25, 38-39; Martin, *Histoire de l'esclavage dans les colonies françaises* (Paris, 1948), 130-42, 164-65, 189-90, 251-59.

[21] Martin, *Histoire de l'esclavage*, 190, 209-26; McCloy, *Humanitarian Movement*, 114-25. Abolition became associated with the worst excesses of the French Revolution. See *Parliamentary History of England*, XXXI (House of Lords, 1794), 467-70; Clarkson, *History*, II, 208-12; Robert I. Wilberforce and Samuel Wilberforce (eds.), *The Correspondence of William Wilberforce* (2 vols., London, 1840), I, 89-90; Lafayette to Clarkson, January 27, 1798 (photostat in Rhodes House, Oxford); Louis Gottschalk, *Lafayette between the American and French Revolution* (Chicago, 1950), 380-81.

[22] Wilberforce, *Correspondence*, I, 328-29; Robert I. Wilberforce and Samuel Wilberforce, *The Life of William Wilberforce* (5 vols., London, 1838), III, 30-33, 198-200; [James Stephen], *The Crisis of the Sugar Colonies: or an Enquiry into the Objects and Probable Effects of the French Expedition to the West Indies* (London, 1802), 121-28, 151-95; *Report of the Committee of the African Institution . . . July, 1807* (London, 1807), 15; *Fifth Report of the Directors of the African Institution . . . March, 1811* (London, 1811), 1-2; Thomas Morton Birtwhistle, "The Development of Abolitionism, 1807-1823" (M.A. thesis, University of London, 1931), 19-30.

[23] This had been proposed in 1788 by the Reverend F. Randolph, *A Letter to the Right Honourable William Pitt . . . on the Proposed Abolition of the African Slave Trade* (London 1788), 44-46. The scheme was later championed by James Stephen. See [James Stephen], *Reasons for Establishing a Registry of Slaves in the British Colonies* (London, 1815); letter of James Stephen, April 14, 1815, Add. MSS, 38,416, fols. 364-71; Lowell J. Ragatz, *The Fall of the Planter Class in the British Caribbean, 1763-1833* (New York, 1928), 389-94.

[24] The gradualism, however, was combined with a sense that slavery was the ultimate of all evils. See Society for the Mitigation and Gradual Abolition of Slavery Throughout the British Dominions, *Prospectus* (London, 1823), v-vii; James Cropper, *A Letter Ad-*

Between British and American antislavery men there was a bond of understanding and a common interest in suppressing the international slave trade and finding a home in Haiti or western Africa for free Negroes.[25] But in America the antislavery movement was given a distinctive color by the discouraging obstacles that stood in the way of even gradual emancipation. While states like New York and Pennsylvania provided tangible examples of gradual manumission, they also showed the harsh and ugly consequences of racial prejudice.[26] Americans, far more than the British, were concerned with the problem of the emancipated slave. Even some of the most radical and outspoken abolitionists were convinced that colonization was the inescapable prerequisite to reform. Others stressed the importance of education and moral training as the first steps toward eventual freedom.[27]

In America the gradualist frame of mind was also related to the weakness and limitations of political institutions. British abolitionists could work to enlist the unlimited power of a central Parliament against colonies that were suffering acute economic decline. But slavery in America was not only expanding but was protected by a sectional balance of power embodied in nearly every national institution. A brooding fear of disunion and anarchy damped down the aspirations of most American abolitionists and turned energies to such local questions as the education and legal protection of individual Negroes. Antislavery societies might call for the govern-

dressed to the Liverpool Society for Promoting the Abolition of Slavery (Liverpool, 1823), 31-32.

[25] Twelfth Report of the Directors of the African Institution . . . April, 1818 (London, 1818), 35-37, 130-40; Fourteenth Report of the Directors of the African Institution . . . May, 1820 (London, 1820), 33-37, 84-97; Fifteenth Report . . . March, 1821 (London, 1821), 39-41; Wilberforce, Correspondence, I, 118; William Allen, Life of William Allen, with Selections from his Correspondence (3 vols., London, 1846), I, 114-15, 136-40. Thomas Clarkson to James Monroe, March 18, 1817 (photostat in Rhodes House, Oxford); Earl Leslie Griggs and Clifford H. Prator (eds.), Henry Christophe and Thomas Clarkson: A Correspondence (Berkeley, 1952), 124-25, 141-42; Zachary Macaulay to Mrs. Clarkson, March 31, 1823, Add. MSS, 41,267A, fols. 134-35.

[26] Edward R. Turner, The Negro in Pennsylvania (Washington, 1911), 143-68; Charles H. Wesley, "The Negroes of New York and the Emancipation Movement," Journal of Negro History, XXIV (January, 1939), 65-103; Wesley, "The Concept of Negro Inferiority in American Thought," ibid., XXV (October, 1940), 540-60; Thomas Branagan, Serious Remonstrances, Addressed to the Citizens of the Northern States (Philadelphia, 1805), passim; Branagan, Political and Theological Disquisitions on the Signs of the Times (Trenton, 1807), passim.

[27] Emancipator (reprint), vii, ix-x; "Appeal of American Convention," Journal of Negro History, VI, 215-18; Drake, Quakers and Slavery, 114-15; Turner, Negro in Pennsylvania, 210-12; [William Griffith], Address of the President of the New Jersey Society for Promoting the Abolition of Slavery (Trenton, 1804), 8-9.

ment to outlaw slavery in the District of Columbia or even to abolish the interstate slave trade, but in the end they had to rely on public opinion and individual conscience in the slave states. While British abolitionists moved with the circumspection of conservative pragmatists, their American counterparts acted with the caution of men surrounded by high explosives. For many, the only prudent solution was to remove the explosives to a distant country.

But if British and American abolitionists were gradualist in their policies and expectations, they did not necessarily regard slavery as simply one of many social evils that should be mitigated and eventually destroyed. The policy of gradualism was related to certain eighteenth-century assumptions about historical progress, the nature of man, and the principles of social change; but we have also noted a subjective, moral aspect to antislavery thought that was often revealed as an immediate consciousness of guilt and a fear of divine punishment. During the British slave trade controversy of the 1790's the entire system of slavery and slave trade became identified with sin, and reform with true virtue.[28] Though antislavery leaders adopted the gradualist policy of choosing the slave trade as their primary target, they bitterly fought every attempt to meliorate or gradually destroy the African trade. It was the determined opponents of the slave trade who first gave popular currency to the slogan, "immediate abolition," which became in the early 1790's a badge of moral sincerity.[29] When uncompromising hostility to the slave trade became a sign of personal virtue and practical Christianity, the rhetoric of statesmen acquired the strident, indignant tone that we associate with later American abolitionists. Charles James Fox made scathing attacks on those who pled for moderation; he even said that if the plantations could not be cultivated without being supplied with African slaves, it would be far better for England to rid herself of the islands. "How shall we hope," asked William Pitt, "to obtain, if it is possible, forgiveness from Heaven for those enormous evils we have committed, if we refuse to make use of those means which the mercy of Providence

[28] Clarkson, History, I, 1-29, 158-66; II, 119-20, 347, 581-86; Society Instituted in 1787 [Report], 2; [William Belsham], Remarks on the African Slave Trade (London, 1790), 18-19; Granville Sharp, Serious Reflections on the Slave Trade and Slavery (London, 1805), 8-38; Sharp, "The System of Colonial Law" Compared with the Eternal Laws of God (London, 1807), 13; Stephen, Crisis in Sugar Colonies, 174-76.
[29] William Wilberforce, A Letter on the Abolition of the Slave Trade (London, 1807), 301-302; Wilberforce, Life, I, 345-46, 351; Debate on the Motion for Abolition of Slave Trade ... 1792 (Wilberforce speech), 47-48.

hath still reserved to us for wiping away the guilt and shame with which we are now covered?"[30]

This sense of moral urgency and fear of divine retribution persisted in British antislavery thought and was held in check only by a faith in the certain and predictable consequences of indirect action.[31] Whenever the faith was shaken by unforeseen obstacles or a sense of crisis, there were voices that condemned gradualism as a compromise with sin. Granville Sharp, who interpreted hurricanes in the West Indies as supernatural agencies "to blast the *enemies* of *law* and *righteousness*," called in 1806 for direct emancipation by act of Parliament, and warned that continued toleration of slavery in the colonies "must finally draw down the Divine vengeance upon our state and nation!"[32] When William Allen, Zachary Macaulay, and James Cropper became disillusioned over the failure to secure an effective registration scheme and international suppression of the slave trade, they pressed for direct though gradual emancipation by the British government.[33] The British Anti-Slavery Society remained officially gradualist until 1831, but individual abolitionists, particularly in the provinces, became increasingly impatient over the diffidence of the government and the intransigence of colonial legislatures.[34] From 1823 to 1832 the British Caribbean planters violently attacked the government's efforts to meliorate slavery. They not only devised schemes to nullify effective reform but threatened to secede from the empire and seek protection from the United States.[35]

[30] *Debate on the Motion . . . 1792*, pp. 116-17, 132-34, 164-65.

[31] Granville Sharp, *The Case of Saul, Shewing that His Disorder was a Real Spiritual Possession* (London, 1807), preface to 1807 ed., iii-iv; [Anon.], *The Horrors of the Negro Slavery Existing in Our West Indian Islands* (London, 1805), 4-5, 36; James Stephen, *A Defence of the Bill for the Registration of Slaves* (London, 1816), 36-55; Wilberforce, *Correspondence*, II, 495-96.

[32] Sharp, *Serious Reflections*, 38; Sharp, "*Systems of Colonial Law*," 13.

[33] For the formation of the British Anti-Slavery Society, see David B. Davis, "James Cropper and the British Anti-Slavery Movement," *Journal of Negro History*, XLV (October, 1960), 241-58.

[34] MSS Minutes of the Society for the Mitigation and Gradual Abolition of Slavery Throughout the British Dominions (Rhodes House, Oxford), I, 34-36, 133-35, 139, 141; II, 1-8, 18-21, 49-52, 81, 132-41; III, 4-6, 20-27; Society for the Mitigation and Gradual Abolition of Slavery, *Second Report* (London, 1825), *passim; Anti-Slavery Monthly Reporter* (London), I (January 31, 1826), 80; I (May 31, 1826), 185-88; III (June, 1830), 239-63. In the 1830's American abolitionists claimed that the British Anti-Slavery Society had adopted the principle of immediatism in 1826, and later historians have repeated the same error. It was only in 1831 and 1832 that immediatism gained widespread support, and even then the more conservative leaders looked to the government for an effective but gradual working plan.

[35] Ragatz, *Fall of the Planter Class*, 287, 332, 412-48; Claude Levy, "Barbados: The

Though the evils of West Indian slavery were probably mitigated in the 1820's, the planters' resistance convinced many abolitionists that gradual improvement was impossible.

The most eloquent early plea for immediate emancipation was made in 1824 by a Quaker named Elizabeth Heyrick, who looked to the women of Great Britain as a source of invincible moral power, and who preached a massive consumers' crusade against West Indian produce. The central theme in Mrs. Heyrick's pamphlet, *Immediate, Not Gradual Abolition*, was the supremacy of individual conscience over social and political institutions. Since antislavery was a *"holy war"* against "the very powers of darkness," there was no ground for compromise or for a polite consideration of slaveholders. Like the later American immediatists, she excoriated gradualism as a satanic plot to induce gradual indifference. It was a delusion to think that slavery could be gradually improved, for "as well might you say to a poor wretch, gasping and languishing in a pest house, 'here will I keep you, till I have given you a capacity for the enjoyment of pure air.' "[36] For Mrs. Heyrick the issue was simple and clear-cut: sin and vice should be immediately exterminated by individual action in accordance with conscience and the will of God.

In 1824 such views were too strong for British antislavery leaders, who still looked to direct government action modeled on the precedent of the Canning Resolutions, which had proposed measures for ameliorating the condition of West Indian slaves as a step toward ultimate emancipation.[37] Abolitionists in Parliament continued to shape their strategy in the light of political realities, but by 1830 several prominent reformers had adopted the uncompromising stand of Elizabeth Heyrick. The shift from gradualism to immediatism is most dramatically seen in James Stephen, who possessed a mind of great clarity and precision and who, having practiced law in the West Indies, had acquired direct experience with slavery as an institution. For a time Stephen adhered to the principle of gradualism, transferring his hopes from the slave registration scheme to a "di-

Last Years of Slavery, 1823-1833," *Journal of Negro History*, XLIV (October, 1959), 316-22.

[36] Elizabeth Heyrick, *Immediate, Not Gradual Abolition; or, An Inquiry into the Shortest, Safest, and Most Effectual Means of Getting Rid of West Indian Slavery* (London, 1824), 8, 14-18.

[37] But on June 8, 1924, the General Committee of the Anti-Slavery Society instructed its secretary to procure a dozen copies of the Heyrick pamphlet for distribution to interested members; and some of the Society's members were reported at the same time to favor immediate abolition. Minutes, I, 111-12.

gested plan" of abolition by stages, beginning with domestic servants. By 1830, however, he was convinced that debate over alternative plans merely inhibited action and obscured what was essentially
a question of principle and simple moral duty. It would be a tragic
mistake, he felt, for the abolitionists to propose any measure short
of "a general, entire, immediate restitution of the freedom wrong-
fully withheld." Lashing out at the moral lethargy of the government, he denounced the principle of compensation to slaveowners
and rejected all specific gradualist measures such as the liberation of
Negro women or the emancipation of infants born after a certain
date. Stephen's immediatism was based ultimately on a fear of divine
vengeance and an overwhelming sense of national guilt. "We sin
remorselessly," he said, "because our fathers sinned, and because
multitudes of our own generation sin, in the same way without
[public] discredit."[38]

On October 19, 1830, the Reverend Andrew Thomson, of St.
George's Church in Edinburgh, delivered a fire-and-brimstone
speech that provided an ideology for George Thompson and the
later Agency Committee.[39] Beginning with the premise that slavery
is a crime and sin, Thomson dismissed all consideration of economic
and political questions. When the issue was reduced to what individual men should do as mortal and accountable beings, there was no
possibility of compromise or even controversy. The British public
should "compel" Parliament to order total and immediate emancipation. With Calvinistic intensity he exhorted the public to cut down
and burn the "pestiferous tree," root and branch: "You must annihilate it,—annihilate it now,—and annihilate it forever." Since
Thomson considered every hour that men were kept in bondage
a repetition of the original sin of man-stealing, he did not shrink
from violence: "If there must be violence, . . . let it come and rage its
little hour, since it is to be succeeded by lasting freedom, and prosperity, and happiness."[40]

Taking its cue from men like Stephen, Thomson, and Joseph
Sturge, the Anti-Slavery Society reorganized itself for more effec-

[38] James Stephen, *The Slavery of the British West India Colonies Delineated* (2 vols.,
London, 1824-1830), II, 387, 390-401; Minutes, III, 132-33.

[39] Raymond English, "George Thompson and the Climax of Philanthropic Radicalism, 1830-1842" (unpublished dissertation, Cambridge University), 33. I am indebted
to Mr. English for lending me a copy of his manuscript.

[40] Andrew Thomson, *Immediate Emancipation: Substance of a Speech Delivered at the
Meeting of the Edinburgh Society for the Abolition of Slavery* (Manchester, 1832), 4,
11, 24.

tive action and focused its energies on raising petitions and arousing public feeling against slavery.[41] While Thomas Fowell Buxton sought to make the fullest use of public opinion to support his campaign in Parliament, he found himself under mounting pressure from abolitionists who refused to defer to his judgment. People's principles, he told his daughter, were the greatest nuisance in life.[42] When the government finally revealed its plan for gradual and compensated emancipation, the Anti-Slavery Society committed itself to vigorous and aggressive opposition.[43] But once the law had been passed, the antislavery leaders concluded that they had done as well as possible and that their defeat had actually been a spectacular victory. They had achieved their primary object, which was to induce the people to support a tangible act that could be interpreted as purging the nation of collective guilt and proving the moral power of individual conscience.

In America the developing pattern was somewhat similar. Despite the conservatism of most antislavery societies, a number of radical abolitionists branded slaveholding as a heinous sin, which, if not immediately abandoned, would bring down the wrath of the Lord. A few early reformers like Theodore Dwight, David Rice, Charles Osborn, and John Rankin, were well in advance of British

[41] Many historians have been misled by Sir George Stephen's *Antislavery Recollections* (London, 1854), which states that the Agency Committee was an independent body formed by the democratic "young England Abolitionists" after the conservative Anti-Slavery Society had vehemently rejected the plan of employing itinerant agents (pp. 128-29). Actually, the Society had accepted the plan in principle in 1828. In large meetings of May 25 and June 1, 1831, the Society unanimously approved the Agency program and appointed a subcommittee which included such outsiders as George Stephen, Emmanuel Cooper, and Charles Stuart (Minutes, III, 93-100). Dissension did not arise over the wisdom of arousing public opinion, as Stephen claimed, but over the control of such efforts and the co-ordination of policy by a central authority. The Agency subcommittee remained a part of the parent society until July 4, 1832, when a rupture came over the General Committee's assertion of its right to inspect all antislavery documents prior to publication (*Ibid.*, 142-52). While many members of the parent society favored immediate emancipation, it was the Agency Committee that popularized the doctrine. See *The Tourist: A Literary and Anti-Slavery Journal* (London), I (1832-1833), 16, 94, 108, 124, 173, 231, 266, 308; *Report of the Agency Committee of the Anti-Slavery Society* (London, 1832), 3-4; Charles Stuart, *The West India Question* (London, 1832), 4-6; George Thompson, *Three Lectures on British Colonial Slavery, Delivered in the Royal Amphitheatre, Liverpool* (Liverpool, 1832), 57-64, 76-77.

[42] Frank Carpenter Stuart, "A Critical Edition of the Correspondence of Sir Thomas Fowell Buxton, Bart., with an Account of his Career to 1823" (2 vols., M.A. thesis, Institute for Historical Research, London, 1957), II, 24-29, 45-46, 244.

[43] Society for the Abolition of Slavery Throughout the British Dominions [Circular Letter to Provisional Organizations], April 4, 1833, pp. 1-2; [Anon.], *Some Remarks on Mr. Stanley's Proposed Bill for the Abolition of Colonial Slavery* (n.p., 1833), 1-7; Minutes, IV, 54-55, 61; Richard, *Joseph Sturge*, 106-107.

antislavery writers in their sense of moral urgency and their mistrust of gradualist programs. As early as 1808, David Barrow, although he denied favoring immediate abolition, anticipated the later doctrine of the American Anti-Slavery Society by refusing to recognize the lawfulness of slavery or the justice of compensation. Holding that slavery was the crying sin of America, he urged a prompt beginning of manumission in order to avert the retribution of God.[44] Three years earlier Thomas Branagan, who opposed "instantaneous emancipation" if the freed Negroes were to remain within the United States, contended that his plan for colonization in the West would bring a speedy end to slavery and avert the divine judgment of an apocalyptic racial war.[45] In 1817 John Kenrick showed that colonization could be combined with a kind of immediatism, for though he proposed settlement of free Negroes in the West, he went so far as to suggest that the powers of the central government should be enlarged, if necessary, in order to abolish slavery. "If slavery is 'a violation of the divine laws,'" Kenrick asked, "is it not absurd to talk about a gradual emancipation? We might as well talk of gradually leaving off piracy—murder—adultery, or drunkenness."[46]

The religious character of this radical abolitionism can best be seen in the writings of George Bourne, an English immigrant who was to have a deep influence on William Lloyd Garrison. In 1815 Bourne condemned professed Christians who upheld the crime of slavery. "The system is so entirely corrupt," he wrote, "that it admits of no cure, but by a total and immediate, abolition. For a gradual emancipation is a virtual recognition of the right, and establishes the rectitude of the practice." But while Bourne associated slavery with the very essence of human sin, his main concern was not the plight of Negroes but the corruption of the Christian church:

> Had this compound of all corruption no connection with the church of Christ; however deleterious are the effects of it in political society, however necessary is its immediate and total abolition, and however pregnant with danger to the *Union,* is the prolongation of the system; to Legislators and

[44] David Barrow, *Involuntary, Unmerited, Perpetual, Absolute, Hereditary Slavery, Examined; on the Principles of Nature, Reason, Justice, Policy and Scripture* (Lexington, Ky., 1808), 13-14, 42.
[45] Thomas Branagan, *Serious Remonstrances,* 35, 64; Branagan, *Buying Stolen Goods Synonymous with Stealing* (2nd ed. [printed with *The Penitential Tyrant*], Philadelphia, 1807), 233-39.
[46] John Kenrick, *Horrors of Slavery* (Cambridge, Mass., 1817), 38-39, 58-59.

Civilians, the redress of the evil would have been committed. But *Slavery* is the *golden Calf*, which has been elevated among the Tribes, and before it, the Priests and the Elders and the *nominal* sons of Israel, *eat, drink, rise up to play, worship and sacrifice.*[47]

Thus for Bourne "immediatism" meant an immediate recognition of the sin of slavery and an immediate decision on the part of Christians to purge their churches of all contamination. He was far more interested in the purification of religion than in slavery as an institution.

In 1825 the Boston *Recorder and Telegraph* published a long correspondence that further clarifies the origins of immediatism. After arguing that slavery was unlawful and suggesting that slaves might have a right to revolt, "Vigornius" [Samuel M. Worcester] asserted that *"the slave-holding system must be abolished;* and in order to the accomplishment of this end, immediate, determined measures must be adopted for the ultimate emancipation of every slave within our territories."[48] This was the position of the later Kentucky and New York abolitionists, but Vigornius combined it with strong faith in the American Colonization Society. He was bitterly attacked by "A Carolinian," who accused him of believing in "an entire and immediate abolition of slavery." "Philo," the next contributor, said he opposed immediate emancipation on grounds of expediency, but recognized the right of slaves to immediate freedom; he advocated, therefore, "immediate and powerful remedies," since "We are convinced, and if our Southern brethren are not convinced, we wish to convince them, and think with a little discussion we could convince them, that to postpone these prospective measures a day, is a great crime . . . and moreover, we wish to state directly, that this postponement is that, in which we consider the guilt of slavery, so far as the present proprietors are concerned, to consist."[49]

A Southerner, who called himself "Hieronymus," defended Vigornius and tried to avoid the ambiguities that were later to cloud discussions of immediate abolition. Vigornius, he wrote,

[47] George Bourne, *The Book and Slavery Irreconcilable: With Animadversions upon Dr. Smith's Philosophy* (Philadelphia, 1816), 7-8, 16-19, appendix. Bourne's appeal for unconditional emancipation attracted the attention of William Allen, the English philanthropist who was later instrumental in founding the British Anti-Slavery Society. See William Allen (ed.), *The Philanthropist: or Repository for Hints and Suggestions Calculated to Promote the Comfort and Happiness of Man* (London), VI (1816), 334-50.
[48] [Samuel M. Worcester], *Essays on Slavery: Re-Published from the Boston Recorder & Telegraph, for 1825, by Vigornius, and Others* (Amherst, 1826), 24-25.
[49] *Ibid.*, 32-33.

pleads, it is true, for *speedy* emancipation, and immediate preparatory steps. But immediate and speedy are not synonimous [*sic*] expressions. One is an absolute, the other a relative or comparative term. An event may in one view of it be regarded as very speedy, which in another might be pronounced very gradual. If slavery should be entirely abolished from the United States in 30, 40, or even 50 years, many . . . will readily admit, that it would be a speedy abolition; while every one must perceive, that it would be far, very far, from an immediate abolition. In a certain sense abolition may be immediate; in another, speedy; and in both, practicable and safe. There are not a few blacks now at the South, qualified for immediate emancipation, if Legislatures would permit, and owners would confer it.[50]

Hieronymus, who had read and been impressed by Elizabeth Heyrick's pamphlet, agreed with Vigornius that colonization was the only practicable solution to the nation's most critical problem.

These ardent colonizationists believed that slavery was a sin that would increase in magnitude and danger unless effective measures were adopted without delay. Yet by 1821 Benjamin Lundy and other abolitionists had come to the opinion that the American Colonization Society was founded on racial prejudice and offered no real promise of undermining slavery. Lundy thought that slavery could not be eradicated until his fellow Americans in both North and South were willing to accept the free Negro as an equal citizen.[51] But in the meantime the institution was expanding into the Southwest and even threatening to spread to such states as Illinois. In the face of such an imposing problem, Lundy called for the swift and decisive use of political power by a convention of representatives from the various states, who might devise and implement a comprehensive plan for emancipation.[52]

The American antislavery organizations absorbed some of this sense of urgency and mistrust of palliatives. The Pennsylvania Society for the Abolition of Slavery was cautious in its approach to the national problem, but in 1819 it approved a declaration that "the practice of holding and selling human beings as property . . . ought to be *immediately* abandoned."[53] In 1825 the Acting Committee of

[50] *Ibid.*, 46-47.
[51] *Genius of Universal Emancipation* (Greeneville, Tenn.), I (September, 1821), 33; (October, 1821), 49-52.
[52] *Ibid.*, I (September, 1821), 35; (February, 1822), 118-20; (March, 1822), 135. Lundy favored colonization at public expense of Negroes wishing to leave the country, but he also called on the North to receive emancipated slaves without restriction, and exhorted the South to repeal laws discriminating against free Negroes.
[53] Turner, *Negro in Pennsylvania*, 216. In 1819 the Pennsylvania Society sent a mes-

the American Convention for Promoting the Abolition of Slavery advocated the "speedy and entire" emancipation of slaves, a phrase later used by the British Society.[54] The Convention showed little confidence in any of the specific proposals for gradual abolition but at the same time rejected direct emancipation by act of Congress as an impossibility. Alert always to the need for conciliating the South and remaining within the prescribed bounds of the Constitution, the Convention considered every conceivable plan in a rationalistic and eclectic spirit.[55] In the South, however, there was an increasing tendency to see the most conservative antislavery proposals as immediatism in disguise.[56] By 1829 the gradualist approach of the American Convention had reached a dead end.[57]

It is a striking coincidence that both the British and American antislavery movements had come to a crucial turning point by 1830.[58] In both countries the decline of faith in gradualism had been marked in the mid-1820's by enthusiasm for a boycott of slave produce, a movement which promised to give a cutting edge to the moral testimony of individuals.[59] In both countries the truculence and stubborn opposition of slaveholders to even gradualist reforms brought a sense of despair and indignation to the antislavery public. To some degree immediatism was the creation of the British and American slaveholders themselves. By accusing the most moderate critics of

sage to the American Convention, calling for the "total and most early abolition of slavery, consistent with the interest of the objects of your care." American Convention, *Minutes of the Sixteenth Session of the American Convention* (Philadelphia, 1819), 6-8.

[54] American Convention, *Minutes of the Nineteenth Session of the American Convention* (Philadelphia, 1825), 30.

[55] "Appeal of American Convention," *Journal of Negro History*, VI, 235-40; "American Convention Documents," *ibid.*, *passim*.

[56] Glover Moore, *The Missouri Controversy, 1819-1821* (Lexington, Ky., 1953), 303-304; [Worcester], *Essays on Slavery*, 29; William S. Jenkins, *Pro-Slavery Thought in the Old South* (Chapel Hill, 1935), 67-80.

[57] This is perhaps most clearly seen in the memorial drawn up by a committee of the American Convention on December 11, 1829. See "American Convention Documents," *Journal of Negro History*, VI, 351-57. Also, Drake, *Quakers and Slavery*, 134-39; Alice Dana Adams, *The Neglected Period of Anti-Slavery in America* (Boston, 1908), 116-17, 154-57, 175-76.

[58] This parallel development of British and American antislavery movements was recognized by Benjamin Lundy. See *Genius of Universal Emancipation*, New Series (Baltimore), III (November, 1832).

[59] *The Philanthropist: A Weekly Journal* (Mount Pleasant, Ohio), II (August 21, 1819), 297-99; II (September 4, 1819), 324-25; Norman B. Wilkinson, "The Philadelphia Free Produce Attack upon Slavery," *Pennsylvania Magazine of History and Biography*, LXVI (July, 1942), 297-99; Adams, *Neglected Period*, 127, 149-51; Minutes of the Society for the Mitigation and Gradual Abolition of Slavery, II, 1-52; James Cropper, *The Support of Slavery Investigated* (London, 1824); Heyrick, *Immediate, Not Gradual Abolition*, *passim*.

radical designs and by blocking the path to many attempted reforms they helped to discredit the gradualist mentality that had balanced and compromised a subjective conviction that slavery was sin.[60] The sense of crisis between 1829 and 1831 was also accentuated by an increasing militancy of Negroes, both slave and free.[61] In 1829 David Walker hinted ominously of slave revenge; grcups of free Negroes openly repudiated the colonization movement; and in 1831 bloody revolts erupted in Virginia and Jamaica. In that year a new generation of American reformers adopted the principle of immediatism, which had recently acquired the sanction of eminent British philanthropists.[62] But while American abolitionists modeled their new societies and techniques on British examples, the principle of immediatism had had a long and parallel development in both countries.

In one sense immediatism was simply a shift in strategy brought on by the failure of less direct plans for abolition. Earlier plans and programs had evoked little popular excitement compared with parliamentary reform or Catholic emancipation in England, or with tariff or land policies in the United States. As a simple, emotional slogan, immediate abolition would at least arouse interest and perhaps appeal to the moral sense of the public. As a device for propaganda it had the virtue of avoiding economic and social complexities and focusing attention on a clear issue of right and wrong.[63] If the public could once be brought to the conviction that slavery was wrong and that something must be done about it at once, then governments would be forced to take care of the details.

[60] William B. Hesseltine, "Some New Aspects of the Pro-Slavery Argument," *Journal of Negro History*, XXI (January, 1936), 8-13; *Philanthropist, A Weekly Journal*, VII (April 20, 1822), 353-55.

[61] Aptheker, "Militant Abolitionists," *Journal of Negro History*, XXVI, 444-48; Wesley, "Negroes of New York," *ibid.*, XXIV, 68-81; Bella Gross, " 'Freedom's Journal' and the 'Rights of All,' " *ibid.*, XXVII (July, 1932), 241-62; Herbert Aptheker, *The Negro in the Abolitionist Movement* (New York, 1941), 33-36, 40-42. The crisis was also intensified by the tariff and nullification controversy in America and by the mounting pressure for political reform in Britain.

[62] Barnes, *Antislavery Impulse*, 32-33, 42-44; Roman J. Zorn, "The New England Anti-Slavery Society: Pioneer Abolition Organization," *Journal of Negro History*, XLII (July, 1957), 159-73; David M. Ludlum, *Social Ferment in Vermont, 1791-1850* (New York, 1939), 142-44.

[63] See, for example, the letter in *The Liberator* (Boston), I (January 22, 1831), 13, suggesting that a special juvenile department would help correct prejudice in adults: "For there is, perhaps, no better way of removing error, than by leading the mind back to the first simple view of a subject, which you would present to a child." Also, Barnes and Dumond (eds.), *Weld-Grimké Letters*, I, 95-97, 100, 118, 125-28; *Report of the Agency Committee* (London), 2-3; Letter of James Stephen to Anti-Slavery Society, April 3, 1832, Minutes, III, 131-35.

But immediatism was something more than a shift in strategy. It represented a shift in total outlook from a detached, rationalistic perspective on human history and progress to a personal commitment to make no compromise with sin. It marked a liberation for the reformer from the ideology of gradualism, from a toleration of evil within the social order, and from a deference to institutions that blocked the way to personal salvation. Acceptance of immediatism was the sign of an immediate transformation within the reformer himself; as such, it was seen as an expression of inner freedom, of moral sincerity and earnestness, and of victory over selfish and calculating expediency.[64] If slaveholders received the doctrine with contempt and scathing abuse, the abolitionist was at least assured of his own freedom from guilt. He saw the emergence of immediatism as an upswelling of personal moral force which, with the aid of God, would triumph over all that was mean and selfish and worldly.[65]

There are obvious links between immediate emancipation and a religious sense of immediate justification and presence of the divine spirit that can be traced through the early spiritual religions to the Quakers, Methodists, and evangelical revivals.[66] The new abolitionism contained a similar pattern of intense personal anxiety, rapturous freedom, eagerness for sacrifice, and mistrust of legalism, institutions, and slow-working agencies for salvation. It was no accident that from the late seventeenth century the boldest assertions of antislavery sentiment had been made by men who were dissatisfied with the materialism and sluggish formality of institutionalized religion, and who searched for a fresh and assuring meaning of

[64] Barnes and Dumond (eds.), *Weld-Grimké Letters*, I, 97-103, 116, 132-35, 140-46; *Liberator*, I (January 8, 1831), 7; *Philanthropist, A Weekly Journal* (Mount Pleasant, Ohio), II (September 4, 1819), 324-25; *The Philanthropist* [an earlier journal published by Charles Osborn] (Mount Pleasant, Ohio), I (December 5, 1817), 114; Bourne, *The Book and Slavery*, 20-21, 58, 74-75, 139-40, Appendix; Heyrick, *Immediate, Not Gradual Abolition*, 34-36.

[65] "Letters of William Lloyd Garrison to John B. Vashon," *Journal of Negro History*, XII (January, 1927), 36-38; Thompson, *Three Lectures on British Colonial Slavery*, 4-5, 7; *Tourist*, I, 84, 124; William Allen to Charles Babbage, December 1, 1832, Add. MSS, 37,187, fols. 255-56.

[66] Rufus M. Jones, *Spiritual Reformers in the 16th and 17th Centuries* (Boston, 1959 [1st ed. 1914]), xviii-xlvii, 44-45, 234, 288-98; William C. Braithwaite, *The Beginnings of Quakerism* (London, 1955 [1st ed. 1912]), 49-50; Rufus M. Jones, *The Later Periods of Quakerism* (2 vols., London, 1921), I, 23-37, 78, 81-83; Wade C. Barclay, *Early American Methodism* (2 vols., New York, 1949-1950), I, xxii-xxiii; William G. McLoughlin, *Modern Revivalism* (New York, 1959), 103-105. It should also be noted that the issue of gradual versus immediate emancipation followed a long religious controversy over gradual versus immediate, instantaneous conversion.

Christian doctrine in a changing world.[67] To the extent that slavery became a concrete symbol of sin, and support of the antislavery cause a sign of Christian virtue, participation in the reform became a supplement or even alternative to traditional religion.[68] As a kind of surrogate religion, antislavery had long shown tendencies that were pietistic, millennial, and anti-institutional. By the 1830's it had clearly marked affinities with the increasingly popular doctrines of free grace, immediate conversion, and personal holiness. According to Amos A. Phelps, for example, immediatism was synonymous with immediate repentance: "All that follows is the carrying out of the new principle of action, and is to emancipation just what sanctification is to conversion."[69]

Immediate emancipation was also related to a changing view of history and human nature. Whereas the gradualist saw man as at least partially conditioned by historical and social forces, the immediatist saw him as essentially indeterminate and unconditioned. The gradualist, having faith in the certainty of economic and social laws, and fearing the dangers of a sudden collapse of social controls, was content to wait until a legal and rational system of external discipline replaced the arbitrary power of the slaveowner. The immediatist, on the other hand, put his faith in the innate moral capacities of the individual. He felt that unless stifling and coercive influences were swept away, there could be no development of the inner controls of conscience, emulation, and self-respect, on which a free and Christian society depended.[70] His outlook was essentially romantic,

[67] For an expression of the religious motives of antislavery, see Wilberforce, *Life*, V, 156-59. There is a clear relationship between antislavery and religious anxiety in the lives of many abolitionists. Obviously, most religious anxiety found other outlets than antislavery; but the writings of abolitionists in both Britain and America show that the cause satisfied religious yearnings that could not be fulfilled by the traditional institutions of the church.

[68] This point is made convincingly by Barnes, *Antislavery Impulse*, 104-107. See also, Granville Sharp, *The Law of Retribution* (London, 1776), 250-52; Locke, *Anti-Slavery in America*, 59-60; Branagan, *Political and Theological Disquisition*, 22-30; Kenrick, *Horrors of Slavery*, 40; Parrish, *Remarks*, 2-9, 34-36; Branagan, *Penitential Tyrant*, vi-xi; Bourne, *Book and Slavery*, 135-41.

[69] Amos A. Phelps, *Lectures on Slavery and Its Remedy* (Boston, 1834), 179. For the relation between antislavery and revivalism, see Barnes and Dumond (eds.), *Weld-Grimké Letters*, I, 40-52, 94-97; McLoughlin, *Modern Revivalism*, 23-31, 53-54, 86, 107-12; Charles C. Cole, *The Social Ideas of the Northern Evangelists, 1826-1860* (New York, 1954), 101-25, 196, 231-38.

[70] For the rise of new values concerning work, authority, and the development of inner disciplinary controls, see Reinhard Bendix, *Work and Authority in Industry: Ideologies of Management in the Course of Industrialization* (New York, 1956), 34, 60-62, 72-73; Adam Smith, *An Inquiry into the Nature and Causes of the Wealth of Nations* (Modern Library ed., New York, 1937), 364-66.

for instead of cautiously manipulating the external forces of nature, he sought to create a new epoch of history by liberating the inner moral forces of human nature.[71]

It falls beyond the scope of the present essay to show how immediatism itself became institutionalized as a rigid test of faith, and how it served as a medium for attacking all rival institutions that limited individual freedom or defined standards of thought and conduct. It is enough to suggest that immediatism, while latent in early antislavery thought, was part of a larger reaction against a type of mind that tended to think of history in terms of linear time and logical categories, and that emphasized the importance of self-interest, expediency, moderation, and planning in accordance with economic and social laws. Immediatism shared with the romantic frame of mind a hostility to all dualisms of thought and feeling, an allegiance to both emotional sympathy and abstract principle, an assumption that mind can rise above self-interest, and a belief that ideas, when held with sufficient intensity, can be transformed into irresistible moral action.[72] If immediate emancipation brought misunderstanding and violent hostility in regions that were charged with racial prejudice and fear of sectional conflict, it was nevertheless an appropriate doctrine for a romantic and evangelical age.

[71] See Hoxie Neale Fairchild, *The Noble Savage; a Study in Romantic Naturalism* (New York, 1928), 404-405; Lois Whitney, *Primitivism and the Idea of Progress* (Baltimore, 1934), 21-22, 82-85; Margaret T. Hodgen, "The Negro in the Anthropology of John Wesley," *Journal of Negro History*, XIX (July, 1934), 308-23; Branagan, *Serious Remonstrances*, 32-35; Sharp, *Just Limitation*, 36-37, 65-67; William Roscoe, *The Wrongs of Africa* (London, 1787), 9-12; James Anderson, *Observations on Slavery* (Manchester, 1789), 3-5; New York City Anti-Slavery Society, *Address to the People of the City of New York* (New York, 1833), 3-12; George Allen, *Mr. Allen's Report of a Declaration of Sentiments on Slavery* (Worcester, Mass., 1838), 10-11; Barrow, *Involuntary . . . Slavery*, 45. For the relation between this romantic anthropology and the liberal theology of men like Nathaniel W. Taylor and Albert Barnes, see McLoughlin, *Modern Revivalism*, 45-69. Stanley Elkins correctly discerns the anti-formal and anti-institutional character of immediatism (*Slavery*, 189-92), but he relates it to the fluid social structure in the United States; the same characteristics had been present in British and French antislavery literature from the eighteenth century, and their accentuation by the 1830's would seem to have been part of a major ideological development.

[72] Walter J. Bate, *From Classic to Romantic* (Cambridge, Mass., 1946), 176-77; Walter E. Houghton, *The Victorian Frame of Mind* (New Haven, 1957); Meyer H. Abrams, *The Mirror and the Lamp* (New York, 1953).

Notes and Documents

New Sidelights on Early Antislavery Radicalism

David Brion Davis*

SIXTY years ago Russell P. Jameson published a masterful study of Montesquieu's influence on French antislavery thought. Quite rightly, he singled out the Chevalier Louis de Jaucourt's article, "Traite des Nègres," published in the *Encyclopédie* in 1765, as a forceful and trenchant extension of Montesquieu's antislavery arguments, and as the most important statement on the subject until the later 1770s.[1] In a recent study of my own, I observed that "de Jaucourt was able to rise above the qualifications engendered by Montesquieu's tolerance for institutional differences," and after quoting the central passage, I termed the argument "one of the earliest and most lucid applications to slavery of the natural rights philosophy . . . [which] succeeds in stating a basic principle which was to guide the more radical abolitionists of the nineteenth century."[2] Neither Jameson nor I suspected that Montesquieu's ideas had earlier been refracted by the Scottish Enlightenment, or that de Jaucourt had merely copied someone else's words.

In an article on Montesquieu and English antislavery opinion published in 1933, F. T. H. Fletcher briefly mentioned a "brilliant pre-Blackstonian" jurist, George Wallace, whose massive tome, *A System of the Principles of the Law of Scotland,* quoted extensively from Book XV of the *Esprit des lois* and applied Montesquieu's antislavery arguments to Scotland. Fletcher said nothing about the nature of Wallace's arguments, adding merely that the treatise was expensive, weighted down with legal abstractions, and thus little read.[3] Wallace never carried the work beyond "Volume I," published in Edinburgh in 1760. This lone volume, now very rare, apparently had no influence on Scottish jurisprudence.

* Mr. Davis is a member of the Department of History, Yale University.

[1] Russell Parsons Jameson, *Montesquieu et l'esclavage: étude sur les origines de l'opinion antiesclavagiste en France au XVIII° siècle* (Paris, 1911), 345-346.

[2] David Brion Davis, *The Problem of Slavery in Western Culture* (Ithaca, N. Y., 1966), 416.

[3] F. T. H. Fletcher, "Montesquieu's Influence on Anti-Slavery Opinion in England," *Journal of Negro History,* XVIII (1933), 416-417.

Nevertheless, a comparison between Wallace's text and de Jaucourt's influential article in the *Encyclopédie* reveals astonishing similarities. Following Montesquieu, Wallace denied all the classical grounds for justifying enslavement and asserted that no man has a right to purchase Africans or any other human beings: "Men and their liberty are not *in commercio;* they are not either saleable or purchaseable." De Jaucourt mentioned an unidentified Englishman, "full of humanity and enlightenment," who had demonstrated that human beings cannot be the objects of trade and cannot be bought or sold at any price. This premise led to the following radical conclusions:

Wallace	De Jaucourt
For these reasons, every one of those unfortunate men, who are pretended to be slaves, has a right to be declared to be free, for he never lost his liberty; he could not lose it; his prince had no power to dispose of him. Of course, the sale was *ipso jure* void. This right he carries about with him, and is entitled every where to get it declared. As soon, therefore, as he comes into a country, in which the judges are not forgetful of their own humanity, it is their duty to remember that he is a man, and to declare him to be free.	Il n'y a donc pas un seul de ces infortunés que l'on prétend n'être que des esclaves, qui n'ait droit d'être déclaré libre, puisqu'il n'a jamais perdu la liberté; qu'il ne pouvoit pas la perdre; et que son prince, son pere, et qui que ce soit dans le monde n'avoit le pouvoir d'en disposer; par conséquent la vente qui en a été faite est nulle en elle-même: ce negre ne se dépouille, et ne peut pas même se dépouiller jamais de son droit naturel; il le porte partout avec lui, et il peut exiger par-tout qu'on l'en laisse jouir. C'est donc une inhumanité manifeste de la part des juges de pays libres où il est transporté, de ne pas l'affranchir à l'instant en le déclarant libre, puisque c'est leur semblable, ayant une ame comme eux.[4]

It is clearly a mistake to attribute this radical antislavery position to the rationalism or secular humanitarianism of the French Enlightenment. Montesquieu may have prepared the way for Wallace's uncompromising

[4] George Wallace, *A System of the Principles of the Law of Scotland,* I (Edinburgh, 1760), 95-96; *Encyclopédie, ou dictionnaire raisonné des sciences, des arts et des métiers* . . . , XVI (Neufchâtel, 1765), 532.

argument, but his own position on colonial slavery was shrewdly ambiguous.[5] But who, then, was George Wallace, and why should he have asserted the universal illegality of slavery in a scholarly treatise on Scottish law?

Unfortunately, Wallace remains a curiously obscure figure, although he gained local prominence in Edinburgh at a time when the city flourished as one of the most culturally exciting centers of Europe. His father, the Reverend Robert Wallace, left a far more indelible impression. The elder Wallace was the author of *A Dissertation on the Numbers of Mankind in Ancient and Modern Times* . . . (1753), which was translated into French within a year of its initial publication; this and a later work, *Various Prospects of Mankind, Nature, and Providence* (1761), were said to have anticipated and influenced Thomas Malthus.[6] Robert Wallace belonged to an urbane, latitudinarian group that was gaining power and patronage in the Church of Scotland, in opposition to the evangelicals. He was also a prophet of modernity and a member of Edinburgh's literary and social elite. It is hardly surprising that his son should have become a member of the Scottish bar (the Faculty of Advocates) and of such organizations as the Rankenian Club, the Select Society, and the Revolution Club. George evidently admired and respected his father, since he referred, in his discussion of slavery, to "the learned, the ingenious, and the virtuous Author of a 'DISSERTATION ON THE NUMBERS OF MANKIND.'" But a few years before George Wallace published his treatise on the laws of Scotland, when he was not yet thirty, he became embroiled in the bitter "*Douglas* affair"—a controversy over the staging of a play, *Douglas,* which the evangelical party angrily denounced. Whatever else contributed to Wallace's later obscurity, this scandal had complex political consequences and apparently made him a victim of the rising and powerful Dundas family.[7]

The section on slavery in Wallace's *Law of Scotland* seems out of step

[5] See Fletcher, "Montesquieu's Influence," *Journal Negro Hist.,* XVIII (1933), 414-426; Jameson, *Montesquieu et l'esclavage,* 306-307, 340-347; and Davis, *The Problem of Slavery,* 394-396, 402-409.

[6] Edinburgh, 1753; London, 1761. It is said in Robert Wallace's biographical sketches that his *A Dissertation on the Numbers of Mankind* was translated under the personal supervision of Montesquieu; Elie de Joncourt was the actual translator of the 1754 edition of *Essai sur la différence du nombre des hommes dans les tems anciens et modernes* (London). Marc-Antoine Eidous translated a 1769 edition, *Dissertation historique et politique sur la population de l'ancien tems comparée avec celle du nôtre* (Amsterdam). I have found no evidence of a French translation of George Wallace's *A System of the Principles of the Law of Scotland.*

[7] For information on George Wallace I have relied heavily on Mr. Nicholas Phillipson, of the University of Edinburgh, whose detailed knowledge of 18th-century Scotland has richly supplemented the lean accounts of Wallace in standard reference works.

with the rest of the work. A book which sought to place Scottish law within a broad theoretical framework derived from Montesquieu, Kames, and Hume had no obvious need for a lofty digression on American slavery. Wallace's attack may have had some bearing on local political conflicts, especially if he knew that some of his orthodox opponents had interests in the slave colonies. Yet the *Esprit des lois* had set a precedent for such rhetorical excursions on slavery as a means of defining barbarous custom, natural law, and historical progress. Moreover, Wallace related his seeming digression to three specific goals.

First, he was concerned over the probability that colonial masters would bring slaves back to Scotland and appeal to Scottish courts to uphold their rights as owners of human property. Well over a decade before the Somerset and Knight cases resolved this problem in England and Scotland by denying slaveholders any legal claim, Wallace insisted that human bondage could find no protection from the law of Scotland. That law had either abolished or had never recognized the institution. Judges, therefore, were "in *no case,* to adjudge one to be the slave of another."[8]

But Wallace found the question of slavery important and "interesting to humanity" for even broader reasons. As a disciple of the Enlightenment, he took it as axiomatic that "all that inequality, which is to be found among the individuals of human race, is derived from political and arbitrary institutions alone." From the principles of natural liberty and equality, it followed "that all inequality, all dependence, all servility, all superiority, all subjection, all pre-eminence, which is not *necessary* to the welfare of Society, is unnatural; and that, if it could, it ought to be destroyed." Unlike most of his contemporaries, Wallace doubted whether the necessities of social welfare could ever be permanently defined, since history showed "that many unexpected revolutions have

[8] Wallace, *Law of Scotland,* 88-89, 95-96. In a footnote, p. 97, Wallace mentioned a 1757 case: "One *Montgomery Shedden,* a niger boy, being in Edinburgh, refused to return to his master, because he said he was, like every other British subject, a free man in Britain. Council were ordered to argue the point both in writing and *viva voce.* But during the very time when the Court of Session was *hearing* them plead at the bar, notice came, that the boy was dead. So Judgment was not pronounced." Wallace anticipated some of the main issues and arguments of the Somerset case of 1772 and the Knight case of 1777. Though he admitted that slavery was part of the ancient written law of Scotland, he also pointed out that "it may have been the case, that any thing like slavery, such as it is described in these ancient books, never took place in Scotland." In any event, laws, Wallace held, "may be repealed by Custom. The same principles, which seem to have determined us to abolish servile tenures, oppressive jurisdictions, and lawless attachments, have induced us totally to abolish the inhuman usage of slavery. So far as I have been able to learn, no vestige of it remains in Scotland. Indeed, it has been disused, and has been unknown for several generations past. So that there is not any remembrance of the establishment of it now remaining among us." (p. 89)

happened, and that things have existed so contrary to all expectation, that he would, indeed be a rash man, who should pronounce decisively, any thing, which is not naturally to be absolutely impossible." Wallace could even entertain the possibility, though hardly the probability, of an eventual abolition of private property, "that bane of human felicity," and of the emergence of a society of perfect and universal equality, like that described in Thomas More's *Utopia*. By emphasizing man's capacity for change and by elevating the goal of possible perfectibility, Wallace opened the way for more immediate and tangible improvement: "But, tho the condition of human affairs may never arrive at ideal perfection, we ought not to abandon them out of peevishness or out of despair. We ought to use our endeavours to make them approach as near it, as possible. In the same manner, we ought not, because we cannot reduce mankind to an *absolute* equality, therefore to abandon them; but ought to do all, which we can do, to reduce them as near it, and to make them as independent of one another, as may be. From hence it follows, that an institution, so unnatural and so inhuman as that of Slavery, ought to be abolished."[9]

For Wallace, then, colonial slaver · symbolized an extreme of social inequality which was the precise antithesis of the ideal toward which mankind should strive: "It makes the bulk of mankind dependent on the few; and that not only for their bread and for life, but for the enjoyment of it, for ease, for tranquillity, and for a momentary felicity." He recognized, of course, that like any institution, lawful or unlawful, slavery might be "attended with some accidental advantage." Alarmists would warn that any tampering with slavery would ruin the colonies. Wallace's initial response was virtually the same as that of the Abbé Raynal a decade later: "Be it so; would it from thence follow, that the bulk of mankind ought to be abused, that our pockets may be filled with money, or our mouths with delicates? The purses of highwaymen would be empty, in case robbery were totally abolished. Let, therefore, our colonies be ruined, but let us not render so many men miserable."[10]

But this moral rhetoric merely prefaced Wallace's third major point, which was a prediction of the material blessings that abolition would entail. Clearly Wallace was not thinking of a gradual emancipation. "It might," he admitted, "occasion a stagnation of business for a short time. Every great alteration produces that effect." Yet slavery itself had inhibited the growth of population and civilization in the New World:

[9] *Ibid.*, 89-91.
[10] *Ibid.*, 91, 96. De Jaucourt copied these passages in the *Encyclopédie*, which may have been the source for Raynal's rhetorical outburst in Book X of *Histoire philosophique et politique des établissemens et du commerce des Européens dans les deux Indes* (Amsterdam, 1770), a work which was actually the collaborative effort of several *philosophes*.

"Set the Nigers free, and, in a few generations, this vast and fertile continent would be crowded with inhabitants; learning, arts, and every thing would flourish among them." After acknowledging that the great reformation might damage British commerce, Wallace drew on his father's work, which had supposedly demonstrated "that a nation may be more populous, more wealthy, more virtuous, and more happy without than with an extensive foreign trade." Wallace's antislavery views were thus linked with a hostility toward the old colonial system and with Hume's doctrine that " 'Tis industry, which is the real source of wealth. As long as a nation continues to be industrious, it need not be afraid of poverty." For some reason Wallace failed to develop his economic arguments against slavery, which anticipated those of the Physiocrats, and abruptly concluded his chapter with long quotations, in French, from the *Esprit des lois*.[11]

Wallace's attack on slavery deserves more attention than it has received, not only because of its influence on the Encyclopedists, and perhaps on the Abbé Raynal, but because of its vision of Negro emancipation as a first and practicable step toward the ideal of human equality. While Wallace's arguments were too radical to play a major role in the later British antislavery movement, they had an immediate impact in America, where Anthony Benezet incorporated crucial passages from the *Law of Scotland* in his developing compendium of antislavery literature.

Given the obscurity of Wallace's tome, one is tempted to ask whether de Jaucourt lifted the antislavery argument from Benezet's *A Short Account of That Part of Africa, Inhabited by the Negroes . . . and the Manner by Which the Slave Trade is Carried On*, a pamphlet published in Philadelphia in 1762. It would be a nice irony of international communications if Montesquieu's influence, radicalized by George Wallace, returned to the *Encyclopédie* by way of an American publication. Unfortunately, textual discrepancies rule out this possibility.[12] Yet Benezet, unlike de Jaucourt, identified Wallace as the author of the doctrine that "'every one of those

[11] Wallace, *Law of Scotland*, 96-98. Although de Jaucourt's translation seldom changed Wallace's meaning, the following deviations should be noted: Wallace argued that after the Negroes had been set free, the American continent, "instead of being inhabited by wild beasts and by savages . . . would be peopled by philosophers and by men." De Jaucourt changed the latter phrase to "hommes industrieux," which presumably omitted philosophers. He also added "liberté" to Wallace's "industry" as the real source of wealth. *Encyclopédie*, 533.

[12] Benezet omitted a few lines from Wallace which de Jaucourt translated. As I have already noted, Robert Wallace's writings were known in France as early as 1754, and it is possible that George's volume reached France through his father's literary contacts or by way of an enlightened traveler like Adam Smith. De Jaucourt was a latitudinarian Protestant who knew English well. No doubt Wallace's passages on slavery were a happy find for an encyclopedist burdened with the task of writing a multitude of short articles on a large variety of subjects.

unfortunate men, who are pretended to be slaves, has a right to be declared to be free, for he never lost his liberty." And Benezet further disseminated Wallace's words in 1766, in his *A Caution to Great Britain and her Colonies, in a Short Representation of the Calamitous State of the Enslaved Negroes in the British Dominions.* In 1767 this pamphlet was reprinted in England and translated into French. Benezet was also an indirect source for the antislavery sentiment of the *Ephémérides du citoyen,* which in 1769 heaped praise upon the Pennsylvania Quakers for supposedly emancipating their slaves.[13]

It was as an anthologist and collator of scattered material that Benezet made his major contribution to the early antislavery movement. Many of his pamphlets are little more than hastily compiled collections of quotations and extracts regarding West African culture, the slave trade, and the injustice and inhumanity of Negro slavery. The juxtaposition of such testimonials was novel, and in the 1760s and 1770s many influential Englishmen and Americans first grasped the full horrors of the Atlantic slave system after stumbling upon a Benezet tract. In 1767, for example, Granville Sharp discovered Benezet's *A Short Account* in a London bookstall, and the next year had the work reprinted for further distribution.[14] In 1772 John Wesley encountered Benezet's *Some Historical*

[13] There was no French translation of Benezet's *A Short Account,* although on p. 487 of *The Problem of Slavery* I erroneously said that "even before Sharp had reprinted Benezet's tract in England, it had been translated into French." Evidently I confused *A Short Account* with Benezet's *A Caution to Great Britain,* which was translated in 1767. A related error is to be found in Joseph Sabin, *Bibliotheca Americana,* II (New York, 1869), 63, who repeated a mistake made in Joseph-Marie Quérard, *La France littéraire, ou dictionnaire bibliographique des savants, historiens et gens de lettres de la France, . . .* (Paris, 1827-1839), in which Benezet's *Relation historique de la Guinée, avec une recherche sur l'origine et les progrès de la traite des nègres . . .* (London, 1788), is given an original publication date of 1762, the year of *A Short Account,* instead of the correct date of 1771. *A Short Account* was translated into German in 1763 as *Eine kurtze vorstellung des theils von Africa,* but this edition, printed at Ephrata, Pa., was designed only for the German-speaking inhabitants of Pennsylvania. Although Benezet was not well known in France until the Marquis de Chastellux and Brissot de Warville engaged in a literary controversy over his character in the late 1780s, there had been French translations of two of his antislavery pamphlets as well as his *A Short Account of the People Called Quakers* (Philadelphia, 1780). For the place of the Quakers in French thought, see Edith Philips, *The Good Quaker in French Legend* (Philadelphia, 1932).

[14] However, in 1774 Sharp wrote to Benjamin Rush: "When I reprinted Mr. Benezets acco't. of Africa in 1768, so few Copies were sold that I gave away, by degrees, almost the whole impression being determined to make it as publick as I cou'd; for many well meaning people will read, (and some worthy talk of) Books that are given them, who will not put themselves to the trouble and expence of buying." London, Feb. 21, 1774, in George S. Brookes, *Friend Anthony Benezet* (Philadelphia, 1937), 447.

Account of Guinea (1771) which helped inspire him to write his own *Thoughts Upon Slavery* (1774), plagiarizing liberally from Benezet's pages.[15]

Benezet, then, acted as a kind of middleman of ideas who was led by antislavery zeal to collect and disseminate a radical, secular philosophy. But for a devout Quaker, this role had its hazards. Although American Quakers were gradually absorbing a rationalistic vocabulary of natural rights, Benezet remained an intensely pious, self-effacing man. He held little hope for human happiness or perfectibility in this world. In 1752, for example, he warned that "the only end for which thou wast created in this world is, that by living in a state of obedience, by constant watching and prayer, thy soul may, with the assistance of divine grace, become so purified, as to be fitted to dwell with God for ever." Five years later, after exclaiming over "the weakness, the instability, the Self, the remains of a subtle Pride that hangs about human nature," he wrote Samuel Fothergill that "I hope I am cured from any more dependance and expectation from man."[16] It is noteworthy that he refrained from quoting Wallace on "the superior wisdom and civility of the present age," or on the ideal that "men ought to be reduced to a level [of equality] as much, that is, they ought to be as free, and as independent of one another, as is consistent with the good of Society." At that point in the text where de Jaucourt continued quoting Wallace (and Hume) on industry as the real source of wealth—"As long as a nation continues to be industrious, it need not be afraid of poverty. Industry, like necessity, is inventive, and falls on a thousand ways of employing itself to the profit of the industrious"—Benezet concluded the selection with his own appeals to God and piety, subjects notably absent from Wallace's argument.

Benezet was, in fact, highly selective in his use of radical antislavery literature. Aside from his handling of Wallace, a most interesting instance of this is his treatment in *A Short Account* of "a large extract from a pamphlet, lately published in London, on the subject of the slave trade." The anonymous pamphlet, now exceedingly rare, was entitled *Two Dialogues on the Man-Trade*.[17] It contained, although one would not know this from Benezet's long extract, the most radical antislavery doctrine

[15] Philadelphia, 1771; London, 1774.

[16] Benezet to a Schoolmaster, ca. 1752, and to Samuel Fothergill, Philadelphia, Oct. 17, 1757, in Brookes, *Friend Anthony Benezet*, 210, 223.

[17] Benezet, *A Short Account of That Part of Africa*, 2d ed. (Philadelphia, 1762), 37-63; J. Philmore [pseud.], *Two Dialogues on the Man-Trade* (London, 1760). The name "J. Philmore" appears only at the end of the pamphlet. I have been unable to trace the identity of the author, but perhaps some specialist in anonyms and pseudonyms will be able to solve the mystery. The pamphlet was printed "for J. Waugh in Lombard Street, W. Fenner in Paternoster Row, G. Woodfall at Charing-Cross, W. Owen at Temple Bar, and Mrs. Kingham at the Royal Exchange."

that I have found in any publication that appeared before the French Revolution.

The mysterious author was well informed on the details of the English slave trade. He had read William Snelgrave and other traders' accounts, and had apparently conversed with sailors back from the Guinea coast. Even his estimate of thirty-five thousand blacks transported annually by British ships is not far off the mark.[18] An educated man, the author could sprinkle his text with Latin quotations and draw on the authority of Cicero, Seneca, Juvenal, Locke, and Pufendorf. Although Benezet omitted the "dialogue" format, in the original the arguments were presented in the form of a friendly debate between "J. Philmore," who had all the logic and knowledge on his side, and "Mr. Allcraft," who was financially involved in the slave trade, but whose moral doubts made him a suitable candidate for conversion.

Benezet reprinted most of Philmore's arguments with obvious delight. The devout Quaker might bridle a bit at the statement that man is a "noble Creature, made but a little lower than the Angels, and crowned with Glory and Honour."[19] But he could welcome the assertions, long familiar to Quakers, that enslavement is equivalent to "man-stealing," and that the receiver of stolen goods is as guilty as the original thief. He could endorse the ringing statement, which he later repeated as if it were his own, that "no Legislature on Earth, which is the Supreme Power in every civil Society, can alter the Nature of Things, or make that to be lawful which is contrary to the Law of GOD, the Supreme Legislator and Governor of the World."[20]

But this ancient doctrine's revolutionary potential lay in its direct application to an institution sanctioned by custom and statute. Although Philmore emphasized moral guilt and atonement ("How can you, as some of you do, go to the Sacrament of the Lord's Supper? How can you lift up your guilty eyes to Heaven?"), he also called for physical retribution. George Wallace had exhorted judges to free Negroes illegally and unjustly held down by force. Philmore said that the slaves could rightfully free themselves.

Here are the passages which Benezet, as a peace-loving Quaker, felt constrained to omit:

[18] Philip D. Curtin estimated the "possible volume exported by the English slave trade, by coastal region of origin in Africa," at an annual average of 23,100 for the decade 1751-1760, and at 27,200 for the decade 1761-1770. However, the volume of trade varied greatly from year to year, and 18th-century estimates of British slave exports for separate years range from 42,560 in 1759 (this was the calculated capacity of ships sent out) to 53,100 in 1768. *The Atlantic Slave Trade. A Census* (Madison, Wis., 1969), 150, 146. It should ' e added that Philmore thought that the 35,000 estimate might be too low.

[19] Philmore, *Two Dialogues,* in Benezet, *A Short Account of That Part of Africa,* 33.

[20] *Ibid.,* 41.

And so all the black men now in our plantations, who are by unjust force deprived of their liberty, and held in slavery, as they have none upon earth to appeal to, may lawfully repel that force with force, and to recover their liberty, destroy their oppressors: and not only so, but it is the duty of others, white as well as blacks, to assist those miserable creatures, if they can, in their attempts to deliver themselves out of slavery, and to rescue them out of the hands of their cruel tyrants.[21]

To justify this uncompromising approval of slave violence, Philmore appealed to the "higher law" doctrine of Cicero. And he was prepared to carry the argument still further. Any nation, he affirmed, would be justified in demanding that England should free all her slaves. If England refused, the other could legitimately go to war to liberate the colonial slaves by force:

They would be so [justified], Mr. Allcraft, as, in that case, we might justly be considered as the aggressors; for in truth we are now at war (we Englishmen, we christians, to our shame be it spoken) and have been for above a hundred years past, without any cessation at all, at war and enmity with mankind in general, and in this war we have destroyed every year, at least for some years past, near as many of the human race, who never did us any injury, as have been destroyed in the same time, by the war now carried on in Europe [the Seven Years' War].[22]

Needless to say, this was revolutionary doctrine in 1760, as it would be in America in 1860 (or 1970). But it was also a logical extension of Wallace's doctrine that "every one of those unfortunate men, who are pretended to be slaves, has a right to be declared free, for he never lost his liberty." Though Philmore called on England to set an example to other nations by proclaiming immediate liberty to "those captives now in our plantations," he broke new ground by condemning England and other slave trading countries as aggressor nations that had long been "at war and enmity with mankind in general." This view would never become a part of accepted antislavery doctrine, though it has reappeared in different forms in more recent times. Its open avowal in the mid-eighteenth century might either have inhibited the growth of antislavery movements, or have made them into truly revolutionary forces. But there was, we can see, a screening element in the gathering and transmission of early antislavery pronouncements. While the higher law doctrine would live on in the mainstream of antislavery literature, often in a muted or half-suppressed form, the names of George Wallace and "J. Philmore" were soon forgotten.

[21] Philmore, *Two Dialogues,* 54. This revolutionary utterance came in response to Allcraft's fear of the danger of slave insurrections, evidenced by the timely discovery of a plot for rebellion among the blacks of Antigua.
[22] *Ibid.,* 57.

THE ANTISLAVERY MOVEMENT AND THE PROBLEM OF VIOLENT "MEANS"

JOHN DEMOS

I

FROM the very beginning of the antislavery movement the question of violence was significant and more or less pressing. It arose as a matter of course, whenever "means" were considered. Would the slaves be justified in resorting to insurrection, in order to secure their freedom? What sort of pressure should the North bring to bear upon Southerners? What was the proper reaction to anti-abolition mobs?

The answers which antislavery men gave to these questions reveal much that was essential to the course of the movement, and to nineteenth-century reform in general. At the start abolitionists nearly everywhere tried to disassociate themselves from the idea of a violent overthrow of slavery. By 1836-1837, however, this consensus was beginning to break down. Around their opposition to servile revolt certain abolitionist leaders attempted to build an elaborate philosophical construct, soon to be known as the theory of "non-resistance." These men, like most of their reform colleagues, believed that policy must proceed always from first principles; and in developing such principles they were prepared to be led a great distance from the original point of departure. Indeed they appear, in retrospect, almost to have been imprisoned by their own ideas—so irresistibly were they swept along, against a huge body of accepted institutions and values. In other respects, too, non-resistance may be seen as highly typical of the larger reform effort. Deriving originally from the New Testament, it closely paralleled various contemporary experiments in religious perfectionism; and its long-range expectations were little short of millennial. In fact, one observer who followed its growth from the start was moved to remark that "there is such a thing as

501

115

going beyond the Millennium."[1] Non-resistance was in some ways the most "ultra" of all the nineteenth-century "ultra-isms."

Born within the abolitionist movement, non-resistance never really managed to have a life of its own. Instead, it helped to split antislavery in two. The division after 1840 between the "political action" men and the Garrisonian, or "disunion," abolitionists is a familiar story. Somewhat less well-understood, perhaps, is the source of this cleavage. The usual explanation places heavy emphasis on Garrison's repudiation of a *proslavery* Constitution and government. In actual fact, however, the basis of his opposition to working within the American political system was non-resistance. The Constitution was wrong because it sanctioned "life-taking"—war and capital punishment. The additional evil of its support for slavery was discovered later on.

Those abolitionists who could not stomach non-resistance, the "political action" men, went their own way during the 1840's. Most of them were opposed to the use of violent "means," but they tried to subordinate discussion of this matter to the necessity of nourishing antislavery sentiment. Meanwhile non-resistance, having generated its greatest force in the early 1840's, suffered a steady eclipse during the latter half of this decade.

In the 1850's non-resistance, and the less doctrinaire kinds of peaceful abolitionism as well, completely collapsed. Driven by the rapid pace of events, and even more by the inclinations of vast numbers of new recruits, the antislavery movement became increasingly receptive to violence. By 1859 it was nearly as united in its support for forcible "means" as it had been with regard to the pacifism of its earliest days. How much this change may have worked actually to precipitate violence is a difficult question. But in any event when the violence of all-out war finally came in 1861, the antislavery movement was far

[1] William Ladd, quoted in Henry Steele Commager, *Theodore Parker* (Boston, 1936), 193.

better prepared for it than would have been the case at any previous stage of its development.

II

The period of the first great mushrooming of antislavery societies was, of course, the 1830's. The problem of violence was faced at the outset, and largely in terms of slave insurrections. The constitution of every new society contained a disclaimer such as the following: "This society . . . will never countenance the oppressed in vindicating their rights by resorting to physical force. . . . Our very object precludes the idea of all resort to force. We have no force but the force of truth."[2] William Lloyd Garrison adopted the same position in the first issue of his antislavery newspaper, *The Liberator*. In a stilted little poem addressed to the slaves he declared that

> Not by the Sword shall your deliverance be;
> Not by the shedding of your master's blood.
> Not by rebellion—or foul treachery. . . .[3]

Slave revolt was discouraged as both wrong in principle (though there was as yet little elaboration of this point), and impolitic as well. The Negroes were too few in number and too ill-equipped to fight on even terms with their masters. Furthermore, abolitionists would be able to gain the support of Northerners much faster by urging a peaceful course, than otherwise. Thus in 1835 the Massachusetts Anti-Slavery Society affirmed its belief that "by the patient endurance in their wrongs . . . the slaves will hasten the day of their peaceful deliverance from the yoke of bondage . . . whereas by violent and bloody measures they will prolong their servitude, and expose themselves to destruction."[4]

Yet it must be said that there was something slightly am-

[2] From the Constitution of the New York Anti-Slavery Society, printed in *An Address of the New York City Anti-Slavery Society to the People of the City of New York* (New York, 1833), 22, 46.

[3] *The Liberator*, Jan. 1, 1831, 2.

[4] *The Liberator*, Oct. 10, 1835, 163.

biguous about this advice; for abolitionists also held out the prospect of insurrection as a kind of threat with which to prod the slaveholders into making immediate plans for emancipation. One observer, noting ominously that many Southerners "seem to be incapable of rising . . . to a just sense of the *dangers* of slaveholding," made the facetious proposal that such men be "colonized to St. Domingo, to examine the graves of the whites who fell in one general ruin before the exasperated fury of the colored population, whom they had kept in cruel bondage."[5] Closer to home, the famous Nat Turner rebellion of August, 1831, seemed a dark portent of things to come. Garrison's reaction to this event was compounded of horror ("We have exerted our utmost efforts to avert the calamity"), and the reminder, repeated many times over, that "I-told-you-so."[6] A correspondent of *The Liberator* contributed an article, "Causes of Slave Insurrections," in which he declared that such occurrences were inevitable wherever men were held in bondage. It was basically a matter of human nature: "Negroes, like other men, have a spirit which rebels against tyranny and oppression."[7]

An obvious example of this innate, rebellious spirit could be found in the American Revolution. And the Revolution was a source of continuing concern through the whole course of the antislavery movement. Garrison's early injunctions against slave revolt brought the following question from a reader of *The Liberator:* "Do you mean that only the slaves must forbear from fighting, or do you mean that our Revolutionary fathers were wrong?"[8] The American Anti-Slavery Society grappled with the matter in its first official "declaration": antislavery is "an enterprise . . . without which that of our fathers is incomplete"; antislavery will carry to an appropriate conclusion the principles of liberty announced in the Declaration of Independence. Yet there is an important difference

[5] *The Liberator*, July 12, 1834, 110.
[6] *The Liberator*, Sept. 3, 1831, 143.
[7] *The Liberator*, Sept. 17, 1831, 150.
[8] *The Liberator*, July 8, 1831, 110.

between the two movements: *"Their* principles led them to wage war against their oppressors, and to spill human blood like water, in order to be free. *Ours* forbid the doing of evil that good may come. . . ."[9]

A few words must be said about the alternative to those violent means for which antislavery men expressed such distaste. That the early nineteenth century was an optimistic age is almost a commonplace. An integral part of this optimism was the belief that righteousness and truth, if presented in a straightforward fashion, would inevitably overcome all obstacles. The reformer's job was to make the truth widely known; public opinion would do the rest. Thus Garrison could explain the founding of *The Liberator* as follows: "What is able to overthrow the present system of slavery? An enlightened, consolidated, and wisely-directed *public opinion.* How shall this be secured? By disseminating LIGHT—by preaching the TRUTH. For this purpose we established *The Liberator,* as a medium through which LIGHT and TRUTH might obtain a wide circulation."[10]

Nineteenth-century reformers usually sought to be active on a variety of different fronts, and many leading abolitionists were associated at various times with the effort to promote international peace. In the middle 1830's some of these men began to be impatient with the cautious stand of the orthodox peace organizations; and in this impatience lay the germ of future schism, not only for the cause of peace, but for antislavery as well. As early as January, 1834, Garrison was criticizing the American Peace Society for attempting to distinguish between aggressive and defensive wars, and confining its attention to the former. In the months that followed, this matter received increasing amounts of space in *The Liberator.* As one correspondent wrote: "Among the friends of moral reform . . . the belief is prevailing more and more that our Saviour meant to inculcate the doctrine of never fighting in self-defense."[11]

[9] *The Liberator,* Dec. 14, 1833, 195.
[10] *The Liberator,* Jan. 4, 1834, 2.
[11] *The Liberator,* Apr. 26, 1834, 68.

506 THE NEW ENGLAND QUARTERLY

A year later *The Liberator* reported a public debate, held in Boston, on the question: "Would the slaves be justified in resorting to physical violence to obtain their freedom?" The Rev. Samuel May opened for the negative. "According to the dictates of unenlightened and unsanctified human nature," he said, the slaves would indeed be justified in such a course. "But according to the principles of the Gospel and the precepts of Jesus Christ, . . . (they) had not the right to resort to violence. The spirit of the Gospel was one of forbearance, of long-suffering, of forgiveness."[12] Succeeding speakers expressed exactly the same sentiments. Indeed, there might have been no debate at all had not one "Mr. Weeks" finally risen to argue in favor of "a resort to arms." For this he was roundly attacked on all sides.

The peaceable character of antislavery work was emphasized not only in New England but throughout the country. James Birney, defending abolitionists at a public debate in Ohio, called particular attention to their "peace principles."[13] William Allen told the Michigan Anti-Slavery Society that peaceful agitation was "all the weapon we needed to give the death blow to the monster. We did not want swords of glittering steel. . . ."[14] The Pennsylvania Society, at its first meeting in 1836, passed a strong resolution in support of non-violence. Only one man dissented, and he was subsequently obliged to leave the organization.[15] Thus William Ladd could remark in 1837 that "every antislavery man is a peace man; or at least I have known but two or three exceptions."[16]

These "peace principles" were severely tested during the middle 1830's, the great "mob years" for the abolitionists. In all sections of the country they found themselves subjected to bitter, and sometimes injurious, physical attack. But in nearly every case the response of antislavery men was non-violent.

12 *The Liberator*, Apr. 11, 1835, 59; Apr. 18, 1835, 62.
13 *The Liberator*, Jan. 16, 1836, 9.
14 *The Liberator*, Aug. 25, 1837, 137.
15 *The Liberator*, March 18, 1837, 45.
16 *The Liberator*, Feb. 13, 1836, 26.

Garrison, and many of his colleagues as well, took very great pride in this unflinching commitment to a policy of calm self-restraint under the most trying conditions. "Did they (the abolitionists) return railing for railing and blow for blow?" asked one correspondent in *The Liberator*. "Did they demand blood in return for blood, and violence for violence? No! these are neither the principles nor practices of the abolitionists. *They are men of peace.* They have asserted again and again, and they still re-iterate, that THEY WILL NOT FIGHT."[17]

Inevitably, though, there were at least a few occasions when abolitionists did *not* turn the other cheek. For example, members of the Ohio Anti-Slavery Society, at the time of their annual meeting in 1836, are said to have armed themselves with clubs to repel an unfriendly mob.[18] But the first clear-cut breach of non-violent principles occurred during the events surrounding the murder of Elijah P. Lovejoy at Alton, Illinois, in November, 1837. In attempting to protect the press on which his antislavery newspaper was printed, Lovejoy, or one of his men, shot and killed a local youth named Bishop. Shortly thereafter the mob cut down the intrepid editor in a most brutal fashion; but for some abolitionists the prior resort to arms seriously compromised his "martyrdom."[19]

The reaction of the Garrisonians, for example, was quite ambivalent. They felt a profound sorrow at the death of Lovejoy, and they deplored the mob spirit which had brought it about. But on the other hand, they regretted that the Alton reformers "should have allowed any provocation, or personal danger, to drive them to take up arms in self-defense."[20] "In

[17] *The Liberator*, Aug. 2, 1834, 122.

[18] Benjamin P. Thomas, *Theodore Weld: Crusader for Freedom* (New Brunswick, N. J., 1950), 107.

[19] And there was indisputable evidence that the step had been consciously taken. In a letter, written while events were moving toward their tragic end, Lovejoy had admitted that "a loaded musket is standing at my bedside, while my two brothers, in an adjoining room, have *three others*, together with *pistols*, *cartridges*, etc. I have had inexpressible reluctance to resort to this method of defense. But dear-bought experience has taught me, that there is at present no safety for me, and no defense in this place either in the laws or the protecting aegis of public sentiment." (Quoted in *The Liberator*, Dec. 1, 1837, 194.)

[20] *The Liberator*, Nov. 24, 1837, 191.

the name of Jesus of Nazareth," declared *The Liberator*, "who suffered himself to be unresistingly nailed to the Cross, we solemnly protest against any of his professed followers resorting to carnal weapons under any pretext or in any extremity whatever."[21]

The sadness of certain abolitionists about Lovejoy's attempt at self-defense originated in their sense of the moral character of the movement. The Grimke sisters, for instance, saw reason to fear that "God will (now) take the work of abolishing slavery out of our hands. He gave us a great *moral* enterprise to carry forward. He gave us arms of Heavenly temper to use, the sword of the spirit, prayer, preaching the truth."[22] According to this line of argument, the cause was assured success only if its moral purity were rigorously maintained. Had Lovejoy declined to take up arms, he might not have been killed; or in any case the whole episode would have had "a more thrilling and abiding effect." William Goodell had still other reasons for criticizing the action of Lovejoy. He was afraid, he recalled later, that abolitionists everywhere might be induced to arm themselves in self-defense; that bloodshed would inevitably follow; that the country might then become "a scene of domestic violence in which the abolitionists would be almost certain to be overpowered."[23] There was, here, a more pragmatic sort of concern.

Some of the local antislavery organizations in New England adopted the *Liberator* stand on Lovejoy—that is, sorrow over his death, and sorrow, too, that he did not "die unresistingly." But other New England societies took a somewhat different position; their statements omitted all reference to the question of self-defense. In this they were joined by the central office of the American Anti-Slavery Society, which declared simply that it was "due to the memory of the deceased to state that he was slain . . . whilst engaged in defending his property and his

21 *The Liberator*, Nov. 24, 1837, 191.

22 Letter from Sarah Grimke to Sarah Douglass, Nov. 23, 1837. See Gilbert H. Barnes and Dwight L. Dumond, editors, *Letters of Theodore Dwight Weld, Angelina Grimke Weld, and Sarah Grimke, 1822-1844* (New York, 1934), 440.

23 From the *Friend of Man*. Quoted in *The Liberator*, Sept. 6, 1839, 141.

rights in a manner justified by the laws of the land, and of all other civilized countries."[24]

The most important single effect of the Lovejoy affair was the strengthening of the non-resistant opinions of certain, chiefly "Garrisonian," abolitionists. And in the early months of 1838, Lewis Tappan wrote to *The Liberator*, suggesting that it was "a very suitable time to discuss the Peace question."[25] Tappan declared himself opposed to all use of violent means, but he knew that at least some of his colleagues were doubtful about extending the principle to clear cases of self-defense. The whole matter should be talked out at length, he urged. One wonders if he had any suspicion of the grave difficulties that such discussion would create in the months ahead.

III

In 1838 the "ultraists" and the moderates in the American Peace Society formally parted company. This event may be regarded as a prelude to the similar split within the ranks of the antislavery movement two years later.

The Liberator had begun by this time to carry a more or less regular column under the heading of "Peace." This provided a forum for thrashing out the whole issue, exactly as Lewis Tappan had urged. Biblical sanctions for nonviolence were discussed in full; and "problem situations" from everyday life, to which peace principles might or might not be applicable, were submitted from a variety of quarters in order to stimulate debate. At this time, too, Henry Clarke Wright began his first extended speaking tour in behalf of non-resistance principles. Wright was soon to become the most devoted of all the apostles of the new cause.

At an "anniversary meeting" of the national peace society in May, 1838, Wright, Garrison, and a few others apparently decided that the differences between their own views and those of the rest of the membership warranted bold, new steps. They

[24] Resolution of the Executive Committee, American Anti-Slavery Society. See *The Liberator*, Dec. 1, 1837, 195.

[25] *The Liberator*, Jan. 5, 1838, 2.

secured the passage of a resolution calling for a convention the following September, to discuss the peace question in all its aspects. It was to be open to all the "friends of peace"; but the committee on arrangements was stacked with New Englanders, and Boston was chosen as the site.

Any doubts as to who controlled the convention were dispelled by the first day's proceedings. Garrison submitted a motion urging that women be granted full debating and voting rights, which was promptly passed. Thereupon George Beckwith (secretary to the national peace society) and a number of other "moderates" withdrew. The field was thus left clear for the all-out non-resistants. They proceeded to establish a formal organization in support of their principles, to be called the New England Non-Resistance Society. The key clause in the "constitution" which they drew up is worth quoting in full: "The members of this society agree . . . that no man, or body of men . . . have a right to take the life of man as a penalty for transgression, that no one who professes to have the spirit of Christ, can consistently sue a man at law for redress of injuries, or thrust any evildoer into prison, or fill any office in which he would come under obligation to execute penal enactments—or take part in military service—or acknowledge allegiance to any human government—or justify any man in fighting in defense of property, liberty, life, or religion; that he cannot engage in or countenance any plot to revolutionize, or change by physical violence, any government, however corrupt or oppressive."[26] Garrison himself was deeply moved by this result. He felt sure that the founding of the Non-Resistance Society would soon be regarded as a crucial turning point in the course of all human history. "Mankind shall hail the *twentieth of September*," he prophesied, "with more exultation and gratitude than Americans now do the *fourth of July*."[27]

The great body of non-resistance doctrine was rooted firmly in the Bible. The men who developed it claimed as their ulti-

[26] *The Liberator*, Sept. 28, 1838, 154.
[27] *The Liberator*, Sept. 28, 1838, 155.

mate source of reference such familiar New Testament precepts as: "Thou shalt not kill"; "Resist not evil"; "Love thine enemies"; "Overcome evil with good."[28] The Old Testament, on the other hand, presented a problem with which the non-resistance movement was obliged to grapple from the very start. For the Lord of the Hebrews was truly a "God of Battles." The initial response of most non-resistants to this difficulty was to regard the Bible as a kind of "progressive revelation." According to this view, the Mosaic code ("An eye for an eye, and a tooth for a tooth," etc.) was appropriate to the particular time and place of the Judaic people. The life of Christ, however, signalized the start of a new, higher "dispensation," to which the spirit of non-resistance was essential. Christ simply abrogated the earlier "covenant."[29]

It is quite possible to miss the full significance of non-resistance doctrine; for in some respects the term itself is misleading. Leo Tolstoi recognized the central core of the doctrine when he wrote, in tribute to Garrison: "He denied the right of any man whatsoever, or of any body of men, forcibly to coerce another man in any way."[30] Indeed, "non-coercion" would have been the most appropriate name for the movement. That "non-resistance" became, instead, the operative term is due to the early connection with the larger peace movement. Something was needed to dramatize the difference between the ideas of the "ultra" peace men and those of their more moderate colleagues. And since defensive wars were the original bone of contention, the words "non-resistance" seemed quite to the point.

Reduced to its simplest terms, then, the doctrine affirmed that no man was justified in using any kind of physical force

[28] For a longer list of New Testament references, see *The Liberator*, Aug. 30, 1839, 139.

[29] See, for example, the Preamble to the Constitution of the New England Non-Resistance Society, printed in *The Liberator*, Sept. 28, 1838, 154. Also see a letter from Sarah Grimke to Gerrit Smith, in Barnes and Dumond, *Weld-Grimke Letters*, 549.

[30] See Fanny Garrison Villard, *William Lloyd Garrison on Non-Resistance* (New York, 1924), 47.

to alter the opinions or conduct of his neighbor. And as such, it could be regarded as more or less basic to all other reforms. It militated as clearly against slavery as against war. It lent support to the drive to "emancipate" women. It attacked the "enslavement" of certain men to the "demon rum." And it called in question even the punishment of criminals. Thus Sarah Grimke wrote to Henry C. Wright in March, 1838: "It does appear to me that the Principles of Peace lay at the root of all Reformations, that if the simple precept 'resist not evil' were once entrenched in the hearts and consciences of men, slavery and oppression and war and domestic tyranny and the usurping of authority over one another must wholly cease."[31] "As to anti-slavery" in particular, wrote an "ultra" man from Ohio, "Non-resistance is rock-salt."[32] And the Non-Resistance Society resolved in 1839 that "the abolition of slavery is involved in the doctrines of non-resistance as the unit is included within the aggregate; for if a slaveholder became non-resistant, he could never again *strike* a slave; never *compel* him to labor; never reclaim him if he chose to leave him; in a word, never resort to that law of violence, in which the relation of master and slave originated, and by which it must be continually sustained."[33]

I have already suggested the special character of non-resistance as a religious movement; but the point must be developed further. As one of its staunchest advocates wrote in 1845: "It is in the highest sense an embodying of Christianity—a practical carrying out those peculiarities which render the teaching of Jesus superior to all other religions. It is preparing the way for the full manifestation of the reign of Christ on earth."[34] It is, in fact, not quite sufficient to say that non-resistants referred continually to the teachings of Jesus; more than that, they saw themselves as *imitating* Christ in every particular—down to, and including, if necessary, his martyrdom. Garrison wrote of

[31] Barnes and Dumond, *Weld-Grimke Letters*, 614.
[32] Letter from John Smith, in *The Liberator*, Oct. 31, 1845, 176.
[33] *The Liberator*, Nov. 1, 1839, 176.
[34] Letter from John Smith, in *The Liberator*, Oct. 31, 1845, 176.

their own feelings about the course they had chosen to follow: "They have reached their present position by slow and painful steps. Henceforth they are crucified unto the world, and the world unto them. They feel that they are as lambs in the midst of wolves, but their trust is in the Good Shepherd, who is mighty to save even unto the uttermost."[35] Implicit in this was a clear kind of religious perfectionism: a truly Godlike character might be developed in this life, by an unflinching adherence to the non-resistant way. "The spirit of non-resistance is the highest attainment of the soul," wrote Samuel May. "A true non-resistant must have the same mind that was in Christ. He must have become a dear child of God."[36]

There is, too, an obvious note of millennialism in many of these pronouncements. "We believe," wrote Garrison in *The Liberator,* "(that) the success of the non-resistance enterprise will prove the reconciliation and salvation of a warring and lost world, and that it surpasses in magnitude and importance every other."[37] He looked forward to the "happy time, when swords shall be beaten into ploughshares, and spears into pruning-hooks, and men shall learn war no more, and all rule and all authority shall be put down."[38] The non-resistance millennium, then, would be a kind of glorious anarchy—organized without "priests and rulers," on the principles of love and forgiveness.

Such a bias against human institutions was an inevitable corollary of non-resistance beliefs: nothing must be permitted to fetter the spirit of the individual. Consider the way in which

[35] *The Liberator,* Oct. 26, 1838, 171.

[36] Article from *The Monthly Miscellany of Religion and Letters,* reprinted in *The Liberator,* Dec. 20, 1839, 204.

[37] *The Liberator,* March 28, 1845, 52.

[38] *The Liberator,* Feb. 22, 1839, 31. In the advance toward this "happy time," moreover, America seemed to occupy a peculiarly favorable position. Here there were "abundant elements for progress, and a field of action comparatively free from those obstacles which so impede reform elsewhere." It was true that the only major institutional change in this country was accomplished "through the agency of brute force." Circumstances might lead to similar "physical force resistance" in other countries ("France, for example, or England"); but in America "the better course of effecting reform by moral and intellectual means is more trustingly expected." (*The Liberator,* Sept. 1, 1843, 140.)

an Ohio woman described her "conversion" to non-resistance: "Four years ago the Lord delivered my spirit from all parties, and societies, of whatever name and object; and I have not since recognized myself accountable to any but my Heavenly Father."[39] Thus non-resistants were prominent "come-outers" from the various churches. They decried the influence of priests and ministers over the great mass of lay worshippers; the individual conscience, they felt, should be the only arbiter of right. Furthermore, most churches lent their support to the government; and the latter was notorious in its reliance upon force. Non-resistants were clearly obliged to refrain from all participation in the activities of government. Even voting was proscribed since "every ballot, however gently deposited, encloses, in fact, a bullet, for the heart of the offender against the law to which it may give birth."[40]

Military establishments were, of course, especially vicious; and the famous convention of September, 1838, set up a committee to petition the state to exempt non-resistants from militia duty.[41] All existing penal codes were corrupt, because founded on the principle of physical coercion. Punishment, indeed, was a matter properly left to God. Possessed of beliefs such as these, non-resistants became prominent in various societies organized during the 1840's to work for the abolition of the death penalty.

Non-resistance was in obvious conflict with certain key events and ideas of the American political tradition; and some, at least, of its most fervent supporters had the courage to say so. Garrison at one point called the Revolutionary War "selfish, revengeful, murderous." He suggested that Jesus Christ and George Washington stand at opposite poles as guides to human conduct, and that men are obliged to make a moral choice between them.[42] The principle of majority rule was an-

[39] Letter of Mrs. James Boyle, printed in *The Liberator*, Apr. 5, 1839, 56.
[40] See the proceedings of the fifth annual meeting of the New England Non-Resistance Society, printed in *The Liberator*, Nov. 10, 1843, 179.
[41] *The Liberator*, Oct. 5, 1838, 160.
[42] *The Liberator*, July 14, 1843, 111.

other important part of the American credo which came under attack from non-resistants. In fact, they regarded it as simply "the doctrine that might makes right." No group of human beings, however large, was justified in imposing laws upon a lesser number of its fellows.[43]

In sum, non-resistance may be regarded as a kind of prototype of nineteenth-century "ultraism." The men who used this word rarely, if ever, defined it; yet its meaning is clear enough. It had particular reference to a kind of black-and-white, either-or mentality; and to the penchant for following out a principle wheresoever it might lead. "Slavery is slavery, though no more than a single victim be held in servile chains. War is war, though not more than two individuals be arrayed in deadly hostility against each other. Non-resistance is to the violence that is in the world, what teetotalism is to intemperance, or immediate emancipation to slavery."[44] Thus spoke the ultraist in William Lloyd Garrison.

IV

From the very start there were some antislavery men who could not accept the whole body of non-resistance doctrine. As early as the summer of 1837, James Birney expressed considerable doubt about the effect that the "ultra" peace principles of men like H. C. Wright might have on the movement. And immediately following the convention which organized the Non-Resistance Society, the Rev. Orange Scott, Methodist preacher and staunch friend of antislavery, submitted to *The Liberator* a number of articles strongly condemning the whole business. The debate, which soon widened to include abolitionists everywhere, focussed particularly on the "no government" question. The first impulse of the opponents of non-resistance was to attempt to disassociate the new cause from abolitionism proper. The two movements must be kept apart, these men said; the workings of one must not be allowed to interfere with the other. In March, 1839, Birney, Lewis Tappan, and Henry

[43] *The Liberator,* Oct. 29, 1842, 171.
[44] *The Liberator,* May 27, 1843, 83.

B. Stanton (representing the American Anti-Slavery Society, which would have nothing to do with non-resistance) attempted to force the issue. Carrying the fight to the very heartland of the opposition, they appeared at a meeting of the New England Anti-Slavery Society. Their object was to present a resolution making it incumbent on all abolitionists to use their elective franchise. They implied that the national society might sever all ties with any state or local organization that failed to recognize this obligation. But the New Englanders overwhelmingly (and indignantly) rejected their proposals. Henceforth the battle lines were clearly drawn.

In the months that followed, the question of the proper attitude toward the government continued to be the main source of contention. And this is a good place to emphasize once again the primacy of non-resistance among the issues which were about to divide antislavery in two. Significantly, the New York men referred to the Garrisonians both as the "no-government group" and as "non-resistants." They regarded the terms as interchangeable, and indeed this usage was fair enough. As early as 1837—long before he discovered the connection between *slavery* and the American political system—Garrison was writing that "the governments of this world are all Anti-Christ," inasmuch as "they cannot be maintained except by naval and military power."[45] After certain Massachusetts abolitionists left the state society to form a rival organization, H. C. Wright accused them of supporting "the right to draw 'the sabre of revolution' to overthrow slavery... the right in man to butcher his brother."[46] The charge was much overdrawn, but it does show that the issue between the two groups was non-resistance.

The reaction of the public at large may also be of interest. A more or less typical article, in the *Haverhill Gazette*, regretted that "persons originally associated for the laudable purpose of promoting peace on earth, and good will to man, should have been led by the ultra spirit of the age, into such wild and im-

[45] *The Liberator*, Dec. 15, 1837, 203; "prospectus" for the next volume.
[46] *The Liberator*, Aug. 23, 1839, 136.

practicable hallucinations." The ideas of the non-resistants were, indeed, "more suited to the McLane asylum for the insane, than for the Marlboro chapel."[47] The *Greenfield Gazette* expressed a fear that these "fanatical ultraists" might bring ruin upon the whole cause of antislavery. The *Gazette* itself was on the side of abolition, but still "we are not ... such abolitionists as to destroy all the old landmarks, uproot all government, make men and women of babies, and fools of grown people."[48] In short, the popular image of non-resistance was scarcely flattering. To many men it seemed to aim at a total inversion of the natural order of things; in a more colorful phrase, it proposed to "topsy-turvy all creation."[49]

Non-resistance was essentially a New England movement in its origin; and so it remained throughout the decade of the 1840's. Elsewhere the most significant development during these years was the rise of political antislavery. The political abolitionists were basically unsympathetic to violence, but they refused to mold such an attitude into a larger philosophical system. As early as 1838, Theodore Weld was expressing this resistance to a doctrinaire approach, in letters to the Grimke sisters. Pressed by them for an account of his own opinions about "peace principles," he declared that he practiced a brand of "personal non-resistance." In the course of his efforts for antislavery, he said, there had been many occasions for "turning the other cheek"; but he refused to carry the principle all the way to "no-government," or other such extremes."[50]

An "Address to the Slaves," published by a Liberty Party

[47] Reprinted in *The Liberator*, Oct. 19, 1838, 168.

[48] Reprinted in *The Liberator*, Oct. 19, 1838, 168.

[49] See *The Liberator*, Feb. 15, 1839, 28. An amusing remark by Edmund Quincy several years later is also worth noting. The public, he said, seems to think that "we are in the habit of meeting at midnight with dark lanthorns and slouched hats, like so many Guy Fauxes, to gloat over the future explosion of the mine which we are running underneath the foundations of human society, and which is to blow it 'sky high, sir, sky high.'" (*The Liberator*, Dec. 25, 1846, 150.)

[50] See Barnes and Dumond, *Weld-Grimke Letters*, 513.

convention in 1842, concluded with the following: "Woful as is slavery, and desirable as is liberty, we entreat you to endure the former—rather than take a violent and bloody hold of the latter."[51] The Liberty Party men also stated their reasons for urging this course. They noted that "some persons in our ranks" opposed all violent resistance to tyranny on principle. However, "the great majority of abolitionists justify their forefathers in bloody resistance to oppression; and can therefore dissuade you from resistance to a ten-thousand-fold greater oppression, not on the high ground of absolute morality, but on the comparatively low one of expediency." "Bloody resistance" simply would not work.

Meanwhile, the Garrisonians moved to a total repudiation of the United States Constitution, and began calling for a dissolution of the national union. Political antislavery, of course, attacked this position; and the New England men replied in kind. *The Liberator* for 1844-1845 carried a running debate between the two sides, with Garrison and Gerrit Smith as the chief protagonists. According to Smith, non-resistance opinions alone were responsible for the stand of the "disunionists," but Garrison vigorously denied the charge. "Is it a non-resistance question at all?" Garrison asked—and then replied in the negative. "None but antislavery reasons are urged in favor of a dissolution of the Union."[52] Garrison had, by this time, come to realize the wisdom of keeping non-resistance and antislavery separate. Indeed, in 1839 he had founded a special journal, *The Non-Resistant*—thus shifting the burden of the new cause away from the pages of *The Liberator*. Yet the initial connection between the two movements was clear—and significant. And even in the 1840's telltale signs of non-resistance rhetoric would occasionally show up in antislavery pronouncements. In December, 1844, for example, the Rhode Island state society passed a resolution recommending that abolitionists should "secede from the present blood-cemented government

51 Printed in *The Liberator*, Feb. 11, 1842, 22.
52 *The Liberator*, Oct. 31, 1845, 174. See also Sept. 20, 1844, 150.

of the United States."[53] The phrase "blood-cemented" came straight from the non-resistance lexicon.

The Mexican War was perhaps the most significant event of the 1840's in its long-range implications for antislavery. Yet with respect to the problem of violence alone its effects were minimal. It did provide a specific issue on which abolitionists of all factions could agree, but it did not alter the larger balance between the non-resistants and the political-action men. Both sides opposed the war simply because it seemed designed to extend the area of slavery. A few reformers, it is true, may have been led by the prevailing excitement to denounce *all* war; but this was far from a firm commitment. A good case in point could be found in the career of Charles Sumner, soon to play an important role in the struggle against slavery. Sumner's startling Fourth of July oration to the city of Boston in 1845 revealed him to be an all-out peace man. "In our age," he said, "there can be no peace that is not honorable; there can be no war that is not dishonorable."[54] Theodore Parker, too, at about the same time affirmed that "war is an utter violation of Christianity. If war be right, then Christianity is wrong, false, a lie. Every man who understands Christianity knows that war is wrong."[55] Yet when Europe was swept by a wave of "liberal" revolutions a few years later, both men began to forget their peace principles. They ultimately came to believe that there were some instances in which fighting was justifiable. Thus Parker wrote to Francis Cobbe: "I think we should agree about war. I hate it, I deplore it, yet see its necessity. All the great charters of humanity have been *writ in blood,* and must continue to be so for some centuries."[56]

In fact, after 1845 one can see in certain antislavery quarters the beginnings of a frontal attack on nonviolent principles. The stalwart Kentuckian, Cassius Clay, would never have any

[53] *The Liberator,* Dec. 13, 1844, 199.

[54] Quoted in David Donald, *Charles Sumner and the Coming of the Civil War* (New York, 1960), 108.

[55] See Henry Steele Commager, *Theodore Parker* (Boston, 1936), 192.

[56] Commager, *Theodore Parker,* 193.

part of the "sickly cant" and "mawkish sensibility" of non-resistance. "Moral power," he argued, "must always be backed with cold steel and the flashing blade."[57] In 1847 *The Liberator* regretfully reported a speech by C. L. Remond, wherein it was urged that "the slaves were bound, by their love of justice, to RISE AT ONCE, en masse, and THROW OFF THEIR FETTERS."[58] And as early as 1845 no less a personage than Gerrit Smith began to doubt that slavery "will die a peaceful death." The thought of war did not make him happy, but he resigned himself to its necessity.[59]

The New England Non-Resistance Society, meanwhile, had fallen on hard times. Financial insolvency had forced *The Non-Resistant* to suspend publication in 1842; and two attempts to revive it proved abortive. Attendance at the annual meetings was never very great. Henry C. Wright became a kind of roving ambassador for the movement, and managed to stimulate at least some interest wherever he went. But when he carried the fight overseas to Europe in 1845-1847, there was no one to take his place in New England and the cause languished badly. In addition, the public image of non-resistance was more unfavorable than ever. Generally speaking, this was a period of decline for organized non-resistance; though as individuals, many of its supporters seem to have kept faith—at least in a loose sense.

In terms of its intellectual content, non-resistance was pulled in opposite directions during the 1840's. There was, in the first place, a desire to delimit the movement in certain ways, so as to make it palatable to larger numbers of people. But, on the other hand, it possessed its own peculiar, internal momentum which carried some of its adherents to truly "ultra" extremes.

The "moderates" decided that they were not opposed to all civil government per se—but only to all *existing* govern-

[57] Article reprinted in *The Liberator*, July 18, 1845, 113.
[58] *The Liberator*, July 9, 1847, 109.
[59] See Ralph Volney Harlow, *Gerrit Smith* (New York, 1939), 304. See also *The Liberator*, Jan. 26, 1849, 14.

ments.[60] Moreover, they gave qualified approval to the practice of confining insane persons,[61] and even to the imprisonment of criminals—providing the aim was "cure and restoration," not punishment. But other non-resistants attacked such opinions as mere temporizing. Charles Stearns, for instance, wrote to *The Liberator* in 1845 deprecating any retreat from principle, even in "extreme cases."[62] "Either the principle of violence is right, or it is wrong," declared another one of the faithful; the issue was as simple as that.[63] Here, once again, spoke the ultraist—with his special, almost ruthless intensity in all that relates to principle.

In this case, as always, ultraism bore exotic fruit. The Bible was first to feel its effect, as men like Stearns and Wright continued down the path leading away from orthodox religion. As early as 1845 the former had publicly opined that the Old Testament contained "many lies" and was "no more the work of God than the Koran, or the Book of Mormon."[64] Its most obvious defects, of course, related to the question of "peace." Wright, meanwhile, affirmed that "the writers of the Old Testament were in some instances mistaken," and asked "Shall we sacrifice God to a book?"[65] These men could not remain satisfied with the earlier explanation of Old Testament "problems"; that is, the idea of "progressive revelation," according to which God had ordained the Mosaic law as appropriate to the particular circumstances of the ancient Hebrews. Killing, they said, could *never* have been right; it was an absolute moral law for all time. No matter what the circumstances, God could never have encouraged men to do wrong.

But having sacrificed the "book" to God, these non-resistants now came near to sacrificing God to a kind of abstract moral law. Taking life, they argued, is everywhere and always

[60] *The Liberator*, Oct. 18, 1844, 168.
[61] *The Liberator*, Aug. 23, 1844, 132.
[62] *The Liberator*, Dec. 19, 1845, 204.
[63] *The Liberator*, March 20, 1846, 47.
[64] *The Liberator*, Oct. 10, 1845, 164.
[65] *The Liberator*, Nov. 17, 1848, 181.

wrong; and if the Bible seems to sanction killing, we must discard our belief in its Divine origin. For God can never kill. Nor, for that matter, can he "lie, steal, or enslave."[66] More orthodox Christians argued that such views, in effect, restricted the Lord's omnipotence; and indeed the whole discussion became known as the "rights of God controversy." The non-resistants could reply that God was by definition incapable of killing, stealing, or otherwise transgressing the moral law. Yet it is clear that the moral law itself was what chiefly interested them. God became little more than a name applied to their own perceptions of right conduct. As Henry Wright declared in 1855: "*Humanity before all things*—before all books and all institutions; and God in the soul is the only authority."[67] Non-resistance had thus carried its foremost apostle to a position very close to Transcendentalism.

V

The decline of non-violent abolitionism in the 1850's was nothing short of a total collapse. The process can be traced simply in the defections from the non-resistance movement. Angelina Grimke Weld was one of the first to go. Professing to be herself "amazed" at the transformation in her own beliefs, she nonetheless decided that "slavery is more abhorrent . . . to Christianity than murder. . . . We are compelled to choose between two evils, and all that we can do is to take the *least*, and baptize liberty in blood, if it must be so."[68] Charles Stearns abandoned his "peace principles" under the stress of conditions in "bleeding Kansas," where he went to live in 1854. He had done so, he assured Garrison, only after the most protracted soul searching. He had made a serious attempt to practice non-resistance, and had endured several hard beatings as a result. Indeed, he had "when smitten, literally turned the

66 *The Liberator*, Jan. 12, 1849, 6.

67 *The Liberator*, March 30, 1855, 50.

68 Letter of Angelina Grimke Weld to "a friend" in Brookline, Mass. Reprinted in *The Liberator*, July 7, 1854, 106.

other cheek, and had been smitten on that also."[69] But he felt that further attacks might endanger his life; and he had decided that "if non-resistance is not a safe principle, . . . it cannot be a true one." Garrison would understand if he had "come to Kansas and gone to fighting the Missouri wild beasts." Stearns's letters to *The Liberator* show a considerable measure of guilt over his apostasy from the cause of non-resistance, and an intense anxiety that Garrison should "understand." How bitter, then, it must have been for him to read this comment, which the editor appended to one of his first letters: "It is evident that our impulsive friend Stearns has got thoroughly frightened out of his peace principles, as Peter denied his Lord to save himself from impending danger. We compassionate his weakness."[70]

But Garrison was standing alone more and more, by now, in his support for "peace principles." S. S. Foster and Samuel May had given up the faith in the middle of 1856; and Parker Pillsbury followed their example a year or so later. Pillsbury, indeed, told the Massachusetts Anti-Slavery Society in 1859 that "he longed to see the time come when Boston should run with blood from Beacon Hill to the foot of Broad Street."[71] And Wendell Phillips (whose non-resistance had always been a little uncertain) told the same audience that "he was glad that every five minutes gave birth to a black baby, for in its infant wail he recognized the voice which should yet shout the war cry of insurrection; its baby hand would one day hold the dagger which should reach the master's heart."[72] But the crowning blow, no doubt, was the recantation of Henry Wright himself. In 1859 we find this greatest of all "peace" champions at a Massachusetts antislavery meeting, sponsoring a resolution "that resistance to slaveholders and slavehunters is obedience to God, and a sacred duty to man," and "that it is

[69] *The Liberator*, Feb. 15, 1856, 27.
[70] *The Liberator*, Jan. 4, 1856, 2.
[71] *The Liberator*, Feb. 4, 1859, 19.
[72] *The Liberator*, Feb. 4, 1859, 19.

the right and duty of the North . . . to instigate the slaves to insurrection."[73]

These defections from the principles of non-resistance were important events in the conversion of the antislavery movement to violent "means." But even more important was the accession of new leaders who had *never* been truly non-resistant. Parker has already been mentioned. Thomas Wentworth Higginson and Henry Ward Beecher were equally prominent. Beecher, indeed, did more than anyone else to popularize the cause of "bleeding Kansas." His pledge that his own Plymouth Church would donate twenty-five Sharp's rifles to the embattled antislavery men there, produced a new name for these firearms—"Beecher's Bibles." "You might as well read the Bible to Buffaloes as to those fellows who follow Atchison and Stringfellow," he said. "Moral suasion has always been the better for a little something to stand on."[74] The political leadership of antislavery also contributed to the new attitude—Sumner, whose former interest in the cause of peace had now completely evaporated; and Joshua Giddings, who avowed that "were I a slave, I would escape, if in my power, though compelled to walk upon the dead bodies of slaveholders from Mississippi to Malden."[75]

There were three main factors behind this growing receptivity to violence. The Fugitive Slave Law, for one, served to bring some of the most repugnant features of slavery into the heart of Northern cities and towns. In combatting it, force seemed essential: there was no other way of freeing a fugitive who was guarded by large numbers of police and militiamen. The events surrounding the return of Anthony Burns to slavery, for example, measurably altered the attitudes of New England abolitionists toward violence. At a meeting held two weeks later, many of them voiced approval of the use of force to rescue fugitives. And some who still clung to non-resistance

[73] *The Liberator*, Apr. 15, 1859, 59.
[74] *The Liberator*, Feb. 29, 1856, 36.
[75] *The Liberator*, Nov. 4, 1859, 174.

exhorted those of their colleagues who were *not* so minded, to take up arms at once. Even Garrison pointedly asked the latter group "where was their fidelity to their principles?"[76]

In the second place, the changed attitudes were a natural reaction to the inescapable *fact* of violent conflict over slavery in places like "bleeding Kansas." As Stearns had written from the battleground itself: "Non-resistance is at a great discount here. . . . We have an army of the most valiant fighters in the world."[77] Heretofore abolitionists had honestly believed that slavery could be destroyed by peaceful means, but now that hope was vanishing. Thus Gerrit Smith wrote to Frederick Douglass in 1854: "As you are aware, I went to Congress with very little hope of the peaceful termination of American slavery. I have returned with less."[78]

Finally, the willingness to employ force simply reflected the growing numerical strength of antislavery. Force made sense when there was a large host of men to back it up. Adin Ballou, practically the only non-resistant whose principles never wavered, drew attention to this point in July, 1859, while writing for *The Practical Christian*. "Antislavery zeal is swallowing up the remnant of the peace host," he lamented. "It is a remarkable fact that just in proportion as the old dormant proslavery multitude are getting roused up and enlisted on the Anti-Slavery side, our Peace abolitionists are getting out of patience with their moral weapons, . . . and now think they must resort to the sword."[79]

For reasons such as these, then, many one-time non-resistants went over to "violent means" during the 1850's. But it should also be said that they were, to a considerable extent, carried along by the "old dormant proslavery multitude" of which Ballou spoke. It is interesting, and not a little ironic, that the "ultra" or "radical" position was the pacific one;

[76] *The Liberator*, June 9, 1854, 90.
[77] *The Liberator*, Jan. 12, 1855, 6.
[78] Harlow, *Gerrit Smith*, 305.
[79] Reprinted in *The Liberator*, July 28, 1854, 117.

while the "moderates" were not averse to violence, where necessary. It was the belated commitment to antislavery of large numbers of ordinary citizens which tipped the scale in favor of force. The great majority of Americans still believed in the "right of revolution" when other avenues of redress were closed. Some of the new recruits, indeed, may well have been among the mobs which attempted to use force *against* the abolitionists in the 1830's. Without them the antislavery movement might have continued to look askance at violent measures for some while longer.

The Abolitionists: A Decade of Historiography, 1959–1969

By Merton L. Dillon

Unlike the objects of their concern abolitionists were never "invisible men." Quiet work behind the scenes was not their way. Their function as advocates required them to exert every effort to insert their principles into the public mind. So successfully did they accomplish this purpose that contemporaries seldom doubted their determining influence in the shaping of events. Later, historians of nineteenth-century America, generally agreeing with the ante-bellum assessment of abolitionists, concluded that theirs had been a key role in bringing about the Civil War and in purging the nation of slavery. Of the major interpreters of American history only Charles A. and Mary R. Beard and Frederick Jackson Turner, with their emphases on economics and other impersonal aspects of history, ventured to create a perspective which diminished the abolitionists to trivial consequence.[1]

The nationalist historians writing after the Civil War were inclined to view the abolitionists as moral heroes. But by the 1930's and 1940's a near reversal in attitude had taken place. The revisionists, focusing on Civil War causation, then portrayed them as having been destructive in their effect. Abolitionists were condemned in revisionist writings as fanatics whose agitations had brought about a needless war. By the 1960's historians for the most part had abandoned a methodical search for the causes of the Civil War, and along with it the effort to measure abolitionist responsibility for the events preceding it.[2] Yet this change in interest did not signal a decline in the attention paid to the antislavery movement. In recent years abolitionists have seemed more important than ever before, not because of their relation to the Civil War but because of their concern with race, prejudice, and

---

[1] Staughton Lynd, *Class Conflict, Slavery, and the United States Constitution* (Indianapolis and New York, 1967), 143–44; Charles A. Beard and Mary R. Beard, *The Rise of American Civilization* (2 vols., New York, 1927), I, 695–703, 709–10.

[2] David M. Potter, *The South and the Sectional Conflict* (Baton Rouge, 1968), 91–99; David Donald, "American Historians and the Causes of the Civil War," *South Atlantic Quarterly*, LIX (Summer 1960), 351–55.

Mr. Dillon is professor of history at Ohio State University.

142

justice matches that of today. As the abolitionists' relevance to the contemporary situation became obvious, research and writing on them naturally increased in volume, if not in scope. Most recent works on the subject have taken the form of monographs, biographies, articles, and interpretative essays. Only Dwight L. Dumond and Louis Filler have undertaken comprehensive treatments, although David B. Davis has launched a large enterprise that promises eventually to encompass both the British and American antislavery movements.[3]

By far the largest part of the writings since 1959, in contrast with those of immediately preceding years, express sympathy for both the aims and the style of abolitionists. Their methods may not in every instance be wholeheartedly endorsed, but rarely does one any longer find them dismissed in revisionist terms as fanatics, seekers after martyrdom, or irresponsible agitators. Instead they have again become objects of respect and admiration, much as they were in the writings of nationalist historians of post–Civil War years.[4]

No doubt it places too much faith in the efficacy of historical research to attribute the recent near-revolution in attitude toward abolitionists solely to increased knowledge about them. The comprehensiveness of Dumond's writings on the antislavery movement probably should be given only partial credit for putting Avery Craven's unflattering views of abolitionists into eclipse. Surely more to the point is a New York *Times* report that as the civil rights march from Selma, Alabama, drew near to Montgomery early in 1965 it was to be joined by at least twenty historians, including some of the most prominent students of the Civil War and Reconstruction.[5] The sympathy those historians

[3] Dwight L. Dumond, *Antislavery: The Crusade for Freedom in America* (Ann Arbor, 1961); Louis Filler, *The Crusade Against Slavery, 1830–1860* (New York, 1960); David B. Davis, *The Problem of Slavery in Western Culture* (Ithaca, 1966), the first of a projected three volumes.

[4] Bertram Wyatt-Brown, "Abolitionism: Its Meaning for Contemporary American Reform," *Midwest Quarterly*, VIII (October 1966), 41–55. The fact that some reviewers so sharply criticized Dumond for being uncritical of the abolitionists suggests that attitudes toward them may be less universally sympathetic than the above paragraph claims. See especially C. Vann Woodward, "The Antislavery Myth," *American Scholar*, XXXI (Spring 1962), 312–28, and reviews by David Potter, Louis Filler, and David Donald in *American Historical Review*, LXVII (July 1962), 1064; *New England Quarterly*, XXXV (December 1962), 557; and *Political Science Quarterly*, LXXVII (June 1962), 273. For a late assertion that "many" abolitionists "coveted to become martyrs," see William H. Pease and Jane H. Pease, "Antislavery Ambivalence: Immediatism, Expediency, Race," *American Quarterly*, XVII (Winter 1965), 693.

[5] New York *Times*, March 23, 1965.

manifested for the aims and tactics of the New Abolitionists[6] seems to have been rather widely shared by other historians who did not venture to Alabama. That sympathy must have influenced to some degree their understanding of the antislavery movement.

The modern civil rights movement made the program, tactics, and frame of mind of abolitionists comprehensible to more persons than at any other time since 1865. Events of the 1950's and afterward gave the abolitionists a contemporaneousness not often enjoyed by figures of the past. It was easy for an advocate of civil rights in 1965 to feel kinship with the historical abolitionists and to identify their public activities with his own.[7] For that reason the antislavery movement could be studied with greater perception and depth of understanding than had generally been possible before. While a few naysayers retained the largely discredited antiabolitionist stance of the revisionists into the 1960's[8] and while the new views entered textbooks slowly,[9] most writers on the subject adopted interpretations that would have pleased the abolitionists themselves.

Thus when Fawn Brodie in 1965 published an essay entitled "Who Defends the Abolitionist?" and conveyed the impression that hardly anybody did, she was in effect beating a dead horse;[10] for the editor of the volume in which the essay appeared remarked in his introduction that he had been unable to find any contributor from the younger generation of historians willing to undertake an attack on abolitionists.[11] And even Mrs. Brodie, finding few present-day writers whose hostile views made them subject to castigation, had to focus her complaint of antiabolitionist bias on certain Southern apologists and others who, for the most part, had written decades earlier. Of prominent contemporary scholars exhibiting such bias, she could cite only David Donald (hardly a flagrant example when judged by earlier anti-

[6] The term, of course, is from Howard Zinn, *SNCC: The New Abolitionists* (Boston, 1964).

[7] Zinn, "Abolitionists, Freedom-Riders, and the Tactics of Agitation," in Martin Duberman (ed.), *The Antislavery Vanguard: New Essays on the Abolitionists* (Princeton, 1965), 417–51.

[8] Arnold Whitridge, *No Compromise! The Story of the Fanatics Who Paved the Way to the Civil War* (New York, 1960); although objective in tone, Henry H. Simms, *Emotion at High Tide: Abolition as a Controversial Factor, 1830–1845* (Baltimore, 1960), seemed to imply that the abolitionists had agitated unreal issues, see especially p. vi.

[9] Patrick J. Groff, "The Abolitionist Movement in High School Texts," *Journal of Negro Education*, XXXII (Winter 1963), 43–51.

[10] Duberman (ed.), *Antislavery Vanguard*, 52–67.

[11] *Ibid.*, viii.

abolitionist standards), whose Pulitzer Prize–winning biography of Charles Sumner had appeared in 1960.[12]

It was suggestive of the extent of change in attitude toward abolitionists that Donald's work was vigorously and elaborately challenged from so many quarters. He exhibited excessive complacency toward slavery, it was charged, and presented an "apotheosis of opportunism" as a standard of statesmanship. But his major error, according to his several critics, was to portray a neurotic and somewhat disagreeable Sumner, whose abolitionism apparently had been generated by his own inner tensions and personal inadequacies rather than by revulsion against the horrors of slavery.[13]

Criticism on related counts was not altogether new to Donald, for in the eyes of certain critics he already was under a cloud because of an earlier essay in which he had sought to find psychological roots for the antislavery movement.[14] Although it had once been considered a quite reputable, even an obligatory, task for historians to attempt to discern the motives that account for human action, efforts to interpret the abolitionists in social and psychological terms now generated minor historiographical storms. The problem that called for solution was this: slavery had existed for many centuries, yet abolitionism was a relatively late development. How could this chronological discrepancy be explained? Some students, dissatisfied with an explanation that accounted for the appearance of abolitionism solely as an uncomplicated response to evil, attempted to locate hidden sources of the antislavery movement.

Gilbert H. Barnes, whose work may be said to have laid the foundation for nearly all other modern studies of abolition, had presented in 1933 one of the first and most widely accepted answers to this perplexing problem.[15] He found the antislavery impulse in a great religious revival originating in western New York in the 1820's. In Barnes's work the reform movements were related to a shift in theological emphasis away from Calvinism toward a gospel of benevolence, an intel-

---

[12] Donald, *Charles Sumner and the Coming of the Civil War* (New York, 1960).

[13] Louis Ruchames, "The Pulitzer Prize Treatment of Charles Sumner," *Massachusetts Review*, II (Summer 1961), 749–69 (quote on page 751); Paul Goodman, "David Donald's *Charles Sumner* Reconsidered," *New England Quarterly*, XXXVII (September 1964), 373–87.

[14] "Toward a Reconsideration of Abolitionists," in Donald, *Lincoln Reconsidered* (New York, 1956), 19–36.

[15] *The Antislavery Impulse, 1830–1844* (New York, 1933).

lectual trend that he credited somewhat overgenerously to Charles G. Finney. Some persons saw at once that the connection Barnes had made between abolitionism and what twentieth-century scholars were likely to consider religious fanaticism could be regarded as discreditable to the movement.[16] Thus the revisionists welcomed Barnes aboard, and a student of the historiography of Civil War causation unhesitatingly placed him with that group.[17] Whether this association was altogether fair or correct, Barnes unmistakably had accounted for abolitionism by relating it to a force other than slavery. Yet at the same time he made it possible to view abolitionism as conservative and respectable by showing that most of the vagaries and eccentricities often attributed to its advocates had been characteristic of William Lloyd Garrison and his circle and not of Theodore Dwight Weld and James Gillespie Birney, the Westerners whose activities Barnes emphasized. This qualitative distinction among the personnel of the antislavery movement was made still more explicit in Dumond's *Antislavery Origins of the Civil War in the United States* (Ann Arbor, 1939) and his *Antislavery: The Crusade for Freedom in America* (Ann Arbor, 1961), works that no one would be likely to mistake as belonging to the revisionist camp of Civil War historiography.

Soon after Barnes's work was published, Avery Craven began to relate the antislavery movement as well as other ante-bellum reforms to tensions produced in individuals by the economic upheaval and social flux of the Jacksonian era.[18] According to Craven the unconscious psychological needs and motives of certain hypersensitive Northerners—not the objective problems of slavery and prejudice with their inescapable moral dimension—accounted for the appearance of abolitionism. The effect of such an analysis undoubtedly was to denigrate the abolitionists. When Donald in the 1950's, using concepts drawn from social psychology, attempted specifically to explain the abolitionists in a similar way, he and those few colleagues who accepted his interpretation found themselves grouped with the severest critics of the abolitionists and even with open apologists for slavery, as though to assert that abolitionists were complicated and sometimes hu-

[16] William G. McLoughlin, "Introduction to the Harbinger Edition," in Barnes, *The Antislavery Impulse, 1830–1844* (Harbinger ed., New York, 1964), x–xiv.

[17] Thomas J. Pressly, *Americans Interpret Their Civil War* (Princeton, 1954), 268–70.

[18] His fully formulated view appears in Craven, *The Coming of the Civil War* (New York, 1942), 117–18, 124–30, 150.

manly flawed was to allege that their cause was in some way unworthy.[19]

The fate of Donald's work on the abolitionists did not discourage others from similar attempts at historical analysis. Clifford S. Griffin in 1960 placed the pressures that accounted for reform outside the reformers and made the pressures objective, whereas both Craven and Donald had internalized them and considered them irrational.[20] The reformers, according to Griffin, knew exactly what they were doing and what their motives were. He depicted reformers, including abolitionists, as conservatives with a rage for order rather than as advocates of justice and social change. Reform, he asserted, was a calculated means to preserve the status quo, although he left undefined the precise relationship between conservatism and a reform so radical as abolishing slavery. The import of Griffin's study was to suggest that abolitionists and other reformers had not been unselfishly opposed to the evils they crusaded against, a view quite out of harmony with the prevailing mood of the 1960's.

Despite the pitfalls that laid in wait for those searching for the roots of abolitionism, some historians still refused to be content with a simplistic explanation of the movement. In a wide-ranging enterprise, David B. Davis undertook a comparative history of antislavery movements and in preparation studied the problem of slavery in Western culture. His work exemplified the new interest in intellectual and comparative history as well as the continuing search for an explanation of abolitionism. He traced changing attitudes toward slavery and addressed himself to much the same question Donald had asked: Why, even though it had existed for many centuries, did men oppose slavery only at specific times? He found the answer to lie in major shifts that had occurred in Western culture during the eighteenth century, especially changes within religious sects and denominations.[21] In an influential essay published in 1962 he related the appearance of

[19] See the listing in Anne C. Loveland, "Evangelicalism and 'Immediate Emancipation' in American Antislavery Thought," *Journal of Southern History*, XXXII (May 1966), 172n. Not surprisingly, historians who criticized Donald's thesis because it suggested that abolitionists were imperfect failed to comment on the analogy between their position and that of the Donatists of the fourth and fifth centuries, who insisted that the sacraments' validity depends upon the character of the priest who administers them. See W. H. C. Frend, *The Donatist Church: A Movement of Protest in Roman North Africa* (Oxford, 1952), 319–21, 323–24.

[20] Griffin, *Their Brothers' Keepers: Moral Stewardship in the United States, 1800–1865* (New Brunswick, 1960).

[21] Davis, *Problem of Slavery, passim.*

the doctrine of immediatism in both England and the United States to the development of the romantic and evangelical frame of mind.[22] None of Davis' writings suggested that abolitionists suffered from maladjustment, as Donald's work had done; they rather depicted them as swept forward by irresistible cultural change.

Meanwhile, psychological interpretations of abolition were being further called into question. Robert A. Skotheim pointed out what he regarded as methodological inadequacies in Donald's essay, thereby casting doubt on the validity of the Donald thesis, but his own essay did not attempt to prove the thesis mistaken.[23] Dumond dealt with it in perhaps the most devastating fashion simply by ignoring it. It was left to Larry Gara, Betty Fladeland, and Martin Duberman to challenge Donald's conclusions directly.[24] Gara pointed out the wide occurrence of antislavery sentiment throughout the North and the numerous variations it assumed and showed that it could not be identified with any particular group or class. Fladeland examined the extensive range of persons affiliated with the antislavery movement and concluded from their variety that there was no typical abolitionist who fitted Donald's model, or probably any other. Their only common denominator was antipathy to slavery. Thus the argument was back where it started: Slavery itself, not social and psychological tensions or even cultural change, had generated antislavery. Duberman met Donald on his own ground, as it were, by asserting the impossibility in the existing state of limited historical and psychiatric knowledge of ascertaining the motives of the men who became abolitionists. Generalization was therefore impossible.

Duberman's article on the one hand was an invitation to intensive biographical research; on the other, it could be read as an endorsement of nominalism. In any event his warning apparently achieved its purpose, for fewer historians and biographers ap-

[22] Davis, "The Emergence of Immediatism in British and American Antislavery Thought," *Mississippi Valley Historical Review*, XLIX (September 1962), 209–30.
[23] "A Note on Historical Method: David Donald's 'Toward a Reconsideration of Abolitionists,'" *Journal of Southern History*, XXV (August 1959), 356–65. For Donald's reply to the critique, see *ibid.*, XXVI (February 1960), 156–57.
[24] Gara, "Who Was an Abolitionist?" in Duberman (ed.), *Antislavery Vanguard*, 32–51; Fladeland, "Who Were the Abolitionists?" *Journal of Negro History*, XLIX (April 1964), 99–115; Duberman, "The Abolitionists and Psychology," *ibid.*, XLVII (July 1962), 183–91. Duberman further clarified his views in "The Northern Response to Slavery," in Duberman (ed.), *Antislavery Vanguard*, 406–13.

peared willing to speculate on the psychic maladjustments of abolitionists after it was published. With the possible exception of an earlier article by Arthur M. Schlesinger, Jr., taking issue with revisionists who denied the moral dimension of the Civil War,[25] Duberman's essay was probably reprinted and cited more often than any other recent writing on the antislavery movement. This favorable reception was understandable, since the essay comported with the growing reluctance on the part of many historians to offer large generalizations about the past and with the inclination to focus on the specific and the discrete in human situations. It reflected, too, compassion and forebearance in favorable contrast to the censoriousness and quickness to judge so evident in the work of some earlier critics of the antislavery movement. The essay was written at a time when a considerable part of the academic community was becoming aroused to new activism by racial injustice, and it was obvious that to persist in questioning the motives of earlier reformers was by implication to question one's own.

Duberman's view that abolitionists might be happy, well-adjusted persons was confirmed in his prize-winning biography of James Russell Lowell, whom he portrayed as a balanced individual deserving study as much for his admirable life style as for his worldly accomplishment.[26] In a more modest biographical effort Ira V. Brown reported that J. Miller McKim, a founder of the American Anti-Slavery Society and lifelong abolitionist, was neither neurotic nor fanatical. He was happy in his work and his family life, Brown contended, and "There was nothing eccentric or bizarre about his appearance or his personality."[27] Other biographical studies of antislavery leaders presented similarly favorable portraits of their subjects.[28] Thus the abolitionists, it appeared, were much like present-day reformers—normal men and

[25] "The Causes of the Civil War: A Note on Historical Sentimentalism," *Partisan Review*, XVI (October 1949), 969–81.
[26] *James Russell Lowell* (Boston, 1966), *passim*, but especially xx–xxii.
[27] "Miller McKim and Pennsylvania Abolitionism," *Pennsylvania History*, XXX (January 1963), 56–72 (quote on page 71).
[28] Irving H. Bartlett, *Wendell Phillips: Brahmin Radical* (Boston, 1961); Helen G. Baer, *The Heart Is Like Heaven: The Life of Lydia Maria Child* (Philadelphia, 1964); Merton L. Dillon, *Elijah P. Lovejoy, Abolitionist Editor* (Urbana, 1961); Tilden G. Edelstein, *Strange Enthusiasm: A Life of Thomas Wentworth Higginson* (New Haven, 1968); Gerda Lerner, *The Grimké Sisters from South Carolina: Rebels Against Slavery* (Boston, 1967); Milton Meltzer, *Tongue of Flame: The Life of Lydia Maria Child* (New York, 1965); Bertram Wyatt-Brown, *Lewis Tappan and the Evangelical War Against Slavery* (Cleveland, 1969).

women disinterestedly absorbed in the racial issues of their time. Instead of being driven by maladjustment to espouse reform, they had simply expressed legitimate concern about a genuine problem. What had once seemed to be their deplorable excesses in rhetoric and zeal were now explained variously as an appropriate response to monstrous evil or merely as typical of the florid style of a romantic, unrestrained age.[29]

Admittedly there were a few abolitionists whom nobody was likely to consider as other than eccentric—Abigail Folsom, Parker Pillsbury, and Stephen Symonds Foster among them—but the most conspicuous figure to remain unabsorbed in the new categories of normality and decorum was William Lloyd Garrison. In some sense he had always been the touchstone of antislavery. A center of controversy in his own day, he remained one in the 1960's. Beset with critics inside the antislavery movement while he lived, he encountered hostility also from some modern scholars whose sympathies for abolitionists otherwise were unrestrained.[30] In part this may have been a consequence of their liberal faith that justice could be achieved in racial matters without the necessity of the nation's undergoing the fundamental reconstruction Garrison's agitation implied; in part it may simply have been the result of historiographical accident.

When Gilbert Barnes had the good luck to discover that famous "trunkful of letters . . . in a farmhouse attic near Allston, Massachusetts," he had located the manuscripts upon which he based his influential reinterpretation of the antislavery movement.[31] For the most part the letters had been written by Western abolitionists at odds with Garrison. The new version of abolitionist history, first prepared by Barnes in Ulrich B. Phillips' seminar at the University of Michigan, magnified the antislavery contributions of Theodore Dwight Weld, whose letters they were, and correspondingly diminished the role of Garrison, whom Barnes portrayed as having been not so much ineffectual as positively

[29] Donald G. Mathews, "The Abolitionists on Slavery: The Critique Behind the Social Movement," *Journal of Southern History,* XXXIII (May 1967), 163–82; Zinn, "Abolitionists, Freedom-Riders, and the Tactics of Agitation," 418–26, 430–31.

[30] David A. Williams, "William Lloyd Garrison, the Historians, and the Abolitionist Movement," Essex Institute, *Historical Collections,* XCVIII (April 1962), 84–99; Louis Filler, "Garrison Again, and Again: A Review Article," *Civil War History,* XI (March 1965), 69–75.

[31] Barnes and Dumond (eds.), *Letters of Theodore Dwight Weld, Angelina Grimké Weld, and Sarah Grimké, 1822–1844* (2 vols., New York and London, 1934), I, xix.

150

hurtful to abolitionist efforts. Unfortunately for Garrison's reputation Barnes's account soon became standard. His point of view was given still greater authority when Dumond—also a Phillips' student and his successor at Michigan—discovered the papers of James Gillespie Birney[32] and wrote persuasive histories of the antislavery movement, which were likewise highly critical of Garrison and intensely sympathetic to the Western abolitionists.

Like so many reinterpretations there was little that was revolutionary in the new disparagement of Garrison. Some nineteenth-century writers had similarly disputed his primacy and usefulness to the cause, and Albert Bushnell Hart, together with some of his students, had long ago presented material casting doubt on Garrison's claims of originality and leadership.[33] But among modern historians it was Barnes and Dumond who provided the information that apparently destroyed the Garrison "legend." According to their accounts Garrison's liabilities were many, but the overriding one was his radicalism: he was a Christian anarchist who associated numerous bizarre causes and revolutionary theories with abolitionism, thereby alienating conservative persons who would otherwise have joined the antislavery cause. The true exponents of abolitionism, they averred, were the Western revivalists and advocates of antislavery politics. A number of influential historians of the antislavery movement apparently found most worthy of admiration those abolitionists who could be identified as exponents of conventional, democratic modes of political action to achieve reform within the existing order.

Despite the authoritative and even venerable dismissal of the claims for Garrison's pre-eminence in the antislavery movement, not all historians agreed, and much of the writing on abolitionism in the 1960's had the effect of rehabilitating Garrison and New England abolitionists in general. One of the first such works to appear was Louis Filler's *The Crusade Against Slavery* (New York, 1960). The book related antislavery to politics and a multitude of other reforms and emphasized the influence of Garrison and his circle throughout the narrative. Louis Ruchames' collec-

[32] Dumond (ed.), *Letters of James Gillespie Birney, 1831–1857* (2 vols., New York and London, 1938).
[33] William Birney, *James G. Birney and His Times: The Genesis of the Republican Party with Some Account of Abolition Movements in the South Before 1828* (New York, 1890); Hart, *Slavery and Abolition, 1831–1841* (New York and London, 1906); Mary S. Locke, *Anti-Slavery in America from the Introduction of African Slaves to the Prohibition of the Slave Trade (1619–1808)* (Boston, 1901); Alice D. Adams, *The Neglected Period of Anti-Slavery in America, 1808–1831* (Boston, 1908).

tion of antislavery documents likewise unmistakably placed Garrison at the center of the movement.[34] Two biographies of Garrison, both published in 1963, predictably asserted his importance but without denying the influence of abolitionists outside New England.[35] Yet Garrison's biographers, far from expressing unqualified admiration for their subject, accepted much of the criticism that Barnes and Dumond had made of his personality and tactics. It seemed difficult indeed for the academic temperament to approve of Garrison, even while conceding his significance. John L. Thomas, in particular, found him unpleasant. But Thomas' strictures were not confined to his odd and disagreeable personal qualities. He also required him, and by implication other abolitionists as well, to bear a terrible burden of guilt. According to Thomas, Garrison was chiefly responsible for creating the moral absolutism that Thomas said caused the Civil War. He alleged further that Garrison and his followers were responsible for the nation's failure to solve its racial problems after emancipation because they had not put forward a comprehensive program for dealing with freed slaves.[36]

Even while such accounts were being published, a few unalloyed partisans of Garrison appeared. Two obvious means of coming to terms with his ideology were available to those who sympathized with him. His radicalism could be accepted and approved for what it was, or its existence could be denied. Both approaches were tried. Bertram Wyatt-Brown, writing in a decade acquainted with the possibilities of violence and insurgency in promoting social change, held in 1967 that Garrison should be viewed as a moderate akin to twentieth-century liberals, for when one compared his pacifism and nonresistance with the tactics abolitionists might have advocated to advance their program—guerrilla warfare, assassination, and the like—he and other abolitionists appeared conservative indeed. In utter contrast to the view of Barnes and Dumond, who assumed Garrison's unsavory reputation and deleterious influence, Wyatt-Brown claimed that Garrison's respectability had been an asset to the antislavery

[34] *The Abolitionists: A Collection of Their Writings* (New York, 1963).

[35] Walter M. Merrill, *Against Wind and Tide: A Biography of Wm. Lloyd Garrison* (Cambridge, Mass., 1963); John L. Thomas, *The Liberator, William Lloyd Garrison: A Biography* (Boston, 1963).

[36] Thomas, *The Liberator*, 5, 452, 458. Thomas was freer with psychological interpretations than most recent biographers. He stated that Garrison "transferred his resistance to maternal authority into a hatred of society and a compulsion to tear it down." *Ibid.*, 309.

cause. Further, he had served as a symbol of unity for a movement that otherwise might have been hopelessly fragmented.[37]

Other defenders of Garrison did not consider him moderate at all, but acknowledged his radicalism and praised it. The "extremism" of at least some abolitionists had always constituted an obstacle to efforts to understand them. The indisputably revolutionary strand in antislavery thought was recognized and uniformly deplored by cautious Americans before the Civil War.[38] Afterward it often provided historians with grounds for charging abolitionists with fanaticism. On the other hand their radical aspect was ignored by writers who wished to absorb them into an account of the progress of liberal democracy and who took for granted that American institutions could deal satisfactorily with racial problems. Sometimes, as in the works of Barnes, the abolitionists' radicalism was disposed of by identifying it with Garrison and his followers. More recently, as some forms of extremism have become familiar through daily advocacy and implementation and as democratic institutions have increasingly been called into question, the radical features of abolitionism have received wider notice and understanding. Louis Ruchames, one of the abolitionists' most consistent advocates, defended Garrison against his detractors and also came forward in 1959 to defend John Brown against the charge of insanity and to justify Brown's actions at Harper's Ferry.[39] Several writers analyzed the abolitionists' dilemma concerning the use of violence as a mode of emancipation and of resistance to the "slave power." It is tempting to speculate that historians pursuing this theme have not been unaware of the several tactical choices available to contemporary civil rights advocates.[40]

[37] "William Lloyd Garrison and Antislavery Unity: A Reappraisal," *Civil War History*, XIII (March 1967), 5–24.

[38] Lorman Ratner, *Powder Keg: Northern Opposition to the Antislavery Movement, 1831–1840* (New York and London, 1968). A description of a reformer who shrank from what she construed as the extremism of abolitionists is in Francis E. Kearns, "Margaret Fuller and the Abolition Movement," *Journal of the History of Ideas*, XXV (January–March 1964), 120–27.

[39] Ruchames, "William Lloyd Garrison and the Negro Franchise," *Journal of Negro History*, L (January 1965), 37–49; Ruchames (ed.), *A John Brown Reader* (London and New York, 1959), 16–32. For a criticism of Brown's actions see Tilden G. Edelstein, "John Brown and His Friends," in Hugh Hawkins (ed.), *The Abolitionists: Immediatism and the Question of Means* (Boston, 1964), 71–79.

[40] Lewis Perry, "Versions of Anarchism in the Antislavery Movement," *American Quarterly*, XX (Winter 1968), 768–82; John Demos, "The Antislavery Movement and the Problem of Violent 'Means,'" *New England Quarterly*, XXXVII (December 1964), 501–26; Louis Filler, "Nonviolence and Abolition," *University Review*, XXX (Spring 1964), 172–78.

In an essay expounding the relation between immediatism and revivalism Anne C. Loveland pointed out the extremely radical implications of abolitionist reform, and Truman J. Nelson, using somewhat mystical language, emphasized the revolutionary character of Garrison's theories and approved of it.[41] Perhaps the most thorough exploration of the theme was by Aileen Kraditor in *Means and Ends in American Abolitionism.*[42] Besides being almost the only completely appreciative modern treatment of Garrison (Kraditor even asserted that he had a sense of humor!), it was also a profound analysis of the conflicting opinions and programs advanced by abolitionists. It showed the tensions produced within the antislavery organizations by struggles for ascendancy between a faction which sought to save existing society through reform and another faction which wanted a fundamental reconstruction of the social order. Kraditor treated the ideas of each group with respect and understanding. She conceded to the abolitionists a seriousness of purpose and a degree of intellectual responsibility not always acknowledged elsewhere.

The abolitionists have sometimes been charged with ignorance and impracticality. Thomas in 1963 wrote that they knew very little about slavery. Furthermore, while they crusaded to end slavery, they demonstrated their irresponsibility by giving no thought to the problems abolition would create. Dumond had demolished the first charge many years earlier, and the work of James M. McPherson published in 1964 provided an answer to the second.[43] Abolitionists, according to McPherson, were much more than visionary theorists. They were by no means so devoted to abstractions as Stanley M. Elkins, for instance, had asserted,[44] and they understood the implications and inescapable corollaries of freeing the slaves far better than their critics alleged. They did

[41] Loveland, "Evangelicalism and 'Immediate Emancipation,'" 172–88; Nelson, "The Liberator," *Ramparts,* IV (November 1965), 21–29; Nelson (ed.), *Documents of Upheaval: Selections from William Lloyd Garrison's The Liberator, 1831–1865* (New York, 1966). See also Donald G. Mathews, "Orange Scott: The Methodist Evangelist as Revolutionary," in Duberman (ed.), *Antislavery Vanguard,* 71–101; and Merton L. Dillon, "The Abolitionists as a Dissenting Minority," in Alfred F. Young (ed.), *Dissent: Explorations in the History of American Radicalism* (DeKalb, Ill., 1968), 83–108.

[42] *Means and Ends in American Abolitionism: Garrison and His Critics on Strategy and Tactics, 1834–1850* (New York, 1969).

[43] Thomas, *The Liberator,* 454; Dumond, *Antislavery Origins,* 7–9; McPherson, *The Struggle for Equality: Abolitionists and the Negro in the Civil War and Reconstruction* (Princeton, 1964).

[44] *Slavery: A Problem in American Institutional and Intellectual Life* (Chicago, 1959), 140–206.

not abandon any of their moral fervor after the Civil War began, McPherson wrote, but instead persistently urged the Union government to endorse emancipation as a war aim and to grant equal rights to the freedmen. They were astute and effective critics of governmental policy, and they are largely due the credit for such advances toward racial justice as were made during the Civil War and Reconstruction.

Barnes and Dumond had pictured the antislavery impulse as moving through political channels, but McPherson found important abolitionists in the 1860's and even afterward still acting independently of parties and continuing to apply pressure for social justice to hesitant or recalcitrant politicians. They were advocates of racial equality during the Civil War era, McPherson contended, and they continued to work for that unrealized goal long after Reconstruction had ended. McPherson's study had another unremarked implication. The great majority of abolitionists he found working for equality were Easterners, many of them members of Garrison's circle. This emphasis, perhaps in part the result of the author's selection of research materials, raised once again the question of the relative influence of Eastern and Western abolitionists and of the relative importance during the war years of those abolitionists who adhered to Garrison and those who followed other paths.

Historians of the antislavery movement from Barnes onward recognized that American abolitionists were not immune to influences from abroad. Barnes made much of Garrison's eagerness to secure endorsement by British fellow workers in order to acquire for himself some of their reflected prestige. Barnes emphasized especially the strength of the British example of emancipation in the West Indies and the influence—in part harmful, he decided— of their slogan of immediate emancipation. Dumond also acknowledged the importance in America of the writings of certain British antislavery leaders but nevertheless left the impression that American developments were largely independent of outside influence. More recent studies have emphasized again the close ties and interrelationships between British and American abolitionists. Antislavery in the United States now appears to have constituted part of a strong international concern.[45]

[45] Barnes, *Antislavery Impulse*, 29–37, 140, 142–43; Dumond, *Antislavery: The Crusade for Freedom*, 168–69, 182; Frank Thistlethwaite, *The Anglo-American Connection in the Early Nineteenth Century* (Philadelphia, 1959), 103–20; Thomas F. Harwood, "British Evangelical Abolitionism and American Churches in the 1830's," *Journal of Southern History*, XXVIII (August 1962), 287–306 (but see

It was understandable that most writers on the antislavery movement should concentrate attention on the ante-bellum decades when slavery became a great public issue. Thus, as compared with the thirty years immediately preceding the Civil War, the antislavery movement before 1830 remained a relatively unexplored field, although Dumond dealt with many important aspects of the earlier years and at least four other writers covered themes of the period. In the 1960's Winthrop D. Jordan's *White over Black* included important information on the colonial and early national antislavery movement; Arthur Zilversmit detailed the legal processes that ended slavery in the Northern states; Philip J. Staudenraus prepared a new study of the colonization movement; and Merton L. Dillon's biography of Benjamin Lundy served as the vehicle for the presentation of antislavery developments during the 1820's.[46] But for most historians the accomplishments of the earlier periods apparently seemed too few, the personalities too obscure, and the issues too uncompelling to attract their interest.

Most of the early antislavery organizations still remain unstudied, although the Providence Abolition Society, the Abolition Society of Delaware, and the North Carolina Manumission Society have been subjects of articles.[47] The existence of a number of similar societies in the South, especially during the 1820's, had long provided the factual basis for repeated statements that prior to 1831 there were more antislavery advocates in the South than elsewhere. From these statements came the conclusion that the

---

the critique in Mathews, "Orange Scott," 82n); Harwood, "Prejudice and Antislavery: The Colloquy Between William Ellery Channing and Edward Strutt Abdy, 1834," *American Quarterly*, XVIII (Winter 1966), 697–700; Howard R. Temperley, "British and American Abolitionists Compared," in Duberman (ed.), *Antislavery Vanguard*, 343–61; Douglas H. Maynard, "The World's Anti-Slavery Convention of 1840," *Mississippi Valley Historical Review*, XLVII (December 1960), 452–71; C. Duncan Rice, "The Anti-Slavery Mission of George Thompson to the United States, 1834–1835," *Journal of American Studies*, II (April 1968), 13–31.

[46] Dumond, *Antislavery: The Crusade for Freedom*, 16–157; Jordan, *White over Black: American Attitudes Toward the Negro, 1550–1812* (Chapel Hill, 1968); Zilversmit, *The First Emancipation: The Abolition of Slavery in the North* (Chicago and London, 1967); Staudenraus, *The African Colonization Movement, 1816–1865* (New York, 1961); Dillon, *Benjamin Lundy and the Struggle for Negro Freedom* (Urbana and London, 1966).

[47] James F. Reilly, "The Providence Abolition Society," *Rhode Island History*, XXI (April 1962), 33–48; Monte A. Calvert, "The Abolition Society of Delaware, 1801–1807," *Delaware History*, X (October 1963), 295–320; Patrick Sowle, "The North Carolina Manumission Society, 1816–1834," *North Carolina Historical Review*, XLII (Winter 1965), 47–69.

South once harbored a widespread, flourishing antislavery movement which might have attained success if agitation by Northern abolitionists had not provoked a counterreaction. Some scholars never believed this; yet the myth died hard. But as Southern recalcitrance in racial matters became obvious during the 1950's, the apparent continuity of what Phillips had called "the central theme of Southern history" invited a re-examination of claims to earlier Southern adherence to antislavery principles.

Kenneth M. Stampp in 1966 asserted without qualification that there never had been a Southern antislavery movement, a thesis Dumond had already put forward. But not until publication of Gordon E. Finnie's 1969 article was evidence readily available to demonstrate the fragility and narrow limits of Southern opposition to slavery.[48] Meanwhile, others questioned whether even Southerners of the Revolutionary era had sincerely opposed slavery. Robert McColley struck especially hard at Jeffersonian Virginia, supposedly the very nursery of antislavery thought, by demonstrating that at the time of slavery's supposed decadence and disrepute it had possessed a degree of economic utility and public acceptance among Virginians sufficient to counteract the philosophic objections quietly voiced by a few philanthropists.[49] Don B. Kates, Jr., on the other hand, held that social and political considerations rather than economic interest accounted for the South's failure to end slavery during the Revolutionary era.[50]

That position was vastly strengthened by Jordan's work on the origins of American racial attitudes. Deep-seated psychic and cultural forces supported both slavery and a debased status for free blacks, according to Jordan.[51] His account covered only the period before 1812, but it left the impression that abolitionists in ante-bellum years and later advocates of racial justice worked against obstacles that were far more formidable than had generally been recognized. Staughton Lynd claimed that despite their frequently voiced devotion to natural rights the Founding Fathers, North as well as South, had been quite "ready to compromise the concept that all men are equal." Donald G. Mathews

---

[48] Stampp in Daniel J. Boorstin (ed.), *An American Primer* (2 vols., Chicago and London, 1966), I, 280; Dumond, *Antislavery: The Crusade for Freedom,* 87–88, 173; Finnie, "The Antislavery Movement in the Upper South Before 1840," *Journal of Southern History,* XXXV (August 1969), 319–42.

[49] *Slavery and Jeffersonian Virginia* (Urbana, 1964).

[50] "Abolition, Deportation, Integration: Attitudes Toward Slavery in the Early Republic," *Journal of Negro History,* LIII (January 1968), 33–47.

[51] *White over Black, passim.*

traced the long retreat of the Methodist church from its strong early antislavery stand, and Robert T. Lewit demonstrated the ease with which Protestant missionaries became involved with the defense of slavery.[52] Apparently, slavery was so powerfully chauvinistic in its effects that it either compromised or engulfed most of its Southern opponents and many in the North as well. There was reason to believe that abolition of slavery in the Northern states had left nearly undisturbed the racist views that supported the institution.[53]

The conclusion seemed inescapable that racism, of which slavery was only one of several manifestations, had had a long and tenacious hold on the American people and that the abolitionists had been unable to dispel it. Nonetheless, abolitionist arguments against slavery and prejudice undeniably played a large part in ante-bellum controversy and especially in political developments. The impact of abolitionist agitation against slavery was unclear, but it was nevertheless obvious that in some way the Civil War did come, slavery was destroyed, and the Reconstruction amendments were added to the Constitution. Exactly how these events were related to abolitionism seemed less certain than once had been the case. Both Barnes and Dumond had written of an antislavery impulse originating in the evangelical movement, then working through the antislavery societies, and finally becoming institutionalized in the Liberty, Free Soil, and Republican parties. "I am constrained to the belief . . . that if Weld and Birney were abolitionists, Lincoln was one," Dumond wrote; "and if they had a plan, he had a better one."[54] That some relationship existed between the abolitionists and the antislavery politicians was certain, but exactly what the relationship was remained a matter of dispute.

John L. Myers contended that the agency system used by the antislavery societies had succeeded in disseminating abolitionist ideas through countless small towns and rural areas of the North, thereby laying the base in public opinion on which the later anti-

[52] Lynd, *Class Conflict*, 185–213 (quote on page 213); Mathews, *Slavery and Methodism: A Chapter in American Morality, 1780–1845* (Princeton, 1965); Lewit, "Indian Missions and Antislavery Sentiment: A Conflict of Evangelical and Humanitarian Ideals," *Mississippi Valley Historical Review*, L (June 1963), 39–55.
[53] Stanley I. Kutler, "Pennsylvania Courts, the Abolition Act, and Negro Rights," *Pennsylvania History*, XXX (January 1963), 14–27; Robert M. Spector, "The Quock Walker Cases (1781–83)—Slavery, Its Abolition, and Negro Citizenship in Early Massachusetts," *Journal of Negro History*, LIII (January 1968), 12–32.
[54] *Antislavery Origins*, 107.

slavery political parties would be built.[55] The skilled propagandistic work of the abolitionists, especially their understanding of the predispositions of the audience they sought to reach, was illustrated by their use of such stock figures as the "tragic octoroon" and by their clever tailoring of antislavery arguments to meet the peculiar needs of their audience. Such activity, it was claimed, paved the way for the success of antislavery politicians.[56] Wyatt-Brown demonstrated the effectiveness of the abolitionists' postal campaign of 1835 in associating their cause with civil rights and thereby making it a successful political movement. In 1835 antislavery "had arrived at the national capital to stay," he wrote.[57] McPherson contended, much as Barnes had done, that it was the controversy over the gag rule that opened the way for the creation of an antislavery political party, which presumably embodied abolitionist principles.[58]

Biography served as a convenient medium for illustrating the development of antislavery politics. Studies of John P. Hale, Owen Lovejoy, George W. Julian, Benjamin F. Wade, and others illuminated various facets of a process which nonetheless began to be less clearly defined and less explicable than Barnes and Dumond had contended it was.[59] Kinley J. Brauer's *Cotton Versus Conscience* traced the antislavery political movement in Massachusetts and cautiously used some of the same analytical con-

[55] Myers presented his thesis in these articles: "The Beginning of Anti-Slavery Agencies in New York State, 1833–1836," *New York History*, XLIII (April 1962), 149–81; "Antislavery Activities of Five Lane Seminary Boys in 1835–36," Historical and Philosophical Society of Ohio, *Bulletin*, XXI (April 1963), 95–111; "The Early Antislavery Agency System in Pennsylvania, 1833–1837," *Pennsylvania History*, XXXI (January 1964), 62–86; "The Major Effort of National Anti-Slavery Agents in New York State, 1836–1837," *New York History*, XLVI (April 1965), 162–86; "Organization of 'The Seventy': To Arouse the North Against Slavery," *Mid-America*, XLVIII (January 1966), 29–46.

[56] Jules Zanger, "The 'Tragic Octoroon' in Pre–Civil War Fiction," *American Quarterly*, XVIII (Spring 1966), 63–70; Mathews, "The Abolitionists on Slavery," 165–71; Filler, "Nonviolence and Abolition," 172–78.

[57] "The Abolitionists' Postal Campaign of 1835," *Journal of Negro History*, L (October 1965), 227–38 (quote on page 237).

[58] "The Fight Against the Gag Rule: Joshua Leavitt and Antislavery Insurgency in the Whig Party, 1839–1842," *ibid.*, XLVIII (July 1963), 177–95.

[59] Richard H. Sewell, *John P. Hale and the Politics of Abolition* (Cambridge, Mass., 1965); Edward Magdol, *Owen Lovejoy: Abolitionist in Congress* (New Brunswick, 1967); Patrick W. Riddleberger, *George Washington Julian, Radical Republican: A Study in Nineteenth-Century Politics and Reform* ([Indianapolis], 1966); Hans L. Trefousse, *Benjamin Franklin Wade: Radical Republican from Ohio* (New York, 1963); Frank O. Gatell, *John Gorham Palfrey and the New England Conscience* (Cambridge, Mass., 1963); Martin B. Duberman, *Charles Francis Adams, 1807–1886* (Boston, 1961).

cepts Donald had employed in his study of the abolitionist personality.[60] The only synthesis of the theme of antislavery politics to appear during the decade shared many of the revisionists' presuppositions and for the most part treated the Barnes-Dumond interpretation with skepticism.[61]

Some of these works might be taken as suggesting that both the argument and strategy of the abolitionists had triumphed by converting a Northern majority to their program of freeing the slaves and establishing racial justice. But a troublesome fact intruded to create difficulties for defenders of such a thesis—the same anti-Negro sentiment that Jordan and others showed operating in earlier years still flourished alongside and often even within the antislavery parties. The Free Soil movement, it appeared, was heavily laced with racism, and many leading Republican politicians during the Civil War and Reconstruction displayed anti-Negro prejudices which seemed to reflect faithfully the racist sentiments of broad segments of the Northern population.[62] Whatever their successes may have been in some geographic areas and despite their skill at organization and propaganda, the abolitionists had evidently failed to persuade a majority in the North to relinquish racial prejudice. Perhaps, too, the Republican party itself embodied less of the antislavery impulse than had once been thought.

When the urban North became the focus of racial protest in the mid-1960's, it became difficult to believe any longer that racial bias and injustice in the nineteenth century had been exclusively Southern. The central theme of *American* history appeared to be the determination to keep the *United States* a white man's country. Although the allegation was strongly denied, some began

[60] *Cotton Versus Conscience: Massachusetts Whig Politics and Southwestern Expansion, 1843–1848* (Lexington, Ky., 1967).

[61] Elbert B. Smith, *The Death of Slavery: The United States, 1837–65* (Chicago and London, 1967).

[62] Merton L. Dillon, "The Failure of the American Abolitionists," *Journal of Southern History*, XXV (May 1959), 159–77; Leon F. Litwack, *North of Slavery: The Negro in the Free States, 1790–1860* (Chicago, 1961); Eric Foner, "Politics and Prejudice: The Free Soil Party and the Negro, 1849–1852," *Journal of Negro History*, L (October 1965), 239–56; Foner, "Racial Attitudes of the New York Free Soilers," *New York History*, XLVI (October 1965), 311–29; C. Vann Woodward, "Seeds of Failure in Radical Race Policy," American Philosophical Society, *Proceedings*, CX (February 1966), 1–9; V. Jacque Voegeli, *Free but Not Equal: The Midwest and the Negro During the Civil War* (Chicago and London, 1967); Eugene H. Berwanger, *The Frontier Against Slavery: Western Anti-Negro Prejudice and the Slavery Extension Controversy* (Urbana, Chicago, and London, 1967).

to suspect that the abolitionists themselves had been infected with racist bias.[63] Certainly, it was highly suggestive that most white historians of the antislavery movement had given only minimal attention to the activities of Negro abolitionists, a neglect that is still only partially remedied.[64] As a related theme, one historian claimed in 1961 that abolitionists had deliberately developed the "legend" of the Underground Railroad in an effort to aggrandize themselves, whereas in truth free Negroes had been the principal operators of the system and fugitive slaves its most notable heroes.[65] This interpretation accorded faithfully with contemporary views emphasizing the chauvinistic and self-seeking character of most white Americans, apparently including even the abolitionists to some degree. Perhaps more important, it was related to the frequently expressed opinion that Negroes must achieve their own liberation in a racist society such as America was said to be. A general survey of Negro history published in 1966 seemed to credit most of the gains secured by Negroes during ante-bellum years to their own efforts.[66]

The emphasis scholars have recently given to the pervasiveness of racial prejudice among white Americans had the effect of mak-

[63] Litwack, "The Abolitionist Dilemma: The Antislavery Movement and the Northern Negro," *New England Quarterly*, XXIV (March 1961), 50–73; Litwack, "The Emancipation of the Negro Abolitionist," in Duberman (ed.), *Antislavery Vanguard*, 137–55; William H. Pease and Jane H. Pease, "Boston Garrisonians and the Problem of Frederick Douglass," *Canadian Journal of History*, II (September 1967), 29–48; Pease and Pease, "Antislavery Ambivalence," 682–95; Potter, *South and the Sectional Conflict*, 201–18. For the view that abolitionists championed equality, see James M. McPherson, "A Brief for Equality: The Abolitionist Reply to the Racist Myth, 1860–1865," in Duberman (ed.), *Antislavery Vanguard*, 156–77; Dillon, "Failure of the American Abolitionists," 165–67; John L. Myers, "American Antislavery Society Agents and the Free Negro, 1833–1838," *Journal of Negro History*, LII (July 1967), 200–19. The controversy is discussed in Richard O. Curry, "The Abolitionists and Reconstruction: A Critical Appraisal," *Journal of Southern History*, XXXIV (November 1968), 527–45. The condescension, if it existed, conceivably could work both ways: in a recent conversation with me a black university student dismissed the abolitionists as "white liberals who felt sorry for blacks."

[64] Benjamin Quarles, *Black Abolitionists* (New York, 1969), is a comprehensive treatment, but new studies of individual Negro abolitionists remain to be made. See also Robert C. Dick, "Negro Oratory in the Antislavery Societies, 1830–1860," *Western Speech*, XXVIII (Winter 1964), 5–14. Alma Lutz, *Crusade for Freedom: Women of the Antislavery Movement* (Boston, 1968), ignores Negro women altogether.

[65] Larry Gara, *The Liberty Line: The Legend of the Underground Railroad* (Lexington, 1961).

[66] August Meier and Elliott M. Rudwick, *From Plantation to Ghetto: An Interpretive History of American Negroes* (New York, 1966), 65–122. See also Carleton Mabee, "A Negro Boycott to Integrate Boston Schools," *New England Quarterly*, XLI (September 1968), 341–61.

ing more plausible some of the revisionists' interpretations of the relation of the antislavery movement to the Civil War. Beard's opinion that the abolitionists' moral crusade against slavery had been of only minor influence in producing widespread Northern opposition to the South was echoed in several recent works. It became evident that antislavery and anti-Negro sentiment could co-exist in the same mind. Opposition to slavery, it appeared, might be something quite different from a humanitarian effort to aid oppressed and suffering blacks. The suspicion grew that some persons had opposed slavery only because they recognized it as the key to Southern power. Margaret Shortreed [George] in 1959 portrayed the antislavery politicians as a tightly knit, determined group bent from the first on destroying Southern power. As she interpreted them, their hostility to slavery was not morally derived. The politically oriented antislavery group, she contended, retained its will and cohesiveness from the date of its appearance around 1840 through the consummation of its long-sought revolution during Reconstruction. Thus, she saw political abolitionism as both more and less than single-minded opposition to slavery.[67] In an essay reminiscent of the Beardian view Larry Gara argued in 1969 that it was anti-Southern sentiment rather than antislavery sentiment that gained favor in the North during the 1850's. It was not a humanitarian-derived determination to aid Negroes, either slave or free, but opposition to the "slavocracy's" harmful effects on Northern whites that had been the determinant in Northern antislavery politics.[68]

Recent writing on the antislavery movement has added significantly to knowledge of its relation to American society and to Western culture in general; more is known about its personnel, their characteristics, ideology, and strategy, and their interrelationships. But the research of the decade has made an assessment of the abolitionists little easier than it was in earlier years. The paradox of a North opposed to slavery and yet profoundly racist once more called into question the role and influence of the abolitionists. They were seldom blamed any longer for causing the Civil War, but their actual achievements remained undefined. It

[67] "The Antislavery Radicals: From Crusade to Revolution, 1840–1868," *Past and Present*, No. 16 (November 1959), 65–87. The discussion of the Civil War in Barrington Moore, Jr., *Social Origins of Dictatorship and Democracy: Lord and Peasant in the Making of the Modern World* (Boston, 1966), 142–46, relies heavily on this essay.

[68] "Slavery and the Slave Power: A Crucial Distinction," *Civil War History*, XV (March 1969), 5–18.

seemed undeniable that their activity resulted from intense individual commitment to a noble cause and that their experience might on that account be worthy of study even if their influence could not be precisely measured. But it is unlikely that many historians will be satisfied with such a justification for scholarship, for at least until recently few have been much impressed with unrequited gestures of the human spirit.

Yet recent scholarship has made tangible accomplishment even more difficult to ascertain. It now seems indisputable that despite all the abolitionists' years of religiously inspired agitation against racial prejudice, a majority of their fellow countrymen refused to relinquish such prejudice. Observers of the contemporary scene can hardly fail to perceive that present-day reformers have taken up labors that the abolitionists were unable to complete a century before. Even the supposition that the abolitionists were directly responsible for ending slavery has been called into question. Dumond, who throughout a long and distinguished career probably remained the abolitionists' most vigorous champion, asserted in 1965 that the Union army was the chief instrument of emancipation, an interpretation that would seem to leave the role of the abolitionists vaguer than ever.[69]

If it be true that slavery was ended more or less as an unanticipated consequence of war—or through the fortuitous efforts of individual abolitionists during wartime, as McPherson claimed and not as the result of Northern consensus that justice to blacks required abolition; and if racial prejudice was not generally moderated by antislavery agitation, then what was the historical role of the abolitionists? The effect of such questions, troublesome as they are, need not be to diminish the stature of the abolitionists, but rather to confirm the view that they always were a prophetic element operating in a deeply racist society whose inmost prejudices not even their most dedicated effort proved adequate to dispel. The abolitionists appear only the more remarkable for bravery and clarity of vision as new accounts reveal the extent of racist views in American culture. One might finally be forced to conclude, without astonishment or cynicism, that the abolitionists had indeed failed in their mission and that the crusade for justice which they waged before the Civil War must be renewed with every generation. So negative an assessment need not be taken as denigration, except perhaps by those who persist in assuming the necessity of measuring influence, for in this instance one need not

[69] *America's Shame and Redemption* (Marquette, Mich., 1965), 47–48, 90–93.

be deeply concerned with causal relationships or be distressed if the abolitionists' efforts are found to have encountered rejection and failure more often than success.

What can be discovered in the history of antislavery in the ante-bellum years are struggles and conflicts over deeply held values and loyalties and the spectacle of a few perplexed men who finally rejected some of their culture's ancient assumptions in order to advance the cause of justice. Finally, that history offers a rare opportunity to observe and to take part in the interplay of past and present. Acquaintance with the abolitionists has made more comprehensible some of the events of recent times, and, for some persons, contemporary involvement has reached back to illumine the past.

The Failure of the American Abolitionists

By MERTON L. DILLON

THE PRESTIGE OF THE ABOLITIONISTS ROSE AS THE FEDERAL Government adopted an emancipation policy and as the military resistance of the Confederacy weakened and finally collapsed. As the end of the Civil War drew near, the once despised abolitionists appeared in retrospect to have been early prophets of the future. Northerners, welcoming the destruction of the Old South, granted to William Lloyd Garrison and his associates an honored place among the architects of victory. Consequently, when Secretary of War Edwin M. Stanton made plans to hold a flag-raising ceremony at Fort Sumter in April 1865 on the fourth anniversary of its surrender, he must have thought it peculiarly appropriate to include Garrison among the government's eighty invited guests, for Garrison, better than any other living man, symbolized the abolition movement for Stanton's generation.[1] The abolitionists themselves accepted the new prestige offered them as no more than their due, a rightful vindication of a righteous cause. According to their own interpretation, they had been responsible for the abolition of slavery;[2] and, with the military defeat of the Confederate States of America, their work was completed—or so most of them assumed. "The American Anti-Slavery Society," wrote Garrison to his wife early in 1865, "may reasonably conclude that its specific mission is ended."[3] Few indeed of the veterans of the antislavery movement still living after Appomatox

[1] Wendell Phillips Garrison and Francis Jackson Garrison, *William Lloyd Garrison, 1805-1879: The Story of His Life Told by His Children* (4 vols., Boston, 1885-1889), IV, 136-40.
[2] *Proceedings of the American Anti-Slavery Society at its Third Decade, Held in the City of Philadelphia, Dec. 3d and 4th, 1864 [1863]* (New York, 1864), 3.
[3] Garrison and Garrison, *William Lloyd Garrison*, IV, 137.

questioned Garrison's view. Yet historical accuracy would have been better served had they done so, for in the Civil War and the Thirteenth Amendment the abolitionists had won only a circumstantial victory. They had achieved practically none of their program.

The success of any historical movement, it would seem, ought to be judged by its own terms and values; the extent of its accomplishments ought to be measured against its professed aims and methods. Viewed in such fashion, the antislavery movement must be ranked not as a triumph but as one of the major failures of our history. This is not to depreciate either the sincerity and nobility of the abolitionists or their ultimate effect upon the course of events. It is to say, however, that they failed to carry out their announced mission. The abolitionists—from the gentle Benjamin Lundy to the fanatical John Brown—had much to do with establishing emotional commitments in both North and South.[4] By their remorseless agitation they sharpened sectional antagonisms; by their insistence upon viewing all issues in terms of principle, they transmuted sectional controversies into titanic moral struggles, thus rendering compromise unlikely if not impossible. Southerners, reacting to their verbal attacks, defended slavery and "Southern Rights" more stubbornly. Northerners, accepting at least part of the abolitionist indictment of slavery and slaveholders, thereby became more willing to fight an intersectional war. That the abolitionists in such fashion helped to bring about the Civil War and thus to end slavery few can doubt.[5] But this is by no means the same thing as saying that they succeeded in accomplishing their program.

The comprehensive reform movement of the 1830's, of which the campaign to abolish slavery eventually emerged as the most

[4] The abolitionists, unlike other antislavery advocates, favored (1) immediate, uncompensated emancipation without expatriation and (2) the recognition of the civil and political rights of the freedmen. Lundy, once a gradualist and a colonizationist, had become an abolitionist by 1833, if not before. *Genius of Universal Emancipation*, XIII (May 1833), 118-20.

[5] For the abolitionists' part in events leading to the Civil War, see the contrasting views in Dwight Lowell Dumond, *Antislavery Origins of the Civil War in the United States* (Ann Arbor, 1939) and Arthur Young Lloyd, *The Slavery Controversy, 1831-1860* (Chapel Hill, 1939).

conspicuous part, may be viewed both as a religious crusade to cleanse the earth from sin, and, in its more secular phase, as an effort to reassert the declining influence of New England and the New England clergy. The status motive remained recessive, however. Thus only the first aspect of the antislavery movement was ever clearly articulated, and until at least 1840 the organized opposition to slavery remained primarily a crusade for moral reform, with churches its accustomed forum and religious arguments its most powerful ammunition.[6] Most of the abolitionists belonged, as had their forebears, to the Congregational or Presbyterian churches, where, under the influence of a new revivalistic spirit, they shared the true believer's sense of fevered urgency to aid God in the accomplishing of His plans. It was, indeed, their religious orientation that gave to the abolitionists most of their distinctive qualities—their extraordinary zeal, their steadfastness, their consecration, their willingness to face martyrdom.[7] Characteristically, they viewed their problems in the light of theology and enunciated their program in phrases reminiscent of their intellectual ancestors in Massachusetts Bay: "We view the hand of God afflicting us," confessed the abolitionist members of the Presbytery of Alton, Illinois, during one of their many times of trouble, "& feel called upon to humble ourselves before God; & to inquire earnestly, why he hath a controversy with us."[8]

But in spite of the abolitionists' emphasis on moral and religious reform, the antislavery crusade can not entirely be explained by reference to the religious zeal of its exponents, genuine though

[6]Gilbert Hobbs Barnes, *The Antislavery Impulse, 1830-1844* (New York, 1933), 3-28; Dumond, *Antislavery Origins*, 35; for the secular aspects of reform see Richard Lyle Power, "A Crusade to Extend Yankee Culture, 1820-1865," *New England Quarterly* (Orono, Me.), XIII (1940), 638-53, and Clifford S. Griffin, "Religious Benevolence as Social Control, 1815-1860," *Mississippi Valley Historical Review* (New Orleans), XLIV (December 1957), 423-44.

[7]Hazel C. Wolff, *On Freedom's Altar: The Martyr Complex in the Abolition Movement* (Madison, Wis., 1952).

[8]Minutes of the Presbytery of Alton, November 16, 1837 (McCormick Theological Seminary, Chicago).

that zeal undoubtedly was.[9] The majority of the abolitionists, it appears, were young, New England-born descendants of old Federalist families. They thus belonged to a class which saw its power waning in the face of the changes the nineteenth century had brought. The rapid populating of the Mississippi River Valley filled them with dread that their section would presently lose its political and moral influence to an unschooled, uncouth, and unbelieving West. Particularly they regretted the new Jacksonian democracy and their own declining political and social influence in relation to it. Most of them accordingly could feel little kinship with those politicians and philosophers who assumed that men were naturally good and could be trusted to judge rightly without strict moral and religious guidance. Such guidance the young reformers were prepared to give, much as their ancestors had guided past generations. The difference, however, was that nineteenth century America was in the process of rejecting the theocratic ideal.[10] Regarded in that way, therefore, the reformers' cause may be considered lost from its very start.

To grasp the extent of the failure of these dedicated men, one must first understand the magnitude of their purpose, recognizing at the same time that their failure, great though it was, doubtlessly is magnified for us by the eschatological overtones of the terms in which they formulated their program. God had intended man to cooperate with Him in renovating the world in preparation for the Second Coming, explained the reformers, but most Americans blasphemously denied their duty and ran away from God. Unguided men, left to their own devices, could be expected to do little to fulfill their sacred obligations. Consequently, the reformers had bestirred themselves, they said, to prepare the land for impending judgment and to rescue sinners from the imminent descent of the wrath of God.[11]

[9]David Donald, *Lincoln Reconsidered: Essays on the Civil War Era* (New York, 1956), 19-36; see also the abstract of Avery Craven's paper in *Journal of Southern History*, VII (February 1941), 57-58.

[10]John R. Bodo, *The Protestant Clergy and Public Issues, 1812-1848* (Princeton, 1954), 31-60.

[11]"Motives to Active Benevolence," *Quarterly Christian Spectator* (New Haven), IV (1822), 617-18; "On Public Spirit," *American Baptist Magazine* (Boston), VI (1826), 80-85; Edward Beecher, *Baptism, with Reference to Its Import and Modes* (New York, 1849), 1-2.

Surveying the nation in 1830, the reformers saw (as reformers have always been able to see) vast numbers of people ignoring the ordinary imperatives of morality. This seemed to be true in whichever quarter they looked but in no place quite so flagrantly as the South. There, they concluded, a proud and powerful section of the country flourished in wickedness, quite beyond the pale of New England's moral influence. The Southern practice of slavery provided salient evidence of this fact, the abolitionists believed. For they had pronounced slavery a sin—it was not merely bad policy, it was not merely evil (theologians would understand the distinction), it was a positive sin.[12] The abolitionists, in their role as the dedicated instruments of God, set themselves to destroy this palpable violation of God's law. By so doing, they would fulfill their own religious responsibilities, and they might also in some measure reassert clerical influence over the nation at large.

Not only did the abolitionists believe they were carrying out God's plans to perfect the world, they thought of themselves also as struggling to save the nation from immediate, temporal judgment. Since God is just, they reasoned, He could not be expected permanently to suffer mankind to flout His ordinances. No calamity that might have befallen America could have taken the abolitionists by surprise. They thoroughly expected God momentarily to wreak His awful vengeance upon both the North and the South for their persistence in maintaining slavery, the nation's most conspicuous sin.[13] "Look at the manner in which our sister state, Louisiana, is treating her slaves!" commanded the indignant antislavery editor Elijah P. Lovejoy. "Why, as surely as there is a thunderbolt in Heaven and strength in God's right arm to launch it, so surely will it strike the authors of such cruel oppression."[14] If the holocaust of the Civil War proved such predictions at least circumstantially correct, it also measured the extent of abolitionist failure, for judgment—whether from God or not—came in the form of war, and abolitionist efforts had been powerless to end slavery and thus to avert war.

[12]*Genius of Universal Emancipation*, I (February 1822), 123; XI (February 1831), 165.
[13]*Ibid.*, II (July 1822), 10, 79; V (December 1825), 121-22.
[14]St. Louis *Observer*, April 16, 1835.

The abolitionists' apocalyptic view was by no means a casual or an incidental thing; indeed it came to be generally accepted. The pervasiveness of their interpretation of the Civil War as Divine retribution may be gauged in the vivid conceits of Julia Ward Howe's "Battle Hymn of the Republic," in which God is pictured amidst the carnage of war "trampling out the vintage where the grapes of wrath are stored." The idea appears with equal clarity in the solemn sentences of the penultimate paragraph of Abraham Lincoln's second inaugural address, which are informed by echoes of Lovejoy's prophecy written thirty years before.[15]

Of course none of these gloomy predictions of wrath to come formed a program; they were merely earnests of a point of view. But such a view could easily generate specifics, and almost certainly it would invest its proponents with remarkable energy: one cannot suppose that God's partners often flag.

Thus with motives grand and obligations solemn, the abolitionists inaugurated their crusade to banish slavery from the land. The method they adopted to accomplish this end was simple to the point of being doctrinaire. By speeches and publications they would attempt to persuade all Americans—but especially slaveholders—that slavery was a heinous sin calling for immediate repentance. Since slaveholders, however misdirected, were assumed to be reasonable creatures whose better natures when properly enlightened could be trusted to govern them, the abolitionists hoped they would repent and free their slaves as soon as the incontrovertible fact of their sin had been laid before them.[16]

[15]Ralph L. Woods (ed.), *A Treasury of the Familiar* (New York, 1942), 46; Abraham Lincoln, *Collected Works*, Roy P. Basler, ed. (9 vols., New Brunswick, N. J., 1953), VIII, 333.

[16]Antislavery advocates had early urged efforts to renovate the slaveholder rather than simply to condemn slavery. See *Genius of Universal Emancipation*, IV (June 1825), 142–43, and "Thoughts on the Discussion of Slavery," *Quarterly Christian Spectator*, VII (1825), 405–408. Abolitionists were later encouraged to undertake the program of converting the South by James A. Thome, an antislavery Southerner. *Speech of James A. Thome of Kentucky, Delivered at the Annual Meeting of the American Anti-Slavery Society, May 6, 1834; Letter of the Rev. Samuel H. Cox, against the American Colonization Society* (Boston, 1834), 7–11.

The abolitionists soon realized, however, that the process of enlightenment was not likely, by itself, to end slavery. A formidable obstacle, they concluded, blocked the success of their program. This was the conviction held by most people, North and South, of the Negro's anthropological inferiority.[17] That belief, more than anything else, caused even many Northerners who otherwise accepted the abolitionists' view of slavery to hesitate to espouse their program for ending it. "Whilst the poor black is treated so contemptuously in, what are called, the free states . . . it is not to be wondered at, that the cause of negro-emancipation moves so slowly," commented James G. Birney.[18] Unless racial prejudice might in some way be destroyed, the antislavery crusade could hardly succeed, for adherence to the idea of the Negro's inferiority, the abolitionists discovered, tended to produce not ardent crusaders but half-hearted antislavery "men who would abolish slavery only in the abstract, and somewhere about the middle of the future."[19]

Most Americans in the early nineteenth century considered the presence of large numbers of free Negroes within the community so dangerous to society as to be intolerable. How, then, could prudent men contemplate freeing the slaves, it was often asked, unless some way were found to transport the freedmen out of the country? And that had proved to be a physical impossibility. The American Colonization Society, the major national organization concerned with slavery before 1833, had long worked to send free Negroes to Africa, but it had accomplished little. Few of the objects of its philanthropy desired to leave their homes in order to move to Africa, nor did the society ever have available enough ships or money to transport in significant numbers even that minority of Negroes willing to emigrate. The abolitionists, unlike the colonizationists, denied both the necessity and the morality of attempting expatriation. The slaves, abolitionists

[17]*Genius of Universal Emancipation,* VII (November 3, 1827), 139; X (February 12, 1830), 179; Dwight Lowell Dumond, "Race Prejudice and Abolition, New Views on the Antislavery Movement," *Michigan Alumnus Quarterly Review,* XLI (April 1935), 377, 382.
[18]Birney to Gerrit Smith, July 14, 1835, in Dwight Lowell Dumond (ed.), *Letters of James Gillespie Birney, 1831-1857* (2 vols., New York, 1938), I, 202.
[19]American Anti-Slavery Society, *Sixth Annual Report* (New York, 1839), 103.

insisted, must be freed at once and the freedmen allowed to remain in the United States.[20] The abolitionists made no concessions whatever to the prevailing racial prejudice, which had served as one of the main bulwarks of the American Colonization Society, nor did they become discouraged when they found that prejudice was nearly universal. While readily granting the fact that racial prejudice existed, the abolitionists denied its inevitability. As radical reformers they refused to recognize any view or any institution as unmalleable under the blows of heaven-inspired emotion and logic. "They contended," as Henry B. Stanton, an official of the American Anti-Slavery Society, explained, "that this prejudice was visible; that being a sin it could be repented of, being a folly it could be cured."[21] But verbal onslaughts against the sin of prejudice might not be enough, the abolitionists decided. They must promote repentance by proving prejudice unwarranted. They intended, therefore, to demonstrate to all skeptics that the Negro equaled the white man in every respect; that the degradation of the Negro resulted not from any inherent biological defect but from slavery and oppression. Once freed and granted the opportunities available to other free men, they contended, Negroes could accomplish as much as the members of any other race.

The antislavery organizations established by the abolitionists espoused the removal of racial prejudice as one of their central aims. The constitution of the New England Anti-Slavery Society, formed January 1, 1832, called not only for immediate abolition but also for the use of all means "to improve the character and condition of the free people of color, to inform and correct public opinion in relation to their situation and rights, and obtain for them civil and political rights and privileges with the whites."[22] Every abolitionist is duty bound, said the Society's official journal, to "aid and encourage all the efforts which they [the free Negroes]

[20]*Genius of Universal Emancipation*, VII (December 8, 1827), 181-82; X (September 2, 1829), 8; William Lloyd Garrison, *Thoughts on Colonization: or an Impartial Exhibition of the Doctrines, Principles and Purposes of the American Colonization Society, together with the Resolutions, Addresses and Remonstrances of the Free People of Color* (Boston, 1832).
[21]American Anti-Slavery Society, *First Annual Report* (New York, 1834), 23.
[22]*Abolitionist* (Boston), I (January 1833), 2.

are making to elevate themselves,—to banish from his own mind the unworthy feelings which would lead him to regard any human being with contempt merely on account of his color; and to teach his neighbors to follow his example."[23] The constitution of the American Anti-Slavery Society, formed in December 1833, contained the statement, "This Society shall aim to elevate the character and condition of the people of color, by encouraging their intellectual, moral, and religious improvement, and by removing public prejudice, that thus they may, according to their intellectual and moral worth, share an equality with the whites of civil and religious privileges . . . ."[24]

The abolitionists' two goals—(1) to spread the doctrine of the sin of slavery and (2) to eradicate the nearly universal prejudice—once accomplished would, they supposed, work a moral revolution in the country. They viewed the two goals as inseparable. Indeed, so intertwined were they in abolitionist thought that it is quite impossible to imagine their acceptance of the one without the other. If anything, they believed the ending of prejudice must precede, not follow, the abolition of slavery. As soon as the Negro is "felt to be in *fact* and in *right* our own countryman, the benevolence of the country will be emancipated from its bondage," predicted an early abolitionist. "It will flow out to meet the colored man . . . it will proclaim his rights—and the fetters of the slave will fall asunder."[25] In such a spirit of optimism the reformers began their work, assuming that with the Negro recognized as an equal and slaveholders convinced of their sin, the slaves would be freed. The entire nation would accept this event, the abolitionists supposed, and the freedmen would be welcomed by their fellow countrymen. Thus the caste system would end, justice and harmony prevail, and God's will be done on earth.

That was the heart of the abolitionist program. But pending the

[23]*Ibid.*, I (March 1833), 43.
[24]*Constitution of the American Anti-Slavery Society: with the Declaration of the National Anti-Slavery Convention at Philadelphia, December, 1833, and the Address to the Public Issued by the Executive Committee of the Society, in September, 1835* (New York, 1838), 4.
[25]*Anti-Slavery Record* (New York), I (1835), 32.

achievement of these two major goals, the abolitionists would
seek minor victories. By exerting their influence on Congress,
they would attempt to bar slavery from the territories; they would
seek symbolic victories such as the abolition of slavery and the
slave trade within the District of Columbia; and they would seek
to eliminate such evils as the interstate slave trade. They would
not, however, attempt by national legislation to destroy slavery
within the states where it already existed; for they conceded
slavery to be a local institution subject to the control of the people
of the slave states. Accordingly, its destruction in the South must
await the accomplishment of the abolitionists' moral revolution.[26]

Such were the goals and methods enunciated by the American
Anti-Slavery Society at its formation in 1833; they were the goals
and methods then accepted by a majority of abolitionists everywhere.

The abolitionists directed their program of moral suasion with
equal vigor toward both the North and the South, and it was
rejected with almost equal vehemence by the people of both
sections. The abolitionists perhaps asked too much—and it was
no doubt simple-minded to ask it at all—when they pleaded
with Southerners to relinquish their valuable slave property. In
any event, after 1830 Southerners managed largely to stifle abolitionist efforts to persuade them of their sin. Southern states passed
laws imposing severe punishment on those who circulated antislavery literature or uttered antislavery sentiments.[27] Abolitionists
who ventured into the South were threatened with punishment
so extreme that few dared enter the area,[28] and most of those
native Southerners who opposed slavery either kept their views

[26]*Declaration of Sentiments and Constitution of the American Anti-Slavery Society, together with All Those Parts of the Constitution of the United States Which Are Supposed to Have Any Relation to Slavery* (New York, 1835).

[27]Russel Blaine Nye, *Fettered Freedom; Civil Liberties and the Slavery Contro-versy, 1830-1860* (East Lansing, Mich., 1949), 54-69; Clement Eaton, *Freedom of Thought in the Old South* (New York, 1951), 126-30.

[28]Benjamin Lundy, for example, thought it necessary to travel under an assumed name when he passed through the South on his first trip to Texas. Benjamin Lundy to Elizabeth Chandler, September 6, 1832, in Elizabeth Chandler Papers, (Michigan Historical Collection, University of Michigan).

to themselves or fled to the North.[29] Contrary to abolitionist expectation, few Southerners demonstrated contrition for holding slaves, nor did many give any evidence at all that they intended ever to end their peculiar institution. Indeed, some of them soon defended as a positive good the system the abolitionists branded as unmitigated sin. Clearly the abolitionists had failed to convince slaveholders, whom they had pictured as rational, potentially moral men, of the iniquity of their practices. Nor did they experience greater success in persuading Southerners of the Negro's capacity for improvement. As the years passed, some Southerners denied even that the Negro and the white man belonged to the same human species.[30] Abolitionist failure among slaveholders by that time could be considered complete.

Meanwhile the abolitionists attempted to carry out their program to end racial prejudice in areas and among groups more easily accessible to them. In the Northern states, especially in the cities bordering the Ohio and Mississippi Rivers, lived thousands of free Negroes—most of them social outcasts, economically depressed, and suffering the pressures of legal and extra-legal discrimination. They were living proof, some thought, of the fact of racial inferiority and the dangers inherent in emancipation. The abolitionists, on the other hand, saw in the miseries of the free people of color an opportunity and a challenge. If they could improve the condition of these people, Northern skeptics and perhaps Southerners, too, would be compelled to discard their racial prejudices and admit the feasibility and safety of emancipation.[31] Very early, therefore, the abolitionists began humanitarian work with this group.

[29]*Genius of Universal Emancipation*, VI (April 28, 1837), 193; Samuel G. Ward to Absalom Peters, November 12, 1831, and Gideon Blackburn to Absalom Peters, April 12, May 22, 1833, in American Home Missionary Society Papers (Chicago Theological Seminary).

[30]William Sumner Jenkins, *Pro-Slavery Thought in the Old South* (Chapel Hill, 1935), 242-84; Josiah Clark Nott and George Robins Gliddon, *Types of Mankind: or, Ethnological Researches, Based upon the Ancient Monuments, Paintings, Sculptures, and Crania of Races, and upon Their Natural, Geographical, Philological, and Biblical History* (Philadelphia, 1854), 79-87, 456-60.

[31]On the condition of the free people of color as evidence of the dangers of emancipation, see *African Repository* (Washington), VII (1831-1832), 97-109; on plans to elevate the free Negro, see *Genius of Universal Emancipation*, VI (May 12, 1827), 223.

Because it seemed to them that the most good could be accomplished by demonstrating the intellectual capacity of Negroes, the abolitionists concentrated their efforts on providing them with education. Soon after the New England Anti-Slavery Society was founded, it appointed standing committees to aid in apprenticing colored children to learn trades, to attempt to end school segregation, and to improve the existing schools for colored children.[32] By 1837 the American Anti-Slavery Society had delegated three of its agents to the sole task of "encouraging our colored brethren in the free states, in their laudable efforts to rise, by good education of their children and virtuous industry, above the cruel prejudice which is crushing them in the dust . . . ."[33] Augustus Wattles labored in Indiana as an agent of the American Anti-Slavery Society to aid free Negro farmers. Later, through the philanthropy of Quakers, he founded a school for free Negroes in Mercer County, Ohio.[34] In Indiana, abolitionists founded the Union Literary Institute and other schools for Negroes.[35] At Addison, Michigan, Prior Foster, a free Negro, received abolitionist support for his Woodstock Manual Labor Institute, a school for free Negroes.[36] Not all such schools were designed exclusively for colored children. In Lenawee County, Michigan's earliest antislavery center, the Raisin River Institute, operated by the abolitionist Laura S. Haviland, advertised that it welcomed all applicants "irrespective of *complexion* or condition."[37]

Efforts of this kind produced a strong, hostile reaction in both North and South. When Theodore Dwight Weld and his fellow

[32]Garrison and Garrison, *William Lloyd Garrison*, I, 282.

[33]*Quarterly Anti-Slavery Magazine* (New York), II (July 1837), 348.

[34]Gilbert Hobbs Barnes and Dwight Lowell Dumond (eds.), *Letters of Theodore Dwight Weld, Angelina Grimké Weld and Sarah Grimké, 1822-1844* (2 vols., New York, 1934), I, 90-91; Henry Howe, *Historical Collections of Ohio; Containing a Collection of the Most Interesting Facts, Traditions, Biographical Sketches, Anecdotes, etc., Relating to Its General and Local History; with Descriptions of Its Counties, Principal Towns and Villages* (Cincinnati, 1849), 336.

[35]Newport, Ind., *Free Labor Advocate and Anti-Slavery Chronicle*, September 13, 1845; Levi Coffin, *Reminiscences of Levi Coffin, the Reputed President of the Underground Railroad* (Cincinnati, 1898), 171.

[36]Woodstock Manual Labor Institute Circular in James G. Birney Papers (William L. Clements Library, Ann Arbor).

[37]Ann Arbor, Mich., *Signal of Liberty*, May 23, 1842.

students at Lane Seminary in 1834 undertook to aid the colored people of Cincinnati, school authorities objected, apparently because they saw implications of racial equality in the close interracial relationships which Weld's projects involved. The consequent disciplinary measures imposed by the Lane trustees led some forty students to withdraw from the seminary.[38] Two years later an anti-abolitionist mob in Cincinnati turned their wrath against the Negro section of the city, wrecking and burning as they went.[39] Prudence Crandall's attempts to enroll Negro students in her school at Canterbury, Connecticut, caused so much popular opposition that she abandoned the project.[40] In Jacksonville, Illinois, in 1844, a proposal to allow colored children from the local Sunday schools to participate in the Fourth of July celebration nearly rent the city's churches.[41] It was of course to be expected that among the slaveholding citizens of St. Louis abolitionist activity would produce opposition, but some Missourians refused to tolerate solicitude even for free Negroes. Thus, women in St. Louis who established a school for free colored children were threatened with mob violence and their school was closed.[42] Similar events occurred in Kentucky, where most Sunday schools for Negroes had ceased to operate by the fall of 1835.[43]

Implicit in much of the opposition to educating free Negroes was the suspicion that racial equality would lead inevitably to racial amalgamation.[44] The widespread fear of Negro social equality provided a powerful incentive to riot against abolitionists throughout the North and became a major factor in Northern

[38]Sidney Strong, "The Exodus of Students from Lane Seminary to Oberlin in 1834," *Papers of the Ohio Church History Society*, IV (1893), 10; Theodore Dwight Weld, *A Statement of the Reasons which Induced the Students of Lane Seminary to Dissolve Their Connection with That Institution* (Cincinnati, 1834).

[39]Betty Fladeland, *James Gillespie Birney: Slaveholder to Abolitionist* (Ithaca, 1955), 141-42.

[40]Edwin W. Small and Miriam R. Small, "Prudence Crandall, Champion of Negro Education," *New England Quarterly*, XVII (December 1944), 506-29.

[41]Chicago *Western Citizen*, July 25, 1844.

[42]St. Louis *Observer*, July 31, 1834.

[43]James G. Birney to Joseph Healy, October 2, 1835, in Dumond (ed.), *Birney Letters*, I, 250.

[44]*Genius of Universal Emancipation*, XIV (May 1834), 86. For an abolitionist effort to meet this objection, see *Speech of James A. Thome*, 14.

opposition to them.[45] Years of antislavery activity failed measurably to eliminate racial prejudice, especially in the states of the Old Northwest.[46] "By nature, education, and association, it is believed that the negro is inferior to the white man, physically, morally, and intellectually," asserted a legislative committee in Illinois after more than a decade of abolitionist agitation in that state; "whether this be true to the fullest extent, matters not, when we take into consideration the fact that such is the opinion of the vast majority of our citizens . . . ."[47]

The abolitionists could not change Southern convictions of the Negro's anthropological inferiority, and they had been little more successful in the North. While it is true that in some limited areas, especially in New England, the abolitionists won local victories in altering views toward Negroes,[48] these victories only dented and did not break the wall of prejudice, and the Civil War began with the bulwark essentially intact. The Union Army, which was to be the effective instrument in the destruction of slavery, contained many soldiers who exhibited extreme racial prejudice,[49] and the three earliest settled states of the Northwest Territory—Ohio, Indiana, and Illinois—maintained legal discriminations against free people of color until the eve of the Civil War, and in some instances long after it. [50]

---

[45]See testimony of Webb C. Quigley, participant in the Lovejoy riots of 1837, in William S. Lincoln, *Alton Trials of Winthrop S. Gilman, Who Was Indicted . . . for the Crime of Riot, Committed on the Night of the 7th of November, 1837, while Engaged in Defending a Printing Press, from an Attack Made on It at That Time, by an Armed Mob* (New York, 1838), 115.

[46]Henry Wilson, *History of the Rise and Fall of the Slave Power in America* (3 vols., Boston, 1874), II, 181-89.

[47]*Reports Made to the Senate and House of Representatives of the State of Illinois, at Their Session Begun and Held at Springfield December 2, 1844* (2 vols., Springfield, 1845), II, 247.

[48]Louis Ruchames, "Race, Marriage, and Abolition in Massachusetts," *Journal of Negro History,* (Washington), XL (July 1955), 250-73.

[49]Bell I. Wiley, "Billy Yank and the Black Folk," *Journal of Negro History* XXXVI (January 1951), 35-52.

[50]Henry W. Farnam, *Chapters in the History of Social Legislation in the United States to 1860* (Washington, 1938), 215-17, 220-21, 424-25, 427-29, 458-59; none of Indiana's discriminatory legislation was repealed before the Civil War, and school segregation was not outlawed in that state until 1949. Emma Lou Thornbrough, *The Negro in Indiana, a Study of a Minority* (Indianapolis, 1957), 127.

The antislavery crusade gained numerous recruits in the North in the later 1830's. It may even be true, as some have thought, that as many as 200,000 Northerners belonged to antislavery societies at the height of the movement. But it is surely a mistake to suppose that this figure represents the number of Northerners who were anxious to free the slaves *and* grant them equality. The large accessions to antislavery society membership after 1835 did not, in fact, result solely from a disposition to aid and elevate the Negro. As Catherine Beecher observed at the time, a great many men either declared or implied that in joining the abolitionists "they were influenced, not by their arguments . . . but because the violence of opposers had identified that cause with the question of freedom of speech, freedom of the press, and civil liberty."[51] Miss Beecher's brother Edward, who had been associated in Illinois with the murdered antislavery editor, Elijah P. Lovejoy, made it clear that he joined the abolitionists because of the opposition to them.[52] Each important mob incident brought accessions to the antislavery cause from among those men who believed that popular opposition to the abolitionists imperiled civil liberties.[53] Many antislavery recruits, especially those in the West, entered the movement in order to preserve their own rights; they did not necessarily feel any considerable interest in Negro rights. These adherents to the antislavery cause called themselves abolitionists, and they have been so called ever since, but not all deserved that name. They were indeed eager to end slavery at once; yet they gave little attention to the corollary of emancipation—equal rights for the freedmen. The original abolitionists, therefore, soon found themselves and their aims submerged by the very success of their movement.

The work of the abolitionists as moral reformers had practically ended by 1844. Encountering failure at every turn, many of the antislavery leaders changed their methods in the late 1830's,

[51]Catherine E. Beecher, *An Essay on Slavery and Abolitionism, with Reference to the Duty of American Females* (Philadelphia, 1837), 36.
[52]Edward Beecher, *Narrative of Riots at Alton in Connection with the Death of Rev. Elijah P. Lovejoy* (Alton, 1838), 36-38.
[53]Nye, *Fettered Freedom*, 108-21; James G. Birney to Charles Hammond, Nov. 14, 1835, in Dumond (ed.), *Birney Letters*, I, 270.

frankly adopting political action, with its implied threat of coercion, as the only means offering a possibility of success for their
campaign to end slavery. A shift in that direction had long been
underway. James G. Birney, a leader in the political antislavery
movement, had concluded as early as 1835, "that repentance is
far off, if at all to be expected . . . ."[54] Benjamin Lundy had early
declared his belief that slavery could be ended only at the ballot
box and by the national government.[55] While disenchantment with
moral suasion spread, Garrison and a few of his friends kept up a
lonely, tireless battle along the old lines, but the majority of so-
called abolitionists, especially those in the West, deserted him in
his lofty realm of moral argument to take their places in the
political arena. As the issue became increasingly involved with
politics, those who insisted on using only the old methods to
achieve the old goals gradually found themselves thrust farther
into the background. Although some antislavery societies continued to operate after 1840, they had by that time been largely
superseded by the new political organizations. "The Societies
have done good work in their day," explained Zebina Eastman,
who was later to be an organizer of the Republican party, "and
we can cherish them still, for the love of old associations, if we
choose . . . . But the advanced state of the cause, the political
aspect which it has taken, require a different organization . . . one
which has not the stuffiness and sluggishness of age upon it."[56] Opposition to slavery and to the South continued as vigorously as
ever in the 1840's, but it was henceforth to be expressed primarily
in direct action, with decreasing emphasis upon moral suasion.[57]

This was a momentous change. For one thing, it indicated that
the New England theocracy had lost still another engagement
in its long battle to maintain its influence. The moral reformers
had been overwhelmed by the influx into their movement of men
more practical than they; and their program, in becoming popular,
had lost some of its original features. Furthermore, the change

[54]Birney to Gerrit Smith, September 13, 1835, *ibid.*, I, 243.
[55]*Genius of Universal Emancipation*, XI (September 1830), 81; XIII (May
1833), 120.
[56]Chicago *Western Citizen*, March 30, 1843.
[57]Barnes, *Antislavery Impulse*, 177-90; Dumond, *Antislavery Origins*, 83-97.

constituted a tacit admission by the antislavery group of the failure of the abolitionist program as a moral reform and of the inadequacy of the philosophical basis upon which it had rested. Other appeals, more practical and perhaps more selfish, were recognized to possess greater effectiveness than pleas for conformity to the moral law. Moreover, by failing to maintain its original position, the antislavery movement abandoned all hope of achieving its original goals of ending racial prejudice and persuading slaveholders to abandon their sin. For although force might end slavery, no coercion could possibly end prejudice, and repentance gained by force would not be repentance at all. Since public opinion toward Negroes had not been significantly changed, it became nearly certain that even if the slaves were freed, the freedmen would still be condemned to a long period of depressed status.

Most important at that time, however, was the fact that the refusal of the nation to accept the abolitionists' original program increased the chances for war. Slavery would not be ended voluntarily; yet abolitionists had succeeded in persuading Northerners that the South and its institutions were evil. Even if few Northerners believed in or wanted Negro equality, a great many of them had become convinced that slavery must somehow end. By succeeding to that extent, the antislavery crusade had moved the nation closer to war. A few antislavery advocates had early foreseen this eventuality, even though they usually deplored it. "Perhaps at this moment," one of them speculated in 1822, "the tears of the enslaved children of Africa are watering the seeds of the dissolution of the Union, which may end in consequences more terrible than the scenes of St. Domingo."[58] At the height of the antislavery controversy, the Reverend Charles G. Finney warned Theodore Dwight Weld that abolitionism must lead to civil war.[59] And in 1844, after many Western abolitionists had espoused political action against slavery, the students at the Missionary Institute, an abolitionist college near Quincy, Illinois, announced at their commencement exercises that *"Onward,* is our

[58]*Genius of Universal Emancipation,* I (April 1822), 151.
[59]Barnes and Dumond (eds.), *Weld-Grimké Letters,* I, 318-20.

motto, *Universal Freedom, or death on the battlefield,* is our watchword."[60] But the young men who spoke so belligerently hardly belonged in the tradition of the moral reformers.

"Slavery is such a cruel thing that it must be destroyed," William Stewart had declared in an address before the General Assembly of the Presbyterian Church in 1835, "and still it would be better to have it done by moral influences than by force; by pricking the consciences of slaveholders . . . ."[61] Implicit in Stewart's statement was the assumption that if emancipation could not be accomplished peacefully and with the consent of the slaveowners, it would be accomplished in some other way. Thus the Civil War came, destroying slavery together with much else—all, however, without accomplishing the grand aim of the abolitionists: the creation of a society in which the principles of Christianity, as the abolitionists understood them, would be realized, and in which men of all colors could live together in harmony and equality. Although slavery was ended by the Civil War, racial prejudice was not; for abolition had come through the use of military power, without general willingness to relinquish the idea of racial inequality.[62]

In spite of all their efforts, the abolitionists had failed to create widespread determination in any part of the nation to grant to the freedmen social or political or economic equality. One faction in the American Anti-Slavery Society refused to agitate even for Negro suffrage and, led by Garrison, broke away from the organization in 1865. Wendell Phillips continued to lead the remaining group until 1870 when, with the ratification of the Fifteenth Amendment, it disbanded, on the apparent assumption that constitutional provisions could accomplish what moral agitation had failed to do.[63] Decidedly in the minority were such men as Parker Pillsbury, an early associate of Garrison, who warned the American Anti-Slavery Society at its last annual meeting that "our work

[60]Chicago *Western Citizen,* August 17, 1843.
[61]*Liberator* (Boston), June 27, 1835.
[62]The pervasiveness of racial prejudice is one of the main themes of Rayford W. Logan, *The Negro in American Life and Thought: The Nadir, 1877-1890* (New York, 1954).
[63]*National Anti-Slavery Standard* (New York), April 16, 1870.

is not yet quite done; at least mine is not done, nor will it be done till the blackest man has every right which I, myself, enjoy."[64]

Like most other abolitionists, William Lloyd Garrison accepted the Thirteenth Amendment as the culmination of his life's work. On his trip to attend the Secretary of War's flag-raising ceremony at Fort Sumter in the spring of 1865, he could quite fittingly observe while he stood beside the tomb of John C. Calhoun that "down into a deeper grave than this slavery has gone, and for it there is no resurrection."[65] But he might also have reflected as he watched the Stars and Stripes flying once again over Charleston harbor, that although slavery was dead, the goals of the abolitionists had not yet been accomplished.

[64]Parker Pillsbury, *Acts of the Anti-Slavery Apostles* (Concord, N. H., 1883), 501.
[65]*Liberator,* April 15, 1865.

T W O

TOWARD A RECONSIDERATION OF ABOLITIONISTS

I

ABRAHAM LINCOLN was not an abolitionist. He believed that slavery was a moral wrong, but he was not sure how to right it. When elected President, he was pledged to contain, not to extirpate, the South's peculiar institution. Only after offers of compensation to slaveholders had failed and after military necessities had become desperate did he issue his Emancipation Proclamation. Even then his action affected only a portion of the Negroes, and the President himself seemed at times unsure of the constitutionality of his proclamation.

It is easy to see, then, why earnest antislavery men were suspicious of Lincoln. Unburdened with the responsibilities of power, unaware of the larger implications of actions, they criticized the President's slowness, doubted his good faith, and hoped for his replacement by a more vigorous emancipationist. Such murmurings and discontents are normal in American political life; in every village over the land there is always at least one man who can tell the President how the government ought to be run.

But a small group of extreme antislavery men, doctrinaire advocates of immediate and uncompensated abolition, assailed the wartime President with a virulence beyond normal expectation. It was one thing to worry about the fixity of Lincoln's principles, but quite another to denounce him, as did Wendell Phillips, as "the slave-hound of Illinois." Many Republicans might reasonably have wanted another candidate in 1864, but there was something almost paranoid in the declaration by a group of Iowa abolitionists that "Lincoln, . . . a Kentuckian by birth, and his brothers-in-law being in the rebel army, is evidently, by his sympathies with the owners of slaves, checked in crushing the rebellion by severe measures against slaveholders." A man might properly be troubled by Lincoln's reconstruction plans, but surely it was excessive for a Parker Pillsbury to pledge that, "by the grace of God and the Saxon Tongue," he would expose the "hypocrisy and cruelty" of Lincoln and of "whatever other President dares tread in his bloody footsteps."

The striking thing here is the disproportion between cause and effect—between Lincoln's actions, which were, after all, against slavery, and the abuse with which abolitionists greeted them. When a patient reacts with excessive vehemence to a mild stimulus, a doctor at once becomes suspicious of some deep-seated malaise. Similarly, the historian should be alert to see in extraordinary and unprovoked violence of expression the symptom of some profound social or psychological dislocation. In this instance, he must ask what produced in these abolitionists their attitude of frozen hostility toward the President.

These abolitionist leaders who so excessively berated Lincoln belonged to a distinct phase of American antislavery agitation. Their demand for an unconditional and immediate end of slavery, which first became articulate around 1830, was different from earlier antislavery sentiment, which had focused on gradual emancipation with colonization of the freed Negroes. And the abolitionist movement, with its Garrisonian deprecation of political action, was also distinct from political antislavery, which became dominant in the 1840's. The abolitionist, then, was a special type of antislavery agitator, and his crusade was part of that remarkable American social phenomenon which erupted in the 1830's, "freedom's ferment," the effervescence of kindred humanitarian reform movements—prohibition; prison reform; education for the blind, deaf, dumb; world peace; penny postage; women's rights; and a score of lesser and more eccentric drives.

Historians have been so absorbed in chronicling what these movements did, in allocating praise or blame among squabbling factions in each, and in making moral judgments on the desirability of various reforms that they have paid surprisingly little attention to the movement as a whole. Few serious attempts have been made to explain why humanitarian reform appeared in America when it did, and more specifically why immediate abolitionism, so different in tone, method, and membership from its predecessors and its successor, emerged in the 1830's.

The participants in such movements naturally give no adequate explanation for such a causal problem. According to their voluminous memoirs and autobiographies, they were simply convinced by religion, by reading, by reflection that slavery was evil, and they pledged their lives and their sacred honor to destroy it. Seeing slavery in a Southern state, reading an editorial by William Lloyd Garrison, hearing a sermon by Theodore Dwight Weld—such events precipitated a decision made on the highest of moral and ethical planes. No one who has studied the abolitionist literature can doubt the absolute sincerity of these accounts. Abolitionism was a dangerous creed of devotion, and no fair-minded person can believe that men joined the movement for personal gain or for conscious self-glorification. In all truth, the decision to become an antislavery crusader was a decision of conscience.

But when all this is admitted, there are still fundamental problems. Social evils are always present; vice is always in the saddle while virtue trudges on afoot. Not merely the existence of evil but the recognition of it is the prerequisite for reform. Were there more men of integrity, were there more women of sensitive conscience in the 1830's than in any previous decade? A generation of giants these reformers were indeed, but why was there such a concentration of genius in those ten years from 1830 to 1840? If the individual's decision to join the abolitionist movement was a matter of personality or religion or philosophy, is it not necessary to inquire why so many similar personalities or religions or philosophies appeared in America simultaneously? In short, we need to know why so many Americans in the 1830's were predisposed toward a certain kind of reform movement.

Many students have felt, somewhat vaguely, this need for a social interpretation of reform. Little precise analysis has been attempted, but the general histories of antislavery attribute the abolitionist movement to the Christian tradition, to the spirit of the Declaration of Independence, to the ferment of Jacksonian democracy, or to the growth of romanticism. That some or all of these factors may have relation to abolitionism can be granted, but this helps little. Why did the "spirit of Puritanism," to which one writer attributes the movement, become manifest as militant abolitionism in the 1830's although it had no such effect on the previous generation? Why did the Declaration of Independence find fulfillment in abolition during the sixth decade after its promulgation, and not in the fourth or the third?

In their elaborate studies of the antislavery movement,[1] Gilbert H. Barnes and Dwight L. Dumond have pointed up some of the more immediate reasons

[1] Gilbert H. Barnes, *The Antislavery Impulse, 1830–1844* (1933); Barnes and Dwight L. Dumond, eds., *Letters of Theodore Dwight Weld, Angelina Grimké Weld and Sarah Grimké, 1822–1844* (2 vols., 1934); Dumond, ed., *Letters of James Gillespie Birney, 1831–1857* (2 vols., 1939); Dumond, *Antislavery Origins of the Civil War in the United States* (1939).

for the rise of American abolitionism. Many of the
most important antislavery leaders fell under the influence of Charles Grandison Finney, whose revivalism
set rural New York and the Western Reserve ablaze
with religious fervor and evoked "Wonderful outpour-
ings of the Holy Spirit" throughout the North. Not
merely did Finney's invocation of the fear of hell and
the promise of heaven rouse sluggish souls to renewed
religious zeal, but his emphasis upon good works and
pious endeavor as steps toward salvation freed men's
minds from the bonds of arid theological controversies. One of Finney's most famous converts was
Theodore Dwight Weld, the greatest of the Western
abolitionists, "eloquent as an angel and powerful as
thunder," who recruited a band of seventy antislavery
apostles, trained them in Finney's revivalistic techniques, and sent them forth to consolidate the emancipation movement in the North. Their greatest successes were reaped in precisely those communities
where Finney's preaching had prepared the soil.

Barnes and Dumond also recognized the importance
of British influence upon the American antislavery
movement. The connection is clear and easily traced:
British antislavery leaders fought for immediate emancipation in the West Indies; reading the tracts of Wilberforce and Clarkson converted William Lloyd Garrison to immediate abolitionism at about the same
time that Theodore Weld was won over to the cause
by his English friend Charles Stuart; and Weld in turn
gained for the movement the support of the Tappan

brothers, the wealthy New York merchants and philanthropists who contributed so much in money and time to the antislavery crusade. Thus, abolition had in British precedent a model, in Garrison and Weld leaders, and in the Tappans financial backers.

Historians are deeply indebted to Professors Barnes and Dumond, for the importance of their studies on the antislavery movement is very great. But perhaps they have raised as many questions as they have answered. Both religious revivalism and British antislavery theories had a selective influence in America. Many men heard Finney and Weld, but only certain communities were converted. Hundreds of Americans read Wilberforce, Clarkson, and the other British abolitionists, but only the Garrisons and the Welds were convinced. The question remains: Whether they received the idea through the revivalism of Finney or through the publications of British antislavery spokesmen, why were some Americans in the 1830's for the first time moved to advocate immediate abolition? Why was this particular seed bed ready at this precise time?

II

I believe that the best way to answer this difficult question is to analyze the leadership of the abolitionist movement. There is, unfortunately, no complete list of American abolitionists, and I have had to use a good deal of subjective judgment in drawing up a roster of leading reformers. From the classified indexes of the *Dictionary of American Biography* and the old Appleton's *Cyclopaedia of American Biography* and from important primary and secondary works on the reform generation, I made a list of about two hundred and fifty persons who seemed to be identified with the antislavery cause. This obviously is not a definitive enumeration of all the important abolitionists; had someone else compiled it, other names doubtless would have been included. Nevertheless, even if one or two major spokesmen have accidentally been omitted, this is a good deal more than a representative sampling of antislavery leadership.

After preliminary work I eliminated nearly one hundred of these names. Some proved not to be genuine abolitionists but advocates of colonizing the freed Negroes in Africa; others had only incidental interest or sympathy for emancipation. I ruthlessly excluded those who joined the abolitionists after 1840, because the political antislavery movement clearly poses a different set of causal problems. After this weeding out, I had reluctantly to drop other names because I was unable to secure more than random bits of information about them. Some of Weld's band of seventy agitators, for instance, were so obscure that even Barnes and Dumond were unable to identify them. There remained the names of one hundred and six abolitionists, the hard core of active antislavery leadership in the 1830's.

Most of these abolitionists were born between 1790 and 1810, and when the first number of the *Liberator* was published in 1831, their median age was twenty-nine. Abolitionism was thus a revolt of the young.

My analysis confirms the traditional identification of radical antislavery with New England. Although I made every effort to include Southern and Western leaders, eighty-five per cent of these abolitionists came from Northeastern states, sixty per cent from New England, thirty per cent from Massachusetts alone. Many of the others were descended from New England families. Only four of the leaders were born abroad or were second-generation immigrants.

The ancestors of these abolitionists are in some ways as interesting as the antislavery leaders themselves. In the biographies of their more famous descendants certain standard phrases recur: "of the best New England stock," "of Pilgrim descent," "of a serious, pious household." The parents of the leaders generally belonged to a clearly defined stratum of society. Many were preachers, doctors, or teachers; some were farmers and a few were merchants; but only three were manufacturers (and two of these on a very small scale), none was a banker, and only one was an ordinary day laborer. Virtually all the parents were stanch Federalists.

These families were neither rich nor poor, and it is worth remembering that among neither extreme did abolitionism flourish. The abolitionist could best appeal to "the substantial men" of the community, thought Weld, and not to "the *aristocracy* and fashionable worldliness" that remained aloof from reform. In *The Burned-Over District,* an important analysis of reform drives in western New York, Whitney R. Cross has confirmed Weld's social analysis. In New York, antislavery was strongest in those counties which had once been economically dominant but which by the 1830's, though still prosperous, had relatively fallen behind their more advantageously situated neighbors. As young men the fathers of abolitionists had been leaders of their communities and states; in their old age they were elbowed aside by the merchant prince, the manufacturing tycoon, the corporation lawyer. The bustling democracy of the 1830's passed them by; as the Reverend Ludovicus Weld lamented to his famous son Theodore: "I have . . . felt like a stranger in a strange land."

If the abolitionists were descendants of old and distinguished New England families, it is scarcely surprising to find among them an enthusiasm for higher education. The women in the movement could not, of course, have much formal education, nor could the three Negroes here included, but of the eighty-nine white male leaders, at least fifty-three attended college, university, or theological seminary. In the East, Harvard and Yale were the favored schools; in the West, Oberlin; but in any case the training was usually of the traditional liberal-arts variety.

For an age of chivalry and repression there was an extraordinary proportion of women in the abolitionist movement. Fourteen of these leaders were women who defied the convention that the female's place was at the fireside, not in the forum, and appeared pub-

licly as antislavery apostles. The Grimké sisters of
South Carolina were the most famous of these, but
most of the antislavery heroines came from New England.

It is difficult to tabulate the religious affiliations of
antislavery leaders. Most were troubled by spiritual
discontent, and they wandered from one sect to another seeking salvation. It is quite clear, however, that
there was a heavy Congregational-Presbyterian and
Quaker preponderance. There were many Methodists,
some Baptists, but very few Unitarians, Episcopalians,
or Catholics. Recent admirable dissertations on the
antislavery movement in each of the Western states,
prepared at the University of Michigan under Professor Dumond's supervision, confirm the conclusion
that, except in Pennsylvania, it is correct to consider
humanitarian reform and Congregational-Presbyterian-
ism as causally interrelated.

Only one of these abolitionist leaders seems to have
had much connection with the rising industrialism of
the 1830's, and only thirteen of the entire group were
born in any of the principal cities of the United States.
Abolition was distinctly a rural movement, and
throughout the crusade many of the antislavery leaders seemed to feel an instinctive antipathy toward the
city. Weld urged his following: "Let the great cities
alone; they must be burned down by *back fires*. The
springs to touch in order to move them *lie in the
country*."

In general the abolitionists had little sympathy or

understanding for the problems of an urban society. Reformers though they were, they were men of conservative economic views. Living in an age of growing industrialization, of tenement congestion, of sweatshop oppression, not one of them can properly be identified with the labor movement of the 1830's. Most would agree with Garrison, who denounced labor leaders for trying "to inflame the minds of our working classes against the more opulent, and to persuade men that they are contemned and oppressed by a wealthy aristocracy." After all, Wendell Phillips assured the laborers, the American factory operative could be "neither wronged nor oppressed" so long as he had the ballot. William Ellery Channing, gentle high priest of the Boston area, told dissatisfied miners that moral self-improvement was a more potent weapon than strikes, and he urged that they take advantage of the leisure afforded by unemployment for mental and spiritual self-cultivation. A Massachusetts attempt to limit the hours of factory operatives to ten a day was denounced by Samuel Gridley Howe, veteran of a score of humanitarian wars, as "emasculating the people" because it took from them their free right to choose their conditions of employment.

The suffering of laborers during periodic depressions aroused little sympathy among abolitionists. As Emerson remarked tartly, "Do not tell me . . . of my obligation to put all poor men in good situations. Are they *my* poor? I tell thee, thou foolish philanthropist,

that I grudge the dollar, the dime, the cent I give to
such men. . . ."

Actually it is clear that abolitionists were not so
much hostile to labor as indifferent to it. The factory
worker represented an alien and unfamiliar system
toward which the antislavery leaders felt no kinship or
responsibility. Sons of the old New England of Fed-
eralism, farming, and foreign commerce, the reformers
did not fit into a society that was beginning to be
dominated by a bourgeoisie based on manufacturing
and trade. Thoreau's bitter comment, "We do not ride
on the railroads; they ride on us," was more than the
acid aside of a man whose privacy at Walden had been
invaded; it was the reaction of a class whose leadership
had been discarded. The bitterest attacks in the journals of Ralph Waldo Emerson, the most pointed denunciations in the sermons of Theodore Parker, the
harshest philippics in the orations of Charles Sumner
were directed against the "Lords of the Loom," not
so much for exploiting their labor as for changing the
character and undermining the morality of old New
England.

As Lewis Tappan pointed out in a pamphlet sug-
gestively titled *Is It Right to Be Rich?*, reformers did
not object to ordinary acquisition of money. It was instead that "eagerness to amass property" which made
a man "selfish, unsocial, mean, tyrannical, and but a
nominal Christian" that seemed so wrong. It is worth
noting that Tappan, in his numerous examples of the

197

vice of excessive accumulation, found this evil stemming from manufacturing and banking, and never from farming or foreign trade—in which last occupation Tappan himself flourished.

Tappan, like Emerson, was trying to uphold the old standards and to protest against the easy morality of the new age. "This invasion of Nature by Trade with its Money, its Credit, its Steam, its Railroads," complained Emerson, "threatens to upset the balance of man, and establish a new universal monarchy more tyrannical than Babylon or Rome." Calmly Emerson welcomed the panic of 1837 as a wholesome lesson to the new monarchs of manufacturing: "I see good in such emphatic and universal calamity. . . ."

Jacksonian democracy, whether considered a labor movement or a triumph of laissez-faire capitalism, obviously had little appeal for the abolitionist conservative. As far as can be determined, only one of these abolitionist leaders was a Jacksonian; nearly all were strong Whigs. William Lloyd Garrison made his first public appearance in Boston to endorse the arch-Whig Harrison Gray Otis; James G. Birney campaigned throughout Alabama to defeat Jackson; Henry B. Stanton wrote editorials for anti-Jackson newspapers. Not merely the leaders but their followers as well seem to have been hostile to Jacksonian democracy, for it is estimated that fifty-nine out of sixty Massachusetts abolitionists belonged to the Whig party.

Jacksonian Democrats recognized the opposition of the abolitionists and accused the leaders of using slavery to distract public attention from more immediate economic problems at home. "The abolitionists of the North have mistaken the color of the American slaves," Theophilus Fisk wrote tartly; "all the real Slaves in the United States have pale faces. . . . I will venture to affirm that there are more slaves in Lowell and Nashua alone than can be found South of the Potomac."

III

Here, then, is a composite portrait of abolitionist leadership. Descended from old and socially dominant Northeastern families, reared in a faith of aggressive piety and moral endeavor, educated for conservative leadership, these young men and women who reached maturity in the 1830's faced a strange and hostile world. Social and economic leadership was being transferred from the country to the city, from the farmer to the manufacturer, from the preacher to the corporation attorney. Too distinguished a family, too gentle an education, too nice a morality were handicaps in a bustling world of business. Expecting to lead, these young people found no followers. They were an elite without function, a displaced class in American society.

Some—like Daniel Webster—made their terms with the new order and lent their talents and their family names to the greater glorification of the god of trade. But many of the young men were unable to overcome their traditional disdain for the new money-grubbing class that was beginning to rule. In these plebeian days they could not be successful in politics; family tradition and education prohibited idleness; and agitation allowed the only chance for personal and social self-fulfillment.

If the young men were aliens in the new industrial society, the young women felt equally lost. Their mothers had married preachers, doctors, teachers, and had become dominant moral forces in their communities. But in rural New England of the 1830's the westward exodus had thinned the ranks of eligible suitors, and because girls of distinguished family hesitated to work in the cotton mills, more and more turned to schoolteaching and nursing and other socially useful but unrewarding spinster tasks. The women, like the men, were ripe for reform.

They did not support radical economic reforms because fundamentally these young men and women had no serious quarrel with the capitalistic system of private ownership and control of property. What they did question, and what they did rue, was the transfer of leadership to the wrong groups in society, and their appeal for reform was a strident call for their own class to re-exert its former social dominance. Some fought for prison reform; some for women's rights; some for world peace; but ultimately most came to make that natural identification between moneyed aristocracy, textile-manufacturing, and Southern slave-grown cotton. An attack on slavery was their best, if quite unconscious, attack upon the new industrial system. As

Richard Henry Dana, Jr., avowed: "I am a Free Soiler, because I am . . . of the stock of the old Northern gentry, and have a particular dislike to any subserviency on the part of our people to the slave-holding oligarchy"—and, he might have added, to their Northern manufacturing allies.

With all its dangers and all its sacrifices, membership in a movement like abolitionism offered these young people a chance for a reassertion of their traditional values, an opportunity for association with others of their kind, and a possibility of achieving that self-fulfillment which should traditionally have been theirs as social leaders. Reform gave meaning to the lives of this displaced social elite. "My life, what has it been?" queried one young seeker; "the panting of a soul after eternity—the feeling that there was nothing here to fill the aching void, to provide enjoyment and occupation such as my spirit panted for. The world, what has it been? a howling wilderness. I seem to be just now awakened . . . to a true perception of the end of my being, my duties, my responsibilities, the rich and perpetual pleasures which God has provided for us in the fulfillment of duty to Him and to our fellow creatures. Thanks to the A[nti]. S[lavery]. cause, it first gave an impetus to my palsied intellect. . . ."

Viewed against the backgrounds and common ideas of its leaders, abolitionism appears to have been a double crusade. Seeking freedom for the Negro in the South, these reformers were also attempting a restora-

201

tion of the traditional values of their class at home. Leadership of humanitarian reform may have been influenced by revivalism or by British precedent, but its true origin lay in the drastic dislocation of Northern society. Basically, abolitionism should be considered the anguished protest of an aggrieved class against a world they never made.

Such an interpretation helps explain the abolitionists' excessive suspicion of Abraham Lincoln. Not merely did the President, with his plebeian origins, his lack of Calvinistic zeal, his success in corporate law practice, and his skill in practical politics, personify the very forces that they thought most threatening in Northern society, but by his effective actions against slavery he left the abolitionists without a cause. The freeing of the slaves ended the great crusade that had brought purpose and joy to the abolitionists. For them Abraham Lincoln was not the Great Emancipator; he was the killer of the dream.

The Antislavery Movement in the Upper South Before 1840

By Gordon E. Finnie

Benjamin Lundy, the abolitionist editor of the *Genius of Universal Emancipation*, estimated that there were in 1827 a total of 106 antislavery societies with 5,150 members in the slave states, whereas there were no more than 24 such organizations with 1,475 members in the free states.[1] These statistics have frequently been used by scholars to support the thesis that there was a strong antislavery movement in the South before an alleged reaction in the 1830's repressed a rising tide of antislavery feeling and transformed it into a positive defense of the institution of slavery.[2] Since most Southern antislavery sentiment was in the upper slave states, this paper seeks to determine the validity of this interpretation by a survey and analysis of the antislavery movement in these states.

[1] *Genius of Universal Emancipation*, October 14, 1827. The *Genius of Universal Emancipation* (hereafter cited as *GUE*) was published in Greeneville, Tennessee, from 1821 to 1825. It was published with variations in title in Baltimore from 1825 to 1831, in Washington from 1831 to 1833, and in Philadelphia from 1834 to 1836. There is an overlapping with the *Genius of Universal Emancipation and Baltimore Courier* (cited hereafter as *GUEBC*) from 1825 to 1827.

[2] Among the most important works published before World War II are Stephen B. Weeks, *Southern Quakers and Slavery* (Baltimore, 1896); John Spencer Bassett, *Anti-Slavery Leaders of North Carolina* (Baltimore, 1898); Mary Stoughton Locke, *Anti-Slavery in America from the Introduction of African Slaves to the Prohibition of the Slave Trade, 1619–1808* (Boston, 1901); Alice Dana Adams, *The Neglected Period of Anti-Slavery in America, 1808–1831* (Boston, 1908); Asa Earl Martin, *The Anti-Slavery Movement in Kentucky Prior to 1850* (Louisville, 1918); Martin, "The Anti-Slavery Societies of Tennessee," *Tennessee Historical Magazine* [cited hereafter as *THM*], I (December 1915), 261–81; Theodore M. Whitfield, *Slavery Agitation in Virginia, 1829–1832* (Baltimore, 1930); Ruth Scarborough, *The Opposition to Slavery in Georgia Prior to 1860* (Nashville, 1933); Joseph Clarke Robert, *The Road from Monticello: A Study of the Virginia Slavery Debate of 1832* (Durham, 1941). A few recent publications have raised serious questions about the validity of the thesis that a strong antislavery tradition existed in the South before the alleged reaction of the 1830's. For example, see Louis Filler, *The Crusade Against Slavery, 1830–1860* (New York, 1960); Dwight L. Dumond, *Antislavery: The Crusade for Freedom in America* (Ann Arbor, 1961); Robert McColley, *Slavery and Jeffersonian Virginia* (Urbana, 1964).

Mr. Finnie is assistant professor of history at West Georgia College.

In Delaware, most northeastern of the slave states, the gradual abolition movement before 1800 was principally confined to the Society of Friends, the Nicholites, a few Methodists and Presbyterians, and two abolition societies. The first of these societies was organized at Wilmington in 1788 and was so frail that it faded away in 1795. The second was also established at Wilmington in 1788 and was quite small, having about fifty members in 1796. Since support for the organization was so paltry, it disbanded in 1800.[3]

After 1800 the antislavery movement in Delaware was dominated by the Delaware Society for Promoting the Abolition of Slavery. This society was organized at Wilmington in December 1800 and drew its membership almost exclusively from prosperous Quaker merchants, manufacturers, and tradesmen in the Wilmington and Brandywine area. During the first four years of its existence the society managed to add a few members to its meager roll, but it was unable to set up auxiliary societies among the Methodists at Duck Creek, Dover, and Milford. Interest in the society's program began to wither in 1805, and by 1807 the organization lost much of its original enthusiasm and former support. By the summer of 1811 it had become so feeble that it held only one meeting between then and January 1, 1816. There was some thought of disbanding at that time, but a decision was made to continue, and the society was reorganized in the following November. Little is known about the society after its reconstruction, except that it continued to meet regularly and send delegates to the annual meetings of the American Convention for Promoting the Abolition of Slavery. The society also persisted in its efforts to abolish slavery gradually and to help the free Negro. Moreover, it expanded its objectives in 1826 by supporting the deportation and free-produce movements.[4]

The Delaware Society for Promoting the Abolition of Slavery

---

[3] *The Constitution of the Delaware Society for Promoting the Abolition of Slavery* . . . (Philadelphia, 1788); The American Convention for Promoting the Abolition of Slavery, and Improving the Condition of the African Race, *Minutes of the Proceedings, 1796* [cited hereafter as ACPAS, *Minutes*] (Philadelphia, 1796), 37–38; Monte A. Calvert, "The Abolition Society of Delaware, 1801–1807," *Delaware History*, X (October 1963), 299–300; John A. Munroe, *Federalist Delaware, 1775–1815* (New Brunswick, 1954), 160–61, 217; Kenneth L. Carroll, "More About the Nicholites," *Maryland Historical Magazine* [cited hereafter as *MHM*], XLVI (December 1951), 282–83, 288–89.

[4] ACPAS, *Minutes, 1804*, p. 14; *ibid.*, *1805*, p. 19; *ibid.*, *1819*, pp. 4, 15–27; *ibid.*, *1823*, pp. 14–16, 24; *ibid.*, *1826*, p. 42; Calvert, "Abolition Society of Delaware," 300–301, 305–306, 317–19; Munroe, *Federalist Delaware*, 217.

received assistance from four other antislavery organizations in Delaware during the nineteenth century. The first of these was established in Sussex County in November 1809 and the second in Kent County in 1817. The Wilmington Society for the Encouragement of Free Labor was set up in 1826 for the purpose of encouraging the production and consumption of goods produced by free labor, and in 1838 the Delaware Anti-Slavery Society was organized at Wilmington as an auxiliary to the American Anti-Slavery Society. These organizations were Lilliputian in size, languished shortly after their formation, and endured for no more than three years.[5]

There was also an inconsequential deportation movement in Delaware during the third decade of the nineteenth century. Two deportation societies were organized in 1824 at Wilmington, and in the winter of 1827 the Delaware legislature adopted a resolution commending the American Colonization Society. Between that date and the summer of 1833 the movement encountered chilling apathy in Delaware. Some interest was awakened as a result of abolitionist attacks upon the Colonization Society, but the great majority of Delawareans were so indifferent to the deportation movement that it never achieved more than a precarious existence.[6]

Although Delawareans were reluctant to support the organized antislavery movement, they voluntarily manumitted a sizable number of slaves. Except for the decade 1810–1820 the number of free Negroes in Delaware increased consistently from 1790 to 1840. In 1790 the federal census reported a free Negro population of 3,899, and in 1800 the number of free Negroes increased to 8,268. The number grew to 13,136 in 1810, to 15,855 in 1830, and to 16,919 in 1840. The total number of slaves in the state declined from 8,887 in 1790 to 2,605 in 1840.[7]

These remarkable population trends, coupled with the disin-

[5] ACPAS, *Minutes, 1809*, p. 20; *ibid., 1818*, p. 6; *ibid., 1821*, pp. 3–4; American Anti-Slavery Society, *Annual Report, 1838* [cited hereafter as AAS, *Annual Report*] (New York, 1838), 5, 16, 45; *ibid., 1839*, p. 34; Calvert, "Abolition Society of Delaware," 320n; Munroe, *Federalist Delaware*, 217–18; Adams, *Neglected Period*, 156–57; Ruth Ketring Nuermberger, *The Free Produce Movement* (Durham, 1942), 13–14.

[6] American Society for Colonizing the Free People of Color, of the United States, *Annual Report, 1824* [cited hereafter as ACS, *Annual Report*] (Washington, 1824), 166; *ibid., 1827*, pp. 65–67; *African Repository*, IX (December 1833), 318–19.

[7] U. S. Bureau of the Census, *Negro Population, 1790–1915* (Washington, 1918), 57; cited hereafter as *Negro Population*.

clination of Delawareans to back the antislavery movement, seem to indicate that a great number of persons in Delaware seriously questioned the merits of the institution of slavery but were unwilling to espouse an organized movement to destroy it. These phenomena also suggest that the overwhelming majority of persons in Delaware adhered to a position on slavery comparable to the one expressed anonymously by "A Plain Citizen" in 1798: "I abhor," he declared, "the slave trade, [but] I neither conceive [slaveholding] inconsistent with my Conscience, nor derogatory to the Christian religion, the rights of mankind, or the different orders of subordination; yet have no objection to its gradual abolition."[8]

A similar attitude was probably shared by many who lived in Maryland, where the antislavery movement won little support before 1800. Prior to that date organized sentiment in favor of gradual emancipation was mainly confined to the Quakers, Nicholites, and Methodists,[9] and to the Maryland Society for Promoting the Abolition of Slavery. This society had about six members at the time of its organization at Baltimore in September 1789 and encountered widespread suspicion and hostility. In spite of this unfavorable reaction, it succeeded in forming three auxiliary societies in 1790–1791 and in expanding its membership to about 250 in 1797. But these momentary gains were not enough to keep the society alive, and it dwindled away by 1798.[10]

After the degeneration of the Maryland Society, the antislavery movement in Maryland made little progress. The Quakers and Nicholites persevered in their attack upon the institution of slavery, but emigration and their minority position within an expand-

---

[8] Quoted in Munroe, Federalist Delaware, 162; see also pages 164–65, 218.
[9] Kenneth L. Carroll, "Maryland Quakers and Slavery," MHM, XLV (September 1950), 222, 224; Carroll, "Religious Influences on the Manumission of Slaves in Caroline, Dorchester, and Talbot Counties," ibid., LVI (June 1961), 176–97; Carroll, "Joseph Nichols and the Nicholites of Caroline County, Maryland," ibid., XLV (March 1950), 47–61; Carroll, "More About the Nicholites," 282–83, 288–89; Thomas E. Drake, Quakers and Slavery in America (New Haven, 1950), 81–82, 96–97; Donald G. Mathews, Slavery and Methodism: A Chapter in American Morality, 1780–1845 (Princeton, 1965), 8–14, 18.
[10] "Constitution of the Maryland Society, for Promoting the Abolition of Slavery . . . ," American Museum, VII (January–June 1790), Appendix II, 6–8; Memorials Presented to the Congress of the United States of America, by the Different Societies Instituted for Promoting the Abolition of Slavery . . . (Philadelphia, 1792), 23–27; Constitution and Act of Incorporation of the Pennsylvania Society for Promoting the Abolition of Slavery . . . (Philadelphia, 1820), 7–8; ACPAS, Minutes, 1797, pp. 37–38; ibid., 1804, pp. 16, 20; [John S. Tyson], Life of Elisha Tyson, the Philanthropist (Baltimore, 1825), 23–35, 50–51, 53, 58.

ing slaveholding population impaired their effectiveness. The Methodists tried to stand by their rules on slavery; but the exigencies of institutional life, the inclination toward compromise within the church, and the growth of proslavery feeling made fidelity more and more difficult.[11] From time to time a few courageous individuals also begged the state legislature to destroy the domestic slave trade, to eradicate slavery gradually, and to improve the condition of the slave. But each appeal met with callous indifference, outright rejection, or carefully reasoned arguments for retaining the status quo. Moreover, emancipationists confronted such an adverse climate of opinion that a quarter century passed before they established a single organization devoted primarily to the abolition of slavery itself.[12]

This body was formed at Baltimore on August 25, 1825, and was known as the Maryland Anti-Slavery Society. Its fundamental purpose was to promote the gradual abolition of slavery, but it also advocated the deportation of the free Negro. The society hoped to achieve these ends by setting up auxiliaries throughout Maryland and by participating in political activity designed to further its objectives.[13] During its first three years the society organized eleven auxiliaries and recruited about five hundred members. But it suffered devastating defeats at the polls when it ran antislavery candidates for the state legislature in 1825 and 1826. And support was so meager thereafter that the society held its last meeting in September 1830.[14] Nothing is known of it after

[11] ACPAS, *Minutes, 1804*, p. 25; "Memorial of the Religious Society of the Friends . . . to Congress, 1817," Mt. Pleasant (Ohio) *Philanthropist*, December 19, 1817; Carroll, "Religious Influences," 183, 186; Carroll, "More About the Nicholites," 286; Carroll, "Quakerism in Caroline County, Maryland: Its Rise and Decline," Friends Historical Association, *Bulletin*, XLVIII (1959), 91, 93–94; "Some Account of the Religious People Called 'Nicholites,'" *Friends' Miscellany*, IV (September 1833), 243–45, 250; Drake, *Quakers and Slavery*, 114–15, 134–35; Mathews, *Slavery and Methodism*, 19–29, 33, 34, 36–37, 54–55.

[12] Mt. Pleasant (Ohio) *Philanthropist*, March 13, 1819; April 20, 1820; GUE, July 1821; March 1822; January 20, 27, February 24, 1827; August 1830; April 1832; GUEBC, February 4, 1826; ACPAS, *Minutes, 1804*, p. 25; *ibid., 1817*, pp. 13–15; Jeffrey R. Brackett, *The Negro in Maryland: A Study of the Institution of Slavery* (Baltimore, 1899), 55–56; Adams, *Neglected Period*, 49.

[13] GUE, August and September 1825; October 7, 21, December 23, 1826; GUEBC, September 5, October 1, 8, 1825; February 4, April 29, 1826; ACPAS, *Minutes, 1826*, pp. 27, 30, 31; *ibid., 1827*, pp. 51–52; Merton L. Dillon, *Benjamin Lundy and the Struggle for Negro Freedom* (Urbana, 1966), 109–11.

[14] GUEBC, September 17, 24, October 1, 8, 1825; April 29, September 2, 1826; GUE, September 16, October 7, December 23, 1826; March 31, December 22, 1827; February 23, May 24, 1828; ACPAS, *Minutes, 1827*, p. 51; Dillon, *Benjamin Lundy*, 111–14, 115–17.

that date. In all likelihood the organization was dissolved and its auxiliary societies merged with the American Colonization Society. Most of its members probably redirected their activity into the deportation movement.

This movement began in Maryland in June 1817, when the Baltimore Colonization Society was established. In the following January the Maryland legislature unanimously endorsed the idea of removing free Negroes, and a state deportation society was organized at Baltimore in August 1818. During the next decade ten auxiliary societies were formed, and Episcopalians, Roman Catholics, Methodists, and Quakers periodically lauded projects for getting rid of the free Negro.[15] In spite of these somewhat encouraging developments, sentiment in favor of the deportation movement waxed and waned unspectacularly in Maryland until the autumn of 1831, when the tragic events associated with the Nat Turner insurrection catalyzed hitherto lukewarm deportationists and quickened Negrophobia in the state.[16]

This ominous episode in Southampton County, Virginia, and the ghastly fear it engendered infused new life into the deportation movement in Maryland and led to a series of actions that were calculated to reduce Maryland's expanding Negro population.[17] In December 1831 the legislature passed a law providing for the appointment of three commissioners to supervise the removal of free Negroes from the state. This law also appropriated $20,000 to assist in deporting free Negroes, arranged for funding in the future, and authorized judicial officials to furnish the commissioners with lists of manumitted slaves to be removed. In addition, the law required that sheriffs deport free Negroes out of the state if they refused to go to Liberia. Shortly thereafter the languid state deportation society was revived, and in April 1833 the Board of Managers of the Maryland State Colonization Society decided to establish a colony of free Negroes on the coast of

---

[15] ACS, *Annual Report, 1818*, p. 25; *ibid., 1819*, pp. 121–24, 126–27; *ibid., 1819* (2d ed.), 104; *ibid., 1820*, p. 144; *ibid., 1822*, p. 114; *ibid., 1824*, p. 171; *ibid., 1827*, pp. 68, 97; *ibid., 1828*, pp. 85, 110–11; GUE, November 1824; November 3, 1827; GUEBC, July 4, 1825; *African Repository*, I (August and December 1825), 191–92, 318; III (April 1827), 60; P. J. Staudenraus, *The African Colonization Movement, 1816–1865* (New York, 1961), 25, 38–39.

[16] ACS, *Annual Report, 1828*, pp. 78–79; *African Repository*, III (October 1827 and February 1828), 250–51, 368–69; V (October 1829), 251; VI (May, June, and July 1830), 73, 125, 155; John H. B. Latrobe, *Maryland in Liberia* (Baltimore, 1885), 10–12, 14–15.

[17] Negro population in Maryland increased from 111,079 in 1790 to 155,932 in 1830. *Negro Population*, 45.

Africa. They also took a step which was unprecedented in the history of the deportation movement: they declared that the purpose of the Maryland State Colonization Society was "the ultimate extirpation of slavery, by proper and gradual efforts . . . ."[18] This radical action on the part of the board evidently alienated many deportationists in the state. As a result, the state society's efforts to establish new auxiliaries met with little success throughout the remainder of the decade. Nevertheless, the society did succeed in planting a colony of free Negroes at Cape Palmas in February 1834, and it continued to receive the financial support of the state legislature.[19]

Maryland legislators had no humanitarian illusions about their partnership with the Maryland State Colonization Society. They regarded their patronage as a device to rid the state of an unwanted free Negro population. In their view the deportation movement was merely a way of assuring themselves that "in process of time, the relative proportion of the black to the white population, will hardly be matter for serious or unpleasant consideration."[20] They also tried to make it clear that their support for the movement should not be interpreted as abolitionist in nature. Indeed, they were so intent on making this position known that they expunged two petitions for gradual abolition from the General Assembly's journal a few months after the state society indicated it favored the gradual abolition of slavery.[21]

Such actions were only to be expected. By 1836 radical opposition to slavery was so unpopular in Maryland that the Baltimore Annual Conference of the Methodist Episcopal Church, which had formerly contained a sizable number of emancipationists, condemned the abolition movement. And the situation was so bad by 1838 that Maryland Hicksite Quakers even refused to allow their members to become "entangled" in any way with the antislavery movement.[22]

---

[18] Quoted in *African Repository*, IX (May 1833), 91; see also *ibid.*, XVII (June 15, 1841), 184; *GUE*, April 1832; June 1833; Latrobe, *Maryland in Liberia*, 12, 15–16; *The Maryland Scheme of Expatriation Examined* (Boston, 1834), 6–12.

[19] *African Repository*, IX (November 1833), 280; XI (January and October 1835), 58, 296; XII (April 1836), 132; XVII (February 15, September 15, 1841), 54, 276; Latrobe, *Maryland in Liberia*, 45–46, 67–68, 74, 84.

[20] Quoted in *African Repository*, VII (March 1831), 30; see also *ibid.*, VIII (April 1832), 52–55.

[21] *Maryland Scheme of Expatriation Examined*, 13.

[22] L. C. Matlack, *The Antislavery Struggle and Triumph in the Methodist Episcopal Church* (New York, 1881), 82; Drake, *Quakers and Slavery*, 144.

Conditions were slightly better in Virginia, but the antislavery movement made little headway there. Before 1800 organized support for gradual abolition was limited primarily to the Society of Friends, the Methodists, and two manumission societies in Henrico and Frederick counties. There was also sporadic opposition to slavery on the part of a few isolated individuals, the most radical of whom were James O'Kelly and David Barrow. But these persons represented an insignificant minority in Virginia. Indeed, proslavery sentiment was so widespread by the turn of the century that Francis Asbury soberly predicted that slavery would endure in Virginia for ages.[23]

After 1800 the gradual abolition movement in Virginia became more and more feeble. The Society of Friends, a small number of Methodists, and a few radical Presbyterians doggedly tried to block the onrushing tide of slavery, but they constantly lost ground. Moreover, no more than ten weak antislavery societies were established during the first three decades of the nineteenth century, and they were all confined to Loudoun and Frederick counties. They were also dominated by men who were principally concerned with extricating white Virginians from the baneful effects of slavery and with promoting the deportation of the free Negro. Six of these societies met in August 1827 and attempted to organize a permanent convention devoted to gradual abolition and deportation, but their efforts met with little success, and the convention was disbanded sometime in 1828.[24]

The decline of sentiment in favor of gradual abolition was accompanied by the growth of the deportation movement in Virginia. In 1817 a "small but opulent society of slave-holders" was organized as an auxiliary to the American Colonization Society.[25] Between that date and 1820 nine more auxiliaries were estab-

[23] ACPAS, *Minutes, 1796,* p. 10; *ibid., 1797,* pp. 37–38; *ibid., 1798,* p. 10; *ibid, 1800,* pp. 9–11; [David Barrow], "*Circular Letter. Southampton County, Virginia, February 14, 1798*" (Richmond, 1798); James O'Kelly, *Essay on Negro Slavery* (Philadelphia, 1784); Elmer T. Clark *et al.* (eds.), *The Journal and Letters of Francis Asbury* (3 vols., Nashville, 1958), II, 151; McColley, *Slavery and Jeffersonian Virginia,* 2–3, 4, 5, 35–36, 81, 114–75, 180–89; Weeks, *Southern Quakers,* 213.

[24] ACPAS, *Minutes, 1804,* pp. 16, 20, 25; *GUE,* October 1824; June and September 1825; May 5, August 18, September 29, 1827; April 26, May 3, October 18, 1828; John D. Paxton, *Letters on Slavery . . .* (Lexington, Ky., 1833); Mathews. *Slavery and Methodism,* 37–39; McColley, *Slavery and Jeffersonian Virginia,* 152–53.

[25] Early Lee Fox, *The American Colonization Society, 1817–1840* (Baltimore, 1919), 53.

lished, and the society obtained such popularity by 1825 that the General Assembly appropriated five hundred dollars for its support and officially approved its purposes. In 1828 the number of auxiliaries in the state increased to twenty-nine, and the Colonization Society of the State of Virginia was organized at Richmond. A heated dispute in Congress over the federal government's constitutional authority to acquire an African colony momentarily crippled the deportation movement in Virginia after 1828, but the prolonged furor following the Nat Turner insurrection in the summer of 1831 revitalized the movement almost overnight. Languid auxiliaries returned to life, a few new ones sprang up, and many former opponents of the movement endorsed it.[26] Indeed, the revival flourished to such an extent by 1832 that some deportationists even tried to secure the enactment of a bill providing for the gradual deportation of Virginia's entire Negro population.[27] This determined effort was defeated on January 25, 1832, when the legislature adopted a resolution stating that it was "inexpedient" to take such a step at that time.[28] Nevertheless, sentiment in favor of deportation persisted, and support for the movement was so widespread by 1833 that the editor of a Virginia newspaper asserted that "there is very little opposition felt or manifested to the scheme of African Colonization. Men, of all creeds in politics and of all sects in religion, cooperate in advancing its interests."[29]

Humanitarians in North Carolina were not so fortunate. In 1804 the American Convention for Promoting the Abolition of Slavery asserted

that public opinion in that state, is exceedingly hostile to the abolition of slavery, that every attempt towards the emancipation of people of colour is regarded with an indignant and jealous eye; that at present, the inhabitants of that state, consider the preservation of their lives, and all they hold dear on earth, as depending on the continuance of slavery; and are even riveting more firmly the fetters of oppression.

[26] ACS, *Annual Report, 1819*, p. 128; *ibid., 1819* (2d ed.), 101–103, 139; *ibid., 1820*, pp. 130–31, 140, 142–44; *ibid., 1825*, p. 43; *ibid., 1828*, pp. 101–108; *African Repository*, I (March and June 1825 and February 1826), 5, 124, 370; III (March 1827), 22–23; VI (October 1830), 241; Staudenraus, *African Colonization Movement*, 106–10, 177–80.

[27] Virginia's Negro population almost doubled during the years 1790–1830, growing from 305,493 in 1790 to 517,105 in 1830. *Negro Population*, 45.

[28] Virginia, *Journal of the House of Delegates, 1831–1832* (Richmond, 1831–1832), 15, 93, 110.

[29] Quoted in Fox, *American Colonization Society*, 92; see also Staudenraus, *African Colonization Movement*, 181.

. . . that no language the Convention could use, would have the smallest tendency to promote a relaxation of that rigorous severity, which the great body of the citizens believe necessary to preserve them from insurrection and massacre.[30]

Under conditions such as these the gradual emancipation movement made little progress in North Carolina. Before the organization of the Manumission Society of North Carolina in the summer of 1816 the movement was dominated by Quakers and Nicholites, and it embraced only a minute proportion of the total white population.[31] The Manumission Society contained few non-Quakers, encountered almost insurmountable difficulties from the moment of its establishment, frequently failed to muster a quorum of fifteen at its annual meetings, and was hampered by the awareness of the unpopular nature of its cause. It was also weakened by a split within the society between incorporationists and colonizationists and by a controversy over the question of establishing segregated Negro schools under the direction of the society. At the height of its influence in 1826 the society's membership was approximately sixteen hundred persons; and it had no more than forty auxiliary societies, all of which were confined to seven or eight counties of western North Carolina. After 1826 support dwindled, and by 1831 criticism of its activities reached such intensity that the society cautiously refused to petition the legislature for the repeal of a law prohibiting the education of slaves. By July 1834 the General Association, with twelve members present, adopted a resolution authorizing the president "to use such means as in his judgment may seem expedient to arouse the sleeping Branches."[32] With this, the General Association adjourned, never to meet again as the Manumission Society of North Carolina.

[30] ACPAS, *Minutes, 1804,* pp. 25–26.

[31] Weeks, *Southern Quakers,* 220–27; Kenneth L. Carroll, "The Nicholites of North Carolina," *North Carolina Historical Review,* XXXI (October 1954), 453–62; D. L. Corbitt, "Freeing Slaves," *ibid.,* I (October 1924), 449–50; Emma King, "Some Aspects of the Work of the Society of Friends for Negro Education in North Carolina," *ibid.,* 403; John Spencer Bassett, *Slavery in the State of North Carolina* (Baltimore, 1899), 66–67.

[32] H. M. Wagstaff (ed.), *Minutes of the N[orth]. C[arolina]. Manumission Society, 1816–1834* (Chapel Hill, 1934), 13, 19–20, 21–22, 29, 32, 35–38, 42, 44–45, 47, 58–63, 65, 66, 68–69, 74, 84, 93–94, 97, 99, 112, 162, 168, 170, 173–74, 178, 181–82, 186–87, 192–93, 197–200, 202–208 (the quotation is on page 208); Levi Coffin, *Reminiscences of Levi Coffin . . .* (Cincinnati, 1876), 75–76; ACPAS, *Minutes, 1826,* p. 37. Compare this analysis of the Manumission Society with Patrick Sowle, "The North Carolina Manumission Society, 1816–1834," *North Carolina Historical Review,* XLII (January 1965), 47–69.

Deportationists in North Carolina experienced a similar disappointment. When the American Colonization Society first began its propaganda campaign there in 1818 it discovered that a considerable amount of good will toward the society prevailed. This was particularly true at Raleigh, Fayetteville, and Chapel Hill, where auxiliary deportation societies were set up in 1819. In spite of this auspicious beginning, the deportation movement advanced at a snail's pace. During the next seven years well-meaning North Carolinians occasionally uttered evanescent endorsements of the Colonization Society, and additional auxiliaries were established at Greensboro and Hillsboro and in Hertford County. In December 1827 a state deportation society was organized at Raleigh, and by the end of 1828 the number of auxiliaries increased to nine. But deportation sentiment began to crumble in 1828. As a result, only one auxiliary society was established during the next three years, and the movement almost faded into oblivion.[33] By 1835 persons advocating an antislavery position constituted a hopeless minority in North Carolina, even when they restricted their activity to the deportation of Negroes who were already free.[34]

A comparable situation existed in Tennessee, where the gradual abolition movement was pathetically weak. Before the organization of the Manumission Society of Tennessee in 1815 the movement was principally confined to the Quakers of Greene, Jefferson, Washington, Blount, and Grainger counties and to the Methodists of eastern Tennessee.[35] After 1815 the movement was chiefly restricted to three small and ineffectual antislavery organizations: the Manumission Society of Tennessee, the Humane

[33] ACS, *Annual Report, 1819* (2d ed.), 139, 146–47; *ibid., 1820*, p. 129; *ibid., 1822*, p. 117; *ibid., 1825*, p. 67; *ibid., 1827*, p. 73; *ibid., 1828*, pp. 117–19; *ibid., 1831*, Appendix; *ibid., 1832*, Appendix; *African Repository*, I (July and September 1825), 158, 222; II (November 1826), 284–85; III (May 1827), 65–73; Minnie Spencer Grant, "The American Colonization Society in North Carolina" (unpublished M.A. thesis, Duke University, 1930), 22, 26–28, 29–38, 41–57; see pages 58–81 for the work of the society in North Carolina after 1840.

[34] Carter G. Woodson, "Freedom and Slavery in Appalachian America," *Journal of Negro History*, I (April 1916), 143; see also Bassett, *Slavery*, 95–106; *African Repository*, XII (July 1836), 217–18.

[35] Weeks, *Southern Quakers*, 322, 333, 337, 339; Chase C. Mooney, *Slavery in Tennessee* (Bloomington, 1957), 65; Mathews, *Slavery and Methodism*, 45–56; Asa Earl Martin, "Anti-Slavery Activities of the Methodist Episcopal Church in Tennessee," *THM*, II (June 1916), 100; James W. Patton, "The Progress of Emancipation in Tennessee, 1796–1860," *Journal of Negro History*, XVII (January 1932), 83.

Protecting Society of Greene County, and the Moral, Religious, Manumission Society of West Tennessee.[36] With the exception of the Manumission Society of Tennessee, none of these organizations existed for more than three years or experienced any growth.[37]

The Manumission Society was organized in Greene County on November 21, 1815. The number of branch societies grew from seven to sixteen during the next year, and the membership increased to 474, all of whom were residents of the eastern counties of Greene, Sullivan, Washington, Blount, Grainger, and Cocke. By September 1823 the auxiliaries numbered twenty, and the membership expanded to more than six hundred. The society reached its maximum strength in 1824, when the total number of societies increased to twenty-two and the membership swelled to approximately eight hundred.[38]

Despite this apparent growth the Manumission Society of Tennessee was never so "strong" as its North Carolina counterpart. Although it managed to escape the internal controversies which plagued the North Carolina organization in its early years, the Manumission Society of Tennessee was forced in 1820 to plead with the branch societies for financial support. Moreover, local auxiliaries increasingly neglected to send delegates to the annual convention. The state of affairs was so bad by August 1825 that the delegates to the annual convention lamented "the want of zeal, the want of energy, and the want of exertion, in many of their branches, and members." In the following year the president of the society asserted that the condition of the organization was beginning to be critical because many of the members were so "luke-warm and indifferent." Matters continued to worsen, and

[36] "West" Tennessee is really a misnomer. The Moral, Religious, Manumission Society of West Tennessee was organized at Columbia in Maury County, which lies south of Nashville in Middle Tennessee.

[37] The Manumission Society was organized in Greene County on November 21, 1815, and for all practical purposes died by December 1821. The Humane Society, which was made up of persons who also belonged to the Manumision Society, was established in November 1820 and faded out of existence sometime in 1823. The West Tennessee group was formed in December 1824 and was probably dissolved in 1826 or shortly thereafter. Martin, "Anti-Slavery Societies of Tennessee," 266, 272, 276. See also Jonesborough *Emancipator*, April 30, 1820; "Compacts and Rules of the Humane Protecting Society [November 1820]," GUE, November 1821; "Constitution of the Moral, Religious, Manumission Society [December 1824]," *ibid.*, February 1825.

[38] Jonesborough *Emancipator*, April 30, 1820; ACPAS, *Minutes, 1823*, p. 17; GUE, July 1825; Martin, "Anti-Slavery Societies of Tennessee," 266.

by December 1831 the society was practically, if not actually, defunct.[39]

It is hardly surprising that the Manumission Society of Tennessee languished. The desire to inhibit the growth of the free Negro population had become so pronounced in Tennessee by December 1831 that the General Assembly passed a law forbidding the further immigration of free Negroes into the state. This statute also made it unlawful for a slave to be manumitted except on the explicit condition that he be immediately removed from Tennessee.[40] Indeed, antislavery sentiment was so weak in Tennessee by 1834 that there were less than two thousand persons, out of a total estimated white population of 550,000, who openly advocated the gradual abolition of slavery, even if accompanied by the immediate deportation of the entire free Negro population. Of these persons, more than one-third lived in Washington and Greene counties.[41]

The deportation movement was also limited in scope and effectiveness in Tennessee. In 1817 the Presbyterian Synod of Tennessee officially sanctioned the American Colonization Society, and in the following year Andrew Jackson was elected a

---

[39] Jonesborough *Emancipator*, September 30, 1820; *GUE*, September 1822; August 15, 1823; July and September 1825; December 2, 1826; March 31, December 22, 1827; November 1830; Martin, "Anti-Slavery Societies of Tennessee," 272. Quotations are from "Address of the Eleventh Annual Convention of the Manumission Society of Tennessee to the Respective Branches [August 1825]," *GUE*, September 1825, and "President's Address to the Members of the Manumission Society of Tennessee [August 1826]," *GUEBC*, December 2, 1826.

[40] The law of 1831 was also designed to inhibit manumission itself. For example, it required that the owner give bond equal to the value of the slave as a guarantee that the liberated Negro would be sent out of the state and that he would be provided for until he left. Caleb Perry Patterson, *The Negro in Tennessee, 1790–1865* (Austin, 1922), 154–55, 157 .

[41] By 1834 antislavery sentiment was confined almost entirely to the eastern section of the state, where slavery could not be profitably adapted to the economic and agricultural mode of life. Moreover, the antislavery movement in Tennessee was almost completely dominated by those who favored deportation. Every antislavery petition presented to the constitutional convention of 1834 sought the deportation of the free Negro, and the most radical members of the convention asserted that they would not support any plan for the gradual abolition of slavery which failed to provide for the immediate deportation of the liberated Negro. *Journal of the Convention of the State of Tennessee, Convened for the Purpose of Revising and Amending the Constitution Thereof* (Nashville, 1834), 26, 31, 33, 48, 52, 70, 71–73, 79, 81, 82, 85, 98–99, 102–105, 108, 125–30, 145, 147–51, 209, 222–28, 256, 349. See also Chase C. Mooney, "The Question of Slavery and the Free Negro in the Tennessee Constitutional Convention of 1834," *Journal of Southern History*, XII (November 1946), 487–509, for an excellent and comprehensive discussion of the struggle over slavery in the convention.

vice-president of the society. Moreover, the state legislature authorized Tennessee's representatives in Congress to seek federal assistance for procuring a colony in Africa where free Negroes might be sent. Sentiment in favor of deportation gradually increased during the next decade, and in 1829 a state deportation society was organized. By May of the following year the number of auxiliaries in the state had increased to twenty, and an agent for the society reported that ministers of all denominations were giving the movement their support. In spite of these promising developments, the deportation movement was unable to gain momentum in the Volunteer State. In July 1831 a member of the state society lamented that deportationists had made little, if any, progress in Tennessee.[42] This judgment was confirmed several months later when an agent of the parent society reported that Tennesseans were so hostile toward the Colonization Society that the most he could do was "to communicate correct information as to the design and operations of the Society, and remove prejudice and suspicion . . . ."[43] By 1832 the number of auxiliaries in the state began to diminish, and in October 1833 the state society reported that there had been "very limited interest hitherto taken in the cause, by the people of this State."[44] After 1833 the deportation movement in Tennessee declined rapidly.[45]

Following the loss of public support for deportation, a few Tennesseans continued to oppose slavery in a radical manner. In 1835 a society advocating the immediate abolition of slavery was organized at Rock Creek in East Tennessee. This frail organization had nine members at the time of its establishment and dwindled away two years later. In 1836 fifty-five Rhea County citizens sent a petition to the state legislature protesting the enactment of a law making the receipt of abolitionist literature a penitentiary offense. The following year there was some radical antislavery activity at Maryville College, a Presbyterian institution in Blount County. About the same time Elijah Eagleston, a Presbyterian minister at Madisonville, expelled two of his most prominent members from the church because they had partici-

---

[42] ACS, *Annual Report, 1818*, pp. 19, 24–25; *African Repository*, I (March 1825), 5; III (February 1828), 372–77; V (December 1829), 301; VI (May 1830), 72, 78; VII (July 1831), 145–46.

[43] *African Repository*, VII (January 1832), 346.

[44] *Ibid.*, IX (December 1833), 319–20; see also ACS, *Annual Report, 1831*, Appendix; *ibid., 1832*, Appendix.

[45] Compare Mooney, *Slavery in Tennessee*, 73–76; Patton, "Progress of Emancipation in Tennessee," 102.

pated in the slave trade in the preceding year. Such expressions of antislavery sentiment were rare in Tennessee after 1834. Nevertheless, a small number of emancipationists continued to challenge the status quo.[46]

Radical opposition to slavery was also uncommon in Kentucky. Before 1800 there was only sporadic criticism of the institution of slavery, and most of this was associated with David Rice, a Presbyterian minister. Shortly before the Kentucky constitutional convention of 1792 Rice published an antislavery treatise which unequivocally condemned slavery as being inconsistent with the law of nature and the Christian ethic.[47] Although Rice and a small group of antislavery delegates to the convention persistently attempted to make the Negro's inalienable right to freedom a social and political reality in Kentucky, the proslavery majority triumphed. This in turn intensified the determination of the antislavery faction and eventually led to the organization of an abolition society. Nothing is known of this society, except that it existed in 1797 and was probably organized by Rice.[48]

During the years 1800–1823 organized support for gradual abolition in Kentucky was largely confined to a small group among the Methodists, Baptists, and Presbyterians.[49] Although there were occasional indications of a growing sentiment among some slaveholders that neither the financial well-being nor the personal safety of the white population was enhanced by slavery, the abolition movement never embraced more than a small fraction

[46] AAS, *Annual Report, 1838*, p. 53n; Martin, "Anti-Slavery Societies of Tennessee," 277–78; Patterson, *Negro in Tennessee*, 195–97; Woodson, "Freedom and Slavery in Appalachian America," 148; Patton, "Progress of Emancipation in Tennessee," 97.

[47] [David Rice], *Slavery Inconsistent with Justice and Good Policy* (Lexington, 1792). Rice delivered the text of this pamphlet as an address before the convention.

[48] ACPAS, *Minutes, 1797*, pp. 37–38; Martin, *Anti-Slavery Movement in Kentucky*, 13–17, 24–25.

[49] William Warren Sweet (ed.), *The Rise of Methodism in the West: Being the Journal of the Western Conference, 1800–1811* (New York, 1920), 147–48, 184; Sweet (ed.), *Religion on the American Frontier* (4 vols., New York, 1931–1946), I, 328–30, 508, 564–67; II, 169–70, 378–80, 382; [John Finley Crowe], "The Apologist," *Abolition Intelligencer and Missionary Magazine*, I (October 1822), 82–84; John M. Peck, "Kentucky Baptists," *Baptist Memorial and Monthly Chronicle*, I (February 15, 1842), 44; J. H. Spencer, *A History of Kentucky Baptists from 1769 to 1885* (2 vols., Cincinnati, 1885), I, 182–86; Walter B. Posey, "The Baptists and Slavery in the Lower Mississippi Valley," *Journal of Negro History*, XLI (April 1956), 118, 120; Martin, *Anti-Slavery Movement in Kentucky*, 19–20, 23, 35, 36, 38–41.

of Kentucky's population, and it never had more than a transitory existence.[50] The antislavery society organized by David Rice in 1797 had only a handful of members and disappeared shortly after its establishment. The Baptized Licking-Locust Association Friends of Humanity experienced a similar history. This association was principally restricted to the counties of Nelson, Nicholas, Bourbon, Mason, Montgomery, Woodford, and Shelby; and at the time of its formation in September 1807 it had about 190 members. In September of the following year the association was reorganized and became the Kentucky Abolition Society. This society maintained a feeble existence until its dissolution in 1823. Like the Friends of Humanity, the Abolition Society had only a small number of members and a few thinly scattered auxiliaries. At no time in the society's history did its membership exceed one hundred nor the number of auxiliaries go beyond four. Indeed, the society was so weak that it never attracted more than twelve delegates to any one of its annual meetings.[51]

After the disbanding of the Kentucky Abolition Society in 1823 the antislavery movement in Kentucky was increasingly dominated by men who were chiefly interested in deporting the free Negro. By that date the major religious bodies in the state had endorsed the objectives of the deportation movement, and sentiment in favor of deportation grew to such an extent in January 1826 that the General Assembly unanimously passed a resolution urging Kentucky's congressmen to use their efforts to promote the shipment of free Negroes to Africa. The following year the legislature formally sanctioned the American Colonization Society and reiterated its instructions to the state's representatives in Washington.[52] In December 1828 the Kentucky State Colonization Society was organized at Frankfort for the purpose of relieving Kentuckians of "the serious inconveniences resulting from the existence among them, of a rapidly increasing number of free persons of colour, who are not subject to the restraints of slav-

[50] *GUE*, September 8, 15, 29, October 6, 14, 1827; October 18, 25, 1828; April and July 1833; Martin, *Anti-Slavery Movement in Kentucky*, 64–68, 88–97, 102–38.
[51] Sweet (ed.), *Religion on the American Frontier*, I, 564–65; *GUE*, August 1, 1823; Kentucky Abolition Society, *Minutes, 1809–1823*, *passim*; Martin, *Anti-Slavery Movement in Kentucky*, 39–41.
[52] *Abolition Intelligencer and Missionary Magazine*, I (October 1822 and February 1823), 86–87, 158; ACS, *Annual Report, 1823*, p. 70; Robert Davidson, *History of the Presbyterian Church in the State of Kentucky* (New York, 1847), 337–38; Martin, *Anti-Slavery Movement in Kentucky*, 52–53.

ery . . . ."[53] Shortly thereafter the parent society appointed four agents to disseminate information concerning the deportation movement, and this resulted in the creation of at least twenty-five auxiliary societies during the next three years. But an epidemic of Asiatic cholera struck Kentucky in the summer of 1833, and the growth of the deportation movement was somewhat retarded thereafter. Nevertheless, a considerable amount of support for the movement continued, and the American Colonization Society became the primary channel through which Kentuckians expressed their opposition to slavery during the remainder of the 1830's.[54]

Although deportationists dominated the antislavery movement in Kentucky during the third decade of the nineteenth century, a few persons continued to believe in more drastic types of antislavery activity. During the years 1831–1833 gradual emancipationists made three unsuccessful attempts to establish antislavery organizations, and in March 1835 James G. Birney organized the Kentucky Anti-Slavery Society at Danville. This organization was an auxiliary of the American Anti-Slavery Society and was dedicated to the immediate abolition of slavery. But hostility toward the society was so intense that Birney was forced to leave Kentucky the following October. His departure marked the disappearance of the Kentucky Anti-Slavery Society and clearly revealed that Kentucky's proslavery majority would not tolerate the presence of men who were unequivocally opposed to slavery.[55]

A similar attitude prevailed in Missouri. Before 1820 sentiment in favor of slavery was so pervasive that only a small number of persons in Saint Louis, Jefferson, Washington, Lincoln, and Cape Girardeau counties even dared to question the propriety of continuing the institution of slavery in the state. Moreover, not a single restrictionist was elected to the Missouri constitutional con-

[53] Quoted in *African Repository*, IV (January 1829), 351. The number of free Negroes in Kentucky almost doubled during the years 1820–1830, increasing from 2,759 in 1820 to 4,917 in 1830. *Negro Population*, 57.
[54] Kentucky State Colonization Society, *Annual Report, 1834*, p. 3; ACS, *Annual Report, 1831*, Appendix; Martin, *Anti-Slavery Movement in Kentucky*, 53, 62; J. Winston Coleman, Jr., "Henry Clay, Kentucky, and Liberia," Kentucky State Historical Society, *Register*, XLV (October 1947), 315; see also Coleman, "The Kentucky Colonization Society," *ibid.*, XXXIX (January 1941), 4–9, for the details of the deportation movement in Kentucky after 1840.
[55] Kentucky Anti-Slavery Society, *Proceedings, 1835* (n.p., n.d.); Martin, *Anti-Slavery Movement in Kentucky*, 68–69, 70–72, 74–75; Betty Fladeland, *James Gillespie Birney: Slaveholder to Abolitionist* (Ithaca, 1955), 113–23.

vention in 1820; and only one delegate to the convention, Benjamin Emmons from Saint Charles, voted against the slavery clauses of the constitution. According to the historian of the antislavery movement in Missouri, Emmons' vote was the only trace of antislavery sentiment in the convention.[56]

During the years 1820–1840 proslavery sentiment grew rapidly in Missouri. The number of slaves increased from 10,222 in 1820 to 58,240 in 1840,[57] and hostility toward any kind of antislavery activity was so bitter by the summer of 1833 that emancipationists were severely flogged, repeatedly intimidated, and frequently forced to leave the state. Furthermore, sentiment in favor of proscribing free speech grew to such an extent by October of that year that a Saint Louis newspaper asserted that "no man has the right to discuss the abstract question of slavery where it is calculated to jeopardize the life and property of his fellow citizens." Indeed, in January 1837 the state legislature unanimously adopted a law prohibiting any kind of antislavery activity in the state. By 1840 Missourians had such a hatred of abolitionists and the principles they advocated that the word "abolitionist" was used as "an epithet which signified . . . the sum of all villanies . . . ."[58]

Under such inimical circumstances the antislavery movement failed to make any real progress in Missouri. From 1820 to 1840 a few fitful expressions of antislavery sentiment were uttered in sparsely distributed communities throughout the state, and a small number of emancipationists in Saint Louis made two feeble attempts to begin a gradual abolition movement, the first in 1827–1828 and the second in 1835. Some antislavery activity was also associated with a group of Mormons in Jackson County in 1831 and 1832 and a small number of Baptists in Saint Louis County in 1834. Moreover, a few immediate abolitionists tried to proselytize in parts of central and northeastern Missouri after 1835. A group of German immigrants who settled in Saint Louis and

[56] Benjamin Merkel, "The Antislavery Movement in Missouri, 1819–1865" (unpublished Ph.D. dissertation, Washington University, 1939), 4, 6, 10, 12, 14, 18–26.

[57] *Negro Population,* 57.

[58] Merkel, "Antislavery Movement in Missouri," 50, 53, 54, 56–58, 59, 60–71, 78–81, 84–88 (quotations are on pages 59, 87–88); Merkel, "The Abolition Aspects of Missouri's Antislavery Controversy, 1819–1865," *Missouri Historical Review,* XLIV (April 1950), 238; F. A. Sampson, "Marion College and Its Founders," *ibid.,* XX (July 1926), 486–87; Lyle Wesley Dorsett, "Slaveholding in Jackson County, Missouri," Missouri Historical Society, *Bulletin,* XX (October 1963), 27–28.

Warren counties in 1837 also evinced some hostility toward slavery but made no particular efforts to destroy it. Indeed, the climate of opinion in Missouri was so antagonistic to abolitionists, immediate or gradual, that they failed to establish a single antislavery society in the state before 1840.[59]

Conditions were somewhat more favorable for deportationists. In March 1817 an editorial in the *Missouri Gazette* lauded the deportation of free Negroes as "a means of protection for the white race."[60] During the next decade sentiment in favor of deportation grew sufficiently to make possible the establishment of a small auxiliary deportation society at Saint Louis in 1826. Nevertheless, a sizable number of Missourians feared that congressional support for deporting free Negroes might open the door for federal interference with the institution of slavery. The deportation movement therefore languished until the spring of 1833, when the Saint Louis Colonization Society experienced a momentary revival and began an intensive campaign to overcome prejudice against the movement. This effort resulted in the creation of four new auxiliaries late in 1833 and in the growth of some support among the Methodists of Missouri. But resentment toward the movement continued to persist, and it received little support thereafter.[61]

Viewing the antislavery movement in the upper South in retrospect, several conclusions concerning its nature and its supporters seem warranted. To begin with, there never was a single antislavery movement in the upper South. Instead, there were at various times and places in the upper slave states at least three antislavery "movements." The first was carried on by an infinitely small number of *immediate abolitionists*. These persons insisted that "slaveholding is a great crime in the sight of God . . . [and] that the best interests of all concerned require its immediate

[59] *GUE*, September 1821; *Abolition Intelligencer*, I (November 1822), 100–101; Merkel, "Antislavery Movement in Missouri," 2–3, 10, 11–14, 17–22, 32–33, 35–36, 39–44, 53–54, 71–79, 89; Dorsett, "Slaveholding in Jackson County, Missouri," 27–28; A. A. Dunson, "Notes on the Missouri Germans on Slavery," *Missouri Historical Review*, LIX (April 1965), 355, 358–61; G. Hugh Wamble, "Negroes and Missouri Protestant Churches Before and After the Civil War," *ibid.*, LXI (April 1967), 322, 334, 345–47.
[60] Quoted in Merkel, "Antislavery Movement in Missouri," 5–6.
[61] ACS, *Annual Report, 1827*, pp. 81–100; *ibid., 1828*, pp. 97–120; *ibid., 1829*, p. 79; *African Repository*, III (August 1827), 186–87; IX (May 1833 and January 1834), 91, 349; XI (December 1835), 371; Staudenraus, *African Colonization Movement*, 136, 170, 186; Merkel, "Antislavery Movement in Missouri," 37–38, 80.

abandonment." They also demanded that legal steps be taken to ensure the Negro's rightful place in American society.[62]

The second movement was conducted by a small number of *gradual emancipationists*, who tended to be either incorporationist or colonizationist in outlook. The *incorporationists*, who represented only a small proportion of gradual emancipationists, were utterly opposed to slavery itself, condemned it as being inconsistent with the Declaration of Independence and the Christian religion, and sought to abolish it gradually. Since they were convinced that justice could not be done to the Negro through emancipation alone, and inasmuch as they were opposed to making expatriation a condition of freedom, the incorporationists urged that steps be taken to prepare the enslaved Negro for assimilation into society as a full and permanent citizen of the United States.[63]

The *colonizationists* were also opposed to slavery in principle and sought to abolish it gradually. But they did not think it would be possible or desirable to incorporate the emancipated slave into American society. Many colonizationists, particularly the Quakers, were genuinely concerned with the welfare of the free Negro and had learned from long experience that most Southern states failed to provide the legal and social immunities that would protect him from abuse, degradation, and probable re-enslavement. Moreover, a large number of colonizationists were profoundly skeptical of the Negro's capacity for moral and intellectual growth, and they asserted that such an "inferior" being could not be peaceably incorporated into society. Many colonizationists were also persuaded that the free Negro was a fruitful source of lawlessness and crime, of social and political insecurity; and others were afraid that the free Negro would ultimately seek social and political equality with the whites and that amalgamation would be the inevitable result of his continued residence in the United States. Colonizationists therefore

[62] Kentucky Anti-Slavery Society, *Proceedings*, 1835, pp. 1–2, 6; the quotation is on pages 1–2. See also James G. Birney, *Letter on Colonization* . . . (New York, 1834) and James Duncan, *A Treatise on Slavery* (Vevay, Ind., 1824), which exemplify the most radical expressions of antislavery sentiment ever uttered by Southern abolitionists.

[63] For typical incorporationist writings see David Barrow, *Involuntary, Unmerited, Perpetual, Absolute, Hereditary Slavery Examined* . . . (Lexington, 1808); "To the People of Tennessee, *GUE*, July 1822; John Rankin, *Letters on American Slavery* (Boston, 1833); O'Kelly, *Essay on Negro Slavery*.

generally insisted that the free Negro be removed from the South immediately after manumission.[64]

The third movement was carried on by *deportationists.* A few of these persons sincerely believed that the deportation of the free Negro would eventually lead to the ultimate abolition of slavery, which they regarded as being contrary to every principle of morality and religion. But the overwhelming majority of deportationists neither opposed slavery in principle nor sought to abolish it. Instead, they opposed only the evil effects the white man had to endure when slavery was not properly controlled. Moreover, they were principally interested in liberating themselves from the threats inherent in the rapidly multiplying Negro population. Unlike the colonizationists and the few deportationists who genuinely supported gradual abolition, the great majority of deportationists—who were in most cases members of the American Colonization Society—constantly asserted that their only purpose was to rid the country of an unwanted free Negro population. They carefully and openly disclaimed any intention whatever of interfering with the rights of property or of promoting the abolition of slavery; and they declared that such a purpose would be incompatible with the interests the deportation movement was designed to promote. They therefore limited their "antislavery" activity to the deportation of Negroes who were already free or who might be freed for the purpose of deportation.[65]

William H. Roane, one of the leaders of the "antislavery" faction in the Virginia legislature during the slavery debate of 1832, was typical of many deportationists. During the debate Roane asserted that he would never go into abstract questions concerning "the metaphysical doctrines of the natural equality of man, or the abstract moral right of slavery." He emphatically stated that

[64] See the following, which are representative colonizationist writings: "Letter from Jeremiah Hubbard of Guilford County, North Carolina . . . to a Friend in England," *African Repository,* X (April 1834), 33–43; Paxton, *Letters on Slavery;* "Address of Moses Swaim to the General Association," Wagstaff (ed.), *Minutes,* 124–33.

[65] See the following, which are typical deportationist writings: "Resolution of the Powhatan Colonization Society to the General Assembly of Virginia, 1829," *African Repository,* V (March 1829), 15–23; "Address of James T. Morehead to the Kentucky State Colonization Society, January, 1834," Kentucky State Colonization Society, *Annual Report, 1834,* pp. 13–32; and an extract from the Leesburg, (Va.) *Genius of Liberty* in *GUE,* November 1821; see also ACS, *Annual Report, 1828,* pp. 14–19; *ibid., 1833,* xiii–xvi; *African Repository,* VI (September 1830), 193–209; VIII (January 1833), 331–36; ACPAS, *Minutes, 1818,* pp. 47–54, 60–68.

he had never "revolted at the idea or practice of slavery . . . . It has existed," he declared, "and ever will exist, in all ages, in some form, and to some degree." Moreover, he asserted that history, experience, observation, and reason had taught him "that the torch of liberty has ever burnt brightest when surrounded by the dark and filthy, yet nutritious atmosphere of slavery." He also insisted that he did not "believe in that Fan-faronade about the natural equality of man." Indeed, he said: "I do not believe that all men are *by nature* equal, or that it is in the power of human art to make them so. I no more believe that the flat-nosed, woolly-headed black native of the deserts of *Africa*, is equal to the straight-haired white man of Europe, than I believe that the stupid, scentless greyhound is equal to the noble, generous dog of *Newfoundland*." Roane therefore stated that he would support "a *slow, gradual, certain,* and energetic system for the removal of all *emancipated* or *purchased* slaves from the Commonwealth, till the *ratio of population* between them and the whites, attains, at least, that equilibrium, which, in all future time, will give to every *white man* in the State, that *certain* assurance that *this* is *his* country . . . and . . . that his SLAVE IS HIS OWN PROPERTY."[66] Thus he would support the deportation of the free Negro and, if absolutely necessary, allow the state to purchase and remove enough slaves to reduce the threat to white supremacy. Beyond that he would not go.[67]

Roane's attitude could hardly be called "antislavery." But it accurately reflects the nature of the position many so-called "antislavery" Southerners adopted during the nineteenth century. Before the organization of the American Colonization Society in 1816 the antislavery movement in the upper South was dominated by men who were fundamentally dedicated to the gradual abolition of slavery. Thoroughly convinced that all men were equally entitled to freedom in the social order and that slavery was utterly inconsistent with the Christian ethic, a handful of incorporation-

[66] This discussion of Roane's position is based upon an extract from the Richmond *Enquirer*, February 4, 1832, which is quoted in Robert, *Road from Monticello*, 80–81.

[67] See also James McDowell, Jr., *Speech of James M'Dowell, Jr., . . . in the House of Delegates of Virginia, on the Slave Question* (Richmond, 1832); Philip A. Bolling, *The Speeches of Philip A. Bolling . . . in the House of Delegates of Virginia, on the Policy of the State in Relation to Her Colored Population* (Richmond, 1832); Charles James Faulkner, *The Speech of Charles James Faulkner . . . in the House of Delegates of Virginia, on the Policy of the State with Respect to Her Slave Population* (Richmond, 1832).

ists and a few colonizationists struggled against overwhelming opposition in their attempts to exterminate slavery. But as the nineteenth century advanced, death and wholesale emigration systematically stripped the gradual emancipation movement of its most radical leaders and loyal supporters. As a consequence, the antislavery movement was left in the hands of an increasing number of Roane-type deportationists. Under their leadership the movement lost much of its essential character as an *abolitionist* crusade and was ironically transformed into an undertaking that was in essence *deportationist, proslavery,* and *anti-Negro*.

After 1816 a few abolitionists, immediate and gradual, continued to oppose slavery in a radical manner; and some deportationists genuinely regarded their activity as a means of promoting the ultimate extinction of slavery. But a large majority of deportationists absolutely denied that they, under the specious pretext of removing a "vicious" and "noxious" population, were secretly undermining the rights of property and declared that they would withdraw their support from the deportation movement if such charges could be proved.[68] Any deportationist who admitted such a purpose would be a "base traitor" to the movement and its "worst enemy." Such an individual, they asserted, should be tried by "an outraged community" and, if found guilty, should be branded as "a traitor to his country and the cause of humanity."[69] Deportationists who shared these views probably contributed some support to the gradual abolition movement in the upper South before 1840, but they did so inadvertently and in violation of their most cherished convictions.

Since Roane-type deportationists played an increasingly larger role in the antislavery movement in the upper slave states during the nineteenth century, historians need to be extremely cautious when making generalizations about the extent to which *antislavery* sentiment actually existed in the upper South. Many mistakes in historical judgment can be avoided if scholars will make a clear-cut distinction between Southerners who were *genuinely opposed to the principle of slavery itself* and those who were *opposed only to the adverse effects white men had to endure when slavery was not properly controlled.*

If this distinction is made, historians are not likely to make the

[68] For example, see "Memorial of the Auxiliary Society of Powhatan County, Virginia, to the General Assembly of Virginia," in Philip Slaughter, *The Virginian History of African Colonization* (Richmond, 1855), 16–17.
[69] Quoted, *ibid.,* 25–26.

dubious claim that there was a widespread antislavery movement in the upper South before the so-called "Great Reaction of the 1830's." Instead, they will see that there were at various times and places in the upper slave states a minute number of abolitionists who advocated the immediate abolition of slavery, a few incorporationists who promoted the gradual abolition of slavery and the incorporation of the Negro into American society, and a somewhat larger number of colonizationists who supported programs for gradual abolition when they were accompanied by the immediate removal of the liberated Negro from the South. At no time in the history of the upper South did these persons represent more than a small fraction of the white population. Furthermore, only a small number of feeble and thinly scattered abolition societies ever existed in the upper slave states. These organizations never achieved more than a tenuous existence, they were generally dominated by Southerners who urged that the Negro be removed from the South immediately upon manumission, they were in most instances confined to geographical localities where the use of slave labor was relatively limited in scope, and they never received any substantial support from non-Quakers. Most Southern churchmen with a proclivity for humanitarian reform usually became deportationists and joined the American Colonization Society.

This organization received a considerable amount of support in the upper South. But its influence was principally limited to areas where relatively large numbers of persons were engaged in non-agricultural employment, to counties where the number of Negroes often exceeded 40 per cent of the total population, and to other areas where white Southerners were especially apprehensive about the deleterious influence of slavery on the white man. Although the Colonization Society managed to establish a substantial number of auxiliary deportation societies in the upper South, these organizations were quite small, they were dominated by slaveholders and those who had a profound aversion to the Negro, most of them usually languished a short time after they were formed, and they were most active in times of real or imagined threats of insurrection.

REVISIONISTS VS. ABOLITIONISTS: THE HISTORIOGRAPHICAL COLD WAR OF THE 1930s AND 1940s

Betty L. Fladeland

When Charles M. Andrews gave his 1925 presidential address to the American Historical Association on the subject of the American Revolution, he began by defending his choice of topic on grounds of "the pleasure that comes from harping on an old string."[1] I defend my harping on my old string of antislavery by saying it was not my decision. Professor Robert McColley convinced me that as one of the oldest survivors of the antislavery historians, I owed it to the younger generation to recount something of the course of antislavery history which reached a point of take-off when Gilbert H. Barnes and Dwight L. Dumond discovered the Weld-Grimké and the Birney letters and published them in the 1930s. This paper, then, is something of a subjective, personal approach, starting with things I was told by Professor Dumond with whom I did my Ph.D. at the University of Michigan.

It is hard to believe that, academically speaking, Ulrich B. Phillips was my grandparent for, paradoxically, it was his work on slavery that stimulated the antislavery studies that followed. In his graduate

Ms. Fladeland is recently retired from the Department of History at Southern Illinois University at Carbondale. This paper was delivered on July 26, 1985, as the presidential address of the Society for Historians of the Early American Republic during its seventh annual conference at Gunston Hall, Lorton, Virginia.

[1] Charles M. Andrews, "The American Revolution: An Interpretation," *American Historical Review*, 31 (Jan. 1926), 219-232, quotation, 219. I wish to thank Professors Thomas D. Clark, Richard N. Current, Merton L. Dillon, John Hope Franklin, Paul Gaston, LeRoy P. Graff, Robert G. Gunderson, Robert Johannsen, August Meier, Thomas J. Pressly, James W. Silver, Kenneth M. Stampp, A. Elizabeth Taylor, C. Vann Woodward, and James Harvey Young for responding to my queries in preparation of this paper.

JOURNAL OF THE EARLY REPUBLIC, 6 (Spring 1986). © Society for Historians of the Early American Republic.

seminar at Michigan in the late 1920s, two of the students were Barnes and Dumond who, according to Dumond, began to react against what they considered Phillips' too sympathetic portrayal of slavery in the Old South and his dismissal of the abolitionists as critics who knew not of what they spoke. However, Merton Dillon, who has just completed a study of Phillips, has evidence that as early as 1915 Phillips had approved an outline for Barnes's study of the antislavery movement.[2] Historians Fred Landon and Wendell Stephenson have asserted that it was Phillips himself who urged Barnes to make his study, having long believed that the history of the antislavery movement needed revision.[3] Perhaps Phillips and Barnes were more compatible in their thinking than Phillips and Dumond, but I am inclined to think that Dumond's differences of interpretation from those of his mentor developed later in the 1930s.[4]

In any case, Barnes and Dumond decided to collaborate in their search for more raw material on the antislavery movement, so they made lists of all the abolitionists they could identify and began systematically to track down family descendants. As we know, their persistence paid off handsomely. They found not one, but two, amazing and related collections. It was Barnes who experienced the excitement of opening a trunk in a farmhouse attic in Massachusetts which contained the fading letters of Theodore Weld, Angelina Grimké Weld, and her sister, Sarah Grimké. Meanwhile Dumond was on the trail of the descendants of James G. Birney, whose only daughter, Florence, had married into a Michigan family by the name of Jennison. The trail eventually led to a house in Bay City where an elderly woman, in response to inquiries, allowed that they had some boxes with ''old

---

[2] G. H. Barnes to U. B. Phillips, Nov. 21, 1915, Phillips Papers (Sterling Library, Yale University, New Haven, Conn.).

[3] Fred Landon, ''Ulrich Bonnell Phillips: Historian of the South,'' *Journal of Southern History*, 5 (Aug. 1939), 364-371; and Wendell H. Stephenson, ''A Half Century of Southern Historical Scholarship,'' *ibid.*, 11 (Feb. 1945), 3-32, esp. 23-26.

[4] Dillon tells me that in 1929 when Phillips declined a professorship at Cornell he suggested Barnes for the position. But when Phillips moved to Yale in 1930 he expressed satisfaction that Dumond was chosen to succeed him at Michigan. Phillips to Arthur Aiton, Mar. 21, 1930, Misc. MSS. (Clements Library, University of Michigan, Ann Arbor, Mich.). In this letter, Phillips said he hoped the Michigan Department of History would add Barnes to the staff as well. In an earlier letter it appears that Avery Craven had been Phillips' first choice. Phillips to Claude Van Tyne, Aug. 8, 1929, Van Tyne Papers (Bentley Library, University of Michigan). See also Phillips to Craven, Feb. 23, 1933 (Dunn Library, Simpson College, Indianola, Iowa), which suggests that Michigan did make an offer to Craven. I am indebted to Merton Dillon for referring me to these letters.

stuff'' in them, she didn't know just what. Under the basement steps they found a large wooden box filled with the Birney papers.

But once Mrs. Jennison realized that she was the possessor of valuable historical documents, she was reluctant to let go of them. It took all of Dumond's diplomacy and charm to persuade her what an important contribution she could make to American history if she allowed the material to be deposited at the University of Michigan. Learning in the course of their conversation that she was a great admirer of Senator Albert Beveridge of Indiana, Dumond's strategy was to ask the American Historical Association to finance publication of the Birney letters through its Beveridge Fund, and quite pleased at this tie between the Birney and Beveridge families, Mrs. Jennison capitulated.[5] The papers were deposited at the William L. Clements Library of the University of Michigan where Professor Dumond could keep an eye on them and on any scholars who came to use them.

As most of you know, the publication of the *Weld-Grimké Letters* in 1934 and the *Birney Letters* in 1938 added a whole new dimension to the history of the antislavery movement by informing us of the role of New York and the West and of western leaders.[6] Assimilating the opinions and attitudes of Theodore Weld, the Tappan brothers, the Grimké sisters, James G. Birney, Henry Stanton, and a host of their correspondents, the two editors concluded not only that William Lloyd Garrison's leadership had been much overemphasized, but that his belligerent manner had done more harm than good for the cause. They succumbed to the all-too-human tactic of elevating their own new heroes by putting down Garrison. The result was that they stimulated a major historical war over Garrison's role.

Of more historiographical significance for the immediate period of the 1930s and 1940s, Barnes and Dumond had reopened an old question that dated back to the antebellum period itself: were the abolitionists fanatics and therefore outside the mainstream of American society, or were they reformers who operated much as did leaders of other reform movements such as those for temperance, labor, or free public education? Inherent in this argument was the idea which became

---

[5] The papers were legally owned by George Birney Jennison, who agreed to the arrangement. The negotiations to have the Weld-Grimké letters deposited at the Clements Library were also carried on by Dumond, not Barnes. See exchanges between Dumond and L. D. Weld, Mar. 8, Apr. 13, 18, June 7, Sept. 1, 1939, Dec. 17, 1940, Jan. 21, 1941, Dumond Papers (Bentley Library).

[6] Gilbert H. Barnes and Dwight L. Dumond, eds., *Letters of Theodore Dwight Weld, Angelina Grimké Weld and Sarah Grimké, 1822-1844* (2 vols., New York 1934); Dwight L. Dumond, ed., *Letters of James Gillespie Birney, 1831-1857* (2 vols., New York 1938).

the thesis of the revisionist historians: that abolitionist fanaticism, not slavery itself, accounted for the northern vs. southern hysteria and hatred that made it impossible to settle sectional disputes peaceably. While they conceded that southern "fire-eaters" were extremists also, they held the antislavery crusaders chiefly responsible because they were the inciters, the fire-eaters only the responders to northern attacks.

Revisionists found support for their side in Barnes's and Dumond's emphasis on Garrisonian extremism and, ironically, neglected the very point Barnes and Dumond were trying to convey: the relative insignificance of the Garrisonian radicals as compared with the moderate, mainstream Weld-Tappan-Birney group. True, the revisionists noted the distinction in the reviews they wrote as the Weld-Grimké and Birney letters were published, but in their writings about the "blundering generation" that allowed the Civil War to happen, it was Garrison who still emerged most often as one of their models of an abolitionist. I say "one of" because they gained from Barnes and Dumond a second abolitionist model who, though different from Garrison, served the revisionists' purpose equally well: the religious zealot of the Great Revival who applied his own moral proscriptions to slavery and became dedicated to imposing his values on the South. Charles W. Ramsdell praised Barnes's *The Antislavery Impulse* for "throw[ing] a bright light upon the origins and character of the abolition crusade," some of whose leaders "looked forward with pious exaltation to the prospect of civil war with 'the stealers of men.' "[7]

Merle Curti, not a revisionist and certainly sympathetic to the antislavery cause, wrote in his review of the *Weld-Grimké Letters* that, "From these letters it is clear that the abolitionists were intelligent, high-minded and morally courageous," but he observed that they failed not only to understand the southern point of view, they also failed to understand each other. "And," he concluded, "at times these religious and moral zealots were almost morbid in their mutual criticisms and their self-analyses," thus foreshadowing the psychohistorical approach of a later generation, some of whom branded the abolitionists as neurotic or psychotic misfits.[8]

---

[7] Gilbert Hobbs Barnes, *The Antislavery Impulse, 1830-1844* (New York 1933); Charles W. Ramsdell, "The Changing Interpretation of the Civil War," *Journal of Southern History*, 3 (Feb. 1937), 3-27, quotation, 16.

[8] Curti's review of the *Weld-Grimké Letters* is in the *Journal of Southern History*, 1 (May 1935), 224-226. For an example of a book portraying the abolitionist leaders as having martyr complexes, see Hazel Catherine Wolf, *On Freedom's Altar: The Martyr Complex in the Abolition Movement* (Madison 1952).

While Arthur C. Cole suggested that perhaps Barnes labored with too much "gusto" to displace Garrison, his reading of *The Antislavery Impulse* convinced him that even so Barnes admitted Garrison's "real and persistent influence." Avery Craven seems to have accepted Barnes's conclusion that Garrison was a "hindering factor" in the antislavery movement. He advised that the book deserved serious attention although it was over-simplified and "a bit overdrawn," adding that "iconoclasts are inclined that way." Apparently Craven was reluctant to relinquish his radical model. James G. Randall's review hailed Barnes's book as "the revisionist interpretation of the antislavery crusade," and in 1937, when he published his *Civil War and Reconstruction*, he claimed in a footnote that his account of the antisalvery movement was based on the revisionist point of view as presented by Barnes and Dumond.[9] A source of the claim that Barnes was himself a revisionist lay in his introduction to the *Weld-Grimké Letters* where he summarizes the translation of antislavery opinion into political power. He describes how insurgent antislavery congressmen eventually formed a bloc which became the nucleus of a new movement in national affairs. "Session by session," Barnes observed, "their numbers grew, and upon each issue with an antislavery aspect they spoke with increasing authority for the abolition host. Inevitably they divided their party and the nation."[10]

What the revisionists did not pick up, and neither did Thomas Pressly when he classified Barnes as a revisionist in *Americans Interpret Their Civil War,* was an important distinction: while Barnes was critical of some abolitionists, he looked on "his" abolitionists positively. "Their names make up a roll of heroes," he affirmed admiringly. William G. McLoughlin's interpretation of Barnes in his introduction to the 1964 edition of *The Antislavery Impulse* corroborates Dumond's statements to me of Barnes's growing sympathy for the antislavery people he was learning to know and for their cause.[11] Since Barnes was an economist, it was natural that he began his thinking on sectional differences with an economic interpretation, but he moved to a recognition of religion

---

[9] Cole's review is in the *Mississippi Valley Historical Review*, 21 (June 1934), 96-98; Craven's is in the New York *Herald Tribune* Book Review Section, April 22, 1934; and Randall's is in the *Journal of Southern History*, 1 (Feb. 1935), 96-98; see also J. G. Randall, *The Civil War and Reconstruction* (Boston 1937), 102n.

[10] Barnes and Dumond, eds., *Weld-Grimké Letters*, I, xvi.

[11] Thomas J. Pressly, *Americans Interpret Their Civil War* (Princeton 1954), 268-270; Barnes and Dumond, eds., *Weld-Grimké Letters*, I, xvii; Barnes, *The Antislavery Impulse* (New York 1964), vii-xxx; McLouglin to Dumond, Jan. 25, 1964, Dumond Papers (Bentley Library).

as furnishing the major impulse of the antislavery movement. A last piece of evidence for Barnes's increasing identification with the abolitionists is the review he wrote of Arthur Young Lloyd's book, *The Slavery Controversy*. Lloyd was a student of Frank Owsley, one of the Old South's most ardent defenders, with no use at all for abolitionists. "Unfortunately," Barnes criticized, "the author's selection and interpretation of documents . . . are not always such as to establish confidence in his conclusions." He charged Lloyd with using sources out of context and of choosing the most extreme examples that were not representative of any but the "lunatic fringe" of the abolitionists. Moreover, on the biblical argument over slavery, Barnes went on, "the author's sympathies are even more dangerously engaged." All of Lloyd's abolitionists were infidels, anarchists, and free-lovers. And here Barnes repeated his belief that, on the contrary, most of them were "embodiments of Christian piety."[12]

Although Barnes lived until 1945 he wrote nothing more and never engaged the revisionists in debate. That was left for Dumond who, to a greater degree than his older colleague, had enshrined the abolitionists in his pantheon of heroes. Although he termed them, as well as the fire-eaters, extremists, and gave in his lectures what was basically the revisionist version of emotions engendering the war spirit, there was no doubt about where he believed the blame for the war really lay. His argument was that the first step toward sectional conflict was taken when the South suppressed free discussion of the slavery question. Free discussion might have led to gradual emancipation, or at least "would have prevented the political contest . . . from becoming sectional in character." War would not have come, Dumond concluded, "had the South shown the slightest disposition to reason." But the slave system had become so rooted that its adherents were willing to plunge the nation into "internecine strife" to preserve it.[13]

His indictment of the South quickly provoked the full wrath, first of southern historians such as Frank Owsley, J. G. de Roulhac Hamilton, Charles W. Ramsdell, and E. Merton Coulter, and second of northern revisionists, Craven and Randall. You will notice that I categorize Craven as a northern historian, for that is what he was, contrary to popular assumption. True, he was born in North Carolina, but only because at the time of his birth his mother was visiting relatives there, but then returned home to Iowa. As a matter of fact, Craven

---

[12] Arthur Young Lloyd, *The Slavery Controversy, 1831-1860* (Chapel Hill 1939); review by Barnes in *Journal of Southern History*, 6 (May 1940), 271-273.

[13] Dwight Lowell Dumond, *Antislavery Origins of the Civil War in the United States* (Ann Arbor 1939), 84, 121, 130.

was descended from Quaker forebears who had moved out of North Carolina because of their objections to slavery—a bit of information which makes Craven's attitude toward the abolitionists even more paradoxical and interesting.[14]

Dumond's unequivocal denunciation of the South hit with something of a shock effect because up to that time his credentials had been good as far as southern and revisionist historians were concerned. His dissertation on the secession movement, written under the direction of U. B. Phillips, was published in 1931 and was followed within the year by his edited work, *Southern Editorials on Secession*.[15] Reviewers noted that Dumond seemed to put the responsibility for secession on the Republicans more than on any other group because of their refusal to compromise and their failure to reassure the South that its constitutional rights would be recognized. One can only smile now at Roulhac Hamilton's praise of *The Secession Movement*: "The study is an excellently documented narrative and . . . there is manifest in it, fairly clearly, strong sympathy with the point of view of the South in the period treated."[16] In his preface Dumond had written, "It has been my constant concern to detach myself from the tradition that the Civil War was irrepressible."[17] When the Southern Historical Association was organized in 1934 and its *Journal* established in 1935, Dumond was among those chosen for its first Board of Editors. But between the early 1930s when he was working on secession, and 1938-39 when he published the *Birney Letters* followed by his *Antislavery Origins of the Civil War*, Dumond had been immersed in abolitionist materials and had become nothing less than a convert to the cause, with all the zeal of a convert.

It would be misleading to give the impression that vitriolic exchanges began only with Barnes's and Dumond's work on the antislavery movement. They entered the lists in the midst of fierce disagreements over a set of essays written by twelve southerners and published in 1930 as the book, *I'll Take My Stand*. The essays extolled the virtues of the agricultural South before it had been corrupted by northern capitalism. The group, known as the Nashville Fugitives and centered at Vanderbilt, included, along with major southern poets,

---

[14] Avery Craven to Merton Dillon, Jan. 1, 1970, in possession of the addressee.
[15] Dwight Lowell Dumond, *The Secession Movement, 1860-1861* (New York 1931); and *Southern Editorials on Secession* (New York 1931), which won the first award for publication given by the American Historical Association's Beveridge Fund Committee.
[16] *Mississippi Valley Historical Review*, 19 (Dec. 1932), 430-432. See also *American Historical Review*, 37 (July 1932), 772-773, for review by Frank Maloy Anderson.
[17] Dumond, *Secession Movement*, v.

two historians, Frank Owsley and H. C. Nixon. Rupert B. Vance at the University of North Carolina declared *I'll Take My Stand* to be a "poetic and passionate attack" which ignored facts, once again put the blame on the Yankees, and if its advice were to be followed would "lead a return to the abyss."[18] Among historians who came down hard on the book was William Hesseltine at the University of Wisconsin, himself southern born. He termed the Fugitives "the Young Confederates," who "in the most humorless series of essays that has been published for many a day, take up the cudgels in defense of the agrarian tradition." "At no time in its history . . . ," Hesseltine snorted, "has the American South been other than a horrible example of the spiritual failure of agrarianism." He went back to one of the old abolitionist contentions that the antebellum South had produced no great sculptors, poets, or architects; and philosophers, scholars, and thinkers were "pitifully few." It had produced politicians and army officers in abundance—men whose careers were directed into "anti-social channels," "not particularly worthy of praise."[19] These debates regarding an accurate portrayal of the Old South comprised the matrix out of which also emerged the new controversy over the abolitionists and their role in the coming of the Civil War. A current southern scholar, Joel Williamson, in his recent book, *The Crucible of Race*, refers to the 1920s and 1930s as a time when southerners "imagined a past that never was," and had covered over its "profound fissures" with "a heavy plastering of myth."[20]

To go back to my statement about harping on an old string, let me remind you that a harp has forty-six strings; and the rival historical camps found at least that many to pluck, often using the pedals to produce half-tones as well. And some, one must admit, remind one of harpies rather than harpists, using their talons to seize the food of their victims and to carry off the souls of the dead. It was the vigor of the contest that led to the founding of the Southern Historical Association in 1934; and the meetings of that organization as well as those of the Mississippi Valley Historical Association abounded in programs

---

[18] Twelve Southerners, *I'll Take My Stand: The South and the Agrarian Tradition* (New York 1930); review by Rupert B. Vance in *Mississippi Valley Historical Review*, 18 (June 1931), 116-117.

[19] Hesseltine's review appeared originally in the *Sewanee Review*, 39 (Jan.-Mar. 1931), 97-103, and is reprinted in Richard N. Current, ed., *Sections and Politics: Selected Essays by William B. Hesseltine* (Madison 1968), 3-11.

[20] Joel Williamson, *The Crucible of Race: Black-White Relations in the American South Since Emancipation* (New York 1984), 459-460.

devoted to the ongoing debates. It seems particularly ironic that the very historians who were so vehemently denouncing the emotional extremism which led to the Civil War in 1861 were now themselves becoming so emotional that they provoked their own civil war within the profession.

Frank Owsley led off against Dumond in his review of the *Birney Letters*. While praising the editorial work, he found Dumond's "conception of the slavery controversy" to be "lacking in scope and in objectivity." "Indeed, one feels," said Owsley, "that the editor has become a member of the Weld-Grimké-Tappan-Finney Holy Band." He "completely failed to comprehend the Southern situation with reference to slavery." E. Merton Coulter followed in much the same vein in reviewing *Antislavery Origins*, pronouncing it "as uncompromising in position and as dogmatic in statement as the abolitionists whom it seeks to explain and defend." Coulter was particularly horrified by Dumond's sentence, "Would that the historian might somehow recover the emotions which surge through men's hearts and alter civilizations"—a statement Coulter took to mean praise for the emotional appeals of the abolitionists and a call for the same approach on the part of historians. Likewise, he was insulted by Dumond's labeling the South "intellectually moribund" because of its violations of freedom of speech and press, which Coulter denied.[21] Not surprisingly, Carter G. Woodson had only praise for Dumond's *Birney Letters*; and James B. Browning, also writing for the *Journal of Negro History*, had equal praise for Dumond's *Antislavery Origins* as "a crowning achievement, in courageous interpretation of new material" which told historians they "have not justification for ignoring abolition literature," or concentrating only on plantation records.[22]

Meanwhile Arthur C. Cole of Ohio State University also became a target of the defenders of the Old South. In a session of the MVHA in 1930 he and Roulhac Hamilton crossed swords over whether or not Lincoln's election had been an "immediate menace" to the South. Hamilton said yes, because Lincoln and the Republican party had been abolitionized, and he quoted with evident relish a statement of Caleb Cushing's that described the abolitionists as "monomaniacs of ferocious philanthropy, teachers and preachers of assassination and

---

[21] Owsley's review is in the *Journal of Southern History*, 5 (May 1939), 263-264; Coulter's in *ibid.*, 6 (May 1940), 270-271.

[22] For the Woodson and Browning reviews see *Journal of Negro History*, 24 (Jan. 1939), 113-114, and 25 (Jan. 1940), 120-122.

treason." Hamilton was quite ready to accept the *DeBow's Review* definition of Yankees as "that species of the human race who foster in their
hearts lying, hypocrisy, deceit, and treason."[23]

Charles W. Ramsdell supported Hamilton's position in his review
of Coles's book, *The Irrepressible Conflict*. His verdict was that it "betrays
an attitude too closely akin to that of the anti-slavery propagandists
of 1860." Moreover, in his presidential address to the SHA in 1936,
Ramsdell contended that U. B. Phillips had "thoroughly exploded the
abolitionist charge that the slave was systematically or usually over-
worked or otherwise treated with brutality," and that Phillips' work
was "so conclusive that it would be impossible for any respectable
historian today to describe the institution as did von Holst or Rhodes."[24]
Ramsdell was spared living through the 1960s, but he surely must
have been dismayed by the appearance, the year after his speech, of
Bell Wiley's first book, *Southern Negroes, 1861-1865*. Although a
southerner and a student of Phillips at Yale, like Barnes and Dumond
before him, Wiley began to veer away from the traditional Phillips
line. He refuted the stereotype of the loyal slave, showing that during
the war most of them fled if they had a chance, or in other ways
demonstrated attitudes of greater independence. In short, "the faithful
slave of postwar panegyrics was almost wholly fictional."[25]

While not completely satisfied with Wiley's treatment of blacks,
Charles H. Wesley and Carter Woodson were quick to praise his study
as being in advance of most historical literature in presenting the truth
rather than in perpetuating preconceived ideas and traditions. Thomas
Robson Hay, a northern historian, welcomed Wiley's support for the
old abolitionist claims and threw a satirical barb at historians "whose
idealistic conceptions derived from inheritance or self-delusion" were
now destroyed by Wiley's shattering of the old "shibboleth of slave
loyalty." Francis B. Simkins, a southern historian, accepted Wiley's
thoroughly researched evidence, including "that the master was as
capable of disloyalty to the accepted obligations of slavery as were the

---

[23] Report of Annual Meeting, *Mississippi Valley Historical Review*, 17 (Sept. 1930),
300-311. The papers by Cole and Hamilton, both under the title "Lincoln's Election
an Immediate Menace to Slavery in the States?," were published in the *American
Historical Review*, 36 (July 1931), 740-767, and 37 (July 1932), 700-711, quotations,
702, 710.
[24] Arthur Charles Cole, *The Irrepressible Conflict, 1850-1865* (New York 1934).
For Ramsdell's review see *Mississippi Valley Historical Review*, 21 (Sept. 1934), 279-281;
Ramsdell, "The Changing Interpretation of the Civil War," 3-27, quotation, 13.
[25] Bell Irvin Wiley, *Southern Negroes, 1861-1865* (New York 1938). The quotation
is from the Report of the Annual Meeting, *Journal of Southern History*, 5 (Feb. 1939), 67.

slaves themselves," but his phrasing implies that slaves had acquiesced in some form of contractual agreement.[26]

Historians defensive of the Old South sustained still another shock in 1940 when Clement Eaton's *Freedom of Thought in the Old South* supported Dumond's contention of censorship, and it was necessary to add Eaton's name to that of Wiley as a renegade in his own section. As Owsley had objected to Dumond's claims of suppression of free speech and publication, he now confronted Eaton's. "It did not seem to occur to Mr. Eaton," he retaliated, "that the abolitionists and their political allies were threatening the existence of the South as seriously as the Nazis threaten the existence of England, and that their language was so violent, obscene, and insulting that even Dr. Goeb[b]els in all his flights has seldom equaled and never surpassed it." "Mr. Eaton returns periodically to his thesis in a manner reminding one of the air compressor on a streetcar, which breaks out every now and then, even when the car is sitting quietly on a sidetrack, and pumps furiously for no apparent reason."[27] R. S. Cotterill seemed to admit the censorship of free speech by joining Owsley in defending the need to rein in the abolitionists on grounds of public danger: "[Cassius] Clay and Birney were neither debaters nor critics; they were purveyors of vituperation and abuse and they were dealt with as such. . . . Those who were suppressed were the inciters of servile insurrection, the advocates of slave confiscation, and the preachers of racial equality."[28]

On the pro-abolitionist side, Merle Curti was distressed by Ralph V. Harlow's lack of objectivity in his portrayal of the antislavery leaders as presented in his biography of Gerrit Smith: he was "influenced by an underlying assumption . . . that the abolitionists were specialists in exaggeration and abuse, lacking brain power and wisdom, and unpardonably devoid of a sense of humor wherever the slave was concerned."[29] Carter Woodson was bitterly disappointed that U. B. Phillips' unfinished *Course of the South to Secession*, edited by E. M. Coulter, still clung to the old interpretation so blinded by sectional bias.[30] But more controversial than either of those was Arthur Young

---

[26] See Carter Woodson's review in *Journal of Negro History*, 23 (July 1938), 370-371; Charles H. Wesley's in *American Historical Review*, 44 (Apr. 1939), 657-658; Thomas Robson Hay's in *Journal of Southern History*, 4 (Nov. 1938), 530-531; and Francis B. Simkins' in *Mississippi Valley Historical Review*, 25 (Dec. 1938), 425-426.

[27] Clement Eaton, *Freedom of Thought in the Old South* (Durham 1940); Owsley's review in *Journal of Southern History*, 6 (Nov. 1940), 558-559.

[28] *Mississippi Valley Historical Review*, 27 (Sept. 1940), 299-300.

[29] *Ibid.*, 26 (Sept. 1939), 267-268.

[30] *Journal of Negro History*, 25 (Apr. 1940), 238-239.

Lloyd's *The Slavery Controversy*. Carter Woodson declared that it "could have been written in 1870 by R. M. T. Hunter or James M. Mason." "Hitler and his Aryans," he was persuaded, "will doubtless be glad to have such justification for their racialism. The author lost time studying modern historiography except so far as he has learned to prostitute it to propoganda."[31] Woodson was pointedly responding to Owsley's reference to the Nazis and turning the argument on its head. Hesseltine unleashed his charactristic acerbity on Lloyd: "If Dr. Lloyd does not quite defend slavery, he certainly defends the southern defenders. The volume comes very near satisfying the well-known southern desire to have the truth of history told from the southern stand-point."[32] The veteran author of *Parties and Slavery*, Theodore Clarke Smith, reviewed Lloyd's and Dumond's books as a pair and called a plague on both for their biases.[33]

Craven's answer to Arthur Cole's *The Irrepressible Conflict*, and at the same time his rebuttal of Dumond, was contained in his Walter Lynwood Fleming lectures, published in 1939 as *The Repressible Conflict*. He argued that southern nationalism was defensive, stemming from the abolitionist offense, that the abolitionists—"these fanatics" he called them—who knew little of the reality of slavery, nonetheless "unrestrained by fact, were creating clear-cut pictures of slavery, slaves, slaveholders, and southern . . . life . . . ." "Slavery as a reality . . . ," he believed, "could be almost ignored in our study of sectional conflict had it not become the symbol of all sectional differences." That the war was "inevitable" or "irrepressible" "was to be an artificial creation of inflamed minds."[34] Ramsdell approvingly interpreted Craven as saying that the abolitionists had "launched into a perfect ecstasy of vilification" of slavery; while Coulter suggested that Craven had presented a new interpretation by making a "clever distinction" between the Negro and Negro slavery, holding that much that was argued against slavery was in fact inherent in the Negro. E. R. Thomas, writing for the *Journal of Negro History*, saw Craven as aspiring to do for the coming of the war what U. B. Phillips had done for plantation slavery and what Dunning did for Reconstruction. He seems to account for Craven's point of view by mentioning not only his birth in North

---

[31] *Ibid.* (Jan. 1940), 110-112.

[32] *Mississippi Valley Historical Review*, 26 (Dec. 1939), 419-421.

[33] *American Historical Review*, 45 (Apr. 1940), 663-664.

[34] Avery Craven, "The Repressible Conflict," in *An Historian and the Civil War* (Chicago 1964), 46-63, quotations on 54, 52, 46.

Carolina but also his marriage into a branch of the family of Tom Watson, the "Negro-baiting demagogue of the 'Nineties."[35]

I get the impression that Craven was being typed as a racist, was accepted in that role by Coulter, and despised for it by Thomas. In fact, it seems to me that by the mid-thirties there was something of a feud developing between Craven and the leading black historians. For the most part the work of W. E. B. DuBois, as that of Herbert Aptheker, had been dismissed out of hand by reviewers because of their Marxist orientation; but Craven went further. Writing for the *American Journal of Sociology*, Craven scorned DuBois' *Black Reconstruction* as being "in large part, only the expression of a Negro's bitterness," besides being "based on abolition propaganda and the biased statements of partisan politicians." "The temper is as bad as the sources," he criticized. "The result is not history but only a half-baked Marxian interpretation of the labor side of Reconstruction and a badly distorted picture of the Negroes' part in Southern life." In another review for the same journal, Craven dismissed Charles H. Wesley's book, *The Collapse of the Confederacy*, in eighteen lines, ending with "he [Wesley] has only demonstrated again how difficult it is for a Negro to write sanely of a period in which his race suffered such great injustice."[36]

It was a surprise to discover in the *Journal of Negro History* for 1936 an article on the proslavery argument written by Hesseltine which takes issue with Craven's insistence that the South's defense of slavery occurred only as a reaction to the antislavery crusade—a surprise because of Hesseltine's own cynical view of the abolitionists and because he has usually been considered a revisionist himself. In this article he insists that all of the proslavery arguments were in place before Garrison ever appeared, that they were formulated simultaneously with the beginnings of slavery in the colonies. He takes issue with Phillips, too, by asserting that "the real central theme of Southern history seems to have been the maintenance of the planter class in control." One wonders if this article influenced Craven's review of Hesseltine's *History of the South*, which also appeared in 1936 and which Craven pronounced

---

[35] Ramsdell's review in *Journal of Southern History*, 5 (Nov. 1939), 553-554; Coulter's in *Mississippi Valley Historical Review*, 26 (Sept. 1939), 265-266; and Thomas' in *Journal of Negro History*, 24 (July 1939), 345-348.

[36] *American Journal of Sociology*, 41 (Jan. 1936), 535-536; and 44 (Mar. 1939), 775. I am told that Craven's black students got on very well with him. There is evidence of good personal as well as professional relationships in student letters in the Craven Papers.

to be a "smug oversimplification" of the slavery controversy.[37] Woodson, on the other hand, thought it constituted a long step toward a well balanced history of the South because it took into account "all the elements of the population." Later Woodson again praised Hesseltine for not being "a partisan or propagandist" despite his birth and education in the South. He had been, Woodson reported, "belittled by the pro-slavery historians of the Lloyd-Craven school; in fact . . . literally damned" because he "violated the canons of Southern historical writing."[38]

For Woodson there was a distinct difference between Hesseltine on the one hand and Craven and Randall on the other when it came to racism. When Randall's *Civil War and Reconstruction* came out, Woodson allowed as how Randall "occasionally treats the Negro as a human being"; but he had repeatedly reiterated prejudicial, stereotypical characterizations of blacks, and had accepted Phillips' view of slavery despite the documentary refutations recently put forward by Frederic Bancroft and especially in Helen T. Catterall's multi-volumed study of judicial cases.[39]

I was again surprised when I read Craven's review of Randall for I had always coupled their names as practically indivisible, something like Mason and Dixon, never mentioned separately. Craven begins by saying that *Civil War and Reconstruction* is hard to classify although it has the "form and style" of a textbook. "Yet," he puzzled, "its

[37] William Hesseltine, "Some New Aspects of the Pro-Slavery Argument," *Journal of Negro History*, 21 (Jan. 1936), 1-14, quotation, 14. There is an interesting letter from William E. Dodd to Avery Craven. Apr. 25, 1932, Craven Papers, in which Dodd, also, dissents from Craven's assignment of so much blame to the abolitionists. He, like Hesseltine, believed that southern leaders had already decided against all "schemes" of emancipation, even gradual ones, long before the abolitionists began their attacks. The abolitionists were gadflies, Dodd conceded, but basically not the cause of anything. "However," he concludes, "I am the only southerner who has ever acknowledged this and you, like Phillips, may simply put it down to perversity." Frank Owsley confided to Craven that while he thought Dodd should have written more for the South, it was perhaps fortunate that he did not, because he had little sympathy for the Old South and such leaders as Ruffin, Calhoun, and Rhett. Sue Owsley to Craven, Apr. 27, 1933, Craven Papers. For Craven's review of Hesseltine's *History of the South* (New York 1936) see *Mississippi Valley Historical Review*, 24 (June 1937), 88-89.
[38] *Journal of Negro History*, 22 (Apr. 1937), 240-246, and 28 (Oct. 1943), 485-488. While appreciative of what Hesseltine had done, Woodson remained critical of him for presenting slavery as more benevolent and patriarchal than it actually was, and for neglecting the humanitarian motives of the abolitionists.
[39] *Journal of Negro History*, 22 (July 1937), 372-377; Frederic Bancroft, *Slave-Trading in the Old South* (Baltimore 1931); Helen Tunnicliff Catterall, ed., *Judicial Cases Concerning American Slavery and the Negro* (5 vols., Washington 1926-1937).

959 pages of plodding detail will prevent any wide use in college classes. On the other hand, it is lacking in most of the qualities supposed to attract the general reader. . . . As a study of the sectional struggle which culminated in civil war the work is quite inadequate. As a study of Reconstruction from a national angle it is sadly incomplete. The real value of the work lies, therefore, in the war period itself, an adequate treatment of which draws the book out to quite unnecessary length for any of the uses suggested."[40] Unity within the revisionist ranks was obviously a misconception on my part.

In view of all this hostility, one wonders which brave—or devilish—member of the MVHA program committee arranged a session at the Omaha meeting in 1940 that had Dumond in the chair, Lloyd reading a paper on "The Militant Abolitionists," and with Craven as one of the commentators. Unfortunately for our sense of curiosity, Professor Hesseltine stuck to the bare facts in reporting the sessions.[41] It was at that same 1940 meeting that Randall gave his presidential address on "The Blundering Generation." War is "too much dignified," he declaimed. One should rather consider "the despairing plunge, the unmotivated drift, the intruding dilemma, the blasted hope, the self-fulfilling prediction, the push-over, the twisted argument, the frustrated leader, the advocate of rule or ruin, and the reform-your-neighbor prophet." If one word had to be selected to account for the war, he concluded, it would have to be not "slavery" but "fanaticism."[42] Randall was expressing his pacifism in regard to the coming of World War II as well as the Civil War, but his phrases about the "reform-your-neighbor prophet" and not slavery but fanaticism were a hit at those in his audience whom he considered to be neo-abolitionists. He had said much the same thing in a paper at the previous November gathering of the SHA, and in both he seemed to be directly answering Dumond's *Antislavery Origins*. Randall held that it was too extreme to say that the dispute over slavery was vital to the extent of justifying war. Because so few slaves escaped, he did not think the Fugitive Slave Law could have aroused much emotion. The issue of slavery in Kansas was a fabricated one, therefore the whole question of slavery in the territories was a trivial, not a substantial one. He answered Bell Wiley even more directly by resurrecting Phillips

---

[40] *Mississippi Valley Historical Review*, 24 (Sept. 1937), 263-264.
[41] Report of the Annual Meeting, *Mississippi Valley Historical Review*, 27 (Sept. 1940), 247.
[42] J. G. Randall, "The Blundering Generation," *ibid.* (June 1940), 3-28, quotation, 11.

on the slavery issue thus: "The actual antebellum fact as to the attitude of Negro slaves toward their masters is that of docility and faithfulness . . . ."[43]

In his presidential address to the SHA that same year, Professor Owsley charged that the abolitionists, with no ifs, ands, or buts, were the fundamental cause of the Civil War. Starting in the Missouri debates they had begun the "violent, denunciatory, insulting language" that launched the "so-called" antislavery crusade, which was, "in fact," "a crusade against the southern people." "Indeed," he protested, "as far as I have been able to ascertain, neither Dr. Goebbels nor Virginio Gayda nor Stalin's propaganda agents have as yet been able to plumb the depths of vulgarity and obscenity reached and maintained by George Bourne, Stephen Foster, Wendell Phillips, Charles Sumner, and other abolitionists of note." Although insisting that they were much too indecent to quote, Owsley did cite Wendell Phillips on the South being "one great brothel."[44] Along with Owsley's address, that SHA conference included a session on "The Antislavery Crusade," at which Albert Simpson of Georgia suggested that in interpreting the origins of the movement one must "admit the possibility that the crusade might have received an initial impetus because it offered such a splendid outlet for the activities of pornographic minds."[45]

Reading between the lines of Thomas D. Clark's report of the SHA program committee for the following year, one's impressions of the growing tensions in the organization are reinforced. The committee for 1941, he reported, intended to give more attention to aspects of southern history other than the Civil War. When I asked him recently if there had been a conscious design to get away from the intense controversies, he readily corroborated my suspicion. But the committee for 1941 had no control over the presidential address, presented by B. B. Kendrick, who accounted for the antislavery movement as "a handy and, in most cases, a relatively inexpensive method for members of a conscientious nonslaveholding middle class to pay their debts to God." As the descendants of seventeenth century English Puritanism, they allied themselves with the financial and industrial interests to split asunder the union through a "Holy War" to which they marched

[43] J. G. Randall, "The Civil War Restudied," *Journal of Southern History*, 6 (Nov. 1940), 439-457, quotation, 445.

[44] Frank L. Owsley, "The Fundamental Cause of the Civil War: Egocentric Sectionalism," *ibid.*, 7 (Feb. 1941), 3-18, quotations, 15-16.

[45] This quotation is from the Report of the Annual Meeting, *ibid.*, 56-57.

singing the "Battle Hymn of the Republic."[46] Kendrick had touched
on another theme that was picked up by later historians of the
movement.

Although the SHA and the MVHA did not convene in 1942 and
1943 because of travel problems during World War II, jostling by
pro- and anti-abolitionists continued in their journals throughout the
1940s. Henry H. Simms, a native of Virginia who taught at Ohio
State, met Owsley's standard of "cold detachment" in his presentation of *A Decade of Sectional Controversy*; but Charles Sydnor displeased
his sectional colleagues by admitting that the South's defensive attitude
toward slavery closed minds and eyes to the faults of southern society.[47] Herbert Aptheker was brought to task by Frank J. Klingberg
for labeling slavery a "barbarous tyranny" without proper consideration for the "positive" aspects such as "the beneficial influences of
white civilization upon the Negro race," including Christianity.[48]
Fletcher Green of North Carolina, who often played the role of mediator
between the chief contenders, was decidedly upset with Allan Nevins
for whom it was always the South that was "weighed and found wanting." "Like the abolitionists of the period of which he writes, Nevins
seems to be blinded by his sense of moral values," Green accused.
But he was equally critical of what he took to be Avery Craven's distortion of the abolitionists' distorted picture of slavery.[49]

I attended my first national convention in 1949, the year that Dumond was president of the MVHA. I recall being rather apprehensive
because I knew his address was a ringing defense of the abolitionists
and might not sit well with everyone present. Dumond was a big man
with a commanding voice and presence, forceful and eloquent in his
lectures, and could be counted on to stir his audience. Ray Billington,
in his report of the annual meeting, pronounced, "The presidential
address by Dwight L. Dumond . . . was the high point of the program. For more than an hour he held his listeners spellbound as he

[46] *Ibid.*, 8 (Feb. 1942), 63-74; B. B. Kendrick, "The Colonial Status of the
South," *ibid.*, 3-22, quotation, 13-14.

[47] Owsley's review of Henry H. Simms, *A Decade of Sectional Controversy, 1851-1861*
(Chapel Hill 1942), is *ibid.*, 9 (Feb. 1943), 119-120; his review of Sydnor's *Development of Southern Sectionalism, 1819-1848* (Baton Rouge 1948) is *ibid.*, 15 (Feb. 1949),
108-110.

[48] Herbert Aptheker's *Essays in the History of the American Negro* (New York 1945)
was reviewed by Frank J. Klingberg, *ibid.*, 12 (May 1946), 280-281.

[49] Fletcher Green's review of Allan Nevins, *Ordeal of the Union* (New York 1947),
is in *Mississippi Valley Historical Review*, 35 (June 1948), 128-129; and his review of
Avery Craven, *The Coming of the Civil War* (New York 1942), is in *Journal of Southern
History*, 8 (Nov. 1942), 564-565.

spoke . . . ." Dumond's thesis was that the abolitionists were the true conservatives of the philosophy of the Declaration of Independence and the first amendment. They were the cultural heroes of the antebellum period when the freedoms of speech and press were being violated by Jackson's government, by state legislatures, in theological circles, and in institutions of higher learning. Gag laws and mob violence were pervasive in the North as well as in the South. To insist on discussing slavery was an "assertion of an individual right not contrary to, but actually in harmony with, the social interest." Dumond tied past to present. Our historic freedoms were once more endangered in the 1940s and public apathy prevailed as freedom of inquiry and discussion were circumscribed by teachers' oaths, restrictions by administrators and boards of regents. Public leaders were "almost completely paralyzed" in "their ability to make sound judgments."[50] Spellbound his audience was, and he sat down to thunderous applause and then a standing ovation. Caught up in the emotional surge myself, I failed to notice if there were some dissenters who remained seated.

I am inclined to think that the frustrations of the dissenters may have had some bearing on a session the following day, entitled "The Mississippi Valley and the Civil War." James G. Randall presided, with papers delivered by Paul Gates, Thomas Pressly, and Kenneth Stampp. Who said what I do not recall, nor can I find any real clue in the convention report. But it was Pressly's paper on "The Peace Interpretation" that set off an angry discussion from the floor—so vehement that Owsley and Craven stalked out. Paul Gates then responded to Craven's bitter criticisms of Pressly, prefacing his remarks by saying something to the effect that if Craven did not want to stay and hear the comments, that should not inhibit them from refuting mistakes in what he had said.[51]

Rereading and rethinking Dumond's address now, I can see his strategy. He made no attack whatsoever on the historical academy; he appealed to it as victim rather than as perpetrator of intolerance. No contemporary historian was named, no colleague's interpretation of slavery or of abolitionism was directly challenged. Who could denounce him for upholding the Declaration of Independence and the

---

[50] Dwight L. Dumond, "The Mississippi: Valley of Decision," *Mississippi Valley Historical Review*, 36 (June 1949), 3-26, quotations, 17, 25; Report of the Annual Meeting, *ibid.* (Sept. 1949), 291.

[51] Report of the Annual Meeting, *ibid.*, 297-299; Thomas Pressly to Betty Fladeland, Feb. 4, 1985. Thomas D. Clark also corroborates my memory of the walk-out.

first amendment? Where Dumond had warily circled his opponents, however, Arthur Schlesinger, Jr., made a frontal assault. In an article published in the *Partisan Review* in October of that year, he attacked Owsley, Randall, and Craven by name. He thought the Nashville "cult" of which Owsley was representative lived in a fantasy world to be equated with that of *Gone with the Wind*. "Yet I cannot escape the feeling," Schlesinger wrote, "that the vogue of revisionism is connected with the modern tendency to seek in optimistic sentimentalism an escape from the severe demands of moral decision." He saw revisionism as a historical school which "evades the essential moral problems in the name of a superficial objectivity . . . ." "By denying themselves insight into the moral dimension of the slavery crisis . . . ," he challenged, "the revisionists denied themselves a historical understanding of the intensities that caused the crisis."[52]

At the fall meeting of the SHA in Williamsburg, a southerner took up Schlesinger's theme in a paper which reviewed past presidential addresses of that body. Herman Clarence Nixon, a Craven student, a political scientist, and director of the Vanderbilt University Press, and whom I mentioned before as one of the Nashville Fugitives, had made a dramatic switch from southern conservatism to radicalism, and seems to have felt no qualms about delivering his criticisms of the past presidents with several of them sitting in the audience. The presidential addresses of Owsley in 1940, Kendrick in 1941, and A. B. Moore in 1942 "sound high notes and ring clear bells of regional patriotism. Let's sing 'Dixie'!" he scoffed, agreeing with Schlesinger that these southern historians had "won the battle of words with a strong assist from *Gone with the Wind*." Nixon proposed a debate between Owsley and Schlesinger at the next convention, with a "supporting cast" of Craven and Randall in Owsley's corner, and Hesseltine in Schlesinger's. He admitted that he had no nominee for an impartial moderator. "My composite president, synthetic author, and compound straw man has given a peculiar twist or sequel to what U. B. Phillips emphasized as 'The Central Theme of Southern History,' " Nixon declared. "Unlike Phillips, he has sought to conceal the southern Negro in a woodpile of constitutional abstractions, ignoring him statistically and spiritually. . . . He writes of southern democracy and democratic rights with little or no consideration of ten million colored citizens. . . . In an oversimplification of the complex, he seems to reach

---

[52] Arthur Schlesinger, Jr., "The Causes of the Civil War: A Note on Historical Sentimentalism," *Partisan Review*, 16 (Oct. 1949), 969-981.

a wishful conclusion that the South must be left alone to solve its own
problems and then not solve them.'' Unlike Dumond, Nixon lectured
his contemporaries directly: the historian ''cannot take time to rectify
the defects of his society, but he should take pains not to personify
these defects. He should support no iron curtain against the inter-
change of ideas and provide no fuel for the Nordic signal fire which
sometimes burns on Stone Mountain.''[53] Much to my dismay, no one
whom I have asked remembers the reception given Nixon's paper at
that meeting.

The 1949 conventions seem to have reached a sort of climax in
the cold war. Beginning in the 1950s, and of course in the 1960s,
the times were changing and also the histories of slavery and antislavery.
In the last years of his life even Avery Craven retreated from his revisionist interpretation, seemed even to forget what he had earlier written, and clearly wanted to be remembered as in step with the times.
He told Robert Johannsen that he had not chosen the title, *The Repressible Conflict*, for his Fleming lectures, but that LSU Press did, and expressed annoyance that he had been unfairly labeled as a consequence
of that title.[54] After reading Merton Dillon's article of 1969 on abolitionist historiography, Craven wrote him a letter objecting to his
categorization. He denied the reputation allotted to him of being ''a
biased Southerner and a defender of slavery, a critic of abolitionists.''
''So if you will read the sections you quote,'' he admonished Dillon,
''you will see that the prejudice is on your side not mine.'' Then he
ends his letter with a poignant appeal: ''Only recently did I, with
one of my former students, seek out the grave of Charles Osborn,
one of the great abolitionists, found it in an abandoned Quaker
graveyard, cleaned the ground and erected a suitable marker at our

---

[53] H. C. Nixon, ''Paths to the Past: The Presidential Addresses of the Southern
Historical Association,'' *Journal of Southern History*, 16 (Feb. 1950), 33-39. Thomas
D. Clark told me of Nixon's switch in stance on the Old South. See also Report
of the Annual Meeting, *ibid.*, 40-47.

[54] Robert Johannsen to Betty Fladeland, Nov. 29, 1984. A letter from Arthur
Cole to Craven of June 29, 1935, Craven Papers, indicates an interesting coincidence.
Evidently Craven had objected to Cole's title, *The Irrepressible Conflict*, and Cole replied
to explain that he had intended to call the book *The House Divided*, but that his series
editor, A. M. Schlesinger, Sr., preferred to use Cole's second choice. There is also
a terse note from Schlesinger to Craven (Mar. 14, 1935) in which Schlesinger writes:
''Even if you are correct in finding an alternative contemporary meaning for 'irrepressible conflict,' I still do not think you were justified in fathering this particular
meaning on Cole. Nowhere in the book does he argue that bloody war was inevitable.''

own expense. That is a sample of 'unflattering views of abolitionists.' Can you match it?"[55]

Since the 1960s one has been tempted to claim a final victory for the abolitionists and for pro-abolitionist historians, as Ramsdell in his time did for U. B. Phillips; but having studied history for half a century, I am not about to fall into that trap. Perhaps some day I shall be turning over in my grave as Grandfather Phillips must have been doing many a time in the decades since his passing.

---

[55] Merton L. Dillon, "The Abolitionists: A Decade of Historiography, 1959-1969," *Journal of Southern History*, 35 (Nov. 1969), 500-522; Avery Craven to Merton Dillon, Jan. 1, 1970. In his later years Craven wrote many letters complaining of being misinterpreted. See letters to Craven from Kenneth Stampp, Mar. 17, 1965; from David B. Davis, July 27, 1967; from Richard O. Curry, Jan. 31 and Feb. 23, 1970; from Hans Trefousse, Jan. 19 and Feb. 3, 1970; and from Eric Foner, Apr. 18, 1971. There is also one from Ralph Gabriel as early as Dec. 31, 1942. Instead of trying to defend himself or placate Craven, Gabriel gives back Craven quotations and asks him bluntly what they mean.

"Historical Topics Sometimes Run Dry": The State of Abolitionist Studies

By

Lawrence J. Friedman*

BEFORE, during, and after the Civil War those who had worked for immediate emancipation and civil rights for blacks were vitally interested in conveying the "true" history of their movement. William Goodell, Parker Pillsbury, James Freeman Clarke, Thomas Wentworth Higginson, John Greenleaf Whittier, Austin Willey, and others penned and publicized general histories of abolitionist efforts.[1] Henry B. Stanton, Samuel J. May, and Henry C. Wright wrote personal memoirs that closely resembled general histories.[2] Abolitionists, in addition, were anxious to write biographies of each other. Oliver Johnson wrote on Garrison, Lewis Tappan wrote about his brother Arthur, Elizur Wright, Jr., wrote on Myron Holley, Luther Marsh told the story of his father-in-law Alvan Stewart, Beriah Green took up James Gillespie Birney, John White Chadwick published on Sallie Holley and Samuel May, Jr., while Thomas Wentworth Higginson wrote on Wendell Phillips.[3] Although Garrison never completed

---

*The author is Professor of History at Bowling Green State University. He wishes to thank Professors Merton L. Dillon and Jane H. Pease for perceptive criticisms of early drafts of this essay.

[1]See, e.g., William Goodell, *Slavery and Anti-Slavery; a History of the Great Struggle in Both Hemispheres; with a View of the Slavery Question in the United States* (New York: William Harned, 1852); Parker Pillsbury, *Acts of the Anti-Slavery Apostles* (Concord, N.H., 1883); James Freeman Clarke, *Anti-Slavery Days: A Sketch of the Struggle which Ended in the Abolition of Slavery in the United States* (New York: R. Worthington, 1884); Thomas Wentworth Higginson, "Anti-Slavery Days," *Outlook* 60 (3 September 1898): 47–57; John Greenleaf Whittier, *The Conflict with Slavery, Politics and Reform: The Inner Life Criticism* (New York: Houghton Mifflin, 1889); and Austin Willey, *The History of the Antislavery Cause in State and Nation* (Portland, Maine: Brown Thurston, 1886).

[2]Henry B. Stanton, *Random Recollections* (New York: Henry B. Stanton, 1885); Samuel J. May, *Some Recollections of Our Antislavery Conflict* (Boston: Fields, Osgood, 1869); Henry C. Wright, *Human Life: Illustrated in My Individual Experience as a Child, a Youth, and a Man* (Boston: Bella Marsh, 1849).

[3]Oliver Johnson, *William Lloyd Garrison and His Times* (Boston: B.B. Russell, 1880); Lewis Tappan, *The Life of Arthur Tappan* (New York: Hurd and Houghton, 1870); Elizur Wright, *Myron Holley; and What He Did for Liberty and True Religion* (Boston: Elizur Wright, 1882); Luther Marsh, "Alvan Stewart," unpublished ms., n.d., Alvan Stewart Collection, New York State Historical Association; Beriah Green, *Sketches of the Life and Writings of*

177

plans to write a history of the movement, from the 1840s on his private letters tended, more and more, to romanticize the antislavery past.[4] National, state, and local antislavery societies held regular anniversary conventions and yearly gatherings to recount the turbulent but successful historic progress of the cause.[5]

The theme that abolitionist historical endeavors were intended to convey was the clear if gradual emergence of a hated minority into shapers of a broad-based Northern antislavery conscience which, in turn, demanded and secured the eradication of Southern slavery. Whether in formal histories or, more often, in personal letters, abolitionists took great pains to stress this fruition of their efforts—this "growth of a dissenting minority."

Interestingly, "the growth of a dissenting minority" theme was first articulated in the 1830s. This was a decade when initial immediatist abolition efforts evoked contemptuous slogans and mob responses. But it was also a decade in which some abolitionists entertained expectations that they might become a majority. Indeed, perhaps hopes of ultimate victory had to be kept alive amidst widespread hostility. "What have the abolitionists *done?*" Garrison asked in 1832, only one year after he had launched the *Liberator.* "They are reforming and consolidating public opinion, dispelling the mists of error, inspiring the hearts of the timid, enlightening the eyes of the blind, and disturbing the slumbers of the guilty." Oliver Johnson, Garrison's colleague, concurred: "The cause is marching forward to a speedy triumph." Despite antiabolitionist mobs, Lewis Tappan was also optimistic. "The anti-s[lavery] cause is surely advancing," he charged, for "the antislavery doctrines have pervaded large portions of the [Northern] community." Whittier concurred: "The cause *is* progressing. I want no better evidence of it than the rabid violence of our enemies."[6]

James Gillespie Birney (Utica, N.Y.: Jackson and Chaplin, 1844); John White Chadwick, *A Life of Liberty: Antislavery and Other Letters of Sallie Holley* (New York and London: G.P. Putnam's Sons, 1899); *idem*, "Samuel May of Leicester," *New England Magazine* (April 1899): 201–14; Thomas Wentworth Higginson, *Wendell Phillips* (Boston: Lee and Shepard Publishers, 1884).

[4]For a brilliant commentary on the historical and ritualistic nature of Garrison letters since the 1840s, see James Brewer Stewart, "Garrison Again, and Again, and Again . . . ," *Reviews in American History*, December 1976, 539–45.

[5]See, e.g., the annual reports of the American Antislavery Society; *Proceedings of the First Annual Meeting of the New York State Anti-Slavery Society, Convened at Utica, October 19, 1836* (Utica, N.Y., 1836); and *Fourth Annual Report of the Board of Managers of the Massachusetts Anti-Slavery Society with Some Account of the Annual Meeting, January 20, 1836* (Boston: Isaac Knapp, 1836).

[6]William Lloyd Garrison, *Thoughts on African Colonization* (reprint ed., New York: Arno Press, 1968), part 1, pp. 56–57; Oliver Johnson, untitled ms., 10 June 1838, Album, Western Antislavery Society MSS, Library of Congress; Lewis Tappan to Gerrit Smith, 15 February 1836, Gerrit Smith Papers, Syracuse University; Lewis Tappan Journal, 14

178

Abolitionist Studies

Throughout the 1840s abolitionists continued to maintain that they were making significant inroads on Northern public opinion— that antislavery doctrine was advancing from hated minority status. Setbacks in Texas and in the Mexican War hardly seemed to discourage them. "It is no longer the difficult task it once was, to open the eyes of the [Northern] people to the pro-slavery frauds practiced upon them," noted Samuel May, Jr. "I never felt more assured than I do now, of the downfall of Slavery—and that at no very distant day." According to James Russell Lowell, abolitionists had surmounted "immense odds"; they had transformed Northern attitudes "in a wonderfully short space of time." Lewis Tappan, Gerrit Smith, and Edmund Quincy also celebrated the many bright "signs of the time."[7]

The sectional polarization of the 1850s and the intensification of Northern focus upon a Southern "slave power conspiracy" provoked more frequent and ebullient abolitionist espousals of "the growth of a dissenting minority" theme. Samuel May, Jr., Lewis Tappan, and William Goodell noted that Northerners were no longer antagonistic to militant antislavery slogans but seemed to thrive on abolitionist doctrines. To Joshua Leavitt, Lincoln's presidential victory in 1860 represented the final triumph of abolitionist principles: "What a growth since 1840. . . . It is a joy to have lived to this day."[8]

The Emancipation Proclamation and ratification of the Thirteenth Amendment provided abolitionists with legal proof that victory had been achieved—that they had indeed set into motion a chain of events that had mobilized the North and destroyed slavery. They noted "the great triumph of truth and justice" brought about by the "anti-slavery phalanx." Together with Gerrit Smith, Lewis Tappan, and other leading immediatists of the 1830s, Garrison was honored in the postwar years for carrying freedom through the land. The path running from

November 1837, Lewis Tappan Papers, Library of Congress; Ellis Gray Loring to Elizur Wright, Jr., 22 February 1837, Ellis Gray Loring Letterbook, Houghton Library, Harvard. Whittier is quoted in James Brewer Stewart, *Holy Warriors: The Abolitionists and American Slavery* (New York: Hill and Wang, 1976), 73.

[7]Samuel May, Jr., to R.D. Webb, 6 February 1849, Boston Public Library (BPL). See also May, Jr., to Webb, 7 March 1848, BPL. Lowell in *The Anti-Slavery Papers of James Russell Lowell* (Boston and New York: Houghton Mifflin, 1902), 2:56; Lewis Tappan to Seth Gates, 10 March 1840, to Joseph Sturge, 31 August 1842, and to Benjamin Tappan, 14 October 1844, all in Lewis Tappan Papers, Library of Congress; Gerrit Smith to Nathaniel Crenshaw, 30 December 1841, Letter Copy Book 1827–1843, Gerrit Smith Papers, Syracuse University; Edmund Quincy Journal, 28 January 1842, Edmund Quincy Papers, Massachusetts Historical Society.

[8]Samuel May, Jr., to Richard D. Webb, 8 February 1859, BPL; Lewis Tappan to Benjamin Tappan, 12 May 1855, Lewis Tappan Papers, Library of Congress; Goodell, *Slavery and Anti-Slavery*, 466; Joshua Leavitt to Salmon P. Chase, 7 November 1860, Salmon P. Chase Papers, Library of Congress.

179

the immediatist abolitionists of the 1830s to Lincoln in the early 1860s was direct and clear.[9]

To be sure, abolitionists were not the first group of reformers who constructed a historical perspective to celebrate the triumph of their efforts. But what distinguished them from many other reform groups was that their perspective—"the growth of a dissenting minority"—has become the governing paradigm for modern-day antislavery scholarship. In large measure, posterity has accepted their account of growing Northern influence and ultimate success.

This is not to say that all historians have uncritically accepted "the growth of a dissenting minority" paradigm. To the contrary, there have always been historians who have sharply discounted it.[10] Through their extensive work with abolitionist materials, Irving H. Bartlett, Lewis C. Perry, Ronald G. Walters, and Bertram Wyatt-Brown have even pointed to the need for an altogether new paradigm.[11] But for every historian who has disputed the alleged abolitionist success in molding antebellum Northern public opinion, many more may be

[9]Whittier, *Conflict with Slavery*, 146; Wendell Phillips Garrison and Francis Jackson Garrison, *William Lloyd Garrison, 1805–1879* (New York: Century, 1885–89), 4:128–29. For data on the honoring of leading abolitionists during the postwar years, see James M. McPherson, *The Abolitionist Legacy: From Reconstruction to the NAACP* (Princeton: Princeton University Press, 1975), 32–33; Henry Wilson, *History of the Rise and Fall of the Slave Power in America* (Boston and New York: Houghton Mifflin, 1872), 1:262; Garrison and Garrison, *Garrison*, 4:181–82; Larry Gara, "A Glorious Time: The 1874 Abolitionist Reunion in Chicago," *Journal of the Illinois State Historical Society* 65 (Autumn 1972): 28.

[10]See, e.g., Charles A. and Mary R. Beard, *The Rise of American Civilization* (New York: MacMillan, 1927), 1: 700, 709; J.G. Randall. *The Civil War and Reconstruction* (Boston: D.C. Heath, 1937), 103; Roy F. Nichols, *The Disruption of American Democracy* (New York: Macmillan, 1948); John Higham, *From Boundlessness to Consolidation: The Transformation of American Culture, 1848–1860* (Ann Arbor: William L. Clements Library, 1969), 23; Eric Foner, *Free Soil, Free Labor, Free Men: The Ideology of the Republican Party before the Civil War* (New York: Oxford University Press, 1970), 219–25; Eugene H. Berwanger, *The Frontier against Slavery: Western Anti-Negro Prejudice and the Slavery Extension Controversy* (Urbana: University of Illinois Press, 1967); Elbert B. Smith, *The Death of Slavery: The United States, 1837–65* (Chicago: University of Chicago Press, 1967), 37–38; Harold M. Hyman, *A More Perfect Union: The Impact of the Civil War and Reconstruction on the Constitution* (New York: Knopf, 1973), 320; Michael F. Holt, "Antislavery and the Law: The Story of a Reciprocal Relationship," *Reviews in American History* 6 (December 1978): 516–17.

[11]Irving H. Bartlett, *Wendell Phillips: Brahmin Radical* (Boston: Beacon Press, 1961); Lewis Perry, *Radical Abolitionism: Anarchy and the Government of God in Antislavery Thought* (Ithaca: Cornell University Press, 1973); Ronald G. Walters, *The Antislavery Appeal: American Abolitionism after 1830* (Baltimore: Johns Hopkins University Press, 1976); Bertram Wyatt-Brown, "New Leftists and Abolitionists: A Comparison of American Radical Styles," *Wisconsin Magazine of History* 53 (Summer 1970): 267; Bertram Wyatt-Brown, *Lewis Tappan and the Evangelical War against Slavery* (Cleveland: Press of Case Western Reserve University, 1969).

cited who have endorsed it. Indeed, there is no other clearly and fully articulated paradigm to explain the abolitionist role in the chain of events that led to Civil War.

Besides forging the interpretive framework for much subsequent historiography, abolitionists developed three alternative explanations for their alleged "growth" in influence over Northern attitudes and actions. Each of these, although at least mildly in conflict with the other two, has likewise found a significant following among professional historians.

The first abolitionist explanation centers on the role of civil liberties. Abolitionists of all factions repeatedly maintained that their influence grew whenever their freedom to espouse antislavery doctrines was infringed upon. Denials of civil liberties drew diverse Northerners to their aid in defense of traditional Northern rights. Thus, men and women who might otherwise have had nothing to do with antislavery became comrades of abolitionist crusaders; the ranks of the movement swelled. Thomas Garrett, an abolitionist from Wilmington, Delaware, put the proposition most clearly: "The North has been made to see the chains which the South has been Forging for their necks . . . and they have rebelled." J. Miller McKim, Samuel May, Jr., Joshua Leavitt, and others offered identical claims for the source of abolitionist strength.[12]

Historian Russel B. Nye drew upon these abolitionist claims when he wrote his influential book, *Fettered Freedom: Civil Liberties and the Slavery Controversy, 1830–1860* (1949). Much like abolitionists recounting their own antislavery experiences, Nye maintained that "the abolition movement became inextricably bound up with the preservation of civil liberties, and that the relationship strengthened it and helped it to insure its final victory by mobilizing Northern opinion on its side." Nye detailed instances where abolitionists were denied the right of petition, the use of the mails, freedom of the press, and other fundamental rights. Northerners sided with them out of apprehensions that precedents were being set for eradication of their own liberties.[13] In the decades since Nye's study, this white civil liberties argument that the abolitionists forged and Nye perpetuated has received almost unquestioning acceptance within the historical profession.[14]

[12]Thomas Garrett, untitled essay, 8 September 1854, Album, Western Anti-Slavery Society MSS, Library of Congress; J. Miller McKim to William Lloyd Garrison, 8 December 1860, BPL; Samuel May, Jr., to J.B. Estlin, 8 January 1848, BPL; *Emancipator and Weekly Chronicle* (Boston), 16 December 1844 (Leavitt).

[13]Russel B. Nye, *Fettered Freedom: Civil Liberties and the Slavery Controversy, 1830–1860* (East Lansing: Michigan State College Press, 1949), 250–51, 32–69, 121, 218, chap. 5.

[14]See, e.g., Louis Filler, *The Crusade against Slavery 1830–1860* (New York: Harper, 1960), 100; James M. McPherson, "The Fight against the Gag Rule: Joshua Leavitt and Antislavery Insurgency in the Whig Party, 1839–1842," *Journal of Negro History* 48 (July 1963): 177; Larry Gara, "Slavery and the Slave Power: A Crucial Distinction," *Civil War*

181

The Historian

Although all sorts of abolitionists propounded the civil liberties argument, only those who had supported the Liberty Party tended to endorse a second explanation for expanding abolitionist influence. The main lines of this second explanation were simple. After a decade of floundering, abolitionists forged the Liberty Party, which paved the way for the Free Soil Party, and it in turn evolved into the Republican Party of Lincoln which freed the slaves. As John White Chadwick put it, the Liberty Party was "the first party to make anti-slavery a matter of partisan politics, a party which developed in 1848 into the Free Soil party . . . and in 1856 the Republican party, the instrument by which slavery was abolished." Old-time Liberty Party men like Elizur Wright, Luther Marsh, Henry Stanton, and Austin Willey marked this same route for the "growth" of Northern anti-slavery opinion.[15]

A substantial number of historians who have acquiesced in "the growth of a dissenting minority" paradigm have echoed this Liberty Party-Free Soil-Republican Party explanation.[16] But the writings of Dwight L. Dumond, Merton L. Dillon, and Richard H. Sewell have developed it most fully.[17]

Still a third explanation for "growth" of abolitionist influence was advanced by Garrison and his followers long before it was adopted by historians. It justified Garrisonian abstention from third-party politics. Because they steered clear of the Liberty Party and agitated from outside the formal party process, Garrisonians maintained, they were able to force the Northern wings of the major parties to respond to vital moral issues. Indeed, through their pressure upon Northern

---

History 15 (March 1969): 5–18; and Leonard L. Richards, *"Gentlemen of Property and Standing": Anti-Abolition Mobs in Jacksonian America* (New York: Oxford University Press, 1970), 162–63.

[15]Chadwick, *Sallie Holley*, 25; Wright, *Myron Holley*, 234–36; Marsh, "Alvan Stewart"; Stanton, *Random Recollections*, 92; Austin Willey, *The History of the Antislavery Cause in State and Nation* (Portland, Maine: Brown, Thurston, 1886).

[16]See, e.g., John L. Thomas, *The Liberator: William Lloyd Garrison* (Boston: Little, Brown, 1963), 251; Carleton Mabee, *Black Freedom: The Nonviolent Abolitionists from 1830 through the Civil War* (New York: Macmillan, 1970), 246–47; Arthur Young Lloyd, *The Slavery Controversy, 1831–1860* (Chapel Hill: University of North Carolina Press, 1939), 56; and Kenneth M. Stampp, *And the War Came: The North and the Secession Crisis, 1860–1861* (Baton Rouge: Louisiana State University Press, 1950), 148.

[17]Dumond most clearly delineates this explanation in *Antislavery Origins of the Civil War in the United States* (Ann Arbor: University of Michigan Press, 1939). Dillon's *The Abolitionists: The Growth of a Dissenting Minority* (DeKalb: Northern Illinois University Press, 1974) contains his fullest development of the explanation. Sewell provides his most developed version in *Ballots for Freedom: Antislavery Politics in the United States, 1837–1860* (New York: Oxford, 1976). It should be noted that Dumond, Dillon, and Sewell also incorporate the civil liberties explanation for "growth" of influence, although it is not central to their argument.

182

politicians, the Free Soil and Republican Parties were compelled to become far less equivocal on the slavery controversy.[18]

Since the early 1960s, historians have generally been much less hostile to Garrison and his followers than they had been in earlier decades. Several of the more sympathetic have elaborated upon the Garrisonian strategy for wielding influence over Northern society that he and his followers had espoused.[19] Drawing heavily upon the writings of the Garrisonians, Aileen S. Kraditor and James Brewer Stewart have provided the fullest and most profound elaboration of Garrisonian strategy.[20]

These, then, are the three explanations that abolitionists propounded and that historians have elaborated to sustain the claim of gradually increasing abolitionist influence in Northern society. Reflecting the antebellum conflict between political abolitionists and Garrisonians, the Liberty-Free Soil-Republican evolutionary explanation is obviously at odds with the Garrisonian outside-agitator explanation. One claims that abolitionists were influential because they participated in a political party; the other claims influence because they refused to take part in party political activity. The abolitionist civil liberties explanation does not logically conflict with either of these two explanations. But it does conflict in emphasis. If the preponderance of

[18]Samuel May, Jr., to Richard D. Webb, 6 November 1860, BPL. Lydia M. Child is quoted in the *National Anti-Slavery Standard*, 24 June 1841. For similar pronouncements by other Garrisonians, see, e.g., Thomas Wentworth Higginson, *Contemporaries* (Boston, 1899), 246–47; Oliver Johnson, *William Lloyd Garrison and His Times* (Boston: Russell, 1880), 306; Clare Taylor, ed., *British and American Abolitionists: An Episode in Trans-atlantic Understanding* (Edinburgh: Edinburgh University Press, 1974), 332; Wendell Phillips to Elizabeth Pease, 25 January 1846, BPL; Wendell Phillips, *Speeches, Lectures and Letters*, 1st ser. (Boston, 1863), 135; William Lloyd Garrison to Samuel May, Jr., 2 December 1848, BPL; Garrison and Garrison, *Garrison*, 3: 236; and Edmund Quincy to R.D. Webb, 30 January 1845, Quincy-Webb Correspondence, BPL.

[19]See, e.g., Wyatt-Brown, *Lewis Tappan*, 271, 282n.2; Robert MacDougal, "William Lloyd Garrison and the Role of the Moral Extremist," *Social Studies* 67 (January/February 1976): 33–34.

[20]Aileen S. Kraditor, *Means and Ends in American Abolitionism: Garrison and His Critics on Strategy and Tactics, 1834–1850* (New York: Pantheon Books, 1967, 1969), chaps. 6, 7; Kraditor, "American Radical Historians on Their Heritage," *Past and Present* 56 (August 1972): 149; James Brewer Stewart, "The Aims and Impact of Garrisonian Abolitionism, 1840–1860," *Civil War History* 15 (September 1969): 203; Stewart, *Holy Warriors*, 107–8; Stewart, "Garrison Again," 539–45; Stewart, "Politics and Belief in Abolitionism: Stanley Elkins' Concept of Antiinstitutionalism and Recent Interpretations of American Antislavery," *South Atlantic Quarterly* 75 (Winter 1976): 94–97. Because Kraditor's major study of abolitionist strategy, *Means and Ends*, concluded at 1850 with the Free Soil movement, she did not comment on Garrisonian impact upon the Republican party. In *Holy Warriors*, 102, differently than in his earlier publications, Stewart finds some credence not only in the Garrisonian explanation for abolitionist "growth" but also in the Liberty Party explanation.

183

abolitionist appeal in the North derived from the suppression of their civil liberties, the tactics abolitionists used *vis-à-vis* the two major parties (third party or Garrisonian outside agitation) dwarf in significance. Thus, adherents to "the growth of a dissenting minority" have differed rather sharply on what caused "growth" of abolitionist influence. This alone affords some cause for questioning the validity of the paradigm.

In fairness to historians who have espoused the paradigm, however, it is important to recognize that several have been quite circumspect in the way they have embraced it. Although Russel Nye maintained, for example, that repression of abolitionist rights brought Northerners to regard the abolitionists as champions of white liberties as well as black freedoms, he continually guarded against asserting that positive acts of the abolitionists themselves caused this transformation in public opinion. Of the three major exponents of the Liberty Party abolitionist explanation of the movement's expanding influence, only Dwight L. Dumond dogmatically asserted the "growth" paradigm without qualification. Richard Sewell and Merton Dillon, in keeping with the judicious tone of their own scholarship, were considerably more hesitant about claiming a direct causal relationship between the actions of political abolitionists and the ultimate abolition of slavery. Aileen Kraditor and James Stewart, the leading exponents of the Garrisonian explanation for the "growth" paradigm, also took care to sharply qualify their appraisals of abolitionist influence. Thus, save for Dumond, the major exponents of the paradigm have not felt confident to state, unequivocally, that it was the actions of the abolitionists which turned the North against slavery and the Southern "slave power conspiracy."

In some measure, historians have espoused the "growth" paradigm with restraint because the sources themselves are ambiguous. Several seem to have picked up on vague and periodic abolitionist references to the limitations of their movement—references designed to supplement rather than to question the "growth" paradigm. Consider, for example, John A. Collins's introduction to his 1842 anthology, *The Anti-Slavery Picknick*, a collection of poems, songs, and short stories designed to assure children that abolitionism was certain to triumph. "Our principles are not now confined to 'a few fanatics'," Collins wrote, "but have, in consequence of the agitations of the last twelve years, taken a deep and lasting hold on the sympathies and affections of a great body of the people in the free States." But in the very next sentence of his introduction, Collins cast doubt upon the triumph of abolitionist principles. Those principles had been "misrepresented by our opponents" and the result was antiabolitionist "prejudice in the minds of many." Unfortunately, Collins implied but never clearly stated that "a great body of the people in the free States" who favored abolitionism exceeded "the minds of many" who did not. A year later, Nathaniel Peabody Rogers recounted the progress of

184

abolitionism in Concord, New Hampshire, in similarly equivocal terms: "We seem to make progress—but I at times incline to think we are making the mistake folks sometimes do—who are moving by fixed bodies & suppose them in motion—when all the motion is in themselves." By 1849 Whittier boasted to Lewis Tappan that it had become as difficult to find a proslavery man in the North as it used to be to find an abolitionist. But almost instantly Whittier modified his opinion: "I have scarcely charity enough to suppose that this marvelous conversion is altogether genuine & heartfelt."[21]

To accurately incorporate abolitionist pronouncements such as these, historians have obviously felt compelled to qualify but not to drastically overhaul or replace "the growth of a dissenting minority" paradigm. By perceptively noting abolitionist ambivalence regarding the success of the movement, the historian is apt to bring an equivocal tone into his own study. This may explain the movement of many scholars, since the early 1960s, away from questions of abolitionist influence—away from even suggesting the abolitionist role in the coming of the Civil War.[22]

But we can never hope to understand the most vital aspects of the abolitionist experience unless we arrive at a better understanding of their precise influence and power during the sectional crisis and the outbreak of the war. Rather than sidestepping the issue of influence, scholars must determine whether they need to drastically modify if not totally replace the "growth" paradigm. This is the most fundamental question facing abolitionist historiography. Until we can come to a reasonable response, there is little point in researchers diligently compiling new information on the evolution of abolitionism. "Like oil wells," Bertram Wyatt-Brown has noted, "historical topics sometimes run dry" and antebellum abolitionism seems to be one such topic.[23] Unless we can decide precisely how to refine or replace the governing "growth" paradigm, fresh data on the abolitionists will rarely furnish useful insights. As many current researchers on antebellum abolitionism will openly acknowledge, there does not seem to be much more of fundamental importance that can be said about the topic. This desperate state of affairs will remain until historians can make some basic determination regarding the "growth" paradigm.

[21]Collins, ed., Anti-Slavery Picknick, 3; Nathaniel P. Rogers to Henry C. Wright, 19 April 1843 (copy), BPL; Whittier in Wyatt-Brown, Lewis Tappan, 328.

[22]Merton L. Dillon, "The Abolitionists: A Decade of Historiography, 1959–1969," Journal of Southern History 35 (November 1969): 500, notes this movement by some scholars away from questions of abolitionist influence. Lewis Perry and Michael Fellman, eds., Antislavery Reconsidered: New Perspectives on the Abolitionists (Baton Rouge: Louisiana State University Press, 1979), evidences the perpetuation of this trend.

[23]Bertram Wyatt-Brown, review of The Abolitionists: The Growth of a Dissenting Minority by Merton L. Dillon, in American Historical Review 83 (June 1976): 662.

185

The Historian

II

The case for total abandonment of the paradigm is substantial. First, there is the matter of paltry abolitionist supportive resources. In the only systematic study of abolitionists' funding sources, Benjamin Quarles has concluded that they were the most underfunded of all antebellum reformers. The average state and local antislavery society ran on a shoestring—less than $3,000 annually. Two of the most active organizations—the Massachusetts Anti-Slavery Society and the Pennsylvania Anti-Slavery Society—were each able to garner only about $6,000 a year. Between 1833 and 1839 the American Anti-Slavery Society collected no more than $160,000, less than the *yearly* budget of some evangelical missionary organizations. Every weekly antislavery society newspaper operated at a loss. Thus, few of them continued to publish for any length of time. Most significant, Quarles has found no *growth* in funding sources between the 1830s and the Civil War.[24] Unfortunately, no systematic study of the number of members in abolitionist societies for the 1831–61 period has been conducted. But membership probably never exceeded the 250,000 who, according to the American Anti-Slavery Society, belonged to the sundry abolition societies that existed in 1838. This is because the number of state and local abolition societies never increased beyond a July 1837 peak while abolitionist activities after 1840 came increasingly to be conducted on the state and local levels.[25]

Influence, of course, can be exerted with scarcities in material resources. Money and memberships are not indispensable. A second and at least equally serious challenge to "the growth of a dissenting minority" paradigm is posed by the ethnocultural approach to Jacksonian politics. Practitioners of this approach have insisted that antebellum Americans perceived local issues as more important than national issues because the federal government rarely entered into crucial areas of their lives: state, county, city, and town governments took charge of most important matters affecting a citizen's existence. One must therefore turn to the local level and the nature of economic, social, cultural, and religious factors in a specific locality to grasp what motivated citizens. Thus, a North-South sectional issue like antislavery could have had a decided impact on most Northerners only if it linked tightly to issues closer to home.[26] Local-level analysis has convinced

[24]Benjamin Quarles, "Sources of Abolitionist Income," *Mississippi Valley Historical Review* 32 (June 1945): 63–76.

[25]Gerald Sorin, *Abolitionism: A New Perspective* (New York: Praeger, 1972), 17; Mabee, *Black Freedom*, 37; Quarles, "Sources of Income," 75; Richards, *"Gentlemen of Property and Standing,"* 159.

[26]Joel H. Silbey provides a clear statement of the assumptions of the ethnocultural school in "The Civil War Synthesis in American Political History," *Civil War History* 10 (June 1964): 130–40.

186

most ethnocultural historians that "antislavery" (in the egalitarian, nonracist, abolitionist sense of the term) did not link closely with vital local concerns in specific Northern communities. Michael F. Holt, for example, has found that increasing Republican electoral strength in Pittsburgh during the 1850s had little to do with abolitionism, much less with antislavery sentiment. Rather, the native-born Protestant working class and the middle class that, together, forged Pittsburgh's Republican majority were primarily motivated by antiimmigrant and anti-Catholic sentiments. They also voted Republican to protest against the railroads and against new taxes to pay the interest on bonds issued to railroad companies.[27] Ronald Formisano arrived at the same sort of conclusion for sparsely settled Michigan that Holt came to for Pittsburgh. For the most part, Michigan's Republican Party grew because large and influential groups of evangelical Protestants in diverse localities saw in it the hope of Christian unity and the dissolution of religious sectarianism. Indeed, Michigan Republicanism was not even mildly antislavery, much less abolitionist, and Republican leaders rejected pleas for black enfranchisement.[28] In 1972, Lee Benson summarized the findings of Holt, Formisano, and other ethnocultural historians: "Had Northerners held a referendum in November, 1860, solely on a proposition requiring the Federal government to require Southern state governments to abolish slavery by some form of legislative action, probably no more than 2 percent, almost certainly no more than 5 percent, of the Northern electorate would have voted 'Aye'." Antislavery simply had no meaningful impact on the crucial local level.[29]

This sort of conclusion by ethnocultural historians is lacking in one essential. There was a Civil War, two sections (North and South) fought that war, and slavery had something to do with Northern and Southern sectionalism. A preponderantly local focus does not reveal what commonalities (however superficial) drew Northerners together and which ones drew Southerners together so that a sectional war could be fought.[30] But if ethnocultural historians have not adequately accounted for the coming of the Civil War, their systematic local-level analyses of Northern voter behavior make one point clear. The abolitionist campaign for immediate emancipation and full civil rights for

[27]Michael Fitzgibbon Holt, *Forging a Majority: The Formation of the Republican Party in Pittsburgh, 1848–1860* (New Haven: Yale University Press, 1969).

[28]Ronald P. Formisano, *The Birth of Mass Political Parties: Michigan, 1827–1861* (Princeton: Princeton University Press, 1971), especially 269, 287, 289–324.

[29]Lee Benson, "Explanations of American Civil War Causation," in *Toward the Scientific Study of History* (Philadelphia: Lippincott, 1972), 246.

[30]For a useful critique of the ethnocultural school on this score, see Eric Foner, "The Causes of the American Civil War: Recent Interpretations and New Directions," *Civil War History* 20 (September 1974): 200–201.

187

blacks never commanded the support of many Northern voters. In an important 1964 essay, "The Nature of Belief Systems in Mass Politics," Philip E. Converse found this result altogether understandable and suggested that substantial portions of the antebellum Northern population "were only dimly aware that slavery or a controversy about it existed." This, Converse argued, was because of the vast gulf between the complex, abstract, and functionally interdependent elements in the antislavery belief system of the abolitionists and the more concrete thoughts of Northern masses several days' journey from slavery. What abolitionist ideas reached ordinary Northerners were shorn of abstraction and functional interdependence. They bore little resemblance to the belief system that the abolitionists were trying to propagate.[31]

Not only does analysis of abolitionist material resources and local-level ethnocultural study pose problems for "the growth of a dissenting minority" paradigm; it runs into a third and perhaps even more serious obstacle. None of the three varieties of the paradigm explaining abolitionist "growth" in influence (a civil liberties crisis, the appeal of the Liberty Party, or the pressure of the Garrisonians) deals with Northern churches. Given the patently moralistic nature of the abolitionists' appeal, their close association with diverse religious-benevolent societies, and the very large proportion of ordained ministers within the movement, this is a most serious mistake. We must, therefore, take note of the state of knowledge concerning abolitionist impact upon Catholics and upon the diverse Protestant denominations in the North to see whether abolitionists influenced the religious community toward which much of their effort was directed.

Although there is no modern analytic study of abolitionist impact upon the Catholic Church as a whole, what scholarly publications we do have demonstrate no more than very slight traces of positive influence. With very few exceptions, American Catholics, North and South, viewed abolitionism as contrary to Catholic ideals and ethics and in unholy association with European radicalism. Indeed, Catholic publications regularly opposed the abolitionists as unlawful revolutionaries.[32]

The absence of significant abolitionist influence upon the Protestant Episcopal Church and the Lutheran synods also seems readily apparent. Hardly any organ of either denomination acknowledged slavery as a religious problem that merited attention. The few Northern evangelical (Low Church) Episcopalians with antislavery feelings

[31]Philip E. Converse, "The Nature of Belief Systems in Mass Publics," in *Ideology and Discontent*, ed. David E. Apter (Glencoe: Free Press of Glencoe, 1964), 249–52.

[32]Madeline Hooke Rice, *American Catholic Opinion and the Slavery Controversy* (New York: Columbia University Press, 1944); Richard Roscoe Miller, *Slavery and Catholicism* (Durham, North Carolina, 1957); Benjamin J. Blied, *Catholics and the Civil War* (Milwaukee: Benjamin J. Blied, 1945).

188

felt they had to remain silent in order to secure support from Southern evangelicals in averting High Church Episcopal dominance. Similarly, save for the Franckean Synod of upstate New York and eventually the Pittsburgh Synod, local Lutheran bodies were unwilling to enter the slavery controversy.[33]

Thanks to Donald G. Mathews's *Slavery and Methodism* (1965), the situation in the Methodist Episcopal Church is also clear. In 1836 antislavery moderates advocating missions to Christianize Southern slaves and to colonize free blacks in Africa had forged the dominant posture of the church. But in the years that followed, abolitionist pressures upon the denomination's Northern congregations increased. By 1838 approximately six of the church's sixteen Northern conferences had abolitionist-sympathizing antislavery majorities; three other conferences had large antislavery minorities. By then there may have been as many as 50,000 abolitionists in the Methodist Church. Their pressures persisted, and by 1844 church moderates in the North had come to assume unequivocal antislavery postures. The result was a schism, with a Northern antislavery and a Southern proslavery branch of the church. Thus, the experience was different than that with the Catholic, Protestant Episcopal, and Lutheran churches, and the abolitionists exerted substantial influence upon the numerically large Methodist Episcopal Church.[34]

The situation of five other Protestant denominations—the Presbyterians, Congregationalists, Baptists, Quakers, and Unitarians—is considerably less clear. This is largely owing to the absence of high-caliber studies like that of Mathews. Most modern historians have asserted that the Northern wings of each of these denominations came to embrace only very mild and vacillating antislavery postures while they rejected and even castigated immediatist abolitionists. However, there were significant attitudinal variations among antislavery moderates. One therefore wonders whether most moderates drew closer to immediatists as time transpired—as they did in the Methodist Church. That is, even if immediatist abolitionism did not totally prevail within these five denominations, it is crucial to know how close to that goal

---

[33]For one of the few adequate discussions of the Protestant Episcopal Church posture on slavery, see Conrad James Engelder, "The Churches and Slavery: A Study of the Attitudes toward Slavery of the Major Protestant Denominations" (Ph.D. diss., University of Michigan, 1964), especially 260–63. For analyses of the Lutherans, see Robert Fortenbaugh, "American Lutheran Synods and Slavery, 1830–60," *Journal of Religion* 13 (January 1933): 72–92, and Douglas C. Stange's case study of the Franckean Synod, *Radicalism for Humanity: A Study of Lutheran Abolitionism* (St. Louis: Oliver Slave, 1970).

[34]Donald G. Mathews, *Slavery and Methodism: A Chapter in American Morality, 1780–1845* (Princeton: Princeton University Press, 1965), especially 86–87, 113–47, 168, 212–82.

189

it came. But those historians who have studied the five have not been able to answer that question with any precision. This is because they have offered generalizations based on national events like the 1837–38 schism within the Presbyterian Church and the 1844–45 controversy over the two national Baptist missionary societies. At the same time, they have acknowledged that the most important church activities took place at the local level because of the quasi autonomy of most local congregations. But they have not conducted very many local-level investigations. Consequently, it has been impossible to determine precisely what type of impact abolitionists had upon their more moderate antislavery colleagues, even if they fell short of converting those colleagues to immediatism.[35]

The consensus of historians, then, is that abolitionists did not win over the Catholic Church or the major Protestant denominations to immediatism—with the Methodists standing out as the sole exception. But because most scholarship on the topic is altogether inadequate and because there are too few studies at the local level, we must regard this as only a preliminary conclusion. On the other hand, there is certainly no basis, at the present time, to apply "the growth of a dissenting minority" paradigm to most churches or church-goers in the antebellum North.

In addition to problems posed by the dearth of abolitionist material resources, by ethnocultural scholarship, and by knowledge of abolitionist activity in Northern congregations, "the growth of a dissenting minority" paradigm suffers from a fourth fundamental defect. It

---

[35]For analysis of the Presbyterian Church, see C. Bruce Staiger, "Abolitionism and the Presbyterian Schism of 1837–1838," *Mississippi Valley Historical Review* 36 (December 1949): 391–414; George M. Marsden, *The Evangelical Mind and the New School Presbyterian Experience: A Case Study of Thought and Theology in Nineteenth-Century America* (New Haven: Yale University Press, 1970), 93–99; Andrew E. Murray, *Presbyterianism and the Negro: A History* (Philadelphia: Presbyterian Historical Society, 1966), especially 88–89, 104; Victor B. Howard, "The Anti-Slavery Movement in the Presbyterian Church, 1835–1861" (Ph.D. diss., Ohio State University, 1961), 1–88; and Robert W. Doherty, "Social Bases for the Presbyterian Schism of 1837–1838: The Philadelphia Case," *Journal of Social History* 2 (Fall 1968): 69–79. For studies of the Congregationalists, see Engelder, "Churches and Slavery," 92–117; W.D. Weatherford, *American Churches and the Negro* (Boston: Christopher Publishing House, 1957), 199–217; Clifton Herman Johnson, "The American Missionary Association, 1846–1861: A Study of Christian Abolitionism" (Ph.D. diss., University of North Carolina, 1958); and Robert Cholerton Senior, "New England Congregationalists and the Anti-Slavery Movement, 1830–1860" (Ph.D. diss., Yale University, 1954). For literature on the Baptists, see Mary Burnham Putnam, *The Baptists and Slavery, 1840–45* (Ann Arbor: George Wahr, 1913); and Engelder, "Churches and Slavery," 53–91. Thomas E. Drake, *Quakers and Slavery in America* (New Haven: Yale University Press, 1950), and Douglas C. Stange, *Patterns of Antislavery among American Unitarians, 1831–1860* (Cranbury, New Jersey: Fairleigh Dickinson University Press, 1977), are the major studies of these liberal denominations.

190

assumes that abolitionists set out to convert the North to antislavery and effected their goal. But events may not have transpired so precisely as the abolitionists had hoped. Instead of converting the North, they may have aroused the South to an aggressive defense of slavery. This Southern defense may have cultivated anti-Southern, antislavery feelings through the North.

There is a certain logic and some grounding in fact for what is really a Southern-based alternative to the "growth" paradigm—an alternative that views the abolitionists as comparatively uninfluential actors in a larger sectional drama. We know that a few abolitionists like Gamaliel Bailey and Samuel Lewis upset a great many slaveholders through their ineffectual efforts to win over the nonslaveholding South. We also know that subsequent proslavery Southern pressure upon the North was direct and substantial—that if there had been no Southern sectionalism or secession, there would have been no Civil War. Conversely, it is apparent that by the 1850s most Northern elites were considerably more anti-Southern than proabolitionist.

It is necessary, of course, to bear in mind that Southerners began making sharp attacks and heavy demands upon the North for a complex variety of reasons. Since some of these Southern attacks and demands were made even before the crusade for immediatist abolitionism commenced, several of the reasons for them had nothing to do with immediatism. Nevertheless, it is certainly time to seriously test a hypothesis that historians have toyed with since George Fort Milton and Henry H. Simms in the 1930s and early 1940s—to determine whether abolitionists quite unintentionally contributed to Northern antislavery by stirring up the animosities of the proslavery South. If this is roughly valid, it could move us from "the growth of a dissenting minority" to an abolitionist "push"-Southern "shove" paradigm. The Southern "shove" would become more central than the initial abolitionist "push" in cultivating widespread Northern antagonism to the South and to its peculiar institution.

III

Given the present state of historical research, what should be done with the "growth" paradigm for antebellum abolitionism? Many of the abolitionists who forged it and the historians who espoused it have been ambivalent on the extent of abolitionist influence in the North. Abolitionists were always short on material resources. They had little electoral success at the crucial local level. To be sure, they had decided influence upon Northern Methodists, but minimal impact upon Catholics, Protestant Episcopalians, or Lutherans. Considerable research on the local level is required before we can assess their precise impact upon Northern Presbyterians, Congregationalists, Baptists, Quakers, or Unitarians. Finally, the most important consequence of their con-

191

duct may have been a negative Southern response which, in turn, served to cultivate both anti-Southern and antislavery feeling in the North.

From these observations, we can conclude, as Aileen Kraditor once did, that we simply do not know what general impact abolitionists had upon Northern public opinion.[36] This conclusion would require at least tentative abandonment of "the growth of a dissenting minority" paradigm. But given the poor state of our knowledge of the abolitionists' church activities and the dearth of systematic research on their role in the anti-Northern militancy of the South, total if tentative abandonment of the paradigm seems premature.

It is certain that the abolitionists exerted some influence at certain times and in certain places. They were among the articulate elites of Jacksonian society and intimate exchanges among disparate elites was a fact of antebellum life. Thus, the abolitionists were not anonymous to the power figures of the North. Daniel Webster knew Lewis Tappan. Horace Greeley knew Oliver Johnson. By the mid-1840s, even Garrison rubbed shoulders with "Boston respectability." Thus, in a situation unlike contemporary mass society, the abolitionists were able to see and to communicate their views to sundry Northern power brokers. By 1838 there may have been as many as 250,000 abolitionists operating within perhaps 1,350 antislavery societies. They were extraordinarily energetic in trying to propagate their views. In addition to countless conversations and letter exchanges, from mid-1837 to mid-1838 activists in the American Anti-Slavery Society published 7,877 bound volumes, 47,250 tracts and pamphlets, 4,100 circulars, and 10,490 prints. The Society's weekly newspaper, the *Emancipator,* had an annual circulation of 217,000, *Human Rights* enjoyed a yearly circulation of 189,000, the *Slave's Friend* reached 131,050, and the *Quarterly Anti-Slavery Magazine* ran at 9,000. Combined with this, the A.A.S.S. had a well-organized agency system that sent abolitionists to all areas of the North to make converts.[37] In view of the task that the abolitionists had undertaken, Benjamin Quarles was correct to note that their resources were quite limited. Yet it is certain that most powerful Northerners had perused at least one or two abolitionist publications while some had direct verbal exchanges with local abolitionists. Indeed, by the 1850s many Northern power brokers were so disturbed by the Southern "slave power conspiracy" that they became considerably less antagonistic to the abolitionists. If their ears were still not fully open to immediatist

[36]Aileen S. Kraditor, "The Abolitionists Rehabilitated," *Studies on the Left* 5 (Spring 1965): 103–6.

[37]Dumond, *Antislavery Origins,* 84–85; John L. Myers, "The Agency System of the Anti-Slavery Movement, 1832–1837, and Its Antecedents in Other Benevolent and Reform Societies" (Ph.D. diss., University of Michigan, 1960).

192

Abolitionist Studies

ideas, they had ceased to assume that abolitionist words were invariably those of "the enemies of the people."[38]

Moreover, as Ronald G. Walters has demonstrated in his brilliant 1976 study, *The Antislavery Appeal*, there was a cultural dimension to immediatism that made abolitionists kindred spirits with many other antebellum reformers. Abolitionists manifested and championed a pervasive reformist goal of cultural voluntarism—the notion that the good society consisted of individuals who acted on their own initiative while conforming to society's need for moral conduct. Like many other Americans with reformist inclinations, they believed that individual emotion was the surest guide to right and wrong while they insisted that "civilized" society suppress the immoral animalistic qualities of individual impulse. Desirous of both spontaneous quest for individual desires and "proper" moral restraints, the abolitionists viewed black bondage as invidious: it curbed spontaneous pursuits and it eliminated moral restraints. Whereas many other adherents to cultural voluntarism did not apply it so rigorously to slavery, their basic cultural values were still similar to those of the abolitionists. Thus, other Northerners with broad reform disposition were not only in physical proximity to the abolitionists; their basic cultural values were similar, so that meaningful dialogue could ensue.

In addition to having at least some rapport with influential Northerners, especially those with broad reformist sympathies, it is clear that abolitionists changed the course of events in the North at certain very specific points in time. Clearly there could have been no antiabolitionist mobs in Northern communities in the mid-1830s had there been no abolitionists. Nor would the intense Congressional controversy over the Gag Rule have ensued had there been no abolitionists to flood Congress with antislavery petitions. Consider more specific examples. Had immediatist Abishai Scofield failed to attend a session of the Chenango, New York, Presbytery early in 1846, a resolution placing that body on record against slavery would have received little support. The resolution passed by a single vote—Scofield's.[39] More important, recall that although Liberty Party presidential candidate James G. Birney received only 62,300 votes in 1844, the 15,000 he drew in New York State were enough to throw the state's electoral votes to Polk over Clay. Had Clay won in New York, he would have won the presidency.[40]

[38]Lorman Ratner develops this point regarding Northern attitudes of the 1850s in *Powder Keg: Northern Opposition to the Antislavery Movement, 1831–1840* (New York: Basic Books, 1968), 140–41.

[39]Amasa Foote to Abishai Scofield, 6 April 1846, Abishai Scofield MSS, Burton Historical Collection, Detroit Public Library.

[40]Hugh H. Davis, "The Reform Career of Joshua Leavitt" (Ph.D. diss., Ohio State University, 1969), 276.

193

One can cite many such examples of abolitionist influence, as one can cite many more situations where abolitionists had no influence. The point is that abolitionists certainly had some influence in the North. But until we learn more about Northern churches at the local level, we have no basis to say that their influence was either growing or substantial during the antebellum decades. Rather than speak of "the growth of a dissenting minority," it is more accurate to refer to the *constant presence* of an articulate dissenting minority. Sectional conflict, Civil War, and legal emancipation would probably have occurred even if there had been no active abolition movement, although certain specific aspects of these occurrences might have been different. Often, as in the case of Northern antiabolitionist mobs and Southern fears of an abolitionized North, their contribution was unintentional. But on certain specific occasions, their precise intentions were effected. In January of 1839 Horace Bushnell issued a warning to the abolitionists that, despite its unfairly antagonistic tone, seems to accurately reflect the state of current knowledge on the movement:

> I turn on the other hand, to our Anti-Slavery brethren, and say, do not regard yourselves too hastily, as the beginning of a movement for liberty, or assume too much consequence to yourselves in the organization you have raised up. Neither conclude, too hastily, that what you are doing is a real advantage. The destruction of slavery will be accomplished; either with you, or without you; or, if you make it necessary, in spite of you.[41]

[41]Horace Bushnell, *A Discourse on the Slavery Question. Delivered in the North Church, Hartford, January 10, 1839* (Hartford, 1839), 11.

194

CHAPTER VI

WENDELL PHILLIPS:

THE PATRICIAN AS AGITATOR

❁

COLLEGE *bred men should be agitators to tear a question open and riddle it with light and to educate the moral sense of the masses.*
WENDELL PHILLIPS

THE historical reputation of Wendell Phillips stands very low. With the single exception of V. L. Parrington, the standard writers have been handling him roughly for over forty years. Finding him useful chiefly as a foil to Abraham Lincoln, historians have stereotyped him as the wrongheaded radical of the Civil War crisis—an emotional person, lacking in responsibility, but quick to condemn those who had it, standing always for extremes that public opinion would not sustain, reckless, mischievous, and vindictive.

But conventional historians in condemning men like Phillips have used a double standard of political morality. Scholars know that the processes of politics normally involve exaggeration, mythmaking, and fierce animosities. In the pursuit of their ends the abolitionists were hardly more guilty of these things than the more conventional politicians were in theirs. Somehow the same historians who have been indulgent with men who exaggerated because they wanted to be elected have been extremely severe with men who exaggerated because they wanted to free the slaves.

And Phillips is vulnerable. He was an agitator by profession, and the agitator is always vulnerable. Horace Greeley cleverly—but untruthfully—said of him that he was so lacking in largeness of views that "he cannot conceive of a tempest outside of a teapot." Dozens of irresponsible utterances can be combed out of his speeches. "The South," he once said, "is one great brothel,

267

where half a million of women are flogged to prostitution," and the sentence has made its way into innumerable histories of the slavery controversy as an illustration of the abolitionist mentality.[1] The generation of historians that has condemned this as a distortion has also chosen to ignore the vital subject of miscegenation and the light it throws upon the slave system and its caste psychology. It is hard to say which distortion is the more serious, but the advantage in controversy will always rest with the academic historian who can fall back upon the pose of scholarly impartiality to substantiate his claims.

Phillips was in some ways more sophisticated than those who condemn him. Certainly he had attained a higher level of intellectual self-awareness. Both historians and agitators are makers of myths, a fact of which Phillips was intensely conscious, but while few historians of the slavery controversy have had a reasoned philosophy of history, Phillips had a reasoned philosophy of agitation. The work of the agitator, he saw, consists chiefly in talk; his function is not to make laws or determine policy, but to influence the public mind in the interest of some large social transformation. His role in society is vastly different from the responsible politician's, and rightly so:

> The reformer is careless of numbers, disregards popularity, and deals only with ideas, conscience, and common sense. He feels, with Copernicus, that as God waited long for an interpreter, so he can wait for his followers. He neither expects nor is overanxious for immediate success. The politician dwells in an everlasting NOW. His motto is 'Success'—his aim, votes. His object is not absolute right, but, like Solon's laws, as much right as the people will sanction. His office is not to instruct public opinion, but to represent it. Thus, in England, Cobden, the reformer, created sentiment, and Peel, the politician, stereotyped it into statutes.

The agitator is necessary to a republican commonwealth; he is the counterweight to sloth and indifference.

> Republics exist only on the tenure of being constantly agitated. The antislavery agitation is an important, nay, an essential part of

---

[1] The qualification with which Phillips's sentence ends: "or, worse still, are degraded to believe it honorable," is generally omitted when he is quoted.

the machinery of the state. . . . Every government is always growing corrupt. Every Secretary of State . . . is an enemy to the
people of necessity, because the moment he joins the government,
he gravitates against that popular agitation which is the life of a
republic. A republic is nothing but a constant overflow of lava. . . .
The republic which sinks to sleep, trusting to constitutions and
machinery, to politicians and statesmen, for the safety of its liberties,
never will have any.

Like many other Americans of his period, Phillips had an un-
conquerable faith in moral progress. He believed that he was
living in an age of ideas—a democratic age, in which the ideas
of the masses were the important thing. There was no higher
office, he felt, than exercising the moral imagination necessary
to mold the sentiments of the masses into the form most suitable
for the next forward movement of history. "The people always
mean right, and in the end they will have the right." The man
who launches a sound argument for a just cause is certain to
win in the long run. "The difficulty of the present day and with
us is, we are bullied by institutions. . . . Stand on the pedestal
of your own individual independence, summon these institutions about you, and judge them."

Phillips's career illustrates the principle that the agitator is
likely to be a crisis thinker. In periods of relative social peace
the agitator labors under intellectual as well as practical restraints, for he thinks in terms of the *ultimate potentialities* of
social conflicts rather than the immediate compromises by which
they are softened. His moral judgments are made from the stand-
point of absolute values, with which the mass of men cannot
comfortably live. But when a social crisis or revolutionary
period at last matures, the sharp distinctions that govern the
logical and doctrinaire mind of the agitator become at one with
the realities, and he appears overnight to the people as a plausible and forceful thinker. The man who has maintained that all
history is the history of class struggles and has appeared so wide
of the mark in times of class collaboration may become a powerful leader when society is seething with unresolved class conflict; the man who has been vainly demanding the abolition of
slavery for thirty years may become a vital figure when emancipation makes its appearance as a burning issue of practical politics. Such was the experience of Wendell Phillips: although he

never held office, he became one of the most influential Americans during the few years after the fall of Fort Sumter.

Phillips is by far the most impressive of the abolitionists. Although he shared most of the foibles of the abolitionist movement, he was a keener observer and had a more flexible mind than most of his colleagues, and in the end he rose high above the intellectual limitations of Garrisonism. He was also the only major figure who combined in one career the abolition ferment of the prewar period with the labor movement of the postwar industrial epoch. When he began his agitations, he was steeped in the moral transcendentalism of the age of Emerson, Parker, and Thoreau; when he died, in 1884, he was a militant partisan of labor who spoke in the phrases—though he could never fully assimilate them—of economic realism. Often mistaken, he had often been utterly right when others were terribly wrong. A man of conscience and keen perceptivity, he represented the priceless provincial integrity that can be found in midcentury America wherever the seed of the Puritans had been sown.

The first of the Phillipses came to America in 1630; the family prospered through the generations, always producing large numbers of merchants and Congregational clergymen. Wendell's father, a wealthy lawyer with excellent mercantile connections, became the first Mayor of Boston under the city charter of 1821. Life gave the son everything a Boston boy could want— family, good looks, wealth, brains, and an education at the Boston Latin School and Harvard. At the university he was a social lion, a darling among the aristocrats; Thomas Wentworth Higginson recalled many years later that Phillips was the only undergraduate for whom the family carriage was habitually sent out to Cambridge on Saturday mornings to fetch him to Boston for Sundays. When Beacon Street turned its back on him for joining the abolitionists, Phillips could indulge in the snobbery of calling his detractors "men of no family."

In 1835, after a course of study at Harvard Law School under Justice Joseph Story, Phillips opened a law office in Court Street. It was then only four years since William Lloyd Garrison had begun publishing the *Liberator*. Respectable people, although they might express a genteel distaste for slavery, an institution peculiar to the South and long since disappeared from Massachusetts, would have nothing to do with Garrison; solid citizens like Edward Everett could publicly express pleasure at the capture of fugitive slaves. State and Milk Streets hummed with Southern trade.

One afternoon, not long after Phillips began his practice, a mob rushed down Court Street dragging Garrison by a rope. When the lawyer ran to the street and inquired why the Boston regiment was not called out to protect the victim, a bystander pointed out that most of the regiment was in the crowd. Phillips, born within sight of Bunker Hill and nurtured on the traditions of the Revolution, was an intense Boston patriot, and this violation of civil liberty in the old town revolted him. He soon drew close to the abolition movement, and in little more than a year married Anne Terry Greene, daughter of a wealthy Boston shipper, a stern militant among the early abolitionists. "My wife made me an out and out abolitionist," he declared in later years, "and she always preceded me in the adoption of the various causes I have advocated." For a short time he played only a small part in the abolition movement, but this was enough to burn the bridges that bound him to Beacon Street. He became an outcast to the Boston aristocracy and lost his prospects as a lawyer. His family concluded that he was insane and thought seriously of putting him in an asylum.

In 1837, at the age of twenty-six, Phillips really found himself. Elijah Lovejoy, a newspaper editor, had been murdered by a mob in Alton, Illinois, for insisting upon his right to attack slavery. William Ellery Channing called a protest meeting at Faneuil Hall, and Phillips was standing among the crowd when Attorney General William Austin rose to defend the slayers of Lovejoy by comparing them to the mob that managed the Boston Tea Party. Nothing could have been better calculated to arouse the provincial patriot in Phillips. He leaped to the platform and denounced Austin in a remarkable extemporaneous speech which was cheered enthusiastically. He had felt his power over an audience, and it was natural now that he should throw himself wholeheartedly into abolitionist agitation.

Phillips was the most valuable acquisition of the New England abolitionists. He brought to the movement a good name, an ingratiating personality, a great talent for handling mobs and hecklers, and, above all, his voice. He was probably the most effective speaker of his time. Chauncey Depew, when over ninety, declared that he could recall hearing all the leading speakers from Clay and Webster to Woodrow Wilson, and that Phillips was the greatest. In casual intercourse not everyone found him an impressive man; Emerson even said that he had only a "platform existence." But if this was true, his platform personality at least was incomparably genuine. His manner, informal and direct in contrast to the pompous pedestal oratory that was so common, warmed his audiences. Listeners, sympathetically disposed, could achieve a feeling of identification with him that was impossible with formal orators like Webster and Edward Everett. As he himself said of Daniel O'Connell, his speech was effortless—"like picking up chips." Where other speakers indulged in long periods and complex metaphors, he understood the rhythms of speech best adapted to the needs of agitation. His talk was familiar, often homely, but his inspired passages throbbed with the heady moral rhetoric of transcendentalism, and grew nervous and staccato in their impassioned climaxes, sustained only by their continuous moral thunder and lightning. When he spoke, Emerson testified, "the whole air was full of splendors." "Phillips goes to the popular assembly as the others go to their library. Whilst he speaks, his mind feeds. Animal spirits, enthusiasm, insight, and decision." Speakers refused to follow him on the platform; if he were not last, everything would be anticlimax.

Phillips's own wealth, and his wife's, would have released him from the cramping necessity of sober work, but he turned his talents into money. Not long after joining the abolitionists, Phillips closed his law office and devoted himself to speaking and lecturing. His income from this source ranged from $10,000 to $15,000 a year; one of his standard lectures, called "The Lost Arts," which seems today in cold print a rather feeble performance—"not worth hearing" was his own judgment—was repeated over two thousand times from Portland to St. Louis and earned him by his estimate $150,000 over a period of forty-five years. He exerted pressure on lecture societies by charging high fees for his formal talks but speaking against slavery free of charge. Charity became a kind of vocation with him; his generosity was almost pathological. An old memorandum book listing his charitable donations between 1845 and 1875 was found among his effects after his death. The personal gifts, always itemized by recipients, as "John Brown . . . a poor Italian . . . Mrs. Garnaut . . . poor . . . refugee," came to over $65,000.

During the troubled years following the murder of Lovejoy, Phillips went on dozens of "abolitionizing" trips through neighboring towns in Massachusetts or beyond the borders of the state. He would return each time to report to his wife, a nervous invalid seldom able to leave her couch, whose famous injunction: "Wendell, don't shilly-shally!" rang in the memories of their friends. And Phillips did not shilly-shally. He followed Garrison through his most intransigent phases, cursed the Constitution, and defied mobs by calling for the dissolution of this "Union with Slaveholders." He stood for a multitude of causes, demanding equal rights for women, temperance, freedom for Ireland, justice for the American Indian, abolition of capital punishment, kinder treatment of the mentally ill.

The life of agitation had its dangers. Mobs followed him about, and Phillips, who had once been welcome at the elegant doors of the most exclusive homes in Boston, learned to slip out of the rear exits of churches and lecture halls and make his way to safety through side streets and narrow alleyways. He became the favorite target of the brokers' clerks and cotton traders' minions who often packed his meetings for sport. In the winter of 1860–1 he was mobbed three times within a month and might have been killed but for a bodyguard of husky young Turnvereiners who formed a cordon around him. At one of these meetings, as his guards stood impassive below, Phillips remained on the platform for an hour waiting to be heard while a hostile crowd bellowed and stamped in the galleries. Then he spoke quietly to the reporters sitting directly beneath him in the pit until the hecklers demanded that he raise his voice for them to hear. He made of agitation an art and a science. "Wendell Phillips," complained a Virginia newspaper, "is an infernal machine set to music."

II

The abolitionist movement was based upon a moral frenzy, not an economic discontent. After about 1830 almost all abolitionists were resident in the North. For the most part they were middle-class people who had no material stake in the conservation or destruction of the slave system, which was in the most literal sense none of their business. Since slavery was a moral offense rather than an economic injury to them, they came to look upon it not as an economic institution but as a breach of the ordinations of God. Abolitionism was a religious movement, emerging from the ferment of evangelical Protestantism, psychologically akin to other reforms—women's rights, temperance, and pacifism—which agitated the spirits of the Northern middle classes during the three decades before the Civil War. Its philosophy was essentially a theology, its technique similar to the techniques of revivalism, its agencies the church congregations of the towns. "Our enterprise," declared Phillips, "is eminently a religious one, dependent for success entirely on the religious sentiment of the people." Again: "The conviction that SLAVERY IS A SIN is the Gibraltar of our cause." Theodore Weld, one of the most effective leaders of the Western wing of the movement, once wrote:

> In discussing the subject of slavery, I have always presented it as pre-eminently a moral question, arresting the conscience of the nation. . . . As a question of politics and national economy, I have passed it with scarce a look or a word, believing that the business of the abolitionists is with the heart of the nation, rather than with its purse strings.

The rarefied moral atmosphere in which the abolitionists treated slavery was heightened by the fact that, unable to agitate or discuss the subject in the South, they were closed off from direct observation of the institution and from contact with those who were defending it. All they could do, in effect, was to go among the people of the North who were not slaveowners and persuade them that slavery was an evil thing from which they should divorce themselves. They had, to be sure, originally planned to make their campaign an appeal to the conscience of the slaveowners themselves, but sober observation of the Southern mind soon showed the hopelessness of such an effort. The minds of the masters were closed, and the abolitionists had precious little access to the minds of the slaves—nor did they want to incite insurrection. As a result they were driven inward intellectually, and their thinking on slavery assumed an increasingly theological and millennial cast. They dealt of necessity in wholesale condemnations and categorical imperatives, which offended many who sympathized with their purposes. James Russell Lowell thought that the abolition leaders "treat ideas as ignorant persons do cherries. They think them unwholesome unless they are swallowed stones and all."

It was understandable, then, that the abolitionists should not have had too clear a conception of how the slave was to be freed nor how an illiterate, landless, and habitually dependent people were to become free and self-sufficient citizens in the hostile environment of the white South. The Garrisonian abolitionists were also misled by the heartening case of abolitionism in England. In the British Empire slavery had been abolished by law in 1833; the system of postponed emancipation provided in the law had proved inferior to immediate liberation, which was adopted with considerable success in Antigua. Taking inspiration from the English precedent, the Americans concluded that the only possible strategy for them was to demand "immediate" abolition. This conclusion, of course, took additional strength from their theological prepossession: slavery was a sin, and one does not seek to purge oneself of sinfulness by slow degrees—one casts it out. Abolition was a question of right, not expediency, said Garrison, "and if slaves have a right to their freedom, it ought to be given them, regardless of the consequences."

Other abolitionists, feeling that it would be impossible to make a quick jump from slavery into freedom, and realizing that slavery in the United States was not legally a national but a state institution, which might be dropped in one place while it was flourishing in another, played with the metaphysics of "immediatism" by calling for "immediate emancipation which is gradually accomplished." Gradual methods, in short, should be immediately begun. Thus James Thome receded from the high ground of the Garrisonians: "We did not wish [the slaves] turned loose, nor even to be governed by the same Code of Laws which are adapted to intelligent citizens." To Garrison's followers this sounded like a proposal to leave the Negroes in some kind of subject condition, like a plan for forced labor—"the substitution of one type of slavery for another." Further, there were few people of any liberal cast of mind who would not agree that somehow, some time, in the distant future, the slaves ought surely to be free—Lincoln, for example, became one of these— and it was important to the militants to dissociate themselves from such Fabian abolitionism. They felt, therefore, that they must cling to the dogma of immediatism even though they could not translate it into a plan of action. Their solution of this propagandistic and doctrinal dilemma took a theological form: slavery was a sin, and one needs no plan to stop sinning. "Duty is ours and events are God's," blared Garrison. ". . . All you have to do is to set your slaves at liberty!" "To be without a plan," cried his followers, "is the true genius and glory of the Anti-Slavery enterprise!"

The abolitionists were even less clear on how the Negro was to become an independent human being after he was freed. Southern proslavery apologists were quick to seize upon this weakness of the abolition case; they grasped all too well the anticipated difficulties of emancipation, and expounded them with the tenacity of the obsessed. Lincoln, who struggled con- scientiously to imagine what could be done about slavery, con- fessed sadly that even if he had full power to dispose of it he would not know how. The abolitionists likewise did not know, but they did not know that they did not know. The result was that when formal freedom finally came to the Negro, many abo- litionists failed entirely to realize how much more help he would need or what form it should take. Phillips, however, had learned to transcend Garrisonian thought. In the critical hour of Recon- struction he dropped the veil of dogma and turned to the reali- ties.

His long acceptance of William Lloyd Garrison's leadership was the greatest handicap that Phillips carried into his abolition activities. Recent historical research, especially that of Gilbert Hobbs Barnes, has shown that Garrison does not deserve his historical reputation as the towering figure of American aboli- tionism. Abolitionism was not a centrally organized movement. Its largest effective units were the state societies, not the national ones. Garrison was not only not the leader of the movement at large, but he was not even accepted as its leader in New Eng- land. The American Anti-Slavery Society, which he captured in

1840 and controlled thereafter, existed chiefly in name.[2] The question has been raised whether he did not do the movement more harm than good, especially in the period after 1840. A harsh and quarrelsome fanatic with an unnecessarily large number of irrelevant peripheral enthusiasms—among them anti-Sabbatarianism, women's rights, and nonresistance—which he insisted on intruding into his abolition activities in the most damaging way, Garrison estranged many potential friends. The influential Western abolitionists who held Phillips in considerable esteem found Garrison intolerable. ("I wonder," wrote James G. Birney to Elizur Wright in 1844, "how such a man as Phillips can quietly stomach all the wretched stuff he has to receive from his associates.")[3]

The secular philosophy of the abolitionists, in so far as they had one, was taken from the Declaration of Independence. They wanted natural rights for the colored man. This philosophy had a particularly strong voice in Phillips. James Otis, John Hancock, Sam Adams, and Colonel Warren were all but contemporaries of his, and he enlisted them in his campaigns as naturally as he did his audiences in the lyceums. But the natural-rights philosophy, as well as his Christian training, led logically to the higher law doctrine. When Garrison, during the 1840's, turned upon the Constitution and urged abolitionists to call for the dissolution of the Union—"No Union with Slaveholders"—Phillips followed his lead, closed his law office because he could not be an attorney without swearing an oath of allegiance, and in 1845 wrote a pamphlet for the American Anti-Slavery Society entitled *Can Abolitionists Vote or Take Office under the United States Constitution?* The answer, of course, was in the negative.

---

[2] "Probably not one in a hundred of even the New England abolitionists ever accepted the special views which the Garrisonian organization adopted after 1843," concludes Jesse Macy in *The Antislavery Crusade*. After Garrison captured the American Anti-Slavery Society in 1840, its annual income fell from $47,000 to $7,000, and did not rise above $12,000 until 1856.

[3] Cf. Thoreau on Phillips in a letter, March 12, 1845: "He stands so firmly and so effectively alone, and one honest man is so much more than a host that we cannot but feel that he does himself an injustice when he reminds us of the American [Anti-Slavery] Society, which he represents. . . . Here is one who is at the same time an eloquent speaker and a righteous man."

Every compromise with evil, reasoned Phillips, is fatal. Any man who votes thereby supports the Constitution, since he consents to appoint as his political agent an officeholder who must swear to uphold the Constitution of the United States. That Constitution is a proslavery instrument; in its very apportionment of representation for Congress it sanctions Southern slaveholding. The common military forces of the Union can be called upon to suppress a revolt of slaves. To support such an instrument of government would be to participate in the moral guilt of slavery. Although Phillips did not suggest that the abolitionists support no human government at all (the position preferred by Garrison), he insisted that they must not support *"this* Government based upon and acting for slavery." Every man is a free moral agent who must bear responsibility for his political acts. It is the bounden duty of the individual not to give even indirect sanction to slavery. "Immoral laws are doubtless void, and should not be obeyed."

Following this creed, the Garrisonians called upon the Northern states to separate from the South. This demand was characteristic of their religious psychology: it was doubtful how much disunion through Northern secession would have accomplished for the slaves, but by dissolving the Union the abolitionists could wash away *their* personal sin of participating in a slaveholding commonwealth. Garrison's flamboyant and inflammatory device of tearing up or burning the Constitution in public probably did the cause considerable harm. But the most damaging aspect of the Garrisonians' attitude toward the Union was that it cut them off from the possibilities of propagandizing through political action. Other abolitionists made excellent propagandistic use of the right of petition by demanding that Congress abolish slavery in the District of Columbia.

After 1840 the non-Garrisonian abolition movement became increasingly political, and although it never gathered much numerical strength as an independent political force, it had an appreciable effect on the major parties. When James G. Birney, running on the Liberty Party ticket in 1844, took enough votes from the New York State Whigs to cost Henry Clay the state's electoral votes, and with them the presidency, the lesson was obvious: abolition sentiment was strategically important. It became increasingly so as the years went on. Thus it was men like

Birney who helped to convince men like Lincoln that the moral revulsion from slavery could not be "safely disregarded." Moreover, the abolitionists themselves learned much from participation in politics, not the least of which was the lesson that a strategy dictated by absolute moral intransigence, however defensible in logic, was not so effective in reality as a strategy qualified by opportunism. They learned that the abolition of slavery must be linked with other, more material issues to reach its full political strength.[4] Political abolitionism, as it became more and more dilute in principle, somehow became stronger and stronger as an actual menace to slavery. The Liberty Party disappeared after two campaigns, but was superseded by the Free-Soil Party, which, in 1848, again held the critical balance in New York State and again determined the outcome of a national election. At length the Free-Soil principle became the central issue of the Republican Party. Misled by Garrison's antipolitical point of view, Phillips failed until the last moment to appreciate the contribution of political friction to the growth of antislavery sentiment. He saw only the fact that the antislavery emphasis of the political parties grew weaker with time and less defensible in abstract principle. "The Liberty party," he declared in 1858, "was on the defensive, the Free Soil party was on the defensive, the Republican party is on the defensive, and each one of them has been driven back, back, back, until now the Republican party has nothing to defend." Only after Lincoln's election did he begin to perceive the possibilities of the major political party as an abolition vehicle. "The Republican party," he then correctly predicted, "have undertaken a problem the solution of which will force them to our position."

At one point Phillips parted company with Garrison. There was an inconsistency between the Garrisonian philosophy of nonresistance and the natural-rights doctrine of the Declaration of Independence. Natural rights meant the right to resist, the

---

[4] One of his colleagues, Theodore Foster, wrote to Birney, December 7, 1845: "I am more and more convinced by reflection that the antislavery feeling alone will never bring over to the Liberty party a majority of all the voters of the United States. We must have some other motives to present to people, which will appeal directly to their own interests. Unless we secure support from other considerations, we shall never, as a party, become a majority, and our *principles* will find some other channel of operation than the Liberty Party."

right to rebel. If the Fathers could revolt, so could the Negro. The Fugitive Slave Law should be resisted by force, Phillips believed, and he would defend the murder of a slave-catcher by a slave. As to slave insurrection:

> I do not believe that . . . we shall see the total abolition of slavery, unless it comes in some critical conjuncture of national affairs, when the slave, taking advantage of a crisis in the fate of his masters, shall dictate his own terms. . . . The hour will come—God hasten it!—when the American people shall so stand on the deck of their Union, "built i' the eclipse, and rigged with curses dark." If I ever live to see that hour, I shall say to every slave, Strike now for Freedom! . . . I know what anarchy is. I know what civil war is. I can imagine the scenes of blood through which a rebellious slave-population must march to their rights. They are dreadful. And yet, I do not know that to an enlightened mind, a scene of civil war is any more sickening than the thought of a hundred and fifty years of slavery. . . . No, I confess I am not a non-resistant. The reason why I advise the slave to be guided by a policy of peace is because he has no chance.

Even after the execution of John Brown, however, Phillips asserted his belief that slavery would "not go down in blood": "I believe in moral suasion. The age of bullets is over." Even during the secession crisis he still vested his hopes in the general sweep of progress, which he pointed out had a firm material basis.

> You see exactly what my hopes rest upon. Growth! . . . You perceive my hope of freedom rests upon these rocks: 1st, mechanical progress. First man walked, dug the earth with his hands, ate what he could pick up . . . then sewing machines lift woman out of torture, steam marries the continents, and the telegraph flashes news like sunlight over the globe. Every step made hands worth less, and brains worth more; and that is the death of slavery. . . . I am sure you cannot make a nation with one-half steam-boats, sewing-machines and Bibles, and the other half slaves. Then another rock of my hope is these Presidential canvasses,—the saturnalia of American life,—when slaves like Seward . . . fling all manner of insult on their masters. Then the ghost of John Brown makes Virginia quick to calculate the profit and loss of slavery. Beside this, honest men, few, but the salt of the times. . . .

Phillips joyously welcomed the crisis caused by Lincoln's election:

> If the telegraph speaks truth, for the first time in our history the *slave* has chosen a President of the United States. . . . Not an abolitionist, hardly an anti-slavery man, Mr. Lincoln consents to represent an antislavery idea. . . . He seems to govern; he only reigns. . . . Lincoln is in *place,* Garrison in power.

Precisely how Lincoln's victory would further the cause he did not know. It was enough that the country now had a major political party which "dares to say that slavery is a sin—in *some* places!"

With other abolitionists, Phillips persisted in saying that the South should be allowed to secede in peace. For almost twenty years he had been advocating disunion; it made little difference whether the North or the South should be first to bow out. The Union had been a moral failure; only the money interests wanted to save it. In fact, however, the North would be materially better off by itself. We might have a right to prevent secession, but why exert ourselves to save an artificial and unprofitable Union? The rest of the slave states would follow South Carolina out of the Union, he foresaw, but the Gulf states in the new Confederacy would open the slave trade and bring ruin upon the slave-breeding states and North Carolina, which then would "gravitate to us free." The standing army, maintained at Northern as well as Southern expense, helped to secure the Southern states from insurrection; let them go free and insurrection would break out. In the end, economic progress would undermine slavery—a strong new note in Phillips's propaganda:

> What is the contest in Virginia now? Between the men who want to make their slaves mechanics for the increased wages it will secure, and the men who oppose, for fear of the influence it will have on the general security of slave property and white throats. Just that dispute will go on, wherever the Union is dissolved. Slavery comes to an end by the laws of trade. . . .
>
> Indeed, the Gulf States are essentially in a feudal condition, an aristocracy resting on slaves,—no middle class. To sustain government on the costly model of our age necessitates a middle class of trading, manufacturing energy. The merchant of the nineteenth century spurns to be subordinate. The introduction of such a class will

create in the Gulf States that very irrepressible conflict which they leave us to avoid,—which alive now in the Border States makes these unwilling to secede,—which once created will soon undermine the aristocracy of the Gulf States and bring them back to us free.

Phillips was confident that the Confederacy would be too weak to attack the North "for the only annoyance we can give her—the sight and influence of our nobler civilization." But less than a month later, when the Confederacy did strike at Sumter, he saw the situation in a new light. This was a defensive war, therefore justified; and out of it emancipation might come. The abolitionists, he confessed in his first post-Sumter address, had imagined that everything could be settled by freedom of thought and discussion.

> Our mistake, if any, has been that we counted too much on the intelligence of the masses, on the honesty and wisdom of statesmen as a class. Perhaps we did not give weight enough to the fact we saw, that this nation is made up of different ages; not homogeneous, but a mixed mass of different centuries. The North *thinks*,—can appreciate argument,—is the nineteenth century,—hardly any struggle left in it but that between the working class and the money kings. The South dreams,—it is the thirteenth and fourteenth century,— baron and serf,—noble and slave. . . . Our struggle is therefore between barbarism and civilization. Such can only be settled by arms.

For Phillips the great goal of the war was not to save the Union but to free the slave. Lincoln's delay stirred Phillips to those tirades which have done so much to cloud his reputation. Like the Radicals in Congress, he saw the futility of waging a conservative war. The South was fighting to save slavery; the North was fighting "not to have it hurt." Lincoln doubtless meant well, but he was no leader—"he is a first-rate second-rate man . . . a mere convenience waiting like any other broomstick to be used." But if the agitator was hard on the President, he was sound in his estimation of Lincoln's strategy. "The President never professed to be a leader. The President is the agent of public opinion. He wants to know what you will allow and what you demand that he shall do." Lincoln was waiting to see if public opinion would sustain emancipation. Very well, then,

Wendell Phillips would see to it that public opinion would sustain nothing else.[5] In July 1861 he said:

> I put my faith in the honesty of Abraham Lincoln as an individual, in the pledge which a long life has given of Chase's love for the antislavery cause; but I do not believe either of them, nor all their comrades, have the boldness to declare an emancipation policy, until, by a pressure which we are to create, the country forces them to do it. . . .

Phillips was impatient with the idea that the war could be waged in a static, defensive political mood. Every drop of blood was shed without purpose until the slaves were declared free. Was the government determined to conduct the war in such a way as to preserve slavery? How could the social basis of the Southern oligarchy, which waged the war, be cut away without freeing its labor? "No social state is really annihilated except when it is replaced by another."

The abolitionist saw the complex relationship between emancipation and diplomacy. England and France stood for the South, he said in 1861. England wants to divide the United States, to "undermine the manufacturing and commercial supremacy of the North." The English middle classes lack the virtue to resist the call of imperial ambition. Ultimately the European governments and the silent masses of slaves will take an active hand in the war, and it is a matter of great moment which moves first.[6] Lincoln must hurry before Europe intervenes; Cameron must arm the Negroes; McClellan must go.

In his desperate eagerness to force a more vigorous conduct

---

[5] This was how Phillips saw his own function: "I must educate, arouse, and mature a public opinion which shall compel the administration to adopt and support it in pursuing the policy I can aid. This I do by frankly and candidly criticising its present policy, civil and military. . . . My criticism is not, like that of the traitor presses, meant to paralyze the administration, but to goad it to more activity and vigor."

[6] Later Phillips stressed the role of American wheat in staving off intervention on behalf of the Confederacy. "Today," he said in July 1863, "the logic of events is that we may save the nation from English and French interference because Illinois is full of wheat, and English harvests are very barren; because France starves, and the valley of the Mississippi is loaded with grain, and she dares not interfere." He once suggested that if Napoleon III tried to plant thrones in the Western Hemisphere, the United States should subsidize European republicans like Garibaldi to overturn the European system.

of the war Phillips dropped the old emphasis on the formality of sin and turned his attention to economic issues. To the horror of many old comrades, he supported Lincoln's practical proposal to abolish slavery among loyal slaveholders through compensated emancipation. No longer did he disdain the economic appeal for the Union—its disruption would "defraud us of mutual advantages relating to peace, trade, national security." In March and April 1862 he went on a six-week lecture tour, which took him to the capital and through New York, Pennsylvania, Ohio, Illinois, and Michigan, where he spoke in several cities. At Washington he lectured twice and visited Congress. Vice President Hamlin left the presiding seat in the Senate to greet him; he dined with the Speaker of the House, and had an interview with Lincoln. At a time when emancipation was the order of the day he had become the outstanding abolitionist in the country, the field agent of the Radicals in Congress. Greeley's *Tribune* estimated that 50,000 people heard his lectures and speeches during the winter of 1861-2, and that almost 5,000,000 read them. Returning from his trip, Phillips was convinced that the West was stronger than the East for emancipation. The President, he reported, was honest, and desirous of seeing an end to slavery. In good time he was to say of the President he had pilloried: "Lincoln was slow, but he got there. Thank God for him."

Phillips had few illusions about the completeness of emancipation under Lincoln's Proclamation, much as he rejoiced in it. "That proclamation," he said, "frees the slave but ignores the negro." To declare the Negro free was one thing, to arm and employ him another. The Republicans were not thorough enough. They had been educated as Whigs, and the Whig Party "had no trust in the masses." When the South began to feel exhausted, Phillips predicted, she would free the Negro and try to use him. He proposed that 10,000 Negro troops be sent east from Louisiana, then occupied by Union troops, not primarily to fight, but to carry word of emancipation. They would soon draw around them a menacing force of 200,000, and the South would be unable to keep her white men at the front. Where lands were captured, the government should confiscate them,

break them up into farms of one hundred acres, and sell those farms to the sons of Vermont and New York, with a deed from the Union guaranteeing the title, and guaranteeing compensation if the owner be evicted, and you have commenced a State. . . .

Presumably these white Northerners would employ free Negro labor. But by 1864, when he started to criticize Lincoln's plan of Reconstruction, Phillips began to look upon the land as the key to the Negroes' welfare and to advocate, with Congressional Radicals like Sumner and Stevens, that the land be turned over to the freedmen themselves. Now that tendency to look to the economic basis of politics which had become marked in him at the beginning of the crisis ripened into fruition. Lincoln's plan, which would allow slaveholders to return to their estates, would not sufficiently change the structure of political power in the South, he argued.

What does that mean? Every man knows that land dictates government. If you hold land, every man his own farm, it is a democracy; you need not curiously ask of the statute book. If a few men own the territory it is an oligarchy; you need not carefully scan its laws. . . . Daniel Webster said, in 1820, the revolution in France has crumbled up the nobles' estates into small farms; the throne must either kill them or they will kill out the throne. . . . Now while these large estates remain in the hands of the just defeated oligarchy, its power is not destroyed. But let me confiscate the land of the South, and put it into the hands of the negroes and white men who have fought for it, and you may go to sleep with your parchments.

It was Phillips's idea that the country owed the Negro "real freedom—not merely technical freedom." For this he must have land, citizenship, education, and the vote. "The moment a man becomes valuable or terrible to the politician, his rights will be respected. Give the negro a vote in his hand, and there is not a politician from Abraham Lincoln down to the laziest loafer in the lowest ward of this city who would not do him honor." The Negro must be free to bargain for a wage contract. To those who argued that gradual progress would be made in the future toward Negro equality Phillips prophetically replied that there would soon be a loosening of tension, a conservative reaction, and that if a good bargain was to be made for the Negro, it must be struck now.

When the war closes the South it is to be made like a garden. . . . Welcome labor there from the North, the East, and the West, and you keep wages high throughout the nation. . . . Disgrace labor down there, make the negro, worth $100 a month, work for $8, and no white man will go there to compete with him. You dam up the labor of the North; you leave the South aristocratic, labor depressed and discredited, and an aristocratic class thrown upward into being above it inevitably.[7]

In June 1865 Garrison and Phillips broke decisively at a meeting of the National Anti-Slavery Society. Garrison proposed that since the purpose of the society had been fulfilled in the thirteenth amendment, it should dissolve. Phillips insisted that the society must continue to work for suffrage for the freedman. Garrison held that it was not reasonable to expect that Southern states give suffrage to the Negro before they should be readmitted to the Union; on the same principle, many Northern states, like Illinois, would have to be put out of the Union.[8] Phillips carried the day, and the society voted to remain in being and elected him president. Keenly aware of the limitations of what had been done, he continued to demand a thoroughgoing Reconstruction policy. In October 1865 he delivered a speech in Boston entitled "The South Victorious," in which he asserted that the Negro still endured every characteristic of slavery except the legal fact of permanent bondage. Race subordination, "the great principle of the South," still survived. In 1868, summarizing the progress of Reconstruction, he pointed out that of the three great aims he had set down for the black and white masses of the South, land, education, and the ballot, the Negro had only the ballot, and this insecurely. He fought on for ratification of the fifteenth amendment, which was meant to provide

---

[7] Cf. Thaddeus Stevens in his Lancaster speech of September 7, 1865: "The whole fabric of southern society *must* be changed, and never can it be done if this opportunity is lost. . . . How can republican institutions, free schools, free churches, free social intercourse exist in a mingled community of nabobs and serfs; of the owners of twenty-thousand acre manors with lordly palaces, and the occupants of narrow huts inhabited by 'low white trash'? If the south is ever to be made a safe republic let her lands be cultivated by the toil of the owners or the free labor of intelligent citizens. This must be done even though it drive her nobility into exile."

[8] This was typical of Garrison's formal style of reasoning. It made no difference to him either that Illinois was firmly in the Union and the Southern states were firmly out, or that there were a few thousand Negroes in Illinois and hundreds of thousands in the Southern states.

the Negro with the ballot; but he sensed the ebb of the radical tide. "Immediate" emancipation had come, and the more closely it was examined, the more "gradual" it seemed. In the kernel of victory he had found the bitter nut of defeat.

III

The abolitionists had received little aid from the fledgling American labor movement in the years before the war. Labor leaders, approached by the middle-class folk or wealthy philanthropists of the cause, tended to reply that they would do well to bestow as much sympathy on the wage slave as the chattel slave, and turned abruptly to their own problems.[9] Abolitionists, in turn, were wont to reply that there was a world of difference between the situation of the free and the slave laborer; that the peculiar sinfulness of the subjection of the Negro more than justified giving him special concern. Phillips agreed. In 1847, challenged by a Utopian socialist in the *Harbinger* on the subject of "wage slavery," he declared:

> There are two prominent points which distinguish the workers in this country from the slaves. First, the laborers, as a class, are neither wronged nor oppressed: and secondly, if they were, they possess ample power to defend themselves by the exercise of their own acknowledged rights. Does legislation bear hard upon them? Their votes can alter it. Does capital wrong them? Economy will make them capitalists. . . . To economy, self-denial, temperance, education, and moral and religious character, the laboring class and every other class in this country must owe its elevation and improvement.

Twenty-four years later Phillips was calling for "the overthrow of the whole profit-making system."

When the Civil War ended, most of the abolitionists returned to their workday pursuits, content to rest upon their formal suc-

---

[9] Ely Moore, the first president of the National Trades Union, told the House of Representatives in 1839 that emancipation would bring the Negro slave into the labor market in competition with the Northern white worker. Should that happen, "the moral and political character, the pride, power and independence of the latter are gone forever."

cess and to luxuriate in their new roles as respected citizens who had once been the prophets of a great moral reform. But Phillips, who had been an agitator by profession, had no other occupation. He was only fifty-four in 1865, and it was natural for him to look for another cause in which to expend his talents.

The success of the Republican Party in 1860 and the few preceding years had begun a change in Phillips's style of thought, which became complete during the Civil War. The moral and religious agitation of the abolitionist movement had awakened men's minds, but of itself had not been sufficient to shape a practical movement to free the slave. In spite of Garrisonian theories, slavery had become a major issue in the American consciousness only as a subject of political action, the theme of a major political party, which drew strength from other issues like free land and protective tariffs. In several speeches delivered before the attack on Sumter, Phillips expressed hope that economic progress, not war, would end slavery—"Slavery comes to an end by the laws of trade"—and began to interpret American history as a series of class struggles. He reached back into the eighteenth century to point out that the American Revolution was fought because American merchants wanted direct trade with the West Indies and planters "wanted to cheat their creditors." The American Revolution gave the people independence and nationality. But the North remained conservative, was "bound in the aristocracy of classes." Then

> Virginia slaveholders, making theoretical democracy their passion, conquered the Federal Government, and emancipated the working classes of New England. Bitter was the cup to honest Federalism and the Essex Junto. Today, Massachusetts only holds to the lips of Carolina a beaker of the same beverage.[10]

Phillips soon came to look upon the Civil War as a Second American Revolution, a contest between bourgeois and feudal civilization. Once a moralist pure and simple, he was becoming a moralist with a philosophy of history.

During Reconstruction, Phillips's attention was focused upon the land. He saw that if the Negro was to win political and per-

---

[10] This interpretation Phillips borrowed, with some of his language, from Richard Hildreth, the Yankee historian, whose work he acknowledged. Cf. the passage in Hildreth's interesting little volume, *Despotism in America* (Boston, 1854), pp. 16–26, 32–3.

sonal freedom he must have possession of the means of production. He was forced to think of slavery not merely as a sin to be purged but as a labor system that must be replaced by some new economic order. The demand for confiscation of the aristocracy's land fixed his attention on property and the relation of its distribution to human rights and political democracy, while the emergence of the ex-slave as a potential agricultural wage worker brought the problems of wage labor into the center of his consciousness.

On November 2, 1865, when he made his first important speech on behalf of labor in Faneuil Hall at a demonstration in favor of the eight-hour day, Phillips declared:

> The labor of these twenty-nine years has been in behalf of a race bought and sold. The South did not rest their system wholly on this claim to own their laborers; but according to Chancellor Harper, Alexander H. Stephens, Governor Pickens, and John C. Calhoun, asserted that the laborer must necessarily be owned by capitalists or individuals. The struggle for the ownership of labor is now somewhat near its end; and we fitly commence a struggle to define and to arrange the true relations of capital and labor.

Karl Marx, looking upon slavery as a socialist, had said that white labor could never be free while black labor was in bondage. Phillips, approaching socialism as an abolitionist, was arriving at the conclusion that black labor could never be truly free until all labor was released from wage slavery. "We protected the *black* laborer, and now we are going to protect the Laborer, North and South, labor everywhere."

Long in revolt against the values of Massachusetts capitalism, Phillips now saw in the money power a menace to republican government. "I confess," he said, "that the only fear I have in regard to Republican institutions is whether, in our day, any adequate remedy will be found for this incoming flood of the power of incorporated wealth." New Jersey was no more than "a railroad station," the laws of New York were being made "in Vanderbilt's counting house," Tom Scott owned the legislature of Pennsylvania, and in his own state it was impossible to get a railroad-dominated legislature to pass laws for the safety of train passengers or to vote a trivial sum for a factual inquiry into the condition of the workers. This was not his conception of democracy. He had always maintained that each separate interest in society must have its own representation in the councils of state. No man can properly vote in behalf of a woman, no white for a Negro, no lawyer or capitalist for a manual laborer. The principle of the Founding Fathers was that "no class is safe unless government is so arranged that each class has in its own hands the means of protecting itself. That is the idea of republics." If corporations can buy legislatures, equality of suffrage is useless and the republican principle is dead. The only force sufficiently numerous, and capable of uniting against the threat of corporate capital, is united labor. "The labor movement," said Phillips, ". . . is my only hope for democracy."

Phillips now became as stoutly devoted to political action as he had been to political inaction during his career as an abolitionist. In 1865 he even attributed the success of the abolitionists to their force at the ballot-box. He was sure that the ballot was the only alternative to a violent outcome of the class struggle. One could not simply wait and discuss while people were hungry; it was just this sort of thing that would lead to an explosion. "We rush into politics because politics is the safety valve." "Avoid all violence," he advised the workers. "Appeal to discussion and the ballot. You outnumber the capitalists at any rate. The ballot was given for just such crises as these." The strike was useful as a tactic—"Never let a man say a word against strikes"—but, for the time being, labor's motto should be: "NEVER FORGIVE AT THE BALLOT BOX!"

In politics, however, there was no place to go. Phillips rapidly became disillusioned with the Republican Party, which he finally described in 1878 as no more than a tool of the capitalist class. He encouraged labor to form its own party and joined the Massachusetts workingmen in their political experimentation from 1869 to 1871. He was the labor party's candidate for governor in 1870 and narrowly missed being nominated by the National Labor Union for the presidency in 1872. But these experiments were all doomed to failure. Phillips's association with the unsavory Benjamin F. Butler in his campaign for the governorship of Massachusetts in 1871 cost him many friends. At last, it was believed, Phillips had soiled himself, and Emerson, who had admired him for thirty years, made it clear that he did not wish to see him in Concord.

V. L. Parrington, in his sympathetic account of Phillips, found "pretty much all of Marxianism" in the philosophy of his later period; but except for his reliance upon the working class and his general economic interpretation of politics, there was little of the Marxist in the American labor reformer. Phillips's socialism was a homespun Yankee product, woven out of several strains of native reform ideology, not the least of which was that of the co-operative movement. "Inaugurate cooperative industry," he urged in 1868:

> Let the passengers and the employees own the railway. Let the operatives own the mill. Let the traders own the banks. Make the interests of Capital and the Community identical. In no other way shall we have free, self-government in this country.

The most militant and most famous expression of his views came in resolutions presented at the Labor-Reform Convention at Worcester in 1871:

> We affirm, as a fundamental principle, that labor, the creator of wealth, is entitled to all it creates.
> Affirming this, we avow ourselves willing to accept the final results of the operation of a principle so radical,—such as the overthrow of the whole profit-making system, the extinction of all monopolies, the abolition of privileged classes, universal education and fraternity, perfect freedom of exchange, and best and grandest of all, the final obliteration of that foul stigma upon our so-called Christian civilization,—the poverty of the masses. . . . We are still aware that our goal cannot be reached at a single leap. We take into account the ignorance, selfishness, prejudice, corruption, and demoralization of the leaders of the people, and to a large extent, of the people themselves; but still we demand that some steps be taken in this direction: therefore,—
> *Resolved,*—That we declare war with the wages system . . . war with the present system of finance, which robs labor and gorges capital, makes the rich richer and the poor poorer, and turns a republic into an aristocracy of capital. . . .

The author of these resolutions had no economic theory. His realism was incomplete because it was not supplemented by any conception of economic evolution, and the few ventures that Phillips made into explaining his economic point of view were lamentable. Although he was a city man, he had been

born at a time when Boston was hardly more than an over-
grown village and the Common was still used as a pasture. He
never accepted urban life or industry, and never squared his
socialist sympathies with the facts of the Industrial Revolution.

> What we need is an equalization of property,—nothing else. My
> ideal of a civilization is a very high one; but the approach to it is a
> New-England town of some two thousand inhabitants, with no rich
> man and no poor man in it, all mingling in the same society, every
> child at the same school, no poorhouse, no beggar, opportunities
> equal, nobody too proud to stand aloof, nobody too humble to be
> shut out. That's New England as it was fifty years ago. . . .

The activities of the First International were sympathetically
reported in Phillips's paper, the *National Standard*. When the
test of the Paris Commune came, Phillips refused to join the
general condemnation in America and hailed the Communard
movement. He held Thiers responsible for the bloodshed in
France, declared: *"There is no hope for France but in the Reds,"*
and described the Communards as "the foremost, the purest and
the noblest patriots of France."

Such sentiments forced him into a deeper and deeper isolation. As an exponent of socialism in the Gilded Age, Phillips was
deprived even of the consolation that the abolitionists had had
of the company of churchmen, poets, millionaires, and the marginal allegiance of some distinguished men and women of good-
will. In 1881, however, he was invited to give the Phi Beta Kappa
address at Harvard. This at least was an opportunity for the
aging orator to heal the old breach with the scholarship of Cambridge, which had spurned him and his causes for forty years.
Instead he flung his last challenge at respectability. He chose
as his topic "The Scholar in a Republic." His theme was an ar-
raignment of American learning for its lack of social leadership
and its moral cowardice.

The duty of the scholar, he began, "is to help those less favored in life," and to educate the mass of the people. And yet
very few of the great truths about society had grown out of
scholarly inquiry, "but have been first heard in the solemn protest of martyred patriotism and the loud cries of crushed and
starving labor." The world makes history in anguish, and scholars write it in half-truths, blurring and distorting it with their

prejudices. The people learn deeply from the agitations of life, and timid scholars shrink from these agitations or denounce them. "A chronic distrust of the people pervades the book-educated class of the North." They do not even scruple to defend the principle of free speech. American scholarship, in truth, had not given its hand to aid in the solution of a single great social question of the age. It had denounced the slavery crusade, spurned the reform of penal legislation, ignored intemperance, and laughed at women's rights. It had never shown sympathy for the victims of oppression abroad—for the Irish or (here Phillips grew particularly shocking) for the Nihilists of Russia, whom it was then condemning so strongly. Seizing upon the Nihilists as an extreme symbol of resistance and rebellion, Phillips launched into an impassioned defense of them and lashed out at "that nauseous hypocrisy which, stung by a threepenny tea tax, piles Bunker Hill with granites and statues, prating all the time of patriotism and broadswords, while, like another Pecksniff, it recommends a century of dumb submission and entire non-resistance to the Russians, who for a hundred years have seen their sons by thousands dragged to death or exile . . . and their maidens flogged to death in the marketplace." It was time, he concluded, that scholarship fulfill its duties, time at last that it take the side of the wage worker and the woman in their coming campaigns for justice. "Sit not, like the figure on our silver coin, ever looking backward."

"It was a delightful discourse," remarked one of his hearers, "but preposterous from beginning to end." Conventional history has been less charitable than Phillips's contemporaries, finding him always preposterous and never delightful. But the agitator who had given no quarter expected none, and perhaps sensed that the scholarship of the future would treat him in the same spirit as had the scholarship of his time. He returned from Cambridge to Boston, exhilarated and grimly satisfied, we may imagine, at the thought that as long as anyone in the old town could remember, he had been a thorn in the side of complacency.

THE ABOLITIONIST DILEMMA:

THE ANTISLAVERY MOVEMENT AND THE NORTHERN NEGRO

LEON F. LITWACK

CONSISTENCY demanded that abolitionists move against racial oppression in both the North and the South. Slaveholders and their spokesmen repeatedly defended the "peculiar institution" on the ground that Negroes were unfit to enjoy the rights and privileges exercised by whites, and they pointed to northern treatment of the free Negro as substantial proof of the real benevolence of slavery and the hypocrisy of antislavery arguments.[1] Abolitionists did not ignore the plight of northern Negroes; indeed, they contended that slaves and free Negroes shared a similar plight. After surveying the condition of Negroes in northern states and cities, they could come to no other conclusion.

Although fundamental differences existed between a con dition of legal servitude and freedom, municipal, state, and federal statutes relegated northern Negroes to a position of legal inferiority, while custom and prejudice reduced them to a subservient economic and social status. Disfranchised in nearly every state, denied the right to settle in some, confined to a diminishing list of menial employments, northern Negroes found themselves systematically separated from the white community. They were either excluded altogether from railway cars, omnibuses, stage coaches, and steamboats, or assigned to special "Jim Crow" sections; they sat in secluded and remote corners of theaters; they could enter most hotels, restaurants, and resorts only as servants; and they prayed in "Negro pews" in the white churches. Moreover, they were educated in segregated schools, punished in segregated prisons, nursed in segregated hospitals, and buried in segregated cemeteries. The public burying ground or "Potter's Field" in Cincinnati sym-

---

[1] See, for example, *Register of Debates*, 21 Cong., 1 Sess., 47, 215; *Congressional Globe*, 30 Cong., 1 Sess., 602, *Appendix to the Congressional Globe*, 29 Cong., 2 Sess., 349.

50

bolized the tragic plight of the Negro—even in death. White bodies were laid east to west; Negroes north to south.[2]

As long as northern laws, institutions, and customs rendered "the freedom of the colored people but an empty name—but the debasing mockery of true freedom," abolitionists confessed that it would be difficult indeed to condemn the practices of the South. Abolitionists, in short, must strike at the roots of slavery, show the Negro's capacity for self-improvement, and demonstrate the sincerity of their own professed sympathy for his plight.[3] Improving the condition of northern Negroes thus formed an integral part of the antislavery movement. In the first issue of *The Liberator*, William Lloyd Garrison advised his "free colored brethren" that the struggle for equal rights in the North constituted "a leading object" of abolitionism.[4] In no other way, agreed James Russell Lowell, could abolitionists more effectively serve "their holy cause."[5]

By 1860 the antislavery societies could point to some important achievements in the North. What made them especially noteworthy was not only the existence of powerful public hostility but dissension and prejudice within the abolitionist movement itself.

I

While deploring racial prejudice and endorsing the Negro's claim to full citizenship, many white abolitionists hesitated to carry their views to the point of social intercourse with their Negro brethren. Since racial mixing flouted the prevailing so-

[2] Edward S. Abdy, *Journal of a Residence and Tour in the United States of North America, from April, 1833, to October, 1834* (London, 1835), III, 7.

[3] For examples of this sentiment, see the address of William Goodell before the Lewis County Anti-Slavery convention, January 10, 1837, in *Human Rights*, February, 1837; *Second Annual Report of the American Anti-Slavery Society . . . 1835* (New York, 1835), 6, 69; *Proceedings of the First Annual Meeting of the New York State Anti-Slavery Society . . . 1836* (Utica, 1836), 57; address of Gerrit Smith before the second annual convention of the New York Anti-Slavery Society, in *The Friend of Man*, October 11, 1837; Sophia Davenport to Anne Warren Weston, June 30, 1838, Weston Papers, Boston Public Library.

[4] *The Liberator*, January 1, 1831. See also issues of January 15, May 28, 1831.

[5] James Russell Lowell, *The Anti-Slavery Papers of James Russell Lowell* (Boston and New York, 1902), I, 21-22.

cial code and might easily lead to mob action, antislavery advocates faced a real dilemma. If an abolitionist fought for equal rights, some argued, it did not necessarily follow that he must also consort with Negroes socially. Indeed, such an act might endanger the effectiveness of the antislavery cause. "May we not find it more efficient to go for their improvement in . . . civil privileges," James Birney asked, "leaving their introduction to *social* privileges out of the public discussion? Would it not be better to leave this . . . matter rather more at rest for the present time than to press it upon the whole community? May not urging it *now* be throwing too much in our way the prejudice against it, and defeat the elevation of the Col'd people to *civil* privileges?"[6]

Although several Negroes actively participated in the organization and activities of the antislavery societies, white abolitionists continued to disagree on the expediency of Negro membership. In 1835, for example, Garrison criticized William Ellery Channing, an antislavery sympathizer, for expressing the belief that "we ought never to have permitted our colored brethren to unite with us in our associations."[7] The following year Charles Follen admitted before the Massachusetts Anti-Slavery Society that abolitionists had been advised "not unnecessarily to shock the feelings, though they were but prejudices, of the white people, by admitting colored persons to our Anti-Slavery meetings and societies. We have been told that many who would otherwise act in union with us, were kept away by our disregard of the feelings of the community in this respect." However, Follen added, excluding Negroes would not only deprive the movement of some effective workers but it would comply with "inhuman prejudice," sanction the principle of slavery, and "give the lie to our own most solemn professions." While abolitionists should select their

[6] James G. Birney to Theodore Weld, July 26, 1834, in Gilbert H. Barnes and Dwight L. Dumond, editors, *Letters of Theodore Dwight Weld, Angelina Grimké Weld, and Sarah Grimké, 1822-1844* (New York, 1934), I, 163.

[7] William Lloyd Garrison to Lewis Tappan, December 16, 1835, quoted in Charles H. Wesley, "The Negro's Struggle for Freedom in its Birthplace," *Journal of Negro History*, XXX, 74 (1945).

social friends according to their own principles, "how can we have the effrontery to expect the white slaveholders of the South to live on terms of civil equality with his colored slave, if we, the white abolitionists of the North, will not admit colored freemen as members of our Anti-Slavery Societies?"[8]

But such liberal sentiments did not always prevail. When abolitionist leaders met in New York on March 9, 1836, to arrange a program for the anniversary meeting of the American Anti-Slavery Society, Lewis Tappan proposed that a Negro minister be invited to deliver one of the addresses. However, considerable opposition thwarted such a bold plan. "This is a ticklish point," Tappan wrote that night. "I insisted upon it as we must act out our principles, but it was said the time has not come to mix with people of color in public. So to prevent disunion I submitted."[9] A month later an even more heated discussion occurred at a meeting of the executive committee of the Society, and one member threatened to resign if "true abolitionism" required social intercourse between Negroes and whites. "I have observed," Tappan wrote after the meeting, "that when the subject of acting out our profound principles in treating men irrespective of color is discussed heat is always produced. I anticipate that the battle is to be fought here, & if ever there is a split in our ranks it will arise from collision on this point."[10]

The meetings of a Philadelphia antislavery society vividly demonstrated the division in abolitionist ranks on the questions of Negro membership and social intercourse. Organized in 1836, this society dedicated itself to arrest the progress of slavery and to strive for eventual abolition. One year after its formation, however, the organization found itself spending

[8] *Fourth Annual Report of the Board of Managers of the Massachusetts Anti-Slavery Society. . . . January 20, 1836* (Boston, 1836), 50.

[9] MSS Diary of Lewis Tappan, February 23, 1836 to August 29, 1838, Papers of Lewis Tappan, Library of Congress; Lewis Tappan to Theodore Weld, March 15, 1836, in Barnes and Dumond, editors, *Weld-Grimké Correspondence*, I, 276-277.

[10] MSS Diary of Lewis Tappan, February 23, 1836 to August 29, 1838, Papers of Lewis Tappan, Library of Congress.

five sessions to discuss the question, "Is it expedient for colored persons to join our Anti-Slavery Societies?" After hearing speakers on both sides, the members finally decided in the affirmative by a margin of two votes. Subsequent meetings discussed such questions as, "Ought Abolitionists to encourage colored persons in joining Anti-Slavery Societies?" and "Is it expedient for Abolitionists to encourage social intercourse between white and colored families?" While resolving at its 1837 quarterly meeting to remove public prejudice and encourage the intellectual, moral, and religious improvement of Negroes, the members debated and eventually tabled a resolution which declared that social intercourse with Negroes would strengthen the bitterness of public prejudice, retard the acquisition of civil and religious privileges, and fasten the chains of bondage even tighter, and which condemned "the conduct of those who feel it their duty to encourage such intercourse, as a necessary consequence of their profession of Anti-Slavery principles." Instead, the convention resolved that it was neither "our object, or duty, to encourage social intercourse between colored and white families." However, they agreed by a margin of ten votes that it would be expedient to accept Negroes as members of antislavery societies.[11]

Such problems apparently confronted foreign as well as American antislavery societies. Edward Abdy, a staunch English abolitionist who visited the United States in the years 1833-1834, later wrote to an American friend, "We cannot, I am ashamed to say, claim exemption from the prejudice of color. . . . [Gustave?] De Beaumont, when asked why Bisette was not a member of the Committee of the French abolition society replied—'Why! he is a colored man.' Here we have a religious man and a liberal expressing sentiments opposed to every rational idea of what we owe to God and humanity. Thus it is that Benevolence is employed to foster Pride—we humiliate while we relieve. . . . It really seems as if many considered an African . . . as entitled to the same sort of sympathy and sub-

11 Minutes of the Junior Anti-Slavery Society of Philadelphia, 1836-1846, Historical Society of Pennsylvania, Philadelphia.

scribed to the anti-slavery society as they subscribe to the society for the prevention of cruelty to animals."[12]

While abolitionists searched their conscience for a way out
of these perplexing problems, Lewis Tappan engaged in a bitter controversy with the revivalist leader and antislavery sympathizer Charles G. Finney, over the wisdom of mixing Negroes and whites in public functions. When, for example, Negro and white choirs shared the same platform at the first anniversary meeting of the American Anti-Slavery Society in May,
1835, some abolitionist sympathizers, including Finney, apparently intimated that such intercourse had helped to provoke the July anti-Negro riots in New York City. But "the
choirs sat separately in the orchestra," Tappan explained, "the
whites on one side and the colored on the other!" Having
"been cruelly *slandered* about attempts to mix black and white
people," Tappan asserted that the seating of the two choirs
was "the only attempt I ever made to mix up the two colors in
any public assembly or elsewhere," and "this I did by order
of a committee of which I was chairman." However, Tappan
admitted that he had once dined with two Negro members of
the executive committee of the American Anti-Slavery Society
and occasionally with "a few colored 'gentlemen' " but this
constituted "the [head] and front of my offending. . . . And yet
many abolitionists have talked about efforts at amalgamation,
etc."[13]

Acting as an intermediary in the Tappan-Finney dispute,
Theodore Weld, the leading western abolitionist, expressed
his own views on the delicate subject of social intercourse.

[12] Edward Strutt Abdy to Maria (Weston) Chapman, May 24, 1844, Weston
Papers, Boston Public Library.

[13] Lewis Tappan to Theodore Weld, March 15, 1836, in Barnes and Dumond, editors, *Weld-Grimké Correspondence,* I, 275-276. References to this dispute are also included in Weld to Tappan, November 17, 1835, March 9, April
5, October 24, 1836, *Weld-Grimké Correspondence,* I, 242-243, 270-274, 289, 345;
MSS Diary of Lewis Tappan, February 23, 1836 to August 29, 1838, Papers of
Lewis Tappan, Library of Congress, especially the entries for February 25 and
March 19, 1836. "I am satisfied CSF [Charles S. Finney] is wrong," Tappan
wrote in his diary, "and has unjust suspicions of me. Last year, in another matter, he accused me of 'pious fraud' wh I thot wholly unmerited."

"Take *more pains* to treat with attention, courtesy, and cordiality a colored person than a white," Weld advised, "from the *fact* that he *is* colored." But in mixing the two races on a social basis, abolitionists should first ask whether its effect on the general public would be "a *blessing* or a *curse* to the Colored people?" Weld felt that his own feelings toward Negroes had been sufficiently demonstrated by his actions while attending the Lane Seminary in Cincinnati. "If I attended parties," he declared, "it was *theirs—weddings—theirs—Funerals—theirs— Religious meetings—theirs—*Sabbath schools—Bible classes— theirs." It did not necessarily follow, however, that he would walk arm-in-arm with a Negro woman at midday down the main street of Cincinnati. Such an act "would bring down a storm of venge[a]nce upon the defenceless people of Color, throw them out of employ, drive them out homeless, and sur‑ render them up victims to popular fury"; indeed, such "an ostentatious display of superiority to prejudice and a *blister‑ ing bravado defiance*" would misconstrue the true motives and objectives of abolitionists and turn public attention from their major goal—the destruction of slavery—to a "collateral" point. While it would be sinful to manifest any unkindness toward Negroes, abolitionists must realize, Weld concluded, that "there are times when we *may refrain* from making *public visible demonstrations* of feelings about differences of color in practical exhibitions, when such demonstrations would bring down persecutions on them."[14]

Charges of racial mixing also deeply annoyed Arthur Tappan. Defending his conduct as late as 1863, the New York abolitionist leader and philanthropist wrote to an English friend regarding his past views and actions. While Christian conduct had bound him to treat Negroes without respect to color, Tappan explained that he had always felt that public sentiment on the subject required "great prudence" on the part of abolitionists. Although he had consistently shown his willingness "*publicly*" to associate with "a well educated and refined colored

[14] Theodore Weld to Lewis Tappan, March 9, 1836, Barnes and Dumond, editors, *Weld-Grimké Correspondence*, I, 270, 272-274.

person," he considered it best to refrain from social intercourse until "the public mind and conscience were more enlightened on the subject." It was thus a "malignant falsehood" to accuse him of "any gross assault on the fastidiousness of the age." As to charges that he or any member of his family "have ever put arms into the hands of colored men or women in New York or anywhere else, it is without the slightest foundation."[15]

The problems of Negro membership and social intercourse also aroused considerable discussion among the women's anti-slavery organizations. When two Quaker women formed a Female Anti-Slavery Society in Fall River, Massachusetts, and invited several interested Negroes to join, it "raised such a storm among some of the leading members that for a time, it threatened the dissolution of the Society." Although the opposition denied any objections to Negroes attending their meetings, they considered it improper to invite them to become members of the Society, "thus putting them on an equality with ourselves."[16] While the Fall River group finally decided in favor of admission, "wicked prejudices about colour" prevented Negro membership in the New York women's anti-slavery society.[17] Delegates to the national convention of anti-slavery women approved, although not unanimously, a resolution by Sarah M. Grimké calling upon abolitionists to associate with their oppressed brethren, to sit with them in churches, to appear with them on the streets, to grant them equal rights in steamboats and stages, and to visit them in their homes and receive them "as we do our white fellow citizens."[18] Less than a

[15] Arthur Tappan to A. F. Stoddard, August 27, 1863, quoted in Lewis Tappan, *The Life of Arthur Tappan* (New York, 1870), 201-202.

[16] Malcolm R. Lovell, editor, *Two Quaker Sisters. From the Original Diaries* (New York, 1937), 119-120. (Elizabeth Buffum Chace and Lucy Buffum Lovell)

[17] Anne Warren Weston to Deborah Weston, October 22, 1836, Weston Papers, Boston Public Library. "Every body has their own troubles and the New York brethren have theirs. Mrs. Cox is the life and soul of the New York Society and she is in a very sinful state of wicked prejudices about colour; they do not allow any coloured woman to join their society. . . . The Tappans have none of this prejudice therefore they and Mrs. Cox are hardly on speaking terms."

[18] *Proceedings of the Anti-Slavery Convention of American Women, . . . 1838* (Philadelphia, 1838), 8. For additional sentiments on this question, see *Proceedings of the Third Anti-Slavery Convention of American Women, . . . 1839* (Philadelphia, 1839), 22, 24; *Proceedings of the Anti-Slavery Convention of American Women, . . . 1837* (New York, 1837), 13, 17.

month after the convention, two Philadelphia abolitionists wrote that the recently passed resolution had "greatly alarmed" some of "our timid friends" who unsuccessfully attempted to expunge it from the published convention report. Not content with this setback, these "pseudo-abolitionists" endeavored to induce leading Philadelphia Negroes to deny publicly any desire to mix socially with whites; only such a disavowal, they warned, would avert "destruction and bloodshed."[19] In Cincinnati, meanwhile, several of the women teachers at the Negro school complained to Weld that some "halfhearted" abolitionist co-workers expressed alarm "if perchance we lay our hands on a curly head, or kiss a coloured face." Since such actions seemed to "offend their nice taste," it became increasingly difficult to work with these prejudiced women in the company of Negroes. "Dear Br.[other]," they pleaded, "do pray the Lord to send us co-workers instead of anti-workers."[20]

Regardless of public opposition and personal doubts, some abolitionists considered social intercourse with Negroes a demonstration of true devotion to the cause. While admitting that one could advocate "the civil emancipation of those whom he would still be unwilling to associate with," the American Anti-Slavery Society warned in its 1837 annual report that its members yielded too readily to prejudice. If color or public opinion alone explained an abolitionist's reluctance to associate with Negroes, then "he wrongs the cause in which he is engaged."[21]

[19] James and Lucretia Mott to Anne Warren Weston, June 7, 1838, Weston Papers, Boston Public Library. "[I]t is only our half-way Abolitionists," Mrs. Mott explained, "and some timid ones like Dr. Parrish who have never joined our societies and who are now quaking with fear—These it is to be regretted are not well understood by the colored people whom they attempt to influence. They think them wholly identified with us and confiding in them as their best advisers they are in danger of being led astray." See also Lucretia Mott to Edward M. Davis, June 18, 1838, in Anna Davis Hallowell, *James and Lucretia Mott. Life and Letters* (Boston, 1884), 130.

[20] Phebe Mathews, Emeline Bishop, Susan Lowe and Lucy Wright to Theodore Weld, March? 1835, in Barnes and Dumond, editors, *Weld-Grimké Correspondence*, I, 217.

[21] *Fourth Annual Report of the American Anti-Slavery Society, . . . 1837* (New York, 1837), 107. For similar abolitionist criticism, see *Proceedings of a Meeting to Form the Broadway Tabernacle Anti-Slavery Society* (New York, 1838), 28, and *The [9th] Annual Report of the American and Foreign Anti-Slavery Society, . . . 1849* (New York, 1849), 68.

When abolitionists did mix with Negroes, it became almost fashionable to tell others about this novel experience, treating it as a personal triumph over the amassed forces of prejudice and evil. Weld, for example, related at great length his daily intercourse with Negroes in Cincinnati. When Negro ministers and friends mixed with whites at the Weld-Grimké wedding, the new bride explained, "They were our invited guests, and we thus had an opportunity to bear our testimony against the horrible prejudice which prevails against colored persons."[22] Both Negroes and whites attended the funeral of James Forten, a prominent Philadelphia Negro leader, and one white participant proudly described it as "a real amalgamation funeral."[23]

But such intercourse was, after all, novel and often dangerous in the ante-bellum United States. In facing this annoying problem, many abolitionists did, indeed, appear hesitant, careful, apprehensive—but always curious. "I hear that Mrs. [Lydia] Child has had a party lately," a Massachusetts woman abolitionist wrote, "and invited colored persons, do write me about it."[24]

II

The aversion to social relations with Negroes might be ascribed in part to the fact that most whites, whether abolitionists or not, acknowledged the existence of vast differences—physical and mental—between the two races. Some abolitionists, for example, failed to question the validity of commonly accepted stereotypes of the Negro character; they contended instead that these peculiar racial qualities constituted no just grounds for denying Negroes freedom or equal political rights. On the other hand, abolitionists such as William Lloyd Garrison argued that the Negro could unfortunately do nothing

[22] Sarah Grimké to Elizabeth Pease, May 20?, 1838, Barnes and Dumond, editors, *Weld-Grimké Correspondence*, II, 679.

[23] Lucretia Mott to Richard and Hannah Webb, February 25, 1842, in Hallowell, *James and Lucretia Mott*, 232.

[24] Sophia Davenport to Caroline Weston, June 5, 1836, Weston Papers, Boston Public Library.

about the color of his skin and this alone perpetuated prejudice. "The black color of the body, the woolly hair, the thick lips, and other peculiarities of the African," Garrison's *Liberator* remarked, "forms so striking a contrast to the Caucasian race, that they may be distinguished at a glance. . . . They are branded by the hand of nature with a perpetual mark of disgrace."[25]

Nevertheless, abolitionist literature contributed its share to the popular conception of the Negro, frequently referring to his meek, servile, comical, minstrel-like qualities. For example, William Ellery Channing, writing in an antislavery tract, described the Negro as "among the mildest, gentlest of men"; his nature is "affectionate, easily touched" and therefore more open to religious impression than the white man's; the European races manifest "more courage, enterprise, invention" but the Negro "carries within him, much more than we, the germs of a meek, long-suffering, loving virtue"; if civilized, the African would undoubtedly show less energy, courage, and intellectual originality than the Caucasian but would surpass him in "amiableness, tranquillity, gentleness and content"; he may never equal the white man "in outward condition" but he would probably be "a much happier race."[26] The Ohio Anti-Slavery Society found that Negroes "endure with more patience the scorn and wrong under which they are pressed down—are more grateful for the favors which they receive— more tractable than persons of like information and intelligence among the whites."[27] Abolitionist author Charles Stuart reported that Negroes were guilty of fewer "atrocious crimes" because they were "less ferocious, less proud, and passionate and revengeful, than others."[28] Accepting this composite pic-

---

[25] *Liberator*, January 22, 1831.

[26] William Ellery Channing, "The African Character," John A. Collins, editor, *The Anti-Slavery Picknick: A Collection of Speeches, Poems, Dialogues and Songs; intended for use in Schools and Anti-Slavery Meetings* (Boston, 1842), 56-58. See also Edward Abdy's interview with Channing in Abdy, *Journal of a Residence and Tour*, III, 217-237.

[27] Ohio Anti-Slavery Society, *Condition of the People of Color in the State of Ohio* (Boston, 1839), 4.

[28] Charles Stuart, "On the Colored People of the United States," *The Quarterly Anti-Slavery Magazine*, II, 16 (October, 1836).

ture of the Negro character, abolitionists might well argue that social intercourse with the blacks not only seemed impolitic but unnatural.

Negro efforts to break away from this stereotype did not always win acclaim within the abolitionist movement. Frederick Douglass, for example, proved to be a formidable antislavery orator. But some abolitionists became concerned over Douglass' rapid intellectual development; perhaps people would no longer believe that he had ever been a slave. "The public have itching ears to hear a colored man speak," antislavery agent John A. Collins pointed out to Garrison, "and particularly *a slave*. Multitudes will flock to hear one of this class speak. . . . It would be a good policy to employ a number of colored agents, if suitable ones can be found." By 1841, however, Douglass' suitability seemed to be in question. "People won't believe you ever was a slave, Frederick, if you keep on this way," one abolitionist told Douglass. Collins added, "Better have a little of the plantation speech than not; it is not best that you seem too learned." [29]

In battling prejudice while at the same time accepting certain popular notions about the Negro, abolitionists frequently exhibited a curious racial attitude. They might, for example, refer to their African brethren—innocently or otherwise—as "niggers" or emphasize some alleged physical or mental characteristic. At times they seemed to sense this dual attitude. When a prominent Massachusetts woman abolitionist described a recent antislavery fund-raising fair in New Bedford, she wrote to her sister, "All the fashionables of the town were there and all the 'niggers' (dont let this letter get into the Mass ab.[olitionist])." [30] Usually, however, abolitionists appeared unaware that they might be using offensive language in describing Negroes. Arnold Buffum, a New England antislav-

[29] Frederick Douglass, *Life and Times of Frederick Douglass* (Hartford, Conn., 1884), 269-270.

[30] Deborah Weston to Mary Weston, January 5, 1840, Weston Papers, Boston Public Library. The "Mass Ab" refers to a weekly abolitionist newspaper edited by Elizur Wright, Jr., which generally disagreed with the Garrisonian position, especially concerning political action. Deborah Weston was a Garrisonian.

ery leader, thus informed Garrison about his activities in be-half of a school "where honors may be dispensed to woolly heads."[31] Abolitionist James W. Alvord, after visiting a school in Clifton, Connecticut, wrote to Weld that one Negro girl sat with the white students. "Cant tell how it will go," he re-marked. "Should not be surprized if some of the white parents should smell her very bad, tho I could not perceive the girls on either side were at all aware of her niggerly odour." At the same time, however, Alvord asked Weld what more he could do for "the salvation" of the Negro. "To this object," he de-clared, "I *would dedicate my life.*"[32]

III

While Negroes demonstrated their appreciation of the ef-forts and accomplishments of the antislavery societies, they did not hesitate to condemn prejudice within the abolitionist movement. "Even our professed friends have not yet rid them-selves of it," a Negro teacher lamented; "to some of them it clings like a dark mantle obscuring their many virtues and choking up the avenues to higher and nobler sentiments." As an example, she cited the comment of "one of the best and least prejudiced men" in the antislavery cause: "Ah said he, 'I can recall the time when in walking with a colored brother, the darker the night, the better Abolitionist was I.' " While this person no longer expressed such feelings, she feared that simi-lar sentiments "oftentimes" manifested themselves among the white friends of the Negro. However, she added, "when we recollect what great sacrifices to public sentiment they are called upon to make, we cannot wholly blame them. Many, very many anxious to take up the cross, but how few are strong enough to bear it."[33]

[31] Arnold Buffum to William Lloyd Garrison, October 23, 1832, in Francis and Wendell P. Garrison, *William Lloyd Garrison, 1805-1879* (Boston, 1894), I, 327.

[32] James W. Alvord to Theodore Weld, August 29, 1838, Barnes and Dumond, editors, *Weld-Grimké Correspondence*, II, 697.

[33] Sarah Forten to Angelina Grimké, April 15, 1837, Barnes and Dumond, editors, *Weld-Grimké Correspondence*, I, 380.

Several Negro leaders complained that white abolitionists devoted so much time to fiery condemnations of southern slavery that they tended to overlook the plight of northern Negroes. One Negro newspaper charged in 1839 that making "abolition in the North" an objective of secondary importance clearly constituted "a primordial defect" in the antislavery movement.[34] Even when white abolitionists turned their attention to the condition of northern Negroes, it appeared to some that they stressed only political rights and education. Was it not "strange," a Negro leader asked, that the Constitution of the American Anti-Slavery Society failed to mention social equality as an objective?[35]

But while some Negro leaders criticized the apathy of white abolitionists, others contended that Negroes had placed too much reliance on the efforts of outside forces, thus actually hampering the struggle for equal rights. The antislavery societies, Martin R. Delany charged, have always "presumed to *think* for, dictate to, and *know* better what suited colored people, than they know for themselves." While he applauded the constructive work of these societies, he felt that Negroes placed too much faith in the "miracle" of abolition and demonstrated too little confidence in their own efforts. After the appearance of some white abolitionists at the 1831 national Negro convention to propose a manual labor college, it seemed to Delany that Negroes suddenly ceased their independent activities, "and with their hands thrust deep in their breeches-pockets, and their mouths gaping open, stood gazing with astonishment, wonder, and surprise, at the stupendous moral colossal statues of our Anti-Slavery friends and brethren, who in the heat and

[34] *Colored American*, May 18, 1839. "They [the American Anti-Slavery Society] make secondary and collateral what ought to have been the primary object of all their efforts. . . . At this moment more is known among abolitionists of slavery in the Carolinas, than of the deep and damning thralldom which grinds to the dust, the colored inhabitants of New York. And more efforts are made by them to rend the physical chains of Southern slaves, than to burst the soul-crushing bondage of the Northern states."

[35] James McCune Smith to Gerrit Smith, March 1, 1855, quoted in Howard Holman Bell, *A Survey of the Negro Convention Movement, 1830-1861* (Ph.D. dissertation, Northwestern University, 1953), 41.

zeal of honest hearts, ... promised a great deal more than they have ever been able half to fulfill, in thrice the period in which they expected it." Awaiting a practical application of abolitionist dogma, Negroes had been disappointed. Instead, "we find ourselves occupying the very same position in relation to our Anti-Slavery friends, as we do in relation to the pro-slavery part of the community—a mere secondary, underling position, in all our relations to them, and any thing more than this, is not a matter of course ... but ... by mere sufferance."[36]

In assessing the weaknesses of the antislavery movement, Negro critics referred particularly to the economic depression of their people and the failure of abolitionists to offer Negroes decent jobs in their business establishments or even in the antislavery offices.[37] After all, abolitionist speeches and editorials could not correct the prevailing prejudices of white society—this required a demonstration of Negro economic improvement. "Our white friends are deceived," a Negro newspaper charged, "when they imagine they are free from prejudice against color, and yet are content with a lower standard of attainments for colored youth, and inferior exhibitions of talent on the part of colored men."[38] Abolitionists possessed the means to assist Negro laborers, these critics maintained, and yet few of them showed any willingness to train or hire Negroes. This prompted one Negro delegate to a convention of the

[36] Martin R. Delany, The Condition, Elevation, Emigration, and Destiny of the Colored People of the United States (Philadelphia, 1852), 10, 24-25, 27.

[37] See, for example, Delany, The Condition ..., 26-28. "It is true," Delany remarked, "that the 'Liberator' office, in Boston has got ... a colored youth, at the cases—the 'Standard,' in New York, a young colored man, and the 'Freeman,' in Philadelphia, ... another, in the publication office, as 'packing clerk'; yet these are but three out of the hosts that fill these offices in their various departments, all occupying places that could have been, and as we once thought, would have been, easily enough, occupied by colored men. Indeed, we can have no other idea about anti-slavery in this country, than that the legitimate persons to fill any and every position about an anti-slavery establishment are colored persons." In addition to this criticism, a delegate to a meeting of the National Council of the Colored People in 1855 charged that "[t]hose who professed to be the strongest abolitionists have refused to render colored people anything but sympathy.... [T]hey might employ a colored boy as a porter or packer, but would as soon put a hod-carrier to the clerk's desk as a colored boy, ever so well educated though he be." Frederick Douglass' Paper, May 18, 1855.

[38] Colored American, November 4, 1837, July 28, 1838.

American and Foreign Anti-Slavery Society to charge that attempts to induce members of the executive committee to admit Negroes into their commercial houses or into the antislavery offices had met with no success. Replying to a specific charge that he used Negroes only in menial employment, delegate Arthur Tappan, owner of a large New York City department store, claimed that he had recently hired a Negro porter but that this person had left his job before being qualified for a clerical position. In any case, Tappan declared, he would not ask "an Irishman sawing wood in the street, and covered with sweat" to dine with his family; neither would be ask a Negro in a similar condition. He only required that his associates be gentlemen, irrespective of color. While regretting that erroneous stories had been circulated among Negroes concerning his conduct, he was still pleased that delegates had alluded to them for this should "put all abolitionists on their guard, and induce them to act out, at all times, the principles they professed."[39]

IV

In view of the prevailing economic outlook among abolitionists, Negro expectations of substantial economic progress under the impetus of the antislavery movement were unwarranted. Abolitionists gave no indication of encouraging Negro workers to combine among themselves or with white workers for economic gains. Inasmuch as Garrison and other reformers had expressed no sympathy with the efforts of white workers to organize into trade unions, this attitude is not surprising.

However, abolitionists did consider the economic plight of the northern Negro. In their appeals to the Negro community, antislavery leaders stressed the importance of economic advancement and independence. Accumulate money, Garrison told a Negro audience in 1831, for "money begets influence, and influence respectability."[40] This became standard abolitionist advice throughout the ante-bellum period. "A colored

[39] The [12th] Annual Report of the American and Foreign Anti-Slavery Society, ... 1852 (New York, 1852), 29-30.

[40] William Lloyd Garrison, An Address Delivered before the Free People of Color, in Philadelphia, New York, and other Cities, during the month of June, 1831 (Boston, 1831), 10.

man who makes a thousand dollars," a Unitarian clergyman
and abolitionist declared in 1859, "does more to put down
prejudice, than if he made a thousand moderately good speeches against prejudice, or wrote a thousand pretty fair articles
against it. No race in this country will be despised which makes
money. If we had in Boston or New York ten orang-outangs
worth a million dollars each, they would visit in the best society, we should leave our cards at their doors, and give them
snug little dinner-parties."[41]

Antislavery organizations encouraged a program of economic uplift. They cheered Negro efforts to shift from menial to
agricultural and mechanical employments and called upon
sympathetic merchants and master mechanics to hire Negro ap-
prentices.[42] In Pennsylvania, abolitionists established a register
of Negro mechanics available for work, and in New England
they moved to establish a manual labor college to train Negro
youths.[43] Gerrit Smith, an antislavery leader and philanthropist, decided to promote the Negro drive for economic independence by distributing approximately 140,000 acres of his
land in northern New York (much of which was poor and
unfit for cultivation) to 3,000 Negroes.[44]

[41] James Freeman Clarke, "Condition of the Free Colored People of the
United States," *The Christian Examiner*, LXVI, 5th Series, IV, 263-264 (1859).

[42] *The Fifth Annual Report of the American Anti-Slavery Society, . . . 1838*
(New York, 1838), 127; *Proceedings of the Third Anti-Slavery Convention of
American Women*, 8; Executive Committee of the American Anti-Slavery Society, *Address to the People of Color, in the City of New York* (New York, 1834),
5; Theodore Weld to Lewis Tappan, February 22, 1836, Barnes and Dumond,
editors, *Weld-Grimké Correspondence*, I, 264-265.

[43] Minutes of the Committee for Improvement of the Colored People, Pennsylvania Abolition Society, 1837-1853, Historical Society of Pennsylvania [24-25];
Liberator, September 29, 1832.

[44] Several factors, however, resulted in the failure of this project. In addition to the poor quality of the land, the cost of moving, settling, seeding, and
waiting for the first crops compelled many Negroes to abandon their grants. In
1848, two years after the inauguration of the plan, less than thirty Negro
families had settled on the new lands. See *An Address to the Three Thousand
Colored Citizens of New-York, who are the owners of one hundred and twenty
thousand acres of land, in the State of New York, given to them by Gerrit Smith,
Esq. of Peterboro, September 1, 1846* (New York, 1846); *North Star*, January 7,
February 18, 1848, January 5, March 2, June 1, 1849; Ralph V. Harlow, *Gerrit
Smith* (New York, 1939), 244-245, 250-252.

But abolitionist efforts consisted largely of advice and encouragement and failed to achieve any measurable economic advance. This partly stemmed from the abolitionists' adherence to orthodox middle-class economics. Garrison, for example, believed that an employer's sense of profit would override his racial prejudices. "Place two mechanics by the side of each other—one colored, and the other white," and "he who works the cheapest and best, will get the most custom. In making a bargain, the color of a man will never be consulted."[45] In a similar vein, an antislavery New England journal declared that Negro merchants would attract customers when they sold goods cheaper than their white neighbors, and Negro mechanics would be more frequently employed when they showed a willingness to work for lower wages than whites. The voice of interest, the journal concluded, speaks "louder and more to purpose than reason or philanthropy."[46]

In 1851 three prominent antislavery sympathizers—Cassius M. Clay, Horace Mann, and Benjamin Wade—communicated their recommendations to a convention of Ohio Negroes. Clay advised the delegates to sacrifice social equality, which he considered impossible to attain even in the free states, and immediate political rights in order to concentrate on the accumulation of wealth. "The blacks should 'get money,'" he declared. "Let them go into the trades—become farmers—manufacturers —where capital and employment are wanting—let them combine, and thus diminish the expense of living, and increase their productive power." According to Mann, however, Negroes could advance economically only by forming separate communities apart from the whites where they could "rise from domestic labor and mere chance-service, from being ditchers and delvers, into farmers, mechanics, artizans, shopkeepers, printers, editors or professional men." Separation would afford all Negroes an equal opportunity to compete for the highest political and economic offices. Wade arrived at al-

[45] Garrison, *Address Delivered before the Free People of Color,* 10.
[46] *New England Magazine,* January, 1832, quoted in *Liberator,* January 21, 1832.

most an identical conclusion; he advised Negroes to withdraw from all menial employments, form separate communities, cultivate the soil, enter the mechanical arts, and thereby attain economic independence. "While scattered about among the white people," this objective could not be realized. Independence, however, would compel whites to grant them respect and recognition, thus forever destroying the doctrine of racial superiority. "The colored skin is nothing," Wade concluded: "When was it ever known that virtue, industry and intelligence were not respected?"[47]

However, abolitionist moral encouragement did not break down the economic barriers confronting northern Negroes. As a result, the Negro entered the Civil War period as an unorganized and unskilled worker competing with newly arrived immigrants for the menial employments.

V

Economic orthodoxy and the aversion of some abolitionists to intimate social relations with Negroes did not prevent the antislavery movement from registering some important victories in the realm of equal rights. Perhaps the most spectacular of these was the successful integration of Negro and white students in the public schools of Boston.

Education constituted the foremost aspiration of the northern Negro. But the possibility of Negroes mixing with white children in the same classroom aroused even greater fears and prejudices than those that consigned them to an inferior place in the church, theater, and railroad car. This, indeed, was virtual amalgamation. Although Negroes sometimes gained admittance to white schools, most northern states either excluded them altogether from the public schools or established separate schools for them.[48]

[47] *Proceedings of the Convention of the Colored Freemen of Ohio, . . . Cincinnati, . . . 1852* (Cincinnati, 1852), 15-25. For the reaction of the Negro community to these recommendations, see *Frederick Douglass' Paper*, October 22, 1852, and *Liberator*, November 26, 1852.

[48] The means by which Negroes were excluded from white schools varied only slightly from state to state. In New England, local school committees usually

Excluded from white schools, Negroes endeavored to establish their own educational institutions and enlisted the support of abolitionists. The education of the emancipated slave had formed a major goal of the early abolition societies, particularly in New York and Pennsylvania.[49] After 1831 the revived abolitionist movement sought to assist Negro education. The constitution of the American Anti-Slavery Society urged the encouragement of the "intellectual, moral, and religious improvement" of Negroes, and Garrison praised Negro efforts to improve his condition through education.[50] Convinced "that faith without *works* is death," Cincinnati abolitionists provided instruction for the Negro community. Other antislavery societies moved to duplicate the achievements of the Cincinnati group.[51]

However, even exclusively Negro schools frequently en-

---

assigned Negro children to separate institutions, regardless of the district in which they resided. Pennsylvania and Ohio, although extending their public school privileges to all children, required district school directors to establish separate facilities for Negro students whenever twenty or more could be accommodated. The New York legislature authorized any school district, upon the approval of a town's school commissioners, to provide for segregation. The newer states also consented to separate instruction. In the absence of legal restrictions, custom and popular prejudices prevented Negroes from entering white schools. For a general survey of state policies regarding Negro education, see U. S. Commissioner of Education, *Special Report of the Commissioner of Education on the Condition and Improvement of Public Schools in the District of Columbia, Submitted to the Senate June, 1868, and to the House, with additions, June 13, 1870* (Washington, 1871), Part II: Legal Status of the Colored Population in Respect to Schools and Education in the Different States, 301-400; and Carter G. Woodson, *The Education of the Negro Prior to 1861* (New York, 1915), 307-335.

[49] Minutes of the Committee for Improving the Condition of Free Blacks, Pennsylvania Abolition Society, 1790-1803, Historical Society of Pennsylvania [1-2, 113, 219-220]; Edward Needles, *An Historical Memoir of the Pennsylvania Society, for Promoting the Abolition of Slavery, the Relief of Free Negroes Unlawfully Held in Bondage, and for Improving the Condition of the African Race* (Philadelphia, 1848), 40, 43, 68, 69-70, 104-105; Charles C. Andrews, *The History of the New-York African Free-Schools, from their establishment in 1787, to the present time* (New York, 1830).

[50] *The Declaration of Sentiments and Constitution of the American Anti-Slavery Society* (New York, 1835), 8; *First Annual Report of the Board of Managers of the New-England Anti-Slavery Society, presented January 9, 1833* (Boston, 1833), 7.

[51] Barnes and Dumond, editors, *Weld-Grimké Correspondence*, I, 132-135, 178-180, 211-218; Abdy, *Journal of a Residence and Tour*, II, 388-389.

countered strong opposition from the white community. The identification of abolitionism with the cause of Negro education provided whites with a convenient excuse for resisting such institutions. In New Haven, Connecticut, for example, Garrisonian abolitionists failed to establish a Negro manual labor college in the face of strenuous local opposition. Such an institution, city officials declared, would propagate antislavery sentiments, prove incompatible with the existence and prosperity of Yale and other notable schools, and be "destructive to the best interests of this city." Attempts to establish a Negro girls school in Canterbury, Connecticut, and to enroll Negro students in a Canaan, New Hampshire academy met even more violent resistance, and failed.

White abolitionists joined Negroes in assailing school segregation, and soon questioned their own efforts to establish exclusively Negro institutions. When some white colleges indicated a willingness to admit Negroes, an abolitionist leader asked Garrison in 1834 if it would not be preferable to patronize those institutions rather than build new ones since "the object we aim at, the destruction of caste, will be the sooner gained."[52] Two years later an abolitionist convention confirmed this opinion by resolving henceforth to oppose separate schools.[53]

Boston was the major focal point of the Negro-abolitionist attack on segregated schools. In Massachusetts, Negroes achieved virtual political and legal equality by 1845, and their children were admitted to public schools, without discrimination, in Salem, New Bedford, Nantucket, Worcester, and Lowell. Only Boston maintained a policy of separation, and it was there that Negroes launched the most concerted and suc-

[52] Elizur Wright, Jr., to William Lloyd Garrison, June 30, 1834, Garrison Papers, Boston Public Library, and Wright Papers, Library of Congress. A New Bedford, Massachusetts abolitionist wrote in 1837 that "it is hardly desirable that there should be an exclusively coloured school established, for the public schools are all open, and black children admitted on terms of the most perfect equality." Deborah Weston to Maria (Weston) Chapman, April, 1837, Weston Papers, Boston Public Library.

[53] *Liberator*, November 19, 1836.

cessful attack on "caste" schools in the North. White abolitionists, convinced that local segregation practices were incompatible with their antislavery efforts, joined the campaign. "It is useless for us to prate of the conduct of South Carolina," a segregation foe declared in 1845, "so long as we maintain—*illegally* maintain—a practice here which at least incidentally sanctions it."[54] The following year the Massachusetts Anti-Slavery Society resolved that "the friends of the cause" residing in those communities which provided separate educational facilities should immediately inform Negroes of their legal rights, and "afford them all possible aid in securing the full and equal enjoyment of the public schools."[55]

While Garrison's *Liberator* assailed the Boston school committee, local Negroes met regularly to prepare new appeals and methods of attack.[56] Rejected by the school committee and the courts, they turned to legislative action and secured in 1855 the enactment of a bill to prohibit distinctions based on race, color, or religious opinions in determining the qualification of students to be admitted into any of the public schools.[57] Negroes and white abolitionists celebrated their triumph for equal rights in a mass meeting.[58] The foes of integration appeared disappointed and fearful. "Now the blood of the Winthrops, the Otises, the Lymans, the Endicotts, and the Eliots,

[54] *Liberator*, June 27, 1845.

[55] *Fourteenth Annual Report presented to the Massachusetts Anti-Slavery Society, by its Board of Managers, January 28, 1846* (Boston, 1846), 91-92.

[56] *Liberator*, August 21, 1846, August 10, September 7, November 9, December 14, 1849, February 8, 1850.

[57] *House Report*, Massachusetts House of Representatives, No. 167 (March 17, 1855).

[58] *Triumph of Equal School Rights in Boston. Proceedings of the Presentation Meeting held in Boston, December 17, 1855; including addresses by John T. Hilton, Wm. C. Nell, Charles W. Slack, Wendell Phillips, Wm. Lloyd Garrison, Charles Lenox Remond* (Boston, 1856). "The best thing learned by these struggles," Wendell Phillips declared, "is, how to prepare for another. . . . He should never think Mass. a State fit to live in, until he saw one man, at least, as black as the ace of spades, a graduate of Harvard College. (Cheers) . . . When they had high schools and colleges to which all classes and colors were admitted on equal terms, then he should think Mass. was indeed the noblest representative of the principles that planted her."

is in a fair way to be amalgamated with the Sambos, the Catos, and the Pompeys," one newspaper declared. "The North is to be Africanized. Amalgamation has commenced. New England heads the column. God save the Commonwealth of Massachusetts!"[59]

The Boston victory encouraged Negroes and abolitionists in other states to increase their agitation, but they had less success. Some small and scattered communities consented to admit both races to the same schoolhouse, but the larger cities such as Philadelphia, New York, Cincinnati, Providence, and New Haven, held firmly to a segregated school system and hoped to stem increasing agitation by promises to correct existing abuses and provide separate but equal facilities for Negro and white children.

In addition to their efforts on behalf of the economic and educational advancement of the northern Negro, abolitionists supported Negro attempts to secure equal political and legal rights with whites and to break down the segregation barrier in public places. The Garrisonian abolitionists, for example, achieved phenomenal success in Massachusetts as they combined with Negroes to secure the repeal of the ban on interracial marriages, the abandonment of "Jim Crow" seating in railroad cars, and the organization of integrated lyceums, as well as the integration of Boston's public schools.

By 1860 the antislavery societies could point to some noteworthy achievements. In assessing the weaknesses and inconsistencies of the abolitionist movement, historians must not overlook these important contributions to the cause of human freedom in the North. Abolitionists did indeed suffer from factionalism, extreme partisanship, narrow class attitudes, prejudice, and even hypocrisy, but they shared these weaknesses with nearly every organized movement and political party in ante-bellum America. The fact that abolitionists did not allow

[59] New York *Herald*, quoted in *Liberator*, May 4, 1855. Subsequent testimony of Boston school officers and teachers praised the results of integration. Although a few white parents withdrew their children and some Negroes suffered insults, integrated schools resulted in neither racial violence nor amalgamation.

these weaknesses to interfere materially with their struggle for civil rights is a tribute to their sincerity. Forced at times to endure mob violence, severe public censure, frustration and defeat, these dedicated agitators displayed an ability to apply theoretical arguments about equal rights to concrete situations. Although frequently hesitant and uncertain in their own social relations with Negroes, abolitionists nevertheless attempted to demonstrate to a hostile public that environmental factors, rather than any peculiar racial traits, largely accounted for the degradation of the northern Negro.

Evangelicalism and "Immediate Emancipation" in American Antislavery Thought

By ANNE C. LOVELAND

Few HISTORIANS OF THE AMERICAN ANTISLAVERY MOVEMENT HAVE appreciated the connection between evangelicalism and the demand for immediate emancipation which emerged in the late 1820's and early 1830's.[1] In the past thirty years immediatism has been variously interpreted as an outgrowth of sectionalism, an imitation of British antislavery efforts, a product of social and institutional disintegration, the anguished protest of a "displaced social elite," or the work of "fanatical" or "crackpot" reformers.[2]

[1] No one recognized the connection between evangelicalism and immediatism more clearly than the abolitionists. Writing in 1852, William Goodell recalled that "There were moral, religious and social influences at work." The missionary enterprise, revivals of religion, "an increasing spirit of inquiry in respect to Christian ethics"—all focused attention on the system of slavery. "Whatever our missionary and evangelizing orators intended, whatever *they* were thinking of, they were God's instruments for putting into the minds of others 'thoughts that burned,' for the emancipation of the enslaved," Goodell wrote. Revivals of religion, he continued, gave prominence to "the old doctrine of Hopkins and Edwards, demanding 'immediate and unconditional repentance' of all sin, as the only condition of forgiveness and salvation." This was urged, Goodell explained, "in direct opposition to the vague idea of a gradual amendment, admitting 'a more convenient season'—a prospective, dilatory, indefinite breaking off from transgression—an idea that had been settling upon the churches for thirty or forty years previous,—an incubus upon every righteous cause, and every holy endeavour." At the same time, Goodell observed, Christians began to consider "the bearing of the religious principle upon the social relations and political duties of man." Goodell concluded: "How short-sighted are those who think that the agitation originated only with a few 'fanatics,' and that all would be quiet if they could be silenced or crushed!" William Goodell, *Slavery and Anti-Slavery; a History of the Great Struggle in Both Hemispheres; with a View of the Slavery Question in the United States* (New York, 1852), 387-89.

[2] See, for example, Arthur Young Lloyd, *The Slavery Controversy, 1831-1860* (Chapel Hill, 1939); Gilbert Hobbs Barnes, *The Antislavery Impulse, 1830-1844* (New York, 1933); Stanley M. Elkins, *Slavery: A Problem in American Institutional and Intellectual Life* (Chicago, 1959); David Donald, "Toward a Reconsideration of Abolitionists," in Donald, *Lincoln Reconsidered: Essays on the Civil War Era* (New York, 1956); Merton Lynn Dillon, "The Failure of the American Abolitionists," *Journal of Southern History,* XXV (May 1959), 159-77; Avery O. Craven, *Civil War in the Making, 1815-1860* (Baton Rouge, 1959), *The Coming of*

Miss LOVELAND is instructor in history at Louisiana State University.

The evolution of evangelical doctrines of sin and ability, repentance and benevolence, and their application to the slavery issue have received only superficial attention.[3]

As a result, historians have usually misconstrued the immediatist slogan, interpreting it as a temporal rather than a moral and religious requirement.[4] They have read into it a deadline for emancipation that misses the point and purpose of the abolitionist demand. The thesis of Gilbert H. Barnes, that the doctrine of immediate emancipation was a British import lacking real meaning and application in American society, has had wide acceptance. According to Barnes, quoting contemporary sources, the British slogan admitted of at least two interpretations: it might be gradually interpreted to mean " '*immediate* emancipation . . . gradually accomplished,' " or it might be literally interpreted to mean the " 'duty of every slave-holder . . . to emancipate his slaves at once without regard to the peculiar circumstances of the case and without inquiring as to the probable consequences which may result from the act.' " Either reading posed an "inescapable dilemma" for American abolitionists. The first interpretation was little more than gradualism under another name, substituting one form of slavery for another; the latter was Garrisonian extremism and " 'nothing less than insanity.' " The doctrinal dilemma was resolved, according to Barnes, only when

---

the *Civil War* (New York, 1942), "Coming of the War Between the States: An Interpretation," *Journal of Southern History*, II (August 1936), 303-22, and *The Repressible Conflict, 1830-1861* (University, La., 1939); James G. Randall, "The Blundering Generation," *Mississippi Valley Historical Review*, XXVII (June 1940), 3-28, and *The Civil War and Reconstruction* (Boston, 1937).

[3] A number of historians have advanced the thesis that revivalism was behind the antislavery impulse, but none has explored the assumptions of evangelicalism and its relation to immediatism. See Barnes, *Antislavery Impulse;* Dwight L. Dumond, *Antislavery Origins of the Civil War in the United States* (Ann Arbor, 1939), 35, 47, 49, and *Antislavery: The Crusade for Freedom in America* (Ann Arbor, 1961), 154, 158, 179; Clifford S. Griffin, "Religious Benevolence as Social Control, 1815-1860," *Mississippi Valley Historical Review*, XLIV (December 1957), 423-44; Alice Felt Tyler, *Freedom's Ferment: Phases of American Social History to 1860* (Minneapolis, 1944), 2-3, 33, 41, 44-45, 489, 497; Whitney R. Cross, *The Burned-Over District: The Social and Intellectual History of Enthusiastic Religion in Western New York, 1800-1850* (Ithaca, 1950), 28-29, 165-66, 168, 217-20; Charles C. Cole, Jr., *The Social Ideas of the Northern Evangelists, 1826-1860* (New York, 1954), 217-20; John L. Thomas, *The Liberator, William Lloyd Garrison: A Biography* (Boston, 1963), 5, 64-65, 104, 453-54.

[4] For exceptions see David Brion Davis, "The Emergence of Immediatism in British and American Antislavery Thought," *Mississippi Valley Historical Review*, XLIX (September 1962), 209-30; and Dillon, "Failure of American Abolitionists." Dwight Dumond hints briefly at a moral reading of the slogan in *Antislavery Origins*, 27.

the Lane Seminary rebels "revived" the doctrine that slavery was a sin and ought immediately to be abandoned.[5]

The effect of the Barnes thesis has been to distort the meaning of immediate emancipation as originally understood by the abolitionists. In his attempt to "revise" William Lloyd Garrison out of the abolition crusade, Barnes ignored the religious and moral heritage which Garrison shared with other abolitionists and which supplied the doctrine of immediate emancipation.[6] The Lane Seminary rebels did not "revive" the doctrine that slavery was a sin and ought immediately to be abandoned. Immediate repentance and abandonment of the sin of slavery was the common creed of early abolitionists, who derived the doctrines and methods of immediatism from evangelicalism and who prosecuted the antislavery movement as a religious and moral enterprise.

Immediatism signaled a change of disposition, not of discourse, in the American antislavery movement. Like many colonizationists and gradual emancipationists, abolitionists articulated their stand in the traditional religious vocabulary. What gave their appeal a special import and urgency was a new view of reform, the product of religious developments of the eighteenth and early nineteenth centuries. These developments infused the traditional vocabulary with new meaning which in turn compelled a new view of man's relation to God and his fellow creatures—one that emphasized ability rather than inability, activity rather than passivity, benevolence rather than piety. Such changes were fundamental to the emergence of the immediatist disposition and view of reform; it will therefore be helpful to consider them in some detail.

During the eighteenth century New England ministers turned

[5] Barnes, *Antislavery Impulse*, 49, 101-103; see also 31, 34, 42-44, 48-49, 59, 60, 66, 77, 79, 83, 90.

[6] "Immediate emancipation"—immediate repentance and abandonment of the sin of slavery—was preached in Garrisonian territory at least a year before Lane Seminary rebels "revived" the doctrine. In April 1833 Amos A. Phelps, pastor of Boston's Pine Street Church and, according to Barnes, spokesman for the New England Anti-Slavery Society, delivered a series of lectures applying the doctrine of immediate repentance to the sin of slavery. The New England Society published them a year later as *Lectures on Slavery and Its Remedy*. Garrison himself learned the doctrine of immediate repentance from Boston's Lyman Beecher and was convinced that the sin of slavery demanded nothing less than immediate repentance and immediate emancipation. Oliver Johnson, *William Lloyd Garrison and His Times; or, Sketches of the Anti-Slavery Movement in America, and of the Man Who Was Its Founder and Moral Leader* (Boston, 1879), 45; Thomas, *The Liberator*, 5, 59, 64-65, 72-73.

their efforts to reviving and strengthening orthodox religion against the attack of secular, rationalistic beliefs. In the process, many of them qualified strict Calvinist doctrines. The theological speculations of Joseph Bellamy, Samuel Hopkins, Timothy Dwight, Nathaniel William Taylor, and Lyman Beecher resulted in a peculiar synthesis of Calvinist and liberal doctrines. Retaining traditional concepts of divine sovereignty, infinite sin, and imperfect sanctification, these men gradually, if unwittingly, adopted certain humanistic, Arminian doctrines of their opponents.

The primary issue for these theologians was man's role in the drama of salvation. Calvinism accentuated the absolute, arbitrary sovereignty of God by contrasting it with the inability and passivity of man.[7] It preached that repentance and conversion were the gifts of God, not the acts of sinful man. This view began to break down when Jonathan Edwards' followers elaborated on his distinction between natural and moral inability. Ironically, they raised the very specter of Arminianism which Edwards had tried to destroy. Joseph Bellamy deemed sin the consequence of moral, not natural, inability, claiming that "all mankind are capable of a perfect conformity to God's law . . . all our inability arises merely from the bad temper of our hearts, and our want of a good disposition . . . ."[8] Samuel Hopkins made a further discrimination between regeneration and conversion which confirmed man's ability in the religious experience. While men remained passive in regeneration, they played an active role in conversion, according to Hopkins. Conversion was an act of the will "in which men, being regenerated [by God], turn from sin to God in the exercise of repentance . . . and faith . . . ." Moreover, conversion was "instantaneous"; the change from sin to God was "wrought not gradually, but at once."[9]

At the beginning of the nineteenth century a new generation of religious leaders, many of them Edwardseans, unwittingly continued the tendency toward Arminianism, all the while preaching against it. Timothy Dwight, Edwards' grandson, encouraged

[7] Frank Hugh Foster, A Genetic History of the New England Theology (Chicago, 1907), 26.

[8] Ibid., 110.

[9] "The human heart is either a heart of stone, a rebellious heart, or a new heart," wrote Hopkins. "The man is either under the dominion of sin, as obstinate and vile as ever, dead in trespasses and sins; or his heart is humble and penitent; he is a new creature and spiritually alive. There can be no instant of time, in which the heart is neither a hard heart, nor a new heart, and the man is neither dead in trespasses and sins, nor spiritually alive." Ibid., 135, 183-84.

a spirit of revivalism and benevolence at Yale Seminary. Avoiding theological controversy and technical jargon, he preached a common-sense religion which combined "dependence upon God and personal responsibility."[10] Similarly, Nathaniel Taylor and Lyman Beecher, defending orthodox Calvinism against the Unitarian attack, stamped the "New Haven Theology" with qualified assertions of man's moral responsibility and free will and defined sin as voluntary rather than inherent in man.[11]

Along with the shift from inability to ability went a changing definition of virtue, or holiness, and benevolence. In *The Nature of True Virtue* Jonathan Edwards had defined "true virtue" as "*benevolence* [or love] *to being in general.*" For him, true virtue was properly exercised in seeking the glory of God; "benevolence to being in general" meant the worship and service of God. But Edwards' followers tended to ignore the spiritual, pietistic sense in which he had defined virtue. Samuel Hopkins, for example, commenting on Edwards' treatise in the *Inquiry into the Nature of True Holiness,* reinterpreted "love to being in general" to mean "universal benevolence, or friendly affection *to all intelligent beings.*"[12] In this respect, Hopkins marks the transition from a religion of piety centered on God, to one of humanitarianism and benevolence toward mankind.[13]

The theological innovations of New England clergymen had a practical analogue in the revivals or "awakenings" of the eighteenth and nineteenth centuries. Whatever their creed or confession, revival preachers proceeded on the assumption that every individual had free will and moral ability to work out his own salvation. They concentrated on reviving apathetic congregations by calling upon sinners to repent and submit to God, without clearly defining their terms or elaborating on doctrine.[14]

Charles Grandison Finney, the leading revivalist of the early nineteenth century, preached virtually the same doctrines in

[10] William Warren Sweet, *Religion in the Development of American Culture, 1765-1840* (New York, 1952), 199.

[11] Foster, *Genetic History,* 242, 246-48, 370; William G. McLoughlin, Jr., *Modern Revivalism: Charles Grandison Finney to Billy Graham* (New York, 1959), 8-10, 12, 31-33; Bernard A. Weisberger, *They Gathered at the River: The Story of the Great Revivalists and Their Impact upon Religion in America* (Boston, 1958), 63 ff., 82-85.

[12] Jonathan Edwards, *The Nature of True Virtue* (Ann Arbor, 1960), 3-5; Foster, *Genetic History,* 95 ff., 152, italics mine.

[13] Joseph Haroutunian, *Piety Versus Moralism: The Passing of the New England Theology* (New York, 1932), 82, 86-87.

[14] Charles Grandison Finney, *Lectures on Revivals of Religion,* edited by William G. McLoughlin, Jr. (Cambridge, 1960), xiii-xiv.

New York's "Burned-Over District" that Lyman Beecher and others were preaching in New England.[15] Finney's revival theology was not original; it merely spelled out explicitly the subtle modifications and compromises that had occurred within Calvinism over several decades. In a more general sense, Finney's theology defined the religious frame of mind of many Americans in the 1820's and 1830's. The fact that Finney was able to evoke an immediate and widespread response suggests that the views he articulated were already familiar and acceptable to his audiences, though perhaps held unconsciously. Seen in this light, Finney's theology was an expression of religious and moral beliefs which had developed over the years and which had wide currency at the very time an increasing number of Americans were demanding immediate emancipation.

Finney approached religion from an experiential, commonsense viewpoint. He defined free will as "the power of originating and deciding our own choices . . . upon moral questions." From free will he derived man's moral responsibility, arguing that "unless the will is free, man has no freedom; and if he has no freedom, he is not a moral agent."[16] Finney specifically repudiated the Calvinist notion of man's inability in conversion. Believing that the individual was free to save himself without the direct aid of the Holy Spirit, he required an immediate decision from the sinner to accept or reject Christ. The sinner could "repent and be converted immediately" according to Finney. The urgency of such action was conveyed in the warning, "Another moment's delay and it may be too late forever."[17]

Finney defined a change of heart as "a change from selfishness to benevolence," from self-interest to a desire for the "glory of his sovereign [God] and the good of the public . . . ."[18] Moreover, the individual was required to translate his benevolent spirit into good works. Benevolence was more than emotion or sentiment; it was a tendency to action, or action itself. As such, it constituted the proper test and evidence of love for God and mankind. Converts were told to strive for "*usefulness*" in religion. They were advised to "set out with a determination to *aim at being useful in the highest degree possible*." "When a man is converted," Finney

---

[15] *Ibid.*, xx; see also McLoughlin, *Modern Revivalism*, 64.
[16] Foster, *Genetic History*, 253; see also Weisberger, *They Gathered at the River*, 111.
[17] McLoughlin, *Modern Revivalism*, 28-29, 68, 73.
[18] *Ibid.*, 70.

explained, "he comes into a new world, and should consider himself as a new man."[19]

The typical convert to evangelicalism underwent a "tidal wave of feeling," which telescoped the traditionally slow cycle of guilt, despair, hope, and assurance into an agonizing experience of a few days or hours.[20] Even then, assurance was short-lived. Conversion often sharpened an individual's sense of sin and guilt, and salvation remained distressingly uncertain despite the fact that it was within the reach of all. To the extent that evangelical Protestantism retained the Puritan notion of imperfect sanctification, it committed converts to endless soul-searching and self-examination, constantly seeking "perfect holiness" and striving to remake the world in the image of the millennium.

In effect, evangelicalism nurtured a utopian, reformist disposition. It influenced the emergence of immediatism in two ways. First, many radical abolitionists were early converts to evangelical Protestantism. To the extent that the religious experience crystallized certain vague notions about sin and responsibility and compelled active benevolence, evangelicalism exercised a direct and positive influence on immediatism. Second, and more important, as a system of belief which articulated religious developments and innovations of past decades, evangelicalism justified an immediatist approach to reform and provided the vocabulary and method of immediatism.

To be sure, not all converts to evangelical religion became radical abolitionists. Many remained socially conservative. For them, as for the majority of evangelical preachers, including Finney and Beecher, revivalism was the primary "reform," salvation the primary goal. Oriented toward the individual rather than society, conservative evangelicals concerned themselves with personal moral reform rather than social and political evils. In their eyes, slavery was a social and political evil, not a personal sin, and abolition was therefore secondary to and derivative from the primary goal of moral and spiritual reformation.

Yet conversion to evangelicalism frequently crystallized vague reformist and humanitarian convictions. Finney himself, who displayed a hesitating and ambivalent attitude toward social reform, suggested "that because true Christians 'supremely value the highest good of Being, they will and must take a deep interest in

[19] Finney, "Instructions to Converts," in Finney, *Lectures on Revivals of Religion*, 404.
[20] Weisberger, *They Gathered at the River*, 28.

whatever is promotive of that end. Hence their spirit is necessarily that of the reformer. To the universal reformation of the world they stand committed.' "[21] Extending the reform impulse of evangelical Protestantism beyond the spiritual and religious realms, men like Theodore Dwight Weld, Arthur and Lewis Tappan, and James Gillespie Birney made revivalism a pragmatic, activistic force for social good. They channeled their religious energies into educational, peace, and temperance movements as well as into Bible, tract, and missionary societies.[22] Eventually they turned to antislavery as a field for benevolent action. A concern for the salvation of masters as well as slaves compelled them to urge the immediate abolition of slavery. In their eyes, emancipation was an important—perhaps the most important—step in the coming of the millennium.

The failure of evangelicalism as a reform of religion also impelled converts into abolitionism. Many converts did not find in evangelical Protestantism the purity and intensity of faith they had anticipated.[23] Others were disappointed by the ambivalent attitude of revivalist ministers toward slavery and other social evils. In the eyes of such men the sin of slavery was a sin of the church as well as society. They proposed to extend the reforming impulse beyond ecclesiastical and doctrinal spheres to the church as a social institution. They preached immediate emancipation as a reform not only of society but of religion. Denouncing organized religion, they proposed to restore Christianity to its original perfection, untainted by the principle of slavery.[24]

Whether prosecuted as an extension of evangelicalism or as a reform of traditional faith, immediatism functioned "as a kind of surrogate religion."[25] It channeled religious and reforming energies outside the domain of organized religion. Abolitionists taught that "Christianity does not consist in conformity to a creed, or in the observance of forms, but in purity of life and de-

[21] McLoughlin, *Modern Revivalism*, 106.
[22] Benjamin P. Thomas, *Theodore Weld: Crusader for Freedom* (New Brunswick, 1950), 15-16, 20-25, 31-33; Betty L. Fladeland, *James Gillespie Birney: Slaveholder to Abolitionist* (Ithaca, 1955), 31-37, 38; Lewis Tappan, *The Life of Arthur Tappan* (New York, 1870), 62, 64, 66-67, 73-74.
[23] Weld to Finney, April 22, 1828, in Gilbert H. Barnes and Dwight L. Dumond (eds.), *Letters of Theodore Dwight Weld, Angelina Grimké Weld, and Sarah Grimké, 1822-1844* (2 vols., New York, 1934), I, 14-15.
[24] Johnson, *Garrison and His Times*, 368; Charles K. Whipple, "Relations of Anti-Slavery to Religion," in *Platform of the American Anti-Slavery Society and Its Auxiliaries* (New York, 1855), 1, 14.
[25] Davis, "Emergence of Immediatism," 229.

votion to the welfare of mankind." They promised a "new and higher spiritual life" to converts to immediatism.[26] The cause of immediate emancipation was described as the pursuit of "a Christian end by Christian means."[27] Abolition was presented as a kind of "calling" which proved one's benevolent affections and in which one might work both for the glory of God and the welfare of mankind. In sum, immediatism was an exhilarating, practical faith which defined sin in concrete terms, demanded weapons to fight it, and optimistically predicted its abolition as the final step toward the millennium.

As a surrogate religion, immediatism fulfilled certain needs and alleviated vague frustrations. It appealed to minds and hearts troubled by flux and disorder and disturbed by the apparent irrelevance of traditional values in a changing society. It injected a sense of purpose and direction into lives thwarted by inadequate religions or unrewarding professions. Above all, it satisfied religious yearnings and humanitarian, reforming impulses that traditional institutions could not fulfill. At the same time, by employing evangelical doctrines in the antislavery context, immediatism gave concrete meaning to abstract notions of benevolence and ability, sin and repentance.

Abolitionists interpreted the evangelical concept of benevolence in humanistic, pragmatic terms. According to Beriah Green, the exercise of benevolence consisted in "cordially embracing the rights and interests of all, whether above or around us, to whom as moral agents, we are related." "The regard which we manifest for man is a fair test and just measure of our regard for God," Green observed. "Professed piety towards God is base and spurious if not united with benevolence for men."[28]

For abolitionists, benevolence meant more than mere sympathy for the slave. Action was the infallible test of true benevolence and charity. "We have an unerring rule by which to judge of men—not by their words, but by their actions—not by their profession, but by their practice," declared one immediatist.[29] In-

[26] Johnson, *Garrison and His Times,* 371, italics mine.
[27] Whipple, "Relations of Anti-Slavery," 3.
[28] Beriah Green, *Four Sermons, Preached in the Chapel of the Western Reserve College, on Lord's Days, November 18th and 25th, and December 2nd and 9th, 1832* (Cleveland, 1833), 41-52; see also 30-40.
[29] Evan Lewis, *Address to the Colored People of Philadelphia. Delivered at Bethel Church, on the Evening of the 12th of the 3rd Month, 1833* (Philadelphia, 1833), 3, 7; see also John Greenleaf Whittier, "Justice and Expediency; or, Slavery Considered with a View to Its Rightful and Effectual Remedy, Abolition" (1833),

deed, positive, forthright action opposing sin and evil was the only prudent course for the true believer. Evangelicalism taught that man was not powerless to prevent evil, that he had the ability to recognize and renounce sin, and that, unless he acknowledged its existence and attempted to eliminate it, he remained guilty in the eyes of the Lord. Contemporary doctrines of ability and moral responsibility constrained abolitionists to "act out" their religious beliefs in a social context. Theodore Weld declared that "as long as I am a moral agent I am fully prepared to *act out* my belief [immediate abolition] in that thus saith the Lord— '*Faith without WORKS is dead*.'"[30]

Evangelical notions of benevolence and ability in turn shaped a new concept of sin which abolitionists applied to slavery. Once benevolence was defined as a concern for "our fellow creatures" or the rights of others, sin acquired a social connotation. Anything that militated against human happiness or the general welfare might be termed sinful.[31] Thus persuaded of the social signification of sin, as well as man's guilt with regard to it, immediatists attacked slavery as sin and slaveholders as sinners. The Reverend Amos A. Phelps advised members of his congregation that they "must assail [slavery] in its true character—as a moral evil, for the existence of which, moral agents are responsible and guilty." The efficacy and truth of the doctrine of immediate emancipation, Phelps argued, lay in the fact that it attacked slavery in its "true character, as a moral, rather than a physical evil . . . . [as] a sin—a crime, and not a mere undefined evil, or calamity, or misfortune."[32]

---

in *The Writings of John Greenleaf Whittier* (7 vols., Boston, 1888-1889), VII, 9-10.

[30] Weld to Elizur Wright, Jr., January 10, 1833, in Barnes and Dumond (eds.), *Weld-Grimké Letters*, I, 99.

[31] Haroutunian, *Piety Versus Moralism*, 151.

[32] Amos A. Phelps, *Lectures on Slavery and Its Remedy* (Boston, 1834), 160-63, 166. See also Elizur Wright, Jr., *The Sin of Slavery and Its Remedy; Containing Some Reflections on the Moral Influence of African Colonization* (New York, 1833), 3. Attacking slavery on moral grounds, abolitionists professed to stand above the divisive issues of politics and religion. At the same time they wooed citizens of every party and sect. They recognized, as evangelical preachers did, the importance of an antisectarian, nondenominational approach, and they avoided the political arena for fear of precipitating sectional or constitutional disputes. *The Liberator*, March 4, 1831, p. 39; Lydia Maria Child, *An Appeal in Favor of That Class of Americans Called Africans* (Boston, 1833), 132; Andover Theological Seminary Anti-Slavery Society, "Apology," *Liberator*, September 28, 1833, p. 153; James G. Birney, "Address of the Kentucky Society for the Gradual Relief of the State from Slavery," in Dwight L. Dumond (ed.), *Letters of James Gillespie Birney, 1831-1857* (2 vols., New York, 1938), I, 109; *Address of the New-York*

The sin of slavery consisted primarily in allowing the system to persist when it could be abolished. Man's ability (both spiritual and physical) to abolish slavery determined his responsibility for it. Slavery could have been eliminated when the colonies won their independence from Great Britain, Lydia Maria Child pointed out. "It could have been done easily, at the time of our confederation; it *can* be done now," she insisted. "The plain truth is, the continuation of this system is a sin; and the sin rests on us."[33]

Because they recognized man's responsibility and ability with regard to the sin of slavery, abolitionists denounced the sinners as well as the system. Gradualists and colonizationists looked upon slavery as an abstract evil. Radical abolitionists not only declared slavery sinful in both principle and practice; they placed the blame for it squarely on individual men.[34] According to abolitionists, slavery was a "national sin" in which Northerners as well as Southern slaveholders participated.[35] The very nature of sin determined that everyone was equally implicated and equally responsible. The notion of degrees of sin or crime was completely alien to the abolitionist ideology.[36] Amos Phelps observed that any

City Anti-Slavery Society to the People of the City of New-York (New York, 1833), 26; Wright, *Sin of Slavery*, 9; Samuel J. May, *Some Recollections of Our Antislavery Conflict* (Boston, 1869), 241; "To the Public," *Liberator*, January 1, 1831, p. 1; May, "Sermon on Slavery," *ibid.*, July 23, 1831, p. 118; "Consistency," *ibid.*, July 30, 1831, p. 123.

[33] Child, *Appeal*, 76.

[34] *Liberator*, March 26, 1831, p. 49; see also Child, *Appeal*, 34; Joseph Anthony Del Porto, "A Study of American Anti-Slavery Journals" (unpublished Ph.D. dissertation, Michigan State University, 1953), 117; William Lloyd Garrison, *Thoughts on African Colonization: or, An Impartial Exhibition of the Doctrines, Principles and Purposes of the American Colonization Society. Together with the Resolutions, Addresses and Remonstrances of the Free People of Color* (Boston, 1832), 1-3; *Liberator*, July 28, 1832, p. 117; Samuel J. May, *Defence of Abolition Principles* (Providence, 1833), 2.

[35] See, for example, the article reprinted from the *Horn of the Green Mountains* (Manchester, Vermont) in the *Liberator*, February 5, 1831, p. 21; Samuel J. May, *A Discourse on Slavery in the United States, Delivered in Brooklyn*, [Connecticut], *July 3, 1831* (Boston, 1832), 8.

[36] "Since wrong was a specific quality, regardless of quantity, and since an offense against the infinite good automatically became itself infinite, any departure whatsoever from divine rule constituted an absolutely enormous crime." Cross, *Burned-Over District*, 208. See also Phelps, *Lectures on Slavery*, 160-63. The notion of degrees of crime or sin may have been a crucial point of conflict between Benjamin Lundy, editor of the *Genius of Universal Emancipation*, and Garrison. While Lundy admitted the universality and (presumably) the equality of guilt as applied to slaveholder and nonslaveholder, he maintained that there were "degrees of crime" as between holding slaves and advocating slavery. Garrison, however, maintained that sin was sin, pure and absolute, and he distinguished only between those who were against slavery and those who were for it, that is, all

person "abetted" the sin of slavery who adopted opinions and pursued practices which, if adopted and pursued by others, would perpetuate the system. Indifference, silence, and affected neutrality involved many nonslaveholders in a "common guilt" with slaveholders.[37] "The very circumstance of remaining inactive, leagues those who are so, to the cause of the oppressor, and weakens the hands of the supporters of emancipation," wrote another abolitionist.[38] "It is useless to mince the matter," Garrison insisted, "the people must be divided into two classes only, on the subject of slavery. All who do not lift up a warning voice against the infernal system, or who cravenly skulk away from the conflict, or who expend their whole philanthropy in groans,— whether they know it or not, whether they believe it or not,—are directly the advocates of oppression; and they alone are its enemies, whose practices correspond with their professions."[39]

Given the evangelical assumptions of most early abolitionists, the slogan "immediate emancipation" had both a normative and a descriptive function in the American antislavery movement. That slavery was a sin and therefore ought to be abolished seemed self-evident to abolitionists. That it ought to be abolished immediately also followed. To attack slavery as a false moral principle was to expose the fallacy of gradual emancipation. If slavery were admitted to be a sin, then it was a sin now and ought to be abolished now. There could be no excuse for continuing it a day or even an hour. "If we believe . . . that slavery is an evil *now*," reasoned one abolitionist, "why should we delay in abolishing it? If it is a sin and a crime, the commands of God imperatively demand its immediate relinquishment. . . . Does not every principle that requires that it should be abolished at all, prove that it ought to be abolished now?"[40]

---

those who were not against it. "Advocates of Slavery," *Genius of Universal Emancipation*, March 1831, pp. 177-78; "Strange Inconsistency," *ibid.*, November 27, 1829, p. 90; see also Child, *Appeal*, 3.

[37] Phelps, *Lectures on Slavery*, 14; May, *Discourse*, 8; Whittier, "Justice and Expediency," 11.

[38] "Neutrality," *Genius of Universal Emancipation*, August 1831, p. 58. Compare the statement by "S.R.J.": "There is no medium here. What is not virtue must be vice—and that which is not justice must be injustice. We must be on one side or the other." *Ibid.*, September 1830, p. 86.

[39] "Strange Inconsistency," *ibid.*, November 27, 1829, p. 90. Compare Garrison's observation, "Everyone who comes into the world, should do something to repair its moral desolation, and to restore its pristine loveliness; and he who does not assist, but slumbers away his life in idleness, defeats one great purpose of his creation." "Individual Duty," *Liberator*, January 8, 1831, p. 7.

[40] Robert B. Hall, "Slavery and the Means of Its Removal. An Address Pro-

But the call for immediate emancipation was something more than a simple "ought" proposition. It established more than a merely temporal requirement for the abolition of slavery. In preaching the doctrine of immediate emancipation, abolitionists assumed, as evangelicals did, man's free will and moral responsibility. These underlying assumptions explain the descriptive nature of the phrase. When abolitionists demanded immediate emancipation, they were not merely saying that slavery should be abolished or that it should be abolished "now"; they were also arguing that abolition was fully within man's power and completely dependent upon his initiative. This dual meaning of the appeal for immediate emancipation is revealed in Lydia Maria Child's statement: "The abolitionists think it a duty to maintain at all times, and in all places, that slavery *ought* to be abolished, and that it *can* be abolished."[41] Other abolitionists employed evangelical doctrines of free will and moral responsibility to prove to the American people that they were "bound" to abolish slavery and that they were "capable" of such action.[42]

Viewing man as a moral agent capable of choosing freely between good and evil, many abolitionists concluded that individuals avoided the duty of immediate emancipation from a lack of will, not ability. According to one abolitionist, the main obstacle in the way of abolition was "THE AVERSION OF HUMAN WILL."[43] The answer to such perversity was regeneration. Preached in terms of evangelical assumptions about sin and ability, immediate emancipation signified immediate repentance of the sin of slavery. Elizur Wright argued that the only way appointed by God to abolish the sin of slavery was through "direct repentance, confession, and reparation of injury."[44] "Under the government of God, as exhibited in this world," he explained, "there is but one remedy for sin, and that is available only by a repentance, evi-

nounced at the Request of the New-England Anti-Slavery Society on the Evening of March 26, 1832 . . . ," *Liberator,* April 14, 1832, p. 57; see also Letter to Editor, Sadsbury, Pennsylvania, October 6, *Genius of Universal Emancipation,* October 16, 1829, p. 41; Johnson, *Garrison and His Times,* 28; *Liberator,* February 18, 1832, p. 25.

[41] Child, *Appeal,* 149.

[42] "What Shall Be Done?" *Liberator,* July 30, 1831, p. 121.

[43] *Ibid.,* June 22, 1833, p. 98; see also "The Opinion of One-Hundred and Twenty-four Clergymen. To the Public," in Phelps, *Lectures on Slavery,* v-xi; *ibid.,* 64-65; *Genius of Universal Emancipation,* July 4, 1828, p. 157.

[44] Wright, *Sin of Slavery,* 24; see also "Nullification," *Liberator,* December 29, 1832, p. 206; Samuel Crothers, *Strictures on African Slavery* (Rossville, Ohio, 1833), 27.

denced by reformation."⁴⁵ "In the way of repentance and reformation there is hope, and in no other," observed another aboli-
tionist.⁴⁶

Repentance of the sin of slavery consisted in giving up as a
basis for action the principle that man may have property in
man and adopting in its place the principle of immediate emancipation. It represented emancipation for sinner as well as slave.
Abandoning the false moral principle of slavery, the sinner freed
himself from sin. At the same time, since action was the test for
belief, true repentance virtually entailed the abolition of slavery.
According to Amos Phelps, immediate emancipation meant for
everyone concerned, *"a yielding up of the* PRINCIPLE *of slavery
as a practical principle—a basis of action, and the adoption of
its opposite.* This one act is emancipation from slavery. All that
follows is the carrying out of the new principle of action, and is
to emancipation just what sanctification is to conversion."⁴⁷

Phelps maintained that the immediatist principle would operate on the community like the doctrine of immediate repentance.
"Indeed, the doctrine of immediate emancipation is nothing more
or less than that of immediate repentance applied to this particular sin; and therefore . . . its actual operation on the community as such, may be gradual. It may in point of fact *become
the power of God to the actual repentance of one here and
another there, and not of the whole community at once."*⁴⁸

Abolitionists readily admitted the likelihood of a temporal gap
between individual repentance and abandonment of the sin of
slavery and total abolition. Although they urged that slavery
ought to be and could be immediately and entirely abolished,
few expected that it would be.⁴⁹ Oliver Johnson compared the
abolitionist to the minister of the Gospel in this respect, pointing
out that the latter "does not cease to proclaim the duty of immediate repentance for sin because he knows that his message
will not be immediately heeded. It is his duty to contend for
sound principles, whether his auditors 'will hear or forbear.'"

⁴⁵ Wright, *Sin of Slavery,* 39.
⁴⁶ "Address to the Churches by the Synod of Cincinnati [December 2, 1831]," in
Dyer Burgess, *The Anti-Conspirator, or, Infidelity Unmasked; Being a Development of the Principles of Free Masonry; to Which Is Added, Strictures on Slavery,
as Existing in the Church* (Cincinnati, 1831), 214.
⁴⁷ Phelps, *Lectures on Slavery,* 179.
⁴⁸ *Ibid.,* 154-55.
⁴⁹ "What Would be the Consequence?" *Genius of Universal Emancipation,* April
1833, p. 89; May, *Defence,* 4; Whittier, "Justice and Expediency," 26.

The fact that slaveholders were not ready at once to obey the dictates of justice and divine law was no criticism of the soundness of the doctrine of immediate emancipation or its power as a "practical working principle."[50] Elizur Wright observed that "all the gradual reformation in practice, which has blessed the world, has been the fruit of stern immediatism in doctrine."[51]

Because they admitted the possibility of a time lag between the individual decision to abolish slavery and total abolition, immediatists were able to co-operate with the more cautious abolitionists who demanded only an immediate decision to work for abolition or immediate preparation for future abolition. The New York City Anti-Slavery Society was willing to call an "important and complex measure an immediate one, if it be promptly commenced with the honest determination of urging it on to its completion."[52] David Lee Child argued, "To make an *immediate beginning* is all that I mean, or that our Society means, by 'immediate abolition.' *Immediate* inquiry, to be followed by action, as soon as inquiry has pointed out the way—these, and these only, are 'immediate abolition' in any rational sense."[53]

But although immediatism was susceptible of a variety of interpretations, under no conditions did it countenance gradual emancipation or colonization. In fact, abolitionists often defined immediate emancipation by contrasting it with gradual solutions. "We use the *definite* phraseology, because we believe nothing but immediate abolition will meet the exigencies of our situation," explained Edwin P. Atlee. "By this we do not mean that the shackles of slavery shall be instantly severed, and the slaves cast out upon the country without the restriction of wholesome laws. . . . The term is to be used *relatively,* as contrasted with *gradual.*"[54]

[50] Johnson, *Garrison and His Times,* 111.

[51] Wright, *Sin of Slavery,* 20-21; May, *Discourse,* 26; Garrison, replying to a review by the *Connecticut Observer* of May's *Discourse, Liberator,* February 11, 1832, p. 23. The quotation from Wright has a semicolon after "world" in the original; this has been changed to a comma in the text.

[52] *Address of the New-York City Anti-Slavery Society,* 5.

[53] Child, *The Despotism of Freedom; or, The Tyranny and Cruelty of American Republican Slave-Masters, Shown to Be the Worst in the World; in a Speech Delivered at the First Anniversary of the New-England Anti-Slavery Society, 1833* (Boston, 1833), 67; see also Birney, "Address of the Kentucky Society," 104, 108-109; *Genius of Universal Emancipation,* November 1832, p. 1.

[54] Edwin P. Atlee, *An Address to the Citizens of Philadelphia, on the Subject of Slavery. Delivered in the Hall of the Franklin Institute, on the 4th of the 7th Month, A.D. 1833* (Philadelphia, 1833), 10; see also "Immediate Emancipation," *Genius of Universal Emancipation,* September 1833, p. 161; Whittier, "Justice and Expediency," 25-26; *Address of the New-York City Anti-Slavery Society,* 11.

Less cautious abolitionists took a more positive approach, asserting the inconsistency of defining slavery as sin and advocating gradual emancipation. "I cannot conceive it possible to join two [propositions] . . . more contradictory to each other," wrote Garrison.[55]

According to abolitionists, the great failure of gradual methods was their inability to deal effectively with the problem of sin. Not only were colonization and gradual emancipation impractical and "visionary"; they rested on a compromise with evil.[56] By denying the duty of present, immediate emancipation, they virtually asserted that slaveholding was not a sin and that the slaves had no right to freedom.[57] At the very least they counseled "everlasting procrastination."[58] Such doctrines fostered "fatal delusion" and baneful prejudice that worked against the change of heart necessary to abolition.[59]

The *sin* of slavery demanded nothing less than immediate repentance and emancipation. Abolitionists preached immediate emancipation and immediate repentance of the sin of slavery because no moral or religious authority countenanced "gradual repentance" or the "gradual abolition of wickedness." John Greenleaf Whittier explained, "We do not talk of *gradual* abolition, because, as Christians, we find no authority for advocating a *gradual relinquishment of sin.* We say to slaveholders—'Repent NOW—*today*—IMMEDIATELY;' just as we say to the intemperate—'Break off from your vice *at once*—touch not—taste not —handle not—from henceforth forever.' . . . Such is our *doctrine of immediate emancipation.* A doctrine founded on God's eternal Truth—plain, simple and perfect. The doctrine of immediate,

[55] "Strange Obliquity of Moral Vision," *Liberator*, November 12, 1831, p. 183.
[56] "Immediate Abolition, IV," *ibid.*, May 5, 1832, p. 69; January 22, 1831, p. 13.
[57] Phelps, *Lectures on Slavery*, 156-58; *Genius of Universal Emancipation*, January 1832, p. 133; see also correspondence of "S.R.J.", *ibid.*, September 1830, p. 86; Green, *Four Sermons*, 3-4; Garrison, *Thoughts*, 78, 87; Eugene P. Southall, "Arthur Tappan and the Anti-Slavery Movement," *Journal of Negro History*, XV (April 1930), 168; William Lloyd Garrison, *An Address Delivered Before the Free People of Color, in Philadelphia, New-York, and Other Cities, During the Month of June, 1831* (Boston, 1831), 22; *Liberator*, July 14, 1832, p. 111.
[58] Wright, *Sin of Slavery*, 20-21.
[59] Phelps, *Lectures on Slavery*, 156-58; Garrison, *Thoughts*, 79; *Genius of Universal Emancipation*, January 1832, p. 133; Green, *Four Sermons*, 3-4; Birney to Gerrit Smith, November 14, 1834, in Dumond (ed.), *Birney Letters*, I, 147-48; *Address of the New-York City Anti-Slavery Society*, 4-5; [Benjamin Bussey Thatcher], *Remarks on the American Colonization Society. From the Christian Examiner and General Review* [No. 53, November 1832] (Providence, 1833), 29; Child, *Appeal*, 133; *Liberator*, July 14, 1832, p. 111.

unprocrastinated repentance applied to the *sin of slavery.*"[60] "I know not by what rule of the gospel men are authorized to leave off their sins by a slow process," Garrison argued.[61] He berated the Reverend Lyman Beecher for supporting colonization while denying his congregation the luxury of gradually leaving off alcohol, adultery, and stealing.[62]

Abolitionists preached immediate, not gradual, repentance and emancipation in an effort to persuade the American people of their duty and ability to abolish slavery immediately. They called for immediate repentance of the sin of slavery, believing that repentance would ultimately result in total abolition. Because abolitionists were willing to admit that immediate emancipation might in fact be gradually accomplished, their program appeared deceptively moderate. Actually, its purpose was a reform of society and individuals far more radical and thoroughgoing than has been imputed even to Garrison—not turning the slaves loose without any restriction whatever, regardless of consequences, but raising the moral tenor of a nation and changing the minds and hearts of white Americans with regard to the Negro, slavery, and abolition. It did not propose to use the method of judicial or legislative decree, but to effect the wholesale regeneration of the American people. In this respect the immediatist solution to the problem of slavery was typically evangelical. Confronted with a frustrating and burdensome evil, abolitionists approached it through the familiar experience of heart-searching, repentance, and conversion. They proposed to dispel human wickedness and moral evil by individual regeneration, and they believed that repentant sinners would turn from selfishness to active benevolence on behalf of the slaves. Preached in evangelical terms, "immediate emancipation" was very often indistinguishable from "immediate repentance."

[60] *Liberator,* August 17, 1833, p. 129; see also Wright, *Sin of Slavery,* 20-21; "Immediate Abolition," *Liberator,* January 7, 1832, p. 2; Garrison, *Thoughts,* 79; Atlee, *Address to the Citizens of Philadelphia,* 10-11.
[61] "Strange Obliquity of Moral Vision," *Liberator,* November 12, 1831, p. 183.
[62] *Ibid.,* July 9, 1831, p. 111.

The Abolitionists on Slavery: The Critique Behind the Social Movement

By Donald G. Mathews

THE ABOLITIONISTS AS AGITATORS AND MORALISTS TRIED TO change the mind of the American democrat. They appealed to his better nature and thundered against his fallen condition in pulpit, press, and petition in order to obtain for Negroes the same opportunity that white men had to participate in the nation's destiny. The goal was noble indeed, but the movement which tried to change American society was, as all human enterprises, compromised by the diverse motives, ideologies, and activities of its adherents. Historians have remarked upon the abolitionists' ambivalence towards Negroes and reminded us that radical anti-slavery men were not always and everywhere social egalitarians. Even as they tried to change prevailing attitudes, some aboli-tionists apparently shared in various degrees many of the preju-dices of their contemporaries—scarcely an earth-shaking dis-covery. And there are other supposed internal contradictions cherished by students of ante-bellum America: abolitionists were involved in a religious crusade that became political; they empha-sized pietistic perfection and individual voluntarism while searching for a valid social ethic that took into account a kind of pristine environmentalism; they agitated against slavery where it did not exist, etc., etc. Part of the ambiguity that supposedly shrouds antislavery history involves the assumption of many scholars that, since abolitionists were trying to destroy slavery, they could not have understood it. Careful investigation, how-ever, will show that this assumption is untrue.

Considering the many contrasts already on a long list, it may seem tiresome to add another. Nevertheless, in reading what abolitionists said about slavery and slaveholders, one gets the dis-tinct impression of exaggerated rhetoric and elaborate condem-nation on the one hand combined with astute insight, humane sympathy, and wide knowledge on the other. In fact, if one takes Herbert Butterfield's advice to practice "imaginative sympathy"

Mr. Mathews is assistant professor of history at Princeton University.

in dealing with the past,[1] he may almost conclude that abolitionists were right when they claimed to be able to understand
slavery better than anyone else since they were "uncorrupted by
a bribe." In any event, behind the flamboyant rhetoric and beyond the vicious allusions of popular oratory there was a legitimate critique of slavery.[2] In order to discuss this critique it will
not do to make distinctions between rational and irrational, sensi-
ble and nonsensical, sober and emotional abolitionists, since these
categories are too vague and invidious for serious discussion. But
it might be useful for the historian to make a distinction between
the various functions of abolitionism, between its functions as a
social movement, as a large-scale agitation, and finally as a
legitimate and thoughtful critique of the institution of slavery.
Once these distinctions are made, it may be easier to see that
abolitionists held a balanced view of slavery even as they attempted to change prevalent attitudes towards it.

- Gilbert H. Barnes first emphasized the intimate relationship between abolitionism and revivalism.[3] Since the publication of his
book in 1933 it has been generally accepted that the same kind of

---

[1] See Herbert Butterfield, "Moral Judgments in History," in Butterfield, *History and Human Relations* (New York, 1952), especially 116-17.

[2] There are many books on the antislavery movement, but few devote a significant section to a discussion of abolitionists' ideas. One exception is the general
analysis in Stanley M. Elkins, *Slavery: A Problem in American Institutional
and Intellectual Life* (Chicago, 1959). Another survey reads like an abolitionist
tract in places; see Dwight L. Dumond, *Antislavery: The Crusade for Freedom
in America* (Ann Arbor, 1961), especially 69-71, 99-100, 252, 255, 357-58. Gilbert H. Barnes, *The Antislavery Impulse, 1830-1844* (New York, 1933), has no
analysis of what abolitionists said about slavery. Rather the book leaves one with
the impression that slavery was condemned out of moral urgency alone and that
Theodore Dwight Weld's *American Slavery as It Is* was the primary statement
of the abolitionists' view of slavery. Louis Filler, *The Crusade Against Slavery,
1830-1860* (New York, 1960), has a few scattered paragraphs concerning the
abolitionists' ideas on the subject of their agitation. Russel B. Nye, *Fettered
Freedom: Civil Liberties and the Slavery Controversy, 1830-1860* (East Lansing,
1949), has one of the best short descriptions of the abolition movement in Chapter 1, but is not greatly concerned with what abolitionists said about slavery.
Even a specialized monograph such as Herman Muelder's *Fighters for Freedom: The History of Anti-Slavery Activities of Men and Women Associated
with Knox College* (New York, 1959), has no discussion of the content of abolitionist thought. Willie Lee Rose, *Rehearsal for Reconstruction: The Port Royal
Experiment* (Indianapolis, 1964), is an exception, but she weaves her analysis
of abolition ideas in with another story. The author of this article has only a few
references to abolitionist ideas in his *Slavery and Methodism: A Chapter in
American Morality, 1780-1845* (Princeton, 1965). Henry H. Simms, "A Critical
Analysis of Abolition Literature, 1830-1840," *Journal of Southern History* (August 1940), 368-82, is too superficial.

[3] Barnes, *Antislavery Impulse.*

preaching which forced men to their knees in religious revivals enticed many of them into the antislavery movement. The social strain resulting from the great changes in American society during the first forty years of the nineteenth century made many people susceptible to the evangelicalism that increased the number of Methodists, Baptists, and even Presbyterians throughout the nation.[4] Along with the revivalistic fervor in the churches came movements which enlisted people in various causes. Each had its prophets, its special vocabulary, its fears, enemies, and ideal vision of society. Each in some way catered to the special needs of people.[5]

Whatever those special needs might have been, thousands of people joined the abolition movement in some capacity. They were encouraged to do so by itinerant organizers who built up a network of local and state agencies and saw to it that the ideas of the movement were broadcast and perpetuated by subscription to one of the many antislavery periodicals. Slogans such as "immediate emancipation without expatriation" emerged from the endless discussions and articles which poured forth from the publicists who shaped the ideas of the movement. Along with the slogans often came the same lack of humor and viciousness of language which characterized the Great Revival's attack upon sin, the Democrat's attack upon Whig, and the rhetoric of many social movements which aimed at conversion either in religion or politics.[6] Thus, when reading abolition literature, one is not called upon to explain away its exaggerations, but to understand them as a function of a movement which existed to perpetuate itself regardless of the value of its goals. As revivalists had been taught to be specific and harsh and to allow no "false comforts for sinners,"[7] so abolitionists acted in relation to slaveholders and slav-

[4] The latest and one of the best discussions of the churches' role in developing the new American society of the nineteenth century is T. Scott Miyakawa, *Protestants and Pioneers: Individualism and Conformity on the American Frontier* (Chicago, 1964). Whitney R. Cross, *The Burned-Over District: The Social and Intellectual History of Enthusiastic Religion in Western New York, 1800-1850* (Ithaca, 1950), is a classic in church and social history, placing the revivals in their social context.

[5] For a discussion of social movements in general see Hadley Cantril, *The Psychology of Social Movements* (New York, 1941); C. Wendell King, *Social Movements in the United States* (New York, 1956); and Hans Toch, *The Social Psychology of Social Movements* (Indianapolis, 1965). A most suggestive study of the mechanics of indoctrination is found in William Sargant, *Battle for the Mind: A Physiology of Conversion and Brain-Washing* (New York, 1957).

[6] Sargant, *Battle for the Mind*, 131-65.

[7] Charles Grandison Finney, *Lectures on Revivals of Religion*, edited by William G. McLoughlin (Cambridge, Mass., 1960), 333-60, especially 359-60.

ery as they labored to build a movement. When they addressed those whom they hoped to convert they were as uncompromising as William Lloyd Garrison promised to be in the first edition of his *Liberator*.[8] Unconditional attack was simply the approved method of the temperance reformation and the revivals; abolitionist crusaders saw no reason to discard weapons that had been so successful in previous sallies against evil.

In reading controversial literature, the historian is under an obligation not to be too easily offended and to appreciate the shocking impact which disputants wanted to create with their propaganda. For even behind rhetoric characteristically "vicious" is a meaning which the true believer would grasp rather easily and which the student should understand. Stephen Symonds Foster was infamous for his pamphlet, *The Brotherhood of Thieves*, in which he accused the Methodist Episcopal Church of possessing less virtue than all the brothels in New York City. Although the statement was not especially delicate (William Lloyd Garrison thought it especially inappropriate in the Methodist stronghold of Syracuse, New York), neither it is prima facie evidence of irrationality. By clearly defining the virtuous and nonvirtuous (abolitionists and antiabolitionists), it not only bound the faithful together but also highlighted one of the main tenets of abolitionist belief by calling into question the respectability of an organization which prided itself on its respectability. Quite apart from the form in which the words came from Foster's outraged pen, he was attacking the Methodist clergy for hypocrisy. Those good men supposedly opposed prostitution and yet refused to condemn a system in which women were bought and sold with no legal rights either as people or as wives and mothers. The point Foster was trying to make in his own peculiar way was that a morality which condemned one kind of prostitution and not another was a false morality What he demanded was a transvaluation of middle-class values.[9]

By making such a demand, Foster and his colleagues were adherents of a peculiar kind of social movement—one that made them into agitators. As agitators they were not attempting to reconstitute American values but to extend the normative power of those values to a group of people hitherto considered beyond the

---

[8] *Liberator*, January 1, 1831.

[9] Stephen Symonds Foster, *The Brotherhood of Thieves: or, A True Picture of the American Church and Clergy* . . . (Boston, 1844), 9 ff.; William Lloyd Garrison to his wife, November 27, 1842, in William Lloyd Garrison Papers (Boston Public Library).

pale. Abolitionists, or at least their articulate spokesmen, were fully aware that they would have to overstate their case in order to move the balky, stubborn American democrat. The master agitator William Lloyd Garrison explained his situation quite succinctly: "In demanding equal and exact justice we may get partial redress; in asking for the whole that is due us, we may get a part; in advocating the immediate, we may succeed in procuring the speedy abolition of slavery. But, if we demand anything short of justice, we shall recover no damages; if we ask for a part, we shall get nothing . . . ."[10] Had the abolitionists relied upon sweet reason and careful analyses presented to the proper authorities, their efforts would have been as proper and pathetic as the quietistic witness of Southern Quakers. As agitators abolitionists knew that the dispassionate understanding of a problem was of interest only to intellectuals and that most Americans scarcely fit into that category. That the abolitionists used passionate and disruptive agitation to gain their ends is not evidence that they did not understand slavery; rather, it is proof that they understood Americans.

The problem was not only agitation, but agitation across most of the lines which divided Americans into smaller communities. Wendell Phillips spoke for the entire abolition movement when he outlined the problems of communication he and his comrades faced. If the nation had been merely a market, abolitionists would talk in dollars and cents, if a college, they would load their "cannons with cold facts," if a church, they would talk of "righteousness, temperance, and judgment to come." But since abolitionists lived in the world of "thought and impulse, of self-conceit and self-interest, of weak men and wicked," they would have to be able to speak to each man in words that would make him respond favorably to antislavery goals.[11] This of course poses a problem for anyone who wants to know what abolitionists said about slaveholders and slavery. Because as agitators the abolitionists spoke in so many different ways to so many different people, no consistently held, clearly defined view of the masters and their system readily emerges from the literature.

Nevertheless, when one takes into account how much aboli-

10 Garrison, *An Address Delivered Before the Old Colony Anti-Slavery Society at South Scituate, Mass., July 4, 1839* (Boston, 1839), 17.
11 Wendell Phillips, *Speeches, Lectures, and Letters* (Boston, 1863), 110. See also Howard Zinn, "Abolitionists, Freedom-Riders, and the Tactics of Agitation" in Martin B. Duberman (ed.), *The Antislavery Vanguard: New Essays on the Abolitionists* (Princeton, 1965), 417-51.

tionist rhetoric had to accomplish and goes behind the functionally angry words to investigate what the historical evidence
reveals, he finds a balanced, intelligent, and sometimes sophisticated understanding of the world which the antislavery radicals
were trying to change. Historians divide abolitionists into Garrisonians, New Yorkers, denominationalists, and many more sub-
groups beloved of the specialist. But whether one does this or
simply takes them straight as noncolonizationist, antislavery
moralists (not politicians or nonextensionists), he will see that
abolitionists (1) thought of slaveholders not merely as sinners
but also as good men; (2) thought slavery a complex institution;
but (3) understood it primarily as arbitrary and absolute power.

One of the basic charges leveled against abolitionists has been
that they were morally simplistic in their condemnation of slaveholders. Repudiating social complexity as a legitimate vindication of slaveholding, they demanded that the abolition of slavery
be begun at once. Years of waiting for conscientious Southerners
to find a way to ease slavery out of existence had produced nothing to convince radical antislavery men that Negro servitude
would die without purposeful action. The matter was made urgent for the revivalistically oriented abolitionists by their conviction that slavery was a sin: it was not a moral evil which everyone
could regret and for which no one was responsible; it was not a
political evil to be left to compromising politicians; it was not an
economic evil to be left to self-interested slaveholders to manage
—it was a sin. It broke the laws of God. It made man into mer-
chantable property and deprived him of his humanity—his freedom to make of himself what he would. Thus, anyone involved
in slavery as a master was culpably responsible to God. This conclusion put abolitionists in the position of calling decent, churchgoing Southerners sinners. Even though they worshiped three
times a day, attended prayer meeting on Wednesday night, took
their slaves with them to camp meeting, paid their debts, and
gave money to foreign missions, slaveholders were sinners. This
view became for many contemporaries as well as for historians
the hallmark of abolitionist attitudes towards the South: abolitionists thought of slaveholders and their advocates as evil people

In reaction to what they supposed was moralistic simplicity,
antiabolitionists and later-day historians committed what could
be called "the fallacy of misplaced righteousness." That is, by
implication they attributed the personal moral respectability of
individual Southerners to the institution of slavery. They pointed

out that abolitionists were disastrously overstating their case by neglecting the complexities of the historical process, human motivation, and institutional entrenchment. Actually, the South was peopled, not by sinners as abolitionists so self-righteously assumed, but rather by good men caught in a difficult situation Many Southern slaveholders were decent people, it was said, who secretly regretted the deep injustices of slavery, who treated their slaves well, and sent them to church on Sunday. Some Negroes even attained some status within the system. One ought not to curse good masters who were unfortunately involved in slavery, but praise them for responsibility in the midst of unjust institutions. These good men—reluctant and kindly slaveholders trying to make slavery as easy as possible for the slaves—were the tragic victims of a cruel and unjust fate.[12] Furthermore, those people who believed the abolitionists irresponsible pointed out that slavery was not so bad as Theodore Dwight Weld claimed it to be in his pamphlet of 1839, *American Slavery as It Is*. As all sections, the South had its evil men (such as slave traders) who gave its peculiar institutions a bad name. The good, however, should not be confused with them and called sinners.

The "fallacy of misplaced righteousness" obscures what reformers are talking about in times of social change. Good men, abolitionists pointed out, were the chief vindicators of American Negro slavery. Had the antislavery vanguard been totally unaware of the moral character of slavery and its relationships, they could justly be accused of being irrelevant fanatics. But the abolitionists were not content with middle-class morality as some historians have been. The simple assumption that abolitionists thought of Southern slaveholders only as unregenerate sinners needs to be challenged to reveal what they did in fact say and simply to set the story straight.

[12] For varying discussions of the "good people" of the South and commissions of "the fallacy of misplaced righteousness," see Avery O. Craven, *Civil War in the Making, 1815-1860* (Baton Rouge, [1959]), 35-63; Robert F. Durden, "The Establishment of Calvary Protestant Episcopal Church for Negroes in Charleston," *South Carolina Historical Magazine*, LXV (April 1965), 63-84, especially 84; Charles Grier Sellers, Jr., "The Travail of Slavery" in Sellers (ed.), *The Southerner as American* (Chapel Hill, 1960), 40-71; Ulrich Bonnell Phillips, *American Negro Slavery: A Survey of the Supply, Employment and Control of Negro Labor as Determined by the Plantation Régime* (New York, 1918), 282-90, 293 ff., 309-30; Samuel Eliot Morison and Henry Steele Commager, *The Growth of the American Republic* (2 vols., New York, 1951), I, 533-44; Henry H. Simms, *A Decade of Sectional Controversy, 1831-1861* (Chapel Hill, 1942),, 14-15; and Arthur Young Lloyd, *The Slavery Controversy, 1831-1860* (Chapel Hill, 1939), *passim*.

The Missouri controversies had educated thoughtful Southerners to believe that Northern interest in slavery was primarily political. Therefore, they were in no mood to appreciate the care with which some abolitionists attempted to explain that slavery was a national problem and that sectional power or virtue was not really at issue. Abolitionists did maintain, however, that their not being from the South was an aid in gaining perspective. Mrs. Lydia Maria Child wrote in her pamphlet on slavery in 1833:

It would be very absurd to imagine that the inhabitants of one State are worse than the inhabitants of another, unless some peculiar circumstances, of universal influence, tend to make them so. Human nature is everywhere the same; but developed differently, by different incitements and temptations. . . . If we were educated at the South, we should no doubt vindicate slavery, and inherit as a birthright all the evils it engrafts upon the character. If they lived on our rocky soil, and under our inclement skies, their shrewdness would sometimes border on knavery, and their frugality sometimes degenerate into parsimony. We both have our virtues and our faults, induced by the influences under which we live. . . .[13]

Abolitionists were willing to admit the obvious: that people accustomed to slavery would be inclined to vindicate it.

In spite of this fact, there were Southerners to whom antislavery men thought they might effectively appeal—the responsible, churchgoing, humane slaveholders who would be sensitive to an honest discussion of slavery. Wrote a Methodist: "I sincerely sympathize with the slave, and as truly with many masters. I believe that northern men would be southern men in their circumstances; and that southern men would be northern men in ours, where moral principle was equally felt."[14] The operative words were "where moral principle was equally felt." Abolitionists believed (or at least a great many of them did) that the moral regeneration of America institutionalized by steady increases in church membership would be the energizing force of abolition. They had seen this moral regeneration become moral action in the creation of new benevolent societies, and they saw no reason why slaves could not be helped just as much as drunkards, prostitutes, and the heathen. Thus they preached a new gospel because, as Orange Scott, the Methodist antislavery leader, wrote, it was "by preaching against great and destructive evils, *particu-*

[13] Child, *An Appeal in Favor of That Class of Americans Called Africans* (Boston, 1833), 27-28.
[14] *Zion's Herald*, May 6, 1835.

larly, pointedly, and *perseveringly,* that the world [was] to be re-formed."[15]

Preaching even to "good men" did not work. James G. Birney's special pilgrimage demonstrates what it did not take abolition-ists everywhere long to find out: that the so-called good people of the South would not listen. As a colonization agent in the South in 1833, Birney, the owner of several slaves and heir to many others, found that the more he condemned slavery the less en-thusiasm he engendered among his listeners. Nevertheless, he persisted in his efforts to convince the respectable portion of the community that it ought to think about abolishing slavery as soon as humanly possible. After his own conversion to abolitionism, Birney tried to convince the Kentucky Presbyterian clergy to urge abolition—but the result was a mild and evasive answer. He then tried to reach the community by reasonable discussion in an antislavery paper—but he was driven from Kentucky as a traitor. Even in the North, Birney's appeal to the churches as America's great moral institutions was repudiated by those whom he had hoped to convert. Not surprisingly, Birney and most of his abolitionist confreres were convinced that the good people were the bulwarks of slavery.[16]

The morality ascribed to responsible people in the South did not impress abolitionists. Some conservative antislavery men tried to develop theories of moral responsibility which allowed for "moral men in immoral society," but most insisted that all slaveholders would have to be held responsible for their status.[17] In this conclusion they denied the relevance of explanations de-riving from the "fallacy of misplaced righteousness." Abolition-ists admitted that slaveholders might be humanely motivated, that they might treat slaves well, that they might preach the Gospel (however mutilated) to them; but, in all cases, the Ne-groes were still slaves. This fact alone ran contrary to any con-

[15] Orange Scott, *An Appeal to the Methodist Episcopal Church* (Boston, 1838), 45.

[16] See [James Gillespie Birney], *The American Churches, the Bulwarks of American Slavery* (Boston, 1843), *passim;* Betty Fladeland, *James Gillespie Birney: Slaveholder to Abolitionist* (Ithaca, [1955]), 90-124; John Devins Lamkin, "James Gillespie Birney: Portrait of a Reformer" (unpublished B.A. thesis, Princeton University, 1965), 175 ff.

[17] See Robert Merideth, "A Conservative Abolitionist at Alton: Edward Beecher's *Narrative," Journal of Presbyterian History,* XLII (March and June 1964), 39-53, 92-103. Beecher explained that although slavery was sinful, the guilt rested upon the community instead of the individual. Amos A. Phelps and the Garrisonians dissented.

cept of freedom, human dignity, and Christian love. Slavery was too evil in principle to be vindicated by the heroic sadness of a conscience-stricken master or by the sympathy of the most gentle mistress. "In the hand of a good man or a bad man . . . *this principle is the same;*" wrote one abolitionist, "it [slavery] possesses not one redeeming quality."[18] In other words, the fact that Southern slaveholders were good men was not relevant in the discussion of slavery.

Abolitionists thus found that their most inveterate enemies were not evil men who defended slavery as a positive good, but good men who could live with it. They were not so simple-minded as to overlook the historical any more than the moral facts of slavery, and as master propagandists they undoubtedly knew that Weld's pamphlet, *American Slavery as It Is*, told the *significant* facts about slavery rather than the whole story. Americans who generally accepted the efficacy of moral living would not be persuaded to hate slavery because it was a mixture of good men and evil institutions. They would be convinced only if slavery in some way affronted their own morality. By thus emphasizing the immoralities associated with slavery, abolitionists acquired a reputation for violent condemnation; but they knew their enemy well. He was not only the proslavery extremist whose absurd abstractions, abolitionists believed, would antagonize the North. Rather, abolitionists understood their major opponents to be the good people of the South.

True, abolitionists called these people sinners, but they were not thought of simply in those terms. An eloquent example of the attitude of antislavery men towards the South can be seen in the address of the executive committee of the American Wesleyan Anti-Slavery Society in 1840. "*The strength of the slave power,*" the Methodists wrote, "*consists in the countenance extended to the system by professedly good men. A practice prevalent only among wicked men, especially one so abominably wicked* as that of enslaving human beings, could not be tolerated in civil society. Hence, it can only exist by seducing professedly good people to believe that 'circumstances' render it necessary for them to adopt it, or justify the practice by those with whom they are connected."[19] Thus, to those who tried to counter abolitionist criticism of slaveholders and slavery with a defense of the good Southern people, the abolitionists replied that the argument was irrelevant.

[18] Orange Scott in *Zion's Herald*, February 24, 1836.
[19] *Zion's Watchman*, October 31, 1840.

They explained, "It is of little consequence to us whether the man who robs us of our money be polite or complacent or otherwise."[20] Decent, philanthropic slaveholders were nevertheless people who deprived other men of their freedom.

When abolitionists turned from the slaveholder to the system he represented they were no more simplistic behind their bombastic rhetoric than when they were dealing with the Pollyanna propriety of the "fallacy of misplaced righteousness." They could all agree that slavery was a complex, well-developed social and economic institution which could not be destroyed in one day.[21] In fact, it would take so long to extinguish the psychological, moral, and cultural scars of slavery that its abolition should be begun immediately. Whether the abolitionist wanted "immediate emancipation gradually accomplished" or "immediate uncondi-

[20] *Ibid.*, June 8, 1836.

[21] The following account is difficult to annotate. Essentially the material upon which this interpretation is based came from the *Liberator*, the *Friend of Man*, the *Herald of Freedom*, the *Philanthropist*, the *Emancipator*, *Zion's Watchman*, Orange Scott's articles in *Zion's Herald* for January and February 1835 and the following pamphlets: the annual reports of the American Anti-Slavery Society; [George Bourne], *Picture of Slavery in the United States of America* (Boston, 1838); William I. Bowditch, *Slavery and the Constitution* (Boston, 1849); Child, *An Appeal in Favor of That Class of Americans Called Africans;* William Goodell, *American Slavery. A Formidable Obstacle to the Conversion of the World* (New York, 1854); Goodell, *The American Slave Code in Theory and Practice: Its Distinctive Features Shown by Its Statutes, Judicial Decisions, and Illustrative Facts* (New York, 1853); [Richard Hildreth], *Despotism in America: or, An Inquiry into the Nature and Results of the Slave-Holding System in the United States* (Boston, 1840); William Jay, *An Inquiry into the Character and Tendency of the American Colonization, and American Anti-Slavery Societies* (New York, 1835); Horace Mann, *Speech of Hon. Horace Mann, on the Right of Congress to Legislate for the Territories of the United States . . . June 30, 1848* (Boston, 1848); Theodore Parker, *A Letter to the People of the United States Touching the Matter of Slavery* (Boston, 1848); Amos A. Phelps, *Lectures on Slavery, and Its Remedy* (Boston, 1834); Orange Scott, *Address to the General Conference of the Methodist Episcopal Church by the Rev. O. Scott, a Member of That Body* (New York, 1836); Scott, *An Appeal to the Methodist Episcopal Church* (Boston, 1838); Seymour B. Treadwell, *American Liberties and American Slavery* (New York, 1838); La Roy Sunderland, *Anti-Slavery Manual, Containing a Collection of Facts and Arguments on American Slavery* (New York, 1837); [Theodore Dwight Weld], *American Slavery as It Is: Testimony of a Thousand Witnesses* (New York, 1839). For reasons suggested above the sources do not "speak for themselves," and careless exegesis of these materials would produce nothing but florid examples to be filed under the superficial categories of "irrationality" and "fanaticism." That the thesis of this article has merit is partially supported by the balanced collections of antislavery arguments edited by Louis Ruchames and especially William H. and Jane H. Pease. See Louis Ruchames (ed.), *The Abolitionists: A Collection of their Writings* (New York, 1963), and William H. and Jane H. Pease (eds.), *The Antislavery Argument* (Indianapolis, [1965]).

tional emancipation," he had no intention of irresponsibly turning the slaves loose without some guidance. From the beginning of their agitation abolitionists could agree with William Lloyd Garrison's plea that Negro slaves be emancipated according to carefully worked out and equitably executed legal procedures which would in the end guarantee Negroes the equality they had been so long denied.[22] The immediacy in immediate emancipation referred to the revivalist-agitator's desire to begin at once in order that something might be done eventually; but the formula in no way contradicted the abolitionist's belief that slavery was not a simple institution.

For one thing, slavery varied from place to place, and in the variations abolitionists hoped they had found a basic weakness. Since slavery was not so significant a part of the economy in the border states as in the expanding cotton kingdom, it had a less firm hold upon the people in those areas. Encouraging evidence of this was found at first in the open criticism of slavery in Kentucky, Maryland, and even Virginia, where a large number of nonslaveholding farmers resented the power of an aristocracy that rested on an unjust and unequal control of the labor force. Slavery where it did exist in the farms of the border states was believed to be less severe than in the great plantations farther south. Smaller holdings were thought to necessitate more humane relations between masters and slaves, a fact which would not justify slavery but which did demonstrate that it was not monolithic in its cultural aspects.

The complexity of slavery, however, was not thought to consist primarily of its situational variations but of its effect upon Southern people and institutions. Negro servitude was so intricately woven into the fabric of society that it compromised values, institutions, and perspectives by which it might otherwise have been weakened. Christianity, the Revolution, democracy, equality—all the abstractions of American national romanticism existed in varying degrees of subordination to the facts of slavery. The complexity existed not in the quantitative varieties of the experiences of slavery but in the qualitative bondage that perpetuated the institution. That is, everything in the system reinforced everything else.[23] Thus, Theodore Dwight Weld could de-

[22] See the prospectus for the *Liberator* printed in the *Genius of Universal Emancipation*, December 1832.

[23] It was this fact that made abolitionists so scornful of amelioration. There was nothing within the system that a reformer could use against it because slavery

scribe the interaction between slave and master as a frustrating experience which was good for neither. Wrote Weld:

. . . not only is the slave destitute of those peculiarities, habits, tastes, and acquisitions, which by assimilating the possessor to the rest of the community, excite their interest in him, and thus, in a measure, secure for him their protection; but he possesses those peculiarities of bodily organization which are looked upon with deep disgust, contempt, prejudice, and aversion. Besides this, constant contact with the ignorance and stupidity of the slaves, their filth, rags, and nakedness; their cowering air, servile employments, repulsive food, and squalid hovels, their purchase and sale, and use as brutes—all these associations, constantly mingling and circulating in the minds of slaveholders, . . . produce in them a permanent state of feeling toward the slave, made up of repulsion and settled ill-will. When we add to this the corrosions produced by the petty thefts of the slaves, the necessity of constant watching, their reluctant service, and indifference to their master's interests, their ill-concealed aversion to him, and spurning of his authority; and finally, that fact, as old as human nature, that men always hate those whom they oppress, and oppress those whom they hate, thus oppression and hatred mutually begetting and perpetuating each other—and we have a raging compound of fiery elements and disturbing forces . . . .[24]

This was one side of slavery, of course, but Weld's statement shows that even as they condemned the worst aspects of that institution, abolitionists knew that it was extremely complex in its hold upon masters and slaves, victimizing both. One may question the abolitionists' tough-minded expectation that men could or would extricate themselves willfully from such a socially determined predicament as that described above, but no one can seriously doubt that abolitionists thought slavery complex. They simply believed that complexity was no vindication either of slavery or the slaveholder; and it is perhaps this ethical rigor rather than simplicity that has made the abolitionists so unpopular.

They maintained that their agitation and ethical importunity was justified because of slavery's effect upon the Negro and its ultimate character as absolute power. It was understood as absolute power because the slave had no legal claim upon the white man with which he could protect himself and because that most precious of American possessions, the right to one's own labor,

---

had become so involved with everything in the South. See Goodell, *American Slave Code*, 403 ff.

[24] [Weld], *American Slavery as It Is*, 116-17.

was denied him. Slaves worked not because they would be better off if they did, but because they would be worse off if they did not. Force, fear, and fraud made slavery operate, abolitionists charged, and what they meant was that men's labor was extracted from them by an inherited system of bondage which ultimately relied upon brute force. They meant that men faced the future not with the hope and courage of the American Hercules but only with despair. And by fraud they meant that the church's Gospel had been used to enslave not free men's minds, that the law and planned ignorance which perpetuated slavery deprived Negroes of the same kind of advancement enjoyed by other Americans. They meant that the Negro was, for all intents and purposes, completely in the hands of the white man.

The best evidence of this fact, abolitionists thought, was the cruelties inflicted by whites on Negroes. Every discussion of the abolitionist attack on slavery includes an appropriate section for atrocities; and this was certainly a major aspect of antislavery propaganda.[25] Everyone who has read this material is well acquainted with the vivid portrayal of all the infamies men can inflict upon their fellows, a striking method by which antislavery publicists could "clank the chains" of slavery in the ears of indifferent Americans.[26] The atrocity stories, while possibly interesting in themselves to some abolitionists and historians, were printed not merely to arouse hatred of the kindly old slaveholder but also to demonstrate that slavery ultimately meant absolute and unchecked power. Abolitionists knew that some slaves were better treated than others—house servants and artisans were assumed to be safer than slaves less visible to the public—and they admitted that some slaveholders could be kind to their servants. But the significant aspect of slavery was not kind treatment. And cruelty was considered not as an exception to kind treatment, but as the natural result of the power to give or withhold kind treatment. With no effective way to defend themselves against the masters, Negroes bore mutilations, brands, and scars as identification not only of runaways in advertisements but also of the entire slave system. Men owned slaves not for altruistic purposes but to exploit their labor; and since the incentive to work was the thoroughly negative one of force not wages, since Negroes as men would intentionally frustrate the masters, and since men

---

[25] The atrocities committed by slaveholders as abolitionists imagined them are vividly recounted and illustrated in Dumond, *Antislavery, passim.*
[26] [Weld], *American Slavery as It Is,* 7.

with absolute power used it, the natural result of slavery was cruelty. This was of course an abstract argument, but mutilated runaways seemed convincing empirical proof of its truth. Halos there were over the heads of some slaveowners; but scars on the backs of runaways were more significant.

The absolute power which so repelled abolitionists was revealed in many guises. Throughout radical antislavery literature run the complementary themes of white authority and Negro helplessness. The absoluteness of the power consisted not in the fact that force was always used with totalitarian efficiency, but in the inability of Negroes to claim anything for themselves on the basis of their own social and legal integrity. The slave trade was selected as the best institutional example of what the master could do to the slaves. The experience of manacles, iron collars, and auction blocks left psychological scars on Negroes which were bad enough and widely criticized, but what was considered even worse was a total disregard for the inviolability of family life. Abolitionists contrasted the relatively humane laws of Louisiana and South America (which forbade breaking up families) with the lack of such protection in most of the American South. Admittedly some (perhaps even many) masters did not break up families, but even the sensitivities of kind slaveholders could not keep families together when the law forced slave sales to pay the debts of deceased planters. And this was not the only shock the slave family had to endure. It was also grotesquely misshapen by servitude. The Negro man had no legal right to protect his wife against a white man, nor could he assume his proper role as a father since his children as well as his wife belonged to the white man. This kind of helplessness before the master's desires brought the emotion-charged accusation that slavery was a "legalized system of licentiousness."[27] This was exaggerated rhetoric perhaps, but quite correct in pointing out that Negroes were subject to the greatest of desecrations, many had experienced them, and none could do anything about it.

The absolute power observed in calculated cruelty or the side effects of the slave trade affected every aspect of the slave's life from daily bread to daily prayer. Since the masters alone were responsible for food and clothing, *their* interests, not those of the slaves, would dictate the quality of provisions. In this as in all cases, abolitionists admitted variations but were unimpressed

[27] *Zion's Herald*, March 11, 1835.

with the general fare reported from the South. Self-interest would not necessarily make the master treat the slaves well because short-term economic interest might possibly contradict long-range human considerations—it would not have been the first time in history. And abolitionists had little faith in the power of public opinion to protect Negroes since the Southern public was thoroughly accustomed to all the evils of slavery. In fact, the slave could turn nowhere to check the power of the white man. The churches were completely subservient to the masters as they tried to make the Negroes into good, docile slaves rather than dignified men. The slaves heard only one side of the Gospel, and were denied the means to broaden their understanding since they could not be educated. Deprived of evangelical truth, of anything stronger than white sensitivities to protect their families, of an independent control over their lives—deprived therefore of self-respect, the Negroes were ultimately helpless.

The best evidence of the Negro's helplessness was found by abolitionists in the slave codes. Slavery could not be completely understood merely by surveying its legal structure, but antislavery radicals knew that the helplessness of the slave and the power of the master were formalized in Southern legislation. In the first place, the law forbade the slave to do anything which could make him free. He could not learn to read or write. He could not follow whatever profession he chose. He could not own property. Consequently, the Negro was denied the American right of self-advancement. Other slave systems (in ancient Rome and contemporary Brazil) might allow Negroes to have personal property or to gain their liberty by legal processes. But in America, where the future was supposedly boundless for all men, the future was denied slaves. In America, where property was so valuable and powerful that to own some meant personal security, the Negro had no access to the privileges and protection of society.

In the law, charged the abolitionists, as in everything else in slavery, the Negro was acted upon—he could not act on his own. He could not sue in court. He could not testify against the white man. He could not in fact resist a white man lest he lose his life. He could not be tried by his peers. He could not assemble freely. Laws required good treatment of slaves, but white men executed and interpreted those laws, leaving the Negro no protection on his own. Furthermore, the laws demanding good treatment of Negroes revealed in themselves how fragile was the slave's claim to protection: a South Carolina law, for example, allowed punishment by sticks or whips but no *unusual* punishment. That sailors as well as Negroes were whipped did not justify either barbarity. The point was, as abolitionists made it, that Negro slaves possessed nothing other than white philanthropy with which to mitigate their slavery. The law which protected so many Americans, which even protected slaves in other times and places, did not protect the Negro slave. The control of the white man was so absolute that no improvement in the legal code could reform slavery. It corrupted everything it touched, leaving nothing with which to fight it—not the church, not the law, not education, and not even philanthropy, which accepted and therefore fortified slavery. Only complete destruction of the system would be acceptable.

The effect of this absolute system upon the Negro was degradation according to abolitionists. Nothing in slavery encouraged independence and resourcefulness for acceptable social goals such as acquiring property and advancement; rather, all the slave's energies were turned to protect himself from the master in one way or another. Bravery, honesty, and resoluteness which might lead a man to fight his master and the system were often rewarded with punishment so that these qualities were distorted into adaptation, deceit, and vacillation in order to survive. Work became a hopeless task that offered no self-gratification so that laziness became a virtue and a chief character trait in the slave. This mirror effect on values was presumed to be the natural result of a system which contradicted everything necessary to make a man responsible, knowledgeable, reflective. But even though the future was hopeless and life precarious, slaves made the best of their lot. In fact, some were happy; and a happy slave was to an abolitionist one of the best examples of the demonic effects of slavery. He was a symbol of the absolute power of the white man to keep Negroes from knowing the depths of their alienation from all that it meant to be free.

The white man, too, suffered ill effects from slavery. The image of the good slaveholder which was so present in abolition literature was tarnished by the general agreement among antislavery men that in giving absolute and arbitrary power to the masters, slavery tended to make them arrogant, violent, and disdainful of the rights of others. Theodore Dwight Weld wrote: "If there is among human convictions one that is invariable and universal, it is, that when men possess unrestrained power over others . . .

they are under great temptations to abuse it . . . ."[28] Abolitionists believed that Southerners yielded to these temptations. In their flamboyant propaganda abolitionists created the familiar image of a bowie-knife-wielding, lazy grandee who fought duels and kept Negro mistresses. The difference between good masters and profligate dandies is of course great. The abolitionists as propagandists tried to have it both ways in order to emphasize that the natural tendency of unchecked power was to corrupt those who wielded it. Respectable people, too, were corrupted because, instead of fighting slavery, they lent their respectability to a system which created what decent people stood against: licentiousness, disrespect for persons, arrogance, and lust for power.

Corruption of people was a primary concern in the abolitionists' scheme of values, but slavery also corrupted the nation and the South. It became abstracted as diabolical power which stripped Americans of the security of their persons. It deprived them of their rights to petition Congress, to assemble peaceably, to publish freely, to dissent from majority opinion.[29] And when the fugitive slave law was passed in 1850, the South's peculiar institution was interpreted as undermining the security of Northern legal processes. Southerners' fear of slaves, of new ideas, and of other white men was weakening the entire nation. Not only was this insecurity affecting freedom, but also the national defense. For if Americans were ever called to fight a strong foreign enemy, their efforts would be endangered by limiting available manpower to white men and limiting those whites' effectiveness by the necessity of policing slaves.

Slavery had corrupted the American economy even as it had its politics and security. It endangered all property by using arguments based upon property rights to defend holding men as slaves. The repugnancy men had for slavery could conceivably be transferred to property, thus devaluing the foundation of American wealth and stability. This consideration was overshadowed by the much more important concern for the economic disadvantages of slavery. Although an economic argument was never emphasized to the exclusion of others, it was usually present in abolitionist literature. Richard Hildreth was particularly eloquent in his *Despotism in America,* where he argued that slavery was a bad labor system which crippled American economic growth. Labor (the principal source of value) was not free to produce and consume at full capacity in a slave society.

---

[28] [Weld], *American Slavery as It Is,* 116.
[29] See Nye, *Fettered Freedom, passim.*

Slave laborers were presumed to be less productive than free because the former had no positive incentive. Only force and authority kept them at their tasks whereas wages and the hope of advancement would increase productivity if they were free.

Not only were the South and nation deprived of the full labor of the Negroes, but also of the whites. The low status of labor as being proper only to slaves supposedly paralyzed the poor whites as well as enervated the masters, whose disdain for work precluded the full utilization of labor resources. Slavery not only penalized the poor white man by devaluing labor, but also by requiring greater capitalization for expansion in the South than in the North. Since Southerners bought their laborers instead of hiring them, only the rich could increase their power appreciably. These supposed limitations on economic expansion were linked also with the fact that slaves did not consume as much as free laborers since their desires were so curtailed. With consumption at a low point, there was consequently less prosperity.[30] This theory that slavery hindered optimum economic growth was complemented by other economic arguments. Most posited the superiority of industrial over agrarian society or accepted slavery as a single explanation of even those economic problems which derived from a one-crop economy. But in the economic and political sphere as in the personal, abolitionists understood slavery to be an unwarranted delimitation of freedom—arbitrary power.

There are many deficiencies in the arguments that abolitionists directed against slavery. Their data may have been faulty, but not the direction in which their understanding was taking them—towards an emphasis on social justice. Their objectivity was of course compromised by their partisan activity; but with all of the scientific knowledge of the twentieth century they would have come essentially to the same conclusions they reached a hundred years earlier. They would have admitted all the findings of historical investigation because they had a great appreciation for facts. But they would also have insisted that slavery, for all of its variety and complexity, still meant the white man's absolute power over the Negro.

Reflecting upon this view, one is struck by the contrast between the abolitionists' understanding of complexity and social determinism as opposed to their much-emphasized voluntarism. They were impressed by the effects of man's social situation in determining his values, goals, and general understanding, and yet they expected some men somehow to transcend their social

[30] [Hildreth], *Despotism in America*, 83 ff., 111 ff.

context and by a sheer act of will break the chains binding their minds as well as their slaves. Frustrated in this, abolitionists retreated either to politics or to the mental and moral utopia of being "right" in a world that was wrong. Their "realism" in doing this is not so important as their pioneering attempt to understand social determinism and at the same time to thwart it.

While trying to understand absolute power and its effect upon people, they tried to affirm man's freedom. This meant that they had to change the rules of the game called "reform." Whereas reformers had previously accepted the givenness of the present structures of society within which to comfort the sick and dispossessed, abolitionists would not. They began to see in part that some social questions and prejudices were simply not so important as justice. That is, proper social agitation did not aim to care for the victims of society but to change society so that there would be no victims in the first place. Abolitionists did not know all the implications of this tendency when they called not for manumission but abolition. They did not always see the general application of principles that called not for colonization to escape prejudice but laws which could fight it. Nevertheless, the principles they professed and the tendencies they started, even unknowingly, were part of the transition from benevolent philanthropy to social reform. Charity had been the genteel province of the "better people" before the abolitionists began their work; but pitying charity was not enough to break absolute power, the new reformers said. Charity itself might be a form of absolute power. Let Negroes have justice. Give them not better food, fewer whippings, and more clothes, but give them equal laws, free churches, honest education, and a chance to acquire property.

This kind of thinking about slavery, linked as it was with social agitation, personal frustration, civil war, and incomplete understanding was never fulfilled by a purposive and just transition from slavery to freedom. The dialectic of social determinism and voluntarism, appreciation for facts and the use of abstract argument, affirmation of complexity and belief in single causation was not resolved by the cataclysm which has since been seen as the major event in the progress of American freedom. Rather, the dialectic was lost in social frustration and political weariness. But unlike most Americans, the abolitionists had at least tried to understand slavery in a new perspective even if with old formulae. And their attempt made them a vanguard in the fight to abridge the complexity of slavery by willful destruction of its absolute power.

WILLIAM H. PEASE & JANE H. PEASE

University of Alberta, Calgary

Antislavery Ambivalence: Immediatism, Expediency, Race*

OF CONSTANT DISTRESS TO STUDENTS OF THE AMERICAN ANTISLAVERY MOVE-
ment has been its ambivalence, especially its ambivalence over the term
Immediatism. The term had originally defined a means to end British
colonial slavery, but it failed to be similarly applicable to emancipation
in the American South. Therefore the antislavery movement strained to
give new meaning to emancipation *"instant and universal."* Did it not
really mean gradual emancipation immediately begun or, perhaps, immediate emancipation gradually achieved? But no less than over immediatism, antislavery crusaders were beset by a fundamental ambivalence in
their attitude toward the Negro himself. At the simplest level there was
no issue. Slavery was sin; and the crusaders were moved to free the slave
by a humanitarianism too genuine to be doubted.[1] Yet, sympathetic as
they might appear and believe themselves to be toward the Negro, the
abolitionists were, as Leon Litwack and others have shown, in part at
least prejudiced against him.[2] And the variety of their response toward
him demonstrates the ambivalence so characteristic of the antislavery
movement as a whole.

* This article was read, in a slightly modified form, at the annual meetings of the
Mississippi Valley Historical Association, April 1965.

[1] The abolitionists were defined and set off from their contemporaries by their opposition to slavery and their concern for the welfare of the slaves, a concern which usually
embraced the free Negroes as well. This article is not, however, designed to compare
abolitionists as a group with nonabolitionists but rather to explore the variations within
the group.

[2] See, for example, Leon Litwack, "The Abolitionist Dilemma: The Antislavery
Movement and the Northern Negro," *New England Quarterly,* XXXIV (1961), 50-73;
and his *North of Slavery: The Negro in the Free States, 1790-1860* (Chicago, 1961).
See also Larry Gara, Louis Filler, Gerda Lerner, Stanley Elkins for considerations of
prejudice. For psychological probing see David Donald, Hazel Wolf, Clifford Griffin,
Martin Duberman.

356

Endemic was the abolitionists' tendency toward abstraction. Frequently they so abstracted both the "Negro" and the "Crusade" that they dealt not with people in a situation but only with intellectualizations in a vacuum. John Thomas has recently noted that William Lloyd Garrison failed "to understand people, black or white" and used them simply "as counters in the grim business of reform." [3] His analysis echoes publisher James Gordon Bennett's conclusion made one hundred years earlier that to Garrison "nothing [was] sacred . . . but the ideal intellect of the negro race." [4]

This preoccupation with the ideal is reflected by the American Anti-Slavery Society, which, at its inception in 1833, resolved that to guarantee education to the Negro was more important than to end "corporeal slavery itself, inasmuch as ignorance enslaves the mind and tends to the ruin of the immortal soul." [5] And, on the very eve of Emancipation, Philadelphia antislavery leader James Miller McKim, although emphasizing the importance of slave rehabilitation and active in prosecuting it, thought that it was "not the place . . . of [the] abolitionists to descend to the details of th[e] work, teaching, and the like; let this," he added, "be attended to by the neophytes and others. We are to continue to be what we always have been," he concluded, "a wheel within a wheel; an original motive power." [6] Thus for thirty years abolitionists, to a greater or lesser extent, heeded the kind of exhortation which Henry C. Wright enunciated so forcefully:

> Watch, Sister, & pray that you enter not into temptation. *Watch, not* . . . *for Abolition as an Organization*, not even for our millions of crushed & bleeding slaves . . . , but watch *for* the eternal, immutable Principles of Justice & Right—watch for *Humanity*. . . . We are seeking an object that must command the respect of the world—i e *the redemption of man from the dominion of man.* This is Abolition.[7]

The abolitionists did, of course, at least partly understand their own position. They may not have realized just how fully they were depersonalizing the Negroes; but they were quite aware that they had difficulties

[3] John L. Thomas, *The Liberator, William Lloyd Garrison, A Biography* (Boston, 1963), p. 153.

[4] Quoted in Wendell Phillips Garrison and Francis Jackson Garrison, *William Lloyd Garrison, 1805-1879; The Story of His Life as Told by His Children* (4 vols.; New York, 1885-89), III, 283.

[5] American Anti-Slavery Society, *Proceedings of the Anti-Slavery Convention, Assembled at Philadelphia, December 4, 5, and 6, 1833* (New York, 1833), p. 19.

[6] James Miller McKim to Samuel J. May, May 20 [1862], in Samuel J. May Papers, Cornell University.

[7] Henry C. Wright to Maria Weston Chapman, May 2, 1839, in Weston Papers, Antislavery Collection, Boston Public Library.

in matching their protestations to their actions. "We are," said the Connecticut crusader Samuel J. May with a Zolaesque directness, "culpably ignorant of, or shamefully indifferent to the wrongs which are inflicted upon our colored brethren. . . . We are prejudiced against the blacks; and our prejudices are indurated . . . by the secret, vague consciousness of the wrong we are doing them. Men are apt to dislike those most, whom they have injured most." [8] And despite the teaching of the antislavery periodical, the *Abolitionist,* that the antislavery enthusiast ought "to banish from his own mind the unworthy feelings which would lead him to regard any human being with contempt merely on account of his color," New York abolitionist Lewis Tappan admitted "that when the subject of acting out our profound principles in treating men irrespective of color is discussed heat is always produced." [9]

This much, then, the abolitionists themselves perceived. But for the student of the antislavery movement it is also imperative to recognize that prejudice and abstraction were but the obvious symptoms of an ambivalence which gives to the antislavery crusade in the expediency and temporizing of its actions and in the complexity of its thought an architecture baroque in the richness of its variations.[10]

It was, for example, relatively simple to accept the humanity of the Negro; but then how did one account for his patently submerged position vis-à-vis the whites? Abolitionists like Lydia Maria Child of Northampton, Massachusetts, tried to link the two elements by admitting that, while all Negroes were not "Scotts or Miltons," they were *"men,* capable of producing their proportion of Scotts and Miltons, if they could be allowed to live in a state of physical and intellectual freedom." [11] At the other extreme the New York Whig politician, William Henry Seward,

[8] Samuel J. May, Sermon delivered May 29, 1831, in Boston, as reported in *Liberator,* July 23, 1831.

[9] *Abolitionist,* I (Jan. 1833), as quoted in Merton L. Dillon, "The Failure of the American Abolitionists," *Journal of Southern History,* XXV (1959), 167. Lewis Tappan. Diary entry [Apr. 1836], as quoted in Litwack, *North of Slavery,* p. 218. See also Garrison's July 4, 1829 oration *(Garrison,* I, 133-34); Susan Cabot, *What Have We, as Individuals, To Do With Slavery* (American Anti-Slavery Society, *Anti-Slavery Tract No. 15.* New York, 1855), pp. 3-4; Beriah Green, *American Anti-Slavery Reporter,* I (June 1834), 88; and Birney to William Wright, June 20, 1845, in *Letters of James Gillespie Birney, 1831-1857,* ed. Dwight L. Dumond (2 vols.; New York, 1938), II, 947.

[10] This ideological ambivalence is reflected in the cleavages within the antislavery movement over the appropriate courses of action to be pursued. These cleavages have already been well examined in a variety of studies on antislavery published since 1935. Whether to take political action or to regard it as damaging to the requisite moral fervor, whether to expend time and funds on schools, give aid to fugitives and buy freedom for individual slaves or to work exclusively to propagate the antislavery faith are debates not only about means but also about the basic concepts of antislavery.

[11] Lydia Maria Child, *An Appeal in Favor of that Class of Americans Called Africans* (orig. ed. 1833. New York, 1836), p. 171.

defending the mentally deranged William Freeman in 1846, tried to subordinate intellectual lack to simple humanity and to separate it from race. He pleaded with the jury that

> the color of the prisoner's skin, and the form of his features, are not impressed upon the spiritual, immortal mind which works beneath. In spite of human pride, he is still your brother, and mine, in form and color accepted and approved by his Father, and yours, and mine, and bears equally with us the proudest inheritance of our race—the image of our Maker. Hold him then to be a MAN.[12]

In denying, furthermore, that the apparent differences between Negroes and whites were not inherent the abolitionists became environmentalists. John Rankin, ex-slaveholder from Virginia and an ardent abolitionist, asserted with good will but dubious logic that, if racial inferiority were a valid criterion, then all Negroes would be inferior to all whites if but one was. Clearly this was not so. Therefore existing inferiority was explainable only in environmental terms.[13] Slavery it was, asserted German refugee Charles Follen of Boston, that debased and degraded the Negroes and generated among whites an "absurd and cruel prejudice against color." [14] The antislavery solution to prejudice was clear once the cause was thus linked to slavery. Charles Calistus Burleigh of Connecticut optimistically exhorted his fellow whites to "give [the Negro] his liberty, and as strong a motive to exertion as you have;—a prospect of reward as sure and ample; not only wages for his toil, but respect and honor and social standing according to his worth, and see what he can then become." [15]

Yet, for all their exuberance, for all their belief in equality, for all their efforts to raise the Negro above the debilitating influences of adverse environment, the abolitionists were never wholly convincing. Much of what they said betrayed an implicit and at times explicit belief in racial

12 William Henry Seward, *Argument in Defense of William Freeman on his Trial for Murder* . . . (4th ed.; Auburn, N. Y., 1846), pp. 8-9. See also C. T. C. Follen, *Works, with a Memoir of His Life* [by Mrs. E. L. Follen] (5 vols.; Boston, 1841), I, 627-28.

13 John Rankin, *Letters on American Slavery Addressed to Mr. Thomas Rankin* . . . (5th ed.; Boston, 1838), pp. 10-11. See also Lewis Tappan, *The Life of Arthur Tappan* (New York, 1870), p. 131; James A. Thome and J. Horace Kimball, *Emancipation in the West Indies. A Six Months Tour in Antigua, Barbadoes, and Jamaica in the Year 1837* (American Anti-Slavery Society, *Anti-Slavery Examiner No. 7*. New York, 1838), p. 75; and Sallie Holley to Gerrit Smith, Nov. 17, 1865, in the Smith Miller Papers, Syracuse University.

14 Charles Follen, "The Cause of Freedom in Our Country," *Quarterly Anti-Slavery Magazine*, II (Oct. 1836), 65.

15 Charles Calistus Burleigh, *Slavery and the North* (New York [1855]), p. 4. Rankin essentially held the same view, but thought that it would take a long time to raise the Negro; see *Letters on American Slavery*, pp. 10-11.

inferiority. Here again ambivalence emerged. That the abolitionists themselves were usually unconscious of their expression of prejudice and that they denied it when challenged should surprise no one. Nor, indeed, is the thoughtful student surprised to learn that such prejudice did in fact exist. Occasionally crude, more often hidden in underlying assumptions or in appeals to science, prejudice played a more pervasive role than the logic of consistency would admit.

Exasperated by poor printing, inferior paper and numerous misprints, and spurred on by his own literary pride, Edmund Quincy lashed out in a letter to Caroline Weston in 1846 at "Wendell's nigger," whom he held responsible for botching an Antislavery Report. Never, he urged, let the printing out to *"Smart people"*; they get things up so poorly.[16] Here clearly was not only a rather vulgar display of prejudice but also of a value structure in which the typography of a convention's report weighed more heavily than economic opportunity for the free Negro.

The acerbity of these outbursts may be attributed to Quincy alone. The subterranean import, however, was common property among antislavery people. As late as 1860 Theodore Parker, a backer of John Brown, observed that "the Anglo-Saxon with common sense does not like this Africanization of America; he wishes the superior race to multiply rather than the inferior." [17] His neighbor, Samuel Gridley Howe, known for his multiple reform interests, accepted Parker's assumptions but rejected his predictions by observing that, particularly among young Canadian refugee Negroes, many succumbed to "mesenteric and other glandular diseases" and suffered from "phthisical diseases" and a "softening of tubercles." "Many intelligent physicians," he stated, "who have practiced among both [white and Negro] classes, say that the colored people are feebly organized; that the scrofulous temperament prevails among them; that the climate tends to development of tuberculous diseases; that they are unprolific and short-lived." [18]

Whether feebly organized in physique or not, the Negroes were certainly docile in temperament. "It is paying a very poor compliment, indeed, to the courage and superiority of us whites," Richard Hildreth said through the sympathetically portrayed Mr. Mason in *Archy Moore*, "to doubt whether we, superior as well in numbers as in every thing else,

16 Edmund Quincy to Caroline Weston, Feb. 1, 1846, in Weston Papers. A year later Quincy complained about Frederick Douglass' independence (what he thought was Douglass' overcharging the *American Anti-Slavery Standard* for copy supplied) by observing that "These niggers, like Kings, are kittle cattle to shoe behind." Quincy to Caroline Weston, July 2, 1847, in Weston Papers.

17 Theodore Parker, *John Brown's Expedition Reviewed in a Letter from Theodore Parker, at Rome, to Francis Jackson, Boston* (Boston, 1860), p. 14.

18 Samuel Gridley Howe, *The Refugees from Slavery in Canada West. Report to the Freedmen's Inquiry Commission* (Boston, 1864), pp. 21-22.

could not inspire awe enough to maintain our natural position at the head of the community, and to keep these poor people in order without making slaves of them." [19] But, if Hildreth's Mason was fictional, the Lane Rebels were not. They had concluded, in their famous debates on slavery, that *"the blacks are abundantly able to take care of and provide for themselves";* but had added immediately that they *"would be kind and docile if immediately emancipated."* [20] This emphasis on docility is important, for quite openly it reduced the status of the Negro below that of the white man. J. Miller McKim, for example, negated American standards of self-reliance and manly independence when he praised Negroes for "their susceptibility to control." [21]

Not unreasonably, many Negroes actively resented this abolitionist presumption about their "susceptibility to control." During the 1850s, in fact, this resentment was in large part responsible for the growth and activity of the Negro Convention movement, whose purpose it was to do for the Negroes themselves what they feared the whites, at last, would not accomplish for them. Frederick Douglass and Henry Highland Garnet, two Negro leaders of marked undocility, both took umbrage at Maria Weston Chapman for her paternal concern about their appropriate behavior; and Douglass, disillusioned with radical abolitionism in the face of growing political antislavery activity and ambitious himself to assert his independence from white abolitionist domination, defied the Boston hierarchy by establishing his own newspaper in Rochester, New York. Likewise, Martin Delany, a successful Negro doctor, resented the Negroes' exclusion from antislavery leadership and was highly dubious about the abolitionists' touted support of economic opportunity for free Negroes. Delany's disillusionment led him to abandon America as a viable home for the Negro and in the late 1850s to sponsor projects for African colonization.[22]

[19] Richard Hildreth, *Archy Moore: The White Slave* (1st ed.; 1836. New York, 1856), p. 264.

[20] As reported in Henry B. Stanton to Joshua Leavitt, Mar. 10, 1834, in *American Anti-Slavery Reporter*, I (Apr. 1834), 54.

[21] James Miller McKim, *The Freedmen of South Carolina . . .* (Philadelphia, 1862), p. 9. See also *Letters from Port Royal. Written at the Time of the Civil War*, ed. Elizabeth Ware Pearson (Boston, 1906), pp. 102-3, 315-16; The *Anti-Slavery Record* III (Feb. 1837), 15; *Letters of Theodore Dwight Weld, Angelina Grimké Weld and Sarah Grimké, 1822-1844*, eds. Gilbert H. Barnes and Dwight L. Dumond (2 vols.; New York, 1934), II, 524; and Leon Litwack, *North of Slavery*, p. 223.

[22] In the Weston Papers one may find numerous examples of the patronizing antislavery attitude and of Negro response to it. See also Filler, *Crusade Against Slavery*, p. 143. In particular note Frederick Douglass to Maria Weston Chapman, Mar. 29, 1846, Weston Papers; and Martin Robinson Delany, *The Condition, Elevation, Emigration, and Destiny of the Colored People of the United States Politically Considered* (Philadelphia, 1852), pp. 25-29.

Despite concepts of racial inferiority, further borne out by an almost universal preference for the lighter-skinned over the darker-skinned Negro,[23] abolitionists in fact did demand just and equitable civil liberties for colored persons. "The oppressive civil disabilities laid upon them in the non-slaveholding States, and the settled opposition to their education and elevation . . .," said the Andover Theological Seminary anti-slavery society,

> are but glaring indications of the prevalent spirit of slavery. The same contempt of the black man—the same disposition to trample on his rights and to lord it over his person, follows him, whatever *degree* of emancipation he may have obtained, and in whatever part of the nation he takes his refuge. Though we had in view only the wrongs of the colored people in New-England, we should feel ourselves compelled to take our present stand, and vindicate their rights as brethren, as men, and as Americans.[24]

Abolitionists everywhere asserted that Negroes and whites should be judged and treated according to the same standards in the apportioning not only of civil rights but also of economic and educational opportunities. In its Declaration of Sentiments the American Anti-Slavery Society announced in 1833 that

> all persons of color who possess the qualifications which are demanded of others, ought to be admitted forthwith to the enjoyment of the same privileges, and the exercise of the same prerogatives, as others; and . . . the paths of preferment, of wealth, and of intelligence, should be opened as widely to them as to persons of a white complexion.[25]

Schools, like Oberlin College and the Noyes Academy in New Hampshire, which admitted Negroes on equal terms with whites,[26] bore out these principles, as did Charles Sumner's argument in the Roberts Case in 1849 that separate schools were unequal and threatened cleavages in

---

23 Antislavery literature contains many illustrations of the preference for lighter-skinned Negroes. See Samuel May Jr., *The Fugitive Slave Law and Its Victims* (American Anti-Slavery Society, *Anti-Slavery Tract No. 18* [New York, 1855]); George Bourne, *Slavery Illustrated in its Effects Upon Woman and Domestic Society* (Boston, 1837); Hildreth's *Archy Moore;* and William I. Bowditch, *White Slavery in the United States* (American Anti-Slavery Society, *Anti-Slavery Tract No. 2* [New York, 1855]); see also in this connection Theodore Dwight Weld, *American Slavery as it is: Testimony of a Thousand Witnesses* (New York, 1839); and the juvenile [Jonathan Walker], *A Picture of Slavery, for Youth. By the Author of "The Branded Hand"* and *"Chattelized Humanity"* (Boston, n.d.).

24 This is a summary given by D. T. Kimball and F. Laine to *Genius of Temperance,* Aug. 22, 1833, as reported in *Liberator,* Sept. 28, 1833. Similar demands for equality of treatment can be found in Child, *Appeal,* pp. 195-208.

25 American Anti-Slavery Society, *Proceedings of the Anti-Slavery Convention, Assembled at Philadelphia,* contains the Declaration of Sentiments.

26 See *Liberator,* Oct. 25, 1834, for information about the Noyes Academy.

society.[27] And Samuel J. May, summing up the concept in a statement which avoided many of the pitfalls of prejudice into which his colleagues fell, averred that "all we demand for them is that negroes shall be permitted, encouraged, assisted to become as wise, as virtuous, and as rich as they can, and be acknowledged to be just what they have become, and be treated accordingly." [28]

Yet these appeals to the efficacy of education and economic betterment reveal the middle-class values to which almost all abolitionists subscribed and which both compound and explain much of the ambivalence in the antislavery movement. As middle-class Americans, abolitionists, naturally enough, measured the Negroes against middle-class standards, and to those standards they expected the Negroes to conform—Negroes who were generally ex-slaves from the lowest and most abject class in America. Assuredly the American Anti-Slavery Society was eager to uplift them to "an equality with the whites" but only after carefully disclaiming that it approved any such non-middle-class shenanigans as adopting colored children, encouraging interracial marriages or "exciting the people of color to assume airs." [29]

It was expected, then, that the Negroes should adapt themselves to the values of the white community, should, as one abolitionist advised, submit to prejudice "with the true dignity of meekness" so that their critics might be stilled. Thus was fulfilled the stereotype of the malleable, willing and docile colored man. Still, on limited occasions, the same writer observed, the Negroes should take a positive stand. They should demand admission to the public schools, they should organize or join lyceum groups, they should acquire knowledge and education. And, he said in a condensed version of a middle-class *Poor Richard's*, they should organize uplifting visits to their poor and degraded brethren and teach them "temperance . . . cleanliness, neatness, strict honesty, and all that belong to good morality." [30] In addition to these virtues, the American Anti-Slavery Society agents were admonished to instill in the free people of color

[27] Charles Sumner, "Equality before the Law: Unconstitutionality of Separate Colored Schools in Massachusetts. Argument before the Supreme Court of Massachusetts, in the Case of Sarah C. Roberts *v.* The City of Boston . . .," in *The Works of Charles Sumner* (Boston, 1872), II, 327-76.

[28] Samuel Joseph May, *Some Recollections of Our Anti-Slavery Conflict* (Boston, 1869), p. 29. See also Birney, *Letters*, II, 945; and Garrison, *Garrison*, I, 148.

[29] Executive Committee of the American Anti-Slavery Society to Mayor Cornelius Lawrence of New York, July 16, 1834, included in the microfilm printing of *Liberator*, between 1833 and 1834, reel 1.

[30] This entire argument appeared in a series of articles, signed "S. T. U.," which appeared in *Liberator*, Feb. 11, 18, 25, and Mar. 3, 1832. The quotations are from the first and last issues, respectively.

the importance of domestic order, and the performance of relative duties in families; of correct habits; command of temper and courteous manners. Also the duty and advantages of industry and economy; promptness and fidelity in the fulfillment of contracts or obligations, whether written or verbal; and encourage them in the acquisition of property, especially of real estate in fee simple, particularly dwellings for their own families. Present their duties and privileges as citizens, and encourage them to become voters, and to secure equal privileges with other citizens. . . .[31]

Others, varying little from the standard reforming attitudes of the day but less optimistic about raising the Negro to the middle class, urged him to adopt their own conception of lower-class standards. He should learn a trade and become a mechanic. Since these abolitionists categorized the social strata in such a way that the hardy mechanic always fell comfortably below the solid middle class, the Negro was bracketed, at worst, with the Irish hod carrier, and at best only identified with the honest toiler.[32]

Sometimes in the abolitionists' arguments one discovers strong overtones of ordinary self-interest. The *Anti-Slavery Almanac* assured its readers, for example, that emancipated Negroes would not flock to the North. Let no one be perturbed, the *Almanac* urged in unctuous tone. "If the slaves are gradually set free, they must leave the place where they are, (and will be likely to go to the north,) that they may not interfere with the slavery which remains. But if they are all set free at once, they may continue where they are." Putting the argument in other terms, emancipated Negroes would be a great boon to the economy not only in the South but in the North as well.[33] "The southern laborers, when free and paid," C. C. Burleigh had said, "would buy of us many comforts and conveniences not allowed them now . . . which would give new activity

31 Executive Committee of the American Anti-Slavery Society to its agents, n.d. [1834-5?], included in the microfilm printing of *Liberator*, between 1833 and 1834, reel 1.

32 See, for example, the *Anti-Slavery Record*, I (June 1835), 68, urging that Negroes be apprenticed at good trades. And see also the commentary reprinted by *Liberator*, Mar. 31, 1837, from the Bangor *Mechanic*, in which it is made quite clear that the laborer is quite aware that the middle class looks down on the working class. See also, for comparisons with the Irish, Hildreth, *Archy Moore*, p. 264; Sarah Grimké to Elizabeth Pease [May 20? 1838], in *Weld-Grimké Letters*, II, 679; William Allen Diary, Nov. 10, 1863, State Historical Society of Wisconsin.

33 The *Anti-Slavery Almanac* (1837 and 1839). The quotation is from the earlier volume, p. 44. The self-interest showed in other ways as well. Defending what later became Radical Republican doctrine, Maria Weston Chapman wrote to Lizzy (Chapman) Laugel (Sept. 24, 1862) that "black *soldiers* would save our Armies, & black *citizens* our *republican institutions*." (Weston Papers). And Wendell Phillips also unconsciously suggested the same prior self-concern when he spoke at the *Liberator's* 20th anniversary celebration: "My friends, if we never free a slave, we have at least freed ourselves in the effort to emancipate our brother man." (Quoted in Garrison, *Garrison*, III, 320).

to our shops and mills and shipping, and steadier employment, and, most likely, higher wages, to all kinds of labor here."[34] Thus emancipation would not inconvenience the North with a mass of freed slaves; it would rather prove quite profitable.

Still, there was the thorny issue of defining the social position of the Negro in a predominantly white society. Many of the same abolitionists who demanded so unfalteringly no association with slaveholders found it ticklishly difficult to espouse social intercourse with Negroes and almost impossible to champion holy wedlock with those of black skin. In theory and in conscience, of course, they deplored the bans on interracial marriage; yet in practice they as often betrayed an opposite sentiment.[35] For his own part, Garrison defended the ideal goal but reconciled it with practical reality. "At the present time," he said expediently, "mixed marriages would be in bad taste. . . ."[36] Elizur Wright, however, scornfully ridiculed such temporizing over prejudice. "Pray, what is the matter? we ask of a generous and enlightened public," he snapped viciously.

> The reply is couched with quaking apprehension, in the appalling interrogatory; *would you have your daughter marry a negro?* And the utter slavery to which this tyrant prejudice has reduced everything that is noble and good in the land, is evinced by nothing more clearly than by the pains taking of even abolitionists to show that colored men *may be* enfranchised and elevated without bringing on the dreaded consequence.[37]

It seemed necessary, in the end, to plaster over the issue and to allay white fears. Mrs. Child, echoing the frequent antislavery assertion that there were scarcely enough abolitionists in the South to account for the evidences of miscegenation there, insisted that to say that abolitionists wished amalgamation was "a false charge, got up by the enemies of the cause, and used as a bugbear to increase the prejudices of the community." In fact, she added, "by universal emancipation we want to *stop* amalgamation."[38] More reassuring to those who hoped that the issues raised by social equality would fail to materialize was Samuel G. Howe's

---

34 Burleigh, *Slavery and the North*, pp. 8-9.

35 See Birney, *Letters*, I, 397; Garrison, *Garrison*, II, 356; *Anti-Slavery Record*, I (June 1835), 71; and Gilbert H. Barnes, *The Antislavery Impulse, 1830-1844* (New York, 1933), p. 274, note 20. See also Louis Ruchames, "Race, Marriage and Abolition in Massachusetts," *Journal of Negro History*, XL (1955), 250-73, on the fight for repeal of discriminatory marriage laws.

36 *Liberator*, Aug. 13, 1831.

37 [Elizur Wright Jr.], "Caste in the United States: A Review," *Quarterly Anti-Slavery Magazine*, II (Jan. 1837), 177.

38 Lydia Maria Child, *Anti-Slavery Catechism* (Newburyport, 1836), pp. 31-32.

commentary made after a close study of Canadian Negroes. "Upon the whole," he observed,

> . . . the experience of the Canadian refugees goes to show that there need be no anxiety upon the score of amalgamation of races in the United States. With freedom, and protection of their legal rights; with an open field for industry, and opportunities for mental and moral culture, colored people will not seek relationship with whites, but will follow their natural affinities, and marry among themselves.[39]

The social distance decreed by class identification provided perhaps the most common and satisfactory framework for abolitionists' contacts with free Negroes. Thus, steeped in middle-class values and having identified the Negroes with the laboring classes, the antislavery band frequently assumed the patronizing air of the uplifter and the saved toward the downtrodden and unwashed. James G. Birney, speaking from a slaveholding background, observed that without question emancipation would, "where the superior intelligence of the master was acknowledged, produce on the part of the beneficiaries, the most entire and cordial reliance on his counsel and friendship."[40] And Sumner, in the Roberts Case, urged that "the vaunted superiority of the white race imposes corresponding duties. The faculties with which they are endowed, and the advantages they possess, must be exercised for the good of all. If the colored people are ignorant, degraded, and unhappy," he asserted with a fine sense of noblesse oblige, "then should they be especial objects of care."[41]

Such paternalism was, to be sure, most benign. At times, however, it was most insufferable. "The more I mingle with your people," Angelina Grimké wrote to Sarah Douglass in a display of tactlessness as gargantuan as it was overbearing,

> the more I feel for their oppressions and desire to sympathize in their sorrows. Joshua Leavitt threw out a new and delightful idea on this subject on our way to Bloomfield. He said he believed the Lord had a great work for the colored people to do, and that your long continued afflictions and humiliations was the furnace in which He was purifying you from the dross[,] the tin[,] and the reprobate silver, that you might come out like gold seven times refined. I Hav[e] thought of this and fully believ[e] you will after all get up abov[e] us and be the favored instruments [to?] carry pure and undefiled Religion to the Heathen

[39] Howe, *Refugees from Slavery*, p. 33.

[40] Quoted in *The Legion of Liberty and Force of Truth, Containing the Thoughts, Words, and Deeds, of Some Prominent Apostles, Champions and Martyrs* (New York. 1843), n.p.

[41] Sumner, "Equality before the Law," II, 376.

World. May the Lord lift you from the dung hill and set you among princes. . . .[42]

Helping the Lord hoist the poor Negroes off the dung hill was, as it often turned out, an arduous and dangerous chore, but one which gave the abolitionists a chance many of them coveted to become martyrs in the cause. To defend the Negro in court, to speak on his behalf before hostile audiences, to be harried from town after town by the frenzied mob was the stuff of which martyrdom was made. And the genuine joy in the experience of such martyrdom only enhanced the rewards of protective guardianship, as those who braved the mob when Pennsylvania Hall was burned well knew. Confronting the hostile elements, the stalwart women of the Female Anti-Slavery Convention "maintain[ed] the perilled cause to the last." As they adjourned "the colored members of the convention were protected by their white sisters, and Oh! Shame to say," one of the white sisters wrote, "at both were thrown a shower of stones."[43] And then, Oh! Shame to say, the brand new hall was set ablaze and totally destroyed.

In their enthusiasm to elevate the Negro, the abolitionists frequently carried on their shoulders an early version of the White Man's Burden. They taught their children in heavily freighted moral tales that "negroes, even poor, degraded, despised slaves, are not without reason and understanding. [And that] many of them have a large share of sagacity." Go forth, they directed even the toddlers, instruct the poor and ignorant; become teachers, and help train the Negroes themselves to become missionaries that they may enlighten "their countrymen who are in ignorance and darkness."[44] The adults themselves set the initial example. When Helen Benson, daughter of Rhode Island abolitionist George Benson, was married to Garrison, she refused to allow cake at her wedding or to wear fancy clothes lest she be a poor model for the Negroes to follow.[45] Theodore Weld also cast himself as an exemplar of the good. "I attend Church with our colored friends," he wrote; "but," he honestly

[42] In Angelina and Sarah Grimké to Sarah Douglass, Feb. 22, 1837, *Weld-Grimké Letters*, I, 364-65. Gerda Lerner contends that the Grimké sisters were almost if not totally above prejudice in "The Grimké Sisters and the Struggle against Race Prejudice," *Journal of Negro History*, XLVIII (1963), 277-91.
[43] Letter from a New York woman, May 18, 1838, in *Liberator*, May 25, 1838.
[44] From a story in the Juvenile Department, signed "H. Sabbath School Treasury," *Liberator*, Jan. 14, 1832. The Juvenile column was a regular feature in the early years of the *Liberator*. Henry C. Wright was designated American Anti-Slavery Society agent to children.
[45] Garrison, *Garrison*, I, 427.

admitted, "I do it to cast my lot with them; and," he contentedly concluded, "tho not spiritually edified, I find joy and peace in it." [46]

It was, however, a far more difficult thing for the same abolitionists to follow through, unhesitatingly and courageously, the implications of their theories, to work unfalteringly and without equivocation, straight on to free the slave and obtain equality for the free Negro. Certainly the abolitionists were almost universally too forthright and too dedicated to be faithless to their ideals; certainly they did not knowingly forsake their plighted word. Still it was a constant fact of the antislavery crusade that it was clearly marked by the constant temporizing of its participants. [47] In Ohio, some Lane students objected when one of their number took up residence with Cincinnati Negro families while he was working among them because they thought it would be harmful to their project. [48] Throughout the North antislavery societies debated the questions "Ought abolitionists to encourage colored persons in joining Anti-Slavery Societies?" or "Is it expedient for Abolitionists to encourage social intercourse between white and colored families?" And their composite response was at best an equivocal "perhaps." [49]

This political temporizing was not, of course, without its reasons, particularly in the light of mobs and physical violence provoked by extremists. Some abolitionists, of course, merely thought of public relations and how best to draw support to the cause. Birney, for his part, thought it enough to strive for equal civil rights without, at the same time, trying for social equality. Too much too soon, he argued, would mean a denial of all rights to the Negro. [50] So too the American Anti-Slavery Society, after the serious antiabolitionist riots in New York in 1834, rejected charges that they supported amalgamation or attacked the Constitution. "We disclaim, and entirely disapprove," they asserted, "the language of a hand-bill recently circulated in this City the tendency of which is thought to be to excite resistance to the Laws. Our principle is, that even hard laws are to be submitted to by all men, until they can by peaceable means be altered." [51]

---

[46] Weld to Sarah and Angelina Grimké, Dec. 15 [1837], in *Weld-Grimké Letters*, I, 496. A similar viewpoint turns up in Unitarian observations quite frequently as a rejection of emotional-evangelical enthusiasms.

[47] In a letter to Lewis Tappan, Weld, for example, wrote concerning a slave case in Connecticut that "not one of the Abolitionists here [in Hartford] was willing to appear *openly* in the matter as the friend of the compla[i]nant. Brother Tyler and myself who are the only persons known publickly in the case as friends of the compla[i]nant, have been and are still plentifully threatened with mob vengeance." June 8, 1837, *Weld-Grimké Letters*, I, 399.

[48] *Liberator*, Jan. 10, 1835.   [49] From Litwack, *North of Slavery*, p. 218.

[50] Birney to Weld, July 26, 1834, *Weld-Grimké Letters*, I, 163.

[51] *Liberator*, July 19, 1834.

The abolitionists were painfully aware of their actions, yet in good conscience they believed that their course was the better part of wisdom and thus did not compromise their valor. Arthur Tappan for one was so fearful lest his earlier activities be misconstrued that he assured A. F. Stoddard of Glasgow in 1863 that "if . . . you should know of any one's charging me with any gross assault on the fastidiousness of the age, when I became the avowed friend of the colored man, you may set it down to the score of ignorance or malignant falsehood." [52] But Sarah Forten, member of the actively antislavery Negro family of Philadelphia, understood. "How much of this leaven still lingers in the hearts of our white brethren and sisters is oftentimes made manifest to us," she wrote, referring specifically to an abolitionist who was comfortable with Negroes only under cover of night; "but when we recollect what great sacrifices to public sentiment they are called upon to make," she generously added, "we cannot wholly blame them." [53]

Briefly, then, the antislavery movement was beset, throughout its history, by a fundamental ambivalence. Never could the abolitionists decide collectively, and infrequently individually, whether the Negro was equal or inferior to the white; whether social equality for the Negro should be stressed or whether it should be damped; whether civil and social rights should be granted him at once or only in the indefinite and provisional future; whether, in fact, social and civil rights should be granted or whether only civil rights should be given him. The abolitionists, furthermore, were torn between a genuine concern for the welfare and uplift of the Negro and a paternalism which was too often merely the patronizing of a superior class. And their forthright concern for the Negro was still more qualified by an unhappy degree of temporizing.

These are the hallmarks of a critical and fundamental ambivalence. When such a quandary existed over the position and treatment of the free Negro and over the very nature of the beings to be freed, abolitionist temporizing becomes understandable. When immediate emancipation as a plan of abolition was translated to mean only immediate repentance of the sin of slavery, the needs of the human beings who were slaves were ignored. The abolitionists had sought solace in abstractions about humanity. And their hesitancy and confusion about the question of race illuminate much of the contention and indecision within the antislavery movement—a movement baffled and torn by ambivalence.

[52] Arthur Tappan to A. F. Stoddard, Aug. 27, 1863, in Tappan, *Tappan*, pp. 201-2.
[53] Sarah Forten to Angelina Grimké, Apr. 15, 1837, *Weld-Grimké Letters*, I, 380.

ENDS, MEANS, AND ATTITUDES:
Black-White Conflict in the Antislavery Movement

Jane H. Pease and William H. Pease

WHEN HE ESTABLISHED the *North Star* in 1847, Frederick Douglass broke the ties which had bound him to William Lloyd Garrison. Although Douglas had been an officer in New England antislavery circles as recently as May of that year, he was, by late fall, exchanging harsh rejoinders with his erstwhile Boston colleagues. Within months the two editors had become open antagonists, and before long the forces of Garrisonian abolitionism were turned against their former friend. The American Anti-Slavery Society, Douglass averred later, was "exerting its energies, and expending its funds for the purpose, small or great, of silencing and putting to open shame a fugitive slave, simply . . . because that fugitive slave has dared to differ from that Society, or from the leading individuals in it. . . ."[1]

Douglass was not alone in his plight. Throughout the thirty years before the Civil War, Negro activists pursued their goals not only in conjunction with white dominated antislavery organizations but through distinctive race associations as well. Like Douglass, they chose means which demonstrated black self-sufficiency and pursued programs which stressed achieving full civil rights for free blacks as much as liberating the enslaved. Like him, they were often propelled on a separate course by the treatment they received from white abolitionists: Condescending patronage irked them. Prejudice among avowed friends angered them. The slowness and abstraction of the antislavery movement frustrated them. Their response was two-fold: as they established all-black conventions, councils, and vigilance committees, they became increasingly critical of their white colleagues in the antislavery crusade.

* * *

It had not always been thus. When in 1831 the *Liberator* had announced the new wave of abolition, Garrison was welcomed for his disavowal of racial inequality. He publicized black opposition to the American Colonization Society. He fought against Massachusetts' proscription of intermarriage. In response, free Negroes eagerly supported

[1] *Frederick Douglass' Paper*, Jan. 13, 1854.

117

371

his leadership, endorsed the new antislavery societies, and sustained the newspaper.[2]

By the end of the 1830's, however, that early enthusiasm waned as blacks who were active in the American Anti-Slavery Society became increasingly sensitive to the prejudices of their white colleagues. Samuel Cornish, one of the most frequent Negro officeholders in antislavery organizations, smarted under their paternalism and demanded that black "moral and intellectual attainments" be judged by the same standards as white. He resented Lewis Tappan's refusal to consult blacks about the disposition of funds bequeathed for the "education and benefit of colored people." He scorned those who talked of the "sacrifice" they made when they met "colored Americans upon terms of social equality."[3]

Like Cornish, Theodore Wright, a New York Presbyterian clergyman and a member of the executive committee of the American Anti-Slavery Society, expressed doubt about the good faith and intentions of white abolitionists. He was "alarmed" that the constitutions of the auxiliary anti-slavery societies frequently said "nothing . . . about the improvement of the man of color." They "overlooked the giant sin of prejudice," which it was their presumed task to "annihilate." Sarah Forten echoed his concern. Observing white colleagues as guests in her father's Philadelphia home, she unhappily concluded that these "professed friends" had not yet rid themselves of prejudice.[4]

Doubtless some of the criticism stemmed from the different emphases which black and white abolitionists placed on the status of the free Negro in the North. It was indeed American Anti-Slavery Society policy that "all persons of color who possess the qualifications which are demanded of others, ought to be admitted forthwith to the enjoyment of the same privileges, and the exercise of the same prerogatives, as others. . . ."

[2] See Garrison's comment on racial equality, *Genius of Universal Emancipation*, Feb. 12, 1830, quoted in Wendell P. and Francis J. Garrison, *William Lloyd Garrison, 1805-1879; The Story of His Life as Told by His Children* (New York, 1885-1889), I, 148. For colonization and intermarriage see James Forten to William L. Garrison, Aug. 9, 1831, Garrison Papers, Antislavery Collection, Boston Public Library; Louis Ruchames, "Race, Marriage and Abolition in Massachusetts," *Journal of Negro History*, XL (July, 1955), 250-273; and *Liberator*, 1831 *passim*. For black support see George Cary to [Garrison], June 6, 1831, Garrison Papers, and scattered issues of *Liberator*, e.g., Mar. 12, 1831, and Mar. 31, 1832.

[3] *Colored American*, May 27, Nov. 4, 1837; July 1, Dec. 30, 1837; Dec. 16, 1837. For further evidence of white "sacrifice" and black disaffection see Theodore Weld to Sarah and Angelina Grimké, Dec. 15, [1837], in Theodore Dwight Weld *et al.*, *. . . Letters of Theodore Dwight Weld, Angelina Grimké Weld and Sarah Grimké, 1822-1844*, edited by Gilbert H. Barnes and Dwight L. Dumond, (New York, 1934), I, 496; also *Colored American*, Oct. 27, 1838.

[4] From a Wright speech, *Friend of Man*, n.d., as copied in *Liberator*, Oct. 13, 1837. Sarah Forten to Angelina Grimké, Apr. 15, 1837, in *Weld-Grimké Letters*, I, 380. For further evidences of black resentment see the speech of Nathaniel Paul in *Friend of Man*, Mar. 14, 1838; and B. F. Roberts to Amos A. Phelps, June 19, 1838, in Phelps Papers, Antislavery Collection, Boston Public Library.

Still, when confronted by the mob violence which their antislavery efforts engendered in the 1830's, whites temporized and equivocated. James Thome, lecturing in Akron, Ohio, explicitly denied an abolitionist commitment to black suffrage and officeholding in the near future. Theodore Weld, who time and again faced down the screams and brickbats of angry crowds, urged on Lewis Tappan the expediency of avoiding public association with blacks. He would not compromise principles, he said; but, he added, such a demonstration of basic principles might on occasion endanger the Negroes' physical safety and harm the cause of equality. Tappan replied that he already weighed public response and acted accordingly. Not only did whites thus sacrifice racial equality to survival in the antislavery fight, they also established other priorities which placed purging individual souls of the sin of slavery ahead of universal emancipation.[5]

Their caution was understandable; their concern for individual souls a requisite of moral reform. But neither was convincing to freemen denied civil rights or to fugitive slaves unsure even of their freedom. Distressed by the myopia of white abolitionists, James McCune Smith, black New York physician, urged them to give priority to eliminating the vestiges of slavery in the North. Smith's neighbor, David Ruggles, head of the New York City Vigilance Committee, set a more specific model for whites by pointing out his group's concern with everyday cases of "oppression and wrong, inflicted on our brethern." By aiding the fugitive, "in our individual spheres of action," Ruggles wrote, we "prove ourselves practical abolitionists." Likewise, Frederick Douglass exploded when, in 1843, an agent for the American Anti-Slavery Society cancelled antislavery meetings to lecture about communitarianism. And the *Colored American* launched an attack on the black Garrisonian Charles Remond for boycotting the World Antislavery Convention in London in 1840 because it refused to seat women delegates. He should, the editors averred, have retained his seat. He was not there merely as an antislavery delegate; he was the spokesman for black America.[6]

By urging action which specifically aided freemen in the North and by discouraging that which promoted feminism, communitarianism, or other reforms ahead of antislavery, black abolitionists thus made clear both their dedication to practical action and their reservations about multiple reform. And though some of them did join the infighting over

[5] American Anti-Slavery Society, "Declaration of Sentiments," in *Abolitionist*, I (Dec., 1833), 179. James A. Thome and J. W. Alvord to Theodore Weld, Feb. 9, 1836; Weld to Lewis Tappan, [Mar. 9, 1836]; and Tappan to Weld, Mar. 15, 1836; all in *Weld-Grimké Letters*, I, 257, 270-274, 275-276. On priorities and purging the sin of slavery see Sarah and Angelina Grimké to Sarah Douglass, Feb. 22, 1837, *ibid.*, 364-365; and Beriah Green in American Anti-Slavery Society *Reporter*, I (June, 1834), 88.

[6] *Liberator*, June 1, 1838. New York Committee of Vigilance, *The First Annual Report . . . 1837 . . .* (New York, 1837), p. 13. Frederick Douglass to Maria W. Chapman, Sept. 10, 1843, Weston Papers, Antislavery Collection, Boston Public Library. *Colored American*, Aug. 8, 1840.

religious orthodoxy, women's rights, and political action, which split the antislavery movement in 1840, many more deplored the factionalism which distracted attention from abolition and civil rights.

In 1839, for example, only four months after a meeting of New Bedford blacks voted to sustain Garrison against the rival Massachusetts Abolition Society, a second meeting contended that the controversy damaged the cause by "introducing into anti-slavery meetings, subjects foreign to the cause of the slave." Such diversions, they said in "stern rebuke," tended "to cripple the efforts of a large portion of the true friends of the slave, and clog the wheels of the abolition car." Arguing similarly, anti-Garrisonians like Thomas Cole of Boston, Samuel Cornish and Samuel Ringgold Ward condemned the Garrisonians for eschewing political action, because to them political action seemed the most realistic way to combat slavery.[7] At stake were both means and ends. In general blacks applauded all manner of Middle Period reform; but in particular no reform took precedence over their own advancement; and no means was acceptable which qualified that end.

By 1840, therefore, many blacks were eager to chart an independent course. John Lewis gave up his agency for the New Hampshire Anti-Slavery Society to act "as a colored man, and representative of [his] people . . . to make the advocacy of the cause the paramount question." In New York, Samuel Ward, convinced that abolitionists "have not so much regard for the rights of the colored men as they think they have," urged his fellows to "act for themselves," and to participate in a black convention to eliminate the state's $250 suffrage qualification for Negroes. In response, the *National Anti-Slavery Standard,* official journal of the American Society, gave paternal advice. Warning against precipitate action, it urged care lest in their understandable "desire to become freemen," blacks "tear down" what they had already built up. Only when whites respected them, the *Standard* concluded, could the latter hope for equality. But free blacks in the North were unwilling to wait for whites to act for them. Hence, an acting editor of the *Colored American* applauded separate race action. "Where our object is confined to our own purposes and for our own advantage . . . we are doing what no others can do for us. . . ." Later, Charles Ray, the regular editor, saw in the *Standard's* advice a "dictatorial" and "authoritative" spirit. Free blacks must, he argued, uphold their rights without white assistance. Anti-slavery societies were fine for fighting slavery, but black conventions marked the way to civil rights in the North.[8]

[7] *Liberator,* June 21, Oct. 18, 1839. Minutes of the annual meeting of the American Anti-Slavery Society, *ibid.,* May 24, 1839. Thomas Cole to Dear Sir, *Colored American,* n.d., copied in *Liberator,* Dec. 18, 1840. *Colored American,* Aug. 17, 1839. Samuel R. Ward to Editor of *Union Herald,* Aug. 23, 1840, in *National Anti-Slavery Standard,* Sept. 10, 1840. For instances of black support for Garrisonians see *Liberator,* Oct. 6, Nov. 3, 1837, and June 7, 1839; also Thomas Van Rensselaer to Garrison, Mar. 24, 1839, Garrison Papers.

[8] John W. Lewis to Executive Committee of the New Hampshire Anti-Slavery

As free Negroes came to discover that white abolitionists' priorities differed from theirs, and as they adopted separate means to fulfill their own particular needs, they came also to assert that their color and experience gave them a special competence which whites lacked. Theodore Wright reminded the New England Anti-Slavery Convention that "You have never felt the oppression of the slave. You have never known what it is to have a master, or to see your parents and children in slavery." This knowledge, Charles Ray contended, made "colored men . . . more competent to judge in some cases in this cause" than white men. A special correspondent to the Colored American went still further in 1841 when he advocated black control of the antislavery movement. "We occupy a position, and sustain relations which [white abolitionists] cannot possibly assume. They are our allies—OURS is the battle." To this Frederick Douglass added six years later, "The man who has suffered the wrong is the man to demand redress. . . ."[9]

Accordingly, in the 1840's, the Negro convention movement focused on independent effort. Yet sporadic meetings were insufficient to bind the race together and direct it toward persistent action. Nor did attempts to create a black press fare any better. Indeed, since the late 1820's, a series of papers had supplemented the coverage of race activities which the Liberator carried, but none had lasted more than a few years at most.[10] Then, in 1847, Douglass established the North Star. His action precipitated a crisis. Although both the Liberator and the American Anti-Slavery Society had earlier recognized the need for a distinctive black press, now the Liberator, the National Anti-Slavery Standard, and the Anti-Slavery Bugle all feared the competition which Douglass' effort, firmly sustained by English financial support, represented. Douglass, however, ignored their protests. In so doing, he made public the

---

Society, Dec. 28, 1840, Herald of Freedom, n.d., copied in Liberator, Jan. 15, 1841. Samuel R. Ward to Editor, June 27, 1840, National Anti-Slavery Standard, July 2, 1840. Ibid., June 18, 1840. Colored American, June 27, July 18, 1840.

[9] Liberator, June 25, 1836. Colored American, Nov. 9, 1839. Ibid., Mar. 6, 1841. North Star, Dec. 3, 1847. In this regard it is interesting to note that James McCune Smith thought Douglass became a black man only after he began to edit his own newspaper; see Smith to Gerrit Smith, July 28, 1848, in The Life and Writings of Frederick Douglass, edited by Philip Foner (New York, 1950-1955), I, 94.

[10] For a brief discussion of the history of the black conventions see William H. Pease and Jane H. Pease, "The Negro Convention Movement," in Nathan I. Huggins, Martin Kilson, and Daniel M. Fox, eds., Key Issues in the Afro-American Experience (New York, 1971), I, 193-205; also Benjamin Quarles, The Black Abolitionists (New York, 1969), and particularly Howard H. Bell, A Survey of the Negro Convention Movement, 1830-1861 (New York, 1969). For the role of the black press see Bella Gross, "Freedom's Journal and the Rights of All," Journal of Negro History, XVII (July, 1932), 241-286; contemporary comments on its role may be found, inter alia, in Rights of All, May 29, 1829, and Liberator, June 2, 1837, June 8, 1838, and January 3, 1840. Among the papers which appeared were the Mystery (Pittsburgh), Colored Citizen (Cincinnati), Herald of Justice (New Haven), Liberty Herald (Cortland, New York), Northern Star and Freeman's Advocate (Albany), and Ram's Horn (New York).

growing distrust and agonizing suspicion between black and white abolitionists.[11]

The Douglass controversy had deep roots. Early in the 1840's Douglass had been a much-needed asset on the antislavery platform. Literate and well-spoken, he commanded his audience, while as an ex-slave with just enough of the plantation still left, he was an ideal exhibit both of the evils of slavery and of the potential of the free black. But he was also an independent man, talented and ambitious to be more than an exhibit in the antislavery cabinet. It was this independence which made his white colleagues distrust his loyalty and fear that he might join a rival antislavery faction.[12]

Consequently they were made uneasy by Douglass' successful English lecture tour in 1845. Maria Chapman of the American Anti-Slavery Society Executive Committee wrote the Irish abolitionist Richard Webb asking him to watch Douglass lest he succumb to the temptations of popularity. When the singularly inept Webb related this to Douglass, the latter wrote to Chapman in high dudgeon. He assured her of his present loyalty; but he also asserted his independence and rejected well-meaning supervision. "Of one thing I am certain," he wrote, "and that is I never gave you any just cause to distrust me. . . . If you wish to drive me from the Antislavery Society," he warned, "—put me under overseership and the work is done."[13]

It was neither surprising, therefore, that when he returned to America Douglass turned down Boston's advice not to establish a paper, nor illogical that the Garrisonians attacked him for it. Their harassment drove him to comment in an early editorial that he knew "of but few, even among professed abolitionists, who [had] entirely triumphed over their long-cherished prejudices" against blacks.[14] It was not, however, until 1851 when he differed with them over political action and the nature of the Constitution that the Boston Clique and their supporters launched their vituperative attack against his alleged ingratitude, ambition, and dishonesty.

Douglass' response to that attack varied. Sometimes he simply denied

[11] See, for example, Samuel May, Jr., to John B. Estlin, May 29, 1847, Samuel May, Jr., Papers, Antislavery Collection, Boston Public Library; Abby K. Foster to Maria W. Chapman, October 5, 1847, Weston Papers and Foster to Stephen S. Foster, Sept. 28, 1847, Foster Papers, American Antiquarian Society; also Sidney H. Gay to Richard D. Webb, June 17, 1849, typescript copy, Garrison Papers. For a less explicit comment see Chapman to Douglass, Sept. 22, 1848, in *North Star*, Dec. 8, 1848.

[12] The Douglass controversy has been much examined and is indicative of the process which led to the open challenges and clashes of the 1850's. See, for example, the study of Philip Foner, cited above, fn. 9; Benjamin Quarles, "The Breach between Garrison and Douglass," *Journal of Negro History*, XXIII (Apr., 1938), 144-154; and William H. Pease and Jane H. Pease, "Boston Garrisonians and the Problem of Frederick Douglass," *Canadian Journal of History*, II (Sept., 1967), 29-48.

[13] Frederick Douglass to Maria Chapman, Mar. 29, 1846, Weston Papers.

[14] *North Star*, Sept. 1, 1848.

,the charges; sometimes he defended his independent action; and sometimes he hurled back his own charge of racial prejudice. "Had I been ambitious of praise, ambitious of position," he countered late in 1853, "I never would have incurred the displeasure of GARRISONIANS. I should have sought their support, and flattered their pride, acknowledged their claims, prophecied smooth things, withheld distasteful criticism, shaped my course by their wishes, and basked in the sunshine of their smiles." Instead, he undertook to debate with them, invoking their "*prejudice against* [*his*] *race*" until, he said, "the question between me and my old friends would be decided . . . as between *white* and *black*, in favor of the *former*, and against the latter; the *white* man to *rise*, as an injured benefactor; and the *black* to *fall*, as a miserable ingrate."[15]

The feud was bitter and vitriolic, and it was widely aired in the anti-slavery and black press. Not unexpectedly, the Rochester editor received strong support from the Negro community. Early on, when the arguments were still largely over constitutional theory rather than personal integrity, Samuel Ward had noted the American Anti-Slavery Society's demands that "a black man must cast out devils in our way, and he must *follow* us, and then he shan't be treated as a white man; but if he dares to show manliness enough to think for himself, as to his field and mode of labor, he must be denounced." When the contest degenerated into a campaign of personal villification, public meetings of blacks from Providence to Chicago endorsed Douglass and denounced Garrison. What united the race most firmly was Garrison's statement that the anti-slavery crusade had become so complicated that it "transcended the ability of the sufferers from American slavery and prejudice, *as a class*, to keep pace with it, or to perceive what [were] its demands, or to understand the philosophy of its operations." Angry blacks scorned the charge as "insulting to the intelligence of colored men."[16]

Indeed, it was the abolitionist proclivity to rarified abstraction which most frequently alienated black support. Douglass, speaking for his fellows, found nothing "so profound and mysterious" in the theory of anti-slavery "that the colored people of the country [could] not understand it." Their whole experience reinforced their awareness of slavery and prejudice "so that while *theoretically* and *abstractly*, the cause of anti-slavery is the cause of universal man, it is *practically and peculiarly* in this country the cause of the colored men. . . ." Still more pointedly James McCune Smith argued that as long as abolitionist concern with philosophy allowed "prejudice and caste to remain upon the statute

[15] *Frederick Douglass' Paper*, Dec. 9, 1853.

[16] *Impartial Citizen*, May 31, 1851. For various meetings defending Douglass, see *Frederick Douglass' Paper*, Nov. 1853-Jan., 1854, *passim*. For Garrison's attack and the rejoinder, see *Liberator*, Dec. 16, 1853; and *Frederick Douglass' Paper*, Jan. 13, 1854.

books" of the free states, the antislavery movement would be paralyzed.[17]

Nor did impatience with discrimination stop at the statute book.
Many blacks saw in white abolitionists' failure to open employment opportunities to them another example in which concrete performance
fell behind abstract principle.[18] It was only factional feuding in 1839 between the anti-Garrisonian Massachusetts Abolition Society and the Garrisonian Massachusetts Anti-Slavery Society which induced the latter
to assist Boston blacks in their quest for jobs. The Abolition Society
had appointed black clergyman Jehiel C. Beman to aid new arrivals, to
get them into schools, to secure them apprenticeships, and to find them
permanent jobs. The *Liberator's* initial response was to label Beman a
traitor to his race for deserting Garrison. Significantly, however, within
weeks, the Massachusetts Anti-Slavery Society announced that it had recently inaugurated in its offices a job exchange service for blacks.[19]

Two years later, in 1842, the black journal *Northern Star and Freeman's
Advocate* of Albany chastised white abolitionists for not opening "every
avenue and destroying every barrier in their power, which is closed
against us and retards our progression. . . ." It pledged itself to "expose
what we consider downright inconsistency, if not base hypocrisy," until
abolitionists secured or provided the race employment opportunities
and admission to white schools. A decade later the harmony of the annual meeting of the American and Foreign Anti-Slavery Society was disrupted when Edward Clark and James McCune Smith charged that its
white members refused to hire black clerks or lend money to well-
trained Negroes who wished to open their own businesses. In 1855 the
National Council of Colored People aired the same charges. And just
before the Civil War Henry Highland Garnet asserted that those whites
who did hire blacks were generally not abolitionists.[20]

Such charges were as serious as they were harsh; yet neither the records of the antislavery societies nor the actions of white abolitionists do
much to refute them. It was only in 1840 that Garrison hired William
Nell to serve as a clerk in the Massachusetts Anti-Slavery Society office.
And, three years later, when funds ran short, it was he whom the Society discharged to save money. Although Nell did not break with the

[17] Frederick Douglass' Paper, Dec. 9, 1853, and Feb. 9, 1855. For a general discussion of the issue see John L. Thomas, *The Liberator: William Lloyd Garrison*
(Boston, 1963), pp. 152-153. See also James McCune Smith's attack on Garrison
and Oliver Johnson, *Frederick Douglass' Paper*, Oct. 5, 1855.

[18] For a general discussion see Leon Litwack, "The Abolitionist Dilemma: The
Antislavery Movement and the Northern Negro," *New England Quarterly*, XXXIV
(Mar., 1961), 50-73.

[19] *Massachusetts Abolitionist, Sept.* 12, 1839; and *Liberator*, Feb. 28, 1840. For
black support of Garrison see *Liberator*, Apr. 3, 1840; and *Massachusetts Abolitionist*, Apr. 2, 1840.

[20] *Northern Star and Freeman's Advocate*, Mar. 31, 1842. *Frederick Douglass'
Paper*, May 27, 1852, and May 18, 1855. *Weekly Anglo-African*, Sept. 17, 1859.

white Garrisonians, this action touched off a rash of black complaints against antislavery job discrimination. Subsequently Thomas Van Rensselaer, Martin Delany, Samuel Ward, and James McCune Smith, spokesmen for a variety of black factions, all publicized the failure of antislavery organizations to employ blacks. Delany also charged that even the honorific offices in the antislavery societies were seldom offered to Negroes; and the records of the societies bear out his charge.[21]

Blacks also resented compromises made at their expense in the greater interests of reform. Led by Douglass, the National Council in 1855 condemned an abolitionism which denounced "Slavery at the South" while it scouted as "delusive and hurtful all schemes for the moral and social elevation of the free colored people of the North." Likewise Douglass' assistant editor William Watkins challenged the integrity of a Providence anti-slavery meeting because it shunned having a black speaker lest he endanger its fund raising. Finally, when Lucy Stone gave a women's rights address to a Philadelphia audience from which Negroes were excluded, Charles Reason wondered "whether there is a common cause between us and the Abolitionists, or whether, as circumstances demand, they believe it their right to forsake us for the benefit of other reforms."[22]

Black's suspicions were further fed by white criticism of their militant action on behalf of civil rights. When, in 1836, Boston Negroes disrupted judicial proceedings to aid the escape of two women being held as fugitives, the Massachusetts Anti-Slavery Society denounced their "tumultuous conduct" and condemned, with "decided disapprobation," their unseemly behavior. Seven years later, in 1843, Maria Chapman, bluestocking leader of the Boston Clique, chastened Henry Highland Garnet for his Address to the Slaves, in which he urged them to rise against their masters and strike for their freedom. Suggesting that Garnet had been badly counselled by whites thus to dismiss Garrisonian principles of nonviolence, Chapman invited Garnet's incensed retort. Who was

[21] *Massachusetts Abolitionist*, Apr. 2, 1840. [Maria W. Chapman to Maria Child, 1843?], Child Papers, Antislavery Collection, Boston Public Library. *North Star*, Feb. 25, 1848. Samuel R. Ward to Douglass, Mar., 1855, *Frederick Douglass' Paper*, Apr. 13, 1855. Martin R. Delany, *The Condition, Elevation, Emigration, and Destiny of the Colored People of the United States Politically Considered* (Philadelphia, 1852), pp. 24-30.

While one may argue that white leaders of antislavery organizations were predominantly preachers, professional reformers, lawyers, and the like, with few jobs at their disposal, there is little record to show that they made significant efforts to find employment for blacks in the commercial and craft establishments of their followers. Nor do their conventions and annual reports show significant application to the economic problems of free blacks. Indeed the entire antislavery movement, with few exceptions, ignored as well the economics of slavery and economic action which might be taken against it.

[22] *Frederick Douglass' Paper*, May 18, 1855, Mar. 2, 1858, and Feb. 10, 1854. McCune Smith also charged that the *Liberator* looked to its own profit when it chose agents, *ibid.*, Jan. 26, 1855.

she to presume to direct him? What distinguished her abolitionism from "abject slavery"?[23]

By the 1850's, black impatience with the relatively passive role expected by their white colleagues was undeniably clear. Samuel Ward, in reviewing his own life experience, charged many white abolitionists with having "no idea that a black man should feel towards and speak of his tormenters as a white man would concerning his." Presbyterian clergyman J. W. C. Pennington refused to heed the *Pennsylvania Freeman*'s prescription for the kind of antislavery action he should take. He would not be thus directed and used. "I despise, in my soul, the thought of being a rest for the rifle of sharp shooters. In an honest war, let every man load, steady his own muzzle, and pull his own trigger. If I wish to be loaded, and fired into an enemy's ranks, I will do it myself." And, when the antislavery societies refused to support the National Council's plan for a manual labor school, Douglass took it as another instance of pretended friendship from those who would "pat . . . on the back" Negroes who knew their place but who would villify those who "step[ped] beyond" it.[24]

These black perceptions of white attitudes made a separatist response increasingly important in the years before the Civil War. In 1855 William Watkins argued that the time had come for blacks to control the antislavery movement. In the past the Negro had depended on white abolitionists and had acted as a hewer of wood and a drawer of water. Now blacks must take the lead. If, after twenty-five years they had accomplished nothing, then whites could justifiably assume that they were incompetent. At the same time, James McCune Smith asserted that the time had come "when our people must assume the rank of a first-rate power in the battle against caste and Slavery; it is emphatically our battle; no one else can fight it for us. . . ." White abolitionists, Garnet added in 1859, could prepare "the public mind for the full and free discussion of [abolition]"; but that was all. Thereafter it was up to blacks.[25]

[23] *Liberator*, Aug. 6, 1836. *Ibid.*, Sept. 22, 1843; and Henry Highland Garnet to Maria Chapman, Nov. 17, 1843, *ibid.*, Dec. 8, 1843. See also a similar contretemps with Lewis Tappan, Tappan to Douglass, Dec. 6, 1856, Letterpress, Lewis Tappan Papers, Library of Congress. Some white abolitionists did, after the Mexican War and especially in the 1850's, show considerable sympathy with the idea of slave rebellion. This was not so much a response to black arguments as to political circumstances generated by the addition of new slave territory and the operation of the Fugitive Slave Law of 1850. See Jane H. Pease and William H. Pease, "Abolitionists and Confrontation in the 1850's," *Journal of American History*, LVIII (Mar, 1972), 923-937.

[24] Samuel Ringgold Ward, *Autobiography of a Fugitive Negro: His Anti-Slavery Labours in the United States, Canada, and England* (London, 1855), p. 13. *Frederick Douglass' Paper*, May 4, 1855. *Liberator*, July 27, 1855. For bitterness against Garrison on these grounds see also James McCune Smith in *Frederick Douglass' Paper*, Feb. 16, 1855; and Douglass in *Liberator*, Nov. 23, 1855, as copied from *National Anti-Slavery Standard*, n.d.

[25] *Frederick Douglass' Paper*, Feb. 2, 9, 1855 and May 18, 1855. *Weekly Anglo-*

Two years before Martin Delany's 1854 plan for a separate black nation was endorsed by a Negro convention and while free blacks almost universally still rejected migration to Africa, a series of public clashes over the American and Foreign Anti-Slavery Society's tentative advocacy of emigration drove home the meaning of such assertions. George T. Downing, Newport, Rhode Island innkeeper, questioned the rationale of the society's new position. Why, he asked, should the Society aid those who emigrated while it ignored free blacks who remained in the United States. "The colored man," he argued, "does not want you to elevate him," for that he can do himself. But he does want recognition when he rises, and he demands an end to being portrayed as a perpetual menial. Smith was even more blunt. He rejoiced that the Society had taken "the last prop . . . from under the colored people." Now, he continued, "They will . . . be likely to stand forth in their naked manhood to resist oppression, as resist we will. . . ." It looked to the New York physician as though the American and Foreign Anti-Slavery Society was eager for black glory in Africa but hesitant to recognize the "manhood in the colored race here in the United States."[26]

Inevitably antislavery groups vigorously replied to such challenges. The *National Anti-Slavery Standard* was indignant when Smith charged that antislavery societies omitted blacks from their lecture series. It noted that William Wells Brown had appeared in the series in question. Further, it accused Smith and Douglass of acting as Herod and Pontius Pilate to the Christ-like antislavery establishment.[27]

Regularly thereafter *Frederick Douglass' Paper* and the *Standard* exchanged accusations and innuendoes. Smith charged that Garrisonians gave different treatment to blacks and whites who disagreed with them. For the latter, there was gentle chiding; for the former, devastating denunciation. The *Standard's* form of reference for whites was "gentlemen"; for blacks, "coloured men." To this the *Standard's* assistant editor, Oliver Johnson, responded in kind, whereupon Douglass charged him with a "native contempt for negroes."[28]

The dispute revealed not only a high degree of mutual antagonism but also suggested white preference for light-skinned Negroes. In one of his responses to Johnson, Smith asserted, not altogether accurately, that the Garrisonians had no black men in their ranks—only "[William Wells] Brown, [Charles] Remond and [Robert] Purvis [who] are all

---

African, Sept. 17, 1859. For a searing indictment of white abolitionists' obtuseness about black needs see James McCune Smith in *Frederick Douglass' Paper*, Jan. 19, 1855.

[26] These responses are all in *Frederick Douglass' Paper*, May 27, 1852.

[27] *National Anti-Slavery Standard*, Dec. 23, 1854. Smith had written in *Frederick Douglass' Paper*, December 15, 1854, under the pseudonym "Communipaw."

[28] *National Anti-Slavery Standard*, Jan. 13, 1855. *Frederick Douglass' Paper*, Jan. 19, Feb. 2, 1855.

yellow men."[29] Their exact position in the antislavery movement was revealed by the experience of Purvis at the annual meeting of the American Society in 1854. A leader of the Philadelphia black community, he was a man of means and education. Somewhat reluctantly he had agreed to speak on this occasion. Thereupon Garrison, always eager to get maximum mileage from Negro performance, carefully pointed out in his introduction that Purvis was indeed a Negro, despite the lightness of his skin. Somewhat later the prominent Unitarian clergyman, William Furness, commended Purvis for having married a woman darker than he. "MR. Furness," reported the *Liberator*, "said that Mr. Purvis was wealthy enough to purchase connection with a white skin; but, with credit to himself, he saw fit not to do so." Purvis was indignant. Garrison's "allusion" was, he noted forcefully, "unnecessary" and certainly it was "no great compliment . . . to say that he was honest enough to acknowledge his blood." Then, proclaiming his pride in his "blood," he concluded by asserting that Mr. Furness was distinctly out of order, and he "hoped that nothing of the sort would be said again."[30]

For thirty years the tension generated by differing attitudes and priorities of white and black abolitionists strained the antislavery movement. Despite the covert and overt racial antagonism, many Negroes remained faithful to the white dominated societies. But many others rejected both the plans and the personnel of reform organizations. By turning to Negro conventions and separatist action, they strove for practical accomplishment toward ending slavery and achieving civil rights, economic opportunity, and useful education. Their action was prescribed in part by priorities and methods which differed from those of the antislavery societies. But, if pragmatism, political reality, and ideological commitment shaped, in the antebellum years, a self-consciously black movement, so too did the attitudes of white abolitionists.

[29] *Frederick Douglass' Paper*, Jan. 19, 1855. For similar charges see the comments of George T. Downing in *ibid.*, for the same date and for Dec. 22, 1854.

[30] Robert Purvis to William L. Garrison, Apr. 16, 1854, Garrison Papers. *Liberator*, May 19, 26, 1854. *Frederick Douglass' Paper*, May 19, 1854.

128

LEWIS PERRY
State University of New York at Buffalo

Versions of Anarchism in the Antislavery Movement

IN THE LATE 1880s THE FAMOUS RUSSIAN NOVELIST AND CHRISTIAN ANAR-
chist, Leo Tolstoy, tried to recover the history of American anarchism
before the Civil War.[1] Tolstoy's own efforts to live according to the Bible
had led to the repudiation of government, and after the publication of
My Religion in 1884 one of the sons of William Lloyd Garrison wrote
to him about the striking similarity between the views expressed in that
book and those once espoused by the great abolitionist. But in response
to Tolstoy's request for further information the younger Garrison had
to confess that he knew of no reformer who had sustained an interest in
the old doctrine called nonresistance. Five years later, Tolstoy had a
chance to correspond with Adin Ballou, a faithful Christian nonresistant
whom the Garrisonians had forgotten. But Ballou was bitter and argumentative; not much could be learned from him. Judging from the
obscurity into which nonresistance had fallen in America as elsewhere,
the Russian wondered whether the world was determined to ignore the
message of the New Testament. For Tolstoy was interested in the beliefs
of Garrison and Ballou not as the odd inventions of a few Americans but
as possible expressions of a universal Christianity.[2]

Tolstoy did not gain much information about the anarchism of the
abolitionists. He guessed that abolitionists had discarded the doctrines
of anarchism in the belief that they embarrassed the cause of the slave.
Because the country had evaded those doctrines, it went through a fra-
tricidal war which put a superficial end to slavery but left a hideous

---

[1] An earlier version of this paper was presented to the New York American Studies
Association in Rochester, N. Y., May 6, 1967.

[2] Lyof N. Tolstoi, *The Kingdom of God is Within You* (New York, 1899), pp. 4,
11, 19; Count Leo Tolstoy and Rev. Adin Ballou, "The Christian Doctrine of Non-
Resistance . . . Unpublished Correspondence Compiled by Rev. Lewis G. Wilson,"
Arena, III (Dec. 1890), 1-12.

pattern of interracial violence. One thing Tolstoy understood perfectly from his own anarchist perspective: Garrison's followers had been anarchistic not in addition to being against slavery but because they were against slavery. He put the matter succinctly:

> Garrison, a man enlightened by the Christian teaching, having begun with the practical aim of striving against slavery, soon understood that the cause of slavery was not the casual temporary seizure by the Southerners of a few millions of negroes, but the ancient and universal recognition, contrary to Christian teaching, of the right of coercion by some men in regard to others. . . . Garrison understood . . . that the only irrefutable argument against slavery is a denial of any man's right over the liberty of another under any conditions whatsoever.[3]

Since Tolstoy's time the anarchism of the abolitionists has perhaps been rescued from obscurity; at least the term "anarchism" appears regularly in the literature on Garrison. Acknowledgment of the fact that Garrison opposed government, however, has not necessarily meant that the reasons for his opposition to government are understood. Lacking Tolstoy's perspective, historians have not known quite what to make of Garrison's anarchism and have been unable to state its relationship to his antislavery. Those interpretations kindest to Garrison suggest that he became an anarchist solely out of impatience with a particular government which paid no heed to his demands. But the more important point is that Garrison knew, or thought he knew, that no human government could respond to the demands of a Christian. Unkind interpretations choose to suggest that Garrison was mentally unbalanced. A typical attitude is that antislavery sentiment can be explained by the presence of the *social* evil of slavery but that anarchist ideas must be explained by the *personal* psychology of the reformer. Kind and unkind interpretations alike assume that anarchism represented a deviation from antislavery.

I propose to suspend this assumption for a while. I would like to speculate on the possibility that anarchism was, as Tolstoy understood, doctrinally related to antislavery; it would then be no surprise that anarchism emerged in many versions throughout ante-bellum reform. Anarchism, it will appear, was not merely the quirk of a handful of eccentric Bostonians, but was, instead, one logical outcome of the Protestant traditions expressed in antislavery. To advance these speculations, I will first consider the views of Garrison and those closest to him, and then inspect some other varieties of anarchism in the 1840s.

[3] Leo Tolstoy, "Introduction to a Short Biography of William Lloyd Garrison," trans. Aylmer Maude, *Tolstoy Centenary Edition* (London, 1935), XX, 577-78.

Although Garrison's views are often catalogued as Christian anarchism, the theology behind them has not often been discovered. Partly the blame belongs with the abolitionists themselves: the Garrisonians called their most anarchistic organization the New England Non-Resistance Society, and instead of anarchism, a term which they lacked in any favorable sense, they advocated nonresistance. Consequently they focused attention on their commitment to what we call nonviolence rather than on the doctrines underlying that commitment. Nonviolence was not the basic issue: opponents of Garrisonian anarchism—religious abolitionists such as Orange Scott, Theodore Dwight Weld and William Goodell—also preached nonresistance among men. This was "old-fashioned" non-resistance, turning the other cheek. But they abhorred what they named "no-governmentism," the idea that government violated the Biblical injunctions against violence.[4] At this point it should be clear that non-violence was less important than the theology in which it was couched.

For their part, the Garrisonian nonresistants resented and repudiated the name of no-governmentism. Here we must attend to them carefully. They insisted that they were striving for, and placing themselves under, the only true and effective government: the government of God. They insisted that they opposed not government, but human pretensions to govern. I find, sometimes to my regret, little sense of humor among them, and there was seldom much deliberate irony in this insistence. Henry C. Wright, the most dogged nonresistant, was deadly serious when he complained of his audiences that they "seemed to think . . . that all who refuse 'to acknowledge allegiance to *human* governments,' but feel it a duty 'to obey God rather than man,' are 'no-government men' and 'jacobins':—to be under the government of Christ—of *moral principle*— was, as has been taught by the religious and political newspapers of the land, and by the American Peace Society, to be under 'no-government'— to be in a state of anarchy."[5] As far as Wright was concerned, simply to state this view was to refute it. Adin Ballou, the best philosopher among the nonresistants, developed this line of reasoning more fully: "there is," he wrote, "strictly speaking, no such thing as human government." The goal of the nonresistance movement was "true moral order," forcing the physical world into a right and orderly condition. "Therefore, all depends on a supreme moral authority, or government. This must be inherently *divine*. . . . It is not original in any created being." Was it not plain, then, that the direction of nonresistance was not away from

---

[4] Donald G. Mathews, *Slavery and Methodism: A Chapter in American Morality, 1780-1845* (Princeton, 1965), p. 161; Benjamin P. Thomas, *Theodore Weld: Crusader for Freedom* (New Brunswick, N. J., 1950), p. 146; *Liberator*, June 12, 1840, p. 2; June 26, 1840, p. 4.

[5] *Non-Resistant*, Mar. 2, 1839, p. 2.

government but toward a government of the highest authority? Ballou wanted to turn the tables on the assailants of nonresistance. He claimed that only "atheists and *would-be Deicides*— . . . the genuine *no government*—*no government*—*ists"*—believed in any human right to govern; man must be the subject of God.[6]

It has been necessary to quote these turgid writers at length because the temptation to equate their views with those of modern spokesmen for nonviolence has obscured their beliefs. They were not being ironical when they identified themselves with true government and their opponents with no government. On the contrary, they were speaking earnestly from a theological viewpoint that may best be described as antinomian. They were Christians who were concerned for the coming of the millennium and who understood that the millennium was the government of God. How did God govern? Directly, through the human heart. And any intermediary authorities between the individual and God were rivals to God's sovereignty and impediments to the coming of the millennium.

The term antinomian is in some ways more useful than the term anarchist. As the quotations from Wright and Ballou indicate, the Garrisonian nonresistants opposed anarchy and yearned for government. If there is a paradox here, it is a paradox at the heart of their faith. They were anarchists—or, more properly, we would call them anarchists—because they detested anarchy. In their categories, human government, so called, was synonymous with anarchy and antithetical to "true moral order." Once we understand this, we will have no difficulty with the relationship between their kind of anarchism and antislavery.

Bronson Alcott, whose enthusiasm for the reforms is less well known than his oracular presence among the Transcendentalists, caught the spirit of nonresistance more simply and clearly than anyone else, and his speeches stood out at nonresistance conventions. "What guide have I but my conscience?" he asked in 1839.

> Church and State are responsible to *me;* not I to them. They cease to deserve our veneration from the moment that they violate our consciences. We then protest against them. We withdraw ourselves from them. I believe that this is what is now going on. . . . I look upon the Non-Resistance Society as an assertion of the right to self-government. Why should I employ a church to write my creed or a state to govern me? Why not write my own creed? Why not govern myself?[7]

Antinomianism consistently led to this point: the uncontested sovereignty of God meant that the individual must follow his own best light. The

[6] *Christian Non-Resistance, In All Its Important Bearings, Illustrated and Defended* (Philadelphia, 1846), pp. 84-85, 214.
[7] *Non-Resistant,* Oct. 19, 1839, p. 4.

only government which does not violate God's sovereignty is the individual's sovereignty over himself. Thus Alcott urged other delegates to ignore government, rather than combat it, and to fix their attention on the great lawgiver in the human soul.

Similar assumptions may be found in the Declaration of Sentiments that Garrison composed for nonresistants. Most simply he presented the syllogism: the New Testament forbids the use of force; government is upheld by force; therefore a Christian must abstain from government. But more was at stake here than literal obedience to Scripture. Here was a millennial appeal away from human government and toward the "one KING and LAWGIVER, one JUDGE and RULER of mankind." The declaration went on to stress the design of nonresistants to "hasten the time" when Christ shall rule directly. To this end, they accepted in their individual lives the belief that "whatever the gospel is designed to destroy at any period of the world, being contrary to it, ought now to be abandoned." [8]

In short, the goal of the Garrisonians was not to eliminate specific earthly evils. Their goal was to renounce all authoritarian relationships among men; it was the very principle of authority that was sinful. That is why abolitionists would not compromise nonresistance to speed the course of antislavery; such a compromise represented a digression from their quest. Unless we understand this, much of the behavior of the nonresistants must appear quixotic. For example, when the Massachusetts legislature revoked some death penalties, ended some militia allowances and passed resolutions against slavery, nonresistants were not gratified. On the contrary, Edmund Quincy spent an editorial worrying over the soul of the abolitionist legislator, George Bradburn. "We believe he could as well hold a slave innocently, as to exercise the power of making laws enforced by penalties, without detriment to his soul; for both relations spring from the same false principle—the assumed right of man to have dominion over man." [9]

Like statements appear repeatedly. Slavery, government and violence were considered identical in principle: all were sinful invasions of God's prerogatives; all tried to set one man between another man and his rightful ruler. In a sense we might even say that these men opposed slavery more as a symbol than as an institution. Slavery served as a paradigm of all human authority, the condition in which one man takes possession of another and removes him from God's sovereignty. Nor was this all a question of abstract theology. The Garrisonians were intent on the prob-

[8] *Non-Resistant*, Jan. 1839, p. 1. The portion of the Declaration reprinted in *The Era of Reform, 1830-1860*, ed., Henry Steele Commager (Princeton, 1960), pp. 172-74, misleadingly omits some of this argument.
[9] *Non-Resistant*, Apr. 20, 1839, p. 3.

lem of order and security, as their obsession with the most violent and immoral aspects of slavery ought to suggest. In their view, the fact that men tried to rule one another explained the prevalence of violence and bloodshed on this earth. Their logic unfolded categorically: to end slavery was to end all coercion; to end all coercion was to release the millennial power of God; to end coercion, again, was to secure peace and order on earth; and to secure peace was, of course, to realize the millennium. Schematically, slavery, government or coercion was the intermediate stage between self-government and divine government. Self-government and divine government reinforced one another, but the intermediate stage was "anarchy" (in the bad sense of pandemonium) in which men were not under moral law. All that was needed to usher in peace was to expel the intermediaries who pretended to keep the peace. These thoughts struck the Garrisonians with mathematical clarity. Anarchism, in the good sense of self-government, was not a dilution of antislavery, but synonymous with it. Ending slavery by civil law, or any other coercion, was a ludicrous contradiction in terms.

It must be admitted, however, that most of the Garrisonians in time lost sight of the simplicity of these definitions. They had always seemed a trifle uneasy when pressed to demonstrate that their commitment to nonresistance did not neglect the plight of the Negro slave. By the mid-1840s many had joined in what was called disunionism, a movement concentrating its attack on the proslavery Constitution and federal government. This movement, though historians have frequently confused it with nonresistance, actually started from quite different assumptions. Since disunionism was scarcely a version of anarchism, it may be passed over quickly in this article. But certain contrasts may help to clarify nonresistant anarchism.

While nonresistance repudiated all human governments as sinful invasions of God's authority, disunionism assumed a divine obligation for men to institute moral governments. Its specific demand was for the North to withdraw from the union in order to establish a new federation not dirtied by the sin of slavery. Here was not antinomianism but the old intolerance of Massachusetts. The government was tolerating slavery, and it was as true now as it had been in the 17th century that "to authorize an untruth, by a Toleration of State, is to build a Sconce against the walls of Heaven, to batter God out of his Chaire." [10] In the 1840s the implications of this sentiment were separatist; by the 1860s they might well prove authoritarian. Let me repeat, to underscore my present purposes, that, although disunionism was bent on purity and the sovereignty

[10] Nathaniel Ward, as quoted in *The Puritans: A Sourcebook of Their Writings*, eds. Perry Miller and Thomas H. Johnson (paperback, New York, 1963), I, 229.

of God, it was not anarchistic and it was almost antithetical to non-resistance.

In fact, it was only in the minds of political abolitionists that dis-unionism seemed synonymous with nonresistance. Wendell Phillips, the chief spokesman for disunionism and never a nonresistant, ridiculed the logic by which dislike of the present federal government was equated with dislike of all government. It was "arrogance" to assume the Con-stitution so perfect "that one who dislikes it could never be satisfied with any form of government whatsoever." [11] Moreover, there were a number of nonresistants who stayed wary of the new movement. For example, an Ohioan wrote Garrison that he too would be pleased to see "the masses" in the North pull out of their compact with the South "even for the com-paratively unworthy object of establishing another arbitrary government in its stead," but this was nothing that a nonresistant should work for. It was time people learned that, slavery or no slavery, voting is wrong and "genuine government does not come from ballot-boxes." [12] But few abolitionist leaders could keep this distinction in mind: the leading Garrisonians gave to disunionism the energy formerly given to non-resistance, although they did not consider these causes identical. Dis-unionism was a temporary antislavery tactic; nonresistance promised the millennial end of all human bondage to sin.

The only prominent nonresistant to denounce disunionism (a good many obscure men did so) was Nathaniel P. Rogers. Reasoning and moral influence could not take effect, he thought, behind a barrage of threats. In any case, he did not care about the political union; what sus-tained slavery was "the moral union," the "agreement in the hearts of the whole people that the colored man shall not have liberty among us." The Constitution was irrelevant to antislavery. Disunion, furthermore, would mean war and unfavorable circumstances for ending any moral evil. (Rogers still looked forward to a day when the union would dis-integrate because people no longer believed in government—a vision once emphasized by almost all Garrisonians.) Rogers found the dis-unionists now to be "political" in three ways: they voted on slogans to characterize themselves; they could not keep their minds off the Constitu-tion; and their remedy for slavery was a disunity beginning with ballots and bound to conclude with bullets.[13]

Rogers was no ordinary nonresistant. He moved through antislavery and nonresistance to become the most respected prophet of what was widely known as come-outerism. And the term come-outerism, as Thomas

[11] *Can Abolitionists Vote or Take Office Under the United States Constitution?* (New York, 1845), pp. 3-4.
[12] *Liberator,* Nov. 2, 1855, p. 4.
[13] *Herald of Freedom,* June 14, 1844, p. 2; July 12, 1844, p. 2; June 6, 1845, p. 3.

Wentworth Higginson reminded readers at the end of the century, was as familiar before the war "as is that of the Salvation Army today." [14] Yet historians have given the movement little careful attention, perhaps because come-outerism manifested itself in many different ways. If we are interested in the versions of anarchism in ante-bellum reform, however, we should at least enumerate these different manifestations.

The term "come-outer" was familiar from the revivals, where it signified a "new light," one who stepped forward to a public profession of faith. Other significant sources of the term were favorite apocalyptic texts from Scripture, such as the angel's prophecy of Babylon's fall. "Come out of her, my people, that ye be not partakers of her sins, and that ye receive not of her plagues" (Rev. 18:4). The first manifestation of come-outerism, then, was a revivalistic, millennial tendency in rural New England, concerning which we have little first-hand information but which for a while dominated the imaginations of abolitionists. Rural come-outers were reported to strut on fences, to renounce money and property, and even to go naked in the summer. Certainly it was their intention to escape from church, state and every form of "social bondage," and to enter into the condition where the saints were free to recognize one another. [15]

Secondly, the name was appropriated by famed abolitionists, even though they substituted the convention hall for the religious ecstasy of the rural come-outers. Frederick Douglass played skillfully on the religious metaphors of bondage—he was a fugitive "in slavery"—and his audiences saw in his escape to northern freedom the model of their religious purposes of self-discovery. [16] Garrison's example may have been less dramatic, but he too called himself a come-outer from creeds and ceremonies. [17] The term extended, thirdly, to "Jerusalem wildcat" churches arising in imitation of Theodore Parker's society in Boston, free congregations centered around nonaligned ministers. In the mind of Thomas Wentworth Higginson at least, this movement sprang not only from the needs of ante-bellum reform but also from the ancient Puritan concern for the voluntary laying-on of hands. [18] In a fourth version, come-outerism

[14] *Cheerful Yesterdays* (Boston and New York, 1898), pp. 115-17.

[15] Henry C. Kittredge, *Cape Cod: Its People and Their History* (Boston and New York, 1930), pp. 257-60, 288-91; Thomas Low Nichols, *Forty Years of American Life* (London, 1864), II, 45-46; P. Douglass Gorrie, *The Churches and Sects of the United States* (New York, 1850), pp. 224 ff.; John Hayward. *The Book of Religions; Comprising the Views, Creeds, Sentiments, or Opinions, of All the Principal Religious Sects in the World . . .* (Concord, N.H., 1845), pp. 177-81.

[16] *Herald of Freedom*, Feb. 16, 1844, p. 2; Parker Pillsbury, *Acts of the Anti-Slavery Apostles* (Boston, 1884), pp. 161-62.

[17] *Liberator*, Jan. 12, 1844, p. 4.

[18] *Cheerful Yesterdays*, pp. 113-14, 130.

referred to antislavery people who seceded from supposedly proslavery denominations and, in effect, built new ones. There may have been a dozen such ventures, mostly ignored by historians and yet providing interesting connections between the moral problem of slavery and theories of ecclesiastical reform.[19] Confused with these secessions was the idea promoted by New York abolitionists, particularly Gerrit Smith, that there could rightfully be only one church in any locality and that higher bodies might represent geographical areas, but never doctrinal or "sectarian" disagreements.[20] This was known as the "Christian" or "Union" movement, and it reminds us that the general purpose of come-outerism was not the introduction of new sects into the denominational competition but the removal of earthly institutions between religious people and God.

All of these different come-outer tendencies came together in August 1840 at the Groton Convention on Christian Union, with Edmund Quincy one officer, Bronson Alcott one of the most vigorous participants, Theodore Parker an observer, and a motley assembly of about 275 New Yorkers and New Englanders. According to a neutral report: "The house seemed to divide into two general parties—the one maintaining that local Churches were a sort of divine organization, with peculiar authority and prerogatives—and the other that they were a purely human organization, or voluntary association, which could not in the nature of things assume any authority or prerogatives not possessed by the individuals of which they were composed." [21] Both parties rejected notions of outside authority, but within anarchistic doctrines there was plenty of leeway for antagonism. Progress from the revival to the millennium would have to be dialectical.

Compared to come-outerism, nonresistance was safely abstract: it expressed itself mainly in repudiation of the idea of government. Come-outerism focused attention on the role of individuals and organization in society renewed: consequently it was a tougher test of anarchistic tendencies and it ended in the most unmodified anarchist and antinomian statements to be found in ante-bellum reform. The best of these statements were provided by Nathaniel P. Rogers. And Rogers did more than merely separate antislavery from political action or institutionalized religion. He ultimately decided that even the voluntary reform

19 The best treatment of this subject remains that in William Goodell, *Slavery and Anti-Slavery; A History of the Great Struggle in Both Hemispheres* . . . (New York, 1852), pp. 487-516.
20 See Smith's *Abstract of the Argument, in the Public Discussion of the Question: "Are the Christians of a Given Community the Church of Such Community"* (Albany, 1847).
21 *Practical Christian*, Sept. 1, 1840, p. 2.

societies involved too much direction and authority to be free of the taint of slavery.

There were two stages in Rogers' approach to this conclusion. First came the standard antinomian scheme with which we already are familiar: to serve God, men, even when acting together, must be thrown back on their own self-government. Soon, however, Rogers came to suspect even the authority of God. The magic that made free meetings possible had its source in human faculties, and even the demands of God had to meet the test of private judgments. For example, it was a contradiction in terms, according to Rogers, to call for the freedom of the slave on grounds of Scriptural authority.[22] Thus Rogers arrived at the most unmitigated anarchism of all the abolitionists, an anarchism brooking no leadership from any quarter of heaven or earth. Before he died, he fell into bitter antagonism with the Boston Garrisonians.

Rogers drew on support in two places: in New Hampshire where he himself led the antislavery society, and in Lynn, which seems to have been the center of the most radical reform. The come-outers of Lynn, in fact, were known as no-organizationists, and they too suspected any form of association that was not thoroughly spontaneous. It was one of their editorial voices who gave the clearest definition of the paradox of antinomianism. "I know of no more strenuous advocates of 'law and order' than that class of persons called 'no-organizationists,'" wrote Henry Clapp Jr.

It is *because* they love law and hate anarchy, that they resist the unreasonable edicts of self-constituted authority, and deny infallibility to that God of organization, *the popular voice.* They see nothing of the beauty of order in a gathering of men and women, each of whom is bitted, and bridled, and kept in check, by an officious chairman. But they do see the beauty of order, in its highest development, where the same people, attracted together by a common thought, exhibit that true 'peace,' whose only 'bond' is 'unity of spirit.' [23]

But Lynn and New Hampshire together were no match for Boston: Rogers died in bitterness and defeat.

Rogers had taken antinomianism beyond an attack on the federal government. Therefore he had raised questions ducked by most of Garrisonian nonresistance. Specifically, he had questioned the authority of local and voluntary institutions, and thus had pointed out an issue of tremendous significance to all abolitionists. Abolitionists had claimed

22 *A Collection of the Miscellaneous Writings of Nathaniel Peabody Rogers* (Manchester, N. H. and Boston, 1849), pp. 280-84, 311-13.
23 *The Pioneer: Or Leaves from an Editor's Portfolio* (Lynn, 1846), p. 152.

that the end of slavery must be spelled out in the peaceful conversion of the slaveholders as part of the culmination of the history of God's work of redemption. They had claimed, moreover, that the perpetuation of the institution of slavery was due to the existence of sinful dispositions in the North as well as the South. All of this underlay the original declaration of sentiments of antislavery, and it is not hard to see how it was converted into nonresistance, into a disavowal of governmental sanctions. Force cannot work conversion. But these beliefs could also have fostered a kind of defeatism: after all, Southerners defended slavery on the grounds that in the state of man since Adam's fall it was essential to social order that some men control others. Abolitionists could name slavery sin and thereby vilify it, but could they show any present escape from it? Could they clear their own institutions of complicity in sin—enough so as to be able to indicate a way out of slavery? Nonresistance had barely reached this question (it had only issued attacks on the formal sinfulness of coercion), and disunionism, on the other hand, too completely freed the North of intrinsic guilt, guilt not coming from connection with the South. For the come-outers it was presumably only the elect who could be trusted outside of social coercions, while Rogers and the no-organizationists seem to have imputed a sentimental reliability to all men, a conception that finally ceased to be Christian. The central problem—if we regard the movement in terms of Christian anarchism—was, however, to show a way out of sin and slavery that did not ignore or smugly exonerate the institutions of the North, that did not predestine half the world to slavery, and still did not negate the sovereignty of God. Two solutions were given for this problem: one of which had to do with the Hopedale Community and the other with the Liberty Party.

Both of these solutions were millennial, as they had to be, starting as they did from concern with the enslavement of man in sin and human government since Adam's fall. Adin Ballou's solution was community. Unlike the Garrisonians, he did not denounce present-day governments. Rather, he agreed with Southerners that such institutions were necessary evils. It is, he told the nonresistance society, "among the irrevocable ordinations of God, that all who will not be governed by *Him* shall be governed by one another—shall be tyrannized over by one another; that so long as men will indulge the lust of dominion, they shall be filled with the fruits of slavery. . . . So if men will not be governed by God, it is their doom to be enslaved by one another." [24] This did not mean that those who gave their allegiance to God must patiently await the Second Coming. Like all abolitionists, Ballou believed men could desist from

[24] *Non-Resistance in Relation to Human Governments* (Boston, 1839); also available in *Liberator*, Dec. 6, 1839, p. 4; and *Non-Resistant*, Nov. 16, 1839, pp. 1-2.

doing wrong, opt for a superior plane of moral law than prevailed on earth, or, as he put it, find in their hearts "the germ of the millennium." At the point when they made that discovery they needed some place to go and new institutions to enclose them. The millennium, after all, was not solely related to extra-historical forces; it would come through self-exploration, conversion and individual secession. Ballou assigned to the Hopedale Community the function of giving converts a means of signifying their secession from earthly government and slavery.[25]

This viewpoint turned out to mix strengths and liabilities about equally. On the one hand, as Ballou gladly pointed out in later years, his community lasted much longer than such others as Skaneateles and Brook Farm, which had scoffed at his restricted theological and reformist purposes as sectarian.[26] And, having taken the long view, he would remain loyal to nonresistance when Garrison and others forsook it.[27] But on the other hand, Ballou's willingness to have the Negro wait in slavery must have seemed a drawback to other abolitionists, even though he anticipated that any other attitude would probably eventuate in civil war and racial bitterness.[28] Furthermore, the long view could lead toward a rather feeble resignation to the failure of the communitarian scheme itself, once it seemed possible that its moment in history had not arrived.[29]

More satisfactory perhaps—that is, truer to the needs of Christian anarchy in antislavery—was the Liberty Party. This movement has usually been taken as the opposite of anarchism and nonresistance, but, at least in the minds of such of its founders as Beriah Green, William Goodell and Gerrit Smith, it was a solution to the same problem of slavery and sin which beleaguered the New England abolitionists. It was a sort of political come-outerism. In the first place, we should notice that the goal of the party was considered to be neither victory at the polls nor attainment of any balance of power but "disconnection from evil." It provided a way of *not* voting for the parties which sinfully governed. Voting was regarded not as an instrument of majority rule but as a record of individual character. In the second place, it was felt that voting for parties which used politics as a way of simply adjusting moral differences was giving a personal guarantee that the millennial government would never come. For the Liberty Party was designed as a vanguard of the millen-

---

[25] *History of the Hopedale Community*, ed. William S. Heywood (Lowell, 1897).

[26] *Practical Christian*, Jan. 22, 1842, p. 2; Nov. 27, 1841, p. 2; May 17, 1845, p. 3; Ballou, *History of the Hopedale Community*, pp. 24-26.

[27] See the exchange between Ballou and Garrison in 1861, as reported in Ballou, *Autobiography of Adin Ballou*, ed. William S. Heywood (Lowell, 1896), pp. 444-49.

[28] See, for example, his editorial, "Pro-War Anti-Slavery," *Practical Christian*, Dec. 21, 1850, p. 2.

[29] Among others, John Humphrey Noyes scoffed at Ballou's account of his own failure. See his *History of American Socialisms* (Philadelphia, 1870), p. 131.

nium rather than as a tactical machine of abolition. In the third place, in pointing toward the millennium, Liberty Party men paid tribute to the same dialectic of divine government and self-government that captivated Garrisonian nonresistants. That is why they wanted a record of individual character instead of an index to majority sentiment; like Ballou, they believed in an obligation for those choosing the government of God to make special arrangements for themselves so as not to dilute their moral influence in hastening the rule of God on earth. Ultimately it was God, not man, who would supervise consequences.[30]

If there is any element of conservatism that distinguished these men from their New England counterparts, it is that they believed in the availability of natural leaders, provided by God, whose authority would be respected only when the obstructions of human government had been cleared away. Such leadership could only come into view voluntarily, naturally. We are still dealing with a version of anarchism. But we are dealing with a version more concerned with the ranks and tiers of voluntary local authority than with the release of individuals into harmonious equality.

A recent sociological study observes that some ventures into reform politics are more concerned with the symbolic identification of the virtue of reformers than with the alleviation of specific social evils. This may be explained by the existence of threats to the social status of the reference groups from which the reformers are drawn.[31] In the case of the Liberty Party, however, an alternative explanation is available. That party was openly established to enable the virtuous to symbolize their allegiance to God. It may be accounted for as a practical response to the theological necessities of antislavery.

The main conclusion to be drawn from this survey, I believe, is that anarchism was nearly at the heart of antislavery in the 1840s. We may feel uncomfortable with Tolstoy's view that the problem of slavery was eternally bound up in the larger problem of man's tendency to take authority upon himself and thereby stifle the kingdom of God within each man; we may prefer not to conclude that abolitionists were inclined toward anarchism simply to the extent that they were clear-sighted Christians. Another explanation, more limited to time and history, may then

30 Illustrations of these points may be found in William Goodell's marvelous history, *Slavery and Anti-Slavery*, Beriah Green, *Belief without Confession* (Utica, 1844) and recurrently in the *Model Worker* (most strikingly in Beriah Green's address, July 28, 1848, p. 1). A prominent Liberty Party theoretician and a forthright anarchist was Lysander Spooner. Theologically he was a deist. See chap. vii of Lewis Curtis Perry, "Antislavery and Anarchy: A Study of the Ideas of Abolitionism before the Civil War" (Doctoral dissertation, Cornell University, 1967).

31 Joseph R. Gusfield, *Symbolic Crusade: Status Politics and the American Temperance Movement* (paperback, Urbana, Ill., 1966).

be adopted. As has often been recognized, antislavery was an outgrowth of revivalism.[32] Within the revival lay a model in which the most God-forsaken communities might approach a millennial escape from sin, not through institutional coercions but through the spontaneous movements of individual hearts. In the 1830s, then, antislavery made a preliminary application of the techniques of universal escape from sin to the social problem of slavery. This extension of concern is understandable enough, once we are reminded that slavery had long been a powerful metaphor for sin in Christian thought.[33] Division came in the 1840s, a division which the political abolitionist William Goodell recognized as nearly inevitable. "When a large body of the people *were* convinced of the truths abolitionists had taught them, the question arose, How shall they best be led to put their principles in practice?" No one kept to the first applications: now they needed not only to think in terms of broadcasting principles; they had to express those principles in action. And in matters of such unearthly significance demands of conformity would have been vain and sinful.[34] Therefore antislavery in the 1840s spawned a variety of submovements, all retaining the revivalistic hope of securing the kingdom of God by individual conversions, but differing considerably over the methods by which this anarchistic hope might innocently be expressed within social institutions.

In this explanation, furthermore, we may see one reason why antislavery stood preeminent among the reforms. It was most openly involved in the Christian problem at the heart of other reforms. Connections with strivings for peace, communitarianism and church reform have already been pointed out. It would be easy to add campaigns against the imprisonment of urban derelicts and against capital punishment in general. A brief list of other movements showing some concern to substitute innocent conversion for sinful coercion in social conduct beneath the sovereignty of God would include: the women's rights movement, particularly when it emphasized the coercions of marriage rather than the liberties of voting; phrenology, when it sought to substitute natural unions for legal marriages; the individualist anarchists led by Stephen Pearl Andrews, who found in anarchism the most progressive applications of Protestantism; a number of educational experiments; and most especially the temperance movement, which found a less ambiguous image in the reformed drunkard than antislavery did in the fugitive slave.

[32] Anne C. Loveland, "Evangelicalism and 'Immediate Emancipation' in American Antislavery Thought," *Journal of Southern History*, XXXIII (1966), 172-88.
[33] David Brion Davis, "Slavery and Sin: The Cultural Background," in *The Antislavery Vanguard: New Essays on the Abolitionists*, ed. Martin Duberman (Princeton, 1965), pp. 3-31.
[34] *Slavery and Anti-Slavery*, pp. 450-51, 454.

The course of anarchistic ideas in each of these other reforms deserves separate investigation, but it is possible to give an illustration revealing connections among the temperance, anti-imprisonment and urban reforms. The illustration is drawn from *Hot Corn: Life Scenes in New York Illustrated*, a novel about crime and drunkenness which the agrarian reformer, Solon Robinson, serialized in Horace Greeley's *Tribune*. Throughout this very popular novel, Robinson singles out alcoholism as a kind of symbol of the moral blindness and lack of character that lead to vice and poverty in the city. Evils such as these cannot be remedied by prisons or institutional controls; rather, they wait to be combated by powerful sentiments of morality and charity. At one point an exemplary young man explains why he did not kill a man who tried to seduce his sister:

"Why did you not strike the villain dead at your feet?"
"That is *savage* nature."
"Why not arrest and punish him then, for his attempt at rape?"
"That is *civilized* nature."
"What then did you do?"
"I forgave him, and bade him repent, and ask God to forgive him as I did."
"Lovetree, give me your hand, I give you my heart; I stand rebuked. I understand you now, that was *Christian* nature. Let us go." [35]

An anarchistic repudiation of the controls of civilization and a celebration of the spontaneous impulses of the heart were easily generated out of evangelical and millennial traditions in a problem-ridden America.

The anarchism derived from the revival supplied a quite different purpose for reform than that of traditional theocratic agencies of social control. Release took the place of containment and harmony took the place of restraint. Therefore attention to versions of anarchism helps us to understand alterations in American social reform in the 1840s. I think we can also agree that these versions are more interesting and intricate than what we are offered in discussions of abolitionism that simply take political action as a norm and anti-politics as an abnormality.

[35] Robinson, *Hot Corn* (New York, 1854), pp. 266-67. Italics added.

THE FATE OF THE SOUTHERN ANTISLAVERY MOVEMENT

A generation ago an American scholar filled the larger portion of a volume with evidence that the initial impulse of organized antislavery sentiment stemmed from within the South itself.[1] Thus, in the early nineteenth century, it was shown, not a few slaveholders mixed profuse apologies with vague condemnations of the institution in the abstract.[2] A more vigorous dissent emanated from many non-slaveholders in the back country of the upper South where the forces of Jeffersonian liberalism together with a chronic antipathy toward the seaboard planters produced a flourishing manumission movement.[3]

The debate in the Virginia legislature of 1832 following the Southampton insurrection marked the high tide of the Southern attack upon slavery.[4] The defeat of the antislavery forces at that juncture, as subsequent events proved, dissipated the accumulating opposition and roused the planting class to a sense of its peril. Some in Virginia, including the Richmond *Constitutional Whig,* did not regret that the issue had been debated and reckoned it glorious that the spirit of Virginia's sons had not shrunk from grappling with the monster.[5] But the inflexible fact remained that the emancipationists had lacked the power to overthrow the vested interests of the East, and that their movement entered a period of progressive decline. Thomas

[1] A. D. Adams, *The Neglected Period of Anti-Slavery in America, 1808-1832* (Boston, 1908).

[2] See also Clement Eaton, *Freedom of Thought in the Old South* (Durham, N. C., 1940), 18-23.

[3] Benjamin Lundy's *Genius of Universal Emancipation,* October 13, 1827, reported the existence of 130 antislavery societies in the United States. Of these, 106 were in the slave states.

[4] *Cf.* T. M. Whitfield, *Slavery Agitation in Virginia, 1829-1832* (Baltimore, 1930), *passim;* J. C. Robert, *The Road from Monticello: A Study of the Virginia Slavery Debate of 1832, Historical Papers of the Trinity College Historical Society* (Durham, N. C., 1941), Series XXIV, *passim.*

[5] March 6, 1832.

10

R. Dew and a host of other proslavery writers began to forge the dialectic weapons of the dominant militant planter aristocracy which emerged from the wreckage of Revolutionary liberal philosophy.

The complete social and political ascendancy attained by the slaveholders after 1832 invites the assumption that the discontented elements in Southern society were ultimately persuaded to accept the inevitability of the slave system. As time went on, it has been contended, emancipation became more difficult because "the slaves in most slave states bore a steadily increasing ratio to the entire population; and the agriculture of the section was more and more put upon them."[6] Presumably even the non-slaveholders could appreciate this added obstacle to emancipation. In this respect the fact that the planters were inclined to encourage the belief that Southern opposition to slavery had disappeared was of no little significance. J. D. B. DeBow expressed the conviction that all non-slaveholders could be classified "as either such as desire and are incapable of purchasing slaves, or such as have the means to purchase and do not because of the absence of the motive."[7]

It would appear, however, that this convenient, though superficial, generalization oversimplifies the problem of accounting for the waning of antislavery agitation. The need for a more adequate explanation of the alleged change in the attitude of Southern non-slaveholders has led a succession of historians to a re-examination of the documents. In consequence one historian emerged with the conclusion that the unifying force—indeed, the "central theme of Southern history"—has been the determination of the whites of the South to maintain white supremacy.[8] A second historian counters with the thesis that planters secured unity in their

[6] Adams, The Neglected Period of Anti-Slavery, 251.

[7] J. D. B. DeBow, The Interest in Slavery of the Southern Non-Slaveholder (Charleston, S. C., 1860), 5.

[8] U. B. Phillips, "The Central Theme of Southern History," American Historical Review, XXXIV, 30-43.

section through the proslavery argument by "playing upon the race prejudice which the argument inculcated."[9] This device had particular success with reference to the poor whites, and Dew and DeBow exploited it to the utmost.[10]

More frequently, however, the decline of the Southern antislavery movement has been attributed to the rise of the Abolitionists in the North. At first glance this explanation would appear to be sustained by irrefutable logic, for the two events occurred almost simultaneously. "The Southern antislavery men were apparently alienated by what they thought the intolerance of their Northern associates," observed one historian who saw more than mere coincidence in those developments.[11]

This latter view can be fortified by the writings of countless contemporaries who expressed the conviction that the Abolition movement was the sole cause for the decline of antislavery sentiment in the South. Niles' *Weekly Register* contended that the "misguided men who are meddling with the internal affairs of the South, are but riveting more closely the bonds which they seem so anxious to sever."[12] According to DeBow, "A class conscientiously objecting to the ownership of slave property, does not exist in the South, for all such scruples have long since been silenced by the profound and unanswerable arguments to which Yankee controversy has driven our statesmen, popular orators and clergy."[13] "Every northern plan of benevolence to the slave," wrote a Baltimore clergyman, "would be rejected, if for no other reason, yet for this, that it originated in

[9] W. B. Hesseltine, "Some New Aspects of the Pro-Slavery Argument," *Journal of Negro History*, XXI, 12-14.

[10] *Cf.* DeBow, *The Interest in Slavery of the Southern Non-Slaveholder;* T. R. Dew, *Review of the Debate in the Virginia Legislature of 1831 and 1832* (Richmond, 1832); Eaton, *Freedom of Thought in the Old South*, 158-161.

[11] Adams, *The Neglected Period of Anti-Slavery*, 252. See also Eaton, *Freedom of Thought in the Old South*, 118, 161,

[12] August 8, 1935.

[13] DeBow, *The Interest in Slavery of the Southern Non-Slaveholder*, 5.

the wrong quarter.'"[14]   Still another observer abused the "northern fanatics" for the mischief they had wrought:

Abolition was moving over the South like the waves of the sea, till Northern abolition began its crusade. Maryland, Virginia, Kentucky and Tennessee were in action and the elements of Southern society were at the task. But when Northern abolition stepped forth into a field not its own, all was hushed. The halls of Southern legislation, instead of thundering with the call for emancipation, were crammed with bills for public safety and protection against foreign interference.[15]

In no less degree Southern politicians, always prone to exaggerate the influence of the Abolitionists, found a similar explanation for the newly achieved unity which their section supposedly enjoyed. Northern Abolitionists, declared John C. Calhoun, had caused Southerners to "correct many false impressions" that even they had entertained in relation to slavery.[16] In Kentucky, recalled Henry Clay, the number of emancipationists was increasing "until the abolitionists commenced their operations. . . . The people of that state have become shocked and alarmed by these abolition movements, and the number who would now favor a system even of gradual emancipation is probably less than it was in the years 1798-1799.'"[17]   Such views were representative of Southern opinion as expressed in Congress.

Yet, despite the seeming unanimity of this testimony, it is doubtful whether the Abolitionists caused many Southern opponents of slavery to reconsider their position. Nor can justification be found for the contention that the antislavery elements in the South were entirely hostile to the Northern antislavery movement. Certainly few of the Southern opponents were naive enough to seek shelter in

[14] Quoted in E. A. Andrews, *Slavery in the United States* (Boston, 1836), 47.

[15] *Colonization and Abolition Contrasted* (Philadelphia, n. d.), 3.

[16] *Congressional Globe*, 25 Cong., 2 sess., appendix, 61-62.

[17] Thomas H. Benton, *Abridgement of Debates in Congress* (16 vols., 1857-1861), XIII, 743.

the proslavery argument simply because men in the North shared their active hostility toward the slave system.

As early as 1824 the president of the North Carolina Manumission Society defined slavery as a national problem and asserted that its abolition would require the cooperation of all the states to "make a common cause of it for the good of the whole."[18] Twenty-five years later a Fellowsville, Virginia, newspaper pronounced the alleged "mad career" of Northern Abolitionists "all moonshine!" "They neither endanger the existence of the Southern States nor aggress that the South may repel. Theirs is a course backed by honesty of purpose. . . . May not citizens in the North 'agitate' slavery, as well as citizens of the States suffering?"[19] A writer from southern Kentucky went so far as to denounce Northerners who refused to support the antislavery cause:

But may not those in slave States, who are laboring in the good cause of Emancipation, expect the sympathy and cooperation of all those who tread a free soil? . . . It is a most mortifying circumstance that there are Northern men who furnish no evidence that they are opposed to slavery.[20]

Perhaps the most significant result of the rise of the Garrisonian movement, so far as the South was concerned, was the fact that it provided the proslavery element with a vast amount of political capital. It has been asserted that the planter class was "thrown on the defense by the abuse of the Abolitionists."[21] But the Northern movement found greater significance from the indirect aid it gave to the supporters of slavery in their attack upon the opposition within their own section. A basic ingredient of all proslavery propaganda after 1832 was a generous portion of

[18] *Minutes of the North Carolina Manumission Society, James Sprunt Historical Studies*, XXII (1934), 85.
[19] Fellowsville, Virginia, *Democrat*, quoted in Louisville *Examiner*, February 10, 1849.
[20] *Ibid.*, February 19, 1848.
[21] Whitfield, *Slavery Agitation in Virginia*, 58.

bitter abuse directed against the Northern Abolitionists.[22]

At least one contemporary Southerner saw clearly the relationship between the Abolition movement and the techniques of proslavery propaganda. It was his belief that the antislavery advocates in the South were being suppressed chiefly by the "ultraism with which slavery has been upheld in the slave States." The purpose of the "Carolina School," he suggested, was "to deepen the pro-slavery excitement, so that they may band all the slave States in one political union, and thus win power and secure it; and, for this end, they appeal constantly and ably to the pride, passion, sectional prejudice, avarice and fears of these slave States." Their action was designed he concluded, to drive the people of the North "to excess, to madden them and make them as ultra on one side as these perpetualists are on the other. . . . The stormier it becomes, the brighter and surer their political prospects."[23]

Other factors must be considered, then, if the decline of the Southern antislavery movement is to find an adequate explanation. Proslavery propaganda and the exigencies of economic competition removed the danger of effective opposition arising from the class of poor whites, and their names were seldom found on the rolls of emancipation societies.[24] But the effect of the proslavery argument upon the yeoman farmers, from whose ranks came the bulk of antislavery advocates, is not so clear. The weakening of their opposition is probably better explained by the decimation of their numbers through migration to the West and the spread of the slave system into the Piedmont. This trend was illustrated in North Carolina where the southwestern counties of Mecklenburg, Cabarrus, Montgomery, Richmond, Iredell, and Davidson eventually rivaled the

[22] Hesseltine, "Some New Aspects of the Pro-Slavery Argument," 2 *et seq.*

[23] Louisville *Examiner*, June 19, 1847.

[24] Eaton, *Freedom of Thought in the Old South*, 87.

eastern counties in the production of cotton through the utilization of slave labor.[25] Similarly many yeomen in western Virginia abandoned their antislavery views in anticipation of joining the ranks of slaveholding planters.[26] "Precisely in proportion as slavery has become more profitable," observed a contemporary, "attachment to it has increased, and the number of those, where it exists, who seek to abolish it, has diminished. This is an adequate explanation of whatever change in Southern opinion has occurred."[27]

Many of the small farmers, however, exhibited a persistent tendency to resist reconciliation with the dominant planter class. In consequence, force, political manipulation and repressive legislation had to supplement propaganda in removing the threat from this group. The application of such tactics alone would seem to indicate that some had not been won over by the proslavery argument. Legislation prohibiting slavery agitation and mob action against the emancipationists provide additional reasons for the dissolution of Southern antislavery societies.[28] Thus during the slavery debates in Virginia in 1832 the local slaveholders grew more aggressive. Large meetings in Mecklenburg, Essex and Northampton counties condemned the activities of the legislature and resolved not to patronize any newspaper favoring emancipation.[29]

Finally, uneven representation in the state legislatures held in check the political power of the small farmers from the back country. From this there sprang a common complaint that "the apportionment of nearly all the Southern

[25] R. H. Taylor, *Slaveholding in North Carolina, James Sprunt Historical Studies*, XVIII (1926), 45.

[26] C. H. Ambler, *History of West Virginia* (New York, 1933), 221 *et seq.*

[27] G. M. Weston, *The Progress of Slavery in the United States* (Washington, 1857), 185.

[28] Eaton, *Freedom of Thought in the Old South*, 28, 87-88, 126-128, 158.

[29] Richmond *Constitution Whig*, January 22, 24, 1832; Richmond *Enquirer*, March 1, May 4, 1832.

States, retain the power of these States in the hands of the slaveholders.''[30] An investigation of conditions in Maryland carried an observer to the conclusion that a majority of its people favored emancipation.

... but such is the division of political power among the counties, that a small number of white inhabitants, in those counties which possess the most slaves, are able to control the legislature of the state. The counties are all entitled to an equal vote in the legislature, although in some there are not more than eight or nine thousand white inhabitants, and in others, four or five times that many.[31]

Furthermore it is evident that, although their forces may have been diminished and their organization broken, a substantial group of small farmers in the upper South retained its opposition to slavery in the years after 1832. Despite the aggressive hostility of the slaveholders and the work of proslavery propagandists, dissenting opinions occasionally found vigorous expression. The prevailing belief that anti-slavery sentiment was dead in the South prompted Cassius M. Clay to write in his Lexington, Kentucky, *True American* that the Southern press was no criterion of public opinion. ''They are the mouthpieces of the slaveholders, who are the property holders of the country; they hold the bread of the press in their hands. . . . Politicians are no better; where is the man among them, who will sacrifice present power, to the contingency of hereafter rising with the swelling tide of freedom?''[32] A Louisville paper dedicated to the emancipation cause declared that ''it is not *politic* to publish opinions adverse to slavery in slaveholding States, and hence antislavery sentiment in those States is not represented in the newspapers.''[33]

Even the most cursory glance at affairs in the upper tier of slave states—Missouri, Kentucky and Maryland—

[30] Louisville *Examiner*, October 30, 1847.
[31] Quoted in Andrews, *Slavery in the United States*, 79.
[32] July 15, 1845.
[33] Louisville *Examiner*, September 2, 1848.

reveals clearly that in them unity was never achieved in the years after 1832. In those states the Freesoil movement waxed strong,[34] and antislavery agitation was constantly a disturbing element in local politics. Missouri teemed with dissenters, emancipation societies were numerous, and in politics the "Charcoals" (so branded because of their alleged partiality for the Negro) waged relentless war upon the champions of slavery.[35] German and Irish immigrants who poured into the state to build the railroads were almost unanimous in their opposition.[36] In 1852 Frank Blair and Gratz Brown established the *Missouri Democrat* at St. Louis. Avowing that abolition was the magic key to that city's industrial development, the new organ of the emancipationists anticipated the day when "St. Louis shall have the mills of Lowell and the forges of Pittsburg."[37] The antislavery forces crowded their way into the state legislature and agitated the question there. In 1857 Gratz Brown rose to assert that an emancipation act, more certain than any that could be passed by the legislature, was already in operation in Missouri. "Look to the laboring population which is coming into your state; which is crowding your highways; . . . which is building up flourishing towns, laying out fertile farms, planting vinyards in all sections of the state, and you will see the movement to which I refer."[38] The same year a Richmond, Virginia, newspaper confessed: "That a large majority of the people [of Missouri] are in favor of the abolition of slavery

[34] *Ibid.*, April 28, August 5, September 23, 1848; C. M. Clay, *Life, Memoirs, Writings, and Speeches of Cassius M. Clay* (Cincinnati, 1886), 175; W. E. Smith, *The Francis Preston Blair Family in Politics* (New York, 1933), I, 240.

[35] J. F. Hume, *The Abolitionists, 1830-1864* (New York, 1905), 159.

[36] Louisville *Examiner*, November 20, 1847; September 30, 1848; Smith, *The Francis Preston Blair Family in Politics*, I, 292.

[37] Quoted in Washington *National Era*, April 9, 1857. See also Smith, *The Francis Preston Blair Family in Politics*, I, 240.

[38] *Speech of B. Gratz Brown before the Missouri Legislature* (St. Louis, 1857), 7.

... is a fact which we are compelled, however reluctant, to receive.''[39]

In Kentucky the militancy of the slaveholders caused organized antislavery societies to lead a precarious existence; but sentiment against slavery seemed nevertheless to be growing.[40] The proslavery argument not only failed to impress the dissenters, but the indignant slaveholders found it impossible to quell the writers and speakers who continued to discuss the subject. When James G. Birney was virtually driven from the state in 1835,[41] others, especially the irrepressible Cassius M. Clay, came forward to take his place. For a few months in 1845 Clay, whose career epitomized the aims and adversities of the Southern dissenters,[42] published at Lexington the *True American* which he devoted to ''gradual and constitutional emancipation.''[43] His allegedly incendiary appeals incited a proslavery mob, in August, 1845, to invade his office and ship his press to Cincinnati.[44] But within two years friends and followers of Clay had founded the Louisville *Examiner* which continued the antislavery agitation for several more years. The last concerted drive of the opposition occurred at the election of delegates to the constitutional convention of 1849. While not a single emancipationist was elected, they nevertheless managed to poll more than 10,000 votes.[45] During the 1850's antislavery candidates came forward in the state elections, and the question found free expression in

[39] Richmond *South*, quoted in Washington *National Era*, July 16, 1857.

[40] A. E. Martin, *The Anti-Slavery Movement in Kentucky* (Louisville, 1918), 64-66.

[41] William Birney, *Life and Times of James G. Birney* (New York, 1890), 82.

[42] *Cf.* Horace Greeley, *The Writings of Cassius M. Clay* (New York, 1848); A. W. Campbell, *Cassius Marcellus Clay* (Richmond, Kentucky, 1888).

[43] Prospectus of the *True American*, quoted in Greeley, *The Writings in Cassius M. Clay*, 211.

[44] Lexington, Kentucky, *True American*, August 15, 1845; Cassius M. Clay, *Appeal of Cassius M. Clay to Kentucky and the World* (Boston, 1845).

[45] Louisville *Examiner*, September 8, 1849.

the press and at public meetings held in that state.[46]

Similar conditions existed in Maryland where slavery was decidedly a declining institution. As early as 1833 Niles' *Weekly Register* reported that "the march of the slaves is south, south. Already they may be said to have crossed the Potomac—for in Maryland they are not generally esteemed as permanent possessions. . . . Free white laborers are taking their places in our most flourishing counties."[47] This trend made it possible for the Free Soilers, despite repressive legislation, to work vigorously, and for antislavery meetings to assemble with a fair chance of avoiding molestation.[48]

While the threat of violence and the penalties provided in hostile legislation generally sufficed to liquidate the once promising manumission movement in North Carolina and Tennessee, such was not the case in Virginia. Organized antislavery societies disappeared soon after 1832, but the protests of public meetings and of the hostile press beyond the mountains could not be silenced entirely. In western Virginia, exulted one dissenter in 1848, "anti-slavery papers and anti-slavery orators are scattering far and wide the seeds of freedom, and an immense number of persons are uttering vaticinations [*sic*] in contemplation of a day of emancipation."[49] One of the leaders of the opposition in that region showed clearly the continued conflict between the two sections of the state when he wrote :

Letters are pouring in upon us from East Virginia praying us "not now, not now," while letters are coming to us from all quarters of West Virginia, which say "now, now." There is of a surety, no mistake in the feeling here. West Virginia is for freedom—nothing more nor less.[50]

[46] Washington *National Era*, February 12, 1857; Martin, *The Anti-Slavery Movement in Kentucky*, 138.

[47] November 16, 1833.

[48] Louisville *Examiner*, October 18, 1847

[49] *Ibid.*, October 28, 1848.

[50] *Ibid.*, November 27, 1847.

Failing to obtain state action many farmers west of the mountains began to consider the possibility of dividing Virginia. As an alternative to this drastic action another group proposed an act by the legislature which would permit each county to decide the issue of slavery or freedom for itself. In defending this plan one advocate explained that the people of his section had long favored emancipation, but that they had always been outvoted by the East. "They are now advocating a law to permit counties to legislate for themselves in the matter; and thus permit a majority of the people in any one county, to meet at the polls, and declare whether slavery shall be longer permitted therein, or not."[51] Henry Ruffner, a Presbyterian preacher, assumed the leadership of this movement, and others joined him to spread the idea among the citizens of western Virginia. Thus the dissenters again attained at least the semblance of an organization:

From the Ohio to the Blue Ridge they are linked together. They know what they have to do. They know that nothing but the hardest labor can accomplish their object. They have organized—organized thoroughly, effectively—so that they can circulate tracts and papers in every part of Western Virginia.[52]

Early in 1847 the Franklin Society of Lexington debated the desirability of taking steps to bring about a division of the state. Those who advocated such a procedure spoke of slavery as their chief reason. John Letcher and Henry Ruffner both urged immediate action toward this end and contended that it was the only way in which the western section could rid itself of slavery.[53] Upon the request of this society Ruffner composed an *Address to the People of West Virginia*. Printed in pamphlet form it presented an antislavery argument based entirely upon economic principles. Ruffner disclaimed any intention of interfering with

[51] *Ibid.*, December 11, 1847.
[52] *Ibid.*, November 6, 1847.
[53] *To the People of Virginia!* (Richmond, 1859), 5.

slavery in eastern Virginia, but he did advocate its abolition west of the Blue Ridge Mountains. He believed that
the best means of obtaining this end was through a division
of the state, but suggested that such action would be unnecessary if the western section was given the right to
abolish the institution. The eastern slaveholders might
then find security in an amendment to the state constitution protecting them from any hostile legislation arising
from the antislavery principles of the West. Ruffner concluded with a detailed plan for gradual emancipation.[54]

After 1847 agitation for a division of Virginia increased
in the western counties, and the opposition to slavery continued. "I know of no non-slaveholder who is not eager
for emancipation," wrote one farmer from that region.
"The majority," vowed another, "want and will have
emancipation."[55] In 1857 the Wheeling *Intelligencer* condemned slavery as an "unmitigated curse to the soil of
Virginia."[56] By then the Free Soil movement had taken
root in West Virginia,[57] and the agitation went on until,
in 1861, the issue was transferred from the hustings to the
battlefield.

The contention of planter politicians that the South
had achieved social and political unity appears, then, to
have been the sheerest of wishful thinking. Few of the
Southern dissenters were ready to make common cause
with the Northern Abolitionists. But conclusive evidence
that the Garrisonians drove the Southern emancipationists
to espouse the cause of proslaveryism is singularly lacking.

KENNETH M. STAMPP

University of Maryland

[54] Henry Ruffner, *Address to the People of West Virginia* (Lexington,
Virginia, 1847).

[55] Louisville *Examiner*, January 1, 1848.

[56] Quoted in Washington *National Era*, April 30, 1857.

[57] In 1852 a convention at Shenandoah, Virginia, organized the Free
Democratic Club, repudiated the Whig and Democratic platforms, and endorsed
the Pittsburg platform of the Free Soil Party. *Ibid.*, November 11, 1852.

The Aims and Impact of Garrisonian Abolitionism, 1840-1860

James B. Stewart

HISTORIANS GENERALLY HAVE HELD that after 1840 Garrisonian abolitionists contributed little to the sectional conflict. This interpretation,
simple and blunt, pictures utopian, unrealistic William Lloyd Garrison presiding over a truncated version of the American Anti-Slavery
Society bereft of members and lacking funds. Many of abolitionism's
most talented operatives, put off by the Garrisonian insistence on
overthrowing the government, non-resistance and women's rights, had
deserted the Society in 1840 for direct political involvement, the Liberty party. After that date, according to most scholars, the American
Anti-Slavery Society claimed the allegiance of only a few itinerant agitators, who assailed a hostile public with bitter attacks on all political
parties, while broadcasting Garrison's anarchic doctrine of northern
disunion. "Misled by Garrison's antipolitical point of view," one historian has concluded, radical abolitionists "failed . . . to appreciate the
contribution of political friction to the growth of antislavery sentiment."[1] In general, students of the antislavery movement have agreed
with Gilbert Hobbes Barnes' contention that the radicals were 'dead
weights' who had an "even less negligible" effect upon sectional events
during the 1840's and 1850's.[2]

Recently, however, certain scholars have cast some general doubt upon the foregoing interpretation. Several historians have charted some
of the general crosscurrents between Garrisonian radicalism and political events, arguing that pure moral agitation and pragmatic political
developments must not be rigidly separated.[3] A re-examination of the
1840's and 1850's suggests that the Garrisonian approach to northern
politics was not nearly as unsophisticated and unproductive as historians have assumed.

To best understand these matters, one must return to 1840. In that

---

[1] Richard Hofstadter, "Wendell Phillips: The Patrician as Agitator" in *The
American Political Tradition and The Men Who Made It* (New York, 1948), p. 149.

[2] Gilbert Hobbes Barnes, *The Antislavery Impulse* (Washington, 1933), p. 175.

[3] See especially Howard Zinn, "Abolitionists, Freedom Riders and the Tactics of
Agitation" in Martin Duberman (ed.), *The Antislavery Vanguard: New Essays on
the Abolitionists* (Princeton, 1965), pp. 417-451; Louis Filler, *The Crusade Against
Slavery, 1830-1860* (New York, 1960); Aileen Kraditor, *Means and Ends in American Abolitionism: Garrison and his Critics on Strategy and Tactics* (New York,
1969).

year a large minority departed the American Anti-Slavery Society. They disavowed the traditional program of moral suasion as well as Garrison's new, "heretical" doctrines, and plunged into politics by establishing the Liberty party. The violent recriminations that ensued between members of the "old" and "new" organizations reflected poorly on both sides and did much to convince historians of the Garrisonians' "antipolitical" bias.

In attacking the Liberty party experiment, the Garrisonians proceeded from the well-founded assumption, validated by twentieth-century scholarship, that all of American society was uniformly hostile to the cause of the slave.[4] The very structure of the American government, the Constitution, reflected this verity in its many proslavery compromises.[5] So did the Garrisonians' own experiences. Congress, they argued, had simply responded to the dominant opinions of the nation by legislating the censorship of abolitionist literature from the southern mail, and by refusing to consider antislavery petitions in the House of Representatives. "Non-resistants declare that, of all questions which now agitate the land, none can compare in importance, *politically*, with that of slavery," Garrison exclaimed in 1839. "Do the politicians agree with them? No!"[6] How could the Liberty party expect "to make an anti-slavery Congress out of pro-slavery materials?" queried Henry C. Wright. "The nation must be abolitionized, before an abolition Congress can be created. . . . Why not then, lend all their energies to abolitionize the nation [?] Then of necessity, the fruit will appear in an anti-slavery Congress and government."[7]

Implicit in Wright's statement are the assumptions of an effective pressure group member, as well as the dreams of a perfectionist. He affirmed his faith in the malleability of public opinion and stated that elected officials react positively to public pressure. In short, Wright articulated his basic belief that the democratic process would respond at all levels to the Garrisonians' special interest, emancipation of the slave. Parker Pillsbury, the most zealous of non-resistants, once clarified nicely the Garrisonian perception of American politics: "Men do not *go* to Congress, they are carried there. They do not act—they are *acted upon*. The active vote does not belong to Congress at all."[8]

Working from this analysis, the Garrisonians' decision to abstain from voting and third party affairs proved tactically essential for their political potency. Their immediate concerns were the opinions, not the ballots, of the voters, and the actions of established representatives,

[4] See Winthrop Jordan, *White Over Black: American Attitudes Toward The Negro, 1550-1812* (Chapel Hill, 1968); Leon Litwack, *North of Slavery: The Free Negro in The North, 1790-1860* (Chicago, 1961).

[5] Staughton Lynd, "The Abolitionist Critique of The United States Constitution" in Duberman (ed.), *Antislavery Vanguard*, pp. 209-239.

[6] *The Liberator*, Sept. 13, 1839.

[7] *Ibid.*, Aug. 30, 1839.

[8] *Ibid.*, Aug. 29, 1850.

not the creation of separate slates of candidates. Therefore, they correctly assumed that conventional political activities were restrictive and morally dangerous, "narrowing the broad dimension of the anti-slavery platform," as Garrison explained.[9] Liberty men were warned that they would inevitably pre-occupy themselves with party machinations, lose interest in emancipation, and moderate their antislavery platform to suit conventional tastes. Besides, as Garrison shrewdly observed, the act of forming a third party could amount to a sop to conscience, a surrogate for effective political action on behalf of the bondsman. "It has never been a difficult matter," he remarked, "to induce men to go to the ballot box; but the grand difficulty has ever been . . . to persuade them to carry a good conscience thither, and to act as free moral agents, not as tools of party." The Liberty party's faulty tactical presuppositions, and its willingness to work within the proslavery Constitution, would, said Garrison, cause it to fail as a permanent force for abolition.[10]

Of course, Garrison was right. By 1848 Henry B. Stanton and Joshua Leavitt, leaders of the "new organization," had abandoned emancipation for "free soil." The former began a new career as a political trimmer, and the latter henceforth worked to sell non-extension as a plausible cure for the slavery question. Others retired, disillusioned with politics.[11] Garrison was premature in his 1842 announcement that these individuals had all become "paralyzed" by "the sorcery of the new organization."[12] But by 1847, Wendell Phillips was already rejoicing privately at "how exactly" his and Garrison's predictions were being fulfilled.[13] Meanwhile, the Garrisonians had begun mobilizing themselves as a minority lobby around their theory of a responsive democracy, directing their efforts towards both the voters of the North, and elected representatives in Washington.

They found many opportunities to exert pressure between 1840 and 1860. These years were marked by mounting sectional tensions within the Whig and Democratic organizations which eventually produced the Free Soil and Republican parties. The extended Gag Rule controversies of the early 1840's soon merged with the issues of Texas annexation, the Mexican War, the Kansas-Nebraska Act, and the recurring debates over the extension of slavery into the territories. An even greater number of congressmen became indentified with antislavery opinions and began assuming sectional leadership in the political sphere.

[9] *Ibid.*, Sept. 13, 1839.

[10] *Ibid.*, June 28, 1839 (quotation); Mar. 11, 1842.

[11] Filler, *Crusade Against Slavery*, pp. 189, 247; Betty Fladeland, *James Gillespie Birney: Slaveholder to Abolitionist* (Ithaca, 1955), p. 265.

[12] *The Liberator*, Aug. 12, 1842.

[13] Wendell Phillips to Elizabeth Pease, Aug. 20, 1847, William Lloyd Garrison Papers, Boston Public Library.

Although none of these men qualified as an abolitionist,[14] their appearance nevertheless stimulated and heartened the Garrisonians. Radicals distinguished carefully between Liberty men, recreants from the exalted cause of moral suasion, and successful office holders elected from traditional constituencies, whose sectional activities marked not a retreat from, but an advance toward, abolitionism.[15] Free Soil Whigs and Democrats, and the Free Soil party itself, seemed to validate the Garrisonian formula of presenting moral arguments within the context of a responsive democracy, and Garrisonians quickly claimed the antislavery politician as their own creation. "It is not too much to claim these results as largely owing to the labors of the Abolitionists," declared Edmund Quincy in 1848, as he surveyed the havoc wrought within northern politics by proponents of free soil.[16] From the first, the American Anti-Slavery Society took this self-ascribed paternity seriously. Even while hurling invective at the Liberty party, they embarked on a program of supporting and challenging these new antislavery politicians and their constituents.

The Garrisonian criterion for supporting politicians was simple; only office-holders who dramatically publicized antislavery questions and disrupted their parties merited active aid. In November, 1841, for example, Garrison heard that a cabal of antislavery Whigs, directed by Joshua Leavitt, Joshua Giddings, William Slade, Seth Gates, and others, had been fashioned in Washington. Immediately, the *Liberator* reminded the antislavery Whigs that they were "pledged in good faith not to flinch, or to yield one iota," while calling on these congressmen's constituents to support their representatives with antislavery petitions. If the electors remained "faithful to themselves, their representatives will also be faithful," Garrison guaranteed.[17] Clearly, Garrison's "antipolitical" point of view did not blind him to the values of politics as an antislavery device. And soon after, Joshua Giddings resigned his seat after being censured by the House for his antislavery activities. Garrison was among the first to appeal to Giddings' constituents that he "be returned by an overwhelming (it ought to be unanimous) vote. . . ." Garrison would never vote himself, but he often saw the advantage of a properly cast ballot. Radical lecturers Parker Pillsbury and Stephen S. Foster rushed to Giddings' district to rouse the voters.[18]

While isolated incidents less dramatic than the above could be cited

[14] The term "abolitionist" is defined here as one who worked outspokenly for immediate, complete, uncompensated liberation for all American slaves. This definition is offered by James M. McPherson, *The Struggle for Equality: The Abolitionists and The Negro in The Civil War and Reconstruction* (Princeton, 1964), p. 3.

[15] *The Liberator*, Mar. 30, 1840; Sept. 22, 1843; Feb. 20, 1846; July 20, 1847; Feb. 8, 1850; Samuel J. May to Charles Sumner, July 12, 1848, Charles Sumner Papers, Houghton Library, Harvard University.

[16] *The Liberator*, Aug. 11, 1848.

[17] *Ibid.*, Nov. 26, 1841.

[18] James B. Stewart, *Joshua Giddings and The Tactics of Radical Politics, 1795-1864* (Cleveland, 1969), Ch. IV; *The Liberator*, Apr. 1, 1842.

to illustrate moment-to-moment Garrisonian support of congressional activity,[19] more instructive was their role prior to 1848 in fostering sectional splits within the Whig and Democratic parties. The first fissure of real consequence opened in 1845 when Democratic congressmen John P. Hale appealed from party policy to the people in opposing Texas annexation. As the powerful New Hampshire Democratic machine moved to terminate Hale's career, dissident Whigs, Democrats and Liberty men coalesced in his behalf.[20] The Garrisonians proved themselves equally ardent, if still non-voting, Hale men. Parker Pillsbury took over Nathaniel P. Rogers' financially shaky New Hampshire *Herald of Freedom* and began furiously attacking the old-line Democrats. Garrison, who had helped engineer the change of editorship, rejoiced that Pillsbury's columns were "never more needed than in this time of crisis, when New Hampshire is seeking to deepen her pro-slavery infamy by the sacrifice of the fearless and upright *Hale*." Stephen S. Foster stood up loyally for Hale at the state Democratic convention which purged him from the party, and the American Anti-Slavery Society sent agents into the Granite State to stimulate the voters in Hale's defense.[21]

Interesting, too, was the timing of Rogers' replacement by Pillsbury. Rogers, who had pushed perfectionism to the literal conclusion of anarchy, had bitterly assailed the Garrisonians as being "purblind with politics." He thought them sinful for their tending to "hover about the polls, to watch the balloting of others, and about the State House, where they can enjoy the turmoil of legislation." Garrison, clearly unwilling to let absolute perfectionism becloud political stratagems, ultimately purged Rogers from the movement.[22]

The Texas issue also produced party divisiveness in Massachusetts, this time among the Whigs. Here, a cadre of "Conscience Whigs," led by Charles Francis Adams, John G. Palfrey, S. C. Phillips, Charles Sumner, and Henry Wilson, began breaking with the party oligarchy over both annexation and the resulting war with Mexico. Garrison, deeply moved by these promising omens in his home state, willingly appeared with Henry Wilson at a "Conscience Whig" anti-Texas meeting, and began attacking the pro-southern "Cotton" wing of the Massachusetts Whig party in the *Liberator*.[23] Repeatedly, he urged the Conscience men to "snap the cords of party, and stand up untrammeled in the cause

[19] Issues of *The Liberator* during the 1840's and 1850's abound with radicals' endorsements of politicians' speeches, antislavery resolutions submitted in Congress, etc. It is impossible to cite them all, but even a casual perusal of *The Liberator* confirms this practice.

[20] Richard H. Sewell, *John P. Hale and The Politics of Abolition* (Cambridge, 1965), pp. 52-68.

[21] *The Liberator*, Feb. 7, 1845; Sewell, *Hale*, p. 57.

[22] *The Herald of Freedom*, May 2, 1845; John L. Thomas, *The Liberator: William Lloyd Garrison* (Boston and Toronto, 1963), pp. 294-295, 296, 300, 319-320, 343, 373.

[23] *The Liberator*, Sept. 26, 1845; Oct. 9, 1845, Feb. 20, 1846.

of liberty." Garrisonians, he explained, were "anxious" to give every Conscience Whig "a full measure of credit for what he has done, and to sustain him as far as he is disposed to go in his opposition to the Slave Power."[24] Throughout 1846 and 1847, Garrison, Wendell Phillips, and Edmund Quincy publicly fostered a bolter's spirit among the Conscience Whigs, enlisted prominent antislavery politicians from out of the state to speak to Massachusetts voters, and supported the divisive acts of "Conscience Whig" congressmen in Washington.[25] When John G. Palfrey defied his party by refusing to vote for "Cotton" Whig Robert C. Winthrop as Speaker of the House of Representatives, Wendell Phillips was among the first to endorse Palfrey's position. "Could I, consciencously, throw a ballot," he wrote Palfrey, "I would spend one 1st of May at Middlesex & have . . . the pleasure of voting for a man who nails his colors to the mast."[26] Garrison defended Palfrey in the *Liberator* against charges from the enraged Whig orthodoxy, thus nursing the ensuing recriminations along.[27]

When 1848 brought with it a coalition of the Free Soil party, disaffected Whigs and Democrats with Liberty men, the radicals again claimed the movement as their own creation. Garrison, privately "hailing it as a cheering sign of the times," saw in the third party "unmistakable proof of the progress we have made, under God, in changing public sentiment."[28] Feeling definitely responsible for the appearance of the Free Soilers, many Garrisonians proceeded to encourage the movement. Samuel J. May, "deeply interested" in "the new party which seems to be forming," wrote to several of its leaders, trying to arrange rallies and public meetings, and he acted as chaplain when the Free Soil convention opened in Buffalo.[29] Edmund Quincy goaded a hesitant Horace Mann to abandon the "bloodhound candidate" of the Whigs, Zachary Taylor, and to "cast his lot with Palfrey and Giddings."[30] Wendell Phillips put aside his no-government principles long enough to ask Edmund Quincy's help in sponsoring the political aspirations of a young Massachusetts Free Soiler. "What he wants," Phillips explained, "is that you should show him an opening, if there be one, to make a few remarks & show himself. . . ." Any "courtesy you can do for him . . . " he told Quincy, "will not be thrown away."[31]

[24] *Ibid.*, Mar. 6, 1846.
[25] *Ibid.*, Oct. 2, 23, 30, 1846; Wendell Phillips to Joshua R. Giddings, Jan. 16, 1847, Joshua R. Giddings Papers, Ohio Historical Society, Columbus.
[26] Wendell Phillips to John Gorham Palfrey, Dec. 9, 1847, John Gorham Palfrey Papers, Houghton Library, Harvard University.
[27] *The Liberator*, Jan. 28, 1848.
[28] William Lloyd Garrison to Samuel May, Jr., Dec. 2, 1848, Garrison Papers.
[29] Samuel J. May to Charles Sumner, July 12, 1848, Sumner Papers; Samuel J. May to Joshua R. Giddings, July 11, 1848, Giddings Papers; Samuel J. May to Mary A. Estlin, July 16, 1848, May-Estlin Papers, Boston Public Library; *The Liberator*, Aug. 25, 1848.
[30] *The Liberator*, Aug. 4, 1848.
[31] Wendell Phillips to Edmund Quincy (confidential), June 30, 1848, Edmund Quincy Papers, Massachusetts Historical Society, Boston.

The most common Garrisonian opinion, however, held that the best way to promote these political malcontents was by continuing in the program of moral suasion. Edmund Quincy explained the strategy clearly in 1848, regarding the radicals' duty towards the Free Soil party. He called on Garrisonians to act as informal campaign workers, directing them to propagandize the electorate, to make "the conscience uncomfortable." "In nine out of ten cases," he observed, "the person thus acted upon, . . . desirous of relief . . . would seek it, in the first instance, in a Free Soil vote." Quincy vowed that there was no better way "to promote the antislavery movement in its every shape."[32]

Garrison's reasoning, when all but endorsing John C. Frémont in 1856, was little different. While warning his followers to eschew the ballot, Garrison observed that "if there were no moral barrier to our voting, and we had a million ballots to bestow, we should cast them all for the Republican candidate." He judged it inconceivable "that any voter, desirous of frustrating the Slave Power will bestow his suffrage upon either Buchanan or Fillmore." Republicanism had arisen as "the legitimate product of moral agitation" of northern voters by Garrisonians. Radicals could best promote antislavery feeling in all its manifestations by continuing to agitate in the traditional way.[33]

Here, then, was one important facet of the Garrisonian political strategy. By adhering to non-voting while acting on their belief in the responsiveness of American democracy, radicals remained unfettered by formal political ties, avoiding every possibility of proslavery compromise. Their position gave them the widest possible freedom to encourage sectional politicians of all parties as well as the voters who elected such men. Unlike the Liberty party, the Garrisonians' efforts in politics never caused them to abandon their demand for immediate emancipation. Wendell Phillips, while overstating his case, made the radicals' strategy quite clear when, in reference to the Free Soilers, he claimed that the Garrisonian movement "converted these men; it gave them a constituency; it gave them an opportunity to speak, and gave them a public to listen. . . . The antislavery cause gave them their votes."[34]

While the pragmatic promotion of candidates and the building of antislavery constituencies represented a major objective of many Garrisonians, they also pursued a second, more subtle strategy for polarizing American politics. Basically, they attacked northern political organizations by denying the Constitution and demanding the dissolution of the Union. They were most unkind in their attacks upon Free Soilers and Republicans. While, as we have seen, Garrisonians offered such politicians encouragement, they simultaneously scored all officeholders

[32] *The Liberator*, Aug. 11, 1848.
[33] *The National Anti-Slavery Standard*, Oct. 25, 1856; Wendell P. Garrison and Francis J. Garrison, *William Lloyd Garrison* . . . Boston, 1885-1889), III, 443-444.
[34] Wendell Phillips, *Speeches, Lectures and Letters, 1st Series* (Boston, 1863), p. 135.

as temporizers whose support of the Constitution actually made them tools of the slave power, accessories with hands drenched in the blood of the bondsman. Endlessly, the Garrisonians reiterated their claim that the only effective approach to abolition was for everyone to disavow the Constitution, that "covenant with death and agreement with Hell."[35]

To most historians, such assaults on the political system confirm only that Garrisonians were variously threatened by the rise of sectional parties, "ambivalent" towards them, or were simply ineffectual and psychotic individuals.[36] Many Garrisonians, however, had politically sophisticated aims in view when challenging the nation with the cry of "No Union with Slaveholders." Edmund Quincy was emphatic on this point: "The abolitionist who stands aside from the Government . . . does not renounce, but multiplies his political influence. The vote which a man casts is but an insignificant emblem of his political power."[37] Charles C. Burleigh, one of Garrison's most flamboyant radical associates, agreed wholeheartedly with Quincy that the disunion doctrine was framed for political ends. He vowed that "no more effective vote is ever cast, in its bearing upon the politics . . . of this nation, than that which is cast . . . from lips denouncing the Constitution. . . ."[38]

Exactly what Burleigh and Quincy meant by these statements comes clear only when one re-examines some of the Garrisonians' intentions in attacking antislavery politicians on disunionist grounds. Their essential objective was to establish a line of communication which would insure consideration for their radical ideas. In 1853, for example, Wendell Phillips engaged in a vicious press debate over disunion with Horace Mann, antislavery representative from Massachusetts.[39] While blistering Mann's replies with further rebuttals, Phillips assured Edmund Quincy: "I'll teach him [Mann] that the Garrisonians never go out . . . without their 'pockets full of rocks'. . . ." Phillips felt that winning this argument was especially important because Mann seemed to be showing disdain for the ideas of non-voting radicals. "Mann rode a high horse," Phillips told Quincy, "thought little of his foes and said, [']lo! I will ramble these vulgar Garrisonians into the mud.'" If radicals like Phillips hoped to cultivate lines of communication with Washington, they could not allow politicians to ignore their arguments, or simply dismiss them. Phillips, in this instance, had to

[35] Thomas, *Garrison*, pp. 305-337.

[36] David Donald, "Toward a Reconsideration of the Abolitionists" in *Lincoln Reconsidered* (New York, 1961), pp. 19-36; Walter M. Merrill, *Against Wind and Tide: A Biography of William Lloyd Garrison* (Cambridge, 1963) p. 322, and Avery Craven, *The Coming of The Civil War* (New York, 1942), pp. 117-150, reflect, respectively, these various conclusions.

[37] *The National Anti-Slavery Standard*, reprinted in *The Herald of Freedom*, Sept. 6, 1844.

[38] *The Liberator*, June 3, 1853.

[39] *Ibid.*, issues from Feb. 25 through May 6, 1853, contain the Phillips-Mann exchange.

assert and preserve the credibility of his doctrines. "If I floor him [Mann]," Phillips guaranteed, "no man will relish disputing my positions."[40] Referring to the Phillips-Mann encounter, Garrison summarized this dynamic neatly, observing that the quarrel was not seen by radicals as a personal one. Rather, he explained, "it relates to rights which are sacred, and to interests too momentous to be weighed in the scales of expediency." "The more faithful we are to each other," he concluded, "The more 'the enemies of the rights of man' will respect us."[41] Nothing pleased the editor of the *Liberator* more than antislavery politicians who listened carefully to Garrisonian attacks, and who treated their assailants' ideas with intellectual and political open-mindedness. Here were office holders who helped maintain the lines between Congress and the agitator. John P. Hale's "unfailing good temper" in holding himself "amenable to censure" evoked warm praise from Garrison. So did Joshua R. Giddings' "nobility of soul" in responding positively to criticism. Such men, instead of being "abusive and malignant," understood "the intentions and aims of . . . PHILLIPS and QUINCY and PILLSBURY and FOSTER too well to fly into a passion. . . ," and Garrison judged it "a pity" that more public men could not "set such an example or profit by it."[42]

In demanding this respectful attention, nearly all Garrisonians occasionally harbored the forlorn hope of totally converting northern politicians.[43] At other times many developed a more complex appreciation of how the politicians' acceptance of their criticisms could best serve the cause of emancipation. Charles C. Burleigh fell into the latter category, arguing that slavery would ultimately be eradicated through legislation enacted by anti-Garrisonian office holders. A sweeping northern commitment to disunion or even Free Soilism was unnecessary, so long as Garrisonians remained steadfast in communicating with the voter and the congressman. By agitating for disunion, Burleigh said, "The laws will be changed long before . . . an entire majority is ready to come into the Free Soil organization. . . . Men are not converted to the true faith at once. . . . Some will come the whole way, some half way, some a quarter of the way."[44] Wendell Phillips was even more specific: "Our object is not to make every man a Christian or a philosopher, but to induce everyone to aid in the abolition of slavery." By publicizing radical doctrines, he continued, "We expect to accomplish our

40 Wendell Phillips to Edmund Quincy, Mar. 22, 1853, Quincy Papers.

41 *The Liberator*, Mar. 11, 1853.

42 *Ibid.*, May 27, 1853. Marius Robinson made similar observations about the "proper" responses which politicians should manifest toward abolitionist criticism. See *The Anti-Slavery Bugle* reprinted in *The Liberator*, Nov. 21, 1851.

43 See, for example, Henry C. Wright to Richard Houghton in *The Liberator*, Oct. 16, 1948, and Marius Robinson to William Lloyd Garrison, Mar. 30, 1853, Garrison Papers.

44 Burleigh's speech is here transcribed from the third to first person and from the past to the present tense. See *The Liberator*, June 3, 1853.

object long before the nation is converted into saints. . . ."[45] Two logical
questions thus arise. What elements in the disunion arguments were
consciously framed for political impact? How extensive and effective
was the influence of Garrisonian communications with elected officials?

Garrison and most others in his circle spent a great deal of their antebellum careers explaining the meaning and intention of their disunion
creed. Even so, many historians have overlooked its political purposes.
First and foremost, the doctrine was framed to give northerners a reply
of equal strength to southern threats of secession. Long before Garrison
first announced northern disunion, a southern minority had invoked
the right to dismember the national compact in order to protect slavery.[46] Until Garrison, the northern response to such threats had been
entirely defensive and legalistic, merely affirming the Union's perpe-
tuity while denying any anti-slavery motives. But Garrison, who judged
Calhoun as "a man who means what he says, and who never blusters,"[47]
keenly appreciated the deficiencies in northern retorts to fire-eaters.
As early as 1837, he was deeply bothered by the polemical advantages
held by southern radicals.

It is only for some few seditious hot-spurs at the South to brandish their . . .
bowie-knives and shout 'We'll dissolve the Union!', and straightway we turn pale,
our knees smite together, and our tongues cleave to the roofs of our mouths![48]

The demand for "No Union with Slaveholders" was as much designed
to correct this imbalance in the sectional debate as it was to satisfy
the personal demands of perfectionism. "The lines are now definitely
drawn," Edmund Quincy announced in 1847. "Calhoun in the South
and Garrison at the North stand front to front. . . . Every man must
needs be on one side or the other."[49] Wendell Phillips was, as usual, even
more specific about the Garrisonians' intention to polarize national politics: "If, as the South has so constantly contended, Secession is a constitutional right, well, we will commend the poisoned chalice to her
lips."[50] Calhoun could sit in the Senate and appeal through the Constitution to secession in order to protect slavery. In opposing Calhoun's
arguments while not even voting, Garrisonians aimed to make northern
office holders aware of concepts and vocabulary with which to repulse
threats of the "hot-spurs."

To be sure, no politician interested in re-election would openly endorse Garrisonian theories. Nevertheless, as the sectional crisis of the
1840's and 1850's ran its course, many free state congressmen indepen-

[45] Phillips, Speeches . . . , 1st Series, p. 120.

[46] William H. Freehling, Prelude to Civil War: The Nullification Crisis in South
Carolina (New York, 1966).

[47] William Lloyd Garrison to Richard Webb, Mar. 1, 1847, Garrison Papers.

[48] Garrison speech reprinted in Truman Nelson (ed.), Documents of Upheaval
(New York, 1966), p. 120.

[49] The Liberator, Nov. 26, 1847.

[50] Ibid., Mar. 24, 1848.

dently came to appreciate, as had the radicals earlier, slavery's deep institutional power. Such officials usually harbored no desire to abolish slavery, but they did wish to express in the most effective terms possible, their opposition to the "slave power" in politics. Garrisonians had already spent years telling politicians that effective antislavery disputation must reach beyond Union and Constitution. Now these congressmen found themselves provided with words and ideas which increasingly fulfilled their needs. In short, politicians who had first been challenged by the Garrisonians on disunionist terms, ultimately found themselves perforce receptive to the radicals' "higher law" doctrine. Many Garrisonians had long been anxious to diffuse their concepts throughout the North in precisely this fashion. Herein lies a good deal of the motivation behind radical criticism of and communications with the likes of Giddings, Sumner, Hale and Mann.

Illustrative of this dynamic are Wendell Phillips' private remarks to Elizabeth Pease written in January, 1846, describing the heated political debates over free soil: "Men who would have whispered Disunion with white lips a year ago now love to talk about it. Many leading men will talk as we were once laughed at for talking a while ago."[51] Phillips, in fact, was understating the situation. As early as 1843, twelve northern congressmen, led by John Quincy Adams and Joshua Giddings, had issued a public appeal warning that the admission of Texas, with slaves, was tantamount to dissolving the Union.[52] In 1845, the Massachusetts and Ohio legislatures had both threatened to refuse recognition of the Federal laws enabling Texas to assume statehood.[53] By mid-1846, Giddings had released a nationally circulated "dissolution letter" which argued that any further increase in slave states would give northern voters perfect moral cause to sever all relations with the Federal government.[54]

Even on these occasions of the early and mid-1840's, northern congressmen had begun speaking against the South in Garrisonian terms, constructing rationales for non-compliance with enacted law. Obviously, such arguments by politicians in behalf of "free-soil" served far more conservative objectives than the Garrisonian demand for immediate emancipation. Nevertheless, as the sectional debate continued to develop, northern office holders increasingly applied this Garrisonian vocabulary when discussing their positions on issues short of abolition.

By April, 1846, Garrison found himself reflecting hopefully upon this heartening addition to the content of northern political rhetoric. Reminiscing, he remarked that in earlier days the radical cry for immediate emancipation had filled the North with loathing and disgust. But

[51] Wendell Phillips to Elizabeth Pease, Jan. 25, 1846, Garrison Papers.

[52] Ashtabula (Ohio) *Sentinel*, May 27, 1843; *The Philanthropist* (Cincinnati) June 14, 1843.

[53] Thomas, *Garrison*, p. 335.

[54] Stewart, *Giddings*, Ch. VI.

now, after years of arduous abolitionist labor, the slogan had insinua-
ted itself into the vocabulary of most northerners. Even those who presently rejected complete and unhalting emancipation had accommodated
themselves to the existence of the idea, "and the doctrine of *IMME-
DIATISM* no longer occupies the time or demands the energies of the
abolitionist." The same eventual acceptance awaited the dictum of "No
Union with Slaveholders," Garrison asserted. He granted that the doctrine was still "as grossly misunderstood, as basely misrepresented, and
as foolishly rejected" as immediatism once had been. But, he also predicted that hard agitation by the American Anti-Slavery Society one
day would make disregard for Constitutionalism and law a common attitude in northern political minds.[55]

The utterances and actions of nothern politicians during the late
1840's and 1850's strikingly fulfilled Garrisonian's prediction. For instance, arguments posited by radicals to justify non-compliance with
the Constitution were picked up and applied by northern congressmen
opposing enforcement of the 1850 fugitive slave law. Garrison once
stated, when defending disunion against the alternative of constitutional amendment, that "Dissolution may be [the] work of a minority.
... A man, or a State can refuse to recognize a law—it requires many to
change one."[56] When it came to opposing the Fugitive Slave Act, politicians framed their arguments in terms strikingly similar to Garrison's.
"We cannot be Christians and obey it," warned an Ohio Free Soil paper.[57] Before a Massachusetts court in 1851, John P. Hale argued in
behalf of individuals charged with violating the Act. Using a Garrisonian mode of reasoning, Hale's most eloquent statements went beyond
technical legality, defending the actions of the accused with the doctrine of "higher law". Ultimately, all of those indicted were exonera-
ted.[58] Ben Wade, serving as a State Supreme Court Justice in Ohio, affirmed that while he would not recommend armed resistance to the
law, he would still justify and dismiss from his court all acts of non-violent civil disobedience.[59] Joshua Giddings made comprehensive use of
Garrisonian "higher law" arguments while speaking in 1859: "We say
today 'down with the fugitive slave act; . . . it is PIRATICAL, and we
will not obey it!"[60] Horace Mann, Phillips' antagonist, was also intellectually indebted to the Garrisonians when opposing the law. "This doctrine—which is one of the off-shoots of slavery—that there is no higher
law than the law of the state is palpable and practical atheism."[61]

Garrison doubtless understood exactly what Mann and these other

---

[55] *The Liberator*, Apr. 17, 1846.
[56] *Ibid.* Jan. 14, 1848.
[57] Ashtabula *Sentinel*, Sept. 14, 1850.
[58] Sewell, *Hale*, pp. 141-142.
[59] Ashtabula *Sentinel*, Nov. 14, 1850.
[60] *Ibid.*, May 26, June 2, 1859.
[61] Mann quoted in Filler, *Crusade Against Slavery*, p. 202.

political dissenters meant, for his American Anti-Slavery Society had begun circulating the same concept over a decade earlier, arguing that strict legal analysis could not meet the issues of slavery. Oliver Johnson was not indulging in self-justification when he observed, long after the Civil War, that "If Sumner and Wilson and Chase and Hale *did* breathe and do noble work . . . , it was only because they found a way to break through the web which the Constitution wove around them, and thus maintain their allegiance to the Higher Law." "That they were able to do this," Johnson continued modestly, "may have been owing largely to the influence of the Garrisonian movement in diminishing the popular reverence for the Constitution. . . ."[62] William Seward, the essence of conservative Unionism, presented ample documentation for Johnson's claim. The famous "Higher Law Speech" represented one benchmark of Garrisonian influence in northern politics. So did his "Irrepressible Conflict" speech and Sumner's "Crime Against Kansas" oration. Whenever confronted by sectional crisis, northern antislavery congressmen readily availed themselves of the theory which undergirded Garrison's demand for overthrowing the Constitution and applied it instead to the problem of the territories.

Seward, Sumner, Chase, and the others were hardly aware that they were employing antislavery language invented by the disunionists, so successful had the radicals been in making their vocabulary into "household words" appropriate to the perceptions and experiences of northern politicians. In turn, an increasing number of slaveholders came to believe that the American Anti-Slavery Society and the "Black Republicans" were one and the same thing and in 1861 reacted accordingly. Viewed in this fashion, the secession crisis represented the culmination of radical impact in the politics of antebellum America.

* * *

Wendell Phillips once remarked that "It may seem strange to some, this claim for Mr. Garrison of profound statesmanship."[63] Perhaps the suggestion advanced here for the political acuity of radical abolitionists seems equally foreign. Nevertheless, Phillips was correct when he observed that Garrison's own contemporaries had "heard him styled a mere fanatic so long" that they found it impossible "to judge him fairly."[64] Perhaps this comment has, until recently, also held true regarding students of the antislavery movement. Such historians possibly have overstressed the image of the "impractical" Garrisonian and have thus obscured these men's self-conscious attempts to influence American politics in the years after 1840. Many Garrisonians, unlike some of their chroniclers, realized that realistic political activity can mean more than just the building of party structures and collecting of votes.

[62] Oliver Johnson, *William Lloyd Garrison and His Times* . . . (Boston, 1880), p. 339.
[63] Phillips, *Speeches* . . . , *1st Series*, p. 152.
[64] *Ibid.*

Politics and Belief in Abolitionism: Stanley Elkins' Concept of Antiinstitutionalism and Recent Interpretations of American Antislavery

James Brewer Stewart

It is hardly a paradox that Stanley Elkins' *Slavery* seems at once a less challenging and more formidable volume than when it first appeared in 1959. His pioneering approaches to slave societies have naturally become commonplace as the list of studies informed by his book continues to grow. Elkins himself has cautioned against his being made the unwilling founder of a new historiographical orthodoxy, expressing misgivings that descriptions of slave systems have become "too severely limited" by his original categories.[1] By contrast the section of *Slavery* that now offers exceptional utility for current scholarship is the one which a few years ago many historians wholly dismissed—the pages treating American abolitionism.

During the 1960s only a few writers on antislavery gave any explicit support to Elkins' view, elaborated in part four of *Slavery*, that abolitionists harbored deep antiinstitutional tendencies. Until

JAMES BREWER STEWART *teaches history at Macalester College. He has published a biography of Joshua R. Giddings and articles on American abolitionists. He wishes to thank the Macalester College Faculty Activities Committee and the administrative officers and staff of the Newberry Library who have provided financial support for the research and writing of this article. A different version of this article was read in 1973 at the meeting of the Southern Historical Association. The author especially wishes to thank Professor Stanley Elkins for criticisms offered on that occasion.*

1. Ann J. Lane, ed., *The Debate Over Slavery* (Champaign-Urbana, 1971), p. 326.

very recently, most historians contented themselves instead by citing the strong rebuttals of Aileen Kraditor and Nathan Glazer, or by assuming that part four held no pertinence for their own work. With the advent of the 1970s, however, Elkins' conclusions have attracted new attention. Bertram Wyatt-Brown and Lewis Perry have both given the basic elements of his interpretation a vigorous if modified reaffirmation.[2] The reason for these extremes of rejection and acceptance arises in part from the nature of the fourth section itself and are worthy of examination. By so doing some starting points for reevaluating and constructively applying the antiinstitutional theme in light of current historical thinking on antislavery begin to suggest themselves. In the process, the relationships between abolitionism, broader cultural trends, and the politics of race reform may also become more clearly understood.

In the statement just noted Elkins observed further that scholarship on abolitionism, like that on slavery, has also become transfixed by his original terms. He has a good point. Part four of *Slavery* does contain features that seem to allow only one of two impulses—to refute, or to assent. Moderate reactions, as Wyatt-Brown has suggested, are stifled by the nearly whiggish conservatism regarding social movements that Elkins displays in part four.[3] Likewise, the civil rights struggles of the 1960s helped many investigators to see that much could be learned by assessing abolitionism sympathetically in the wide-ranging terms of political reform and social struggle. New theories of abolitionist motivation stressed the agitators' healthy autonomy as reflected in their attempts to renovate a sluggish, con-

2. For these various responses to Elkins' ideas see Willie Lee Rose, " 'Iconoclasm Has Had Its Day': Abolitionists and Freedmen in South Carolina," in Martin Duberman, ed., *The Antislavery Vanguard: New Essays on the Abolitionists* (Princeton, 1965), pp. 178-205; George M. Frederickson, *The Inner Civil War: Northern Intellectuals and the Crisis of the Union* (New York, 1965), especially pp. 7-33; Aileen S. Kraditor, "A Note on Elkins and the Abolitionists," *Civil War History* 13 (1967), 330-39; Nathan Glazer, "Introduction" to Stanley Elkins, *Slavery: A Problem In American Institutional and Intellectual Life,* 1st ed., (Chicago, 1959), pp. ix-xvi; Bertram Wyatt-Brown, "Stanley Elkins' *Slavery*: The Antislavery Interpretation Reexamined," *American Quarterly* 25 (1973), 154-75; Lewis D. Perry, *Radical Abolitionism: Anarchy and the Government of God in Antislavery Thought* (Ithaca, 1973); for typical, rather too easy dismissals of Elkins' ideas see James Brewer Stewart, *Joshua R. Giddings and the Tactics of Radical Politics* (Cleveland, 1970), pp. 86-87; and Gerald Sorin, *The New York Abolitionists* (Westport, Conn., 1971), pp. 120-23.

3. Wyatt-Brown, "Elkins' *Slavery*," pp. 154-57; Lane, *Debate Over Slavery,* pp. 362-63.

servative society.[4] Understandably, such historians felt compelled to reject Elkins' contrary insistence that the abolitionists were fatally shaped by their culture to display a romantic, politically destructive antiinstitutionalism. Just as negatively coercive to some historians as his specific values and interpretations has been Elkins' choice of structure for conveying his ideas. Yet, this same mode of elaboration is one of the main reasons that Elkins' interpretations are also now finding defenders.

In part four of *Slavery,* Elkins attempts to isolate the essence of abolitionism and the culture that informed it. The organizing theme is the fatal weakening of structuring elements in pre-Civil War northern society on the one hand, and the simultaneous antiinstitutional posture of the abolitionists on the other. By 1830, he emphasizes, Americans had jettisoned many restraints which had previously provided orderly ways for solving problems. Stable ecclesiastic and legal arrangements had been overturned by an aggressive materialistic individualism. Once well-established denominations had atomized into a myriad of competing sects. Abstracted transcendentalists had replaced instrumentalist, rationalist Founding Fathers as the symbols of America's attitude toward self and society.

Abolitionists, in turn, were shaped by this sloughing off of controlling precedents in their crusade to end slavery, Elkins continues. Reflecting the Yankee culture around them, they found themselves hopelessly unequipped to view race oppression as "a problem of institutional arrangements." Instead they exhibited guilty self-righteousness and a romantic, individualistic inability to subvert the southern labor system without strangling all chances of structured, permanent, and peaceful reform.[5] So constructed, Elkins' presentation amounts to a complete and compelling system of explanation.

First of all, this closed system prevents Elkins from conveying what many readers trained in history have come to expect—a sense of the impact of events and the meanings of shifting beliefs. One such historian, Aileen Kraditor, is Elkins' most influential critic and some of her dissent reflects this discomfiture. Correctly, she has protested that from the late 1830s through 1860 American abolitionism was

4. For a good analysis of the interpretations of abolitionism that have appeared since the publication of *Slavery,* see Merton Dillon, "The Abolitionists: A Decade of Historiography, 1959-1969," *Journal of Southern History* 25 (1969), 500-22.

5. Elkins, *Slavery,* pp. 140-206.

composed of competing factions, each with a different stance toward institutions.[6] Yet subtitles in part four, like "Institutions and Insights," "Intellectuals Without Responsibility," and "The Abolitionist as Transcendentalist," accurately convey Elkins' primary intention. He hopes to build self-contained models which display, regardless of factional differences, abolitionism's basic nature.

So constructed, the chapter challenges the reader to put aside questions about abolitionists' diversity in political perceptions and intellectual predispositions. Instead, Elkins dares the reader to agree to his quintessential judgment—abolitionists of all descriptions were guilt-conscious, moral absolutists, blind to the functions of institutions and hostile to the use of constructive political power. One can hardly blame historians, whatever their civil rights sentiments, for feeling "coerced" by monolithic alternatives like these into rejecting them altogether. Yet other scholars like Wyatt-Brown and Perry have found Elkins' formulations worth accepting in broad form, and for good reasons. Indeed, the self-contained, static explanations found in part four do have powerful ability to clarify cultural unities which remain elusive to the strictly narrative historian.[7] Accordingly, other scholars such as John L. Thomas, David B. Davis and Ronald Walters have also found antiinstitutionalism deep in the abolitionists' intuitive quests for personal redemption and universal moral order.[8] These historians show little of Elkins' distaste for the antislavery hosts and none relies explicitly on part four of *Slavery* for his own explanations. Moreover, all such scholars recognize diversity in abolitionists' thoughts that Elkins' model deemphasizes. Still, each author lends important indirect support to Elkins' propositions.

The net effect is scholarly impasse. Cultural and intellectual historians keep turning up impressive evidence of broad antiinstitutional unities within abolitionism. Students of race reform and sectional

6. Aileen Kraditor, *Means and Ends in American Abolitionism: Garrison and His Critics on Strategy and Tactics, 1834–1850* (New York, 1969), pp. 11-18. For a good look at a roomful of eminent older scholars feeling the same discomfit see "The Question of Sambo," *The Newberry Library Bulletin* 5, no. 1 (1958), pp.14-41.

7. See Bertram Wyatt-Brown, "Stanley Elkins and the Institutional Critique of Ante-Bellum South," unpublished paper delivered in Atlanta, Georgia, at the November, 1973, meeting of the Southern Historical Association.

8. David B. Davis, *The Problem of Slavery in Western Culture* (Ithaca, 1966); John L. Thomas, *The Liberator, William Lloyd Garrison: A Biography* (Boston, 1965); Thomas, "Romantic Reform in America, 1815–1865," *American Quarterly* 17 (1965), 177-203.

politics counter with comprehensive analyses of deep factional divisions which derived from profoundly conflicting attitudes regarding institutions. The former group judges Yankee society most significant for the fragmentation which nurtured the reformers' romanticism. Scholars of the latter persuasion emphasize the conventional wisdom and stubborn racism which the abolitionists shared, but struggled to overcome. To be sure, the division is not as sharp as presented here, and ways around it are suggested in part four of *Slavery* itself where Elkins specifically links political history and larger cultural themes to the abolitionists' behavior. The first task, then, is to overcome the original source of coercion—the "closed" property of Elkins' own explanations.

A good approach to this end may be to return the abolitionists at critical points to the narrative history of sectional conflict from which Elkins has so often removed them, in this case to the period from 1831 to 1840. During this first decade of effort, abolitionists began to develop a number of contradictory judgments while also retaining some common beliefs about the nature of American institutions. These beliefs, in turn, continued to influence their later activities from 1840 until the outbreak of the Civil War. To understand this evolutionary process one must also appreciate the abolitionists' first expectations, their continuing responses to external events, and their shifting perceptions of the choices open to them. Aided by illustrative primary sources and the critical use of recent scholarly conclusions we can then reevaluate Elkins' interpretations and the views of his critics against this process of change within the movement itself.

At the same time, we must also refine Elkins' use of the term "antiinstitutional." Elkins himself is not consistent in his usages. He employs the word in the following three ways—to describe (1) the abolitionists' alienation from established organizations, customs, and sources of authority; (2) their inability to comprehend and exploit organizations and structures per se; and (3) their behavior as clearly subversive of specific transectional parties and religious denominations. Clearly, none of these definitions necessarily complements the other two. Hence, I will try to be more precise than was Elkins while applying his term in all three of these separate senses to the evolution of abolitionism's conservative and radical wings from 1830 onward.[9]

9. These terms for designating various groups of abolitionists are similar to those offered by Kraditor in *Means and Ends*, pp. 8-9, but are less complicated, since my purposes are more general than hers. In her analysis, for example, "Garrisonian" and

But, to begin exploring these issues, one must return first to the early 1830s and the opening campaigns for an immediate, uncompensated end to slavery in the South. Then we can follow, in light of the antiinstitutional theme, abolitionists' situations, ideas, and activities as they began to evolve.

First of all, Elkins is quite correct in insisting that young abolitionists began their efforts possessed of a new, antiformal world view. Historians have since shown convincingly that demands for immediate abolition and the evangelical piety which supported such slogans reflected broad shifts to a vibrant romantic theology in Anglo-American thought. Moreover, parents had trained these youthful recruits to abolitionism with a strong sense of personal uniqueness and with potential for service to God through vocations of social engagement.[10] Such developments alone, however, did not release and shape the spirit of immediatism. The late 1820s and early 1830s witnessed some crucial events, related to slavery and politics, which also influenced nascent abolitionists to interpret their relationships to American institutions in unprecedented ways. One contrast will illustrate this point.

Before 1830, various programs of gradual emancipation and colonization had made no progress toward ending slavery. Yet, such schemes had served a noteworthy function, assuring most concerned, but gradualistically inclined citizens that the problem could be "managed" in rational ways. The response of that generation to disruptive events related to slavery, the Missouri crisis and Vesey slave plot, therefore, had been mild and short-lived.[11] Roughly a decade later,

---

"conservative" are not necessarily antithetical terms. Here, they shall be considered as opposites.

10. David B. Davis, "The Emergence of Immediatism in British and American Anti-Slavery Thought," *Mississippi Valley Historical Review* 49 (1962), pp.209-30; Anne C. Loveland, "Evangelicalism and 'Immediate Emancipation' in American Anti-slavery Thought," *Journal of Southern History* 32 (1966), pp. 172-88; Elkins, *Slavery,* 140-47; Lewis Perry, "Adin Ballou's Hopedale Community and the Theology of Anti-slavery," *Church History,* 39 (1970), 372-89; Gilbert Hobbs Barnes, *The Antislavery Impulse, 1830-1844* (New York, 1933), pp. 3-28 and passim. Bertram Wyatt-Brown, "New Leftists and Abolitionists: A Comparison of American Radical Styles," *Wisconsin Magazine of History,* 53 (1970), 256-68; Lois Banner, "Religion and Reform in the Early Republic: The Role of Youth," *American Quarterly* 22 (1971), 677-95.

11. Merton Dillon, *Benjamin Lundy and the Struggle for Negro Freedom* (Champaign, 1966); Gordon Finnie, "The Antislavery Movement in the Upper South Before 1840," *Journal of Southern History* 35 (1969), 319-42. For an analysis of the thinking of those few and powerless pockets of pre-1830 antislavery radicalism see James Brewer Stewart, "Evangelicalism and the Radical Strain in Southern Antislavery During the 1820's," *Journal of Southern History,* 39 (1973), 379-96.

pious young men and women displayed a stunningly different reaction to the Nullification crisis, David Walker's *Appeal* for armed black resistance, the Jamaica and Nat Turner slave uprisings.

These events, developing with frightening rapidity, now seemed to prove that the approaches of the past were sinful and dangerous, portending race violence and sectional disruption as God's retributive judgments. According to Garrison, Amos A. Phelps, Elizur Wright, Jr., Lydia Maria Child, and many other early writers, the only "safe" and "expedient" solution was the total one.[12] Calls for immediate emancipation, broadcast on the most absolute, unequivocal moral level, alone seemed to provide tangible insurance against an outpouring of the vials of wrath upon the nation and one's own personal damnation.[13] This new opinion offers a constructive application for Elkins' antiinstitutional theme by providing insights into how abolitionists initially perceived the problems of slavery and race, and responded to the personal imperatives of romantic theology.

It is clear, as Elkins maintains, that abolitionists sensed an acute lack of "formalized arrangements" in the early 1830s through which to channel their excruciating concerns.[14] Models that precedent had once sanctioned—gradualist plans—had been stripped of their plausibility by the combined actions of John C. Calhoun, Nat Turner, David Walker, and the abolitionists' own antinomian piety. In this way, the influences of jarring public crises and the romanticism of the culture at large converged on the abolitionists. In other words, American society and politics in the early 1830s played precisely the roles that Elkins assigns to them for the ante-bellum era as a whole. Just as Elkins suggests, the sense of alienation and guilt, the pressures to launch massive, morally absolutist efforts were certainly enormous, given these conditions.[15]

In this same regard, one of Elkins' most heavily criticized subsections, entitled "Choices," helps immeasurably in understanding the

12. See generally Lydia Maria Child, *An Appeal in Favor of that Class of Americans Called Africans* (Boston, 1833); Amos Augustus Phelps, *Lectures on Slavery and its Remedy* (New York, 1834); Elizur Wright, Jr., *The Sin of Slavery and its Remedy* (New York, 1833); William Lloyd Garrison, *Thoughts on African Colonization* (Boston, 1832). On the reinforcing relationship between immediatism and fears of race conflict, see Robert B. Abzug, "The Influence of Garrisonian Abolitionists' Fears of Slave Violence on the Antislavery Movement," *Journal of Negro History* 55 (1970), 15-28.

13. *Liberator*, January 18, 1834.

14. Elkins, *Slavery*, pp. 159-64.

15. Amos A. Phelps to "Wife," 31 August 1835, Antislavery Collection, Boston Public Library.

interplay of culture and events on early abolitionism. In "Choices," Elkins develops a tragic theme for the ante-bellum years by presenting a meditation upon alternative routes toward abolition, other than the bloody civil war which finally freed the slaves, yet ultimately denied equality to the black Americans. These possibilities were theoretically open to abolitionists, but remained nonetheless unexplored. Elkins even offers what he calls a "catalogue of preliminaries—a series of separate short-term reforms rather than root-and-branch abolition" which might have gradually achieved peaceful emancipation.[16]

Barrington Moore, Jr., and Nathan Glazer, as well as Kraditor, have attacked this section for reflecting wistful, reactionary qualities, criticisms which they imply are valid for part four of *Slavery* as a whole. Kraditor, for example, argues that gradualism was an impossible option for abolitionists since "slavery was an integral part of the institutional structure of the nation as a whole." Barrington Moore's criticisms are more sweeping, and similar to others made by Glazer: "In the circumstances of mid-nineteenth-century American society," Moore writes of Elkins' "catalogue," "any peaceful solution, any victory of moderation, good sense, and democratic process would have had to be a reactionary solution."[17]

These statements, perhaps valid in their own right, nevertheless misconstrue Elkins' intentions, for the "catalogue of preliminaries" makes a dramatic point when juxtaposed against the volatile mixture of images which so well describes the years around 1830—those of Calhoun, Turner, Walker, and finally, Garrison. So does another portion of "Choices," wherein Elkins presents eloquent, perhaps purposefully overdrawn contrasts between the nineteenth-century Englishman's businesslike, step-by-step advance toward peaceful emancipation and the Yankee's reflexive conversions to the divisive, "antiinstitutional" slogans. One cannot resist crediting him for pioneering the use of contrafactual propositions to illuminate historical processes. "Moderation was really not an alternative," Elkins abruptly reminds us in the midst of this contemplation of forgotten choices. "The true difficulty lay in the absence of any sense of *limits*

16. Elkins, *Slavery*, pp. 193-206.
17. See Glazer, "Introduction" to Elkins, *Slavery*, 1st ed., pp. xiii-xiv; Barrington Moore, Jr., *Social Origins of Dictatorship and Democracy* (Boston, 1966) pp. 131-32; Kraditor, *Means and Ends*, pp. 8-10.

within which the problem could be handled."[18] His point is that
abolitionists had no choice but to dispense with the inherited "wisdom" of a rationalist age. Kraditor, despite her criticism of Elkins
for overgeneralizing, finds this selfsame conclusion so pertinent that
she closes her book with it. The "real choice for Garrison was not
between . . . fanaticism and reasonable agitation," she observes, "it
was between antislavery agitation and silence."[19] Hers is an apt
characterization of abolitionism's early years, one which also illustrates how Elkins' judgments help to narrow the scholarly impasse
alluded to earlier.

Yet Elkins' model of abstractionism has limits for the 1830s.
Contrary to his emphasis, one which some intellectual historians are
also inclined to reflect, abolitionists *did* act initially on some strong
institutional attachments. Moreover, they employed these loyalties to
develop some well-founded conclusions about slavery as an economic
institution, social system, and as a national political problem. To be
sure, these conclusions served only to reinforce the abolitionists' first
immediatist preachments. But, by the 1840s such preferences were to
have a major influence on the changing relationships of abolitionists
to institutions.

In short, Elkins underrates the abolitionists' ordinary middle
classness.[20] Like many of their stolid nonabolitionist neighbors, they
recommended from the very first the arrangements of their "free
labor" society—vocational independence, family autonomy, unimpeded mobility, and egalitarian governance. In fact, the first calls
made by abolitionists for immediate emancipation should be interpreted, in part, as an expression of their desire to promote the aggressive individualism that Elkins finds so corrosive of inherited structures in the first place. Moreover, these ideas of the "good society"
comport with the views of cultural historians who see such preferences as running through the American imagination generally during
the ante-bellum years. These biases, they stress, reflected a common romantic suspicion of "man-made" artificial authority as dis-

18. Elkins, *Slavery*, p. 194. It is sometimes quite fruitful for persons already knowledgeable about abolitionism to re-read passages in *Slavery* as is suggested here—that is,
for author's literary intentions and their effects on the reader.
19. Kraditor, *Means and Ends*, p. 276.
20. Ibid., pp. 16-17; Bertram Wyatt-Brown, "William Lloyd Garrison and Antislavery Unity: A Reappraisal," *Civil War History* 13 (March, 1967), 5-24.

ruptions of a proper, God-ordered society.[21] Yet, such overarching interpretations, useful in their own right, should not be stressed so as to obscure the discrete political content of abolitionism and its critically important specific relationships to the narrative of sectional disruption.

To be sure, the emphasis of abolitionists on broken slave families, rebellious field hands, listless poor whites, debauched planters, and the retrograde planter economy reflected romantic caricature. Yet, judgments like these were simultaneously grounded in social and political reality, secularly defined. They reflected a clear attempt to understand southern institutions, the people whose lives were shaped by them, and the sectional frictions they generated.[22] For example, Lydia Maria Child referred in 1833 to the Nullification crisis and drew the following conclusions about the ''perpetual clashing'' of free and slave labor civilizations. After sampling them in original form, one could hardly call them products of her ''abstract'' thinking:

There are features in the organization of a society, resulting from slavery, which are conducive to anything but a union of these states. A large (slaveowning) class are without employment, are accustomed to command, and have a strong contempt for the habits of industry. This class, like the nobility of feudal times, are restless, impetuous, eager for excitement. . . . The statesmen of the South have generally been planters. Their agricultural products must pay the merchants . . . the shipowners, the manufacturers and all others concerned in the exchange of manipulation of them. It is universally agreed that the production of raw materials is the least profitable

21. The diversity of studies which reflect this general conclusion is only suggested by this citation, and encompasses ''reform'' and intellectual movements ranging from the forthright by antiabolitionist Jacksonian persuasion through abolitionism itself to the pastoral ideal and the communitarian perfectionism of John Humphrey Noyes. See, for example, J. W. Ward, *Andrew Jackson: Symbol for an Age* (New York, 1962); Marvin Myers, *The Jacksonian Persuasion: Politics and Belief* (New York, 1957), especially pp. 1-142; R. W. B. Lewis, *The American Adam: Innocence, Tragedy and Tradition in the Nineteenth Century* (Chicago, 1955); Ernest R. Sandeen, ''John Humphrey Noyes as the New Adam,'' *Church History* 40 (1971), 82-90. For studies directly relating this theme to antislavery, see two illuminating works: Eric Foner, *Free Soil, Free Labor, Free Men: The Ideology of the Republican Party Before the Civil War* (New York, 1970); and David Brian Davis, *The Slave Power Conspiracy and the Paranoid Style* (Baton Rouge, 1969). I am indebted to Professor Elkins especially for insisting in his criticisms of an earlier version of this paper, on the dynamic, radical properties of Yankee middle-class culture-at-large.
22. Apart from social and economic issues about to be discussed, abolitionists also possessed keen appreciation of the effect of bondage on masters and slaves. See Donald G. Matthews, ''The Abolitionists on Slavery: The Critique Behind the Social Movement,'' *Journal of Southern History* 33 (1967), 163-82.

employment of capital. The planters have always entertained a jealous dislike of those in the more profitable business of manufacture and exchange of products; particularly as the existence of slavery among them destroys ingenuity and enterprise, and compels them to employ merchants, manufacturers, and sailors of the free states.[23]

Child's analyses, oft repeated by other leaders, may seem crudely overdrawn.[24] Imbedded in them, however, were forthright judgments on the institutional sources of sectional conflict, conclusions which in turn arose from Child's own preferences for "free labor." And most of her assertions have since been debated, refined, defended, and seriously criticized by an imposing number of historians, none of whom is given to "abstractionism."[25]

Here then, accompanying Christ-centered attacks on authority, was well-founded social analysis. Blending sacred and profane outlooks with an ease lost to many "modern" minds, abolitionists made few hard distinctions between political perceptions and religious revelations.[26] They judged the race violence and sectional tremors of the early 1830s as omens of divine judgment and, simultaneously, as evidence of institutional disorders. Suspicious of inherited authority and lacking creditable precedents, they expected that massive immediatist activity would quickly allay all of these threats to the nation's spiritual health and organizational strength.[27] Here was the

23. Lydia Maria Child, *An Appeal*, pp. 112, 118-19.

24. See the *Liberator*, 2 February 1833, 4 January 1834, and 23 May 1835, for representative statements by the New England Anti-Slavery Society, Garrison, and Birney, respectively. For Whittier's views, see *The Anti-Slavery Reporter*, September, 1833.

25. Various thoughts expressed in Child's quote have been since explored by many scholars. Just a few are: Foner, *Free Soil*, Eugene Genovese, *The Political Economy of Slavery: Studies in the Economy and Society of the Slave South* (New York, 1965); David Bertelson, *The Lazy South* (Chapel Hill, 1968); John Hope Franklin, *The Militant South, 1800–1861* (Chicago, 1956); C. Vann Woodward, "The Southern Ethic in the Puritan World," *William and Mary Quarterly*, 3d ser., 25 (1968), 343-70; Otto Olsen, "Historians and the Extent of Slave Ownership in the Southern United States," *Civil War History* 18 (1972), 101-16; Stanley Engerman and Robert Fogel, *Time On the Cross: The Economics of American Negro Slavery* (Boston & Toronto, 1974).

26. Mary Douglas, *Natural Symbols: Explorations in Cosmology* (New York, 1970), demonstrates with provocative anthropological arguments how careful one must be in making sharply artificial or anachronistic distinctions between "sacred" and "profane" when discussing a group's collective "worldview."

27. Bertram Wyatt-Brown, "Prelude to Abolitionism: Sabbatarian Politics and the Rise of the Second Party System," *Journal of American History* 58 (1971), 316-41; see also James Brewer Stewart, "Peaceful Hopes and Violent Experiences: The Evolution of Reforming and Radical Abolitionism, 1831–1837," *Civil War History* 17 (1971), 293-309.

primary goal which synthesized their political conclusions and religious predispositions into a common course of action during the early 1830s. As the nation and each citizen earned God's redemption and blessings of Christian peace by rapidly converting to the abolitionist's theology of immediatism, southern residents were also to begin taking on middle-class properties of the North.

Black people in both sections, moreover, were to be fully included in the new bourgeois Christian order. Along with liberated poor southern whites, blacks would exercise the right to improve themselves, unimpeded by economic hierarchy and race suppression. Ex-bondsmen were to become the planters "defenders" as southern lands began to "smile beneath the plough of the freeman—the genial influence of just and equitable wages."[28] The expectation was of a homogeneous America operating on national institutions and common religious values. The Mason-Dixon line and the segregated school would soon be rendered equally obsolete by the irresistible power of moral suasion.[29]

Certainly the expectation was utopian. Moreover, by 1837, this subtle intermingling of politics and theology had been disrupted and was starting to realign itself in contradictory ways. Two new types of events, triggered by the movement but external to it, began to modify abolitionists' perceptions, expectations, and choices. Their goals and relationships to institutions now began to differentiate in response first, to the nation's massive rejection of their initial preachments, and second, to the rise of antisouthern feelings among nonabolitionist northerners.

Leonard Richards, Donald G. Matthews, Russel Blaine Nye, and Elkins himself have analyzed well various aspects of the widespread, sometimes violent opposition to immediate emancipation which mounted during the mid-1830s.[30] Yet historians have generally overlooked the fact that abolitionists could scarcely help but draw from

28. Wright, *The Sin of Slavery*, pp. 39-48.
29. William Lloyd Garrison to Henry E. Benson, August 29, 1831, in Walter Merrill, ed., *The Letters of William Lloyd Garrison* vol. 1 (Cambridge, Mass., 1971), I: *I Will Be Heard! 1822-1835*, 128.
30. Among the best studies are Leonard D. Richards, *Gentlemen of Property and Standing: Anti-Abolition Mobs in Jacksonian America* (New York, 1970); Russel Blaine Nye, *Fettered Freedom: Civil Liberties and the Slavery Controversy, 1830-1860* (East Lansing, 1949); Bertram Wyatt-Brown, "The Abolitionists' Postal Campaign of 1835," *Journal of Negro History* 50, (1965), 227-38; Donald G. Matthews, *Slavery and Methodism, A Chapter in American Morality, 1780-1845* (Princeton, 1965), pp. 113-283.

this broad repressive opposition some painful second thoughts about their original expectations. Consequently, they also discovered some new approaches to the problem of slavery. Elkins' opinion to the contrary,[31] the famous abolitionist schism of 1838 to 1840 resulted from well-defined, conflicting new postures toward institutions which emerged as reformers adjusted their thinking to the facts of mob opposition, southern hostility, and legal proscription. Clearly, the bitter reception made it evident to abolitionists that planters were impervious to moral suasion, and held far greater power in national affairs than had first been suspected. Moreover, American agencies of governance and religion, no matter how defined or otherwise viable, were wholly unequipped to acknowledge the sin of slavery.[32] The antislavery tracts and petitions had not inaugurated an era of Christian repentance and biracial middle-class progress. Instead, by 1838, the abolitionists' only achievements were sectional rancor, repressive legislation, violent disturbances in the North, and notoriety for themselves.

Such results, to be sure, meant publicity for the cause and generated some conversions. Yet, Elkins might with justice point to this outcome as confirming the abolitionists' continuing inability to contemplate rationally the consequences of their actions.[33] At the same time, abolitionists had helped to induce, albeit unintentionally, a rising hostility toward the slave states by nonabolitionist northerners. This development, in turn, caused one part of the movement to begin emphasizing in unprecedented ways the "free labor" loyalties of abolitionist thought. The delicate balance between sacred and profane remained, but the public response to immediatism was causing a rearrangement of its properties. This shift, fully under way by 1838,

31. Elkins, *Slavery*, pp. 180-85.
32. See Matthews, *Slavery and Methodism*, pp. 113-47 and Richard H. Sewell, *John P. Hale and the Politics of Abolition* (Cambridge, 1965), pp. 29-33, for a sampling of the best discussion of religious and political resistance to immediatism in the 1830s. Leon Litwack's *North of Slavery, The Negro in the Free States, 1790-1861* (Chicago, 1961), is one of the earliest and most noteworthy of the many recent studies of ante-bellum American racism. Most currently, see George M. Frederickson, *The Black Image in the White Mind: The Debate on Afro-American Character and Destiny, 1817-1914* (New York, 1971), pp. 1-164.
33. Elkins, *Slavery*, p. 160. The broader crisis of abolitionist aims and hopes was reflected in the open disagreements within the movement over the use of violence which also began in the late 1830s. See John Demos, "The Antislavery Movement and the Problem of Violent Means," *New England Quarterly* 37, (1964), 501-25, and Perry, *Radical Abolitionism*, pp. 231-67.

marked one major departure in the evolving relationships of abolitionists with American institutions and sectional politics. Elkins' presentation describes and assesses this important transition in ways that his critics, as well as those who see broad antiinstitutional unities, have overlooked.

As Elkins, among others, has stressed, the public response to immediatism was ambiguous. Even while most Americans were crying down the abolitionists' fanaticism, influential parts of northern opinion simultaneously began to distrust and oppose the South. The acts of repression themselves and the prospects of incorporating additional slave states into the Union made many nonimmediatist northerners fear for their own civil liberties and "free institutions."[34] All abolitionists shared this concern, but emerging conservative abolitionists, as they have rightly been called, slowly began identifying themselves by responding with special intensity to this rising sentiment. Here were signs of "progress," indications of ways to proceed from the impasse caused by the nation's rejection of original moral suasion. In the minds of conservative leaders like James G. Birney, Elizur Wright, Jr., William Goodell, and Gerrit Smith, these developments meant the opening of new "channels" of activity, to use Elkins' terms, some narrower "boundaries" now offered by the culture within which to approach the problem of slavery.

By 1837 and 1838, conservatives began declaring it imperative for abolitionists to cultivate the rising antisouthern spirit within the North. Thus, they slowly began to redefine their initial religious fears of retributive justice and to reassess their hopes of Christian reconciliation, relating these in new ways to that concrete quality of abolitionist thinking—loyalty to the "free labor" customs of Yankee society. Such reformers were soon engaged in creating a northern consensus on the sin of slavery which would defend and purify "free" and therefore sacred institutions from the menaces of the planter class.

The conservative expressions remained couched in pious beliefs despite what later historians might call their increasingly "earthy" concerns. Northerners, it was maintained, had a clear Christian duty to espouse immediate emancipation and race equality for reasons of personal self-interest, as well as for the good of their souls. By late

34. Elkins, *Slavery*, pp. 185-90; Foner, *Free Soil;* Nye, *Fettered Freedom.*

1836, for example, Birney paid extended tribute to the North's "honest yeomanry" who were, he felt, "as yet untainted with the (pro-slavery) corruption that is at work in other classes, undermining all that is valuable in our government."[35] Or, as William Goodell put it, Yankee Christians must oppose slavery or else "despotism must come." And once it arrived, he prophesied, the *"liberty of the freeman of the North"* would be restored only in "God's . . . terrible drama that will chastise our nation and enfranchise the slaves."[36] By 1838, continuities in evangelical language notwithstanding, conservative abolitionists were turning in more concrete, political directions what had once begun as a "disinterestedly" benevolent quest for sectional reconciliation.

Such expressions of regional loyalty also reflected the conservatives' authentic hostility to long-accepted political conventions. And such views led in turn to activities that were deeply subversive of existing national bodies. To acknowledge that the vast majority of abolitionists adopted the conservative outlook and worked to build antislavery political structures is not, as Kraditor has claimed, to "destroy the validity of Elkins' antiinstitutional charge."[37] To the contrary, the conservatives' strategic emulation of normal political activism reflected romantic assumptions and resulted in divisive programs.

As the sectional crisis ran its course, conservative abolitionists often became deeply involved in Liberty and Free Soil third party campaigns. Each such enterprise required joining political parties and appealing to voters' everyday concerns, including sometimes to racist preferences.[38] So, in certain important respects Kraditor is correct in concluding that conservatives did not display antiinstitutional propensities. Yet, the attempts of conservatives to "purify" party systems

35. James G. Birney to Ezekial Webb, Thomas Chandler, and Darius C. Johnson, October 6, 1836, in Dwight L. Dummond, ed., *The Letters of James Gillespie Birney*, 2 (New York, 1938), I, 363-64.
36. William Goodell to Amos A. Phelps, 23 July 1837, Antislavery Collection, Boston Public Library.
37. Kraditor, *Means and Ends*, p. 15.
38. Eric Foner, "Politics and Prejudices: The Free Soil Party and the Negro, 1849-1852," *Journal of Negro History* 50 (1965), 232-56; John L. Stanley, "Majority Tyranny in Tocqueville's America: The Failure of Negro Suffrage in 1846," *Political Science Quarterly* 74 (1969), 165-88; Eugene H. Berwanger, *The Frontier Against Slavery: Anti-Negro Sentiment and the Slavery Extension Controversy* (Urbana, 1967); Larry Gara, "Slavery and the Slave Power: A Crucial Distinction," *Civil War History* 15 (1969), 5-18; David B. Davis, *The Slave Power Conspiracy*.

also reflected antinomian urgings for a new moral exactitude in everyday politics regarding slavery, an aggressive rejection of long-established values of sectional tolerance and party loyalty. The effect was to further the fragmentation of national organizations. In this process few, if any, ways were suggested by which people might have systematically and peacefully eased the problems of bondage and race oppression. All of these results fall, in one way or another, within Elkins' conceptions of "antiinstitutional."

Elkins, in treating the growth of the antisouthern consensus, employs a narrative strategy for once and analyzes some of these points to good advantage. In referring to what he calls the "democratization" of abolitionism, he even suggests in a prescient footnote that "reformer" (our term is conservative), not "revolutionary," abolitionists were most directly involved.[39] In the text he observes that as more and more northerners "entered the antislavery movement on one level or another, the movement became less and less institutional in character," and ever more individualistic.[40] So it did. The Republican party of 1861, seen as the final product of this dynamic process, was born of institutional fragmentation occasioned, in part, by the efforts of conservative abolitionists in politics. Their insistence that conventional associations embody God-ordained social principles found increasing, if less explicit, support as sectional events played themselves out. Northern candidates, elected by increasingly sectionalized constituencies, came to share such general convictions. Likewise, recent studies of Republican party ideology have emphasized the importance of that broad "free labor" individualism which conservative abolitionists had begun to emphasize twenty years earlier.

Besides stressing a deep belief in each man's God-given right to exercise unlimited authority in fulfilling his destiny, the ideology also contained other antiinstitutional properties. Beliefs in a proslavery conspiracy, for example, reflected widespread distrust of "illegitimate" authority sources. Consequently, the Republican persuasion was versatile in the extreme, and could accommodate a bewildering medley of positions on slavery and on reform in general, not to mention those interested in the party's policies toward such other

39. Ibid., pp. 189 n.94, 189-90 (quotation).
40. Elkins, *Slavery*, pp. 178-90.

"unnatural" forces as immigrants, Catholics, or dealers in "ardent spirits."[41] Without indulging in needless ambiguity, then, one can understand the Republican party as at once reflecting the hard-headed responses of conventional Yankee opinion to temporal issues, and as the agency which best embodied the culture's most widely shared antiinstitutional feelings.

Yet, because conservative abolitionists shared the age's general suspicions of authority and its dominant political preferences, they should not be lumped together either with republicanism or with other factions of abolitionism. Recently, Lewis Perry has suggested otherwise, strongly emphasizing that romantic religious and intellectual affinities are more important than varying political strategies and tactics for understanding the abolitionists as a whole.[42] Such a view overlooks the fact that the conservatives' aim of purifying politics through direct participation guaranteed them a distinctive place in the history of ante-bellum race reform. Unlike the radical Garrisonian faction, conservatives often found their own roles as consistent reformers being subverted and reshaped as the sectional crisis ran its course. They failed to understand the relationship between several of their important goals and the nature of politics itself, even as they contributed to its sectionalization. In this different sense of the term, antiinstitutionalism became increasingly reflected in their own vocational histories.

Except among black political abolitionists such as Henry Highland Garnet or Frederick Douglass, the twin goals of immediate emancipation and ending white supremacy became increasingly difficult to focus on.[43] While manipulating American institutions from

41. Foner, *Free Soil;* Michael F. Holt, *Forging A Majority: The Formation of the Republican Party in Pittsburgh* (New Haven, 1969).

42. Perry, *Radical Abolitionism,* pp. 158-87. Perry, in my judgment, makes a perfectly acceptable and very sophisticated case that certain political abolitionists, at particular times reflected, as did some radical abolitionists, antipolitical, even anarchic views about voting, electioneering and governing. I am not persuaded, however, as Professor Perry seems to be, that such cross-currents were deep, broad, and sustained enough to warrant doing away with distinctions between radical (nonvoting) and conservative (voting) abolitionism, as determined by each group's postures toward and long-term interaction with the course of political events.

43. An instructive case is made by Jane H. and William H. Pease that many black abolitionists, no matter of what faction, almost always had a clearer sense of antislavery purpose than their white colleagues. See "Ends, Means and Attitudes: Black-White Conflict in the Antislavery Movement," *Civil War History* 18 (1972), 117-28. The Peases have also analyzed Garnet with considerable insight in *Bound With Them in Chains: A Biographical History of the Antislavery Movement* (Westport, Conn., 1972), pp. 162-90.

within, the capacity of many conservative abolitionists to act as imaginative, instructive, consistent critics-at-large to the nation, or even to the North, was grievously impaired.[44] Kraditor provides us with a list of exactly fifty-six proposals, some hilariously contradictory to one another, which appeared in the third and fourth party platforms of conservative abolitionists after 1840 as measures for attracting nonabolitionist voters. None of these promises, which dealt with postal rates, tariffs, prohibition, and internal improvements, had anything directly to do with black emancipation even though they reflected a variety of sympathies to other reforms. Instead, they testified to how befuddling and frustrating it was to promote forthright abolition and racial justice by attempting first to collect ballots.[45]

Her list also reminds us that the mobs and general repression of the 1830s caused many conservative abolitionists to explore some genuinely antiinstitutional paths from 1840 to 1861. Elkins' conclusions thus have important uses regarding the portion of the abolitionist movement also most reflective of the drift of ante-bellum northern society. Yet, in this instance the antiinstitutional theme has more complexity to it than its critics, its general defenders, and Elkins himself have thus far indicated. As for William Lloyd Garrison's radical circle, a variegated group which also evolved in response to the antiabolitionism of the 1830s, part four of *Slavery* also has significant value for political and intellectual historians.

During the mid-1830s, Garrison and other like-minded individuals decided, as did the conservatives, that the original aims of the movement—rapid sectional and racial reconciliation—were impossible.[46] Like Birney and other emerging conservatives, radicals were now concluding that existing national denominations and political parties were foully tainted by slavery and needed immediate purging or replacement. But here similarities ended, for Garrison and other radicals did not put increasing emphasis upon the elements of middle-class Yankee social beliefs and did not find reassurance in the North's mounting fears of southern threats to its "free institutions." They refused to equate free expression and "free institutions" generally with existing northern society, and deemed it wrong to modify

44. Joshua Leavitt to Joshua R. Giddings. 6 July 1848. Joshua R. Giddings Papers. Ohio Historical Society.
45. Kraditor. *Means and Ends*, pp. 150-52.
46. William Lloyd Garrison to Elizabeth Pease. November 6. 1837, in Louis Ruchames. ed.. *The Papers of William Lloyd Garrison*. vol. I (Cambridge. 1972) II: *A House Dividing. 1836–1840*. 321.

and "channel" their cause to accommodate nonabolitionist but sectionally sensitized northerners. Instead, reflecting on the antiabolitionist opposition, radicals concluded that all American opinion was uniformly corrupt in its hostility toward emancipation, equality, and free discussion.

In late 1835, for example, Henry C. Wright, one of Garrison's most important associates, began writing down revolutionary conclusions in his journal and in letters to friends, while commenting on antiabolitionist mobs.[47] Garrison, for his part, pronounced "The whole land . . . to be diseased beyond the power of recovery," while citing "the violence of mobs . . . and the madness of their protectors in Church and State" to demonstrate that his conclusions "had been thoroughly proved by a series of tests."[48] Edmund Quincy and Wendell Phillips, both catalyzed by the murder of Elijah Lovejoy by a proslavery mob in 1837, opened their long radical careers with similar statements of the nation's uniform iniquity.[49]

Such assertions, according to Elkins, show abolitionist antiinstitutionalism" reaching the heights of extravagance."[50] In very important respects, he is quite right. Leading radicals, though widely separated on important theological and ideological questions, did share at least one fundamental characteristic which distinguished them sharply from their conservative colleagues. While conservatives were coming to believe that public opinion was expressing its improved tone in political terms, radicals were concluding that officeholders on every level had simply responded to their constituents' unchristian preferences when winking at the mobs and supporting antiabolitionist legislation.[51]

As Kraditor correctly insists, most radicals were not advocates indiscriminately doing away with government in general, especially while citizens remained "unregenerate." Yet Garrison's hope for the substitution of "antislavery for proslavery representatives in every legislative assembly" was laden with antiinstitutionalism. Such a "political reformation," he explained, was to come about "solely by

47. Henry C. Wright, "Journal and Commonplace Book," vol. 26, p. 3; Henry C. Wright to William Lloyd Garrison, 6 April 1837, Antislavery Collection, Boston Public Library.
48. *Liberator,* 8 December 1837.
49. *Emancipator,* 31 April 1838; Wendell Phillips, "The Murder of Lovejoy," in *Speeches, Lectures and Letters,* 1st ser., (Boston, 1864), pp. 2-10.
50. Elkins, *Slavery,* pp. 175-76.
51. *Liberator,* 30 August and 13 September 1839.

a moral change in the vision of the people," not by accepting their sinful opinions, setting up an abolitionist party, and declaring voting essential to one's Christian faith. The "grand difficulty" with political abolitionism, he observed, was that voters acted not "as free moral agents," but as unrepentant "tools of party."[52] A true abolitionist voter was one who had personally transcended the trammels of oppression, not a citizen who simply preferred to vote a straight antislavery ticket. As Elkins might with justice observe, Garrison's view embodied the antithesis of structured political values, a stance which exalted romantic individualism. It would be difficult to disagree.

In making these new formulations, radical abolitionists were now vastly expanding their conceptions of the problem of slavery. As we have noted, Elkins' equation of antiinstitutionalism with a lack of "channels" for concrete action and the reformers' own perceived "limits" seems apt for the movement's earliest years. For the same reasons, the formulation appears doubly pertinent in characterizing the postures of the radicals beginning in the late 1830s. Their initial sense of isolation and feeling of personal responsibility for slavery was certainly intensified by convictions that institutions executed only the heathenish wishes of a corrupt majority. Most of them concluded ultimately that the broad sin of universal oppression was not to be combatted by religious and political "come-outerism," a peaceful abrogation of the United States Constitution, women's rights, and (for a few) a sweeping personal separation from secular constraints in general. It is at this point that Elkins begins marshalling into service adjectives like "fanatical" and "intolerant." Unfortunately, it is also at this point that his specific interpretation loses its pertinence for scholars of both abolitionism and American culture.

For one thing, Elkins' distaste for romanticism prevents him from discerning that radical abolitionism developed a serious body of utopian thought and experimentation. His verdict that American abolitionism, and especially its radical wing, suffered from a general lack of intellectual nourishment[53] actually means only that he disapproves of the assumptions which premised their ideas. One wonders

52. Kraditor, *Means and Ends*, pp. 16-19; Lewis D. Perry, "Versions of Anarchism in the Antislavery Movement," *American Quarterly* 20 (1968), 768-82; *Liberator*, 23 March and 28 June 1839 (quotation).
53. Elkins, *Slavery*, pp. 157-75.

what Elkins might have discovered had he been able to shed this bias, especially so since Perry, who is much more intellectually respectful of extreme romanticism than Elkins, has charted many of antiinstitutionalism's effects on radical abolitionists' beliefs.[54] As noted earlier, some of Perry's judgments on abolitionist faction run counter to those developed here.[55] Yet the point is that even when Elkins himself no longer furnishes insights into the radical Yankee temperament, his concept continues to demonstrate its usefulness.

So, too, the antiinstitutional theme can begin to harmonize the views of the historians of politics and reform on the radicals with those of the students of culture and theology. Here again, however, Elkins himself has made it difficult for scholars to apply his concept since he does not treat the political acts of the radical abolitionists any more respectfully than he does their intellects. The effect is like Kraditor's views regarding the conservative abolitionists. Because of his disdain for "Garrisonianism," Elkins fails to see the positive relationship between the radicals' aims and activities and their antiauthoritarian temperaments. Consequently, the fact remains obscure that radical abolitionists developed a number of very innovative, wholly appropriate approaches to southern slavery and American politics. These things they were able to do precisely because of these qualities of alienation which are explained by cultural and intellectual forces as well as by the impact of sectional events—the radicals' heightened reliance on antislavery theology and their refusals to emulate existing political forms. Political historians, therefore, ought no longer to overlook evidence of deep antiinstitutional proclivities, or feel as Kraditor, Glazer, and others seem to, that Elkins' point of view lacks validity simply because he, himself, showed pronounced biases when discussing abolitionism. Conversely, intellectual historians ought to pay more attention to the political events which helped shape romantic ideas, and to the meaning of such ideas in the larger sectional conflict. In this instance, there is a serious case to be made for the central political importance of Garrrisonian romanticism in the coming of the Civil War.

Most crucially, radical nonvoting abolitionists were continuously able to provide Americans with creative antislavery alternatives to the bloody disruption that finally overtook them. This quality, more than

54. Perry, *Radical Abolitionism.*
55. See n.42 above and accompanying text.

any other, distinguishes them from other factions. To be sure, the radicals' advice had only limited impact in the North, reflected a self-righteous judgmentalism, and did nothing to convert planters in the South. Yet by the 1840s the sectional conflict was developing a momentum of its own, independent of the radicals' cries of "No Union With Slaveholders." Certainly their silence, voluntary or forced, in the 1840s and 1850s would not have heralded the return of national concord. Moreover, radicals now harbored few expectations of achieving immediate or total results. Hence, long-term attempts to transform American opinion and to induce a thorough overhauling of the nation's values seems far more viable an alternative to civil war than the dominant inclinations of compromising with the hegemony of white supremacy, rekindling interest in compensated emancipation, or hoping vaguely for a peaceful solution once a resolute antislavery politician like Lincoln was installed in the White House.[56] The continuing demands for immediate emancipation and disunion were, as Kraditor has demonstrated, attempts to build a common bond of repentance between the sections. Their precise aim was to avoid giving Yankees a false sense of moral arrogance with which to marshal themselves against dangerous southern influences. Individual Republicans and many political abolitionists seriously questioned the nation's white supremacist practices.[57] But unlike the abolitionist radicals, they and their larger party were incapable of the imaginative, even desperately utopian thinking necessary for preparing Americans to dismantle slavery peacefully.

It must also be noted that the personalized antiinstitutional theology of the radical abolitionists generated specific reform techniques as creative and as appropriate to the situation of the 1840s and 1850s as the slogans themselves. Aiming to develop influence as an upopular but nonpartisan minority, radical abolitionists began to perfect the techniques of a modern public service pressure group.[58] They in-

56. For a provocative inquiry into the concept of "hegemony," and well-founded cautionaries about how historians ought to view past movements for American social change, see Aileen Kraditor, "American Radical Historians on Their Heritage," *Past & Present* 56 (1972), 136-53.

57. Kraditor, *Means and Ends*, pp. 206-8; Foner, *Free Soil*, pp. 261-300; Hans L. Trefousse, *The Radical Republicans: Lincoln's Vanguard for Racial Justice* (New York, 1969), pp. 2-167.

58. By "nonpartisan" I do not mean, of course, disinterested regarding the need for emancipation. The term refers only to their refusal to favor one party, section, or sect over another in a moral sense. For analyses of revolutionary abolitionist political activ-

stitutionalized agitation itself as a specialized professional career, exploring for the first time its methods even as many conservatives were sensing confusion regarding their vocational directions and antislavery goals. So considered, several well-known aspects of radical behavior testify to an analytical rigor informed by a clearly romantic perspective.

The obviously antiinstitutional demand for a peaceful overthrow of the Constitution, for example, was based upon research into the American past which displayed anything but an "abstract" approach to history.[59] Since radicals were unencumbered by specific political loyalties, they were free to interpret frankly the records of the 1787 Constitutional convention and to publicize their findings of proslavery compromise without apology. And regardless of later debates over the Founding Fathers' true intentions regarding slavery, the radicals' view of the history itself was reasonably accurate. Calls to dissolve the corrupt, "proslavery" Union thus became vehicles for publicizing historical exposés, challenging Americans of both sections to reexamine their political institutions and the values behind them respecting race and regional chauvinism.[60]

In like manner, the attacks of radicals on all political parties and churches, as well as their exchanges with individual officeholders and clerics comprised essential aspects of intelligent pressure group activity, which was informed by the dictates of perfectionism. Like the National Organization for Women, The Sierra Club, the NAACP, or other special interest groups, they criticized and exposed the noteworthy failures of all persons of importance, regardless of party, sect, or previous acts of sympathy. And, when individual politicians or ministers dramatically publicized moral questions related to slavery, most

---

ity after 1840, see James Brewer Stewart, "The Aims and Impact of Garrisonian Abolitionism, 1840–1860," *Civil War History* 15 (1969), 197-209; Kraditor, *Means and Ends*, pp. 118-77; Howard Zinn, "Abolitionists, Freedom Riders, and the Tactics of Agitation" in Duberman, *Antislavery Vanguard*, pp. 417-52. For a good introduction to the nature of American pressure groups, see Harry R. Mahood, ed., *Pressure Groups in American Politics* (New York 1970).

59. Elkins, *Slavery*, pp. 144-45.

60. Kraditor, *Means and Ends*, pp. 207-12; Staughton Lynd, "The Abolitionist Critique of the United States Constitution" in Duberman, *Antislavery Vanguard*, pp. 209-39; Wendell Phillips, "The Scholar in a Republic," in *Speeches, Lectures and Letters*, 2d ser. (Boston 1891), pp. 330-65; Richard Hofstadter, "Wendell Phillips: Patrician as Agitator" in *The American Political Tradition and the Men Who Made It* (New York, 1948, pp. 135-61; Robert Marcus, "Wendell Phillips and American Institutions," *Journal of American History* 56 (1969), 41-58.

radicals were quick to give strong support. Charles C. Burleigh, a most flamboyant Garrisonian, once explained this tactic well and revealed its highly individualistic premises, observing that "everywhere, in all organizations, there [are] men in favor of freedom. . . . As the antislavery sentiment is held up to the highest point of elevation, it will draw all men up to it."[61] Likewise, in standing apart from the government each radical lost only his vote, Edmund Quincy explained in 1844. Meanwhile, he vastly expanded his capacity to educate the people and to challenge the assumptions of politicians.[62]

In all of these ways, radical abolitionism, because of its deep spiritual alienation, ultimately developed worldly political properties which should not be overlooked. But, to understand better this complicated matter, as well as many other aspects of abolitionism, historians should perhaps look simultaneously to the world of ideas, to the circumstances of culture, and the sequences of narrative politics. In this three-way procedure, Elkins' concept of antiinstitutionalism will, one suspects, continue to illuminate unities and uncover distinctions in America's reform movements and intellectual life. In this regard, perhaps the foregoing pages have helped to relieve somewhat the "coercive" properties which, as Elkins correctly points out, continue to attend the concept of antiinstitutionalism. If so, students of ante-bellum thought and reform ought to reconsider part four of *Slavery*. Elkins' concept represents a valid and versatile insight into the nature of pre-Civil War America, especially when it is applied in a selective, controlled way to the dynamic properties of the age.

61. *Liberator*, 3 June 1852.
62. *National Anti-Slavery Standard*, reprinted in the *Herald of Freedom*, 6 September 1844.

Social events, such as this antislavery tea party sponsored by the Providence Ladies' Anti-Slavery Society, provided income for the movement and encouraged a sense of community among abolitionists. Courtesy of Rhode Island Historical Society Library (Rhi ×3 4506).

No Compromise with Slavery!

ANTI-SLAVERY

Tea Party.

THE LADIES' ANTI-SLAVERY SOCIETY,

Will give a Social Tea Party, at

HOWARD UPPER HALL,

On Wednesday Eve'g Jan. 5, 1853.

The usual attractions presented on such occasions, will be fully displayed.
Friends of the Slave, Lovers of your country's freedom, come and help us!

ADMITTANCE 12 1-2 CENTS.

Tickets for Supper 37 1-2 Cents.

A. C. Greene, Printer, Providence.

"A Determination to Labor . . .": Female Antislavery Activity in Rhode Island

Deborah Bingham Van Broekhoven

Radical abolitionist leader William Lloyd Garrison freely admitted the importance of female support for the antislavery movement. In a letter to one young woman he cited the accomplishments of British female abolitionists, and sought to persuade potential female organizers that "the destiny of the slaves is in the hands of American women, and complete emancipation can never take place without their cooperation." In that same letter Garrison pleaded with women to support his growing movement: "Fully comprehending the horrible situation of the female slaves, how can they [American women] rest quietly upon their beds at night, or feel indifferent to the deliverance of those bonds? Oh, if the shrieks could reach our ears . . . we should shudder and turn pale, and make new resolutions . . . Women of New England—mothers and daughters! if I fail to awake your sympathies, and secure your aid, I may well despair of gaining the hearts and support of men."[1]

If surviving records are indicative, Rhode Island women, from Baptists to Spiritualists, responded with enthusiasm to Garrison's plea. The organization of a "Ladies Anti-Slavery Society" in Providence in 1832—one year before the city's first male antislavery society—encouraged Garrison to hope for "a multitude of similar associations, not only in this but in every other part of the country."[2] Although several recent studies of the abolitionist movement have reexamined women's antislavery activities, the extent of their involvement is still not appreciated. As was true nationwide, in the 1830s and 1840s Rhode Island women activists sponsored public lectures, organized petition drives, and raised funds to support abolitionism. In return, these women received new knowledge and political skills and a sense of participation in a moral community. The contribution of Rhode Island women to the abolitionist movement was significant and deserves greater understanding than it has received in recent studies of Rhode Island abolitionism, which neglect women's associations or characterize one local organization as "only a female society."[3]

In keeping with nineteenth-century assumptions about female character, abolitionists frequently employed emotional appeals to rally women to their cause. "The Slave-Wife," the major piece in *Liberty Chimes*, published by the Providence Ladies Anti-Slavery Society in

Ms. Van Broekhoven is a member of the American Studies Department at Barrington College. An earlier version of this article was presented as part of a lecture series in conjunction with an exhibit at the Museum of Rhode Island History entitled "The Loom & the Lash: Northern Industry and Southern Slavery."

1. William Lloyd Garrison to Harriott Plummer, March 4, 1833, *The Letters of William Lloyd Garrison*, ed. Walter M. Merrill and Louis Rochames, 6 vols. (Cambridge, Mass., 1971), I, 208–209.
2. *Letters of William Lloyd Garrison*, I, 158.
3. John L. Myers, "Antislavery Agents in Rhode Island, 1835–1837," *R.I. History* XXX (1971), 24. See also his "Antislavery Agencies in Rhode Island, 1832–1835," *RIH* XXIX (1970), 82–93. Recent studies that have emphasized the major role of women in the antislavery movement include Ronald G. Walters, *The Antislavery Appeal: American Abolitionism after 1830* (Baltimore, 1977); Blanche Glassman Hersh, *The Slavery of Sex: Feminist Abolitionists in America* (Urbana, 1978); Lawrence J. Friedman, *Gregarious Saints: Self and Community in American Abolitionism 1830–1870* (New York, 1982); and Judith Wellman, "Women and Reform in Antebellum Upstate New York: A Profile of Grassroots Female Abolitionists," in Mabel E. Deutrich and Virginia C. Purdy, eds., *Clio Was a Woman: Studies in the History of American Women* (Washington, D.C., 1980), 113–127.

4. Francis Whipple Green, "The Slave-Wife," in Providence Ladies Anti-Slavery Society, *Liberty Chimes* (Providence, 1845).
5. *Ibid.*, 98.
6. *Ibid.*, 107.
7. *Ibid.*, 100.

1845, typifies this strategy. The story's chief appeal is the character of its female heroine, Clusy Davis, who, at the cost of her life, resists her master's sexual advances and remains loyal to her husband. Written by Rhode Island activist and author Frances Whipple Green, the story is presented as an authentic narrative of one female slave's suffering as recounted by her husband, Laco Ray.[4]

Laco recalls falling in love with Clusy and receiving their "benevolent" master's permission to marry. After the marriage, Laco begins to sense a coldness in his new wife and the couple drifts apart. Returning unexpectedly from an errand one day, Laco discovers the master furtively leaving their slave cabin, and understands the reason for Clusy's reserve. Yet despite repeated lashings, Clusy has resisted the master's advances. At the same time, she informs Laco that she is pregnant, assuring him that the child is his. Despite Clusy's resolve, the master's advances continue, and neither the sympathetic plantation mistress nor the Presbyterian minister who married Clusy and Laco can help. In fact, the minister advises Clusy to "submit" and the sin will be her master's not her own.[5] Meanwhile, each week the master continues to receive communion from this same minister.

The beatings continue; Clusy grows paler and Laco more desperate. One day while Laco is working in the fields, the master ties up Clusy for another beating, during which she faints and suffers a miscarriage. When Laco discovers his dead child and nearly dead wife, they make plans to escape. Still suffering from the abuse inflicted upon her, Clusy dies while they are passing through Maryland. Still, Laco remembers, she had felt the north wind of freedom on her cheek and died confident of a heavenly reward. Laco continues to upper Canada where, when questioned about his grief, he recalls his loss. The narrative concludes with Laco urging the listener to "tell my story. . . . publish it abroad; for if any woman can hear it without a wish—a determination to labor with all her might to abolish THE SLAVERY OF WOMAN, I impeach her virtues—She is not true—she is not PURE."[6]

Like female slaves in many antislavery tracts, the light-skinned Clusy possesses the virtues that northern women most valued, piety and sexual purity. Clusy's faith, for example, remains strong throughout her ordeal. When the minister encourages submission to the master's sexual advances, Laco condemns the religion the clergyman represents. Clusy, however, concludes that the minister "is a liar . . . and the Lord Jesus Christ never sent him." At this point the narrator reminds readers that their own piety requires action: "Think of this, all ye virtuous—all ye pious women of the land; and if your virtue, your piety, are not a mere sham—are not a damning lie—give speedy help to the thousands of women—all of them your sisters in the bonds of Christianity—who are daily prostituted."[7]

Sexual purity was fundamental to the status of true womanhood, and such acknowledgments of the sexual abuse of slave women elicited strong reactions from the public. Clusy's light skin reminded readers that miscegenation had been occurring for generations in the South, emphasizing that unlike Clusy many slave women had been violated. Many Americans, male and female, were shocked that abolitionists would even mention such scandals and joined the anti-abolitionist ranks because of this. Clusy's vulnerability, however, was also sure to engage the sympathy of women who would be alarmed not by the master's lust (sexual purity was considered to be primarily a female virtue) but by her lack of protection. Here too the narrator addresses the reader directly: "Think of it, all ye modest and virtuous women, who have husbands, and brothers and friends, and the laws, to wall around, and protect your purity."[8] Education and literature for middle-class women abounded with moral tales of innocent young women being seduced. The result was always catastrophic to the woman, who usually went insane or died or both. The tragedy of "The Slave-Wife" is that despite her carefully retained purity, Clusy dies.

Having established a sympathetic bond between Rhode Island women and the plight of slaves like Clusy, *Liberty Chimes* then turned to ways women could transform their sympathy into action. In "What Can A Woman Do?" the author admitted that independent thought in a woman was new and often viewed with suspicion, but argued that "the thing becomes more and more common and is fast losing its strangeness."[9] As examples of women's political effectiveness, he cited the women petitioners in Britain who helped end slavery there, the salon keepers in pre-revolutionary France who fostered revolutionary discussions in their parlors, and the influence of Christian women in the church—both as Catholic nuns or saints providing spiritual guidance and as Protestants who financed and managed church projects. Still, the practical question remained: what could women—barred from voting, legislating, and preaching—hope to accomplish? The key means of female influence, this writer and many others argued, was through the education of children. Whether formally as schoolteachers or informally as mothers, any "patient and perseverant" woman could become an "apostle" for abolition. The results, the article suggested, might be twenty, fifty, or one-hundred fold.[10]

While some abolitionist tactics aroused controversy, women could follow most of the advice in *Liberty Chimes* without rebelling against the notion that woman's place was the home and her major role that of mother. Advising women to exert their moral influence on the young involved nothing radical, for large numbers of new schools were established expressly to educate women to be better mothers and teachers of children. This emphasis on the mother's role as educator and transmitter of morals promoted general education for women and allowed, perhaps even required, women to learn about civic matters. As one historian has pointed out, women were considered "mothers of the republic" and as such were responsible for the training of America's future citizens and leaders who would inevitably deal with the slavery issue.[11] Several patriotic articles in *Liberty Chimes* noted the hateful blotch of slavery on the rising glory of America. One decidedly apocalyptic poem predicted that the country would be torn apart by suicidal destruction

8. *Ibid.*, 99.
9. Richard Hildreth, "What Can A Woman Do?" in *Liberty Chimes*, 34–40.
10. *Ibid.*, 40.
11. Linda Kerber, *Women of the Republic: Intellect and Ideology in Revolutionary America* (Chapel Hill, 1980).

12. Eliza Storr, "The Bond-Woman's
Prayer," in *Liberty Chimes*, 53–54. See
also L. H. Price's poem "The National
Destiny," in *Liberty Chimes*, 31–32.
13. *Letters of William Lloyd Garrison,*
I, 221.
14. For references to the formation of
these associations see the *Liberator* July
7, 1832, and April 18 and Dec. 26, 1835;
American Anti-Slavery Society, *Annual
Report of the American Anti-Slavery Society* (New York, 1835), 50–52; and *Proceedings of the Rhode Island Anti-Slavery
Convention* (Providence, 1836), 15.

("The shadow of a coming wrath, just settles around her sons.") because Americans who loved liberty failed to eradicate the injustice of
slavery.[12] The message was clear: if mothers were to secure the future
for their children, abolitionist activity was necessary.

Whether in Providence, Boston, or upstate New York, this type of argument—by orators or writers—won many female hearts. Once persuaded of the need to take action, the next step was to join or form a
female antislavery society, hundreds of which existed across the North
in the 1830s and 1840s. In these associations women could educate
themselves and work to win more female converts. Some women re-
focused or added antislavery activities to established female associations. In Providence, for example, the Colored Female Literary Society
and the Colored Female Tract Society both contributed money to Garrison's newspaper, the *Liberator*.[13] While men at the time, and several
scholars since, have described these women's groups as auxiliaries to
the more dominant male antislavery societies, this label is misleading.
In New England, the women's groups sometimes formed before male societies in their area. As mentioned earlier, a group of young women in
Providence formed New England's first female antislavery society in
June 1832. Boston ladies also organized a small group in 1832, Philadelphia a year later, and others soon followed and multiplied. Young
people formed juvenile emancipation societies in Providence and Pawtucket in 1834 and another group of Providence women, initially over
one hundred strong, formed a more enduring antislavery society in
1835. This group, perhaps the largest and most active in the state, pub-

lished *Liberty Chimes* and encouraged other Rhode Island women to form their own antislavery societies.[14]

The Kent County Female Anti-Slavery Society, also formed in 1835, was perhaps more typical of the hundreds of smaller, yet active female societies across the North. To educate themselves, their families, and friends about the evils of slavery, these women heard speakers when possible, but more often attended public readings of antislavery literature. They also raised money for abolitionist causes, particularly to support the *Liberator*, and organized several petition drives in the villages of Fiskeville, Jackson, Arkwright, Coventry, Phenix, and Washington. At the height of their activities in the 1830s, 263 women "subscribed" to the society's constitution, which made clear the association's purpose:

> We believe that all men are created equal, and are endowed by their Creator with certain inalienable rights among which, are life, liberty, and the pursuit of happiness. We believe that slavery . . . violates these sacred rights, is opposed to the dictates of humanity, and the precepts of Christianity, and ought therefore to be immediately abolished. . . . The object of this society shall be to effect the entire and immediate emancipation of the enslaved people of color within the jurisdiction of the United States, and to obtain for them their inalienable rights.

While these sentiments were not gender based, article one of the by-laws emphasized "the special duty" of women to help other women "to overthrow a system which exposes to outrage and criminal wrong, nearly one million of American females."[15]

Kent County women often drew support and ideas from other anti-slavery women. While male speakers were not excluded, the society's programs more often included literature by women and, occasionally, members gave antislavery speeches. The group listened to selections from such publications as *Right and Wrong in Boston*, the first annual report of the Boston Ladies Anti-Slavery Society, which included a detailed account of a riot by Boston's men "of property and standing" to an announced meeting of the women's group. Despite this opposition, the Boston women emphasized the rightness of their stand against slavery: "It was for our CHILDREN we did it . . . to preserve them 'an inheritance pure and undefiled, and that fadeth not away.'" And so the Kent County women learned of Scripture and precedent that supported their altruism. As the Boston women declared: "we cannot . . . believe that this garment of womanhood . . . debars us from the privileges or absolves us from the duties of a spiritual existence."[16] This sentiment surely reinforced the Kent County women in their conviction, as stated in their constitution, that slavery was an anti-Christian institution.

The women also read Elisabeth Chandler's *An Appeal to the Ladies of the United States*, extracts from Angelina Grimké's *Appeal to the Women of the South*, and Sarah Grimké's *Appeal to the Clergy of the*

1832 Broadside. City of Providence. Courtesy of Rhode Island Historical Society Library (RHi ×3 4672).

15. Constitution of the Kent County Female Anti-Slavery Society, Kent County Female Anti-Slavery Society Records, Rhode Island Historical Society. [Hereafter cited as KFAS Recs.]

16. Minutes, March 5, 1836 and Jan. 15, 1837, KFAS Recs., and Maria Weston Chapman, *Right and Wrong in Boston. Report of the Boston Female Anti-Slavery Society* . . . (Boston, 1836), 38.

17. Minutes, April 30, 1837, and Sept. 19 and Oct. 14, 1838, KFAS Recs.

18. *Ibid.*, Oct. 2, 1837. The Providence ladies statement appeared in the *Liberator*, Nov. 3, 1837, and is quoted in Keith Melder, *The Beginnings of Sisterhood: The American Women's Rights Movement, 1800–1850* (New York, 1977), 89.

19. Minutes, Sept. 9, 1837; June 25, 1837; and Aug. 2, Sept. 2, and Oct. 14, 1838, KFAS Recs.

20. *Ibid.*, July 20 and Dec. 18, 1836; May 28, 1837; and March 30, 1838.

21. Elizabeth J. Chace to Emily A. Winsor, July 27, 1837, Rhode Island Manuscripts, John Hay Library, Providence. Quoted by permission of the Brown University Library.

South. It is clear that the Kent County ladies appreciated the message of these southern sisters, for when the Congregational clergy of Connecticut wrote a public letter censuring the Grimkés for speaking to "promiscuous" (male and female) audiences, these women rallied to support both the Grimkés and Garrison, their sponsor. And despite their religious orientation, the ladies singled out the Congregational clergy for censure and emphasized their "confidence in the integrity and purity of purpose of" Garrison and his radical abolitionist newspaper.[17] In doing this, the Kent County women agreed with the Providence Ladies Anti-Slavery Society which stated: "We deem the self-denying labors of the Misses Grimké worthy of all praise. . . . We totally disapprove of the late 'Clerical Protests,' regarding them as injudicious and unchristian."[18]

Although it seems unlikely that any Kent County women attended the first national convention of abolitionist women in 1837, they did read the report of the proceedings and respond to its request that abolitionist women concentrate their activities on petitioning to block the annexation of Texas and to abolish slavery in the District of Columbia as the most direct and effective method to publicize antislavery issues.[19] If state or regional meetings were rare, letters between female societies kept the women informed and encouraged about the activities of other societies. The Kent County society received letters from the ladies of Putnam, Ohio (accompanied by a petition to circulate), the Fall River Ladies Anti-Slavery Society, and the Providence Ladies Anti-Slavery Society, which also sent books "for lending."[20]

The Providence society seems to have developed a standard letter asking sympathetic individuals to begin a "ladies" antislavery society in their village. A copy has survived, written by Elizabeth J. Chace, the society's corresponding secretary, to Emily Winsor of Greenville in 1837 during the height of the antislavery agitation (see page 45). Chace began with a general greeting and a specific request that Winsor form an antislavery society. She then cited some reasons for this activity: the extra strength women gained through association, both locally and statewide; the immediate threat of Texas, another slave territory, being added to the Union; and finally a plea "for the downtrodden and oppressed in southern bondage and to rouse our own New England women to the discharge of their high responsibility." The letter concluded with an offering of Christian encouragement and future aid from the Providence Society: "I hope you will be enabled to do much 'through Christ strengthening you,' and that you will find many warm hearts and strong hands to cooperate with you."[21] This type of communication not only spurred women to begin new societies, it also kept up morale, conveyed news, coordinated petition drives at crucial moments, and, above all, reinforced members' sense that abolitionist women were part of a national community dedicated to ending slavery.

While the minutes of the Kent County Anti-Slavery Society give us some sense of the activities undertaken by such societies, the publications of Providence and Pawtucket women provide an excellent sampling of the type of literature used to educate people, particularly women, to the evils of slavery and to the virtues and methods of abolitionism. Frances Whipple Green, the most prolific antislavery writer in Providence, authored "The Slave-Wife" in *Liberty Chimes*, and edited *The Envoy: From Free Hearts to the Free* (1840), published by the Pawtucket Juvenile Emancipation Society.[22] Green was typical of many reformers of the time, advocating on issues from abolitionism and Indian rights to factory reform and the extension of the franchise to unpropertied men. (She wrote a history of the Dorr War, siding with Dorr's efforts to further democracy.) Because she was active in many reform and social circles, Green was able to solicit contributions from prominent Rhode Islanders, Elizabeth Buffum Chace, Sarah Chace, Anna Weston, and Sophia Little (Newport) and from more nationally known Massachusetts and Philadelphia abolitionists. Like most of her non-abolitionist works, *The Envoy* is equalitarian in tone and argument, quite as radical as Garrison's *Liberator*. And while she addressed *The Envoy* to both mothers and fathers, the primary argument concerned slave women. Children's antislavery literature was also distributed in Rhode Island, including *The Anti-Slavery Alphabet*, which began "You are very young, tis true / But there's much you can do." It instructed children to join the crusade by pleading with slaveowners, talking with playmates about the evils of slavery, and boycotting products, like sugar, manufactured with slave labor.[23]

While the success of these efforts is impossible to quantify, we do know that the petitioning and literary activity that took place in Rhode Island was extensive. The United States Congress could not deal with the volume of petitions on slavery and so enacted the gag rule, automatically tabling any such petitions, an action that did not stop petitioning, and in fact may have encouraged this activity. Thousands of petitions were sent to Washington and hundreds were directed to state governments, particularly in the North. In Rhode Island the volume of antislavery petitions, plus a good number of anti-abolitionist ones, was so large that a special committee of the state legislature was appointed to deal with them. While antislavery petitions continued to arrive, the legislature clearly did not wish to take a strong abolitionist position. In fact, when Thomas Dorr presented a resolution to accept the petitions against slave trade in the District of Columbia, it was rejected 44–7.[24] The issue remained alive for several years, and in October 1837 the General Assembly passed a resolution against the annexation of Texas and appointed another committee to respond to the petitions. The committee's compromise report affirmed the evil of slavery but also the sovereign rights of southern states.[25]

Women in Rhode Island and elsewhere also provided significant financial support to maintain the movement. They organized an institution especially useful to antislavery societies: the fair or bazaar, held on a very large scale annually in Boston and Philadelphia. These fairs were grand moneymakers, often generating the greatest share of the state antislavery budget. Held during the Christmas season, the local fair was

Sophia Little, antislavery activist and a contributor to Liberty Chimes. *Courtesy of Rhode Island Historical Society Library (RHi ×3 5094).*

22. Frances Whipple Green, ed., *The Envoy: From Free Hearts to the Free* (Pawtucket, 1840).
23. *The Anti-Slavery Alphabet* (Philadelphia, 1847), 3.
24. Rhode Island, House of Representatives, *House Journal*, 1836–1838 (vol. 27), Jan. 1837, #324. See also Feb. 11 and 13, May 5 and 7, June 21, 22, 23, and Oct. 1836. Rhode Island, State Senate, *Senate Journal*, 1837–1841 Rhode Island Schedules, 1836–1838, 62ff.
25. "Report of the Committee on Abolition Petitions," *Olive Leaf and Rhode Island Temperance Herald*, Feb. 12, 1840.

*Elizabeth Buffum Chace
(1806–1899) gained prominence
in the antislavery movement and
later served as president of the
Rhode Island Woman Suffrage
Association. This portrait
appeared as the frontispiece
in volume one of* Elizabeth
Buffum Chace, Her Life and its
Environment *by Lillie Buffum
Chace Wyman and Arthur
Crawford Wyman. Courtesy of
Rhode Island Historical Society
Library (RHi ×3 3388).*

26. Broadside, "No Compromise with
Slavery: Anti-Slavery Tea Party" (Providence, 1853).
27. See, for example, the *Liberator*,
March 3, 1865.
28. American Anti-Slavery Society, *Annual Report of the American Anti-Slavery
Society* (1856; reprint, New York, 1972),
57–58.
29. *Rhode Island Anti-Slavery Convention*, 15.
30. "No Compromise."
31. The *Liberator*, Nov. 8, 1839, quoted
in Walters, *Antislavery Appeal*, 24.

a good place to buy gifts and at the same time help the cause. Smaller towns held scaled-down versions and Providence women seemed to have combined their selling with a formal tea party and supper. The flyer for the 1853 Providence fund-raiser announced "the usual attractions presented on such occasions, will be fully displayed."[26] Also, because the Boston fair was well-established and nearby, some Rhode Island women supported it by sending money or items to sell.[27] Garrison publicly acknowledged the financial importance of these fairs, reporting at one annual meeting:

> To a few energetic women in Boston, Philadelphia, Cincinatti, and other places, it is due that the movement has not been . . . crippled for the want of . . . necessary resources. These have been seconded by the zealous efforts of hundreds of smaller circles in villages and towns, and particularly by the generous and unceasing effort of our friends (abroad) to supply the Fairs with merchandise. . . . The larger proportion of the sum expended annually by this society comes from this source.[28]

Children also helped to raise money for the movement. For example, *The Envoy*, published by the Pawtucket Juvenile Emancipation Society, was intended to be both an educational tool and a fund-raiser, and one year's needlework by a group of Providence girls who met and sewed together netted almost one hundred dollars for the movement.[29]

In addition to raising money, the fairs served other purposes as well. They were educational enterprises to which abolitionists could invite unconverted friends who might imbibe some antislavery sentiment as they sampled refreshments and shopped for gifts. And Ronald Walters has argued that the fairs were a rite of community which affirmed the unity of antislavery supporters. Working at the fair brought women into contact with other parts of the abolitionist community and allowed men and women, young and old, black and white to gather and show their united purpose. Providence women invited "Friend's of the Slave, Lovers of your country's freedom, come and help us!"[30] As Maria Weston Chapman, organizer of the Boston fair wrote of its benefits: "It is the moral power, springing from the exertion to raise [funds]; this increase of light, and energy, and skill, and perseverance, and christian fellowship, and devotedness to our holy enterprise,—and spiritual strength and comfort,—that we value far more than the largest sum."[31] The evidence from their writings and contacts with sisters from Boston and elsewhere indicates that the Providence women at their tea party and supper or the Kent County women gathering signatures agreed wholeheartedly with Chapman.

Although some women's activity continued after 1840, the Rhode Island female abolitionist movement declined markedly, twenty years before the Civil War began. For example, the Kent County Female Anti-Slavery Society apparently dwindled and stopped keeping records. Some reasons seem to have been personal. The corresponding secretary for the Providence Female Anti-Slavery Society died in 1840, while the

Kent County Anti-Slavery Society secretary left to pursue missionary work in the South. But the problem was broader than the loss of a few leaders. Indeed, nationwide male support seems to have diminished at this point, and debate about the nature of this quiet period before the war continues among historians. For some the mob violence of the 1830s, generated by antagonism toward northerners who opposed slavery, led many to wonder if abolitionist's activities were stirring up a worse problem.

While little anti-abolitionist violence occurred in Rhode Island, the Dorr War may have left antislavery supporters like Green concerned, confused, or bitter at the role of local blacks in the conservative victory over the Dorr Democrats. More certainly the Dorr War focused attention on issues of more immediate concern to Rhode Islanders than slavery. As abolitionist A. Fairbanks noted in 1842: "The temperance reform and the abolition also, are all put back . . . owing to the political strife that has been waging between the Government and Dorr parties this past season."[32]

Another reason that women's antislavery activities may have declined so quickly was that most still assumed that woman's place was in the home—not in politics. And while some male abolitionists had allowed women to work for the cause, largely on the grounds of expediency, many retreated from this more equalitarian stance after the violence of the 1830s. Regardless of the approval for rare and bold women like the Grimké sisters, women's place in the political arena had never been clearly established, even within abolitionist ranks. In raising funds to support organizations advocating abolitionism, enlisting popular support in the form of petition signatures, and expanding the ranks of activities by reaching and recruiting other women, female activities seem to have been responsible for much of the movement's success. Their involvement, however, required antislavery advocates to deal with a new criticism—that they were undermining the home and perhaps society by changing women's role—creating accusations that women were hindering the movement. The most radical abolitionists, like Garrison, continued to champion both abolitionism and women's rights, arguing that women were needed and had the right to speak. The more conservative abolitionists split with Garrison over this issue so that after 1840 there were two national associations and many local groups split and feuded with each other.[33]

In Rhode Island many abolitionists deplored this separation and futilely urged unity for the good of the shared goal. The overall effect was that women's rights, an issue which had been clearly, though often inadvertently, raised in the antislavery crusade, was tabled. Many women after 1840 restricted their activities to less controversial support services. Fund-raising was still permissible, since women had been doing that at churches for some time, but more undeniably political participation, like public speaking and petitioning, diminished.

Some women, like Frances Whipple Green and Elizabeth Buffum Chace, refused to compromise. Since the church stood for the present

32. A. Fairbanks to Emily R. F. Winsor, Oct. 16, 1842, Rhode Island Manuscripts, John Hay Library, Providence. Quoted by permission of Brown University Library.

33. Gilbert H. Barnes, *The Antislavery Impulse* (New York, 1964); Eileen Kraditor, *Means and Ends in American Abolitionism: Garrison and His Critics on Strategy and Tactics* (New York, 1969); and Nancy Hewitt, "The Social Origins of Women's Antislavery Politics in Western New York," in Alan Draut, ed., *Crusaders and Compromisers: Essays on the Relationship of the Antislavery Struggle to the Antebellum Party System* (Westport, Conn., 1984), 205–233.

34. Elizabeth B. Chace to Abby Wheaton
Chase, Nov. 26, 1858. Reprinted in the
Liberator.
35. Frances Whipple Green, Shahmah
in Pursuit of Freedom (New York, 1858).
36. Joshua Leavitt, The Emancipator,
Dec. 21, 1833, quoted in Walters, Antislavery Appeal, 102–103.
37. The Liberator, May 21, 1836.

order and therefore against abolitionism, Green abandoned Christian
orthodoxy. Chace resigned from the Providence Meetings of Friends,
the members of which, she argued, were not truly antislavery but rather
apathetic in their support of the status quo. (Interestingly, Chace's husband, also a prominent radical abolitionist, never left the Quaker meeting.) Chace could not take time for other women's causes, such as raising money to restore Mount Vernon: "How can the women of this
nation talk of commemorating that struggle [the Revolution], when,
with their consent, and approval and aid, every sixth woman in the land
is liable to be sold on the auction-block?"[34] And Green continued to
write against prejudice on the eve of the Civil War, publishing her long-
est work, Shahmah in Pursuit of Freedom (1858), the story of an Al-
gerian noble who comes to America to learn about "true human freedom." Of course he is appalled by slavery, and, after a series of stock
adventures, leaves the United States with his bride to seek greater freedom in Brazil.[35]

Petitioning the federal and state governments, educating themselves
and their children, fundraising for national and local associations, Rhode
Island's abolitionist women played a significant role in the fight against
slavery. Despite the diminished visibility after 1840 of female abolitionists, most Americans continued to believe in the superior piety and
moral sense of women. As one of the conservative abolitionists noted:
"the influence of woman under God, is omnipotent."[36] In return, Rhode
Island women, like female activists elsewhere, benefitted personally
from their involvement as their spheres of activity, friendship, and influence broadened. Tens of thousands of American women accepted the
responsibility of moral leadership, which encouraged even conservative
women to expand their roles. Hundreds of women continued their reforming efforts, not just in temperance, education, or abolition, but for
women's rights as well. Green campaigned for factory workers and Chace
against sexual inequality. Other women, too, continued the moral campaign against slavery. As one Providence woman wrote to the Liberator:
"If our gospel teachers will not lead us, we must lead them! Should we
not blush . . . in as much as our sisters are in bonds, and we have not so
much as lifted a hand to save them."[37]

Providence
July 27th 1837

Miss Emily A. Winsor
at Greenville, Smithfield, R.I.

Dear friend,

Having had the pleasure of being informed that you are interested in the cause of truth and humanity I venture to address you a letter to respectfully entreat you to exert your influence in immediately forming a female Anti-Slavery Society in your place. Strength springs from action and actions come from being thrown in our own resources; five or six individuals only associative in this labor of love in assuming this responsibility of a society can produce effect much more than twice that number who feel no such responsibility. However small therefore the material from which you can organize let me entreat you as one united with you in this faerer cause to go on in the holy work—It will gladden the hearts of the Female Society here to know that another Sister brave is at work nearby—who will work in the might of love and the power of truth pleading in trumpet tones for the crushed and fettered.

Now is emphatically the time for the women of our country to labor, if they have the cause of the perishing at heart, if they are loving of their country they will in this time of their Nation's extreme peril put forth their energies to warn her at least from extending the boundaries of her unholy and guilty traffic.

If we are thoroughly imbued with the principles of abolitionism we shall deem it not only a duty but a privilege to engage in this labor of love. What heart would not rejoice to enter into this glorious work. To plead for the downtrodden and oppressed in southern bondage, and to rouse our own New England women to the discharge of their high responsibility.

Will not these arguments urged in love arouse the females of your town to action? We should have Societies organized and petitions going forth not only from every city but every quiet valley and peaceful plain at the North. The voices of New England women should be heard in every breeze crying
    "Shall we behold unheeding,
    Life's holiest feelings crushed?
    When Woman's heart is bleeding,
    Shall Woman's voice be hushed?"
I hope you will be enabled to do much "through Christ strengthening you," and that you will find many warm hearts and strong hands to cooperate with you. Be not discouraged though you meet with strong opposition if you stand the trial you will be all the better prepared for your duties. Our Society here will be happy to give you any advice or assistance in their power and by frequent communicating, enlist the sympathies of both in this common cause—Let us hear from you soon—And may our Heavenly Father grant that it may be such tidings as shall gladden our hearts and give us a new impetus to go on. Let me again urge you to Start a society. Think you number never [sic] so small a list.

Respectfully and truly yours
in the
Cause of Suffering

Eliza J. Chace
Cor. Sec.
P.L.A.S. Society

Miss Emily A. Winsor

461

RONALD G. WALTERS
The Johns Hopkins University

The Erotic South: Civilization and Sexuality in American Abolitionism[1]

AMERICAN ANTISLAVERY SENTIMENT TOOK A VERY DIFFERENT TURN AFTER
1831. Where early abolitionism accepted a gradual end to slavery, after
1831 immediate emancipation became the goal and abolitionism became a
passion driving men and women into lifelong reform careers. Yet slavery
was not new in 1831—it had been present for nearly two centuries. And
slavery did not suddenly become evil in 1831; by abolitionist logic it had
been sinful all along. Still, a number of Northern whites who had little
direct contact with the institution joined blacks in becoming acutely aware
of it, so much so that they felt compelled to seek its instant destruction.
There is a mystery here, a need to account for the rise of a particular kind
of antislavery sentiment at a particular moment in time. The problem,
however, is not fully to be resolved by a search for direct "causes" of post-
1830 abolitionism. There is the related, perhaps prior, task of charting
antislavery's form, a need to determine why it seized upon certain issues
while ignoring others, why its images were so compelling to whites who
might well have ignored slavery, and why those who accepted abolitionism's
call also drifted into a striking and novel variety of other reforms.

Historians attempting to assess the antislavery impulse have sometimes
seized upon the doctrine of "disinterested benevolence," a product of 1820s

[1] An earlier version of this essay, under a different title, was presented at the annual meeting
of the Organization of American Historians in April 1971. Commentators at that session were
Professors William O'Neill and Anne F. Scott, the latter of whom dissented strongly from the
paper's conclusions and methodological assumptions. Other drafts, both before and since,
received numerous helpful assessments from friends and colleagues, most especially from
Professors David Hollinger, Winthrop D. Jordan, Tom and Carol Leonard, Leon Litwack and
from members of the Institute of Southern History seminar at the Johns Hopkins University,
particularly from David Donald.

revivalism and an encouragement for anxious moralists to engage in good works as proof of salvation. Yet such benevolence was anything but emotionally disinterested, as at least one person possessed by it realized. Jane Swisshelm, herself a prominent abolitionist and feminist, cited the zealous commitment of William Lloyd Garrison, pioneer of post-1830 abolitionism. "It is necessary to his existence that he should work," she wrote, "—work for the slave; and in his work he gratifies all the strongest instincts of his nature, more completely than even the grossest sensualist can gratify *his*, by unlimited indulgence."[2] Jane Swisshelm revealed more than she imagined by setting up an antithesis between William Lloyd Garrison and the "sensualist." Antislavery was not simply a result of sexual fears or sexual repression (these, like slavery, existed well before 1831); but antislavery after 1831 gained direction and force from changing, culturally determined attitudes about sex, attitudes which merged with other assumptions to make conditions in the South appear uncomfortably applicable to the North, attitudes which both shaped perception of the problem and guided reformers to a new set of answers in the half-century after 1830, ultimately helping bridge the distance between immediate emancipation and a postwar world in which fit and unfit were presumed to struggle for survival.

Charles K. Whipple described slavery as "absolute, irresponsible power on one side, and entire subjection on the other." Like virtually all abolitionists he grounded his objections to the institution on this relationship of utter submission and total dominance between bondsman and master. There were, of course, other kinds of emphasis possible. Earlier humanitarian reform stressed slavery's suffering and cruelty but, no matter how useful examples of these might be in stirring sentiment, most post-1830 abolitionists finally denied that ill-treatment was what made bondage so terrible. Theodore Dwight Weld, after combing Southern newspapers and exhausting eyewitnesses for horror stories about slavery, asserted that atrocities were not the institution's most basic feature. The "combined experience of the human race," he thought, proved that such "cruelty is the spontaneous and uniform product of arbitrary power. . . ." Abuse was only an effect of submission and dominance. Even those who began by looking at slavery in still another way, in terms of "the chattel principle," came around (like Weld) to a definition which was neither economic, nor institutional, nor based on specific treatment. "Slavery is the act of one holding another as property," a correspondent to the *Philanthropist* declared, add-

---

[2] Julia Griffiths, ed., *Autographs for Freedom*, II (1854; rpt. Miami, Fla.: Research Publications Microfilm, 1969), 231. The connection between "disinterested benevolence" and immediatism was given its earliest sustained formulation in Gilbert Hobbs Barnes, *The Antislavery Impulse: 1830 1844* (1933; rpt. New York: Harcourt, Brace & World, 1964).

ing "or one man being wholly subject to the will of others." In his mind slavery (as a property relationship) resolved itself into a matter of power just as surely as it did for Whipple or Weld.[3]

Slaveholders were not reluctant heirs to their authority, as it appeared to abolitionists; so driving was the urge to dominate that it outdistanced all other possible motives, including greed. Garrison thought "the master-passion in the bosom of the slaveholder is not the love of gain, but the possession of absolute power, unlimited sovereignty." Nevertheless, abolitionists maintained that slaveholders were not peculiar in their failings but rather that they demonstrated what all people should beware of. C. K. Whipple and Theodore Dwight Weld, after detailing in their different ways slavery's devastating effects, each reminded readers that the danger was not confined to white Southerners. "No human being is fit to be trusted with absolute, irresponsible power," claimed Whipple. "If the best portion of our community were selected to hold and use such authority [as masters possess], they would very soon be corrupted." "Arbitrary power is to the mind what alcohol is to the body; it intoxicates," Weld believed. "It is perhaps the strongest human passion; and the more absolute the power, the stronger the desire for it; and the more it is desired, the more its exercise is enjoyed. ... The fact that a person intensely desires power over others, *without restraint,* shows the absolute necessity of restraint."[4] Man might have an innate moral sense, he might at times be molded by his race or environment, but abolitionists were at bottom certain that man also had a deeply implanted drive to tyrannize over others—a drive which required constant vigilance and suppression.

If the slaveholder was not unique in lusting after power, then neither was slavery the only example of coercion and "arbitrary power" disturbing to abolitionists. Few were so extreme as Abby Kelley Foster, who took her nonresistant principles to the point where, an amazed visitor reported, she was "very conscientious not to use the least wordly authority over her child"[5] Other abolitionists, even those less dogmatic (or foolhardy) than Mrs. Foster, were outraged by the tyranny of preacher, politician, corrupt public opinion and institutions.[6] Slavery might be a special case because of

[3]Charles K. Whipple, *The Family Relation, as Affected by Slavery* (Cincinnati: American Reform Tract ... Soc. [1858]), p. 17; [Theodore Dwight Weld], *American Slavery as It Is: Testimony of a Thousand Witnesses* (New York: American Anti-Slavery Soc., 1839), p. 117; *Philanthropist,* Apr. 14, 1840.

[4]*Liberator,* Mar. 1, 1850; Whipple, *Family Relation,* p. 23; [Weld], *American Slavery as It Is,* p. 115.

[5]John White Chadwick, ed., *A Life for Liberty: Anti-Slavery and Other Letters of Sallie Holley* (1899; rpt. New York: Negro Universities Press, 1969), p. 123.

[6]Those abolitionists who were not nonresistants—Christian anarchists—had difficulty determining where authority and power should be used. See, for example, Weld's *American Slavery as It Is.* Weld seems to have spoken of the property aspects of slavery largely as a way of dis-

its magnitude and because it followed racial lines, but the principle could appear elsewhere. Long before antislavery politicians attempted to persuade white Northerners that the Slave Power endangered their own liberties, not merely the slave's, abolitionists warned that arbitrary authority did not stop with master and chattel. "Who is safe?" asked Henry B. Stanton in 1836. "Can you confine the operations of this principle to the black man?"[7] Suppression of civil liberties and stories of whites sold into slavery were only exaggerated reminders that you, in fact, could not do so.

Slavery, then, stood as the virtual distillation of malevolence lurking in the breast of man. The institution, Lydia Maria Child decided, "concentrated the strongest evils of human nature—vanity, pride, love of power, licentiousness, and indolence"—all stemming from man's unrestrained will to dominate. Yet Americans of an earlier generation had also been suspicious of man's ability to wield authority. Such hostility appeared blatantly at the time of the American Revolution and it had even then been applied to slavery. John Woolman, almost a lifetime before Garrison's career began, argued against the institution because "so long as men are biassed by narrow self-love, so long an absolute power over other men is unfit for them." John Adams, in 1765, could write of "the love of power, which had been so often the cause of slavery."[8] But, deep as fear of power had been among the Revolutionary generation, it took on new life after 1830: in addition to bearing an invigorated affinity to a romantic age's "individualism," it regained vitality among antebellum whites who seemed to be losing control over their own destinies, as middle-class moralists well might be in an industrializing nation where the political system was passing into the hands of strange and uncouth men. Also, the concept of "power" was coming by the 1830s to fit into a new web of associations which ensnared some of the deepest and most mysterious forces abolitionists believed to be in all men. These included the deepest, most mysterious, most fearful force of all: human sexuality. For abolitionists the distance was not great from lust for power to mere lust.

---

tinguishing between slavery and "legitimate" uses of power, as in family relations. Lewis Curtis Perry, "Antislavery and Anarchy: A Study of the Ideas of Abolitionism before the Civil War," Diss. Cornell 1967, pp. 101-2, et passim, shows how attacks on slavery easily became attacks upon authority. See also Lewis Perry, "Versions of Anarchism in the Antislavery Movement," *American Quarterly*, 20 (1968), 772, 781.

[7] *Emancipator*, July 21, 1836. Perry, "Antislavery and Anarchy," pp. 12 ff, depicts slavery as a metaphor for denial of freedom.

[8] Child, *An Appeal in Favor of Americans Called Africans* (1836; rpt. New York: Arno Press, 1968), p. 101; Bernard Bailyn, *The Origin of American Politics* (New York: Knopf, 1968), p. 56; Woolman, conveniently quoted in William H. and Jane H. Pease, eds., *The Antislavery Argument* (Indianapolis: Bobbs-Merrill, 1965), p. 7; Adams quoted in Ernest Lee Tuveson, *Redeemer Nation: The Idea of America's Millennial Role* (Chicago: Univ. of Chicago Press, 1968), p. 21.

Abolitionists did not dwell "excessively" on sexual misconduct in the South—their writings have little merit as pornography. Furthermore, for centuries whites had imagined (and cultivated) erotic potential in interracial contact. Nevertheless, this potential could be organized into more than one pattern of perception and antislavery propaganda directly reversed a prevalent assumption by presenting white men, not black men, as sexual aggressors. Early in his career Garrison set the tone. He was accosted by a slaveholder who posed American racism's classic question: "How should you like to have a black man marry your daughter?" Garrison replied that "slaveholders generally should be the last persons to affect fastidiousness on that point; for they seem to be enamoured with amalgamation."[9] The retort was unanswerable and survived down to the Civil War. It was, in part, simply fine strategy, pointing both to an obvious hypocrisy and a very real consequence of slavery.

But abolitionists did not stop with this simple and expedient formula. They were not so opportunistic or unimaginative as to argue that erotic activity was irrevocably bound to be at the instigation of white males. Gerrit Smith believed planters would not fight an insurrection effectively because they would be too "busy in transporting their wives and daughters to places where they would be safe from that worst fate which husbands and fathers can imagine for their wives and daughters." George Bourne pondered "What may be the awful consequences, if ever the colored men by physical force should attain the mastery?" He decided "If no other argument could be adduced in favor of immediate and universal emancipation, that single fact is sufficient. Delay only increases the danger of the white women and augments the spirit of determined malignity and revenge in the colored men." Abolition would lead to forgiveness and to sexual security—for white women as well as female slaves.[10]

Rape, however, was only one form of sexual retribution abolitionists foresaw bondsmen exacting upon the master class. Louisa Barker believed black women lured young slaveholders into illicit attachments as a way of lessening chances that the favored slave might be sold—and to destroy the master's constitution through physical overindulgence. Still another writer

---

[9] *Liberator*, Feb. 5, 1831; for another early example see LaRoy Sunderland, *Anti-Slavery Manual, Containing a Collection of Facts and Arguments on American Slavery*, 2nd ed. (New York: Benedict, 1837), pp. 132-33.

[10] Gerritt Smith to the Jerry Rescue Committee, Aug. 27, 1859, in Octavius Brooks Frothingham, *Gerrit Smith: A Biography*, 2nd ed. (New York: Putnam, 1879), p. 240; [George Bourne], *Slavery Illustrated in Its Effects upon Woman and Domestic Society* (Boston: Knapp, 1837), p. 73. Hints that rape would be a consequence of insurrection were generally delicately phrased. Thomas Wentworth Higginson, *Black Rebellion* (New York: Arno, 1969), pp. 126-27, 175-76, seems to dismiss the possibility. But Higginson was concerned to demonstrate the nobility of slave rebels and was unlikely to acknowledge rape as a feature of their assault on slavery.

argued that "women who have been drawn into licentiousness by wicked men, if they retain their vicious habits, almost invariably display their revenge for their own debasement, by ensnaring others into the same corruption and moral ruin." This placed on female slaves much responsibility for stirring the sensuality of their masters, for degrading the slaveholder as they had been degraded. But there were even more horrifying prospects—lasciviousness did not have to stop with white men and black women enticing each other. "Were it necessary," John Rankin stated primly, "I could refer you to several instances of slaves actually seducing the daughters of their masters! Such seductions sometimes happen even in the most respectable slaveholding families." It was impossible for white girls always to "escape this impetuous fountain of pollution."[11]

Comments like these, besides titillating the imaginations of genteelly horrified readers, touched the South at a sensitive point—its image of itself and of its women. And they moved the argument from the idea that whites were sexual aggressors over to the more comfortable position (for whites) that blacks represented sensuality after all. Yet the key to antislavery descriptions of Southern eroticism was not in any particular combination or aspect, although emotional associations concerning interracial sex undoubtedly played their part; it was in a generalized sense that the South was a society in which man's sexual nature had no checks put upon it.

"Illicit intercourse" was embedded in the very conditions of Southern life, abolitionists believed. For the master "the temptation is always at hand—the legal authority absolute—the actual power complete—the vice a profitable one" if it produced slaves for market ". . . . —and the custom so universal as to bring no disgrace. . . ." In addition, the planter, who had others to work for him, could be indolent and this had a "very debasing" effect on "less intellectual minds." Consequently such men "are driven by it to seek occupation in the lowest pleasures." John Rankin felt that "we may always expect to find the most confirmed habits of vice where idleness prevails." Also, there was scandalous nudity among slaves. One author, using the apt pseudonym, "Puritan," was appalled that "not only in taverns, but in boarding houses, and, the dwellings of individuals, boys and girls verging on maturity altogether unclothed, wait upon ladies and gentlemen, without exciting even the suffusion of a blush on the face of young females, who thus gradually become habituated to scenes of which

---

[11] [Louisa J. Barker], *Influence of Slavery upon the White Population* (New York: American Anti-Slavery Soc., 1855 56), p. 6; [Bourne], *Slavery Illustrated*, p. 71; John Rankin, *Letters on American Slavery, Addressed to Mr. Thomas Rankin, Merchant at Middlebrook, Augusta Co., Va.* (1838; rpt. New York: Arno, 1969), letter 11. Rankin also quoted in *Liberator*, Oct. 20, 1832, and in LaRoy Sunderland, *The Testimony of God against Slavery . . . ,* 2nd ed. (New York: Williams, 1836), p. 87.

delicate and refined Northern women cannot adequately conceive." As if that were not enough, free and easy association between slave children and white children on the plantation spread the depravity of the back cabins (where there was no incentive to virtue) to the big house once again. "Between the female slaves and the misses there is an unrestrained communication," Southern-born James A. Thome explained to the American Anti-Slavery Society. "As they come in contact through the day, the courtesan feats of the over night are whispered into the ear of the unsuspecting [white] girl and posion her youthful mind."[12]

In its libidinousness the South could only be compared to other examples of utter depravity and dissolution. Thome informed an audience of attentive young ladies that "THE SOUTHERN STATES ARE ONE GREAT SODOM" and his account was seconded by another abolitionist who had lived in Virginia and Maryland. "The sixteen slave States constitute one vast brothel," the *Liberator* declared in 1858. Twenty years earlier the *Pennsylvania Freeman* spoke of the "great moral lazarhous of Southern slavery. . . ." Thomas Wentworth Higginson decided that, compared to the South, "a Turkish harem is a cradle of virgin purity." Henry C. Wright preferred comparison with New York's notorious Five Points district, much to its advantage, of course.[13] Like Sodom, brothels or a harem, the South appeared to be a place in which men could indulge their erotic impulses with impunity.

Yet, in the nature of things, there must be retribution. It could be physiological since—the 19th century assumed—sexual excesses ultimately destroyed body and mind. Planters, according to Mrs. Louisa Barker, exemplified the "wreck of early manhood always resulting from self-indulgence." They were "born with feeble minds and bodies, with just force enough to transmit the family name, and produce in feebler characters a second edition of the father's life." Mrs. Barker's comments were consistent with the way other abolitionists viewed the South and with the way her times viewed sex, but they were almost unique in antislavery literature—although the character of the languid but erratic planter was

[12]Whipple, *Family Relation*, p. 8; "Influence of Slavery on Slaveholders," *Quarterly Anti-Slavery Magazine*, 1 (1836), 326; Rankin, *Letters on Slavery*, pp. 62–63 (which also contains comments on the corrupting influence of communication between slave and white children); Puritan, *The Abrogation of the Seventh Commandment by the American Churches* (New York: Ruggles, 1835), p. 5; Thome quoted in *Liberator*, May 17, 1834. Thomas F. Harwood, "The Abolitionist Image of Louisiana and Mississippi," *Louisiana History*, 7 (1966), 298, 299–300, notes abolitionist concern for Southern sexuality.
[13]*Liberator*, May 10, 1834 (comments on Thome's address by "G. B.," undoubtedly George Bourne); Jan. 29, 1858; *Pennsylvania Freeman*, July 4, 1834; Higginson quoted in Tilden G. Edelstein, *Strange Enthusiasm: A Life of Thomas Wentworth Higginson* (New Haven: Yale Univ. Press, 1968), p. 100; *Liberator*, Oct. 8, 1858.

not.[14] The more usual form of retribution predicted for Southern licentiousness was social.

There was a sense among some abolitionists in the 1830s, as immediate emancipation sentiment among them began to take hold, that (in the words of James G. Birney) "from causes now operating, the *South* must be filled in a few years, with blacks and, it may be, that in our lives it will be given up to them." Birney, in a letter marking his public renunciation of colonization as a solution to slavery, detailed the "alarming rapidity" with which the process was operating in his native Kentucky. "In the midst of their oppressions, and in spite of them, the colored population of the South is rapidly increasing," wrote A. A. Phelps in 1834. "Like the Israelites in Egypt, the more they are afflicted, the more they multiply and grow. . . ." Maintain slavery, John Rankin warned, and you will "increase their [slaves'] numbers, and enable them to overpower the nation. Their enormous increase beyond that of the white population is truly alarming." Liberation, however, would disperse blacks and make their population growth "proportionate to the rest of the nation." LaRoy Sunderland quantified the increase, using censuses through 1830, and was not convinced that it all came from promiscuity among slaves. "That the blacks should increase faster than the whites, is easily accounted for," he remarked dryly, "from the fact, that the former class are increased by the latter, but the blacks cannot increase the whites."[15] Such statements seem to have decreased in time and with additional censuses (although complaints about licentiousness persisted), but they and fears of imminent insurrections glare luridly from early abolitionist propaganda, twin expressions of a belief that the South faced an overwhelming chastizing event, that white dominance might in turn become submission.

[14][Barker], *Influence of Slavery*, p. 6. William R. Taylor, *Cavalier and Yankee: The Old South and American National Character* (New York: Braziller, 1961), p. 139, notes that the planter, as a literary figure, was often depicted as lacking vitality and manliness. Taylor felt (I think correctly) that this may reflect the image of John Randolph as well as the 19th century's fascination with Hamlet. In the case of Mrs. Barker, and perhaps in the case of the languid, erratic and unstable Southerner of other antislavery writings, the implications are sexual: the worn-out, enfeebled planter is not Hamlet but the age's concept of a man who has committed sexual excess.

[15]Birney to R. R. Gurley, Dec. 3, 1833 (also, Birney to Gurley, Sept. 24, 1833), in Dwight L. Dumond, ed., *Letters of James Gillespie Birney, 1831-1857* (New York: Appleton-Century, 1938), I, 97, 90; James G. Birney, *Letter on Colonization, Addressed to the Rev. Thornton J. Mills, Corresponding Secretary of the Kentucky Colonization Society* (New York: Office of Anti-Slavery Reporter, 1834), p. 44; Amos A. Phelps, *Lectures on Slavery and Its Remedy* (Boston: New England Anti-Slavery Soc., 1834), p. 209; Rankin, *Letters on Slavery*, p. 108; Sunderland, *Anti-Slavery Manual*, pp. 11-12. *Liberator*, Aug. 13, 1841, noted that by the Census of 1840 blacks showed less than "a fair rate of increase." It was then impossible to maintain that the South was in danger of being overwhelmed. The *Liberator*, alert to an argument, explained that the new figures now proved that slavery had murdered a quarter of a million people who might otherwise have lived.

There were, of course, wonderful propaganda advantages here. The issue of miscegenation forever dogged the antislavery movement and by stressing Southern licentiousness abolitionists could turn on their accusers. They could speak of the slave system's "dreadful amalgamating abominations" and argue that such would "experience, in all probability, a ten fold diminution" with emancipation. They could go as far as Elijah Lovejoy and claim "one reason why abolitionists urge the abolition of slavery is, that they fully believe it will put a stop, in a great and almost entire measure, to that wretched, and shameful, and polluted intercourse between the whites and the blacks, now so common, it may be said so universal, in the slave states."[16] Yet propaganda advantages—if they were the only consideration—would have been greater had abolitionists not also insisted, as they did at times, that "the right to choose a partner for life is so exclusive and sacred, that it is never interfered with, except by the worst of tyrants." Garrison, with his usual tactless boldness, even asserted perfect racial equality and concluded that "inter-marriage is neither unnatural nor repugnant to nature, but obviously proper and salutary; it being designed to unite people of different tribes and nations, and to break down those petty distinctions which are the effect of climate or locality of situation. . . ."[17] Such frontal assaults on antimiscegenation sentiment, if nothing else, show that sexual attitudes were not something merely to be played upon for achievement of social power.

Instead, what abolitionists wrote about Southern sexuality must be put in relation to 19th century assumptions and to conditions in the North which gave urgency to concern for licentiousness, as well as in relation to other reform interests displayed by those involved in the antislavery crusade.

It was possible for abolitionists to perceive the South as a society given over to lust not simply because miscegenation and unhallowed sex occurred under slavery. After all, erotic activity between master class and bondsmen did not originate in 1831 (nor did disgust with Southern morals—New En-

---

[16] *Emancipator*, Sept. 14, 1833; Aug. 10, 1837 (see also Aug. 19, 1834, and issues throughout the summer of 1834 for denials that abolitionists aimed at miscegenation). Leonard L. Richards, *"Gentlemen of Property and Standing": Anti-Abolition Mobs in Jacksonian America* (New York: Oxford Univ. Press, 1970), pp. 31–32, et passim, notes the intense fear of miscegenation which anti-abolitionists fastened onto antislavery men and women.

[17] Sunderland, *Anti-Slavery Manual*, p. 13; *Liberator*, May 7, 1831 (also, Nov. 17, 1832). Child, *Appeal*, p. 133, and Phelps, *Lectures on Slavery*, p. 236, argue that in the future interracial unions might not be scorned and that the present has no right to determine who should marry at a later date. Gerrit Smith, *Letter of Gerrit Smith to Hon. Henry Clay* (New York: American Anti-Slavery Soc., 1839), p. 36, asserts that legal marriages between blacks and whites would increase after freedom but that these were preferable to licentiousness. See also, Bertram Wyatt-Brown, *Lewis Tappan and the Evangelical War Against Slavery* (Cleveland: Case Western Reserve Univ. Press, 1969), p. 177

gland Federalists a generation before had that in abundance). And miscegenation may well have been decreasing at the very time it became a staple of antislavery propaganda.[18] Nevertheless, antebellum Northern sensibility was sharpened by presuming an interchangeability between power and sexuality, by believing that man's nature, if unchained, exhibited fearsome and diverse urges to dominate and possess. Sexuality therefore seemed to exist in the master-slave relationship itself (or, rather, in man himself) not just in the South, which was only an archetype. One abolitionist noted that "Clerical Slave-Holding in Connecticut" some years before had resulted in a "constant illicit intercourse" between ministers and their female slaves. In other words, it could happen anywhere—even with clergymen and even in Connecticut.[19]

Portions of the abolitionist's view possess an eternal validity: some human beings have always turned tyranny into erotic pleasure. But belief that submission and dominance lead to sexual license had much wider currency in 19th century America than in previous centuries or in our own day. Victorian pornography, for instance, exploited situations of power and powerlessness more than the contemporary variety does (despite some lurid exceptions) and probably more than ancient bawdy literature generally did. In one 19th century classic the action took place in a harem where "The Lustful Turk," a darkly sensual being, literally reduced women (even good English women!) to sexual slaves. His power was both political and erotic, and his desires were as unchecked as they were varied. This was strikingly similar to antislavery images of the South and the slaveholder, a similarity increased when one of the lustful Turk's victims made a speech in which she attacked slavery as "the most powerful agent in the degradation of mankind," a charming bit of abolitionism amidst depravity. In more respectable Victorian circles it was thought that servants, another class of underling, were both sexually corrupted and agents of corruption, a matter which later attracted the attention of Sigmund Freud.[20]

[18]Winthrop D. Jordan, *White Over Black: American Attitudes Toward the Negro, 1550-1812* (Chapel Hill: Univ. of North Carolina Press, 1968), p. 137.
[19]W. G. (undoubtedly William Goodell), in *Emancipator*, Sept. 1835.
[20]Anonymous, *The Lustful Turk* . . . (1893; rpt. New York: Zebra Books, 1967; orig. ed. 1828), p. 71; Bernard Wishy, *The Child and the Republic: The Dawn of Modern American Child Nurture* (Philadelphia: Univ. of Pennsylvania Press, 1968), p. 40, notes the belief that servants were corruptors and cites George Combe, an author respected and personally known by many abolitionists; Philip Rieff, *Freud: The Mind of the Moralist* (1959; rpt. Garden City, N.Y.: Doubleday, 1961), p. 166. On Victorian pornography generally see Steven Marcus, *The Other Victorians: A Study of Sexuality and Pornography in Mid-Nineteenth Century England*, rev. ed. (New York: Bantam, 1967). Marcus relates the cult of sensibility, which appeared among antislavery writers, to sexuality. Milton Rugoff, *Prudery and Passion: Sexuality in Victorian America* (New York: Putnam, 1971), is scantily researched but does include a section on the image of the South.

A similar sense that subordination engendered debauchery shaped contemporary anti-Catholic diatribes. George Bourne, an early and important abolitionist, doubled as a Catholic baiter and found his careers easily reconciled. He pictured the South as an erotic society where whites "have been indulged in all the vicious gratifications which lawless power and unrestrained lust, can amalgamate. . . ." Much the same, he believed, prevailed in that other closed society, the convent. There (in Bourne's imagination) the priest's absolute power and unchecked erotic energy replaced the planter's and the seduction and seductiveness of nuns replaced female slaves.[21]

Enough Southern sensuality existed to fuel the minds of men like Bourne and of abolitionists less determined than he to ferret out licentiousness. But in antislavery propaganda Southern sensuality, as much as anything, illustrated a general and not very lovely principle abolitionists held to be true about man and what possession of power did to him. "We know what human nature is; what are its weaknesses, what its passions," the *Philanthropist* asserted confidently, as it remarked upon the plantation's potential for depravity.[22] Plantations, like a moralist's equivalent for the settings of pornographic novels, were simply places where the repressed could come out of hiding. Abolitionists saw both what was actually there—erotic encounters did occur—and what associations of power with sex prepared them to see.

The abolitionist critique's intensity was not just a matter of these associations, nor was it just recognition that sexuality could flourish under slavery. After all, neither possession of power nor of sexual opportunity is innately fearsome; it may be more natural to relish both. The existence of Southern licentiousness and arbitrary will, however, helped abolitionists define the South, slaveholders and slavery in such a way that they became symbols of negation, opposites against which to measure what was good and progressive. And that measurement necessarily reflected a number of firmly held judgments about what man and society should be.

In 1839, unconsciously forecasting the insight of a later and more famous Victorian moralist, Theodore Dwight Weld wrote that "Restraints are the web of civilized society, warp and woof." James G. Birney, musing to his diary in 1850, decided: "The reason that savage & barbarous nations remain so—& unrighteous men, too—is that they manage their affairs by passion—not by reason. Just in proportion as reason prevails, it will control

---

[21] Bourne, letter to Rhode-Island Anti-Slavery Society, in *Liberator*, Feb. 6, 1836; [Bourne], *Lorette, The History of Louise, Daughter of a Canadian Nun, Exhibiting the Interior of Female Convents*, 3rd ed. (New York: Small, 1834), pp. 37–40, 45, stresses the absolute power of the priest—a theme, actually, of the whole novel. Bourne was also a supporter of the notorious Maria Monk and editor of an anti-Catholic newspaper.

[22] *Philanthropist*, quoted in *Emancipator*, Dec. 6, 1838.

& restrain passion, & just in proportion as it prevails, & passion diminishes nations emerge from ignorance & darkness & become civilized." Here was a feeling that civilization, if not its discontents, depended on curbing what another abolitionist called "the fatal anarchy of the lowest passions."[23]

Of course these passions were not exclusively sexual. Birney would not have argued that "savage & barbarous nations" governed themselves by erotic means. But sex was clearly among the most formidable components of the "animal nature" which was to be subdued before humans or their society could be counted as civilized. Theodore Parker decided when a man "is cultivated and refined, the sentiment [of love] is more than the appetite [of sex]; the animal appetite remains but it does not bear so large a ratio to the whole consciousness of the man as before. . . ." The proper gentleman, like the proper lady, triumphed over sensuality. Sarah Grimke, emerging from a different tradition of gentility than Parker's, agreed with his estimate. It was impossible for men and women to enjoy the relationship God intended until "our intercourse is purified by the forgetfulness of sex. . . ." This resonated, almost as a linguistic pun, with an older, basically biblical, tradition which held (as restated by Beriah Green) that "All visible slavery is merely a picture of the invisible sway of the passions."[24] In the minds of

[23][Theodore Dwight Weld], *The Bible Against Slavery. An Inquiry into the Patriarchal and Mosaic Systems on the Subject of Human Rights*, 4th ed. (New York: American Anti-Slavery Soc., 1838), p. 7; James G. Birney MS Diary, May 9, 1850, Birney MSS, Library of Congress; Gilbert Haven, *National Sermons. Sermons, Speeches and Letters on Slavery and Its War . . .* (Boston: Lee & Shepard, 1869), p. 3. Daniel Walker Howe, *The Unitarian Conscience: Harvard Moral Philosophy, 1805-1861* (Cambridge: Harvard Univ. Press, 1970), p. 60: "Unitarians were led to espouse the view that sin consisted of a breakdown in the internal harmony, an abdication by the higher faculties of their dominion over the lower." The theme of control clearly was not confined to antislavery. For other examples see Wishy, *Child and the Republic*, p. 17; Clifford S. Griffin, *Their Brother's Keepers: Moral Stewardship in the United States, 1800-1865* (New Brunswick, N.J.: Rutgers Univ. Press, 1960); and Nathan G. Hale Jr., *Freud and the Americans: The Beginnings of Psychoanalysis in the United States, 1876-1917* (New York: Oxford Univ. Press, 1971). pp. 24-26. Joseph Ambrose Banks, *Prosperity and Parenthood: A Study of Family Planning among the Victorian Middle Classes* (London: Routledge & Paul, 1954), p. 198, notes that about 1830 the English middle class began "applying the theme of control to their own way of life." They did this, in part, by advocating sexual self-restraint. I am aware that the word "passions" had a technical psychological sense which lingered on into the 19th century. But both the context of comments and a check of the *Oxford English Dictionary* have convinced me that abolitionists generally used the word in its more modern sense of "intense emotions," largely sexual. There is information on topics discussed on the following pages, as well as on Victorian sexuality, in John R. Betts, "Mind and Body in Early American Thought," *Journal of American History*, 54 (1968), 787-805.

[24]Parker to Robert White, Oct. 7, 1849, in John Weiss, *Life and Correspondence of Theodore Parker, Minister of the Twenty-Eight Congregational Society, Boston* (New York: Appleton, 1864), I, 386; *Liberator*, Jan. 12, 1838; Green to Weld, July 11, 1841, in Gilbert H. Barnes and Dwight L. Dumond, eds., *Letters of Theodore Dwight Weld, Angelina Grimké Weld, and Sarah Grimké, 1822-1844* (New York: Appleton-Century, 1934), II, 868. On the religious meaning of slavery, sin and bondage see Jordan, *White Over Black*, and David Brion Davis, *The Problem of Slavery in Western Culture* (Ithaca: Cornell Univ. Press, 1966).

Christians slavery had always borne with it imputations of sin and human willfulness, but it took the 19th century, and a millennialistic nation, to transfer these ancient associations from slave to master and to impose upon them a drive for "civilization" and for (what was virtually the same thing) control, particularly control of the inner and lusty man.

Slavery was a guidepost, marking the outer limits of disorder and debauchery; but abolitionist perceptions of human failings neither began nor ended with the South's peculiar institution—reformers defined their own moral responsibilities in much the same terms they applied to slaveholders and other sinners. "And how is slavery to be abolished by those who are slaves themselves to their own appetites and passions?" Beriah Green asked. The *Emancipator* noted "the common acceptance of things" in which "men deem themselves the most happy when they can the most easily set aside known prohibitions and indulge in certain propensities." It contrasted this with the "early propagators of the religion of the cross" who had "no animal passions to gratify" as they were led to martyrdom. The lesson was unmistakable: a man who would do good must first conquer himself.[25]

The courtship of Theodore Dwight Weld and Angelina Grimké, a veritable orgy of restraint, revealed that reformers were willing to practice what they preached. Weld regarded his emotions for Miss Grimké as a challenge to be overcome. "It will be a relief to you," he triumphantly assured Angelina in March 1838, "to know that I have acquired *perfect self-control,* so far as any *expression* or *appearance* of deep feeling is visible to others." Angelina earlier chided him for carrying things too far. "Why this waste of moral strength?" she asked. But she likewise thought of civilization as a repression of mankind's deeper and more mysterious forces. She responded ecstatically upon finding how elevated Weld's views of courtship were—how similar to her own, how unsensual. ". . . I have been tempted to think marriage was *sinful,* because of what appeared to me almost invariably to prompt and lead to it," she wrote. "Instead of the higher, nobler sentiments being first aroused, and leading on the lower passions *captive* to their will, the *latter* seemed to be *lords* over the *former.* Well I am convinced that men in general, the vast majority, believe most seriously that women were made to gratify their animal appetites, *expressly* to

---

[25] *Radical Abolitionist,* I (1856), 101; *Emancipator,* Aug. 24, 1933. See Green to Theodore Dwight Weld, July 11, 1841, in *Weld-Grimké Letters,* II, 868: "We are not fit to plead the cause of Freedom, until we get free from the tyranny of our own passions." Bertram Wyatt-Brown, "Prophets Outside Zion: Career and Commitment in the Abolitionist Movement," paper delivered at the American Historical Association annual convention, Dec. 30, 1970, notes many abolitionists who recalled childhood struggles with self-control. Professor Wyatt-Brown has recast some of his ideas in slightly different form in "The New Left and the Abolitionists: Romantic Radicalism in America," *Soundings,* 44 (1971), 147-63.

minister to *their* pleasure. . . ." The couple's control extended beyond the awkwardness of courtship. A few years after their marriage James G. Birney visited them, remarking to his diary, with a touch of envy, "Their self-denial—their firmness in principles puts me to shame."[26] The Welds, their passions correctly ordered, settled into a long and gently loving life together.

Abolitionists not only controlled their own passional natures, and sought to control the South's, they also detected more general threats which (again) they frequently put in terms of rampant sexuality. "There is not a nation nor a tribe of men on earth so steeped in sexual pollution as this," Henry C. Wright thought. Thomas Wentworth Higginson saw the mass of men "deep in sensual vileness" while William Lloyd Garrison attacked a colonizationist not simply for his views on slavery but also for refusing to believe that "licentiousness pervades the whole land." William Goodell credited the South with an especial licentiousness, but the baneful influence did not stop there; instead it "pollutes the atmosphere of our splendid cities, and infects the whole land with the leprosy of Sodom." Less metaphorical, Stephen Pearl Andrews flatly stated that "Prostitution, in Marriage and out of it, and solitary vice, characterize Society as it is."[27] The South might lead in debauchery but the sin itself jeopardized the North as well.

Once problems were defined in such a way—as loss of moral control and consequent growth of licentiousness—then perception and real conditions fit neatly together. Southern sensuality forecast growing Northern sensuality, and Southern "barbarism," in turn, confirmed abolitionists in their fears about what unbridled human nature could produce anywhere. Even the South's economic state provided proof, for, despite grumblings, abolitionists at heart conceived of Northern industrial growth as a sign of advancing civilization. Moral guidance might well be imperative, but economic diversification itself was good and it was not going on below the Mason-Dixon line—time and again antislavery propaganda pictured the South as an economically backward region, building neither factories nor railroads, seldom even paying its debts. Progress, in fact, could not long continue in a region where man lost control of himself. Only with destruc-

[26] Weld to Angelina Grimké, Mar. 12, 1838; Angelina Grimké to Weld, Feb. 21, Mar. 4, 1838 (see also Weld to Angelina and Sarah M. Grimké, Feb. 16, 1838; and Weld to Angelina Grimké, Feb. 18, 1838), in *Weld-Grimké Letters*, II, 602, 565, 587, 556, 560; Birney MS. Diary, Mar. 14, 1840, Birney MSS. Library of Congress. Birney also thought the Welds and Sarah Grimké to be "the happiest people I know." Weld achieved a Victorian triumph when he was able to exclaim to Miss Grimké, "I forgot utterly that you were not of my own sex," Feb. 8, 1838, in *Weld-Grimké Letters*, II, 534.
[27] *Liberator*, Jan. 29, 1858; Higginson, "Holiness Unto the Lord," *Harbinger*, 3 (1847), 28; *Liberator*, Sept. 17, 1836; *Emancipator*, Jan. 14, 1834; Stephen Pearl Andrews, ed., *Love, Marriage, and Divorce, and the Sovereignty of the Individual* . . . (New York: Stringer & Townsend, 1853), p. 17.

tion of the master's arbitrary power and restoration of moral restraint on all Southerners could the South develop spiritually and economically; only with strengthened restraint could the North continue to develop. Here abolitionism drew directly upon change in Northern society, taking it to be both a cause for anxiety and, more important, a means of weighing the South's lack of progress, its failure to share the benefits of 19th-century civilization.

There were, however, more indirect consequences to industrialization than obvious economic development, and these would likewise conspire to reinforce abolitionist images of Southern depravity and, further, to imply specific cures for general social evils. At first glance some of these consequences seem quite far removed from slavery since they touched society's most pervasive institution—the family. Although the interrelation between family change and economic change is still something of a puzzle, family patterns in America clearly underwent alteration from 1800 onward. The birth rate dropped steadily but appreciably throughout the 19th century (particularly in the Northeast where both industrialization and reform impulses found the atmosphere most congenial). And the home appears to have been declining in economic functions: fewer goods were made in it as a wider variety of products were factory-produced and store-bought; men increasingly commuted to work; and middle-class women seemed to be losing their most apparent economic roles—no longer contributing to a family enterprise, purchasing products rather than making them, and even having immigrant servants available to tend broods of children smaller than those their mothers bore.[28]

Yet what the family lost in economic value it gained in moral prestige, coming (in the antebellum period) to stand as the center for instruction in virtue. Gamaliel Bailey, echoing his contemporaries' sentiments, declared the family to be "the great primal institution, established by the Creator himself, as the first and best school for training men for all social relations and duties."[29] There were good reasons why abolitionists like Bailey, and

---

[28] The best introduction to the literature on antebellum economic change is still Stuart Bruchey, *The Roots of American Economic Growth, 1607 1861: An Essay in Social Causation*, new ed. (New York: Harper & Row, 1968). Population trends can be spotted in J. Potter, "The Growth of Population in America, 1700 1860," in *Population in History: Essays in Historical Demography*, eds. D. V. Glass and D. E. C. Eversley (London: Arnold, 1965), pp. 672-73, 677-78. Wishy, *Child and the Republic*, p. 28, notes a reappraisal of family life after 1830, and the best introduction to the literature of American family history, although now somewhat dated, is Edward N. Saveth, "The Problem of American Family History," *American Quarterly*, 21 (1969), 311-29. Keith E. Melder, "The Beginnings of the Women's Rights Movement in the United States, 1800- 1840," Diss. Yale 1963, pp. 13-14, 19, 34, remarks on the change in woman's economic role, a point several abolitionists also perceived. See Sarah M. Grimké, *Letters on the Equality of the Sexes, and the Condition of Woman . . .* (Boston: Knapp, 1838), p. 54; and Theodore Parker, *Sins and Safeguards of Society*, ed. Samuel B. Stewart (Boston: American Unitarian Ass., n.d.), pp. 182-83.

[29] *National Era*, May 17, 1849.

others eager for moral guidance in a time of flux, would look so fervently at the family—no other social institution seemed half so reliable. American Protestantism was busily dividing into rival denominations, the fragments co-operating briefly during revivals, then going their separate, bickering paths. Unlike the old days, no one clergyman served the community, no one church dominated the landscape. Jacksonian America's political system was even more bewildering because, so moralists thought, it played to the basest instincts of the voter, encouraging demagoguery rather than respectability and virtue. Changing though the family was, there was no other safe haven for morality in such tempestuous times.

And so, in yet another way, Southern sexuality focused what was a matter of immediate concern among abolitionists—the nature of household relationships. Since the slaveholder lacked restraint on his erotic energy, antislavery propaganda assumed he "totally annihilates the marriage institution."[30] Not only did the master fail to sanction or respect marriage among slaves, his uninhibited lustfulness also meant he did not honor his own marriage vows, destroying family relations among whites as well as blacks. Everything converged to deprive the South of a stable family life, robbing that section of the basic mechanism of social control, confirming its status as antithesis of order and civilization. There is no particular evidence that Southern family instability was increasing in the 1830s, nor did abolitionists claim it was. The difference was that by 1830 the family itself was a matter both of anxiety and hope; and anxiety found nightmarish confirmation in the Southern way of life, with its ostensible eroticism and its disdain for the one reasonably dependable moral guardian.

Sexual attitudes, merging with objective conditions and with ideas about power and civilization, guided abolitionists as they looked fretfully southward. But in many of their particular beliefs abolitionists were hardly unique. Antislavery, in fact, moved to much larger rhythms of public concern. If abolitionists worried about licentiousness and the decline of order, then so did men who opposed them in anti-antislavery mobs, fearful that emancipation would upset conventional social relations and promote miscegenation. If abolitionists threw much of their faith for moral training upon the family then, it has to be said, so did defenders of slavery, who portrayed their supposedly patriarchal institution as an alternative to decay of personal ties in the North.[31] It would be a mistake, nevertheless, to dismiss

[30]Stephen S. Foster, *The Brotherhood of Thieves: Or, A True Picture of the American Church and Clergy: A Letter to Nathaniel Barney, of Nantucket* (Boston: Anti-Slavery Office, 1844), p. 9.
[31]Richards, *"Gentlemen of Property and Standing,"* deals with the motivation of anti-abolition mobs. David Donald, "The Proslavery Argument Reconsidered," *Journal of*

patterns of thought as unimportant because they appeared among otherwise very different people, utilized for different purposes. Concern for human sexuality, and equation of civilization with its suppression, was too general to be a direct cause for the rise of antislavery. Rather than make abolitionism inevitable, it made inevitable a certain *kind* of abolitionism; it insured that some Northerners enmeshed in change would be able to see certain things in the South which earlier generations either had not seen or had taken far more lightly. There was, moreover, another kind of importance to assumptions abolitionists applied to Southern behavior, particularly to Southern sexuality: these were threads radiating outward, forming a web of reform commitment much larger than antislavery alone, finally extending beyond the death of slavery.

Abolitionists seem crankish, or quaint, for the various fads and reforms they drifted into. Yet many of these auxiliary causes fit the same mold as antislavery, indicating that abolitionists were driven as much by a generalized desire to control the "animal nature" standing between man and civilization as they were by a specific quarrel with the South, which was only the worst of offenders, the logical extension of human depravity. Time after time abolitionists turned their guns toward the same lack of restraint in the North, or in individuals, as they imagined in the South. In numerous and occasionally subtle ways they betrayed how much of their vehemence stemmed from a pervasive fear that man was giving in too easily to his passionate self. The most frequent attacks of this sort probably were reserved for tyranny of the bottle. But despite near universality of temperance sentiment among abolitionists, they found their most spectacular examples of sin in presumably prevalent Northern sexual immorality, a more literal surrender of man's "higher" qualities (his civilization) to the body's claims than alcoholism.

Abolitionists devoted themselves to sweeping back "the wild sea of prostitution, which swells and breaks and dashes against the bulwarks of society." In fact almost coincident with the rise of antislavery was a Moral Reform movement designed to curb prostitution and to promote purity. It had appeal at antislavery centers such as Oberlin and Western Reserve and many abolitionists became involved in the efforts of one of Moral Reform's chief promoters, the Reverend John McDowall. McDowall's spicy account of sexual depravity in New York City brought tremendous criticism on his sponsor, the local Magdalen Society, and particularly on Arthur Tappan, a prominent member as well as a future president of the American Anti-Slavery Society. A successor to the Magdalen Society, called the American

---

Southern History, 37 (1971), 3–18, analyzes defenders of slavery and makes the point that the proslavery argument bears similarity to abolitionism and other antebellum movements.

Society for Promoting the Observance of the Seventh Commandment, drew upon abolitionists for its officers. Beriah Green was president; three abolitionists, including Weld, were vice-presidents; others, Joshua Leavitt and William Goodell among them, were on the executive committee. Lucretia Mott's support of an organization to redeem fallen women was dampened only by her discovery that it did not offer its services to blacks.[32]

Some abolitionists were convinced that things were drastically wrong even with the institution designed to contain erotic impulses. "The right idea of marriage is at the foundation of all reforms," Elizabeth Cady Stanton decided in 1853. Amidst her suggestions for change was the complaint that "Man in his lust has regulated long enough this whole question of sexual intercourse."[33] Henry C. Wright produced a work on *Marriage and Parentage* which attacked "THE UN-NATURAL AND MONSTROUS EXPENDITURE OF THE SEXUAL ELEMENT, FOR MERE SENSUAL GRATIFICATION" within marriage. He presented as ideal two husbands able to "control all their passional expressions." Stephen Pearl Andrews preached an individualism which bordered on Free Love—except he argued that a liberalization of marriage and divorce practices would actually "moderate the passions instead of inflaming them, and so . . . contribute, in the highest degree, to a general Purity of life. . . ."[34]

So sinister seemed man's erotic nature that it would not be satisfied with

[32]*Sins and Safeguards of Society*, p. 203. Melder, "Beginnings of the Women's Rights Movement," p. 88, notes the coincidence of moral reform and antislavery in time; Robert Samuel Fletcher, *A History of Oberlin College from Its Foundation through the Civil War* (Oberlin College, 1943), I, 296–308, gives material on the appeal of moral reform at Oberlin and Western Reserve. The Magdalen Society affair is recounted several places, most directly in Lewis Tappan, *The Life of Arthur Tappan* (New York: Hurd & Houghton, 1870), pp. 110–20. Data on abolitionist connections with the American Society for Promoting the Observance of the Seventh Commandment can be found in Fletcher, *History of Oberlin*, I, 297, 305; *Emancipator*, Feb. 18, 1834; *Weld-Grimké Letters*, I, 130–31, 136. Otelia Cromwell, *Lucretia Mott* (Cambridge: Harvard Univ. Press, 1958), p. 106, relates the story of Lucretia Mott and the moral reform society. For additional interest in moral reform by abolitionists see the *Friend of Man*, particularly the issues of Dec. 1, 1836, and Jan. 12, 1837; William Lloyd Garrison to Helen Benson, Dec. 17, 1836, Garrison MSS., Boston Public Library; and Henry Steele Commager, *Theodore Parker* (Boston: Little, Brown, 1936), p. 177.

[33]Stanton to Susan B. Anthony, Mar. 1, 1853, in Theodore Stanton and Harriot Stanton Blatch, eds., *Elizabeth Cady Stanton as Revealed in Her Letters, Diary and Reminiscences* (New York: Harpers, [1922]), II, 48 49. Stanton to Anthony, June 14, 1860, in Stanton and Blatch, eds., *Elizabeth Cady Stanton*, II, 82: "Woman's degradation is in man's idea of his sexual rights." For interesting parallels with English reform see J. A. Banks and Olive Banks, *Feminism and Family Planning in Victorian England* (Liverpool: Liverpool Univ. Press, 1964).

[34]Wright, *Marriage and Parentage: Or, The Reproductive Element in Man, as a Means to His Elevation and Happiness*, 5th ed. (Boston: Marsh, 1866), pp. 265, 100; Andrews, ed., *Love, Marriage and Divorce*, p. 20. Wright's book was reviewed by C. K. Whipple in *Liberator*, Sept. 29, 1854 in general, favorably. Perry, "Antislavery and Anarchy," pp. 229 34, discusses Wright's views on marriage and family. Perry plans to analyze Wright's complicated personal attitudes in his forthcoming biography of Wright.

brothel and marriage bed, and abolitionists grasped odd times to warn against the "secret vice" of auto-eroticism. Lewis Tappan interrupted a biography of his brother to urge readers to warn their children that "youthful lusts" could lead to "idiocy, insanity, disfigurement of body, and imbecility of mind." Garrison used the *Liberator* to review a book entitled *Debilitated Young Men,* taking occasion to rail against "the dreadful vice of Masturbation." The vice apparently was prevalent enough, and dreadful enough, to call forth veiled words of warning from Harriet Beecher Stowe and her sister in a book for homemakers they coauthored.[35]

All of this put a terrible burden on the erotic offender. The prostitute spread disease and misery; the lustful husband blighted his wife and transmitted sins to his unborn child; and the masturbator faced self-destruction. One did not even have to be consciously lustful to be harmed by his sexuality. Theodore Dwight Weld badgered his son, suffering both from a mysterious lethargy and an apparently unstimulated loss of semen, by warning "All authorities agree that this drain upon the seminal fluid will . . . lead ultimately to *insanity* or *idiocy.*"[36]

Such beliefs may have bordered on being conventional wisdom; certainly abolitionists were not the only people to think that sexual excess caused insanity and other frightening ills. But abolitionists fit such attitudes into a pattern of social concern, characterized by anxiety over eroticism, North and South. A major part of the pattern resulted from an antebellum turn to find the key to reform within man—not just within man (for others had done that too), but in man's physical nature. A feeling in Jacksonian reform that man's animal self had to be conquered in favor of his immaterial being came around, in circular fashion, to the body once more. Control and liberation were to be found in the same place. Victory lay in the enemy's camp after all.

Still, some ways of reaching that camp were more promising than others. Controlling man's sensual nature implied certain strategies, if one accepted the terms of antebellum culture literally. For one thing, the path cleared for women to participate more openly in reform causes than they had previously. As the middle-class woman retreated from direct and obvious economic support of the family it became common to invest her with other

[35]Tappan, *Life of Arthur Tappan,* p. 121; *Liberator,* Jan. 16, 1846; Catharine E. Beecher and Harriet Beecher Stowe, *The American Woman's Home: Or, Principles of Domestic Science . . .* (New York: Ford, 1869), p. 286. The sisters warned that auto-erotic activity might "terminate in disease, delirium, and death" and that "certain parts of the body are not to be touched except for purposes of cleanliness, and that the most dreadful suffering comes from disobeying these commands."

[36]Weld to Theodore Grimké Weld, July 26, 1860, Weld MSS, Clements Library, University of Michigan. The episode also appears in Gerda Lerner, *The Grimké Sisters from South Carolina: Rebels Against Slavery* (Boston: Houghton Mifflin, 1967), pp. 345-49.

virtues: she was, it seemed, also removed from worldly crassness, more spiritual by nature and by position than man, less sensual. Sarah Grimké, late in life, made explicit what had more commonly been implicit in the antislavery crusade from the beginning. Woman is innately man's "superior," Miss Grimké thought, a fact related to her feeling that "the sexual passion in man is ten times stronger than in woman." Under the right order of things, William Goodell believed, woman serves man as "the chastizer of his desires." Sarah Grimké's sister, Angelina, knew where this argument led, writing of women that "it is through their instrumentality that the great and glorious work of reforming the world is to be done." Of course it can be a dubious blessing to be presumed morally superior—it places shame on sexual impulses and guilt on failure to affect social change. (Sarah Grimké, for instance, felt that female asexuality made women more culpable in sexual transgressions than men, and other abolitionists concluded from woman's moral power that "American mothers are responsible for American slavery.") Yet there was a powerful justification for female activity here, and the point that women had a special role in the drama of redemption was conceded by male abolitionists, even relatively conservative ones who never brought themselves to support the Woman's Rights Movement which grew out of antislavery agitation.[37]

But a drive to control man's animal nature had other implications for antebellum reform besides awakening middle-class women to their obligations and their very real grievances. Virtually simultaneous with the rise of antislavery were still more attempts to subdue licentiousness—less obvious than the Moral Reform movement and less rooted in genuine social evils than antislavery and Woman's Rights. Chief among these peripheral causes was health reform, exemplified by Sylvester Graham, whose memory lives decadently in the Graham cracker. Graham, and men like him, sought to purify the body, to heal it of infirmities, through proper diet. Graham's regimen, which seemed laughable or repulsive to many Americans at the time, found adherents among abolitionists, and not just among Garrisonians (who had a susceptibility to fads). Non-Garrisonians like Henry B. Stanton and Lewis Tappan also found the Graham system enchanting and Oberlin

---

[37]Sarah M. Grimké to [Elizabeth Smith Miller], June 1, 1873, Weld MSS., Clements Library. For statements blaming either American women or Southern women for maintaining slavery see E. L. Follen, *To Mothers in the Free States* (New York: American Anti-Slavery Soc., 1855–6), p. 1; Puritan, *Abrogation of Seventh Commandment*, p. 3; George Bourne quoted in *Liberator*, Feb. 6, 1836; Angelina Grimké, *Appeal to the Christian Women of the South*, 3rd ed. (New York: American Anti-Slavery Soc., 1836), p. 25. For examples of "conservative" abolitionists conceding woman's redemptive influence see *Emancipator*, Dec. 21, 1833; James A. Thome, *Address to the Females of Ohio, Delivered at the State Anti-Slavery Anniversary* (Cincinnati: Ohio Anti-Slavery Soc., 1836), p. 4; and Haven, *National Sermons*, p. 627.

greeted Graham and a fellow dietary reformer, William A. Alcott, with initial enthusiasm. In its heyday the Graham system secured fierce loyalty from such staunch immediate emancipationists as the Welds, Sarah Grimké and William Goodell. LaRoy Sunderland went so far as to claim he owed his life to Graham's diet; Amasa Walker merely achieved regularity from it.[38]

There was also a considerable interest among abolitionists in exercise and gymnastics, programs which, like proper diet, helped in bringing the body under control and in preventing it from interfering with man's spiritual nature. Theodore Dwight Weld had been a missionary for the manual labor school idea before he turned to antislavery. This was a plan designed to mix education and work, both for financial reasons and to put body and spirit into right relation. After his career as an abolitionist had virtually ended, Weld taught in Dio Lewis' gymnastic institute—where William Lloyd Garrison sent at least some of his children and where the Welds themselves sent the son who exhibited signs of excessive loss of seminal fluid. Charles Follen, an early and beloved abolitionist, had been among the first to bring German physical culture ideas to the United States. Although Follen died tragically before Thomas Wentworth Higginson entered the movement, Higginson proved to be his spiritual heir, managing (in New England culture) to glide from antebellum reform to the late 19th century's "vigorous life." So persuasive was Higginson's campaigning for exercise that his efforts, according to one abolitionist, produced an outburst of ice-skating in Worcester, Massachusetts, which earned the title of "Higginson's Revival."[39]

Such activities seem innocent—and innocuous—enough, and, like dietary reform, they appear to have been aimed at an improvement in the quality of life. All that they were. But connected with dietary reform and advocacy of exercise was the familiar drive to subdue man's physical, particularly his sexual, aspects. Health reformers like Graham and William A. Alcott

[38]William B. Walker, "The Health Reform Movement in the United States: 1830–1870," Diss. Johns Hopkins 1955, p. 124; H. B. Stanton and others to Theodore Dwight Weld, Aug. 2, 1832, in *Weld-Grimké Letters*, I, 85; Fletcher, *History of Oberlin*, I, 318–39; *Graham Journal, of Health and Longevity*, 3 (1839), 185; 1 (1837), 5; and 2 (1838), 209. Thomas H. LeDuc, "Grahamites and Garrisonites," *New York History*, 20 (1939), 189–91, reprints with commentary an amusing document about abolitionists who believed in Graham's system.

[39]Walker, "Health Reform Movement," p. 276; Benjamin P. Thomas, *Theodore Dwight Weld, Crusader for Freedom* (New Brunswick, N.J.: Rutgers Univ. Press, 1950), p. 39; Henry Villard, *The Memoirs of Henry Villard, Journalist and Financier: 1835–1900* (Boston: Houghton Mifflin, 1904), II, 52; Thomas Wentworth Higginson, *Out-Door Papers* (Boston: Ticknor & Fields, 1863), p. 142; Sallie Holley to Mrs. Samuel Porter, Feb. 28, 1859, in Chadwick, ed., *A Life for Liberty*. pp. 166–67. Edelstein, *Strange Enthusiasm*, p. 26, writes of Higginson: "The issue of manliness would be very close to many of the social causes he would champion." Walker, "Health Reform Movement," pp. 285–87, considers the "vigorous life" to have been an outgrowth of the health reform movement.

wrote extensively on the terrible effects of sexual excess and presented proper diet as a means of suppressing erotic impulses. Propagandists for physical culture such as Dio Lewis and Russell Trall likewise counseled sexual control and likewise saw their programs as a way of achieving it. "A vigorous life of the senses not only does not tend to sensuality in the objectionable sense," Higginson claimed in an essay on gymnastics, "but it helps to avert it."[40] Dietary reform and the cult of exercise, like antislavery, fastened upon man's erotic nature in order to overcome it.

This was where it led, the concern for excessive sexuality which found some of its more lurid justification in Southern licentiousness and lack of civilization: the other side of fear of man's physical being was a belief that properly understanding it could lead to salvation. The other side of barbarism was true civilization. Certainly Grahamites and gymnastics enthusiasts aimed at a kind of redemption, a freedom from the body's infirmities and corrupt desires. Given the right social engineering, it might even be possible to turn those same desires to the task of regeneration—regeneration of the race, if not the individual. Garrison's tutor in perfectionism, John Humphrey Noyes, produced the clearest example of this in his Oneida Community, where a form of contraception was practiced, as well as plural marriage, in hope that "scientific combination" might be "applied to human generation." The result, Noyes believed, would be increasingly perfect children.[41]

Few, if any, in the antislavery movement were willing to take their ideas to Oneida's scandalous extreme. Yet abolitionists of various sorts did accept Noyes' assumption that regulation of sexuality might go beyond mere suppression of licentiousness and become an active force for human betterment. Henry C. Wright, as usual, wandered as far along the way as any abolitionist. Wright believed that all kinds of antenatal influences shaped human development; that diseases, alcoholism and parents' attitudes at the time of conception passed on to children. But Wright realized possibilities, as well as dangers. Ungoverned sexuality could blight humanity; if libidinousness had power to destroy then, properly regulated, it also had power to produce better men and women. People simply had to use sex wisely, for progress rather than gratification. Wright, ever a visionary, believed, "To the LAW OF REPRODUCTION will human beings, in the future of this world, look as the one great means to expel disease from the body and soul."[42]

---

[40] Higginson, *Out-Door Papers*, p. 139. Walker, "Health Reform Movement," contains information on Trall, Lewis, Graham and Alcott.

[41] "First Annual Report of the Oneida Community" (1848), in Norman E. Himes, *Medical History of Contraception* (1936: rpt. New York: Shocken, 1970), pp. 269–74; Alice Felt Tyler, *Freedom's Ferment. Phases of American Social History from the Colonial Period to the Outbreak of the Civil War* (1944: New York: Harper & Row, 1962), pp. 185 ff.

[42] Wright, *Marriage and Parentage*, pp. 18, 227.

Like Wright, Elizabeth Cady Stanton believed such traits as drunkenness descended to children, and she was impressed by an essay entitled "Cerebral Dynamics" because it "shows so clearly that children are the victims of the vices and excesses of their ancestors." Stephen Pearl Andrews envisioned a time when marriage relations might be changed so that a woman could "accept only the noblest and most highly endowed of the opposite sex to be the recipients of her choicest favors, and the sires of her off-spring, rejecting the males of a lower degree." He suggested "by this means, Nature has provided for an infinitely higher development of the race."[43]

This was eugenics—and hereditarian thought—only in embryonic form. There was, in the antebellum period, no real sense that biological laws might have man in an inescapable iron grip. Even phrenology, which asserted that character was irrevocably revealed in configurations of the skull, allied itself with hygiene, exercise and an interest in the environment. James G. Birney, in his philosophical meditations, thought that "a large, or well developed brain & head" might be partly the product of "early training & sufficiency & good nourishing food." Birney's speculations were consistent with those of professional phrenologists, who tied their craft to ways of improving skulls already in existence and of realizing their full potential, rather than to consigning inferior ones to genetic hell.[44] The mechanisms and social pressures for eugenics were not available before the Civil War: birth control (another attempt to regulate sexuality, dating from the 1830s) was bound up with fears of promiscuity;[45] racialist thought attacked the human unity abolitionists preferred to believe in; and Darwinism lay in the future when Wright, Elizabeth Cady Stanton and Stephen Pearl Andrews formulated their attitudes into opinions. Concern for licentiousness, symbolized most spectacularly by the erotic South, was not, however, product of a universe completely different from that of postwar

[43]Stanton to Susan B. Anthony, Mar. 1, 1853; Stanton to Elizabeth Smith Miller, Sept. 11, 1862, in *Elizabeth Cady Stanton*, II, 48–49, 91; Andrews, ed., *Love, Marriage and Divorce*, p. 20. There was an interesting and significant strain of hereditarian thought expressed by early advocates of Woman's Rights like Henry C. Wright and Mrs. Stanton. Note also that Orson Fowler, who published some of Wright's works, was both a phrenologist and author of *Love and Parentage, Applied to the Improvement of Offspring*. To make the connection even more intriguing, Fowler also published the first edition of *History of Woman Suffrage*.

[44]Birney MS. Diary, Dec. 10, 1850, Birney MSS., Library of Congress. Anne L. Kuhn, *The Mother's Role in Childhood Education: New England Concepts, 1830–1860* (New Haven: Yale Univ. Press, 1947), pp. 114–18; and Walker, "Health Reform Movement," pp. 27–29, see phrenology coupled with an interest in improvement. On phrenology itsef see John D. Davies, *Phrenology, Fad and Science: A Nineteenth Century American Crusade* (New Haven: Yale Univ. Press, 1955).

[45]Henry C. Wright, for instance, actually advocated a form of birth control when he advised abstinence from sexual relations except for procreation—and procreation at intervals of no less than three years. Yet Wright railed against physicians who promoted artificial birth control instead of telling couples to control their passions. *Marriage and Parentage*, pp. 126, 132–33.

America. In their drive to control man's animal nature, particularly his sexuality, abolitionists were part of a continuum from romantic reform, with its emphasis on the individual, to those middle-class moralists at the century's end who valued certain kinds of individualism but who ultimately cast their faith and anxieties onto race and reproduction.

This was a continuum from religiously based perfectionism to physical perfectionism, from enthusiasm to eugenics. Standing midway along it, abolitionists sought to reconcile both ends with each other as well as with human equality. Physical salvation, in these pre-Darwinian days, could not be just a matter of biological necessity. It was God's mandate, not evolution's, which made man's task on earth, according to Theodore Parker, "to unfold and perfect himself, as far as possible, in body and spirit." There was a transition, nonetheless, when Harriet Beecher Stowe, who bore with her the great Revival's seed, exclaimed that "*Perfect* spiritual religion cannot exist without perfect physical religion."[46]

Abolitionism began, and ended, with man. It began with a call for individual outrage and repentance and ended with the Yankee schoolmar'm carrying civilization southward. It sought to liberate men and, at the same time, to control man, to make him moral, eventually to direct his most fearful energies toward his salvation. Abolitionists were not alone in their preoccupations; they were, instead, very much children of antebellum America, less unique in their anxieties and hopes than in the embodiment they found for those anxieties and hopes. The problem of why certain individuals became abolitionists while others, of similar backgrounds, did not is a task for those who can untangle personal motivation. Equally important to understand is the function antislavery played for those captivated by it. For abolitionists slavery summed up discontents which were social, personal and far more general than the South's peculiar institution. The erotic South, like the inhuman and exploitative North of proslavery propaganda, was less a real place than an organizing principle, a culturally planted reference point measuring the dreadful rush of antebellum change. To their credit, antislavery and allied reforms were still too optimistic—perhaps too naïve—to see man, even at his most beastly, imprisoned by biology. There was hope among antebellum reformers that human nature could be over-

---

[46]Parker, *Sins and Safeguards*, p. 53; Stowe, "Bodily Religion," *Atlantic Monthly*, 18 (1866), 92. LaRoy Sunderland, at the time a Methodist minister, argued that religious duty required people to preserve health. *Graham Journal, of Health and Longevity*, 3 (1839), 186-87. For a similar feeling, expressed in a different reform, see Charles E. and Carroll S. Rosenberg, "Pietism and the Origins of the American Public Health Movement: A Note on John H. Grissom and Robert M. Hartley," *Journal of the History of Medicine and Allied Sciences*, 13 (1968), 16-35.

come, that civilization depended on a struggle within man, not a struggle among men.

Yet there was that transition. Younger abolitionists drifted elsewhere. The Garrison children absorbed Darwinism. Moncure Conway went to England, to a friendship with Herbert Spencer and to another kind of revelation. "Darwin's discovery made a new departure in my pilgrimage necessary," he exclaimed. Elizabeth Cady Stanton, shortly after the Civil War, declared that Herbert Spencer's popularization (and socialization) of Darwin had achieved the grand objective of "teaching us to lose sight of ourselves and our burdens in the onward march of the race." Nearing the end of his days, Parker Pillsbury, one of the oldest abolitionists, took satisfaction in Loring Moody's career. Moody had been general agent for the pioneer organization, the Massachusetts Anti-Slavery Society. He went from there to the Society for the Prevention of Cruelty to Animals, and then to "a similar association in behalf of poor children." Yet, according to Pillsbury, Moody's "last labor was doubtless most important of all in his life of nearly seventy years. He originated and organized *The Institute of Heredity*, perhaps, viewed in all its aspects and relations, the most important enterprise to universal human well being of the nineteenth century."[47] The distance from sentimentalism to evolution could be bridged in a lifetime; it was no farther than the erotic South was from Oneida perfectionism. Among antebellum reformers it was virtually the distance between man's moral nature—the universal human being who could be trusted to behave correctly when not corrupted by arbitrary power—and man's animal nature, the passionate creature needing to be kept tightly under control, the physical being over whose body civilization was to triumph.

[47]Conway, *Autobiography, Memories, and Experiences of Moncure Daniel Conway* (Boston: Houghton Mifflin, 1904), II, 350; Stanton to Robert Dale Owen, Apr. 10, 1866, in *Elizabeth Cady Stanton*, II, 113; Parker Pillsbury, *Acts of the Anti-Slavery Apostles* (Boston: Cupples, Upham, 1884), pp. 489-90.

BERTRAM WYATT-BROWN
Case Western Reserve University

Stanley Elkins' *Slavery:* The Antislavery Interpretation Reexamined

NOW THAT SUBURBAN LIBERALISM AND FREEDOM MARCHES HAVE FADED in the Nixonian sun, Elkins' conservative interpretation of 19th century American abolitionism deserves the attention denied it during the civil rights decade. In preparing a critical anthology on Elkins' *Slavery,* Ann J. Lane discovered that after ten years only one article on the antislavery section had appeared, even though that chapter was nearly twice as long as any other in the book. One reason for this neglect was that Elkins had offered no imaginative analogies comparable to those which so provocatively illuminated slave psychology and Latin racial styles.[1] Moreover, the causes of the Civil War, despite numerous centennial commemorations, did not excite the literary battles they once had. Historians of the '60s, like everyone else, were preoccupied with racial tensions, not with the rights and wrongs of sectional disputes. Nevertheless, the antislavery thesis raises too many issues in American social history to be casually put aside.

Elkins' criticism of abolitionism is based on a particular predisposition— for reason over moral passion and faith in ordinary social mechanisms in preference to grand moral absolutes. Either one appreciates the romantic temperament that antislavery exemplified, or, with Elkins, one turns from it in dismay. Northrop Frye once declared, "to say with T. E. Hulme: 'I object to even the best of the Romantics' is much like saying 'I object to even

---

[1] Stanley M. Elkins, *Slavery: A Problem in American Institutional and Intellectual Life* (Chicago: Univ. of Chicago Press, 1959). Aileen S. Kraditor, "A Note on Elkins and the Abolitionists," in Ann J. Lane, ed., *The Debate over "Slavery": Stanley Elkins and His Critics* (Urbana: Univ. of Illinois Press, 1971), pp. 87-101. I am indebted to David Van Tassel, Richard O. Curry, David H. Fischer, Gene Wise and Eugene D. Genovese for their criticism and to the American Philosophical Society for financial aid in preparing this essay.

the best battles of the Napoleonic War.' "[2] Consciously or not, we cannot escape a similarly visceral reaction either to Elkins or to the men and women he disapproved.. But to avoid the dangers of partisanship as much as possible, I will follow this procedure: first, to present the basic argument of Chapter 4; second, to examine the strengths and then the weaknesses of Elkins' strategy; and finally, to ascertain the purpose of the work as a whole.

Despite a familiar stress upon American "frontier" individualism, Elkins presented the case in a highly original way.[3] As he explained it, individual Americans, each struggling against another but sometimes joining in casual unities, swept aside long-standing institutional checks which might otherwise have afforded a structured approach to the "peculiar institution." By 1830, he claimed, whatever stability the country enjoyed was confined to the centrifugal momentum of atoms more or less moving in the same direction.

Elkins drew from these premises the conclusion that Americans were unprepared for dealing with slavery. They not only lacked the institutional means, but they also lacked the proper intellectual frame of mind for reasonable action on any pressing social question. "For Americans of this [1830s] generation," he declared, "the very concept of power—its meaning, its responsibilities, its uses—was something quite outside their experience."[4] Frustrated by the absence of proper channels to effect change, a band of philosophers and abolitionists forced the nation off course. The fragile institutions, which they so ruthlessly denounced, flew apart. Motion became commotion. The nation went to war, a bloody, needless tragedy.

There was a striking parallel between Stanley Elkins' approach to social

[2]"The Drunken Boat: The Revolutionary Element in Romanticism," in Northrop Frye, ed., *Romanticism Reconsidered: Selected Papers from the English Institute* (New York: Columbia Univ. Press, 1963), pp. 2-3. The receptivity of the '60s historians to abolitionism was rather astonishing: see Martin B. Duberman's introductory remarks in his edition, *The Antislavery Vanguard: New Essays on the Abolitionists* (Princeton: Princeton Univ. Press, 1965), p. viii, and Merton L. Dillon, "The Abolitionists: A Decade of Historiography, 1959-1969," *Journal of Southern History*, 35 (Nov. 1969), 500-22. More favorable to Elkins than most scholars was Willie Lee Rose, " 'Iconoclasm Has Had Its Day': Abolitionists and Freedmen in South Carolina," in Duberman, ed., *Antislavery Vanguard*, pp. 188-91. Cf. Oscar Handlin, rev. in *New England Quarterly*, 34 (June 1961), 253-55; Nathan Glazer, intro., *Slavery* (New York: Grosset & Dunlap, 1963), esp. pp. xiii-iv; Bertram Wyatt-Brown, "Abolitionism: Its Meaning for Contemporary Reform," rpr. in Hugh Hawkins, ed., *The Abolitionists: Means, Ends, and Motivations* (Lexington, Mass.: D.C. Heath, 1972), pp. 165-76.
[3]Stanley Elkins and Eric McKitrick, "A Meaning for Turner's Frontier: Democracy in the Old Northwest," in Richard Hofstadter and Seymour M. Lipset, eds., *Turner and the Sociology of the Frontier* (New York: Basic Books, 1968), pp. 120-51.
[4]Elkins, *Slavery*, p. 34.

issues and that of the Founding Fathers of 1789, which a rough characterization of the 18th century view may help to demonstrate. In intellectual terms, the century was typified by a sense of orderliness in human and divine affairs. Men of the Enlightenment thought that selfish instincts could be controlled through ecclesiastical and civil institutions, age-old habits and a general sense of rightness about one's status and allegiances. Under stable conditions, moral progress, humanitarian advance and other noble aspirations were possible, but only so long as the proponents of change deferred to the limitations of power, wisely distributed among neatly adjusted "orders" and institutions. Order, balance, progress were the trinity of Enlightenment hopes. The crumbling of any of these would bring down the others, even to the point of anarchy or tyranny.

Of course, Elkins found this institutional approach congenial not because of an affectation but because of a correspondence with attitudes current in the academic milieu in which *Slavery* was composed, as the following passage illustrates: "Institutions with power produce the 'things' not only upon which one leans but also against which one pushes; they provide the standards whereby, for men of sensibility, one part of society may be judged and tested against another. The lack of them, moreover, removes the thinker not only from the places where power resides but also from the very *idea* of power and how it is used."[5]

Elkins tied the concept of power directly to those institutions which he and other scholars of the 1950s considered the most accessible—the national government, the university centers and the interlocking network of urban social elites. Twenty-five years of growing governmental interest in various scholastic enterprises had encouraged the notion that the most practicable solutions for social ills came through ventures uniting government and intellectual leaders. It was both natural and logical for Elkins to transfer the idea of scholar-as-bureaucrat into 18th century parlance. In a manner of speaking, "brain-trusters," a crude term, became gently translated into the archaic but appropriate designation of "men of sensibility" in the passage above.[6]

Elkins' strategy was well designed for a profound criticism of the romantic temperament in American political reform. He began with these

[5] Ibid., p. 143.
[6] Quoting from Henry James' biography of Hawthorne, Elkins in this section argued that Americans lacked the symbols and resonance of a stable, continental world of cathedrals and regal pomp. Elkins' viewpoint was true enough, but James' meaning was distorted. James spoke of New England as "a plain, God-fearing society . . . not fertile in variations," characteristics common to a provincial society of thin shabbiness. Rustic parochialism, however, should not be confused with anarchistic tendencies. See Leon Edel, *Henry James, The Untried Years, 1843–1870* (Philadelphia: Lippincott, 1953), p. 192; Elkins, *Slavery*, pp. 142–43.

assumptions: that order is preferable to violence; that small gains peaceably won are better than high ambitions leading to shattering disillusionment; that men in their imperfectibility can only delude themselves in zealotry. Given this framework, abolitionism, the most thoroughly romantic of the host of antebellum causes, appeared as the offspring of Byronic impulse and evangelical soulfulness.

Indeed, abolitionists were, as Elkins claimed, inspired with an antinomian vision. In accordance with that theological concept, they stressed the primacy of intuition over intellect, the imperative of immediacy, the commitment to self-discovery through anti-orthodox engagement and finally the justification of deed by direct reference to an absolute ideal, privately ascertained.[7] Although indebted to some of the expansive themes of the Enlightenment, they replaced a faith in traditional mechanisms with a zeal that others either rejected or misunderstood. Like Edmund Burke in his attacks on French Revolutionary enthusiasms, Elkins offered the reasons for the inevitable self-defeat that romantics prepared for themselves. Ironically, his perspective may yet prove more resistant to criticism than his approach to slave psychology, which has met a different fate.[8]

Three major portions of his argument have borne the test of further research in the social sciences and history especially well: first, that American society launched into the 19th century in an iconoclastic, ego-centered and anxious mood; second, that abolitionists and Transcendentalists shared similar moral and intellectual priorities, including a suspicion of conventional attitudes and institutions; third, that both Transcendentalists and abolitionists were opposed to the racial sins of their fathers' and their own generation because of a deep-seated sense of personal guilt.

In regard to American self-serving dynamism, few historians would dispute that the manifold changes in the ways men made their living helped to transform basic ideological patterns during the antebellum period. Most important was the commercializing of agriculture. Subsistence farming and

---

[7] Jacob L. Talmon, *Romanticism and Revolt, Europe 1815–1848* (New York: Harcourt, Brace & World, 1967); Ronald A. Knox, *Enthusiasm, A Chapter in the History of Ideas* (New York: Oxford Univ. Press, 1950); David B. Davis, "The Emergence of Immediatism in British and American Antislavery Thought," *Mississippi Valley Historical Review*, 49 (Sept. 1962), 209–30.

[8] Elkins' stress upon the "anti-institutionalism" of the antebellum reformers has been rigorously attacked, but his understanding of the interplay of ideology and "institution," evinced in Lane, ed., *Debate over "Slavery,"* pp. 361–78, placed his use of the word "institution" squarely within the wide scope of its meaning. See James A. H. Murray, *A New English Dictionary on Historical Principles* (Oxford: Clarendon Press, 1901), 5: 354. This definition also would apply to its use in George M. Fredrickson, *The Inner Civil War* (New York: Harper, 1965), and R. Jackson Wilson, *In Quest of Community: Social Philosophy in the United States* (New York: Wiley, 1968), chap. 1, both of which works conform with Elkins' perspective.

its intimate customs were restricted to backwaters, while cash-crop settlers of North and South developed the vast hinterlands. This transformation made possible the rise of cities, industry and improved means of distribution, travel, education and communication.

Under these circumstances, Americans—always restless—became more mobile, so much so that values could no longer be entrusted to the broken integrity of family and kin, community tradition and outworn elites of tenured clergy and squires. Robert H. Wiebe in *The Search for Order* observed, "Already by the 1870's the autonomy of the community was badly eroded."[9] The process had begun with American independence, but accelerated in the 1830s. The task of cementing society to common aims fell largely to such mass devices as political parties, common schools, benevolent agencies and quickly gathered assemblies for specific objects. Fraternal associations, social clubs and religious activities provided a measure of security. Yet, as Elkins rightly stressed, there was a paradoxical urge for individuality. With some flamboyance but essential truth, Max Lerner in 1957 argued that the archetypal American was the supreme modern man: "Hungering for a sense of personal worth, he is torn between the materialisms he can achieve and the feeling of wholeness which eludes him. . . . He is the double figure in Marlowe, of Tamerlane and Dr. Faustus, the one sweeping like a footloose barbarian across the plains to overleap the barriers of earlier civilizations, the other breaking the taboos against knowledge and experience, even at the cost of his soul." In attempting to master his environment and himself, the antebellum American played so many roles at once and in such rapid sequence (witness Melville's *Confidence-Man*) that loyalties lost former relevance. New and rather unstable ones appeared, sometimes, as David Brion Davis explained, in formulations of a negative character.[10] Occasionally mob action and the rooting out of supposed conspiracies of "aliens" testified to the anxieties that shifts in commitment helped to generate.

Turning to anthropology, we find further support for Elkins' interpretation. Mary Douglas, an English scholar, has worked out a typology rather helpful in understanding the Jacksonian era as Elkins perceived it: when allegiances to a homogenous "group" (a New England village for instance), decline, "grid" or a set of adaptive rules governing the relations between ego-centered individuals offers more meaning than community,

[9]*The Search for Order, 1877–1920* (New York: Hill & Wang, 1967), p. viii. See also, Conrad Arensberg, "American Communities," *American Anthropologist,* 57 (Dec. 1955), 1143–62.

[10]Davis, ed., *The Fear of Conspiracy: Images of Un-American Subversion from the Revolution to the Present* (Ithaca: Cornell Univ. Press, 1971), esp. pp. 9–22. Max Lerner, *America as a Civilization: Life and Thought in the United States Today* (New York: Simon & Schuster, 1957), p. 63.

family custom and routine. As a result of this imbalance between "grid" and "group," she observed, men look upon institutions as temporary agencies to further ambitions and aspirations. Institutions, or more precisely, regulative conventions no longer afford psychic comforts nor do they help the individual to know precisely his relationship to the world around him.

Under these circumstances, Professor Douglas continued, men find anchors of faith in their own bodies and inner feelings while alienating themselves from traditions rapidly losing former sacredness. The immortal self seems to provide surer hooks into "reality" than commitments to family business partnerships, charities or time-honored religious customs. As Mary Douglas explained, preoccupations with personal hygiene, dietary regulations, moral dogmas and introspective yearnings—all newly adopted realms of spirit and body—frequently become replacements for a flagging respectfulness for long-standing authorities in times of social transition. Applying this view to Jacksonian America, one is reminded of the temperance cause, the Grahamite regimen, the sexual asceticism and experimentation of utopians, and the quest for new identities in communitarian fellowship.[11]

Given this context, Elkins was wise to uphold his original observations, though granted an opportunity to retract in Ann Lane's anthology a decade later. "In America," Elkins reaffirmed, "a major cultural fact was the general inability to see any clear relationship, except perhaps a negative one, between institutions and individual character." Institutions (by which Elkins also meant customary usages and conventional ways of thinking as well as formal civil structures) were conceived to be "at best a convenience," and even the family "was not really a given, something that one inherited and in which one assumed a place; it was rather something one created anew . . . and subsequently maintained, as it were, through force of individual will."[12] His commentary has the support not only of other historians but of social psychologists as well.[13]

[11] Douglas, *Natural Symbols: Explorations in Cosmology* (New York: Pantheon, 1970), pp. vii, 19–23, 70–71, 82–83, 149–55; Stephen Nissenbaum, "Sex, Reform, and Social Change, 1830–1840," paper, Organization of American Historians, Washington, D.C., Apr. 6, 1972; Ronald G. Walters, "Antislavery and Sexuality," paper, Organization of American Historians, New Orleans, Apr. 15, 1971; Ernest R. Sandeen, "John Humphrey Noyes as the New Adam," *Church History*, 40 (Mar. 1971), 82–90; Daniel H. Calhoun, *Professional Lives in America: Structure and Aspiration, 1750–1850* (Cambridge: Harvard Univ. Press, 1965), pp. 88–177.

[12] Elkins in Lane, ed., *Debate over "Slavery,"* p. 374.

[13] Douglas, *Natural Symbols*, pp. 33–36, 38; Nathan Adler, "The Antinomian Personality: The Hippie Character Type," *Psychiatry*, 21 (Nov. 1968), 325–38; David C. McClelland, *The Achieving Society* (Glencoe, Ill.: The Free Press, 1961), pp. 13, 48–49. See also David Riesman, *The Lonely Crowd* (New Haven: Yale Univ. Press, 1950); John L. Thomas, "Romantic Reform in America, 1815–1865," *American Quarterly*, 17 (Winter 1965), 656–81.

The second contribution that Elkins offered was a persuasive argument for abolitionist and Transcendental affinities, one that grew out of the cultural setting itself. Antislavery crusaders and the Concord school were part of the same philosophical revolt against Enlightenment rationalism and religious orthodoxy, both of which accepted human weakness as an eternal part of the universal order. Elkins underlined this point in the Lane anthology when he quoted with approval R. Jackson Wilson: "The perfectionism of Garrison and other reformers was, like Transcendentalism, insistently antinomian; both implied a thorough, even ruthless criticism and repudiation of existing institutions."[14] The Boston heresy represented a disillusionment with the prevailing "common sense" theology and seeming hypocrisy, evasions and ordinary muddle of the American churches.

The radical reformer invariably believes that institutions should enfold the ideal, when by their consensual nature, they can only reach for it. In any case, the best minds in the antislavery venture left the denominations and the faiths of their fathers for a more liberating gospel of "free religion," a secular trend in keeping with their stress upon the divinity of the self. No scholar has yet explored this abolitionist trend, one that began in the late 1830s; the phenomenon, however, substantiates Elkins' views. To be sure, Gerrit Smith, La Roy Sunderland, Elizur Wright, the Weld-Grimké family failed to join Garrison's anti-evangelical circle in the 1840s. Yet, they and many others repudiated the theology as well as the formal ecclesiastical structure of contemporary religious life. Instead, they prophesied the need for "a higher, purer theology," as Joshua Giddings exclaimed, to "cast aside" institutions which were "inert, inefficient and worn out." Someone like Giddings, a Congressman from the Western Reserve of Ohio, could hardly have matched the Transcendentalists in learning and sophistication. Yet the kind of abolitionist he represented shared Emerson's and Thoreau's contempt for church conventionalities in the common pursuit of means for glimpsing the future and condemning the present.[15]

Thousands of evangelical Christians and their leaders remained true to the circumspect abolitionism of 1833, but a trend was under way.[16] Even within the evangelical movement of the 1840s, Charles G. Finney's revival

---

[14] Elkins in Lane, ed., *Debate over "Slavery,"* p. 364.

[15] Giddings quoted in James B. Stewart, *Joshua R. Giddings and the Tactics of Radical Politics* (Cleveland: Case Western Reserve Univ. Press, 1970), p. 253. Ralph Waldo Emerson, "New England Reformers," in Edwin C. Rozwenc, ed., *Ideology and Power in the Age of Jackson* (New York: Doubleday, 1964), p. 171: "The fertile forms of antinomianism among the elder puritans seemed to have their match in the plenty of the new harvest of reform."

[16] Bertram Wyatt-Brown, *Lewis Tappan and the Evangelical War against Slavery* (Cleveland: Case Western Reserve Univ. Press, 1969), pp. 310–12; J. R. Jacob, "La Roy Sunderland: The Alienation of an Abolitionist," *Journal of American Studies,* 6 (Apr. 1972), 1–17; Lewis Perry, "Adin Ballou's Hopedale Community and the Theology of Antislavery," *Church History,* 34 (Sept. 1970), 372–90.

doctrine of the sanctification of men in present life transcendentalized, so to speak, Methodist Arminianism. Abolitionists like the Tappan brothers adopted Finney's theology. These and other indications of romantic desires to impute a measure of divinity to mankind showed that Transcendentalism and abolitionism were emphatically moving in the same direction. Elkins, limited by inadequate secondary resources, did not explore the religious tendencies of the age very knowledgeably, but his sketch was consistent with more recent scholarship on the subject.[17]

Likewise, Elkins correctly observed the abolitionists' responsibility for weakening public regard for *some* institutions. Aileen Kraditor disputed this argument, complaining that most crusaders "did not repudiate institutions or institutional means to effect desired change"; they merely sought to replace corrupted ones. Yet, who could argue that these reformers did not seek a radical change in existing relationships between whites and blacks, Yankees and Southerners? This undertaking inevitably clashed with current notions of American nationality, based as they were upon racial hierarchy and sectional parity. In fact, abolitionists were like Reformation Lutherans who rejected the magical assumptions of Catholic ritual, an exercise that inescapably challenged church structure as well.[18] Likewise, Garrison's public burning of the Constitution, for instance, profaned the central icon of romantic patriotism. In that act he consummated what a Reformation sectarian did by proving saint's blood to be nothing more than a vial of colored water. Garrison's contemporaries were horrified or jubilant because they rightly understood its shattering symbolism. Whether reformers remained within a given body to amend it to well-doing or "came out" from corrupted association, they were engaged in a form of institutional subversion. One may feel compelled to approve or repudiate the policy, but the reformers' disruption of accepted norms is a matter of record.

In addition, Elkins saw clearly the tragic costs that were exacted in the practice of romantic antinomianism. Moralists of this kind are often burdened with simple Manichean extravagances and suspicions, intolerance and an abstract way of thinking. They are animated by an individualistic

---

[17]Ernest R. Sandeen, *The Roots of Fundamentalism: British and American Millenarianism, 1830–1930* (Chicago: Univ. of Chicago Press, 1970); Robert Merideth, *The Politics of the Universe: Edward Beecher, Abolition, and Orthodoxy* (Nashville: Vanderbilt Univ. Press, 1968); and Donald G. Mathews, *Slavery and Methodism: A Chapter in American Morality, 1780–1845* (Princeton: Princeton Univ. Press, 1965) are among the noteworthy recent studies in antebellum religious history. Yet historians have only begun the work needed. For instance, there is no good study of spiritualism as it influenced the 19th century transatlantic intelligentsia, including many abolitionists.

[18]Kraditor, in Lane, ed., *Debate over "Slavery,"* p. 92; Douglas, *Natural Symbols*, pp. 48–49.

sense of responsibility for historical conditions and contemporary policies. This moral acuity precludes an orderly approach to power. The stress upon immediacy and national depravity limited the responses of slaveholders and conservatives, no matter how benevolent or open-minded they might have been. A planter could have chosen to join abolitionist forces, as James G. Birney did, or, as Elkins said, "he might simply discharge his sense of guilt by turning on his tormentors."[19] In any event, Southerners predictably closed ranks and turned inward. This form of "consensus" in the South, Elkins observed, withdrew "one kind of liberty" but "conferred in its place another kind which had not previously been there. The mind could now conceive the enemy in any size or shape it chose; specters were utterly free to range, thrive and proliferate."[20]

Meanwhile, abolitionists reworked the definition of a Christian. Slaveholding became the cardinal sin in the antinomian theology, for they judged men solely according to their relationship to slavery, a radical departure in scriptural interpretation. Thereafter it was easy—all too easy—to distinguish the saints from the fallen. Nonslaveholding churchgoers could take refuge from their own spiritual vacuity by condemning others for what environment, circumstance and inclination shielded them from ever doing.[21] Moreover, there were some impoverished efforts to supply new symbols of beatitude and satanism to replace conventional sermon imagery, preoccupied as most clergymen were with submission to Divine Will and neighborly, familial virtues. In contrast, abolitionists stressed distant empathies. Primitive woodcuts of lustful masters and of abject slaves became the gargoyles and relics of a gothic revival. And there was even a kind of Protestant rite of indulgence performed in the purchase of a suitably decorated lamp-mat or a pamphlet from Knapp & Garrison. They were false representations, crude compositions for a complex and highly personal set of relationships in the South. Doubtful churchmen were not simply justifying their own timidity when they reproached abolitionists' portrayals of a Southern purgatory and the blessedness of the antislavery child prattling pieties on her deathbed. In the eyes of some churchmen it seemed that God Himself was soon to be worshiped as a dispenser of tracts. Something of the

---

[19] Elkins, *Slavery*, p. 212.

[20] Ibid., p. 217.

[21] Emerson observed that the antislavery reformer, threatened with church censure, "immediately excommunicated the church in a public and formal process." Worthy though the original act was, it "loses all value when it is copied," he concluded. Emerson in Rozwenc, ed., *Ideology and Power*, p. 171. Elkins, however, grossly overstated the matter when he said, "Our antislavery movement was for practical purposes devoid of intellectual nourishment" (*Slavery*, p. 205). Americans borrowed considerably from foreign sources but they also relied upon traditional Puritan thought, surely a rigorous system. See also, Staughton Lynd, *The Intellectual Origins of American Radicalism* (New York: Pantheon, 1968).

dignity and awesomeness of divinity, as it had been perceived for centuries, was displaced by an identification of sin with certain cultural arrangements and virtue with others.[22]

Proslavery ministers, however, were likewise disposed in behalf of pious slaveholding patriarchalism. Yet pietists could well argue that in the long span of human travail, God had not seen fit to excite men about slavery. Why should He have chosen 1831 for the date of new revelations and the pages of the *Liberator* for a revised Mosaic Law? Like Elkins, conservatives were discomfited by the abolitionists' arrogation of divine authority. Wisely they feared that religion—or religious fanaticism as they saw it—would lead to a blood-bath. It had happened before, and Americans, these critics knew, had not left human passion on the other side of the Atlantic.[23]

Elkins correctly observed that "a gnawing sense of responsibility for the ills of society appears to be experienced most readily in this country by groups relatively sheltered" from the sources of power.[24] Yet, one might question if Americans alone conform to this tendency, for unwittingly Elkins was describing a generational, not a purely national characteristic. Abolitionists and Transcendentalists were generally young men and women at the time of their recruitment or conversion. The young seldom have access to the levers of authority, nor do they fully grasp the mechanisms of governance. Limited in experience and often uncertain of their own untested gifts, they sometimes compensate for such deficiencies with a volatile and abstract idealism. These remarks do not, however, invalidate Elkins' point. Extravagant and naive modes of thought may linger in the American psyche beyond the days of romantic youthfulness chiefly because of the long tradition of religious and moral expectancy in our society. For instance, Frederic C. Howe, a Progressive reformer, recognized that "It was with difficulty that realism got lodgment in my mind; early assumptions as to virtue and vice, goodness and evil remained in my mind long after I

[22]William Ellery Channing, *Slavery* (Boston: James Munroe, 1836), chap. 7. Even Henry Ward Beecher had difficulty straddling the radical implications of antislavery with traditional theology. See William G. McLoughlin, *The Meaning of Henry Ward Beecher: An Essay on the Shifting Values of Mid-Victorian America, 1840-1870* (New York: Knopf, 1970), pp. 185-201.

[23]Southern clerical thinkers naturally relied on strict biblical construction to challenge the intuitional and rationalistic foundations of abolitionism: "The very same spirit of rationalism which has made the prophets and apostles succumb to philosophy and impulse . . . lies at the foundation of modern speculation in relation to the rights of man." The Rev. James H. Thornwell of South Carolina, as quoted in William S. Jenkins, *Pro-Slavery Thought in the Old South* (Chapel Hill: Univ. of North Carolina Press, 1935), p. 237n. "The abolition spirit is undeniably atheistic," declared the Rev. B.M. Palmer of New Orleans. "The demon which erected its throne upon the guillotine in the days of Robespierre and Marat, which abolished the Sabbath and worshipped *reason* in the person of a harlot, yet survives to work other horrors . . ." (ibid., p. 240).

[24]Elkins, *Slavery*, p. 161.

had tried to discard them." As a result, he said, he, like other reformers, had placed faith "in men rather than institutions," spread a gospel of coercive evangelism, and had sought "a moralistic explanation of social problems and a religious solution for most of them." Steeped in the Protestant impulse to mount a pulpit, abolitionists found in reform not only an occasion for pious work but also a means for channeling inner doubts toward morally satisfying ends. These existential fears and hopes were peculiarly associated with the youthful crises of faith and identity about which William James wrote so sensitively in *The Varieties of Religious Experience*. By applying James' insights, Elkins could have added another dimension to his analysis of reform. Instead, his comments about such Transcendentalist figures as William Henry Channing, Margaret Fuller and George Ripley recorded their accustomed gloom without speculation on the inner motives behind it. Having already used psychological theory to explain master-slave relations, Elkins missed an opportunity to do likewise with reform and institutional connections. Nevertheless he was clearly accurate in perceiving a commonality of spirit in Transcendental and reform thought: "its overtone of guilt," abstraction and introspectiveness.[25]

A favorable verdict on many aspects of Elkins' *Slavery* cannot, however, hide a disappointment. His distaste for the antinomian personality was not only historically unfair but also distracting and unessential to his argument. He failed to balance his preference for institutional checks with a discriminating sympathy, one that would have led to greater precision and persuasiveness. After all, these sensitive men and women were caught up in the traumas of the birth of the modern world; they were surrounded by the shifting and perplexing social forces that Elkins himself had so well described. Given these circumstances, it was hardly a wonder that abolitionists were romantics, wracked with feelings they did not fully understand. Even so, the inner compulsions of guilt, ambition and personal despair can hardly explain the entire antislavery movement. A tension between inner doubts and aspirations may have deepened abolitionist convictions, but Elkins did not show how emotional factors were the ultimate determinants of an allegedly irresponsible reform. The causal relationship was implied in a rather mechanistic way. The links between cause and

[25] Howe quoted in Warren I. Susman, "The Persistence of American Reform," *Journal of Human Relations*, 15 (Third Quarter 1967), 97-98; Elkins, *Slavery*, p. 156; William James, *The Varieties of Religious Experience: A Study in Human Nature* (New York: Longmans, Green, 1902). Some recent studies of reform and the generational factor are: Lois W. Banner, "Religion and Reform in the Early Republic: The Role of Youth," *American Quarterly*, 22 (Dec. 1971), 677-95; William J. Gilmore, "The Nature and Context of Reform in America 1815-1835, and the Cultural Generation of 1830," paper, American Historical Association, Boston, Dec. 29, 1970; Bertram Wyatt-Brown, "New Leftists and Abolitionists: A Comparison of American Radical Styles," *Wisconsin Magazine of History*, 53 (Summer 1970), 256-68.

result are ever complex, sometimes unfathomable. Of course, mental anguish played a role, but the examiner of the evidence must resist the temptation of reductionism, a proposition that invariably cheapens the fullness of human experience. Elkins' problem in the final chapter was not an over-application of psychology but a lack of historical charity. The reformers appeared chiefly as victims of their own psychic misfortunes, the reasons for which Elkins morally disapproved. But after all, these earnest thinkers were also fashioners of a destiny for themselves and their world as well.

In any event, abolitionists were better able to cope with conditions around them than he acknowledged. For the most part, the crusaders did not comprehend the exigencies of practical politics, but they did see the potentiality of the mass media as a new weapon of subtle influence. As Aileen Kraditor has so ably shown, they built their reform upon the mechanisms that the sudden rise of mass democracy made available: the national press, mass assembly and mass campaigns, including the postal and petitions efforts. Likewise their programs—even the Garrisonians'— were suited to the needs of instructing the public. Sensationalism was a major way to overcome popular indifference, though hardly one to appeal to those at the center of traditional power. As David C. McClelland observed, "The value of using the mass media for educational purposes lies precisely in the fact that they come to represent a new 'voice of authority' replacing the authority of tradition."[26] Elkins understood the agitational process, but rather than merely describing how abolitionists educated the masses about slavery, he deplored the effort as a creation of pure fantasy from first to last.

In this connection, compare Donald Mathews' explanation for antislavery growth in the Methodist church with Elkins' view of the general procedure. Mathews illuminated the way that Methodist reformers led their Northern brethren to consider themselves " 'responsibly' opposed to slavery," an arduous and lengthy task. "The vagueness and generality of the position," Mathews said, "had the virtue of uniting a maximum number of people under an antislavery banner." Abolitionists were unsatisfied with the meager result, but they had helped to provide Methodists "with a battle hymn in their greatest moment of national crisis."[27] Thus, the radical

---

[26] McClelland, *The Achieving Society*, p. 193. Aileen S. Kraditor, *Means and Ends in American Abolitionism: Garrison and His Critics on Strategy and Tactics, 1834–1850* (New York: Pantheon, 1969); see also Robert D. Marcus, "Wendell Phillips and American Institutions," *Journal of American History*, 56 (June 1969), 41–58.

[27] Donald G. Mathews, "The Methodist Schism of 1844 and the Popularization of Antislavery Sentiment," *Mid-America*, 51 (Jan. 1969), 21–22. See also Larry Gara, "Slavery and the Slave Power: A Crucial Distinction," *Civil War History*, 15 (Mar. 1969), 5–18.

dogma of abolitionism eventually came to serve as a source of comfort and communal security as well as an inspiration for conducting war.

With much less detachment, Elkins described the advance of antislavery ideas as the gradual universalizing of a "fellow-traveler" sympathy. The reference meant an accumulation of corollary issues—the debate over free speech and "gag rules," for example—matters around which moderates rallied as they drew closer to the abolitionist position.[28] The point was valid, but the "fellow-traveler" label demeaned it. Mathews cited the sociological work of Lewis Coser; Elkins borrowed from the rhetoric of anticommunism. Actually, Elkins and Mathews were essentially agreed, for both historians stressed the rise of a new ideology hastened by the expansion of mass communications, the fragmentation of national bodies and the reduction of the antislavery gospel to its lowest common denominator, a murky but visceral dislike of things Southern.

Elkins also failed to concede that much of what abolitionists had to say about the psychic horrors of slavery were points which he himself had so graphically portrayed in other portions of *Slavery*. Nurtured in Calvinism and fed by their own romantic meditations, abolitionists guessed with some precision the effects of total masterhood and bondage. Slavery, they claimed, *could* mold children out of men, broodmares out of women, and disposable chattel from infants. Consistently they attacked the inaccessibility of slaves to normal aspirations. All those institutional restraints and opportunities that Elkins rightly described as needful for healthy psychic development could be found in the reformers' catalog of what was wrong with slavery. Of course, their vision included a gothic terror that granted masters and slaves less than their due as human beings. An antislavery tract was like a novel of the Brontës: a mixture of illuminations into evil and thrusts into popular bathos.

Moreover, Elkins deplored what many others would consider praiseworthy in abolitionist political theory. Exuberant breastbeating and lusty indignation did not exhaust the antislavery reformers' repertoire. They realized that ancient racial folkways were being rapidly incorporated into all those agencies transforming America into a modern state. Abolitionists made war upon both church and party at a time when these institutions were just developing, not when hoary with tradition. Hoping to make changes before the hour passed, abolitionists urged church bodies and political parties to be morally consistent, in conformity with their claims of national representativeness.[29]

[28] Elkins, *Slavery*. pp. 175 93.

[29] John Higham, "From Boundlessness to Consolidation: The Transformation of American Culture 1848 1860," originally published by the William L. Clements Library but most accessible as rpr. (Indianapolis: Bobbs-Merrill, 1969), H-414; Arthur K. Bestor, "Patent-Office

In sum, antebellum reformers were determined to make the country as homogenous and puritanical as possible, to eliminate the evil of folk racism but to strengthen the heritage of Christian idealism. In Talcott Parsons' terms, they were the most comprehensive advocates of a "universalistic-achievement" society in American history. They opposed all compromises with "particularistic-ascriptive" folkways to which Southern culture tenaciously clung. Their doctrines were flavored with the stingy paternalism, sectional chauvinism, suspicion of godless party spirit or "faction," and mustiness of Connecticut Sundays—all aspects of ancient New England custom. Yet abolitionism was eventually, though imperfectly, incorporated into the Northern system of values.[30] Conservatives questioned the fantasies of "higher law," but the ideals reflected were much more appropriate to the secular aspirations of the free-labor North than the old pieties of a bygone day. Given the transfer of power from local squires to national constituencies, it made supreme sense that Americans submit to a single cultural pattern. With communications growing more interstitial, it mattered very much that moral uniformities should keep pace with national growth. Abolitionists simply wanted all blacks included in these nationwide transformations, but especially so in regard to the universal spread of law and the protections of a common, civil religion. Elkins' bias induced him to prefer a deceleration of ideological change even though society was moving rapidly forward.

Intent upon polarizing rational behavior and antinomian vagary, Elkins also took little notice of the conventionalities of 19th century reform. Even antinomians must breathe the common air and accept many of the normal conditions of earthly existence. In the first place, men like Garrison or even an eccentric like Henry C. Wright were not American Jacobins. Antislavery methods were often quite mundane and peaceful. Lewis Tappan's notion of radical behavior was to seize a summer hotel lobby as a forum for antislavery discussion, no matter what fellow vacationers thought.[31] Elkins

---

Models of the Good Society: Some Relationships between Social Reform and Westward Expansion," *American Historical Review,* 58 (Apr. 1953), 505–26; Donald G. Mathews, "The Abolitionists on Slavery: The Critique behind the Social Movement," *Journal of Southern History,* 33 (May 1967), 163–82; Anne C. Loveland, "Evangelicalism and Immediate Emancipation in American Antislavery Thought," ibid., 32 (May 1966), 172–88; Bertram Wyatt-Brown, "Prelude to Abolitionism: Sabbatarian Politics and the Rise of the Second Party System," *Journal of American History,* 58 (Sept. 1971), 316–41.

[30]Talcott Parsons, *Social Structure and Personality* (London: Collier-Macmillan, 1970), and *The Social System* (Glencoe: The Free Press, 1951), esp. pp. 196–200. See also Barrington Moore Jr., *Social Origins of Dictatorship and Democracy: Lord and Peasant in the Making of the Modern World* (Boston: Beacon, 1966), pp. 142–46.

[31]Bertram Wyatt-Brown, "William Lloyd Garrison and Antislavery Unity: A Reappraisal," *Civil War History,* 13 (Mar. 1967), 5–24; Susan A. Tappan to Julia Tappan, June 5, 1848, in private collection, transcript copies in Lewis Tappan MSS, Library of Congress.

made abolitionists' actions seem much more quixotic and flamboyant than could actually have been sustained for the 30 years of the prewar aspects of the crusade. In like manner, Transcendentalists were less consistently opposed to conventional arrangements and values than Elkins suggested. Both groups of reformers seldom quarreled with traditional ideals—family integrity, temperate habits, respect for others. They reasoned that American society was moving away from such ageless goals; they chiefly quarreled with what they discerned as the diminishing quality of American experience. Elkins rightly pointed to an anti-institutional tendency in their criticisms, but qualifications were not supplied in his account. For instance, Emerson's anti-institutionalism bordered on cryptic piety. In his personal life he was jealous of simple comforts of a traditional kind. Sensitive to public opinion, Emerson never spoke against slavery on tour. Unlike the gregarious Lewis Tappan, he submitted only reluctantly to the lucrative lyceum circuit out of a sense of democratic obligation, a duty "to roll with the river of travellers, & live in hotels."[32]

One reason for Elkins' displeasure with the Jacksonian reformers was his own, almost romantic faith in the capabilities of intellectuals. He alleged that "when a society is confronted by a problem" like slavery "one supposes that all the wisdom available . . . should strain toward its solution," a duty that antebellum thinkers irresponsibly shunned.[33] How much wisdom a "solution" may require is always a very subjective matter. Presumably John Adams and the intellectual patriots of 1776 fell short of Elkins' standards, since neither they nor the institutionally minded British leaders were able to settle matters short of war. But the question remains: were the Concord thinkers peculiarly deficient in statecraft? Borrowing Elkins' reliance on analogy for the moment, one might pose them against their English counterparts, the authors of the *Lyrical Ballads*. After a brief, youthful flirtation with French Revolutionary thought in 1790, William Wordsworth and Samuel Taylor Coleridge subsided into poetic repose

[32]Ralph Waldo Emerson to Thomas Carlyle, Apr. 29, 1843, in Joseph Slater, ed., *The Correspondence of Emerson and Carlyle* (New York: Columbia Univ. Press, 1964), pp. 341–42. Both Thoreau and Emerson were rather misrepresented in *Slavery*, esp. pp. 147, 148, 151, 156. While hardly conservative, these men, as well as Orestes Brownson (in his Transcendental phase), Ripley and others, were often ambivalent, even contradictory about the relation of men, morals and society, each to the other. Cf. Wendell F. Glick, "Thoreau of the 'Herald of Freedom'," *New England Quarterly*, 22 (June 1949), 202; Bradford Torrey, ed., *The Writings of Henry David Thoreau: Journal* (Boston: Houghton Mifflin, 1906), 5: 365; Nick A. Adams, "Henry David Thoreau, Abolitionist," *New England Quarterly*, 19 (Sept. 1946), 359–71; Ralph Waldo Emerson, *Miscellanies* (Boston: Houghton Mifflin, 1883), p. 132, a benignly moderate view of the slave issue; Margaret Moody, "The Evolution of Emerson as an Abolitionist," *American Literature*, 17 (Mar. 1945), 5–7. See also Charles R. Anderson, *The Magic Circle of Walden* (New York: Holt, Rinehart & Winston, 1968), pp. 42–48.

[33]Elkins, *Slavery*, p. 140.

without much interest in antislavery or any other philanthropy of the day. Shelley and Byron were more active in politics and radical thought. Yet one would hardly have expected to find them devising committee-room plans for social uplift. Alienation, the Romantic thinker believed, was a function of the poetic temperament. The notion was hardly peculiar to the Concord elite. Like their transatlantic counterparts, the Transcendentalists were concerned with matters of principle, not of power.[34]

Elkins' bias, as the comparison helps to show, led him into errors regarding the chronological setting. One must agree with him that the members of the Concord circle rejected the normal channels of power, but their position was related to the temper of the times, not solely to a unique and tragic American flaw as Elkins suggested. Anachronistic confusion was also evident in Elkins' comparison of British and American emancipation movements. Other critics have noted the inappropriateness of his contrast between the freeing of West Indian slaves by distant Parliamentarians and the American struggle over slavery on native soil. But Elkins also overlooked the parallel chronologies of transatlantic reform. Like the American movement to free Northern slaves, the English endeavor against the slave trade began in the late 18th century along traditional, moderate lines. After 1815, both movements became increasingly romantic, mass-oriented and anti-institutional. Non-Conformists in England replaced the Clapham group in the leadership of the antislavery movement, particularly so after the restructuring of Parliament in 1832. These Dissenters were by no means congenial allies of the Anglican and Tory Establishment, as Elkins asserted, nor did they believe that "the ruling class" was "fluid enough in its recruitment" to satisfy their self-conscious aspirations. In fact, as the English historian Edith F. Hurwitz has observed, "The hostility which the Non-Conformists felt for the [British] state could find direct outlet in the anti-slavery ideology. . . . The anti-slavery movement was a vehicle for bringing to the surface internal strains and conflicts of British society."[35]

The Emancipation Act of July 1833 was intimately connected with various reform causes that challenged aristocratic rule. Quakers and Methodists saw a direct analogy between their civil distresses and restric-

[34]M. H. Abrams, "English Romanticism: The Spirit of the Age," Frye, ed., *Romanticism Reconsidered*, pp. 55 ff. Abrams stressed the impact of the French and American revolutions upon the poetic and philosophical views of this set of young English intellectuals. Wordsworth began, said Coleridge, as "a republican & at least a *Semi*-atheist" (p. 72) in 1790 but he became a staunch Anglican. Emerson, Theodore Parker and Thoreau began as pietists but became more radical in time, thus substantiating, perhaps, Elkins' point about the contrasts between English traditionalism and American masterlessness. Nevertheless, Elkins did not sufficiently qualify and support his position on the Transcendentalists, a rather diverse group.

[35]Elkins, *Slavery*, p. 202. My remarks are largely derived from chap. 2 of Edith F. Hurwitz's forthcoming study, *Politics and Public Conscience: The British Abolitionist Movement and Slave Emancipation*. She has graciously permitted me to quote from an early draft of the text.

tions at home and the more tragic plight of West Indian slaves. Their rhetoric and styles of agitation resembled those of the contemporary American cause; the contexts, though, obviously diverged sharply. Elkins stressed the earlier stage of the English campaigns under the Evangelical members of the Church of England, efforts comparable to the work of Federalist manumissionists in the 18th century and of Whiggish colonizationists in the early 19th century. A more valid analogy for the post-1830 period of reform would have linked Joseph Sturge, the Quaker philanthropist of Birmingham, with the American evangelicals—John Greenleaf Whittier and Orange Scott, for example—and George Thompson, the Scottish leader, with Garrison and Wendell Phillips. Yet, one is forced to agree with Elkins that English reformers *were* more respectful of tradition and privilege than American activists usually were. The very fact that English antislavery became a respectable form of vicarious social protest suggested a caution and obliqueness in the United Kingdom not to be found in Garrison's America.[36]

Nevertheless, Elkins had misread the British reform situation. As a result he treated the American abolitionists more harshly than they deserved. The most telling example was his contrast between the gentle octogenarian William Wilberforce, patriarch of British emancipationism, and William Lloyd Garrison. Evangelicalism of 18th century England belonged to the world of Whig estates and drawing-room prayers. Garrison was a child of romantic zeal and provincial Puritanism. Yet, Elkins asked, "In contrast to these planners, these intellectuals, these men of affairs [of Clapham Commons], what plans had he? what were *his* resources—other than the impotent fury of his poisoned pen?" Garrison was, as Elkins added, very "poor," but he was also very young. (Wilberforce was fifty years his senior when their reform efforts crossed.) Yet Elkins meant "pathetic," not penurious. Adjectives bore the weight of argument.[37]

A truly just evaluation of American immediate emancipationism would have placed it squarely in the context of a romantic spirit abroad in the early 19th century Western world. No country, particularly on the continent, escaped the impact of antinomian, even revolutionary thought. The bastions of feudal institutionalism and particularistic loyalties were inexorably crumbling in France, Germany, Austria and Italy. As in America, economic change, nationalism and mass culture were modernizing the old nations. Tocqueville, to whom Elkins referred for supporting a case for

---

[36]Davis, "Emergence of Immediatism," *Mississippi Valley Historical Review*. 44 (Sept. 1962), 209–30; G.R.S. Kitson Clark, "The Romantic Element, 1830–1850," in John H. Plumb, ed., *Studies in Social History* (London: Longmans, Green, 1955); Elkins, *Slavery*. pp. 202–4. Elkins had to rely on old authorities such as Reginald Coupland and Frank Klingberg in treating British antislavery. (See *Slavery*. p. 204n.)

[37]Ibid., pp. 204–5.

American peculiarities, actually saw America as an example of the European future, one in which traditional ties, intimacies and arrangements surrendered to mass uniformities, restless dynamism, ideological mobilization. America, the French observer believed, was a promise and a warning to the Old World.[38] Elkins, however, reduced Tocqueville's observations to a simple contrast between European stability and American anarchy. By failing to embrace a large vision of romantic intellectualism, Elkins narrowed his theme unduly and provoked his critics to question most of his profound analysis. But the reason why he failed to sustain a strategy of impartiality was perhaps as interesting as anything he said about slaves, comparative institutions and Yankee life.

To understand *Slavery* we must place this brilliant achievement in the context of the period of its composition. Elkins was inevitably influenced by the hopes and disappointments of the Eisenhower era. Historians of that generation have been called "consensus" scholars; the term was vague and somewhat misleading. Yet there was a common mood reflected in their writings, a general mistrust of ideology—and for good reason. The rise of Stalinist Russia, Nazi Germany, militarist Japan and finally Communist China was a wrenching experience. Given the political extremism of mindless McCarthyism at home and cold-war rhetoric in all parts of the world, it seemed to this generation of intellectuals that it mattered little if men willed their own slavery to dictatorships of Right or Left. Both forms of rule achieved the same stultification and horror. As Daniel Bell observed, the academicians of the '50s had once been "intense, horatory [*sic*], naive, simplistic, and passionate, but after the Moscow trials and the Soviet-Nazi pact, disenchanted and reflective; and from them and their experiences we have inherited the key terms which dominate discourse today: irony, paradox, ambiguity, and complexity." Taking chill comfort from the new skepticism, a few rejoiced in an "end of ideology," but most longed "for 'a cause to believe in,' although" self-consciously aware that "the desire for 'a cause' itself is self-defeating."[39] Attention was therefore given to American diversity, pluralism, pragmatic politics and, to a degree, intellectual vacuity—sources of strength for some and of weakness in the eyes of others. To a greater or lesser extent, however, these intellectuals were suspicious of the romantic mode. Thus Elkins' distaste for antinomianism, his almost pessimistic view of man were partly a result of his training at

---

[38] Ibid., p. 160n; J.P. Mayer, *Alexis de Tocqueville: A Biographical Study in Political Science* (New York: Harper, 1960), pp. 29–38.

[39] Daniel Bell, *The End of Ideology: On the Exhaustion of Political Ideas in the Fifties,* rev. ed. (New York: The Free Press, 1965), p. 300.

Columbia under those of the "twice-born" generation, as Bell labeled them, and of his own reactions to the climate of the times.[40]

Elkins' *Slavery* reflected these sentiments in some measure. Man's best chance for progress, the work implied, lay in pragmatic, nonideological and structured benevolence. Chiliasm offered nothing but violence and disillusionment. Blind, unrestrained reaction was self-defeating. Remaining hope focused upon rational social science skillfully coordinated with institutions of power. The promise of that kind of public activity proved illusory a few years after Elkins' work appeared. The mistakes of scholar-bureaucrats and the misfortunes of their foreign and domestic programs may even have hastened the antinomian vagaries that followed. Yet a faith in the concreteness, the seeming substantiality of the social sciences offered Elkins and his contemporaries a reason for creativity and a way for the intellectual to help order and guide the future. A degree of arrogance was involved, but the intentions were inspired and worthy of trial.

Elkins, however, was not merely an echo of contemporary intellectual opinion. Unlike Daniel Boorstin, for instance, he wrestled with the twin problems of slavery and war, subjects Boorstin had rather neglected in his admiration for American good sense. As a result, Elkins was much more sensitive to the tragedies of American history than Boorstin (though less so than C. Vann Woodward and David Potter). Whereas most other leading "consensualists," if the term is appropriate, contrasted European millennialism with a rather stable American culture, Elkins reversed the mirror.[41] Moreover, he was not satisfied with the usual narrative and literary form of history-writing. The strategy he chose offered two advantages, a new way to handle sectional distinctions and a means to avoid the moral and emotional supercharges that so often afflicted scholars of the regional conflict. Con-

[40]John P. Diggins, "Consciousness and Ideology in American History: The Burden of Daniel J. Boorstin," *American Historical Review*, 76 (Feb. 1971), 99–118; Harvey Wish, "The American Historian and the New Conservatism," *South Atlantic Quarterly*, 65 (Spring 1966), 178–91; Irwin Unger, "The 'New Left' and American History," *American Historical Review*, 72 (July 1967), 1237–63; John Higham, "The Cult of the 'American Consensus': Homogenizing our History," *Commentary*, 27 (Feb. 1959), 93–100; Marian J. Morton, *The Terrors of Ideological Politics: Liberal Historians in a Conservative Mood* (Cleveland: Case Western Reserve Univ. Press, 1973). It should be added that Eugene D. Genovese was the first historian to place Elkins' *Slavery* in the context of the Eisenhower period of intellectual conservatism; see Genovese, "The Influence of the Black Power Movement on Historical Scholarship: Reflections of a White Historian," *Daedalus*, 99 (Spring 1970), 477–80.
[41]Louis Hartz, *The Liberal Tradition in America* (New York: Harcourt, Brace & World, 1955); Daniel J. Boorstin, *The Americans: The National Experience* (New York: Random House, 1965); John P. Diggins, "The Perils of Naturalism: Some Reflections on Daniel J. Boorstin's Approach to American History," *American Quarterly*, 23 (May 1971), 153–80 and his "Consciousness and Ideology in American History," *American Historical Review*, 76: 110–11.

vinced that overt moralism blinded men from reality, he did not attack anti-nomian politics and unchecked servitude frontally. Instead he constructed a mediational system which allowed a respectful use of conservative sources like Ulrich B. Phillips and "Southside" Adams. Thus he did not fall into the moral trap of oversimplification in which pro-Southern apologists and such liberals as Kenneth Stampp had been ensnared. Elkins did not wholly avoid emotional reactions, but there were fewer than in the works of Frank L. Owsley, James Randall or Dwight L. Dumond.

Two techniques served to mediate between Elkins' personal convictions and the sectional topic that he chose. The first and most obvious was the adoption of language, style and concepts of a social science derivation and of a morally neutral character: institutions, open systems, social control, power, responsible action, sensibility. These constructions had their opposites in: anti-institutionalism, insensibility, closed systems—rather benign phrases for what some might call fanaticism, bloodthirstiness and the like. The second and more unusual device was the analogy, an elaborate and extended metaphor. Elkins' use of the Nazi experiment in Faustian supremacy illustrated the point. A tone of hardheaded statement of fact disarmed the reader while it highlighted the torment and inner corruption of ideology run amok. A characterization of Southern means of race control was likewise placed next to the appealing portrait of a benevolent, restrained Hispanic culture. In the last chapter, however, Elkins revealed more clearly what his moral purpose was. Therein, the intellectual distance sometimes broke down, partly because the analogies were less gripping in themselves and partly because emotive words appeared more frequently, as evinced in the Garrison-Wilberforce comparison. Thus Elkins banked the fires of conviction, but his moral commitment shone through, especially in Chapter 4.

If hyperbole is permitted, one could say that *Slavery* was a four-chapter sermon. Among other things, *Slavery* was a rational, carefully constructed exposition of the evils of selfish individualism, dogmatism, antinomian self-possession, ideological waywardness and thirst for total power. Elkins' looseness of organization, of which critics have complained, was the result of his decision not to draw these judgments together.[42] To do so would have reversed his nonideological strategy. Nevertheless, he assumed throughout the book that civilization died the moment full authority was vested in the individual actor. He might be an S.S. guard at Dachau, a plantation overlord on the Mississippi River, or a dreamer on the outskirts of Boston. What all three shared was a rejection of institutional restraints. The

---

[42]David Donald, rev. in *American Historical Review*, 65 (July 1960), 921–22; Robert Durden, rev. in *South Atlantic Quarterly*, 60 (Winter 1961), 94–95.

absence of ideological boundaries was the collective failure of their respective societies. Yet it was no less tragic for being so widespread. Elkins implied that each of these antinomian types, so to speak, guard, slaveholder and reformer, represented man out of control, pursuing his uninhibited and devilish ends.

According to this rendering of the historical verdict, men have an inordinate drive for power and a capacity for self-delusion. They will resort to psychological devices of terror to master their fellows and their own destiny. Such mechanisms are possible because men participate in their own humiliation and even learn to enjoy it. Accordingly, "Sambo" was a metaphor in *Slavery*, one representing this trait as well as the consequences of tyranny unchecked by traditions, history, institutions. As symbols, the docile slave and the concentration-camp inmate were luminous images, like figures in stained glass—frozen, one-dimensional, but evocative. Elkins himself seemed a little uncertain about whether he intended a literal characterization or a literary archetype. But metaphors cannot serve a scientifically verifiable function. They are iconographic, not factual. Yet as a means of casting moral light on man's condition, metaphors, whether couched in poetic or scholarly language, can burn the inner consciousness. For that reason alone, *Slavery* must be considered a major achievement. The use of metaphor as a strategy for historiography has seldom been attempted. Elkins' pioneering in the field must be recognized, built upon and improved.

Indeed, historians are still living under the shadow of interpretations and styles offered by social scientists of the 1950s. Their distrust of easy solutions to problems present and past, their sense of irony and their creative yearning for truly workable answers to ancient woes set them apart from their Progressive forebears and a newer, less reflective breed of the sixties.[43] Historians like Elkins explored areas of American experience with rare subtlety and innovation. The articles in the Lane anthology partially testify to our preoccupations even in dissent. They all focus on Elkins' approach in much the same way that Kenneth Stampp's *Peculiar Institution* was shaped by Ulrich Phillips' *Life and Labor in the Old South*.

The one failing that Elkins did not fully overcome was a parochialism that his borrowings from other Western cultures did not assuage. It was a problem that he shared with such major historians as Frederick Jackson Turner. Elkins differed from other post-Progressive historians in some ways, but like them he overstressed American uniqueness. As a result he was too concerned with the American tragedy of civil war to observe that other 19th century nations also bore the weight of moral weakness, ar-

[43]See Aileen S. Kraditor, "American Radical Historians on Their Heritage," *Past & Present*, No. 56 (Aug. 1972), 136-52.

rogance and culpability. For instance, Elkins could be conceded that Latin white colonials faced some modest checks upon masterhood that Americans lacked. Perhaps Brazilian slaveholding was more "open," a pleasant word, and society less racist, as he claimed. Yet, even in imagination, one cannot import the best a society had to offer, without accepting the less attractive corollaries as well. From Elkins' critics we learned that Latin America had its special contributions to make to human travail. Racism, it would seem, was overwhelmed in the utter misery and squalor of practically everybody. Whatever problems Americans have experienced with slavery and prejudice, they have escaped evils present elsewhere. Whatever comforts may be elicited from that state of grace must be balanced against the brutal costs of racial violence and sorrow.

Despite his unwillingness to compare our institutional breakdowns with equally tragic ones in other places, Elkins' moral position is unassailable. If government, laws, history and genial habits were respected because they deserve to be, and if intelligence and responsibility held passion in rein, wars and oppression would cease or at least be subject to less tragic consequences. Elkins sought to demonstrate that the United States had failed to match its potentiality in the antebellum years and his argument was more than a simple moral lesson from the past; it was a study of American character and its romantic tendencies.

Elkins was not so much wrong in his depiction of a fractured and atomistic society, however, as he was incomplete. Indeed, American institutions were undergoing fierce strains, in company with those of Western civilization itself. But the old order, based upon folkways, localistic virtues and simple ties of community and family, had to make way for a new and universalistic system of stateways. The modern industrial nation, as historians have long understood, was formed in the crucible that Theodore Parker and his indignant colleagues helped to fashion. In his final chapter, Elkins pointed mostly to the losses, but surely there were some modest gains as well. Still more important, those gains and defeats were each shaped and distorted, restrained and released in such a way that paradox, both meaningless and profound, formed the texture of the experience. Like the slaveholder who saw only the Sambo in the slave, like the abolitionist who saw only Southern sin and un-Yankee particularism in slavery and not human beings in their infinite varieties, Elkins perceived an experiential aspect of national life, griefs and unrealized possibilities and assumed it was the whole.

We must acknowledge Elkins' bold uses of behavioral techniques. But men, in isolation and collectivity, seldom fit comfortably into the formulae and abstractions provided for comprehending them. A society capable of raising up such complex, admirable men as Emerson, Wendell Phillips and

John C. Calhoun might well have done worse. In the long run, Elkins would be happy to agree. After all, his purpose was not to advocate blind conformity. He did not use Great Britain's institutionalism to advocate a similar social structure for America. Moreover, he did not in any way approve the baser impulses he so tellingly described. To the contrary, he offered his analogies and his strategy of detachment and pragmatic expectancy in the interests of graciousness, equity and racial harmony.

His message resembled that of Hannah Arendt: modern man recognizes no limits to conquest of self, others and environment. Convinced of their own pure motives, both abolitionists and masters demanded unrestrained access to power. There was little humility or reflection on either side of the Potomac. With the bankruptcy of Enlightenment sensibilities, the sacredness of simple obligations, consensual prejudices and social deferences did collapse. A new militance arose with Freedom and Democracy. The march of Northern armies crushed one form of arrogance. Yet it is hard to say that Union victory transformed the American conscience and unfolded a new era of utopian promise.

Elkins' *Slavery* reminds us of some ancient truths of human nature by means of a strategic appeal to reason. Occasionally his bias became too overt. Yet as long as men perceive either war or enslavement as causes for moral outrage, the historian is obliged to indicate his preference for one or the other. Most scholars are so inclined anyhow. Few have dared to leave problems and events of the past unresolved, in a state of tension without message or purpose. Explanations must be offered for the sound in the Marabar Caves, to borrow E.M. Forster's image. Otherwise historians would imply a future as well as a past without meaning. Few if any have yet striven for the kind of experiential truthfulness of a novelist or poet, though Elkins seemed to be working toward this aim. Instead, the historian, like his readers, chooses sides or else serves as referee. The means for making contradictions, wayward irresolutions the essence of historical process have so far escaped us. Glibly expository, we write at our best in the manner of Trollope, not Faulkner. We remain prisoners of moral certitudes and conventions; the humanness of the past fades into grand abstraction. In some measure Elkins is such a prisoner, too, but the situation is common. In any case, the quality of his moral conviction, not his technique alone, has rendered his study the battleground of rewarding contention. A sense of engaged morality made *Slavery* one of the most vigorous, perceptive, haunting volumes in recent American history.

WILLIAM LLOYD GARRISON AND

ANTISLAVERY UNITY: A Reappraisal

Bertram Wyatt-Brown

A RECENT BOOK on current racial tensions is entitled *Who Speaks for the Negro?* One thing is certain: insofar as historical figures are concerned, it is not William Lloyd Garrison.[1] Seldom in American history has any figure been so thoroughly lambasted, by historians and non-historians alike, as the founder of the abolitionist crusade. A popular journalist has called the contents of his *Liberator* "obscene, the sort of self-intoxicated invective that made Senator Bilbo notorious"; and a widely-used college textbook bluntly refers to him as "wayward" and "neurotic."[2] Other scholars have not been much kinder. Despite recent changes in the treatment of abolitionism, Garrison more often than not is still distrusted and sometimes damned,[3] and the cause he

---

[1] Robert Penn Warren, *Who Speaks for the Negro?* (New York, 1965); see, for instance, Warren's interview (p. 274) with Judge Hastie, who said: "There are certain stages . . . when persons like [Garrison] represent the spark to a movement and we can recognize their value as that, without having a necessary admiration for the intemperate, even violent, personality. . . ." This paper was presented at the May, 1966, meeting of the Organization of American Historians in Cincinnati. It is an amplification of the last third of a paper presented to the Society for Religion in Higher Education, Notre Dame University, August, 1963.

[2] J. C. Furnas, *The Road to Harpers Ferry* (New York, 1959), p. 307; Richard Hofstadter, William Miller, Daniel Aaron, *The American Republic* (Englewood Cliffs, N.J., 1959), I, 463.

[3] Louis Filler, book review, *Journal of American History*, LII (1965), 625, notes the lack of a Garrison chapter in Duberman's collection, *Antislavery Vanguard* (see below); see also Filler, "Garrison, Again and Again: A Review Article," *Civil War History*, XI (1965), 70; "Professors have agreed that Garrison was a detriment to the movement." Unfavorable views of Garrison's agitational methods are found in: Stanley M. Elkins, *Slavery, A Problem in American Institutional and Intellectual Life* (Chicago, 1959), Ch. IV; Howard R. Floan, *The South in Northern Eyes, 1831 to 1861* (Austin, 1958), pp. 1-10; Hazel Catherine Wolf, *On Freedom's Altar, The Martyr Complex in the Abolition Movement* (Madison, 1952), pp. 18-31; John L. Thomas, *The Liberator, William Lloyd Garrison, A Biography* (Boston, 1963), a most successful effort but not sympathetic; less critical but perhaps less stimulating is Walter M. Merrill's *Against Wind and Tide: A Biography of William Lloyd Garrison* (Cambridge, 1963); Arnold Whitridge, *No Compromise! The Story of the Fanatics Who Paved the Way to the Civil War* (New York, 1960), pp. 7-11, 85-148; Oliver P. Chitwood, Rembert W. Patrick, Frank Owsley, and H. C. Nixon, *The American People: A*

5

began goes marching on quite well without him. Since it is hard to make a hero of a Yankee editor with a nasal twang, steel-rimmed glasses, and a gift for making enemies, Abraham Lincoln has pre-empted most of the glory and, indeed, most of the monuments. For the Negro rights movement today, who needs a spokesman from history remembered for his disruptive influence in the cause he served?

According to some historians, Garrison's attacks on enemies and friends alike had grown so boisterous by 1840 that he had not only wrecked the movement's cohesiveness, but, by a process of self-combustion had exploded his own authority, too.[4] Other historians have condemned the abolitionists generally and Garrison in particular for being too limited in approach, even, perhaps, insufficiently egalitarian. According to one scholar, Garrison's myopic leadership carried his followers into a labyrinth of religious perfectionism, a fruitless wandering in the byways of extraneous reforms, moral absolutes, and pietistic dreams. As a result, in 1861, the North tragically went to war without a clear moral path to follow toward racial harmony, a path which he could have helped to find. Thus, when emancipation came, he had nothing left to say.[5]

To lay the racial failures of the Civil War generation at the feet of Garrison is not altogether fair, but there is no doubt that his philosophy of agitation was romantic, bizarre, and, for most Americans, indigestible. He spurned the churches because they admitted slaveholders to the altar rail; he denounced the Constitution because of its proslavery clauses. Oath-taking and voting acknowledged that northerners were politically and morally committed to protect the slave system, a complicity with evil which only a peaceful separation of the sections could absolve. According to Garrison, all means of force led to oppression; the only weapon against evil was the testimony of nonresistance. He opposed institutions because these engines of coercion hindered the search for individual perfection. Moreover, he was willing to see "the land filled with the horrors of a civil or a

History (Toronto, New York, and London, 1962), I, 483-485; David Donald, Lincoln Reconsidered: Essays on the Civil War Era (New York, 1961), pp. 19-36.

[4] Filler, "Garrison, Again and Again," 70; Gilbert H. Barnes, The Antislavery Impulse, 1830-1844 (Gloucester, Mass., 1957), pp. 174-175; Dwight L. Dumond, Antislavery: The Crusade for Freedom in America (Ann Arbor, 1961), p. 174; Thomas, Liberator, p. 281; see David Brion Davis, "Abolitionists and the Freedmen: An Essay Review," Journal of Southern History, XXXI (1965), 165, on the abolitionists themselves helping to promote Lincoln's symbolic role.

[5] Thomas, Liberator, p. 408; see the challenge of Louis Ruchames, "William Lloyd Garrison and the Negro Franchise," Journal of Negro History, L (1965), pp. 37-49; also, Davis, "Abolitionists and the Freedmen," 166-167; William H. Pease and Jane H. Pease, "Antislavery Ambivalence: Immediatism, Expediency, Race," American Quarterly, XVII (1965), 682-695, claiming abolitionist equivocation on racial prejudice.

servile war" if slavery did not end peacefully. He would applaud the destruction of the American Union if its existence stood in the way of emancipation. While refusing to encourage rebellion, he tried to frighten southerners with their own nightmare, by probing slavery's instability and threatening God's retribution for the national crime.[6]

It was a hard-hitting, single-minded, and seemingly inflammatory program: dramatic enough to draw widespread attention; romantic enough to enlist the intellectual elite of Boston and Concord; and extreme enough to satisfy the restless urgings of his disciples. Few Americans of that day could imagine a more fanatical approach to the slavery question. Many historians, though by no means all of them, have agreed, stressing its radicalism, waywardness, and demoralizing effect on the antislavery host, most of whom wished to manipulate rather than reject political and ecclesiastical institutions.[7]

What ought to be considered, however, is the moderation by which the movement preserved a unity of agitational method, its factionalism and diversity of personalities notwithstanding. Garrison's opposition to slavery was religious, not political; he required only a theoretical disobedience to national and state government, not a belligerent refusal to obey the law. Even that conservative reformer, Judge William Jay of Westchester, finally understood the meaning of Garrisonian secessionism. In 1857, he declared: "I . . . rejoice in every exposure of the immoral influence exerted by the Union. I rejoice in such exposure, as tending, not to bring about dissolution, but to

[6] Quotation from Larry Gara, "Who Was an Abolitionist?" in Martin Duberman (ed.), *The Antislavery Vanguard: New Essays on the Abolitionists* (Princeton, 1965), p. 37. William Lloyd Garrison to Richard D. Webb, Feb. 28, 1843, William Lloyd Garrison MSS, Boston Public Library (BPL); MS speech before the American Anti-Slavery Society, May 7, 1856, *ibid.* On his reaction to the Nat Turner rebellion, see Wendell Phillips Garrison and Francis Jackson Garrison, *William Lloyd Garrison, 1805-1879: The Story of His Life Told by His Children* (New York, 1885-1889), I, 230-231, 249-250. On the annihilation of the Union, see his "No Compromise with Slavery," *Selections from the Writings and Speeches of William Lloyd Garrison* (Boston, 1852); Garrison and Garrison, *Garrison*, I, 269: "If we deemed it pleasing . . . [to] God . . . we would immediately put ourselves at the head of a black army at the South. . . . Yet, I am for leaving vengeance to God."

[7] Elkins, *Slavery*, pp. 158-164, condemns the New England abolitionists with particular vigor for their anti-institutionalism. It is not suggested that all historians have treated Garrison in this light. Howard Zinn, "Abolitionism, Freedom-Riders, and the Tactics of Agitation," in Duberman, *Antislavery Vanguard*, pp. 417-451, is the latest and most provocative analysis of antislavery policies of action; see also the balanced portrait found in Russel B. Nye, *William Lloyd Garrison and the Humanitarian Reformers* (Boston, 1955); Louis Filler, *The Crusade against Slavery, 1830-1860* (New York, 1960), pp. 120-122, 128-130, points out some interesting weaknesses and strengths of the Garrisonian position; see also David Alan Williams "William Lloyd Garrison, the Historians, and the Abolitionist Movement," *Essex Institute Historical Collections*, XCVIII (1962), 84-99.

render it unnecessary."[8] At times, Garrison thought that once northern protection was withdrawn from the slave masters, rebellion would follow; but generally he pursued its moral imperative, not its revolutionary implications.[9] Admittedly, such an oscillation displayed the romanticism of what Garrison himself called his "foolishness of preaching," but it served his purpose as an agitator—to arouse, alarm, and convert.

Nonetheless, nonviolent disunionism was far from being a concrete program of radical dissent. At it was explained to Adin Ballou in 1844: *"It is not organically political or revolutionary at all; it proposes only conscientious, peaceable, individual and social action."*[10] Among the possibilities *not* explored were: sustained opposition to militia duty; abstinence from the use of government agencies; and refusal to pay taxes. All these things would have dramatized the rejection of proslavery government. Indeed, a few peace men challenged the militia laws, and Charles Stearns and David Cambell went to jail rather than submit. When Stearns asked Garrison to approve his course of action, however, he was advised to pay the requisite fine "rather than *seem* to be rebellious."[11] Subordination to unjust laws,

---

[8] William Jay to Garrison, Phillips, Higginson, Sept. 24, 1857, *Liberator*, Oct. 9, 1857; see also, *ibid.*, Sept. 22, 1843, Adin Ballou's interpretation of disunionism and its results; "Hints for the American People in the Event of a Dissolution of the Union," *ibid.*, Oct. 30, 1846. At first Maria W. Chapman and Garrison both thought political abolitionism was more likely to bring on civil war than moral disunionism; *ibid.*, Sept. 22, 1843, and Garrison's "Massachusetts Abolitionist," *ibid.*, Feb. 22, 1839; Edmund Quincy, "The Life-Taking Principle," *ibid.*, Oct. 30, 1840. "No Union with Slaveholders," was similar to "Immediate Emancipation," in its lack of precision and yet radical coloration; see David B. Davis, "The Emergence of Immediatism in British and American Anti-Slavery Thought." *Mississippi Valley Historical Review*, LXIX (1962), 209-230.

[9] Frederick Douglass, *The Anti-Slavery Movement, A Lecture . . . Before the Rochester Ladies' Anti-Slavery Society* (Rochester, 1855), p. 31, quoting Garrison; cf. Garrison to Elizabeth Pease, July 2, 1842, Garrison MSS, BPL, citing moral purpose of disunion. The nature of a future Yankee republic did not concern him; S. Mitchell to Garrison, October 29, 1856, *Liberator*, Nov. 7, 1856, and editorial reply; editorial, *ibid.*, Dec. 5, 1856; William Henry Channing to Garrison, May 12, 1844, *ibid.*, May 24, 1844; "Address to the Friends of Freedom and Emancipation in the United States," *ibid.*, May 31, 1844; and Garrison and Garrison, *Garrison*, III, 49, 56; Charles E. Hodges, *Disunion: Our Wisdom and Our Duty* (New York, n.d.).

[10] *Liberator*, Nov. 4, 1859, Ballou quoting from a verbal committee report of the American Anti-Slavery Society; also *ibid.*, Dec. 6, 1839, and *Practical Christian*, May 28, 1844: "Let all our friends, especially Non-Resistants, be careful to make this distinction between political, corporate State dissolution of the Union, which is left to take care of itself, and individual moral, peaceable withdrawal from political covenant with slaveholders. . . . The former may be construed as sedition; the latter is at once the duty and privilege of every conscientious man." It is doubtful, however, that even Garrison construed disunionism in quite so pietistic a manner by the 1850's.

[11] Editorial comment on Stearns to Garrison, Jan. 31, 1840, *Liberator*, Feb.

Garrison maintained, was the Christian way to behave. The question of military service was never fully exploited.

From the Stamp Act crisis to the demonstrations against the Viet Nam War, American agitators have sometimes refused to pay taxes to protest what they consider unfair authority. Under Garrison's leadership, however, the issue did not receive the attention it probably deserved. Declared Adin Ballou: "No unnecessary offense is to be given Caesar; but . . . his taxes quietly paid. . . ."[12] The pacifists were open, nevertheless, to the charge of inconsistency. They met their duties to the state, but would not vote or hold office. After his break with Garrison, Frederick Douglass supported Horace Mann's side of a debate with the disunionists by asking: "IS IT CONSISTENT WITH THE DOCTRINE OF 'NO UNION WITH SLAVEHOLD-ERS,' TO PAY TAXES, TO BUY OR IMPORT GOODS, OR TO USE THE POST OFFICE, WHILE THE DOING OF ANY ONE OF THESE THINGS INVOLVES THE MAN WHO DOES SO IN SUP-PORTING THE U.S. GOVERNMENT?" Wendell Phillips gave the standard reply of the Garrisonians; voting was voluntary, taxpaying compulsory. "Suppose I refuse," he said: "Government takes my house, sells it and takes the money. Exceedingly voluntary this!"[13] Using the post office was also voluntary, but the Garrisonians ignored their critics because they felt it "was a most useful instrumentality," cheaper than private postal companies. Of course, their position made practical sense, but in those romantic days of reform "expediency" was more often cursed than applauded, especially on the antislavery rostrum.[14]

Occasionally, however, some isolated reformer tried to reconcile perfectionist thought with actual practice. In 1843, Bronson Alcott refused to pay the unpopular state poll tax; but the incident brought forth just one letter from his friend Charles Lane, published in the

---

14, 1840, petition of Cambell, *ibid.*; see also, "The Militia Laws," from *Mercantile Journal, ibid.*, Aug. 9, 1839, and resolutions against militia system at the annual meeting of the New England Non-Resistance Society, *ibid.*, Nov. 1, 1839; ". . . we deem it unlawful to bear arms, or to hold a military office," declared the signers of the "Declaration of Sentiments adopted by the Peace Convention. . . ." Garrison and Garrison, *Garrison*, II, 231, but outright disobedience was not required or encouraged; *ibid.*, II, 105, 225. There was, however, much grumbling.
[12] At the Non-Resistant Society convention of 1839, *Liberator*, Dec. 6, 1839.
[13] *Frederick Douglass' Paper*, May 6, 1853; *ibid.* (quotation from Douglass), Apr. 23, 29, 1853; Garrison's editorial, *Liberator*, Feb. 14, 1840.
[14] *Ibid.*, Nov. 14, 1856; *Frederick Douglass' Paper*, May 6, 1853. Although the post office was, so to speak, morally neutral, law courts presumably were not. Nonresistants were to settle their differences with others outside the "contaminated" halls of state and national justice; Garrison and Garrison, *Garrison*, II, 225, 232.

Liberator, before the example was forgotten.[15] Only Henry David Thoreau remembered. Some years after his night in the Concord jailhouse for the same offense, he renewed the tax question in his essay on "Civil Disobedience":[16]

I know this well [he said] that if one thousand, if one hundred, if ten men . . . ay, if *one* HONEST man, in this State of Massachusetts, *ceasing to hold slaves*, were actually to withdraw from this copartnership, and be locked up in the county jail therefor, it would be the abolition of slavery in America.

As far as antislavery strategy was concerned, Thoreau's proposal had no impact whatsoever.

Finally, in 1856, Moncure Conway, a young Unitarian clergyman, found the same inconsistencies in nonresistant theory which had worried Douglass and Mann, but he came to a different conclusion. "When we contribute to the treasury of the State," he contended, "we are supporting that which, as a State, supports a Union that is irretrievably given over to the spirit of slavery . . .," a position incompatible with the no-voting principle. Like Thoreau, he believed that a single individual could defy society and set an example which "would shake the whole community," and "a large number . . . would be utterly irresistible." Abolitionists were too "much given to routine, even at Anti-Slavery meetings," he observed. It was time for a new and dramatic approach.[17] No one seconded his motion.

Abolitionists rejected this form of protest for a number of reasons. First of all, none of these advocates was a professional agitator whose ideas could command attention where it counted. Nor were they themselves willing to disobey long and loudly enough to get a hearing. Besides, neither Alcott nor Thoreau were precise about *why* they refused to pay in the first place.[18] In any case, they were in good standing on the revenue books by 1849, if not sooner.[19] The poll tax, moreover, was not an effective device. Its collection was

[15] Lane to Garrison, Jan. 16, 1843, *Liberator*, Jan. 27, 1843; Abigail May Alcott, Jan. 17, 1843, in Odell Shepard (ed.), *The Journals of Bronson Alcott* (Boston, 1938), pp. 150-151. Garrison was away part of Jan., 1843, but he could have commented on the event, had he so desired.

[16] Carl Bode (ed.), *The Portable Thoreau* (New York, 1947), p. 121; cf. Elkins, *Slavery*, p. 169, for a different use of the quotation.

[17] *Liberator*, June 6, 1856, at New England Anti-Slavery Society Convention.

[18] F. B. Sanborn, *Recollections of Seventy Years* (Boston, 1909), II, 446, 447; John Haynes Holmes, "Thoreau's Civil Disobedience," *Christian Century*, LXVI (1949), 787-788. Lane's letter indicates Alcott had in mind the general coerciveness of government rather than slavery in particular; see fn. 15; also John C. Broderick, "Thoreau, Alcott, and the Poll Tax," *Studies in Philology*, LIII (1956), 612.

[19] Shepard (ed.), *Alcott Journals*, pp. 150-151, 164-165, and note 179; Broderick, "Thoreau and Alcott," 623.

haphazard and the levy too small to arouse much indignation, although it was a political issue in the state for a number of years. While some abolitionists, especially during the Mexican War, denounced tax collections for promoting slavery expansion, they had little stomach for confronting lawful authority over an abstraction. The whole tradition of antislavery, once its basic creed was worked out, became primarily an emotional reaction to national events rather than an uninhibited trial of new methods.

Most important of all, however, was the indifference of Garrison and his friends. By the time Thoreau's essay appeared, they had long since ceased the hunt for novel programs, their complacency extending to the Civil War.[20] Using Christ as his measure, Garrison hinged his reformism on New Testament precept. The Romans collected revenues to support idolatrous religion, gladiatorial combats, and other vices, he noted, yet, Christ rendered his accounts to Caesar; and, by implication, so would he.[21] The point is not that such a program would have helped the cause, but rather that, in his hands, there was little experimentation and much more caution than is commonly thought. After his announcement of the disunionist plan in 1842, Garrison made no other innovations, and he discouraged new radical ideas, especially those involving physical force. But if he was unwilling to thrust his policy beyond the realm of stirring manifestoes, other abolitionists in the 1840's began to stir restlessly. Timid though these early signs of extremism were, they eventually culminated in a challenge to Garrison's nonviolence in the following decade.

Any insurrectionary plot had to include the slaves themselves, but, traditionally, the antislavery men, including Garrison himself, had denied any intention of reaching them directly.[22] In 1842, however, Gerrit Smith of New York suggested that abolitionists try to communicate with the slaves and help them to escape. A timid refusal to do so, he thought, would demoralize the cause. But even Smith did not advocate violence at this time. The following year, the New England Anti-Slavery Society issued an address to the slaves (which

[20] Ibid., 617-620; Louis Ruchames (ed.), The Abolitionists: A Collection of Their Writings (New York, 1964), p. 24; Thomas, Liberator, p. 348 and Ch. XVI.

[21] Liberator, Apr. 18, 1856.

[22] See "Declaration of Sentiments of the American Anti-Slavery Society," Ruchames, Abolitionists, p. 79; also William Jay's disclaimer for the American Anti-Slavery Society of 1835 in Bayard Tuckerman, William Jay and the Constitutional Abolition of Slavery (New York, 1890), pp. 67-73; William Jay to Richard Habersham, Feb. 24, 1840, William Jay MSS, Special Collections, Columbia University Library.

few of them probably ever saw), but such sporadic innovations had little effect on abolitionist strategy.[23]

In the 1840's some Negro leaders made a still more militant plea for intervention in the South; but they had to meet the objections of their own people, led by Frederick Douglass, then a Garrisonian, as well as the nonresistant whites. At a colored convention in Buffalo, Henry Highland Garnet called for the violent overthrow of slavery. His resolution was narrowly defeated.[24] Taking up the challenge to white antislavery policy, Maria Weston Chapman, temporary editor of the *Liberator*, felt obliged to spell out for Garnet the chapter and verse of the nonresistant gospel in an offensively patronizing tone.[25] On several other occasions in the 1840's Negroes spoke out for aggressive action. They kept the debate alive, but found few supporters.

Once in a while a Garrisonian such as Francis Jackson protested the use of northern arms and men to protect the southerners' favorite institution, but seldom was there talk of physical resistance to governmental policy. Instead, the slaves were expected "to wait patiently" for peaceful deliverance; they were supposedly too docile to be effective rebels, even if warfare was the right weapon—which the nonresistants claimed it was not.[26]

[23] *Gerrit Smith and the Vigilant Association of the City of New York* (New York, 1860), p. 21, quoting from New York State Abolition Convention Proceedings of Jan. 19, 1842; *Liberator*, Feb. 11, 1842, quoting from *Friend of Man;* "The New England Anti-Slavery Convention Exhorts the Slaves to Direct Action," William H. Pease and Jane H. Pease (eds.), *The Antislavery Argument* (Indianapolis, 1965), pp. 212-223.

[24] Herbert Aptheker (ed.), *A Documentary History of the Negro People in the United States* (New York, 1951, 1963 ed.), I, 226-232; John L. Thomas, *Slavery Attacked: The Abolitionist Crusade* (Englewood Cliffs, N.J., 1965), pp. 99-104.

[25] *Liberator*, Sept. 22, 1843; *ibid.*, Dec. 8, 1843 (Garnet's spirited reply); Aptheker, *Documentary History*, I, 234-236; his "Militant Abolitionism," *To Be Free, Studies in American Negro History* (New York, 1948), pp. 55-56; and his "One Continual Cry" David Walker's Appeal to the Colored Citizens of the World (1829-1830) Its Setting & Its Meaning (New York, 1965), pp. 16-38, all of which find the abolitionists, both white and black, more revolutionary-minded than they really were.

[26] *Anti-Slavery Reporter*, II, Aug. 1, 1854, 171, speech of William H. Furness; Theodore Parker, *The Great Battle between Slavery and Freedom, Considered in Two Speeches Delivered before the American Anti-Slavery Society, at New York, May 7, 1856* (Boston, 1856), pp. 6-7; Garrison's reply, *Liberator*, May 23, 1856; Aptheker, *To Be Free*, pp. 57-58; and notes 56, 57, p. 205; see also "State Convention of Ohio Negroes, 1849," Aptheker, *Documentary History*, I, 278-280 and *Liberator* reprint from New York *Ram's Horn*, 290-291. Garnet continued to speak for insurrection, *Liberator*, Aug. 10, 1849; W. M. Brewer, "Henry Highland Garnet," *Journal of Negro History*, XIII (1928), 44-47; Howard H. Bell, "National Negro Conventions of the Middle 1840's: Moral Suasion vs. Political Action," *ibid.*, XLII (1957), 250-252; George W. Perkins, "Can Slaves Rightfully Resist and Fight?" in Julia Griffiths (ed.), *Autographs for Freedom* (Boston, 1853), pp. 33-39.

In the 1850's, however, a change of mood became apparent. The revolutions in Europe in 1848 and 1849, the passage of the Fugitive Slave Act and the celebrated cases arising from it, the Kansas-Nebraska dispute and other signs of sectional tension brought the Negro advocates of violence and their white allies closer together. Charles Sumner and other sporadic antislavery supporters grew eloquent on the necessity of physical defense of northern and Negro rights. In addition, Henry C. Wright, Charles Stearns, Theodore Parker, and S. S. Foster, all former pacifists, relinquished their condemnation of war, at least to meet these temporary crises.[27] If Garrison were to lead abolitionist opinion, rather than be left behind, his proper move, some might say, would have been to scrap his nonresistant convictions, claiming southern provocation as a convenient excuse. According to one historian, he was in fact guilty of "moral failure and unpardonable folly" in refusing to accept force as a means to abolish slavery, when he could have seen, at least by 1857, that alternatives had vanished.[28] Perhaps he was a dreamer; but so, too, then, were those men, wiser in the political arts than Garrison, who sought pacific solutions to the sectional crises from 1850 to the eve of war.

More importantly, however, what would have been the advantage of such a dramatic about-face after nearly two decades of pacifistic agitation? The unity of the movement would have gained very little. Lewis Tappan, William Goodell, and other leaders of the evangelical wing, hardly less committed to peace than Garrison himself, were also battling against the rising tide of violence. When, for instance, Frederick Douglass adopted Henry Garnet's position, Lewis Tappan, an influential New York abolitionist, threatened to withdraw his support from his journal. "How can I encourage the wider circulation of a paper . . . deserving in most respects as is the Editor, when I believe he is scattering 'firebrands, arson, and death,'" he asked in late 1856. Garrison's apostasy, then, simply would have added this sur-

---

[27] Henry C. Wright, "Death to Kidnappers," *Liberator*, Oct. 4, 1850; Stephen S. Foster, at "Anti-Slavery Convention at Valley Falls, R.I.," *ibid.*, Oct. 11, 1850; Theodore Parker had already proposed forcible resistance to the return of fugitives to the South, *ibid.*, Dec. 4, 1846; Parker to President Fillmore, Nov. 21, 1850, John Weiss (ed.), *Life and Correspondence of Theodore Parker* (New York, 1864), II, 100-102; Charles Sumner, senate speech of Aug. 26, 1852, *The Works of Charles Sumner* (Boston, 1870-1883), III, 191-196; even S. J. May, Garrison's closest supporter, contributed to Kansas arms collection, *Liberator*, May 16, 1856; Charles Stearns to Garrison (from Kansas), Apr. 27, 1856, *ibid.*, May 23, 1856; on the impact of the 1848 uprisings see Frank Preston Stearns, *The Life and Public Services of George Luther Stearns* (Philadelphia, 1907), pp. 70-71.
[28] Thomas, *Liberator*, p. 407.

render of principle to his other crimes, as far as the Tappanites were concerned.[29] They quarreled with his disunionism and his church views, not his nonresistance. Even if one admits that Garrison's influence in the 1850's had declined as his prestige grew, the conversion of the *Liberator* into an organ for Negro and white aggression would have increased the likelihood of more violence and confusion without clarifying the slave issue at all.[30] Paradoxically, Garrison would only have lost much influence by a shift of policy. By embracing conventional views of warfare, he would no longer have retained his reputation as a radical agitator and conservator of the antislavery heritage, which, he always boasted, resided in the old American Anti-Slavery Society. In the tension arising from this dual role, he had found a variety of "extremism" ideally suited to strike a responsive chord in the Yankee conscience—and a note of fear as well.[31]

Anxious to avoid further schisms within the American Anti-Slavery Society, Garrison did not precipitate a fight between the pacifist camp and those who favored the defense of Kansas and the fugitives by force of arms. Nevertheless, he tried to bring them back to traditional nonresistant theory by means of dispassionate argument. When Theodore Parker, as well as the non-Garrisonians Henry Ward Beecher and Gerrit Smith, raised money for Sharp's rifles for Kansas free soilers, Garrison reminded them of their duty as Christians to obey the "Prince of Peace." He also noted their loose grasp of constitutional law, and remarked on the unworthiness of the settlers themselves. The first argument was designed to shame Parker and Beecher, who, as ministers of the gospel, were obligated to reflect the precepts of Christian teaching. Parker, moreover, also misunderstood the nature of the American Constitution. Was the North really able to abolish slavery "peaceably if it can, forcibly if it must." Garrison asked: "does Mr. Parker contemplate an armed invasion of the South . . .?" The Constitution provided no such authority. In answer to Parker's call for a reconstructed Supreme Court, the abolition of slavery in the territories and the District of Columbia, the exclusion of slave masters from holding office, and the prohibition of the inter-

[29] See, for example, William Goodell to Gerrit Smith, Apr. 23, 29, 1856, American Abolition Society letterbook, Oberlin College Library; Lewis Tappan to Gerrit Smith, Aug. 3, 1857, letterbook, Lewis Tappan MSS, Library of Congress (LC); Lewis Tappan to Frederick Douglass, Dec. 19, 1856 (quotation), Frederick Douglass MSS, microfilm, LC; all attempts to preserve the peace principle; cf., *Frederick Douglass' Paper*, Dec. 12, 1856.

[30] C. Vann Woodward, review of Thomas, *Liberator*, New York Times Book Review, June 30, 1963, 6.

[31] Truman Nelson, "The Liberator," *Ramparts*, IV (1965), 21-29, polemical but interesting evaluation; see for example, Howard Zinn's telling example of Garrison at the Douglass speech, Duberman (ed.), *Antislavery Vanguard*, p. 427.

state slave trade, he countered that the "monster Slavery must have suddenly become a very gentle beast, whose roar is like that of a nightingale," if it were to acquiesce. In comparison with his own program, Parker's seemed bloodthirsty and impractical. Its implementation, Garrison warned, would necessitate "an act of usurpation that would lead to civil war, and deluge the land in blood."[32] As for the Kansas free soilers, he observed how inconsistent and even hypocritical these people really were. As he saw it, they cruelly and callously turned their backs on abolitionism, the rights of free colored men, and the fate of fugitives, pursuing "a shuffling and compromising policy throughout. . . ." If these free soilers deserved military aid, he continued, "are not the crushed and bleeding slaves at the South a million times more deserving of pity and succor? . . . Why strain at a gnat, and swallow a camel? . . . Who will go for arming our slave population?"[33] The sarcasm was heavy-handed, as events later proved.

One could argue that Garrison was much more in favor of a vindictive war against the South than his public professions indicated. Certainly there was a constant and intense struggle within his puritan soul between hopes for utopian peace and dreams of a destructive purge of evil. The conflict itself, however, was the very source of his dynamic agitation, and made his pacifism no less sincere. He meant every word when he said: "We have assailed no man unjustly or by violence; we have sought the injury of no slaveholder; we have been law-abiding, in the highest sense of the term; we have not been guilty of treason, nor plotted insurrection; we have sought only a peaceful and voluntary emancipation of those in bondage. . . ."[34] As far as he was concerned, the movement should not depart from this course until victory was achieved, no matter what other Americans chose to do.

Although Garrison remained faithful to his principles throughout the middle 1850's, the assaults against the pacifist citadel grew increasingly virulent. To be sure, such men as James Freeman Clarke, William H. Furness, and O. B. Frothingham supported him, the latter claiming that disunionism was nothing more than a righteous state

---

[32] *Liberator*, Apr. 11, 1856; *ibid.*, Apr. 4, 11, 1856. "You see that such men as Gerrit Smith, Ward Beecher, and Theodore Parker are finding in Sharp's rifles more than in the peaceful Gospel of Christ to aid the cause of right and freedom! They will cause many professed friends of peace to apostatize [sic] from their principles, and give a fresh stimulus to the war principle." Garrison to S. J. May, March 21, 1856, Garrison MSS, BPL; also *Liberator*, Apr. 25, May 3, 1856; Parker in New York *Post*, Mar. 7, 1856, *ibid.*, Mar. 14, 1856; Garrison v. Beecher, *ibid.*, Feb. 29, 1856.

[33] *Ibid.*, Apr. 4, 1856.

[34] Framingham 4th of July address, *ibid.*, July 11, 1856.

of mind leading to "no greater convulsion than is experienced in passing from one frame of temper to another."³⁵ Yet, Thomas Wentworth Higginson, S. S. Foster, and William Wells Brown, among others, demanded what Higginson called a "New Revolution." At the New England Anti-Slavery Society convention of 1857, Higginson said, "You cannot learn men to swim on a table. You have no chance to turn men into freemen by giving them a sense of duty, but by giving them something to defend." Abolitionists, therefore, should prepare to scrap their "disguises and feints," which kept them from the main lesson: the duty of "open" and defiant, not "secret" and passive, treason.³⁶

Garrison, although not remembered for tolerating rival ideas, remained on good terms with these advocates of violence. Undoubtedly age mellowed him, and socially he basked in his role as dean of antislavery, a cause now respectable, in Massachusetts at least. Even if he did not always speak out for peace when others talked of force,³⁷ he did contribute to antislavery unity by welcoming dissent. "We invite persons of all opinions in regard to the matter of resisting evil by physical force," he said of the American Anti-Slavery Society. Surprisingly enough, the old firebrand had become one of the conciliators in the movement, even defending the Republican party against the attacks of his more radical allies.³⁸

His task of holding together the diverse elements in the American Anti-Slavery Society, however, was all the easier because very few

³⁵ *Ibid.*, May 29, 1857; Andrew T. Foss, James Freeman Clarke, at Hopedale meeting, *ibid.*, Aug. 7, 1857; Garrison at same, Aug. 28, 1857; William H. Furness, *ibid.*, May 19, 1854, May 22, 1857.

³⁶ *Ibid.*, June 12, 1857; *ibid.*, May 22, June 5, 1857; see also Thomas Wentworth Higginson, *The New Revolution: A Speech before the American Anti-Slavery Society at their Annual Meeting, May 12, 1857* (Boston, 1857), pp. 1-16, and his speech in *Proceedings of the State Disunion Convention, Held at Worcester, Massachusetts, January 15, 1857* (Boston, 1857), p. 21, a comparatively mild statement, however.

³⁷ See disunion convention, for example, *ibid.*, pp. 31-33, in which Garrison did not challenge the warmongers, who were themselves less aggressive than one might have expected; also the oblique attitude in S. S. Foster, *Revolution: The Only Remedy for Slavery* (New York, n.d.), pp. 1-20, and Parker's *The Aspect of Slavery in America and the Immediate Duty of the North: A Speech Delivered in the Hall of the State House, Before the Massachusetts Antislavery Convention, on Friday Night, January 29, 1858* (Boston, 1858), pp. 41-42.

³⁸ *Liberator*, May 23, 1856; a few days later he said: "Every abolitionist utters his own thought, acts upon his own conviction, whether he has any body to sustain him or not. This it is which makes us strong, vital, fearless, invincible," *ibid.*, June 13, 1856; Thomas Wentworth Higginson, *Contemporaries* (Boston, 1899), p. 249: "I am ready to testify that, at the later period of the contest . . . he seemed wholly patient and considerate with younger recruits," although, he noted, it had not always been so.

of the new activists took up arms themselves.[39] Only one member of the antislavery group in Boston actually made plans for an uprising in the South. Always an individualist, Lysander Spooner had for years recoiled from the "tame, cowardly, drivelling, truckling course pursued by the abolitionists," who wasted their energies "talking to women and children about the churches and the clergy. . . ."[40] His ideas about the antislavery nature of the Constitution were very influential in some antislavery political circles, but his corollary, that slavery could be litigated to death, made no headway. Not only did he claim that the American Constitution provided the legal authority to sue slaveholders for assault and battery, damages, and even the freedom of slave clients, but also that slaves had the right to bear arms and serve in the militia. When Spooner learned that Joshua Leavitt was engaged in the project to get Bibles to southern slaves, he wrote his friend George Bradburn: "Tall business indeed! He had better unite with us in trying to secure to them their natural and constitutional right 'to keep and bear arms.' "[41] With such an active imagination, it was easy for Spooner to justify slave rebellion.

Drawn up in the form of a printed circular sometime in 1858, his plan called upon northerners to prepare for military operations in support of slave rebellions. Southern white nonslaveholders were also to render as much assistance as possible. First would come the creation of Yankee conspiratorial cells, the establishment of newspapers to support their work, the raising of a war chest, and the training of military bands. After gaining the confidence of slaves and white sympathizers in the South, these armed companies would execute a number of simultaneous invasions. With remarkable innocence, he predicted that as soon as this was done, slaveholders would immediately surrender, perhaps without a drop of blood being spilled. If, however, the fighting was not immediately successful, nonslaveholding whites would form "Leagues of Freedom," to punish masters by lynch law or force them to sign emancipation papers. Kidnapped slaveholders, held in mountain retreats, would be used as hostages, and threats of

[39] The exceptions were those in Kansas, acting with John Brown. Wendell Phillips later said: "I like . . . these speeches about insurrection," but he showed little interest in initiating slave rebellion; Higginson, *Contemporaries*, 262-263: "It is doubtful whether he [Phillips] was, in his very fibre, a man of action; but he never discouraged those who were such, nor had he the slightest objection to violating law where human freedom was at stake."
[40] Lysander Spooner to George Bradburn, Jan. 30, 1847, Lysander Spooner MSS, New York Historical Society.
[41] *Ibid.*, Mar. 5, Sept. 14, 1847; to Gerrit Smith, Mar. 14, 1847, Sept. 10, 1857; to S. P. Andrews, Mar. 31, 1847; Spooner influenced Smith as seen in *Letter of Gerrit Smith to S. P. Chase on the Unconstitutionality of Every Part of American Slavery* (Albany, 1847), esp. p. 3.

the destruction of plantation property would compel quick manumissions. Admitting that a general slave uprising would be dangerous without proper planning, he suggested that guerrillas, operating in small bands, "could build forts in the forests, and there collect themselves, and carry on their warfare upon the Slaveholders."[42]

The reaction to the plan was predictable. Wendell Phillips, although one of the leading platform-soldiers, pointed out that such activities "would be treason & the Govt. would at once move & array all its power to crush" it. Daniel Mann and Francis Jackson both repudiated the scheme on the grounds that they were faithful Garrisonian nonresistants, Jackson confessing that he was "loaded down to the gunwales with their apparatus. . . ."[43] Only Stephen S. Foster and Thomas Wentworth Higginson supported his idea. When it came to raising money for it, however, Foster had to decline because of illness in the family and the temporary loss of his "vocal power" owing to the "extraction of all my remaining upper teeth." Even Higginson hedged his enthusiasm. Spooner, he thought, had been too outspoken in announcing the goals of the "Leagues of Freedom." Garrison's opinion apparently was not sought.[44] Thus, while it can hardly be claimed that Garrison alone prevented a more favorable response to Spooner's idea, it is true that his agitational methods, his theories, and above all, his example as a fear-inspiring but pacifist agitator hardly encouraged this sort of innovation. In a sense, Garrison's views of war and the Union were just "radical" enough to dampen enthusiasm for Spooner's kind of extremism.

Even if Spooner found lukewarm support for insurrection in the quiet neighborhoods of Boston, however, John Brown and his band, out on the front lines. so to speak, in Kansas were setting a stirring example for militant abolitionists. His "rescue" of twenty Missouri slaves inspired Wendell Phillips, Parker Pillsbury, and R. J. Hinton of Kansas to speak for this type of action at an antislavery convention in early 1859. With his gift for the picturesque phrase, Pillsbury likened John Brown to Oliver Cromwell and announced that he " longed to see the time come, when Boston streets should run with blood from Beacon Hill to the foot of Broad street.' "[45] Garrison,

---

[42] "A Plan for the Abolition of Slavery," Lysander Spooner MSS, NYHS; Aptheker, *To Be Free*, pp. 62-67, giving a full account of Spooner's project.
[43] Wendell Phillips to Spooner, July 16, 1858; Jackson to Spooner, Dec. 3, 1858; Daniel Mann to Spooner, Jan. 16, 1859; Lysander Spooner MSS, BPL.
[44] S. S. Foster to Spooner, Jan. 8, 1859, *ibid.*; Theodore Parker to Spooner, Nov. 30, 1858; Higginson to Spooner, Nov. 30, 1858; see also Lewis Tappan to Spooner, Oct. 7, 1858; Hinton R. Helper to Spooner, Dec. 18, 1858; Boston *Courier*, Jan. 28, 1859, clipping in Spooner MSS.
[45] *Liberator*, Feb. 4, 1859, meeting of the Massachusetts Anti-Slavery Society, quoted by Holden, of Lynn, Mass.

angry and alarmed, defended nonresistance. In reply to Hinton's unqualified praise for Kansas free soilers, Garrison retorted, "They went
to make money . . . I do not see that Kansas has given us any lessons
of wisdom in regard to the management of the warfare against slavery. I am for going on as we have hitherto done."[46] Other pacifists
rallied around the fading Garrisonian banner, even as the spirit of
aggression reached its climax at Harpers Ferry.[47]

Platform oratory and Spooner's circulars paled into insignificance
with this first and only translation of militant words into direct action
against the South. Faced with the challenge and shock of Brown's
example, Garrison at first reacted by calling it "a misguided, wild,
and apparently insane, though disinterested and well-intended effort.
. . . "[48] The comment drew the instant criticism of Henry Thoreau,
long since an apostate from nonviolence. While beatifying John
Brown, Thoreau had nothing but contempt for "ye Garrisons, ye Bu-
chanans, ye politicians, attorney-generals. . . ."[49] Deserted by so many
former pacifists, Garrison was at this point in danger of becoming a
curious relic of the antislavery past. Understandably, he left all but
nominal adherence to nonviolence behind and quickly joined the
chorus praising Brown.[50]

It would not be the last time an American reformer abandoned
his hatred of war to support a crusade against tyranny. It is ironic,
however, that Thoreau would be much more influential in the history of nonviolent agitation than Garrison, who had served this cause
longer and better. For seventeen years, he had maintained a fairly
consistent, if often equivocal, attitude toward slave rebellion. Still,
a professional agitator, such as he, faced with issues demanding editorial attack, grasps at the shocking sentiment, the belligerent tone,
thereby nullifying objectivity and consistency. Self-righteous though
he was, he had sometimes compromised his position when he thought
it essential or expedient.[51]

[46] *Ibid.*
[47] See Holden's speech in defense of nonresistance, *ibid.*, and debate between
J. Miller McKim and Adin Ballou, *ibid.*, Sept. 30, Nov. 4, 1859.
[48] *Ibid.*, Oct. 21, 1859.
[49] Bradford Torrey (ed.), *The Writings of Henry David Thoreau* (Boston,
1906), XII (Oct. 19, 1859, journal entry) 408.
[50] Garrison to James Redpath, Dec. 1, 1860, Garrison MSS, BPL; also Garrison to LeRoy Sunderland, Sept. 18, 1851, in *Liberator*, Sept. 18, 1857, and
Garrison to R. Wertz, Mar. 7, 1874, Garrison MSS, BPL; these examples reveal
his ambivalent feelings about rebellion, but certainly the Brown affair called
for his condemnation on principle, a pacifist duty he passed by; cf. other former
pacifists reversing themselves, George M. Fredrickson, *The Inner Civil War:
Northern Intellectuals and the Crisis of the Union* (New York, 1965), pp. 36-41.
[51] Thomas, *Liberator*, pp. 388-389, for example of Garrison's change of views
about political action; but see Richard Hofstadter, *The American Political Tra-*

Nonetheless, Garrison's contribution to antislavery unity was his own respectability. Even though he broke with the evangelical and political-minded moderates early in antislavery history, for thirty years he was living proof that even the wildest American radical was seldom the plotter of outright violence. He never sent a *Liberator* to the slaves of the South. He never said: "Slaves, arise, you have nothing to lose but your chains." Nor did he urge military action against the South, until the Civil War came. Instead, his pacifist protests, uncertain as they sometimes were, helped to act as a brake against the use of physical force. Frederick Douglass later reminisced that nonresistance (along with women's rights) "had a depressing effect upon the whole movement."[52] Perhaps he was right; but that was just as well in the light of the grim alternatives.

Some historians might insist that Garrison's pacifism was a hoax, or at best, an obvious impossibility; that since the issue which he raised led to war, he must be held responsible for the consequences. His flaming words were just as dangerous as flaming swords. Certainly his contemporaries frequently said so. It should be remembered, however, that boisterous, uninhibited language was hardly confined to the columns of the *Liberator*, but pervaded the colorful and romantic rhetoric of the times. In addition, even a casual thumbing of the journal would demonstrate that Garrison's vituperative qualities have been somewhat exaggerated.

Of course, it can be said that extremism is a relative matter, and by the standards of his time Garrison qualified as a genuine fanatic. Yet, it was not so much the language he used but the subject to which he applied it that made him seem fanatical. At the end of the nineteenth century, Thomas Wentworth Higginson recalled a point too frequently forgotten: "What such critics overlooked, is that the whole vocabulary of Garrison was the logical result of that stern school of old-fashioned Calvinism in which he was trained." In other words, the same threats of divine judgment delivered from the pulpit would hardly have worried the gentlemen with gold spectacles, but when applied to a volatile and insecure institution it was inflammatory. Under these circumstances, Garrison may be considered a crank, but

---

dition (New York, 1949), pp. 135-161, on the role of the agitator in democratic society. On insurrections, see Garrison to Redpath, Dec. 1, 1860, Garrison MSS, BPL; Garrison and Garrison, *Garrison*, I, "Universal Emancipation," poem, 229-230, and 231, 250n.; *Liberator*, Sept. 18, 1857, Dec. 7, 1860; James M. McPherson, *The Struggle for Equality, Abolitionists and the Negro in the Civil War and Reconstruction* (Princeton, 1964), pp. 33-34; Frederickson, *Inner Civil War*, p. 42.

[52] Douglass to R. J. Hinton, Jan. 17, 1893, *Journal of Negro History*, XXXIII (1948), 471.

hardly outside the main currents of American reform; religious zeal, Biblical language, and Christian pacifism have often been associated with reform movements. In any case, his refusal to advance from pleas for national repentance and disunionist absolution to nonviolent resistance to law or to revolution limits the extent to which he can justly be called extremist. Adin Ballou wisely said: "Mr. Garrison hurts the feelings of the oppressors of men by an application of wholesome truth. Is that to be compared to slitting their ears, breaking their arms, or blowing out their brains?"[53]

Critics of his policy overlook the wealth of alternatives open to the abolitionists in the 1850's. They might have rejected Garrison's paper nullifications, no more outrageous than the public burning of the Fugitive Slave Act and the Constitution, and instead organized guerrilla bands, publicized antislavery among the slaves, or attempted assassinations, kidnappings, and lynchings of proslavery men. There were plenty of European examples to follow, particularly after the 1848 rebellions, and in this country filibusters against Latin countries were then enjoying an unusual vogue. It is remarkable that only a handful of abolitionists supported John Brown's raid, and even more astonishing that after thirty years of agitation, there was only *one* major act of violence against the South. As Abraham Lincoln pointed out: "That affair, in its philosophy, corresponds with many attempts related in history, at the assassination of kings and emperors. . . . Orsini's attempt on Louis Napoleon, and John Brown's attempt at Harpers Ferry were, in their philosophy, precisely the same."[54] The models for violence had long been available. Only the antislavery will and tradition were lacking.

Since that tradition was largely the work of Garrison himself, his unwillingness to go beyond the platform measures of disunionism helped to retain abolitionism within nonviolent bounds. Except for the various abolitionist riots over fugitive slave cases and the defense of Kansas, few abolitionists ever hazarded open civil disobedience. If, on the other hand, he had tried to convert the American Anti-Slavery Society chapters into carbonari or dedicated guerrilla companies, abolitionists might easily have brought on a martyrdom and persecution that would have shocked the nation into either an earlier and more bitter Civil War or an era of rampant tyranny in North and South. If the Garrisonians had been truly destructive, then American

[53] Ballou at the Non-Resistance Convention, Worcester, *Liberator*, Dec. 12, 1856; Higginson, *Contemporaries*, p. 251.
[54] Roy P. Basler (ed.), *Abraham Lincoln, His Speeches and Writings* (New York, 1946, 1962 ed.), Cooper Institute Speech, Feb. 27, 1860, p. 531; Higginson estimated that no more than a dozen abolitionists in Boston "had quite made up their minds to fight," *Contemporaries*, p. 296.

historians might have good reason to question their motives and their sanity.

Yet, it would be a serious mistake to attribute the comparative moderation of Garrison's policy to him alone. The American tradition of reform has generally avoided bloody deeds even if society has been frustratingly slow in righting its wrongs. Garrison and his friends were actors in the last great era of Christian faith, and their appeal naturally focused on the deeply entrenched feelings of a conservative but conscience-minded northern community. This skittishness of revolutionary action was recognized at the time and sometimes lampooned. The editor of the Baltimore *Patriot,* for instance, wrote in 1854: "Perhaps if civil war should come, Mr. Phillips would be surrounded by a life-guard of elderly ladies, and protected by a rampart of whalebones and cotton-padding."[55]

John L. Thomas, in his biography of Garrison, makes brilliantly clear his religious preoccupations, Quaker-like pacifism and his Biblical sense of American destiny. Primarily, however, he and his disciples were liberal nineteenth-century reformers, for all their heady talk of Christian perfection. They were not so very different from others of their kind—Richard Cobden, John Bright, and Daniel O'Connell. In fact, Wendell Phillips, in his famous address to the Harvard Phi Beta Kappa chapter in 1881, pointed out the Anglo-American spirit of nonviolent reform. "In all modern constitutional governments," he said, "agitation is the only peaceful method of progress. Wilberforce and Clarkson, Rowland Hill and Romilly, Cobden and John Bright, Garrison and O'Connell, have been the master spirits in this new form of crusade." Phillips did not rule out the necessity of violence, even in democracies, when free men had their rights disregarded, but he took pride in the lawful approach of Garrison and his small band of crusaders.[56]

Like their British colleagues of reform, whom they much admired, the Garrisonians addressed themselves to the great middle class. In reference to abolitionism, Garrison might have echoed the grand, subtle spirit of Richard Cobden's words about Corn Law repeal:[57]

---

[55] *Patriot,* quoted by *Liberator,* June 2, 1854.

[56] Wendell Phillips, "The Scholar in a Republic," June 30, 1881, in Carlos Martyn, *Wendell Phillips, The Agitator* (New York, 1890), pp. 584, 588.

[57] Quoted by John Morley, *The Life of Richard Cobden* (London, 1903), I, 249. It could be argued that Corn Law repeal agitation derived techniques from abolitionism; see G.R.S. Kitson Clark, "The Romantic Element, 1830-1850," in John Harold Plumb (ed.), *Studies in Social History: A Tribute to G. M. Trevelyan* (London, 1955), p. 232; also, for Anglo-American parallels, Asa Briggs, "John Bright and the Creed of Reform," *Victorian People: A Reassessment of Persons and Themes, 1851-1867* (New York, 1955, 1963 ed.), pp. 197-231, esp. p. 203; Fanny Garrison Villard, *William Lloyd Garrison on Non-Resistance*

We have carried it on by those means by which the middle-class usually carries on its movements. We have had our meetings of dissenting ministers; we have obtained the co-operation of the ladies; we have resorted to tea-parties and taken those pacific means for carrying out our views, which mark us rather as a middle-class set of agitators. . . .

It was a painful, frustrating task to goad that good-intentioned but sluggish lump of consensus into some recognition of antislavery duty. By taking a rhetorically radical stand Garrison gradually helped force stronger antislavery postures among antislavery men outside his faction and, at a slower pace, more conservative Yankees. "He did the work," as Higginson phrased it, "of a man of iron in an iron age." He did not, however, see far enough beyond the extinction of slavery to the racial barriers ahead. As John Jay Chapman said: "That short-sighted element in the philosophy of Abolition . . . ended by putting Slavery to its purgation so quickly and so convulsively that many features . . . of slavery were left behind in the nervous system of the people." Indeed, Garrison offered no "after-cure," but the problems, sufficiently perplexing in our own time, were not easily remedied then.[58]

Even though he had helped to preserve traditional antislavery action in nonviolent channels, he is seldom remembered for it, but only for his intellectual vagaries and belligerent language. Leo Tolstoy, however, once declared that he had been one of the "greatest reformers and promoters of true human progress," and indeed "the first to proclaim" the principle of peaceful resistance.[59] In spite of Tolstoy's claim of indebtedness to his example, in spite of Gandhi's admission of Thoreau's influence, which was largely derived from Garrison, and in spite of Martin Luther King's claimed inspiration from this pacifist heritage, the author of American nonresistant theory has gained little esteem.[60] By remaining faithful, *almost* to the last extremity, to

Together with a Personal Sketch by His Daughter . . . and a Tribute by Leo Tolstoi (New York, 1924), p. 74, finding Garrison's work "wonderfully suited to the sturdy middle-class. . . ." On Anglo-American connections generally see Frank Thistlethwaite, *America and the Atlantic Community, Anglo-American Aspects, 1790-1850* (New York, 1963), pp. 103-133; G. D. Lillibridge, *Beacon of Freedom, The Impact of American Democracy upon Great Britain, 1830-1870* (Philadelphia, 1954), both of which are challenged by David Paul Crook, *American Democracy in English Politics, 1815-1850* (London, 1965).

[58] John Jay Chapman, *William Lloyd Garrison* (Boston, 1921), p. 275; Higginson, *Contemporaries*, p. 256; McPherson, *Struggle for Equality* on later role of Garrison and other abolitionists; Willie Lee Rose, *Rehearsal for Reconstruction, The Port Royal Experiment* (Indianapolis, 1964), for sensitive appreciation of abolitionist difficulties with their preconceptions and Negro realities; see also Ruchames, "Garrison and Negro Franchise," cited fn. 5, above.

[59] Leo Tolstoy, "What I Owe to Garrison," in Fanny Villard, *Garrison on Non-Resistance*, p. 55.

[60] *Ibid.*; and, his "Garrison and Non-Resistance," *The Independent*, LVI (1904),

his Christian principles, Garrison contributed much to the American reform tradition, in his own day and for the future. It can only be hoped that this unity of action, effective for the most part in the trying times before the Civil War, will remain a lively heritage.[61]

Perhaps the time will come when abolitionists of the Garrison persuasion will earn our respect if never our affection. These cantankerous, incorrigible, self-satisfied, moralistic and irascible reformers were tough old birds. They enjoyed their unpopularity. As Garrison once said, "Hisses are music to my ears." Yet, he did expect more recognition than he so far has received: "I look to posterity," he said, "for a good reputation."[62] He still looks in vain.

881-883; "A Message to the American People," *Complete Works of Count Tolstoi.* (New York and Boston, 1904-1905), XXIII, 462; also *ibid.*, 122-123 and XX, 6, 12; Henry Raymond Mussey, "Gandhi the Non-Resistant," *The Nation,* CXXX (1930), 608-610; Wendell Phillips Garrison to L. N. Tolstoi, Mar. 1, 1905, Wendell Phillips Garrison MSS, Houghton Library, Harvard; Gopinath Dhawan, *The Political Philosophy of Mahatma Gandhi* (Amedabad, 1951), pp. 30-31; *The Collected Works of Mahatma Gandhi* (Amedabad, 1958-), VII, 217-218, 228-230, 304-305; George Hendrick, "The Influence of Thoreau's 'Civil Disobedience' on Gandhi's Satyagraha," *New England Quarterly,* XXIX (1959), 462-471; Clarence A. Manning, "Thoreau and Tolstoy," *ibid.,* XVI (1943), 234-243; Richard B. Gregg, *The Power of Non-Violence* (Amedabad, 1960), foreword by Martin Luther King; Mulford A. Silbey (ed.), *The Quiet Battle, Writings on the Theory and Practice of Non-Violent Resistance* (New York, 1958), pp. 76-78, 82-83, 177-178 on Gandhi, and p. 72 on Thoreau.

[61] The best articles on the romantic and religious content of American antebellum reform: John L. Thomas, "Romantic Reform in America, 1815-1865," *American Quarterly,* XVII (1965), 656-681; and his "Antislavery and Utopia," Duberman (ed.), *Antislavery Vanguard,* pp. 240-269; Ralph Henry Gabriel, "Evangelical Religion and Popular Romanticism in Early Nineteenth Century America," in Grady McWhiney and Robert Weibe (eds.), *Historical Vistas, Readings in United States History* (Boston, 1963), I, 407-419; William G. McLoughlin, "Pietism and the American Character," *American Quarterly,* XVII (1965), 163-186.

[62] Quoted by Russel B. Nye, *William Lloyd Garrison and the Humanitarian Reformers* (Boston, 1955), pp. 200-203.

24

Acknowledgments

A.H.R. Forum on Abolition: David Brion Davis, "Reflections on Abolitionism and Ideological Hegemony," John Ashworth, "The Relationship Between Capitalism and Humanitarianism," and Thomas L. Haskell, "Convention and Hegemonic Interest in the Debate over Antislavery: A Reply to Davis and Ashworth," *American Historical Review*, 92, No. 4 (October, 1987): 797-878. Reprinted by permission of the *American Historical Review*.

David Brion Davis, "The Emergence of Immediatism in British and American Antislavery Thought," *Mississippi Valley Historical Review* 49 (1962): 209-310. Reprinted by permission of the *Mississippi Valley Historical Review*.

David Brion Davis, "New Sidelights on Early Antislavery Radicalism," *William and Mary Quarterly*, 3rd Ser. 28 (1971): 585-94. Reprinted by permission of the *William and Mary Quarterly*.

John Demos, "The Antislavery Movement and the Problem of Violent 'Means'," *New England Quarterly* 36 (1964): 501-26. Reprinted by permission of the *New England Quarterly*.

Merton L. Dillon, "The Abolitionists: A Decade of Historiography, 1959-1969," *Journal of Southern History* 35 (1969): 500-22. Reprinted by permission of the *Journal of Southern History*.

Merton L. Dillon, "The Failure of the American Abolitionists," *Journal of Southern History* 25, No. 2 (March, 1959): 159-77. Reprinted by permission of the *Journal of Southern History*.

David Donald, "Toward A Reconsideration of the Abolitionists," in David Donald, *Lincoln Reconsidered : Essays on the Civil War Era* (New York: 1956): 19-36. Reprinted by permission.

Gordon E. Finnie, "The Antislavery Movement in the Upper South Before 1840," *Journal of Southern History* 35(August, 1969): 319-42. Reprinted by permission of the *Journal of Southern History*.

Betty L. Fladeland, "Revisionists vs. Abolitionists: The Historiographical Cold War of the 1930s and 1940s," *Journal of the Early Republic* 6 (1986): 1-21. Reprinted by permission of the *Journal of the Early Republic*.

Lawrence J. Friedman, "'Historical Topics Sometimes Run Dry': The State of Abolitionist Studies," *The Historian* 43 (February, 1981): 177-94. Reprinted by permission of *The Historian*.

Richard J. Hofstadter, "Wendell Phillips: The Patrician as Agitator," in *The American Political Tradition and the Men Who Made It* (1948):

531

135-61. Reprinted by permission of Random House.

Leon F. Litwack, "The Abolitionist Dilemma: The Antislavery Movement and the Northern Negro," *New England Quarterly* 34 (March, 1961): 50-73. Reprinted by permission of the *New England Quarterly*.

Anne C. Loveland, "Evangelicalism and 'Immediate Emancipation' in American Antislavery Thought," *Journal of Social History* 32(May, 1966): 172-88. Reprinted by permission of the *Journal of Social History*.

Donald G. Mathews, "The Abolitionists on Slavery: The Critique Behind the Social Movement," *Journal of Social History* 33 (May, 1967): 163–82. Reprinted by permission of the *Journal of Social History*.

William H. Pease and Jane H. Pease, "Antislavery Ambivalence: Immediatism, Expediency, Race," *American Quarterly* 17 (1965): 682-95. Reprinted by permission of *American Quarterly*.

Jane H. Pease and William H. Pease, "Ends Means, and Attitudes: Black-White Conflict in the Antislavery Movement," *Civil War History* 18 (June, 1972): 117-28. Reprinted by permission of *Civil War History*.

Lewis Perry, "Versions of Anarchism in the Antislavery Movement," *American Quarterly* 20 (Winter, 1968): 768-82. Reprinted by permission of *American Quarterly*.

Kenneth M. Stampp, "The Fate of the Southern Antislavery Movement," *Journal of Negro History* 28 (1943): 10-22. Reprinted by permission of the *Journal of Negro History*.

James Brewer Stewart, "The Aims and Impact of Garrisonian Abolitionism, 1840-1860, " *Civil War History* 15 (1969): 197-209. Reprinted by permission of *Civil War History*.

James Brewer Stewart, "Politics and Belief in Abolitionism: Stanley Elkins' Concept of Antiinstitutionalism and Recent Interpretations of American Antislavery," *South Atlantic Quarterly* 75 (December, 1976): 74-97. Reprinted by permission of *South Atlantic Quarterly*.

Deborah Bingham Van Broekhoven, "'A Determination to Labor. . . . ': Female Antislavery Activity in Rhode Island," *Rhode Island History* 44(May, 1985): 35-45. Reprinted by permission of *Rhode Island History*.

Ronald G. Walters, "The Erotic South: Civilization and Sexuality in American Abolitionism," *American Quarterly* 25 (Summer, 1973): 177-201. Reprinted by permission of *American Quarterly*.

Bertram Wyatt-Brown, "Stanley Elkins' *Slavery*: The Antislavery

Interpretation Reexamined," *American Quarterly* 25 (Summer, 1973) 154–76

Bertram Wyatt-Brown, "William Lloyd Garrison and Antislavery Unity: A Reappraisal," *Civil War History* 13 (1967): 5-24. Reprinted by permission of *Civil War History*.